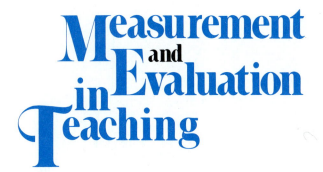

Norman E. Gronlund
UNIVERSITY OF ILLINOIS

Robert L. Linn
UNIVERSITY OF COLORADO

Measurement and Evaluation in Teaching

6th Edition

MACMILLAN PUBLISHING COMPANY
NEW YORK
Collier Macmillan Publishers
LONDON

Editor: Robert Miller
Production Supervisor: Linda Greenberg
Production Manager: Alan Fischer
Text Designer: Patrice Fodero
Cover Designer: Patrice Fodero
Cover illustration: Slide Graphics
Illustrations: Fine Line Illustrations Inc.

This book was set in 10½/12 Electra by Digitype, Inc., and printed and bound by Arcata Graphics/Halliday. The cover was printed by Phoenix Color Corp.

Macmillan Publishing Company
866 Third Avenue, New York, New York 10022

Collier Macmillan Canada, Inc.

LIBRARY OF CONGRESS CATALOGING-IN-PUBLICATION DATA

Gronlund, Norman Edward, 1920–
    Measurement and evaluation in teaching / Norman E. Gronlund,
  Robert L. Linn. — 6th ed.
        p.   cm.
    Bibliography: p.
    Includes index.
    ISBN 0-02-348111-0
    1. Educational tests and measurements.   I. Linn, Robert L.
  II. Title.
    LB3051.G74   1990   88-34632
    371.2'6--dc19   CIP

Printing: 6 7   Year: 2 3 4 5 6

To

Marie A. Gronlund

Joyce E. Linn

Preface

The sixth edition of *Measurement and Evaluation in Teaching* retains the same organization and emphasis as the last edition. It introduces the classroom teacher and prospective teacher to those elements of measurement and evaluation that are essential to good teaching. The main theme throughout the book is that the evaluation of learning plays an important role in the instructional process and that its effectiveness depends largely on the ability to construct and select tests and other evaluation instruments that provide valid measures of the intended learning outcomes.

The book was designed for the introductory course in educational measurement and evaluation, at either the undergraduate or graduate level, and assumes no previous knowledge of measurement or statistics. The writing is direct and numerous examples are used throughout the book to illustrate important concepts, instruments, and procedures. Statistical concepts are introduced only where necessary for understanding the discussion and then the emphasis is on interpretation rather than computation. A special section on elementary statistical computations is provided in Appendix A for those who want to develop a minimum level of computational skill.

Although the organization and emphasis remain the same, this edition includes a number of changes. Some of the more significant ones include (1) shortening of the instructional objectives chapter, with a focus on how to identify and state objectives as intended learning outcomes; (2) revising and updating the material on validity, reliability, and interpreting test scores; (3) rewriting the section on test specifications to describe and illustrate a step-by-step procedure; (4) describing and illustrating new achievement tests (e.g., diagnostic achievement batteries, customized tests) and new editions of aptitude tests (e.g., *Cognitive Abilities Test*, all new *Stanford–Binet*); (5) adding new material on how to locate and evaluate published tests; (6) new sections on accountability, teacher testing, computerized testing, and item response theory in the chapter on trends and issues; (7) revising the section "Elementary Statistics," in Appendix A, to make it more useful with hand calculators; and (8) adding to the appendices lists of professional journals for locating measurement articles and a list of sources for locating objective-item banks for customized testing with a computer. In addition, during revision, boxed material (e.g., Checklist for Reviewing Test Specifications, Steps to Prevent Cheating, Guidelines for Effective Grading) was added to some chapters to highlight important points. The suggested readings at the end of each chapter and the list of published tests in Appendix D were also updated.

As with earlier editions, the focus of the book is best described by a list of general learning outcomes that should result from its use:

1. An understanding of the role of measurement and evaluation in the instructional process.

2. The ability to identify and state instructional objectives as intended learning outcomes.

3. An understanding of the concepts of validity and reliability and their role in the construction, selection, interpretation, and use of tests and other evaluation instruments.

4. The ability to construct classroom tests that measure a variety of intended learning outcomes (from simple to complex).

5. The ability to select the published tests that are most appropriate for a particular situation.

6. The ability to administer tests properly and to use test results effectively (with due regard for the necessary precautions).

7. The ability to interpret test scores (with full awareness of their meaning and the ever-present error of measurement).

8. The ability to construct, select, and use nontest evaluation instruments.

9. An understanding of both the *potentialities* and the *limitations* of the various tests and other evaluation procedures used in the school.

10. An understanding of how tests and other evaluation procedures can contribute to an effective marking and reporting system and to improved educational decisions.

11. An understanding of the educational accountability movement and the role of testing in educational reform.

12. An understanding of current trends and issues in educational measurement.

These understandings and abilities are most likely to be attained when reading of the book is supplemented by other experiences. In the *Student Exercise Manual*, available for use with this book, each chapter contains ten specific learning outcomes and numerous related test items and problems that are intended to help you understand and apply measurement concepts. In addition, or instead, textbook reading can be accompanied by practical projects in test construction, test selection, and test interpretation and the like. In any event, practical application of the material will enhance learning and contribute to competence in using measurement skills.

Our special thanks to the individuals who reviewed the fifth edition of the book and made many valuable suggestions and to the publishers who generously permitted use of their copyrighted materials. We are also grateful for the patience and support of our wives and for the valuable help of the Macmillan editorial staff.

N.E.G.
R.L.L.

Contents

Contents

PART 2

Constructing Classroom Tests

PART 4

Evaluating Procedures, Products, and Typical Behavior

Chapter 15

Evaluating Learning and Development: Observational Techniques

Chapter 16

Evaluating Learning and Development: Peer Appraisal and Self-Report

PART 5

Test Uses and Concerns

Chapter 17

Marking and Reporting

Appendices

Part 1

The Measurement and Evaluation Process

Chapter 1

The Role of Measurement and Evaluation in Teaching

Evaluation of pupil learning requires the use of a number of techniques for measuring pupil achievement. . . . However, evaluation is not merely a collection of techniques—it is a process, a systematic process that plays a significant role in effective teaching. . . . It begins with the identification of the intended learning outcomes and ends with a judgment concerning the extent to which the learning outcomes have been attained.

Informal classroom observation guides many instructional decisions. For example, oral questioning of pupils may indicate the need for a complete review of the material; class discussion may reveal misunderstandings that must be corrected on the spot; and the pupils' obvious interest in a topic may suggest that more time should be spent on it than originally planned. Similarly, in observing individual pupils, a teacher decides that Bill needs help in writing a complete paragraph, that Mary needs more practice in doing math problems, and that George and Betty should be given remedial work in reading. Instructional decisions such as these are repeated innumerably during the process of teaching. Some are based on pupils' oral responses, some on their actual performance of a skill, while still others may be based on a pupil's quizzical look, tone of voice, or physical behavior. In any event, they are all based on the teachers' moment-by-moment observations. Although

3

these observations are informal and unsystematic, they play an indispensable role in effective teaching.

Tests and other procedures for measuring pupil learning are not intended as replacements for teachers' informal observations and judgments. Rather, they are intended to complement and supplement the teachers' informal methods of obtaining information about pupils. The teacher is still the observer and decision maker. Measurement and evaluation procedures merely provide more *comprehensive, systematic,* and *objective* evidence on which to base instructional decisions.

Instructional Decisions Requiring Measurement Data

Numerous decisions are made by teachers that require them to supplement their informal observations of pupils with more systematic measures of aptitudes, achievement, and personal development. Although it would be infeasible to make an exhaustive list of all such decisions, it is possible to identify some of the more common ones. The following list of questions illustrates some of the major instructional decisions teachers are likely to encounter during the course of their teaching. Examples of the types of measurement and evaluation procedures that might be most helpful in answering the questions are included in parentheses.

1. How realistic are my teaching plans for this particular group of pupils? (Scholastic aptitude tests, past record of achievement.)

2. How should the pupils be grouped for more effective learning? (Scholastic aptitude and achievement tests, past record of achievement.)

3. To what extent are the pupils ready for the next learning experience? (Readiness tests, pretests over needed skills, past record of achievement.)

4. To what extent are pupils attaining the minimum essentials of the course? (Mastery tests, class projects, observation.)

5. To what extent are pupils progressing beyond the minimum essentials? (Periodic quizzes, general achievement tests, observation.)

6. At what point would a review be most beneficial? (Periodic quizzes, observation.)

7. What types of learning difficulties are the pupils encountering? (Diagnostic tests, observation, pupil conferences.)

8. Which pupils are underachievers? (Scholastic aptitude tests, achievement tests.)

9. Which pupils should be referred to counseling, special classes, or remedial programs? (Scholastic aptitude tests, achievement tests, diagnostic tests, observation.)

10. Which pupils have poor self-understanding? (Self-ratings, pupil conferences.)

11. Which school mark should be assigned to each pupil? (Review of all evaluation data.)

12. How effective was my teaching? (Achievement tests, pupils' ratings, supervisors' ratings.)

This list of questions highlights the need for various types of information in teaching, but instructional decisions are not that neatly ordered. Within any decision area there are numerous subquestions to be answered, an overlap among the various areas, and many different types of measurement and evaluation data that might be useful in a particular situation. Thus, the teaching–learning process involves a continuous and interrelated series of instructional decisions concerning ways to enhance pupil learning. Our main point here, however, is that the effectiveness of the instruction depends to a large extent on the nature and quality of the information on which the decisions are based.

Test, Measurement, and Evaluation

The terms *test*, *measurement*, and *evaluation* are easily confused because all may be involved in a single process. If we ask students to answer a series of questions concerning science, obtain their scores by counting the number of correct answers, and conclude that the students are making good learning progress, we are concerned with all three concepts. The test is the set of questions, measurement is the assigning of numbers to the test results according to a specific rule (counting correct answers), and evaluation adds the value judgment (*good* learning progress). The specific meaning of each term, as applied to classroom evaluation, is summarized in the box.

Some Basic Terminology

Test	An instrument or systematic procedure for measuring a sample of behavior. (Answers the question "How well does the individual perform —either in comparison with others or in comparison with a domain of performance tasks?")
Measurement	The process of obtaining a numerical description of the degree to which an individual possesses a particular characteristic. (Answers the question "How much?")
Evaluation (classroom)	The systematic process of collecting, analyzing, and interpreting information to determine the extent to which pupils are achieving instructional objectives. (Answers the question "How good?")

Evaluation is a much more comprehensive and inclusive term than *measurement*, and *testing* is just one type of measurement. The term *measurement* is limited to quantitative descriptions of pupils; that is, the results of measurement are always expressed in numbers (e.g., Mary correctly solved 35 of the 40 arithmetic problems). It does not include qualitative descriptions (e.g., Mary's work was neat) nor does it imply judgments concerning the worth or value of the obtained results. Evaluation, on the other hand, may include both quantitative descriptions (measurement) and qualitative descriptions (nonmeasurement) of pupils. In addition, evaluation always includes *value judgments* concerning the desirability of the results. The diagram in Figure 1.1 shows the comprehensive nature of evaluation and the role of measurement techniques and nonmeasurement techniques in the evaluation process. As noted in the diagram, evaluation may or may not be based on measurement, and when it is, it goes beyond the simple quantitative descriptions.

General Principles of Evaluation

As you study the wide array of evaluation procedures used in schools, it is easy to view evaluation as simply a collection of techniques. Instead, evaluation should be seen as an integrated *process* for determining the nature and extent of pupil learning and development. This process will be most effective when the following principles are taken into consideration.

1. Clearly specifying what is to be evaluated has priority in the evaluation process. The effectiveness of evaluation depends as much on a careful description of *what to evaluate* as it does on the technical qualities of the evaluation instruments used. Thus, specification of the characteristics to be measured should precede the

FIGURE 1.1
The role of evaluation techniques and value judgments in evaluation.

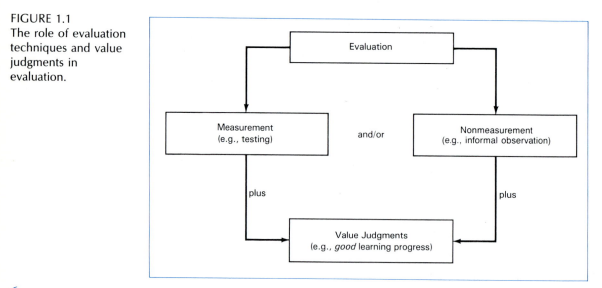

selection or development of evaluation devices. When evaluating pupil learning, this means clearly specifying the intended learning outcomes before selecting the achievement measures to use.

2. An evaluation technique should be selected in terms of its relevance to the characteristics or performance to be measured. Evaluation techniques are frequently selected on the basis of their objectivity, accuracy, or convenience. Although these criteria are important, they are secondary to the main criterion — is this technique the most effective method for measuring the learning or development to be evaluated? Each technique is appropriate for some uses and inappropriate for others. In testing pupil achievement, for example, we need a close match between the intended learning outcomes and the types of test items used.

3. Comprehensive evaluation requires a variety of evaluation techniques. No single type of instrument or procedure can assess the vast array of learning and development outcomes emphasized in a school program. Objective tests of achievement are useful for measuring knowledge, understanding, and application outcomes, but essay tests and other written projects are needed to measure the ability to organize and express ideas. Observational techniques are needed to assess performance skills and various aspects of pupil behavior. And self-report techniques are useful for evaluating interests and attitudes. A complete picture of pupil achievement and development requires combining the results of many different techniques.

4. Proper use of evaluation techniques requires an awareness of their limitations. Evaluation techniques range from very highly developed measuring instruments (e.g., standardized aptitude and achievement tests) to rather crude assessment devices (e.g., observational and self-report techniques). Even our best educational and psychological measuring instruments, however, yield results that are subject to various types of measurement error.

Sampling error is a common problem in educational and psychological measurement. An achievement test may not adequately sample a particular domain of instructional content. An observational measure designed to assess a pupil's *social adjustment* may not sample enough behavior for a dependable index of this trait. Fortunately, sampling error is one kind of error that can be controlled through careful application of established measurement procedures.

A second source of error is caused by chance factors influencing test scores, such as guessing on objective tests, subjective scoring on essay tests, errors in judgment on observation devices, and inconsistent responding on self-report instruments (e.g., attitude scales). Because of these problems, pupils just a few points apart on an educational test should not be considered to be different. In fact, no score on an educational or psychological measure should be treated as a totally accurate measurement of the trait in question. Through the careful use of evaluation techniques, however, we are able to keep these errors of measurement to a minimum.

The incorrect interpretation of measurement results constitutes another major source of error. Test users sometimes interpret test results as more precise than they are (ignoring measurement error) or as an indication of characteristics beyond those the test is designed to measure. For instance, scholastic aptitude scores are sometimes interpreted as measures of innate abilities rather than modifiable abilities or as a measure of general personal worth rather than as a limited measure of verbal and numerical reasoning. Misinterpretation of test results is all too common, but it can be controlled by careful attention to what the test actually measures and how accurately it does so.

This brief introduction to some of the limitations of evaluation techniques should not be viewed as support for the position held by those who are overly skeptical of tests and other evaluation procedures. A healthy awareness of the limitations of evaluation instruments makes it possible to use them more effectively. As a guiding principle it is helpful to keep in mind that the cruder the instrument the greater its limitations and, consequently, the more caution required in its use.

5. Evaluation is a means to an end, not an end in itself. The use of evaluation techniques implies that some useful purpose will be served and that the user is clearly aware of this purpose. To blindly gather data about pupils and then file the information away in the hope that it will some day prove useful is a waste of both time and effort. Evaluation is best viewed as a process of obtaining information on which to base decisions.

Evaluation and the Instructional Process

Broadly conceived, the main purpose of classroom instruction is to help pupils achieve a set of intended learning outcomes. These outcomes should typically include all desired changes in the intellectual, emotional, and physical spheres. When classroom instruction is viewed in this light, evaluation becomes an integral part of the teaching–learning process. The "intended learning outcomes" are established by the instructional objectives, the desired changes in pupils are brought about by the planned learning activities, and the pupils' learning progress is periodically evaluated by tests and other evaluation devices. While the interdependent nature of teaching and learning is beyond dispute, the interdependent nature of teaching, learning, *and* evaluation is less often recognized. The interdependence of these three facets of education can be clearly seen, however, in the following steps included in the instructional process.

Preparing Instructional Objectives

The first step in both teaching and evaluation is that of determining the learning outcomes to be expected from classroom instruction. What should pupils be like at the end of the learning experience? In other words, what kinds of learning product is being sought? What knowledge and understanding should the pupils possess? What skills should they be able to display? What interests and attitudes should they have developed? What changes in habits of thinking, feeling, and doing should have taken place? In short, what specific changes are we striving for, and what are pupils like when we have succeeded in bringing about these changes?

Only by identifying instructional objectives and stating them clearly in terms of intended learning outcomes can we provide direction to the teaching process and set the stage for ready evaluation of pupil learning. This step is so vital to classroom evaluation that the next chapter is entirely devoted to the process of stating instructional objectives in terms of pupil learning.

Preassessing the Learners' Needs

When the instructional objectives have been clearly specified, it is usually desirable to make some assessment of the learners' needs in relation to the learning outcomes to be achieved. Do the pupils possess the abilities and skills needed to proceed with the instruction? Have the pupils already mastered some of the intended learning outcomes? Evaluating pupils' knowledge and skill at the beginning of instruction enables us to answer such questions. This information is useful in planning remedial work for pupils who lack the prerequisite skills, in revising our list of instructional objectives, and in modifying our instructional plans to fit the needs of the learners.

Providing Relevant Instruction

Relevant instruction is the point where course content and teaching methods are integrated into planned instructional activities designed to help pupils achieve the intended learning outcomes. During this instructional phase, testing and evaluation provide a means of monitoring learning progress and diagnosing learning difficulties. Thus, periodic evaluation during instruction provides a type of feedback-corrective procedure that aids in continuously adapting instruction to group and individual needs.

Evaluating the Intended Learning Outcomes

The final step in the instructional process is to determine the extent to which the instructional objectives were achieved by the pupils. This is accomplished by using tests and other evaluation instruments that are specifically designed to measure the intended learning outcomes. Ideally, the instructional objectives will clearly specify the desired changes in pupils and the evaluation instruments will provide a relevant measure or description of the extent to which those changes have taken place. Matching tests and other evaluation instruments to the intended learning outcomes is basic to effective classroom evaluation and will receive considerable attention in later chapters.

Using the Results

Pupil evaluation is often regarded as being essentially for the benefit of teachers and administrators. This attitude overlooks the direct contribution evaluation can make to pupils. Properly used evaluation procedures can contribute directly to improved pupil learning by (1) clarifying the nature of the intended learning outcomes, (2) providing short-term goals to work toward, (3) providing feedback concerning learning progress, and (4) providing information for overcoming learning difficulties and for selecting future learning experiences. Although these purposes are probably best served by the periodic evaluation during instruction, the final evaluation of intended outcomes also should contribute to these ends.

Information from carefully developed tests and other evaluation techniques also can be used to improve instruction. Such information can aid in judging (1) the appropriateness and attainability of the instructional objectives, (2) the usefulness of the instructional materials, and (3) the effectiveness of the instructional methods. Thus, evaluation procedures can contribute to improvements in the teaching–learning process itself, as well as contributing directly to improved pupil learning.

Evaluation results are, of course, also used for assigning marks and reporting pupil progress to parents. The systematic use of tests and other evaluation procedures provides an objective and comprehensive basis for reporting on each pupil's learning progress. In addition to marking and reporting, evaluation results also are used in the school for various administrative and guidance functions. They are useful in curriculum development, in aiding pupils with educational and vocational decisions, and in evaluating the effectiveness of the school program. The simplified instructional model shown in Figure 1.2 summarizes the basic steps in the instruc-

FIGURE 1.2
Simplified instructional model.

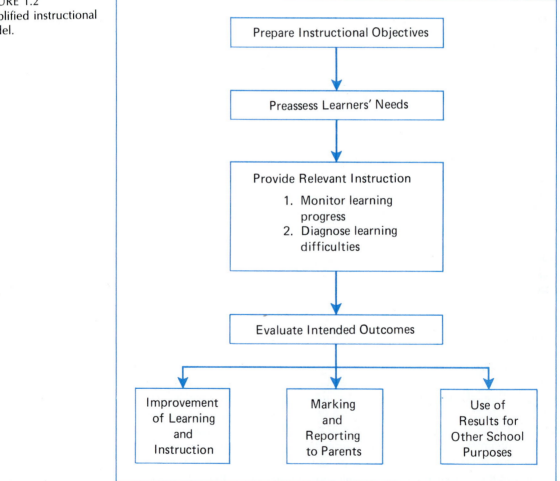

tional process and illustrates the interrelated nature of teaching, learning, and evaluation.

Types of Testing and Evaluation Procedures

One of the distinctive features of the evaluation process is the use of a wide variety of procedures. These may be classified and described in many different ways, depending on the frame of reference used. Here we shall present those bases for classification that are most useful for understanding and using evaluation techniques in teaching. Although the categories are not discrete, they provide a good general overview of evaluation procedures and a useful introduction to some of the basic terminology in the area. The specific techniques used in classroom evaluation will be described and illustrated in later chapters.

Maximum Performance versus Typical Performance

Tests and other evaluation procedures may be placed in two broad categories on the basis of the nature of the measurement. These have been labeled by Cronbach as measures of *maximum* performance and measures of *typical* performance.[1] In the first category are those procedures used to determine a person's *abilities*. Procedures of this type are concerned with how well an individual performs when he is motivated to obtain as high a score as possible. In short, the evaluation results indicate what an individual *can* do when he puts forth his best effort. *Aptitude* and *achievement* tests are included in this category. A distinction between these two types of tests is commonly made in terms of the use of the results rather than of the qualities of the tests themselves. An aptitude test is primarily designed to predict success in some *future learning activity*, while an achievement test is designed to indicate degree of success in some *past learning activity*. Since some tests may be used for both purposes, however, it is obvious that the difference is mainly a matter of emphasis. For example, an algebra test designed to measure achievement at the end of the course also may be used to predict success in future mathematics courses. Such overlapping of function prevents a distinct classification, but the terms *aptitude* and *achievement* provide useful designations for discussions of measures of ability.

The second category in this classification of procedures includes those designed to reflect a person's *typical behavior*. Procedures of this type are concerned with what individuals *will* do rather than what they can do. Methods designed to evaluate *interests, attitudes, adjustment,* and various *personality traits* are included in this category. Here the emphasis is on obtaining representative responses rather than high scores. Although this is an extremely important area in which to appraise pupils, evaluations of typical behavior are fraught with difficulties. Inadequacy of testing instruments in this field has led to wide use of interviews, questionnaires, anecdotal records, ratings, and various other self-report and observational techniques. None of these techniques when used alone provides an adequate appraisal

[1]L. J. Cronbach, *Essentials of Psychological Testing*, 4th ed. (New York: Harper and Row, 1984).

of typical behavior, but the combined results of a number of them enable the teacher to make fairly accurate judgments concerning pupil progress and change in these areas.

Placement, Formative, Diagnostic, and Summative Evaluation

Tests and other evaluation procedures can also be classified in terms of their functional role in classroom instruction. One such classification system follows the sequence in which evaluation procedures are likely to be used in the classroom.[2] These categories classify the evaluation of pupil performance in the following manner:

1. *Placement* evaluation: To determine pupil performance at the beginning of instruction.
2. *Formative* evaluation: To monitor learning progress during instruction.
3. *Diagnostic* evaluation: To diagnose learning difficulties during instruction.
4. *Summative* evaluation: To evaluate achievement at the end of instruction.

The functions of each of these types of classroom evaluation typically require instruments specifically designed for the intended use.

Placement Evaluation. Placement evaluation is concerned with the pupil's entry performance and typically focuses on questions such as the following: (1) Does the pupil possess the knowledge and skills needed to begin the planned instruction? For example, does the beginning reader have the necessary reading readiness skills, or does the beginning algebra student have a sufficient command of computational skills? (2) To what extent has the pupil already mastered the objectives of the planned instruction? Sufficient mastery might indicate the desirability of skipping certain units or of being placed in a more advanced course. (3) To what extent do the pupil's interests, work habits, and personality characteristics indicate that one mode of instruction might be better than another (e.g., group instruction versus independent study). Answers to questions like these require the use of a variety of techniques: readiness tests, aptitude tests, pretests on course objectives, self-report inventories, observational techniques, and so on. The goal of placement evaluation is to determine the position in the instructional sequence and the mode of instruction that is most beneficial for each pupil.

Formative Evaluation. Formative evaluation is used to monitor learning progress during instruction. Its purpose is to provide continuous feedback to both pupil and teacher concerning learning successes and failures. Feedback to pupils provides reinforcement of successful learning and identifies the specific learning errors that are in need of correction. Feedback to the teacher provides information for modifying instruction and for prescribing group and individual remedial work. Formative evaluation depends heavily on specially prepared tests for each segment of instruc-

---

[2]P. W. Airasian and G. J. Madaus, "Functional Types of Student Evaluation," *Measurement and Evaluation in Guidance* 4 (1972):221–233.

tion (e.g., unit, chapter). These are usually mastery tests that provide direct measures of the intended learning outcomes of the segment. Prescriptions for alternative or remedial instruction can be keyed to each item in the test or to each set of items measuring a separate skill. Tests used for formative evaluation are most frequently teacher made, but customized tests made by publishers also can serve this function. Observational techniques are, of course, also useful in monitoring pupil progress and identifying learning errors. Since formative evaluation is directed toward improving learning and instruction, the results are typically *not* used for assigning course grades.

Diagnostic Evaluation.　Diagnostic evaluation is a highly specialized procedure. It is concerned with the persistent or recurring learning difficulties that are left unresolved by the standard corrective prescriptions of formative evaluation. If a pupil continues to experience failure in reading, mathematics, or other subjects, despite the use of prescribed alternate methods of instruction (e.g., programmed materials, visual aids), then a more detailed diagnosis is indicated. To use a medical analogy, formative evaluation provides first aid treatment for simple learning problems and diagnostic evaluation searches for the underlying causes of those problems that do not respond to first aid treatment. Thus, diagnostic evaluation is much more comprehensive and detailed. It involves the use of specially prepared diagnostic tests as well as various observational techniques. Serious learning problems also are likely to require the services of remedial, psychological, and medical specialists. The main aim of diagnostic evaluation is to determine the causes of persistent learning problems and to formulate a plan for remedial action.

Summative Evaluation.　Summative evaluation typically comes at the end of a course (or unit) of instruction. It is designed to determine the extent to which the instructional objectives have been achieved and is used primarily for assigning course grades or for certifying pupil mastery of the intended learning outcomes. The techniques used in summative evaluation are determined by the instructional objectives, but they typically include teacher-made achievement tests, ratings on various types of performance (e.g., laboratory, oral report), and evaluations of products (e.g., themes, drawings, research reports). Although the main purpose of summative evaluation is grading, or the certification of pupil achievement, it also provides information for judging the appropriateness of the course objectives and the effectiveness of the instruction.

Norm-Referenced and Criterion-Referenced Measurement

How the results of tests and other evaluation procedures are interpreted also provides a method of classifying these instruments. There are two basic ways of interpreting pupil performance. One is to describe the performance in terms of the *relative position held in some known group* (e.g., typed better than 90 percent of the class members). The other is directly to *describe the specific performance* that was demonstrated (e.g., typed 40 words per minute without error). The first type of interpretation is called *norm referenced*; the second, *criterion referenced*. When interpretations are each confined to the attainment of a specific objective (e.g., capitalized all proper nouns) they are sometimes called *objective referenced*. This is a criterion-referenced type of interpretation but does not cover as broad a domain of tasks as that typically used in criterion referencing. These three concepts are defined more specifically in the accompanying box.

Some Basic Terminology

Norm-Referenced Test	A test designed to provide a measure of performance that is interpretable in terms of an individual's *relative standing in some known group*.
Criterion-Referenced Test	A test designed to provide a measure of performance that is interpretable in terms of a *clearly defined and delimited domain of learning tasks*.
Objective-Referenced Test	A test designed to provide a measure of performance that is interpretable in terms of a *specific instructional objective*. (Many objective-referenced tests are called criterion-referenced tests by their developers.)

Other terms that are less often used but have meanings similar to criterion referenced: *content referenced, domain referenced,* and *universe referenced.*

Norm-referenced interpretations might be based on a local, state, or national group, depending on the use to be made of the results. Using national norms, for example, we might describe a pupil's performance on a vocabulary test as equaling or exceeding that of 76 percent of a national sample of sixth-graders. Criterion-referenced interpretations can be made in various ways. For example, we can (1) describe the specific learning tasks a pupil is able to perform (e.g., counts from 1 to 100), (2) indicate the percentage of tasks a pupil performs correctly (e.g., spells 65 percent of the words in the word list), or (3) compare the test performance to a set standard[3] and make a mastery-nonmastery decision (e.g., answers correctly *at least* 80 percent of the items measuring "Identification of the main idea in paragraphs").

Although the term *percent* was used in illustrating both types of interpretation, it was used in a distinctly different manner in each. The norm-referenced interpretation indicated the pupil's *relative standing* in a norm group by noting that percent of the pupils in the group who obtained the same score or one lower (called a *percentile* score). The criterion-referenced interpretation focused on the percentage

---

[3]Although a *standard of mastery* can be used in making one type of criterion-referenced interpretation, it is not an essential element of criterion-referenced testing, as illustrated in the first two examples.

of items answered correctly (called a *percentage-correct* score). Although many types of scores are used in testing, the distinction between the percentile score and the percentage-correct score is a significant one because it *illustrates* the basic difference between a norm-referenced interpretation and a criterion-referenced interpretation.

Strictly speaking, norm reference and criterion reference refer only to the method of interpreting the results. These distinct types of interpretation are likely to be most meaningful and useful, however, when tests (and other evaluation instruments) are specifically designed for the type of interpretation to be made. Thus, it is legitimate to use the terms *criterion referenced* and *norm referenced* as broad categories for classifying tests and other evaluation techniques.

Tests that are specifically built to *maximize* each type of interpretation have much in common and it would be impossible to tell which type of test it was from examining the test itself (see box). It is in the construction and use of the tests where the differences can be noted. A key feature in constructing norm-referenced tests is the selection of items of average difficulty and the elimination of items that all pupils are likely to answer correctly. This procedure provides a wide spread of scores so that *discrimination* among pupils at various levels of achievement can be more dependably made. This is useful for decisions based on relative achievement, such as selection, grouping, and relative grading. In contrast, a key feature in constructing criterion-referenced tests is the selection of items that are directly relevant to the learning outcomes to be measured, without regard to the power of items to discriminate among pupils. If the learning tasks are easy, that test items will be easy. No attempt is made to eliminate easy items or alter their difficulty. Here the main purpose is to obtain a *description* of the specific knowledge and skills each pupil can demonstrate. This information is useful for planning both group and individual instruction.

These two types of tests are best viewed as the ends of a continuum, rather than a clear-cut dichotomy. As shown in the following continuum, the criterion-referenced test, at one end, emphasizes *description* of performance and the norm-referenced test, at the other end, emphasizes *discrimination* among individuals. In an attempt to capitalize on the best features of each, many test publishers have attempted to make their norm-referenced tests more descriptive and, thus, to provide for both norm-referenced and criterion-referenced interpretations. Similarly, test publishers have added norm-referenced interpretations to tests that were built specifically for criterion-referenced interpretation. The use of dual interpretation with published tests seems to be an increasing trend that will move many tests more toward the center of the continuum. Although this involves some compromises in test construction and some cautions in test interpretation, the added information may contribute to more effective test use.

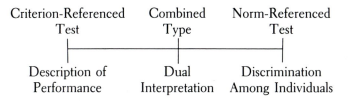

Criterion-Referenced Test	Combined Type	Norm-Referenced Test
Description of Performance	Dual Interpretation	Discrimination Among Individuals

Comparison of Norm-Referenced Tests (NRTs) and Criterion-Referenced Tests (CRTs)*

Common Characteristics of NRTs and CRTs

1. Both require specification of the achievement domain to be measured.
2. Both require a relevant and representative sample of test items.
3. Both use the same types of test items.
4. Both use the same rules for item writing (except for item difficulty).
5. Both are judged by the same qualities of goodness (validity and reliability).
6. Both are useful in educational measurement.

Differences Between NRTs and CRTs (but it is only a matter of emphasis)

1. NRT — Typically covers a *large* domain of learning tasks, with just a few items measuring each specific task.
   CRT — Typically focuses on a *delimited* domain of learning tasks, with a relatively large number of items measuring each specific task.
2. NRT — Emphasizes *discrimination* among individuals in terms of relative level of learning.
   CRT — Emphasizes *description* of what learning tasks individuals can and cannot perform.
3. NRT — Favors items of average difficulty and typically omits easy items.
   CRT — Matches item difficulty to learning tasks, without altering item difficulty or omitting easy items.
4. NRT — Used primarily (but not exclusively) for *survey* testing.
   CRT — Used primarily (but not exclusively) for *mastery* testing.
5. NRT — Interpretation requires a clearly defined group.
   CRT — Interpretation requires a clearly defined and delimited achievement domain.

*When each is built to maximize its type of interpretation.

Both criterion-referenced and norm-referenced measurement are useful in classroom testing. Tests used during instruction (formative tests), typically favor criterion-referenced measurement because of its *descriptive* nature. Each test can be designed to measure such a limited domain of learning tasks that a large number of test items can be included for each task. This makes it possible to use the results to describe specifically what each pupil has learned and what types of learning errors need to be corrected. Tests used at the end of instruction (summative tests), however, typically emphasize norm-referenced interpretations. Such a broad range of learning outcomes is usually covered by the test that just a few items can be included for each outcome. These few items in each area can serve as *indicators* of achievement, and thus help determine each pupil's level of performance, but they provide inadequate *descriptions* of what has been learned specifically.

Summary of Evaluation Categories

A summary of the basic ways of describing classroom tests and other evaluation procedures is presented in Table 1.1. Further discussion of these evaluation categories will be encountered in later chapters.

Other Descriptive Terms

Some of the other terms that are frequently used in describing tests are presented here as contrasting test types but some are simply the ends of a continuum (e.g., speed versus power tests).

Informal versus Standardized Tests.   Informal tests are those constructed by classroom teachers, whereas those designed by test specialists and administered, scored, and interpreted under *standard* conditions are called *standardized tests*.

Individual versus Group Tests.   Some tests are administered on a one-to-one basis using careful oral questioning (e.g., individual intelligence test), whereas others can be administered to a group of individuals.

Mastery versus Survey Tests.   Some achievement tests measure the degree of mastery of a limited set of specific learning outcomes, whereas others measure a pupil's general level of achievement over a broad range of outcomes. Mastery tests typically use criterion-referenced interpretations and survey tests tend to emphasize norm-referenced interpretations, but some criterion-referenced interpretations also are possible with carefully prepared survey tests.

TABLE 1.1
Basic Ways of
Describing Classroom
Evaluation Procedures

Basis for Classification	Type of Evaluation	Function of the Evaluation	Illustrative Instruments
	Maximum performance	Determines what individuals' *can do* when performing at their best.	Aptitude tests, achievement tests
Nature of Measurement	Typical performance	Determines what individuals' *will do* under natural conditions.	Attitude, interest, and personality inventories; observational techniques; peer appraisal
	Placement	Determines prerequisite skills, degree of mastery of course objectives, and/or best mode of learning.	Readiness tests, aptitude tests, pretests on course objectives, self-report inventories, observational techniques
Use in Classroom Instruction	Formative	Determines learning progress, provides feedback to reinforce learning, and corrects learning errors.	Teacher-made mastery tests, custom-made tests from test publishers, observational techniques
	Diagnostic	Determines causes (intellectual, physical, emotional, environmental) of persistent learning difficulties.	Published diagnostic tests, teacher-made diagnostic tests, observational techniques
	Summative	Determines end-of-course achievement for assigning grades or certifying mastery of objectives.	Teacher-made survey tests, performance rating scales, product scales
Method of Interpreting Results	Criterion referenced	Describes pupil performance according to a specified domain of clearly defined learning tasks (e.g., adds single-digit whole numbers).	Teacher-made mastery tests, custom-made tests from test publishers, observational techniques
	Norm referenced	Describes pupil performance according to relative position in some known group (e.g., ranks tenth in a classroom group of 30).	Standardized aptitude and achievement tests, teacher-made survey tests, interest inventories, adjustment inventories

Supply versus Selection Tests.   Some tests require examinees to supply the answer (e.g., essay test), whereas others require them to select the correct response from a given set of alternatives (e.g., multiple-choice test).

Speed versus Power Tests.   A speed test is designed to measure the number of items an individual can complete in a given time, whereas a power test is designed to measure level of performance under ample time conditions. Power tests usually have the items arranged in order of increasing difficulty.

Objective versus Subjective Tests.   An objective test is one on which equally competent scorers will obtain the same scores (e.g., multiple-choice test), whereas a subjective test is one where the scores are influenced by the opinion or judgment of the person doing the scoring (e.g., essay test).

Verbal versus Performance Tests.   Some tests require examinees to make only verbal responses (e.g., vocabulary test), whereas others require some type of motor or manual response (e.g., typing, solving a maze).

Summary

Measurement and evaluation play an important role in the instructional program of the school. Basically, they provide information that can be used in a variety of educational decisions. The main emphasis in classroom evaluation, however, is on decisions concerning pupil learning and development.

From an instructional standpoint, evaluation may be defined as a systematic process of determining the extent to which instructional objectives (i.e., intended learning outcomes) are achieved by pupils. The evaluation process includes both measurement procedures (e.g., tests) and nonmeasurement procedures (e.g., informal observation) for describing changes in pupil performance as well as value judgments concerning the desirability of the changes.

The process of evaluation is likely to be most effective when guided by a set of general principles. These principles emphasize the importance of (1) clearly specifying what is to be evaluated, (2) selecting evaluation techniques in terms of their relevance, (3) using a variety of evaluation techniques, (4) being aware of their limitations, and (5) regarding evaluation as a means to an end, and not an end in itself.

The interrelated nature of teaching, learning, and evaluation can be seen in the following sequential steps in the instructional process: (1) preparing instructional objectives, (2) preassessing learners' needs, (3) providing relevant instruction (monitoring learning progress and diagnosing difficulties), (4) evaluating the intended learning outcomes, and (5) using the evaluation results to improve learning and instruction. In addition to the direct contribution testing and evaluation make to classroom instruction, they also play an important role in marking and reporting, curriculum development, educational and vocational guidance, and evaluating the effectiveness of the school program.

The vast array of evaluation procedures used in the school can be classified and described in many different ways. The following are especially useful designations for describing the various procedures:

NATURE OF THE MEASUREMENT

1. Maximum performance (what a person *can* do).
2. Typical performance (what a person *will* do).

USE IN CLASSROOM INSTRUCTION

1. Placement evaluation (measures entry behavior).
2. Formative evaluation (monitors learning progress).
3. Diagnostic evaluation (identifies causes of learning problems).
4. Summative evaluation (measures end-of-course achievement).

METHOD OF INTERPRETING THE RESULTS

1. Norm referenced (describes pupil performance in terms of the relative position held in some known group).
2. Criterion referenced (describes pupil performance in terms of a clearly defined and delimited domain of learning tasks).

Other terms used to describe tests and other evaluation instruments include the following contrasting types:

- Informal and standardized
- Individual and group
- Mastery and survey
- Supply and selection
- Speed and power
- Objective and subjective
- Verbal and performance

Learning Exercises

1. List several instructional decisions that can be improved by the use of tests.
2. Describe the meaning of the following terms: *test, measurement, evaluation*.
3. Why is it necessary to specify what is to be evaluated before selecting or constructing an evaluation instrument?

4. How should instructional objectives be stated if they are to be most useful in evaluating pupil learning?

5. Give an example of a measure of *maximum performance* and a measure of *typical performance*. Of what value is this distinction in testing?

6. Classify each of the following by indicating whether it refers to *placement* evaluation, *formative* evaluation, *diagnostic* evaluation, or *summative* evaluation.

    a. An end-of-course test used to assign grades.

    b. A test of arithmetic skills on the first day of algebra.

    c. A test in science used to evaluate learning progress.

    d. A device for observing and recording reading errors.

7. List the similarities and differences between criterion-referenced measurement and norm-referenced measurement. For what purposes is each most useful?

8. Which of the following represents a *criterion-referenced* interpretation and which a *norm-referenced* interpretation?

    a. Mary's reading score placed her near the bottom of the class.

    b. John defined 90 percent of the science terms correctly.

    c. Bill can identify all of the parts of a sentence.

    d. Betty surpassed 85 percent of the sixth-graders on the arithmetic test.

9. How would you distinguish between each of the following?

    a. Informal test and standardized test.

    b. Individual test and group test.

    c. Mastery test and survey test.

    d. Supply test and selection test.

    e. Speed test and power test.

    f. Objective test and subjective test.

    g. Verbal test and performance test.

10. From your past school experiences, list some examples of inadequate or inappropriate use of tests or other evaluation instruments. For each example, describe how the action or situation should have been handled.

Suggestions for Further Reading

BLOOM, B. S.; MADAUS, G. J.; AND HASTINGS, J. T. *Evaluation to Improve Learning*. New York: McGraw-Hill, 1981. Chapter 4, "Summative Evaluation," Chapter 5, "Diagnostic Evaluation," and Chapter 6, "Formative Evaluation" provide a comprehensive treatment of these evaluation types.

CRONBACH, L. J. *Essentials of Psychological Testing*, 4th ed. New York: Harper & Row, 1984. Chapter 2, "Varieties of Tests and Test Interpretations," describes tests of maximum performance and typical performance, computer use in testing, and the features of psychometric and impressionistic testing.

NITKO, A. J. "Defining 'Criterion-Referenced Test.'" In R. A. Berk, ed. *A Guide to Criterion-Referenced Test Construction*. Baltimore: Johns Hopkins University Press, 1984, Chapter 1. A comprehensive review of the various meanings of criterion referencing.

PAYNE, D. A. "Measurement in Education." *Encyclopedia of Educational Research*, 5th ed.

New York: Macmillan, 1982, vol. 3, pp. 1182–1190. Provides a historical overview of educational measurement, describes sources of information about educational measurement, and discusses such current issues as test bias, minimum competency testing, testing the disadvantaged, and legal issues.

TEST BULLETIN

MITCHELL, B. C. "A Glossary of 100 Measurement Terms." *Test Service Notebook*, No. 13. New York: The Psychological Corporation. (This glossary has been reprinted in the *Student Exercise Manual* that has been prepared for use with this edition of your textbook.)

Chapter 2

Preparing Instructional Objectives

What types of learning outcomes do you expect from your teaching — knowledge — understandings — applications — thinking skills — performance skills — attitudes? . . . Clearly, defining the desired learning outcomes is the first step in good teaching — it is also essential in the evaluation of pupil learning. . . . Sound evaluation requires relating the evaluation procedures as directly as possible to the intended learning outcomes.

Instructional objectives play a key role in the instructional process. When properly stated, they serve as guides for both teaching and learning, communicate the intent of the instruction to others, and provide guidelines for evaluating pupil learning. These major purposes are illustrated in the following figure.

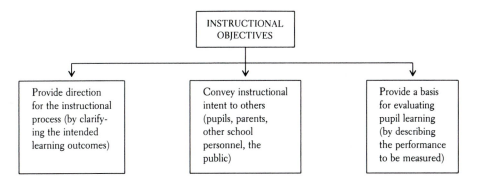

The methods and materials of instruction are likely to be most appropriate and effective if we have first decided what types of performance pupils are expected to demonstrate at the end of the instructional sequence (e.g., unit or course). Describing the intended learning outcomes in performance terms is the main function of properly stated instructional objectives. This clarification of what pupils should be learning and how the learning is to be expressed not only aids the teacher but also helps others understand the focus of the instruction. Our main interest in this book, of course, is in the usefulness of instructional objectives for evaluating pupil learning. As noted in the last chapter, effective evaluation depends as much on a clear description of *what* is to be evaluated as on a determination of *how* to evaluate. Thus, before we develop or select tests and other evaluation instruments to measure pupil learning, we need to clearly specify the intended learning outcomes. That is the main function of well-stated instructional objectives.

Some Basic Terminology

Educational Goal	General aim or purpose of education that is stated as a broad, long-range outcome to work toward. Goals are used primarily in policy making and general program planning (e.g., "Develop proficiency in the basic skills of reading, writing, and arithmetic").
General Instructional Objective	An intended outcome of instruction that has been stated in general enough terms to encompass a *set of specific learning outcomes* (e.g., "Comprehends the literal meaning of written material").
Specific Learning *Outcome*	An intended outcome of instruction that has been stated in terms of specific and observable *pupil performance* (e.g., "Identifies details that are explicitly stated in a passage"). A set of specific learning outcomes describes a sample of the types of performance that learners will be able to exhibit when they have achieved a general instructional objective (also called Specific Objectives, Performance Objectives, Behavioral Objectives, and Measurable Objectives).
Pupil Performance	Any measurable or observable pupil response in the cognitive, affective, or psychomotor area that is a result of learning.

Instructional Objectives as Learning Outcomes[1]

In preparing instructional objectives, it is possible to focus on different aspects of instruction. Some teachers prefer to state the objectives in terms of what they are going to do during instruction. Thus, we might have a statement as follows:

- Demonstrate to pupils how to use the microscope.

Although this statement clearly indicates what the teaching activity is, it is less clear concerning the intended learning outcomes. Literally speaking, the objective has been achieved when the demonstration has been completed—whether or not the pupils have learned anything. A more desirable way to state objectives is in terms of what we expect pupils to be able to do at the end of instruction. After demonstrating how to use the microscope, for example, we might expect pupils to be able to do the following:

1. Identify the parts of the microscope.
2. List the steps to be followed in using the microscope.
3. Describe the precautions in adjusting the microscope.
4. Demonstrate skill in using the microscope.

Statements such as these direct attention to the pupils and to the types of performance they are expected to exhibit as a result of the instruction. Thus, our focus shifts from the teacher to the pupil and from the learning experiences to the learning outcomes. This shift in focus makes clear the intent of our instruction and sets the stage for evaluating pupil learning. Well-stated outcomes make clear the types of pupil performance we are willing to accept as evidence that the instruction has been successful.

When viewing instructional objectives in terms of learning outcomes, it is important to keep in mind that we are concerned with the *products* of learning rather than with the *process* of learning. The relation of instructional objectives (product) to learning experiences (process) is shown by the following diagram:

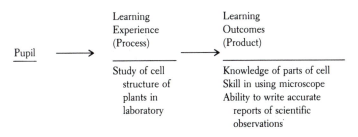

[1]Some of the material in this chapter was adapted from N. E. Gronlund, *Stating Objectives for Classroom Instruction*, 3d ed. (New York: Macmillan, 1985).

This diagram shows several points regarding the role of instructional objectives in teaching–learning situations. First, the objectives establish direction, and when they are stated in terms of learning outcomes, they go beyond knowledge of the specific course content. Note also the distinction between "study of" and "knowledge of" cell structures. The content (study of cell structure) is more aptly listed under process because it is the vehicle through which objectives (knowledge of parts of cell, and so on) are attained.

Second, consider the varying degrees of dependence that the products, "knowledge," "skill," and "ability" have on the course content. "Knowledge of parts of cell" is the most closely related, even though other specific content (i.e., cell structure of animals) could serve the same purpose equally well. In the case of "skill in using microscope" and "ability to write accurate reports of scientific observations," a still greater variety of course content could be used to achieve the same objectives. But this discussion should by no means be construed as an attempt to deemphasize the importance of course content. Course content is extremely important; however, it serves its most useful purpose when viewed as a means of obtaining instructional objectives rather than as an end in itself.

Another point illustrated by the diagram is the degree to which objectives vary in complexity. The first learning outcome, "knowledge of parts of cell," is specific, is easily attained, and can be measured directly by a paper-and-pencil test. The last learning outcome, "ability to write accurate reports of scientific observations," is rather general, cannot be attained completely in a single course, and can be evaluated only by subjective means.

Mastery versus Developmental Objectives[2]

Learning outcomes generally can be divided into those that should be mastered by all students and those that provide for maximum individual development. The mastery outcomes are typically concerned with the minimum essentials of a course —that is, with those learning tasks that must be mastered if the pupil is to be successful at the next level of instruction. The developmental outcomes are concerned with those objectives that never can be fully achieved. Here, we can expect varying degrees of pupil progress along a continuum of development. In arithmetic, for example, we might expect all pupils to demonstrate mastery of certain computational skills but anticipate considerable variation in the development of arithmetical reasoning ability. Similarly, in social studies we might require all pupils to master certain terms, concepts, and skills that are basic to further study in the area, but we would encourage each pupil to go as far as possible in developing application, interpretation, and critical thinking skills. Thus, the instructional emphasis with mastery objectives is to bring all pupils to a uniform level of performance on the minimum essentials of the course, whereas the emphasis with developmental

---

[2]The designations *mastery objectives* and *transfer objectives* also have been used.

objectives is to assist pupils to achieve their maximum development. Both emphases are important to classroom instruction, and this has implications for the specification and use of instructional objectives.

Mastery objectives are typically concerned with relatively simple knowledge and skill outcomes. This makes it possible to analyze each intended learning outcome in considerable detail and to describe the expected pupil performance in very specific terms. The objective to "add whole numbers," for example, might be further defined by a list of specific tasks such as the following:

Adds two single-digit numbers with sums of ten or less $(2 + 5)$.

Adds two single-digit numbers with sums greater than ten $(6 + 8)$.

Adds three single-digit numbers with sums of ten or less $(2 + 4 + 3)$.

Adds three single-digit numbers with sums greater than ten $(7 + 5 + 9)$.

Adds two two-digit numbers without carrying $(21 + 34)$.

Adds two two-digit numbers with simple carrying $(36 + 27)$.

Adds two two-digit numbers with carrying into nine $(57 + 48)$.

Adds two or more three-digit numbers with repeated carrying $(687 + 839)$.

Thus, with mastery objectives it is frequently possible to specify a large representative sample of the specific responses expected of the pupils at the end of instruction. This specification makes it possible to place the learning tasks in sequential order and to teach and test each specific task on a one-to-one basis, as follows:

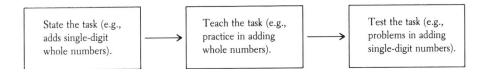

This procedure of stating specific tasks and then teaching and testing them on a one-to-one basis is used in individualized instruction, in training programs, and in those areas of classroom instruction that stress simple learning outcomes (e.g., basic skills). The limited nature of the objectives and the detailed specification of the learning tasks enhance the use of criterion-referenced interpretation.

Instructional objectives at the developmental level are typically concerned with the more complex learning outcomes (e.g., understanding, application, thinking skills). Thus, each general instructional objective tends to encompass many more specific learning outcomes than could possibly be listed for it. All we can reasonably expect to do in defining an objective at this level is to list *as representative a sample* of the specific outcomes as possible. An objective concerned with one aspect of reading comprehension, for example, might be defined by the following sample of specific learning outcomes:

1. Comprehends the literal meaning of written material.
    1.1. Identifies *details* that are explicitly stated in a passage.
    1.2. Identifies the *main thought* that is explicitly stated in a passage.
    1.3. Identifies the *order* in which events are described in a passage.
    1.4. Identifies *relationships* between persons or events that are explicitly stated in a passage.

Although other specific learning outcomes could be listed for this instructional objective, this sample of outcomes provides a fairly good notion of what pupils should be able to do to demonstrate "literal comprehension of written material." It is not expected, of course, that these specific learning outcomes will be taught and tested on a one-to-one basis, as is done with mastery objectives. Instead, a variety of teaching–learning experiences will need to be directed toward the development of literal comprehension skills and the testing will need to be done with various passages of written material that are new to the pupils. Thus, instruction at the developmental level emphasizes complex learning outcomes that result from the cumulative effect of many specific learning experiences and that are expected to *transfer* to a variety of situations.

Teaching at the developmental level must be directed toward the general instructional objective (e.g., literal comprehension) and the total class of responses that it represents, even though we have listed only a sample of them. The list of specific learning outcomes is mainly useful in clarifying the general objective and in providing guidelines for evaluating pupil learning. The role of objectives in teaching and testing at the developmental level can be illustrated as follows:

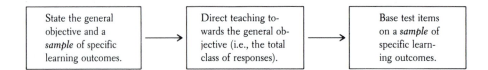

| State the general objective and a *sample* of specific learning outcomes. | Direct teaching towards the general objective (i.e., the total class of responses). | Base test items on a *sample* of specific learning outcomes. |

Because at this level continuous development rather than mastery is intended, norm-referenced interpretation (i.e., comparing the relative performance of pupils) is an appropriate means of describing pupil progress. Some descriptions of the types of learning tasks pupils can perform (criterion-referenced interpretations) are, of course, also useful at the developmental level, but the infinite number of possible outcomes makes such behavior descriptions rather sketchy, cumbersome, and difficult to interpret.

In summary, mastery objectives are typically concerned with simple learning tasks on which pupils are expected to demonstrate a uniformly high level of performance. These objectives tend to be limited enough in scope that all, or nearly all, intended outcomes can be specified for each objective. The learning tasks are typically taught and tested on a one-to-one basis, and criterion-referenced interpretation is especially useful for describing achievement. Developmental objectives are concerned with complex outcomes toward which pupils can be expected to show varying degrees of progress. Because these objectives emphasize high-order learning outcomes that stress the *transfer* of knowledge and skills to new situations, only a relatively few of the infinite number of possible learning outcomes can be specified for each objective. Pupil achievement at the developmental level depends on a variety of learning experiences and is typically tested with items containing some novelty (to measure transfer). Norm-referenced interpretations of pupil achievement are especially appropriate at this level but can be supplemented with some criterion-referenced descriptions of pupil performance.

Selection of Instructional Objectives

In identifying instructional objectives, it is easy to become confused by the seemingly endless array of learning outcomes that might be considered and by the lack of authoritative information concerning which objectives are most valuable for a given course or area of learning. There is no simple method for identifying and selecting instructional objectives, but a systematic approach reduces the confusion and ensures that important learning outcomes will not be overlooked.

Types of Learning Outcomes to Consider

Although the specific learning outcomes resulting from a course of study may run into the hundreds, most of them can be classified under a relatively small number of headings. Any such classification is necessarily arbitrary, but it serves several useful purposes. It indicates types of learning outcomes that should be considered; it provides a framework for classifying those outcomes; and it directs attention toward changes in pupil performance in a variety of areas.

The following list of types of outcomes delineates the major areas in which instructional objectives might be classified. The more specific areas under each type should not be regarded as exclusive; they are merely suggestive of categories to be considered.

1. Knowledge.
   1.1. Terminology.
   1.2. Specific facts.
   1.3. Concepts and principles.
   1.4. Methods and procedures.

2. Understanding.
   2.1. Concepts and principles.
   2.2. Methods and procedures.
   2.3. Written material, graphs, maps, and numerical data.
   2.4. Problem situations.

3. Application.
   3.1. Factual information.
   3.2. Concepts and principles.
   3.3. Methods and procedures.
   3.4. Problem-solving skills.

Begin with a Simple Framework

Starting with a simple framework (Knowledge, Understanding, Application) will help move from factual information to more complex learning outcomes, as illustrated in the following examples:

K = Knowledge
U = Understanding
A = Application

Reading

K — Knows vocabulary.
U — Reads with comprehension.
A — Reads a wide variety of printed materials.

Writing

K — Knows the mechanics of writing.
U — Understands grammatical principles in writing.
A — Writes complete sentences (paragraphs, theme).

Math

K — Knows the number system and basic operations.
U — Understands math concepts and processes.
A — Solves math problems accurately and efficiently.

Science

K — Knows terms and facts.
U — Understands scientific principles.
A — Applies principles to new situations.

Social Studies

K — Knows factual information about social issues.
U — Understands causes of social issues.
A — Applies critical thinking skills to social issues.

Each of these general categories (K, U, A) can then be expanded, with skills and affective outcomes added as needed.

4. Thinking skills.
   4.1. Critical thinking.
   4.2. Scientific thinking.
5. General skills.
   5.1. Laboratory skills.
   5.2. Performance skills.

5.3. Communication skills.
5.4. Computational skills.
5.5. Social skills.

6. Attitudes.

6.1. Social attitudes.
6.2. Scientific attitudes.

7. Interests.

7.1. Personal interests.
7.2. Educational interests.
7.3. Vocational interests.

8. Appreciations.

8.1. Literature, art, and music.
8.2. Social and scientific achievements.

9. Adjustments.

9.1. Social adjustments.
9.2. Emotional adjustments.[3]

Even a cursory glance at this list reveals the many learning outcomes that can be considered when one is developing a list of instructional objectives for a particular course. Not every teacher, or course, will identify objectives in all of these areas. The pupils' age level, the subject-matter area, and the school's philosophy will determine which learning outcomes are to be emphasized in a particular set of instructional objectives. In general, however, we need to expand our view of expected learning outcomes to include all logical outcomes of a course in the final list of objectives.

Taxonomy of Educational Objectives

An especially useful guide for developing a comprehensive list of instructional objectives is the *Taxonomy of Educational Objectives*.[4] This is a detailed classification of objectives that is similar in form to the classification system used for plants and animals. An attempt was made to identify and classify all possible educational outcomes. The system first divides objectives into the following three major areas:

1. *Cognitive Domain*: Knowledge outcomes and intellectual abilities and skills.
2. *Affective Domain*: Attitudes, interests, appreciation, and modes of adjustment.
3. *Psychomotor Domain*: Perceptual and motor skills.

[3]This list of types of learning outcomes is not meant to be exhaustive. For a different set of categories, see the lists of outcomes in Appendix E.

[4]See Appendix E for a detailed summary of the *Taxonomy* categories and a list of the original sources from which the summaries were derived.

Each of the three domains is subdivided into categories and subcategories. The major categories in the Cognitive Domain, for example, are Knowledge, Comprehension, Application, Analysis, Synthesis, and Evaluation. These categories begin with the relatively simple knowledge outcomes and proceed through increasingly complex levels of intellectual ability. This hierarchical pattern of classification is characteristic of all three of the domains.

The *Taxonomy* is primarily useful in identifying the types of learning outcomes that should be considered when developing a comprehensive list of objectives for classroom instruction. One need not use the terminology of the taxonomies when stating outcomes, but a review of the various taxonomy categories will aid in developing a more complete list. The broad range of learning outcomes covered in the *Taxonomy* provides assurance that important types of learning are not overlooked. A helpful guide for the use of the three taxonomy domains in preparing a list of outcomes for classroom instruction is presented in Appendix E. In addition to detailed descriptions of the categories in each domain, illustrative instructional objectives from a variety of content areas are presented, as well as lists of verbs that are useful in stating objectives in terms of pupil performance.

Other Sources for Lists of Objectives

Illustrative instructional objectives for various grade levels and subject-matter areas may be obtained from the following sources.

1. Methods books. Most books on methods of teaching discuss objectives, present examples, and cite references to other sources of objectives in various instructional areas.

2. Yearbooks of educational organizations. The yearbooks and other reports of the National Council of Teachers of English, the National Council of Teachers of Mathematics, the National Council for the Social Studies, and the National Science Teachers Association contain lists of objectives from time to time.

3. Encyclopedia of Educational Research. This publication typically contains an article on each major teaching area, which includes references to sources of instructional objectives.

4. Curriculum guides. Many local and state curriculum guides contain lists of instructional objectives.

5. Test manuals. The manuals accompanying published tests frequently contain lists of objectives that were used in constructing the tests.

6. Banks of objectives. There are various banks of objectives and relevant test items maintained by some organizations and test publishers. See Appendix C for addresses of some objective banks.

In using objectives from these various sources, it is important that the ones selected be relevant to the local instructional program. The selected objectives will also most likely need to be reworded. Many of them will not be stated as intended learning outcomes or in performance terms. Published lists of objectives are probably most useful for obtaining ideas concerning possible outcomes and for evaluating the completeness of a prepared list.

Criteria for Selecting Appropriate Objectives

Our emphasis throughout this section has been on the role of the classroom teacher in the *process* of selecting instructional objectives. We have deliberately avoided discussions concerning which objectives should receive priority at various grade levels and in various subject matter areas. This is a decision for school boards, administrators, curriculum committees, and individual teachers. Our aim has been to clarify how to identify those instructional objectives that will be most useful for teaching and evaluation purposes.

In preparing a list of instructional objectives for a particular course, however, the teacher is still faced with the problem of determining the adequacy of the final list of objectives. The following questions will serve as criteria for this purpose:

1. Do the objectives include all important outcomes of the course? Knowledge objectives are seldom neglected. However, objectives in the area of understanding, thinking skills, attitudes, and the like tend to be slighted unless special efforts are made to consider them. Objectives derived mainly from the methods of instruction and the social experiences of the pupils are also easily overlooked.

2. Are the objectives in harmony with the general goals of the school? The objectives developed by individual teachers must be consistent with the general goals of the school in which they are used. For example, if independent thought, self-direction, and effectiveness of communication are highly valued in the school, these outcomes should be reflected in the teachers' objectives. Similarly, objectives inconsistent with these valued outcomes should be omitted from the list. Part of the difficulty of applying this criterion is that the goals of the school are seldom explicitly stated.

3. Are the objectives in harmony with sound principles of learning? Because objectives indicate the desired outcomes of a series of learning experiences, they should be consistent with sound principles of learning. That is, they should (1) be appropriate to the age level and experiential background of the pupils (principle of readiness), (2) be related to the needs and interests of the pupils (principle of motivation), (3) reflect learning outcomes that are most permanent (principle of retention), and (4) include learning outcomes that are most generally applicable to various specific situations (principle of transfer).

4. Are the objectives realistic in terms of the abilities of the pupils and the time and facilities available? First attempts at identifying objectives for a partic-

FIGURE 2.1
Summary of criteria for
selecting the final list
of objectives.

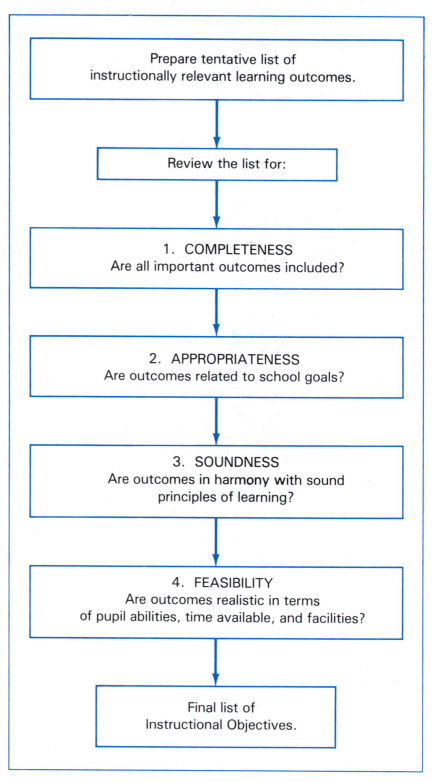

ular course frequently result in an impressive but unattainable list of outcomes. Thus, the final list of objectives should be reviewed in light of the abilities of the group members, the time available for achieving the objectives, and the adequacy of the facilities and equipment available. It is usually better to have a limited set of clearly defined, attainable objectives than a long list of nonfunctional goals.

Make Allowance for Unanticipated Learning Outcomes

No matter how carefully a set of instructional objectives has been selected for a course, there are likely to be some unanticipated effects of the instruction. These effects may be desirable or undesirable, and the majority of them are likely to fall into the affective area. For example, as a result of instruction, pupils may become more dependent or more independent, more conforming or more creative, more critical of printed material or more uncritical, more positive in their self-concept or more negative, and more interested in the subject or less interested. Outcomes of this nature are easily overlooked because they are more likely to result from the method of instruction than from the content of instruction.

In addition to these more global changes in behavior, specific classroom activities may create a need for focusing on outcomes that were not prespecified. An accident in the chemistry laboratory, for example, may indicate a need for special instruction in safety. Similarly, an unanticipated pupil interest in the metric system may create a need to modify instruction in a mathematics class, or an unforeseen international crisis may alter social studies instruction. Thus, although instructional objectives provide a useful guide for instruction, teachers need to be flexible enough in their teaching and testing to allow for unplanned events and unanticipated learning outcomes.

Method of Stating Instructional Objectives

In preparing a list of instructional objectives for a course of study, we have two immediate goals in mind. One is to obtain as complete a list of objectives as possible. This is most likely to occur if we follow the procedures for selecting objectives described in the previous section. The other goal is to state the objectives so that they clearly indicate the learning outcomes that we expect from our instruction.

The task of stating instructional objectives can be simplified if we constantly keep in mind that we are listing intended outcomes of teaching–learning situations. We are *not* describing what we intend to do during instruction but are listing the expected results of that instruction. The point of orientation, then, is the pupil and the types of performance that the pupil should demonstrate at the end of the teaching–learning experience.

Stating objectives in terms of *learning outcomes* rather than the learning process admittedly is easier said than done. Most of us are so concerned with the course content and the ongoing process in the classroom that we find it difficult to concentrate on the results of instruction. The very nature of teaching conditions us

Stating Objectives as Learning Outcomes

Don't state them in terms of

1. *teacher performance*. (e.g., Teach pupils meaning of terms.)
2. *learning process*. (e.g., Pupil learns meaning of terms.)
3. *course content*. (e.g., Pupil studies geometric figures.)
4. *two objectives*. (e.g., Pupil knows and understands terms.)

State them in terms of *pupil performance* at the end of instruction.

1. Knows the meaning of terms.
   1.1 Identifies a definition of the term.
   1.2 Identifies the term that fits a given description.
   1.3 Identifies a synonym of the term.
   1.4 Matches the term to a picture (e.g., types of angles).
   1.5 Differentiates between the term and a second term.

to focus our attention on the learning process. But we can shift this focus if we continually ask ourselves: What should the pupils be able to do at the end of the course or unit of study that they could not do at the beginning? As we attempt to answer this question, always in terms of knowledge, understanding, skills, attitudes, and the like, we shall find that the pupils' terminal performance has almost automatically become the center of focus. We are then in a much better position to state our instructional objectives in terms of *learning outcomes*.

How to Obtain a Clear Statement of Instructional Objectives

A list of objectives for a course or unit of study should be detailed enough to convey the intent of the instruction and yet general enough to serve as an effective overall guide in planning for teaching and testing. You can do this most easily by defining your objectives in two steps: (1) stating the general objectives of instruction as *intended learning outcomes* and (2) listing under each objective a *sample of the specific types of performance* that pupils should be able to demonstrate when they have achieved the objective.[5] This procedure should result in statements of general objectives and specific learning outcomes like the following:

1. Understands scientific principles.
   1.1. Describes the principle in own words.
   1.2. Identifies examples of the principle.
   1.3. States tenable hypotheses based on the principle.
   1.4. Distinguishes between two given principles.
   1.5. Explains the relationship between two given principles.

[5]N. E. Gronlund, *Stating Objectives for Classroom Instruction*, 3d ed. (New York: Macmillan, 1985).

The expected learning outcome is concerned with *understanding*, and the general objective starts right off with the verb *understands*. There is no need to add such repetitious material as "the pupils should be able to demonstrate that they understand." Keeping the statement free of unnecessary words and starting with a verb helps focus on the intended outcome.

There are several things to remember about the *specific learning outcomes* listed beneath the general objective. First is that, like the general objective, each statement begins with a verb. Here, however, the verbs are specific and indicate definite observable responses; that is, responses that can be seen and evaluated by an outside observer. These verbs are listed here to show what is meant by stating the specific learning outcomes in terms of observable pupil performance.[6]

- Describes.
- Identifies.
- States.
- Distinguishes.
- Explains.

Terms such as these clarify what the pupils will do to demonstrate their *understanding*. Such vague terms as *realizes*, *sees*, and *believes* are less useful in defining objectives because they describe internal states that can be expressed by many different types of overt behavior.

Second, the list of specific learning outcomes is merely a sample of the many specific ways that *understanding of scientific principles* might be shown. A pupil who achieved this objective probably could demonstrate many other responses. Because it would be impractical to list all of the specific types of performance that denote understanding, an attempt is made to obtain a *representative sample*. This procedure offers an operational definition of the general objective and still keeps the overall list of objectives and specific learning outcomes within manageable proportions.

Finally, it should be noted that the specific learning outcomes are free of specific course content. Rather than listing the scientific principles the pupils are to understand, they specify the types of pupil performance acceptable as evidence of understanding. Keeping the statements free of specific course content makes it possible to use the same list of learning outcomes with various units of study. Each unit of study will indicate the principles to be understood, and the list of specific learning outcomes will indicate how the pupils are expected to demonstrate their understanding. As we shall see in Chapter 5, a table of specifications is a convenient means of relating the learning outcomes to the various content areas for evaluation purposes.

In planning a unit of instruction for programed learning, or for some limited area of training, it may be possible to list *all*, or nearly all, of the specific outcomes to be

---

[6]See Appendix E for lists of verbs for stating specific learning outcomes in the cognitive, affective, and psychomotor areas.

achieved. In such cases, the intended outcomes are frequently stated as tasks to be performed, rather than as objectives to work toward. Thus, the final list consists of a series of separate, specific statements describing the terminal performance of pupils who have successfully completed the unit. In addition, such statements could also include the conditions under which the performance is to be shown and the standards of performance that are to be accepted.[7] The following statement illustrates this method of describing learning outcomes:

<table>
<tr><td>EXAMPLE</td><td>When given a list of ten United States presidents, the pupil should be able to supply the inauguration dates for at least nine of them.</td></tr>
</table>

In this statement, the *condition* is "when given a list of ten United States presidents," the *performance* is "to supply the inauguration dates," and the *standard of performance* is "at least nine of them." Statements such as these are especially useful when the area of instruction is limited in scope, when simple knowledge outcomes and specific skills are stressed, and when *direct training* is emphasized. When used for regular classroom instruction, however, such statements result in a long, cumbersome list that tends to overemphasize the memorization of factual information and the learning of simple skills. In the more complex areas of achievement (e.g., understanding, application, thinking skills), the specific learning outcomes are so numerous that all we can reasonably expect to do is state a *sample* of them. Thus, stating the general objectives first and then defining each with a representative sample of the specific learning outcomes is a more effective procedure for most classroom instruction.

Stating the General Instructional Objectives

One problem in stating the general instructional objectives is selecting the proper level of generality. The objectives should be specific enough to provide direction for instruction but not so specific that our instruction is reduced to the training level. When we state our major objectives in more general terms, we provide for the integration of specific facts and skills into more complex response patterns. Such general statements also give the teacher greater freedom in selecting the methods and materials of instruction. The "Understanding of Scientific Principles," for example, may be achieved through lecture, discussion, demonstration, laboratory work, or some combination of these methods. Similarly, the objective may be achieved through the use of different textbooks or various other types of instructional material. Stating the general objectives at this level provides a focus for instruction, but it does not restrict the teacher to a particular instructional method or a given set of instructional materials.

The following list of general instructional objectives shows the desired level of generality:

---

[7]R. F. Mager, *Preparing Instructional Objectives*, 2d ed. (San Francisco: Fearon, 1975).

- Knows basic terminology.
- Understands concepts and principles.
- Applies principles to new situations.
- Interprets charts and graphs.
- Demonstrates skill in critical thinking.
- Writes a well-organized theme.
- Appreciates poetry.
- Demonstrates scientific attitude.
- Evaluates an experiment's adequacy.

The verbs at the beginning of each statement are general enough to encompass a range of specific learning outcomes. A sample of the specific outcomes would, of course, need to be added before these general statements would be useful guides for teaching and evaluation. Note that each statement contains a single objective (e.g., *not* "Knows and understands"), and that each statement is relatively free of course content.

The degree of generality may, of course, vary somewhat with the period of instruction for which the list is being prepared. The objectives for a brief unit of instruction are likely to be more specific than those for an entire course of study. In either case, however, selecting from eight to twelve general instructional objectives will usually provide a list that is both manageable and suitable.

Stating the Specific Learning Outcomes

As stated earlier, each general instructional objective must be defined by a sample of specific learning outcomes to clarify how pupils can demonstrate that they have achieved the general objective. Unless the general objectives are further defined in this manner, they will not provide adequate direction for teaching or testing.

Statements of specific learning outcomes for a general objective will be easier to write and will more clearly convey instructional intent if each statement begins with an *action verb* that indicates definite, observable responses (e.g., "Identifies," "Defines"). Such statements specify the types of pupil performance acceptable as evidence that the general instructional objective has been achieved. This assumes, of course, that each specific learning outcome is directly *relevant* to the general objective it is defining. A statement like "Writes the textbook definition of a term" would be appropriate for listing under "Knows Basic Terms," but not under "Understands Basic Terms." For the latter objective, we would need a statement that goes beyond the recall of information, because understanding implies some novelty in the response. Here, a statement like "Defines the term in own words" would be more relevant.

A major problem in defining general instructional objectives is deciding how many specific learning outcomes to list under each objective. It is obvious that a fixed number cannot be specified. Simple knowledge and skill outcomes typically require fewer statements than complex ones. Because it is usually impossible or impractical to list all possible pupil responses for each general objective, the sample should be as representative as possible. In most cases there is not much advantage in listing more than eight specific learning outcomes for each objective, and four or five statements are probably more common. As a general guide, enough should be listed for each objective to show the typical performance of pupils who have satisfactorily achieved the objective.

The following general objectives and specific learning outcomes illustrate a satisfactory level of specificity for stating the intended learning outcomes:

1. Understands the meaning of terms.

    1.1. Defines the term in own words.
    1.2. Identifies the meaning of a term in context.
    1.3. Differentiates between proper and improper usage of a term.
    1.4. Distinguishes between two similar terms on the basis of meaning.
    1.5. Writes an original sentence using the term.

2. Demonstrates skill in critical thinking.

    2.1. Distinguishes between fact and opinion.
    2.2. Distinguishes between relevant and irrelevant information.
    2.3. Identifies fallacious reasoning in written material.
    2.4. Identifies the limitations of given data.
    2.5. Formulates valid conclusions from given data.
    2.6. Identifies the assumptions underlying conclusions.

In addition to illustrating the desired degree of specificity, these statements are good examples of "content-free" objectives. As noted earlier, both the general objectives and the specific learning outcomes should be kept free of specific content so that they can be used with various units of study. In stating our specific learning outcomes, we are attempting to describe what types of pupil performance represent each general objective—*not* what specific content the pupils are to learn.

Keeping the specific learning outcomes content free is, of course, a matter of degree. In some cases all we can do is modify our statements so that they apply to a wider range of course material. The following statements illustrate ways to improve specific learning outcomes in this regard:

Poor: Identifies the last ten United States presidents.
Better: Identifies important historical figures.

Poor: Identifies the parts of a flower.
Better: Identifies the parts of a given structure.

Poor: Distinguishes between a square and a rectangle.
Better: Distinguishes among geometric shapes.

Poor: Describes the main characters in *Silas Marner*.
Better: Describes the main characters in the story.

If we used the first version of each of these specific learning outcomes, we would have to write new statements for each identification, comparison, or description we wanted our pupils to make. The *better* versions can be used with various areas of content and thus free us from the repetitious writing of objectives as each new subject matter topic is considered. The subject-matter topics in each unit of study indicate the content the student is to react to, and the specific learning outcomes specify the types of reactions the pupils are to make to the content.

In some cases it may be desirable or necessary to consult reference books and other relevant materials for the types of performance that might represent an objective. When defining such complex outcomes as *critical thinking, literary appreciation,* and *scientific attitude,* for example, a review of the literature can be very useful. Although you may not find a detailed list of the specific components of each outcome, even general descriptions of the concepts will aid in defining relevant types of performance. In any event, resist the temptation to omit complex outcomes simply because they are difficult to define.

Clarification of Verbs Used in Specific Learning Outcomes

Because the *action verb* is a key element in stating the specific learning outcomes, the selection and clarification of these verbs play an important role in obtaining a clearly defined set of instructional objectives. Ideally, we would like each verb (1) to convey clearly our instructional intent and (2) to specify precisely the pupil performance we are willing to accept as evidence that the general objective has been attained. Unfortunately, some verbs convey instructional intent well (e.g., *identifies*); others are more effective at specifying the pupil responses to be observed (e.g., *labels, encircles, underlines*). When it is necessary to choose between these two types, it is best to select those that most clearly convey instructional intent and, if needed, to clarify further the expected pupil responses in one of the following ways:

1. Add a third level of specificity to the list of objectives.
2. Define the action verbs used in the specific learning outcomes.
3. Use sample test items to illustrate the intended outcomes.

These procedures are probably most useful as guides to test construction and for communicating your intended learning outcomes to others. Each of the procedures will be discussed in turn.

The meaning of each specific learning outcome can be further clarified by listing some of the tasks pupils are expected to perform to demonstrate achievement of the outcome. This would provide three levels for each instructional objective as follows:

1. Comprehends the meaning of written material.
    1.1. Identifies the main thought in a passage.
        1.11 Underlines the topic sentence.
        1.12 Selects the most appropriate title for the passage.
        1.13 Writes the main theme of the passage.

Adding a third level of specificity, like this, might be useful for clarifying come learning outcomes. The specific tasks describe how pupils will indicate that they can "identify the main thought in a passage." But our intended outcome is still *identifying* the main thought. *Underlining*, *selecting*, and *writing* are simply responses we are willing to use as *indicators* of the "ability to identify." Thus, although the third level may be a desirable transition between specific learning outcomes and relevant test items, these specific responses are not instructional outcomes in their own right (i.e., in our example, we are not interested in teaching pupils how to *underline*, *select*, and *write* but, rather, how to *identify*; we assume they already can do the first). This third level of specificity highlights one of the advantages of using levels of objectives rather than only a list of specific tasks to describe the intended outcomes of instruction. With levels, we are less likely to confuse the *intended outcomes* of instruction with the *indicators* of those outcomes.

Another way of clarifying the expected pupil responses is to define or describe each *action verb* used in the list of specific learning outcomes, as illustrated in Table 2.1. (Note the "Types of Responses" and "Sample Test Tasks.") This procedure is especially useful when the teachers in a department or an entire school are developing instructional objectives for each course in the curriculum. Describing the types of responses associated with each action verb gives a uniform meaning from one set of objectives to another and, at the same time, usually eliminates the need for

TABLE 2.1	Action Verb	Types of Responses	Sample Test Tasks
Illustrations of How to Clarify Expected Pupil Responses for Selected Action Verbs	Identify	Point to, touch, mark, encircle, match, pick up.	"Put an X under the right triangle."
	Name	Supply verbal label (orally or in writing).	"What is this type of angle called?"
	Distinguish	Identify as separate or different by marking, separating into classes, or selecting out a common kind.	"Which of the following statements are *facts* (encircle *F*) and which are opinions (encircle *O*)?"
	Define	Supply a verbal description (orally or in writing) that gives the precise meaning or essential qualities.	"Define each of the following terms."
	Describe	Supply a verbal account (orally or in writing) that gives the essential categories, properties, and relationships.	"Describe a procedure for measuring relative humidity in the atmosphere."
	Classify	Place into groups having common characteristics, assign to a particular category.	"Write the name of the type of pronoun used in each of the following sentences."
	Order	List in order, place in sequence, arrange, rearrange.	"Arrange the following historical events in chronological order."
	Construct	Draw, make, design, assemble, prepare, build.	"Draw a bar graph using the following data."
	Demonstrate	Perform a set of procedures with or without a verbal explanation.	"Set up the laboratory equipment for this experiment."

adding third-level *indicators* to each set of objectives. Including examples of test tasks, as shown in Table 2.1, also helps define the meaning of each action verb.

In some cases—for instance, when the test items are to be constructed by others—it is desirable to give one or more model test items for each specific learning outcome. In communicating your instructional intent to others, nothing else can convey the intended outcomes as clearly as illustrative test items. This assumes, of course, that each sample test item is directly relevant to the specific learning outcome that it represents.

Summary of Steps for Stating Instructional Objectives

The final list of objectives for a course or unit should include all important learning outcomes (e.g., knowledge, understanding, skills, attitude) and should clearly convey how pupils are expected to perform at the end of the learning experience. The following summary of steps provides guidelines for obtaining a clear statement of instructional objectives:[8]

I. Stating the general instructional objectives.

   1. State each general objective as an intended learning outcome (i.e., pupils' terminal performance).
   2. Begin each general objective with a verb (e.g., *knows, applies, interprets*). Omit "The pupil should be able to. . . ."
   3. State each general objective to include only one general learning outcome (e.g., *not* "Knows and understands").
   4. State each general objective at the proper level of generality (i.e., it should encompass a readily definable domain of responses). From eight to twelve general objectives will usually suffice.
   5. Keep each general objective sufficiently free of course content so that it can be used with various units of study.
   6. Minimize the overlap with other objectives.

II. Stating the specific learning outcomes.

   1. List beneath each general instructional objective a *representative sample* of specific learning outcomes that describes the *terminal performance* pupils are expected to demonstrate.
   2. Begin each specific learning outcome with an *action verb* that specifies *observable* performance (e.g., *identifies, describes*).
   3. Make sure that each specific learning outcome is *relevant* to the general objective it describes.
   4. Include *enough* specific learning outcomes to describe adequately the performance of pupils who have attained the objective.
   5. Keep the specific learning outcomes sufficiently *free of course content* so that the list can be used with various units of study.

[8]Adapted from N. E. Gronlund, *Stating Objectives for Classroom Instruction*, 3d ed. (New York: Macmillan, 1985). See checklist for evaluating objectives in Appendix A of this book.

6. Consult reference materials for the specific components of those complex outcomes that are difficult to define (e.g., critical thinking, scientific attitude, creativity).
7. Add a third level of specificity to the list of outcomes, if needed.

This procedure for stating objectives does not include the *conditions* under which the pupil performance will be shown (e.g., open book, diagrams will be provided) or the *standards* for evaluating performance (e.g., 90 percent correct). Although some teachers may want to add such information to each objective, there are advantages in stating the conditions and standards separately from the objectives. In many cases, the same conditions and standards apply to all objectives being evaluated at a given time, and thus a statement like the following may be sufficient for an entire set of objectives:

EXAMPLE

Pupil performance will be determined under closed book conditions, but all needed formulas will be provided. Hand calculators may be used. Mastery will be indicated by answering 90 percent of the items correctly.

A statement such as this will prevent the repetitious writing of the same conditions and standards for each objective and also avoid rewriting the list of objectives each time the conditions or standards are changed. We may, for example, use the same objectives for different units of study (e.g., *Knows terms*, *Understands principles*, *Applies principles*) but want to vary the conditions and standards to suit the nature and complexity of the material studied. We may also wish to modify the conditions or standards to match a particular group of pupils (e.g., gifted). Thus, limiting the statements of objectives to concise descriptions of desired pupil performance and stating the conditions and standards separately as needed seem to be desirable for most classroom instruction. The time saved from writing instructional objectives over and over can usually be well spent on other instructional activities.

Summary

Instructional objectives make clear what learning outcomes we expect from our teaching. They describe our instructional intent in terms of the types of performance pupils are expected to demonstrate as a result of instruction. A convenient means of preparing instructional objectives is to follow a two-step process: (1) State the *general instructional objectives* as intended learning outcomes. (2) Define each general objective with a list of *specific learning outcomes* that describes the observable responses that the learners will be able to make when they have achieved the general objective.

When instructional objectives are viewed as learning outcomes and are defined in performance terms, numerous types of intended outcomes might be included. In addition to the more obvious knowledge outcomes, those in the areas of understanding, application, thinking skills, performance skills, attitudes, interests, appreciation, and adjustment should also be considered. Suggestions for objectives in these and other areas may be obtained from Appendix E, "Taxonomy of Educational Objectives," from various published sources, and from objective-item banks that have been prepared for national distribution. The external sources should be used as aids only. Instructional objectives usually are most relevant when teachers develop their own lists, as these take into account the unique features of the local school and community.

The adequacy of the list of objectives for a particular course can be appraised according to the extent to which it (1) includes all important outcomes of the course, (2) is in harmony with the school's general goals, (3) is in harmony with sound principles of learning, and (4) is realistic in terms of the pupils' abilities and the time and facilities available.

No matter how comprehensive a set of instructional objectives may be, there are likely to be some unanticipated outcomes of instruction. Thus, teachers should be alert to this possibility during instruction and should take these unplanned effects into account when evaluating the learning outcomes of a course.

The task of stating instructional objectives is simplified if we keep in mind that we are making a list of intended outcomes of instruction, stated in terms of the types of performance the pupils are expected to demonstrate at the end of the teaching– learning experience. The procedure for stating the objectives for a particular course includes the following steps:

1. State each general instructional objective as an intended learning outcome that encompasses a readily definable domain of pupil responses. Each general objective should begin with a verb (e.g., *knows*, *understands*, *applies*), contain only one general learning outcome, and be relatively content free. Typically, from eight to twelve general objectives will suffice.

2. List beneath each general instructional objective a representative sample of specific learning outcomes stated in terms of pupil performance. Each should begin with an action verb (e.g., *identifies*, *describes*), be relevant to the general objective, and be relatively free of course content so that it can be used with various units of study.

Instructional objectives will require the least rewriting and function most effectively if the *conditions* and *standards* of performance are stated separately.

Learning Exercises

1. What are some of the advantages of stating instructional objectives as learning outcomes?
2. Describe the differences between mastery objectives and developmental objectives. How might testing differ for the two types?
3. Give examples of how ultimate objectives (e.g., good citizenship) might be stated as immediate objectives.
4. Make a list of multiple-course objectives (e.g., study skills) that might be emphasized in your teaching area.

5. Using the summary of steps for stating instructional objectives as a guide, restate each of the following as *general instructional objectives*.

   a. To learn the basic terms in the unit.

   b. Be familiar with the laboratory procedures.

   c. Can show how to write a well-organized paragraph.

   d. Increases his ability to read with comprehension.

6. Using the summary of steps for stating instructional objectives as a guide, restate each of the following as *specific learning outcomes*.

   a. Sees the importance of following safety practices.

   b. Realizes the correct way to spell technical terms.

   c. Is aware of the proper use of laboratory equipment.

   d. Learns the symbols on a weather map.

7. List some of the unplanned effects of instruction (i.e., unanticipated outcomes) that might occur in one of your teaching areas. Which ones would you include in your evaluation of pupil learning? Why?

8. What arguments would you present for and against including the *conditions* of measurement and the desired *standard* of performance in each stated objective?

9. For a unit of instruction in one of your major teaching areas, prepare a list of general instructional objectives and specific learning outcomes following the procedures suggested in this chapter.

Suggestions for Further Reading

BLOOM, B. S.; MADAUS, G. J.; AND HASTINGS, J. T. *Evaluation to Improve Learning*. New York: McGraw-Hill, 1981. See Appendix A for a "Condensed Version of the Taxonomy of Educational Objectives."

GRONLUND, N. E. *Stating Objectives for Classroom Instruction*. 3d ed. New York: Macmillan, 1985. A brief guide describing the step-by-step procedures for stating instructional objectives and for using them in teaching, testing, and marking and reporting. Presents illustrations of instructional objectives, lists of action verbs, and a checklist for evaluating instructional objectives.

TENBRINK, T. D. "Writing Instructional Objectives." In J. Cooper, ed. *Classroom Teaching Skills*, 3d ed. Lexington, Mass.: D. C. Heath, 1986. Describes how to write objectives useful in teaching and testing.

WOOLFOLK, A. E. *Educational Psychology*, 3d ed. Englewood Cliffs, N.J.: Prentice-Hall, 1987. See Chapter 11, "Setting Objectives and Planning," for a discussion of how to state objectives for learning, including the role of the Cognitive, Affective, and Psychomotor Taxonomies.

Chapter 3

Validity

*When constructing or selecting tests and other evaluation instruments,
the most important question is, To what extent will the interpretation
of the scores be appropriate, meaningful, and useful for the intended
application of the results?*

Tests and other evaluation instruments serve a variety of uses in the school. For
example, tests of achievement might be used for selection, placement, diagnosis, or
certification of mastery; aptitude tests might be used for predicting success in future
learning activities or occupations; and appraisals of personal–social development
might be used to understand better pupils' learning problems or to evaluate the
effects of a particular school program. Regardless of the type of instrument used or
how the results are to be used, however, all of the measurements should possess
certain characteristics. The most essential of these are *validity*, *reliability*, and
usability.

   Validity refers to the appropriateness of the interpretations made from test scores
and other evaluation results, with regard to a particular use. For example, if a test is
to be used to describe pupil achievement, we should like to be able to interpret the
scores as a relevant and representative sample of the achievement domain to be
measured. If the results are to be used to predict pupils' success in some future
activity, we should like our interpretations to be based on as accurate an estimate of
future success as possible. If the results are to be used as a measure of pupils'
reading comprehension, we should like our interpretations to be based on evidence
that the scores actually reflect reading comprehension and are not distorted by
irrelevant factors. Basically, then, validity is always concerned with the specific use
of the results and the soundness of our proposed interpretations. As we shall see

later in the chapter, however, this does not mean that validation procedures can be matched to specific test uses on a one-to-one basis.

Reliability refers to the *consistency* of evaluation results. If we obtain quite similar scores when the same test is administered to the same pupils on two different occasions, we can conclude that our results have a high degree of reliability from one occasion to another. Similarly, if different teachers independently rate the same pupils on the same instrument and obtain similar ratings, we can conclude that the results have a high degree of reliability from one rater to another. As with validity, reliability is intimately related to the type of interpretation to be made. For some uses, we may be interested in asking how reliable our evaluation results are over a given period of time and, for others, how reliable they are over different samples of the same behavior. In all instances in which reliability is being determined, however, we are concerned with the *consistency* of the results, rather than with the *appropriateness of the interpretations* made from the results (validity).

The relation between reliability and validity is sometimes confusing to persons who encounter these terms for the first time. Reliability (consistency) of measurement is needed to obtain valid results, but we can have reliability without validity. That is, we can have consistent measures that provide the wrong information or are interpreted inappropriately. The target-shooting illustration in Figure 3.1 depicts the concept that *reliability is a necessary but not a sufficient condition for validity*.

In addition to providing results that possess a satisfactory degree of validity and reliability, an evaluation procedure must meet certain practical requirements. It should be economical from the viewpoint of both time and money; it should be easily administered and scored; and it should produce results that can be accurately interpreted and applied by the school personnel available. These practical aspects of an evaluation procedure all can be included under the heading of usability. The term *usability*, then, refers only to the *practicality* of the procedure and says nothing about the other qualities present.

Nature of Validity

When using the term *validity* in relation to testing and evaluation, there are a number of cautions to be borne in mind.

1. Validity refers to the *appropriateness of the interpretation of the results* of a test or evaluation instrument for a given group of individuals, and *not* to the instrument itself. We sometimes speak of the "validity of a test," for the sake of convenience, but it is more correct to speak of the validity of the interpretation to be made from the results.

2. Validity is *a matter of degree*; it does not exist on an all-or-none basis. Consequently, we should avoid thinking of evaluation results as valid or invalid. Validity is best considered in terms of categories that specify degree, such as high validity, moderate validity, and low validity.

3. Validity is always *specific to some particular use or interpretation*. No test is

FIGURE 3.1
Reliability (consistency)
is needed to obtain
valid results (but one
can be consistently
"off target").

Kit ("Bullseye") Carson
(reliable and valid shooting)

Bill ("Scattershot") Henry
(unreliable and invalid shooting)

Jack ("Rightpull") Armstrong
(reliable but invalid shooting)

valid for all purposes. For example, the results of an arithmetic test may have a high degree of validity for indicating computational skill, a low degree of validity for indicating arithmetical reasoning, a moderate degree of validity for predicting success in future mathematics courses, and essentially no validity for predicting success in art or music. Thus, when appraising or describing validity, it is necessary to consider the specific interpretation or use to be made of the results. Evaluation results are never just valid; they have a different degree of validity for each particular interpretation to be made.

4. Validity is a *unitary concept*. The conceptual nature of validity has typically been described for the testing profession in a set of *Standards* prepared by a joint committee made up of members from three professional organizations that are especially concerned with educational and psychological testing. In the most recent revision of the *Standards*, the traditional view that there are several different "types" of validity has been discarded.[1] Instead, validity is viewed as a unitary concept based on various kinds of evidence.

There are many ways of accumulating evidence to support or challenge the validity of an interpretation of test scores. For convenience, the ways of accumulating evidence are usually grouped together in one of three categories (content, criterion related, and construct). Although these categories help emphasize particular needs for evidence to support specific kinds of interpretations, they are interrelated and all contribute to an overall evaluation of the degree of validity of any given interpretation of scores on a test or other evaluation instrument.

Approaches to Test Validation

The three approaches to test validation are briefly described in Table 3.1. Each of these procedures will be explained more fully in the remainder of the chapter, but for the sake of clarity, the discussion will be limited to the validation of testing procedures. You should be aware, however, that the three categories of validity evidence are also applicable to the other types of evaluation instruments used in the school.

The strongest case for validity can be made when evidence from all of the categories is present. That is, interpretations of test scores are likely to have greater validity when we have a fuller understanding of (1) the test content and the specifications it was derived from, (2) the relation of the test scores to other significant measures, and (3) the nature of the characteristic(s) being measured. However, for many practical uses of a test, it is not practical or necessary to have evidence that ordinarily would be classified in all three of these categories. For example, it is not practical to expect that a teacher would provide evidence that a

---

[1]*Standards for Educational and Psychological Testing* (Washington, D.C.: American Psychological Association, 1985). Prepared by a joint committee chosen from the American Educational Research Association, the American Psychological Association, and the National Council on Measurement in Education.

	Procedure	Meaning	
Content-Related Evidence	Compare the test tasks to the test specifications describing the task domain under consideration.	How well the sample of test tasks *represents* the domain of tasks to be measured.	TABLE 3.1 Approaches to Test Validation
Criterion-Related Evidence	Compare test scores with another measure of performance obtained at a later date (for prediction) or with another measure of performance obtained concurrently (for estimating present status).	How well test performance *predicts* future performance or *estimates* current performance on some valued measures other than the test itself (called a *criterion*).	
Construct-Related Evidence	Establish the meaning of the scores on the test by controlling (or examining) the development of the test, evaluating the relationships of the scores with other relevant measures, and experimentally determining what factors influence test performance.	How well test performance can be interpreted as a meaningful measure of some characteristic or quality.	

classroom test designed to measure student learning is related to other significant measures. Instead, in this case, the primary concern is apt to be with *content-related* evidence, but as we shall see, at least some of the logical analyses of the meaning of the scores that would normally be classified in the *construct-related* category also would be relevant. Similarly, in using a scholastic aptitude test to predict future success in school, *criterion-related* evidence would be a major interest. But we also should be concerned about the appropriateness of the content and the irrelevant factors that influence test performance (e.g., motivation, test anxiety, test-taking skills). Thus, both content- and construct-related evidence would be desirable. It is when test scores are used to measure a specific characteristic or construct (e.g., reading comprehension or mathematical reasoning ability) that all three categories of evidence are of paramount importance. In this case, our focus is on *construct-related* evidence, but both content-related and criterion-related evidence are useful for a fuller understanding of the meaning of the test scores and, therefore, contribute to the validation of our interpretations.

Although there are many types of evidence that can be used in the process of test validation, our discussions of *content-related*, *criterion-related*, and *construct-related* evidence will focus on those procedures that are most useful in practical educational settings.

Content-Related Evidence

Content-related evidence is of special importance when we wish to describe how an individual performs on a domain of tasks that the test is supposed to represent. We may, for example, expect pupils to be able to spell the 200 words on a given word list. Because a 200-word spelling test is too time consuming, we may select a sample of 20 words to represent the total domain of 200 spelling words. Now, if a pupil correctly spells 80 percent of these 20 words, we would like to be able to say that she can probably also spell 80 percent of the 200 words. Thus, we would like to be able to generalize from the pupil's performance on the *sample* of words in the test to the performance that the pupil would be expected to demonstrate on the domain of spelling words that the test represents.

The validity of the interpretation that a test score implies that the pupil *can* probably spell a given percentage of words in the whole domain depends on a number of considerations that go beyond the content-related evidence that is our focus. For example, aspects of construct-related evidence, such as the assumption that the pupil was trying to do her best, that she did not copy her neighbor's spelling words, and that she understood the teacher's pronunciation of the words, influence the validity of the interpretation that she *can* spell a given fraction of the words. Here, however, our concern is with the extent to which our 20-word test constituted a *representative sample* of the 200 words. In this instance, we can obtain a fairly representative sample of spelling words by simply starting with our 200-word list and selecting every tenth word. Having thus assured ourselves that we have a reasonably representative sample, we would have good content-related evidence to support the desired interpretation. As we shall see shortly, judging how adequately a test samples a given domain of achievement is usually much more complex than in this simple example.

The essence of content validation, then, is determining the adequacy of the sampling of the content that the test scores are interpreted to represent. More formally, *content validation is a process of determining the extent to which a set of test tasks provides a relevant and representative sample of the domain of tasks about which interpretations of test scores are made*. In classroom testing, the domains of achievement tasks are determined by the instruction, and test development involves (1) clearly specifying the domain of instructionally relevant tasks to be measured and (2) constructing or selecting a representative set of test tasks. Thus, to obtain a valid measure of learning outcomes, we proceed from the instruction (what has been taught) to the achievement domain (what is to be measured) and finally to the test itself (a representative sample of relevant tasks). As shown in Figure 3.2, content validation requires a judgment that all three are in close harmony.

The evidence obtained from content validation should not be confused with *face* validity, which refers only to the appearance of the test. Based on a superficial examination of the items, does the test appear to be a reasonable measure? A clear distinction between content validation (based on adequacy of sampling) and face validity (based on appearance) can be made with a simple example. If we are giving an arithmetic test to a young child, we might phrase an item as follows: "If you had

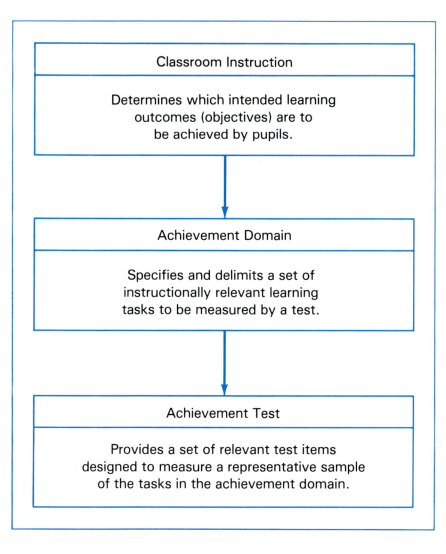

FIGURE 3.2
Content validation in
the testing of
classroom
achievement.

a ten-foot piece of *string* and you cut it in half, how long would the two pieces be?" If the test was to be given to carpenters, we would substitute the word *board* for *string* in this item. Similarly, for plumbers we would use the word *pipe* and for electricians the word *wire*. The problem remains the same, but by phrasing it in appropriate terms, it appears more relevant to the test taker (i.e., has greater face validity). The validity of interpretations of our arithmetic test scores would not be determined by how the test looked, however, but rather by how well it sampled the domain of arithmetic tasks important to each group (i.e., children, carpenters, plumbers, and electricians). Thus, our arithmetic test may provide an adequate measure of content for one group but not another, even though the items were phrased in terms appropriate to each group. Although a test should look like an appropriate measure to obtain the cooperation of those taking the test, face validity should not be considered a substitute for content validation. In fact, the term *face validity* is a misnomer, for it is not really a type of validity evidence at all.

Content Validation and Test Development

Content validation typically takes place during test development. It is primarily a matter of preparing detailed test specifications and then constructing a test that meets these specifications. Although there are many ways of specifying what a test should measure, one widely used procedure in constructing achievement tests uses a two-way chart called a table of specifications. We shall use a brief form of it here to help clarify the process of content validation in preparing a classroom test. More elaborate tables of specifications and other types of test specifications will be described and illustrated in Chapter 5.

Table of Specifications.   The content of a course or curriculum may be broadly defined to include both subject matter content and instructional objectives. The former is concerned with the topics to be learned and the latter with the types of performance pupils are expected to demonstrate (e.g., knows, comprehends, applies). Both of these aspects are of concern in content validation. We should like any achievement test that we construct to produce results that represent both the content areas and the objectives we wish to measure, and the table of specifications aids in obtaining a sample of test tasks that represents both.

A table of specifications, in a very simple form, is presented in Table 3.2 to show how such a table is used in content validation. The percentages in the table indicate the relative degree of emphasis that each content area and each instructional objective is to be given in the test. Thus, if the test is to measure a representative sample of *subject-matter content*, 16 percent of the items should be concerned with plants, 20 percent with animals, 28 percent with weather, 18 percent with the earth, and 18 percent with the sky. Similarly, if the test is to measure a representative sample of the *instructional objectives*, 50 percent of the items should measure "knowledge of concepts," 25 percent should measure "comprehension of concepts," and 25 percent should measure "application of concepts." This, of course, implies that the emphasis on knowledge, comprehension, and application for each

		Instructional Objectives		
Content Area	Knows Concepts	Comprehends Concepts	Applies Concepts	Total
Plants	8	4	4	16
Animals	10	5	5	20
Weather	12	8	8	28
Earth	12	4	2	18
Sky	8	4	6	18
Total	50	25	25	100

TABLE 3.2
Table of Specifications Showing the Relative Emphasis in Percent to Be Given to the Content Areas and Instructional Objectives for a Test in Elementary School Science

content area will follow the percentages in the table of specifications. For example, 8 percent of the test items concerned with plants should measure "knowledge of concepts," 4 percent should measure "comprehension of concepts," and 4 percent should measure "application of concepts."

As noted earlier, the specifications describing the achievement domain to be measured should be in harmony with what was taught. Thus, the weights assigned in this table reflect the emphasis that was given during the instruction. For example, "knowledge" outcomes received twice as much emphasis as did either "comprehension" or "application" outcomes in the instruction and therefore were given twice as much weight in the table. The table, then, indicates the sample of instructionally relevant learning tasks to be measured, and the more closely the test items correspond to the specified sample, the greater the likelihood is of obtaining a valid measure of pupil learning.

The test items must function as intended if valid results are to be obtained. Test items may function improperly if they contain inappropriate vocabulary, clues to the answer, unclear directions, or some other defect. Similarly, items designed to measure understanding and application may measure only the simple recall of information if the solutions to the problems have been directly taught during instruction. In short, a host of factors can influence the intended function of the test items and thus the validity of the test results. Much of what is written in this book concerning the construction of classroom tests is directed toward producing valid measures of achievement.

Content Validation and Test Selection

Evidence obtained from content validation is also of concern when selecting published achievement tests. When test publishers prepare achievement tests for use in the schools, they pay special attention to content validation. Their test specifications, however, are based on what is commonly taught in many different schools. Thus, a published test may or may not fit a particular school situation. To determine whether it does, it is necessary to go beyond the title of the test and to examine what the test actually measures. How closely does the test content correspond to the course content and the instructional objectives in the *local instructional program?* Does the test provide a balanced measure of the intended learning outcomes, or are some areas overemphasized and others neglected? These are the types of questions that need to be asked. A published test may provide more valid results for one school program than for another. It all than depends on how closely the set of test tasks matches the achievement to be measured.

The same types of test specifications used in preparing classroom tests can be used in selecting published tests. The detailed descriptions of course content and instructional objectives and the relative emphasis to be given to each can help us determine which of several published tests is most relevant to our particular situation. It is simply a matter of examining the items in each test and comparing them to our test specifications. The test that provides the most balanced measure of the specified achievement domain is the one that will produce the most valid results. Many test publishers include a detailed description of their test specifications in the test manual. Although this makes it easier to judge the potential validity of the test results, there is no substitute for examining the test tasks themselves and judging how validly they measure the intended learning outcomes in the local instructional program.

Content Validation in Other Areas

Although content validation is of primary interest in achievement testing, it is also of interest in other areas. For example, examining the test content of a scholastic aptitude test aids in understanding the meaning of the scores and provides some evidence concerning the types of prediction for which it might be best suited. Similarly, when constructing or selecting an attitude scale, we are interested in how adequately the items cover those attitudinal topics included in the domain to be measured. In the same manner, an interest inventory should include samples of items that adequately represent those aspects of interest we wish to measure. In these and other situations, the content validation procedure is essentially the same as that in achievement testing. It is a matter of analyzing the content and tasks included in the measuring instrument and the domain of outcomes to be measured and judging the degree of correspondence between them.

Criterion-Related Evidence

Whenever test scores are to be used to predict future performance or to estimate current performance on some valued measure other than the test itself (called a *criterion*), we are especially concerned with criterion-related evidence. For example, reading readiness test scores might be used to predict pupils' future achievement in reading, or a test of dictionary skills might be used to estimate pupils' current skill in the actual use of the dictionary (as determined by observation). In the first example, we are interested in *prediction* and thus in the relationship between the two measures over an extended period of time. This procedure for obtaining evidence of validity calls for a *predictive* validation study. In the second example, we are interested in *estimating present status* and thus in the relationship between the two measures obtained concurrently. A high relationship in this case would show that the test of dictionary skills is a good indicator of actual skill in using a dictionary. This procedure for obtaining evidence of validity calls for a *concurrent* validation study. In the test *Standards*,[2] both the predictive and concurrent designs have been subsumed under the more general category—*criterion-related* validation. This appears to be a desirable arrangement because the method of determining and expressing validity is the same in both cases. The major difference resides in the time period between the two obtained measures, as illustrated in Figure 3.3.

Criterion-related validation may be defined as the process of determining the extent to which test performance is related to some other valued measure of performance. As noted earlier, the second measure of performance (called a *crite-*

[2]*Standards for Educational and Psychological Testing* (Washington, D.C.: American Psychological Association, 1985).

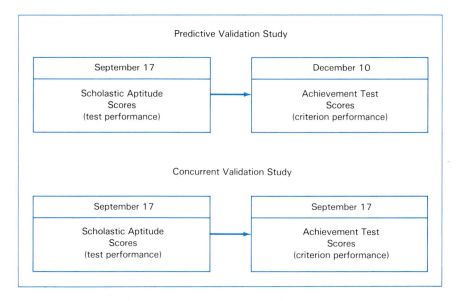

FIGURE 3.3
Types of criterion-
related validation
(based on time
difference only).

rion) may be obtained at some future date (when we are interested in predicting future performance) or concurrently (when we are interested in estimating present performance). First, let us examine the use of criterion-related validation from the standpoint of predicting success in some future activity, and then we shall return to its second use.

Predicting Future Performance

Suppose that Mr. Young, a junior high school teacher, wants to determine how well the scores from a certain scholastic aptitude test will predict success in his seventh-grade arithmetic class. Because the scholastic aptitude test is administered to all pupils when they enter junior high school, these scores are readily available to Mr. Young. His biggest problem is deciding on a *criterion* of successful achievement in arithmetic. For lack of a better criterion, Mr. Young decides to use a comprehensive departmental examination that is administered to the various seventh-grade arithmetic sections at the end of the school year. It is now possible for Mr. Young to determine how well the scholastic aptitude test scores predict success in his arithmetic class by comparing the pupils' scholastic aptitude test scores with their scores on the departmental examination. Do those pupils who have high scholastic aptitude test scores also tend to have high scores on the departmental examination? Do those who have low scholastic aptitude test scores also tend to have low scores on the departmental examination? If this is the case, Mr. Young is inclined to agree that the scholastic aptitude test scores tend to be accurate in predicting achievement in this arithmetic class.

In our example, Mr. Young merely inspected the scholastic aptitude and achievement test scores to determine the agreement between them. Although this may be a desirable preliminary step, it does not provide a very precise notion of the degree of relationship between the aptitude test scores and the scores on the comprehensive departmental examination nor does it provide a very good way of communicating the results. The degree of relationship can be described more precisely by statistically correlating the two sets of scores. The resulting *correlation coefficient* provides a numerical summary of the degree of relationship between the two sets of scores. A correlation coefficient provides a concise, quantitative summary of the relationship for anyone who has learned to understand and interpret this statistical measure. Communication of the meaning of the relationship also can be facilitated by the use of a graphical presentation of the results in the form of a *scatterplot* or by the use of an *expectancy table*. The construction of scatterplots (also known as scattergrams or scatter diagrams) and the calculation and interpretation of correlation coefficients are described and illustrated in Appendix A. Here we confine our discussion to the use and interpretation of these indicators of relationship within the context of criterion-related validation. The construction and interpretation of expectancy tables also will be described here.

Correlation

In order to illustrate the use of correlation coefficients and scatterplots in criterion-related validation, let us consider the exact scores that Mr. Young's pupils received on both the scholastic aptitude test (predictor) and the departmental examination in arithmetic (criterion). This information is provided in the first two columns of Table 3.3. By inspecting these two columns of scores as Mr. Young did, we see that the high scores in Column 1 tend to match the high scores in Column 2. This comparison is difficult to make, however, because the sizes of the test scores in the two columns are different.

The agreement of the two sets of scores can be more easily seen if the test scores are converted to ranks. This has been done in Columns 3 and 4 of Table 3.3. Note that the pupil who was first on the aptitude test ranked third on the arithmetic test; the pupil who was second on the aptitude test ranked fourth on the arithmetic test; the pupil who was third on the aptitude test ranked sixth on the arithmetic test; and so on. Comparing the rank order of the pupils on the two tests, as indicated in Columns 3 and 4 of Table 3.3, gives us a fairly good picture of the relationship between the two sets of scores. From this inspection we know that pupils who had a high standing on the aptitude test also had a high standing on the arithmetic test and that pupils who had a low standing on the aptitude test also had a low standing on the arithmetic test. Our inspection of Columns 3 and 4 also shows us, however, that the relationship between the pupils' ranks on the two tests is not perfect, that there is some shifting in rank order from one test to another. Our problem now is how we can express the degree of relationship between these two sets of ranks in meaningful terms. This is where the scatterplot and the correlation coefficient become useful.

A scatterplot of the pairs of scores for the 20 pupils in Mr. Young's class is shown in Figure 3.4. Each dot represents the two scores that were obtained by an individual pupil. The dots that correspond to the scores received by three of the students (John, Ruby, and Helen) are labeled (see Appendix A for another example and details on the construction of a scatterplot). The scatterplot immediately shows

Pupil	1 Fall Aptitude Scores	2 Spring Arithmetic Scores	3 Aptitude Rank	4 Arithmetic Rank
John	119	77	1	3
Henry	118	76	2	4
Mary	116	72	3	6
Susan	115	67	4	8
Bill	112	82	5	1
Carl	109	63	6	10
Grace	108	60	7	12
Ralph	106	78	8	2
Jane	105	69	9	7
Karl	104	49	10	18
Jim	102	48	11	19
Frank	100	58	12	14
Karen	98	56	13	16
Joan	97	57	14	15
Ruby	95	74	15	5
June	94	62	16	11
Helen	93	46	17	20
George	91	65	18	9
Alice	90	59	19	13
Martin	89	54	20	17

us two important facts about the relationship between scores on the aptitude test that pupils received in the fall and their performance on the comprehensive arithmetic examination the following spring. First, students such as John, who score well above the average in the fall, usually do better than the average on the comprehensive examination in the spring, while most students who score well below average in the fall also score below average in the spring (e.g., Helen). Second, there are some notable exceptions. Ruby, for example, ranked 15th out of 20 on the fall aptitude test, but she obtained the 5th highest score on the comprehensive examination in the spring. Although both facts (that there is a relationship and that it is imperfect) also could be seen from studying the scores in Table 3.3, the scatterplot provides an efficient summary and makes it clear that some of the exceptions to the statement that there is a relationship between the two sets of scores are substantial.

The relationship seen in Figure 3.4 still has not been quantified. For this we need to obtain a correlation coefficient, which is a statistical summary of the relationship between the scores on the two tests. The correlation coefficient that we shall use is known as the *Pearson product–moment* correlation coefficient, and is denoted by *r*. Procedures for calculating this coefficient are described in Appendix A. Here we shall focus on its meaning.

FIGURE 3.4
Scatterplot of test
scores for twenty
junior high school
pupils (scores shown
in Table 3.3).

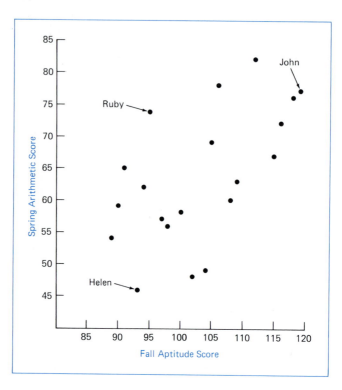

When the procedures for calculating a product–moment correlation coefficient are applied to the scores for the 20 pupils in Mr. Young's class we find that $r = .58$. This correlation coefficient is a statistical summary of the degree of relationship between the two sets of scores in Mr. Young's data. In this instance, it indicates the extent to which the fall aptitude test scores (predictor) are predictive of the spring arithmetic test scores (criterion). This type of correlation coefficient is called a *validity coefficient*.[3]

How good is Mr. Young's validity coefficient of .58? Should Mr. Young be happy or disappointed with this finding? Is this aptitude test a good predictor of future performance in arithmetic?

Unfortunately, there are no simple and straightforward answers to such questions. The interpretation of correlation coefficients is dependent on information from a variety of sources. First, we know that the following correlation coefficients indicate the extreme degree of relationship possible between variables:

1.00 = perfect positive relationship
$.00$ = no relationship
-1.00 = perfect negative relationship

[3] A criterion-related validation study should be based on a larger number of cases than the twenty students used here, but we are simply explaining what a validity coefficient is and how to interpret it.

Because Mr. Young's validity coefficient is .58, we know that the relationship is positive but somewhat less than perfect. Obviously, the closer a validity coefficient is to 1.00, the happier we shall be with it, because larger validity coefficients indicate greater accuracy in predicting from one variable to another.[4]

The three scatterplots in Figure 3.5 show in schematic form how Mr. Young's validity coefficient of .58 compares with correlations of .00 and 1.00. Each dot on the scatterplot indicates an individual's score position on both the predictor and the criterion. Thus, with a correlation of 1.00, each individual falls at the same position on both measures, providing a perfect prediction. At the other extreme, with a correlation of .00, an individual's score on the predictor tells us nothing about the criterion score. At each score level on the predictor, some individuals have high criterion scores, some have low criterion scores, and others fall in between. There is simply no basis for predicting. The scatterplot for a correlation of about .60 indicates that high predictor scores *tend* to go with high criterion scores and that low predictor scores *tend* to go with low criterion scores, but the relationship is far from perfect. As the size of a correlation coefficient increases, the dots on a scatterplot move in the direction of the diagonal series of dots shown for a perfect positive correlation (1.00), indicating increased prediction efficiency.

Another way of evaluating Mr. Young's validity coefficient of .58 is to compare it with the validity coefficients obtained from other methods of predicting performance in arithmetic. If this validity coefficient is larger than those obtained with other prediction procedures, Mr. Young will continue to use the scholastic aptitude test as the best means available to him for predicting his pupils' arithmetic performance. Thus, validity coefficients are large or small only in relation to one another. When prediction is important, we shall always consider more favorably the test with the largest validity coefficient. But in this regard, even aptitude tests with rather low validity may be useful if they are the best predictors available and if the predictions they provide are better than chance.

Estimating Present Performance

Up to this point we have emphasized the role of criterion-related validation in predicting future performance. Although this is probably its major use, there are times when we are interested in the relation of test performance to some other current measure of performance. In this case, we obtain both measures at approximately the same time and correlate the results. This is commonly done when a test is being considered as a replacement for a more time-consuming method of obtaining information. For example, Mrs. Brown, a biology teacher, wondered if an objective test of study skills could be used in place of the elaborate observation and rating procedures she was currently using. She felt that if a test could be substituted for the more complex procedures, she would have much more time to devote to individual pupils during the supervised study period. An analysis of the specific pupil characteristics on which she rated the pupils' study skills indicated that many of the procedures could be stated in the form of objective test questions. Conse-

---

[4]A coefficient of − 1.00 would also give us perfect prediction from one variable to another, but in educational measurements we are most commonly concerned with positive relationships.

FIGURE 3.5
Scatterplots illustrating
different degrees of
positive relationship
between a predictor
and a criterion.

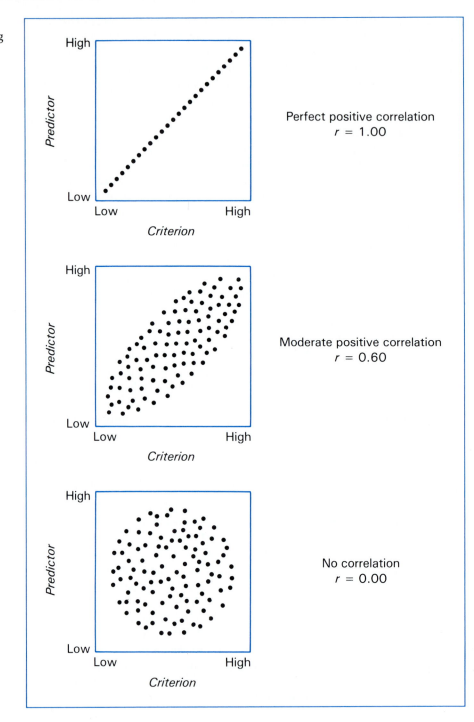

Perfect positive correlation
$r = 1.00$

Moderate positive correlation
$r = 0.60$

No correlation
$r = 0.00$

quently, she developed an objective test of study skills that she administered to her pupils. To determine how adequately the test measured study skills, she correlated the test results with her ratings of the pupils' study skills. The resulting correlation coefficient of .75 indicates considerable agreement between the test results and the criterion measure and represents the concurrent validation of Mrs. Brown's test of study skills.

We might also correlate test performance with some other current measure of performance to determine whether a predictive study is worthwhile. For example, if a set of scholastic aptitude test scores correlated to a sufficiently high degree (e.g., .60) with a set of achievement test scores obtained at the same time, it would indicate that the scholastic aptitude test had enough potential as a predictor to make a predictive study worthwhile. On the other hand, a low correlation would discourage us from carrying out the predictive study, because we know that the correlation would become still lower when the time period between measures was extended. Other things being equal, the larger the time span is between two measures, the smaller the correlation coefficient will be.

Factors Influencing Correlation Coefficients

There are a number of factors that influence the size of all correlation coefficients, including validity coefficients. Knowing these factors can help interpret a particular correlation coefficient — either one we have computed ourselves or one found in a test manual. Some of the basic factors to consider are shown in Figure 3.6. In general, larger correlation coefficients are obtained when the characteristics measured are more alike (e.g., correlating scores from two reading tests), the spread of scores is large, the stability of the scores is high, and the time span between measures is short. As we move along the continuum toward the other end of the scale on any of these factors, the correlation coefficients tend to become smaller. Thus, a small predictive validity coefficient might be explained, in part, by any one of the factors shown on the right side of Figure 3.6 or, more commonly, by some combination of them.

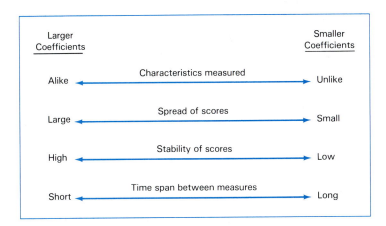

FIGURE 3.6
Some basic factors influencing the size of correlation coefficients.

Expectancy Table

How well a test predicts future performance or estimates current performance on some criterion measure also can be shown by directly plotting the data in a twofold chart like the one shown in Figure 3.7. Here, Mr. Young's data (from Table 3.3) have been tabulated by placing a tally showing each individual's standing on both the fall aptitude scores and the spring arithmetic scores. For example, John scored 119 on the fall aptitude test and 77 on the spring arithmetic test, and so a tally representing his performance was placed in the upper right-hand cell. The performance of all other pupils on the two tests was tallied in the same manner. Thus, each tally mark in Figure 3.7 represents how well each of Mr. Young's 20 pupils performed on the fall and spring tests. The total number of pupils in each cell and in each column and row is also indicated.

The expectancy grid shown in Figure 3.7 can be used as an expectancy table simply by using the frequencies in each cell. The interpretation of such information is simple and direct. For example, of those pupils who scored above average on the fall aptitude test, none scored below 65 on the spring arithmetic test, 2 out of 5 scored between 65 and 74, and 3 out of 5 scored between 75 and 84. Of those who scored below average on the fall aptitude test, none scored in the top category on the spring arithmetic test, and 4 out of 5 scored below 65. These interpretations are limited to the group tested, but from such results one might make predictions concerning future pupils. We can say, for example, that pupils who score above average on the fall aptitude test will probably score above average on the spring arithmetic test. Other predictions can be made in the same way by noting the frequencies in each cell of the grid in Figure 3.7.

More commonly, the figures in an expectancy table are expressed in percentages, which can be readily obtained from the grid by converting each cell frequency to a percentage of the total number of tallies in its row. This has been done for the data in Figure 3.7 and the results are presented in Table 3.4. The first row of the table shows that of the 5 pupils who scored above average on the fall aptitude test, 40 percent (2 pupils) scored between 65 and 74 on the spring arithmetic test, and 60 percent (3 pupils) scored between 75 and 84. The remaining rows should be read in a similar manner. The use of percentage makes the figures in each row and column comparable. Our predictions then can be made in standard terms (that is, chances out of 100) for all score levels. Our interpretation is apt to be a little clearer if we say that Mary's chances of being in the top group on the criterion measure are

FIGURE 3.7
Expectancy grid showing how scores on the fall aptitude tests and spring arithmetic tests are tallied in appropriate cells (from data in Table 3.3).

Fall Aptitude Scores	Spring Arithmetic Scores				Totals
	45–54	55–64	65–74	75–84	
Above Average (over 110)			// 2	/// 3	5
Average (95–110)	// 2	//// 5	// 2	/ 1	10
Below Average (below 95)	// 2	// 2	/ 1		5
Totals	4	7	5	4	20

Fall Aptitude Scores	Percentage in Each Score Group on Spring Arithmetic Test				TABLE 3.4 Expectancy Table Showing the Relation Between Fall Aptitude Scores and Spring Arithmetic Scores*
	45–54	55–64	65–74	75–84	
Above average (Over 110)			40	60	
Average (95–110)	20	50	20	10	
Below average (Below 95)	40	40	20		

*From data in Figure 3.7.

60 out of 100 and that Ralph's are only 10 out of 100 than if we say that Mary's chances are 3 out of 5 and that Ralph's are 1 out of 10.

Expectancy tables take many different forms and may be used to show the relation between various types of measures. The number of categories used with the predictor, or criterion, may be as few as two or as many as seem desirable. Also, the predictor may be any set of measures useful in predicting, and the criterion may be course grades, ratings, test scores, or whatever other measure of success is relevant.

When interpreting expectancy tables based on a small number of cases, like Mr. Young's class of 20 pupils, our predictions should be regarded as highly tentative. Each percentage is based on so few pupils that we can expect large fluctuations in these figures from one group of pupils to another. It is frequently possible to increase the number of pupils represented in the table by combining test results from several classes. When we do this, our percentages are, of course, much more stable, and our predictions can be made with greater confidence. In any event, expectancy tables provide a simple and direct means of indicating the predictive value of test results.

The "Criterion" Problem

In a criterion-related validation study, a major problem is obtaining a satisfactory *criterion* of success. Remember that Mr. Young used a comprehensive departmental examination as the criterion of success in his seventh-grade arithmetic class and that Mrs. Brown used her own ratings of the pupils' study skills. In each instance, the criterion of success was only partially suitable as a basis for test validation. Mr. Young recognized that the departmental examination did not measure all of the important learning outcomes that he aimed at in teaching arithmetic. There was not nearly enough emphasis on arithmetic reasoning; the interpretation of graphs and charts was sadly neglected; and, of course, the test did not evaluate the pupils' attitudes toward arithmetic (which Mr. Young considered to be extremely important). Likewise, Mrs. Brown was well aware of the shortcomings of her rating of pupils' study skills. She sensed that some pupils "put on a show" when they knew they were being observed, and in other instances, she felt that some of the pupils were probably overrated on study skills because of their high achievement in class work. Despite these recognized shortcomings, both Mr. Young and Mrs. Brown found it necessary to use these criterion measures because they were the best available.

The plights of Mr. Young and Mrs. Brown in finding a suitable criterion of success for test validation are not unusual. Selecting a satisfactory criterion is one of the most difficult problems in making a criterion validation study, and for most educational purposes, there is no entirely satisfactory criterion of success. Those used tend to be lacking in comprehensiveness and in most cases produce results that are less stable than those of the test being validated.

The lack of suitable criteria for validating achievement tests has important implications for the classroom teacher. Because statistical types of evidence usually will not be available, teachers will have to depend on procedures of logical analysis to ensure valid test interpretations. This means carefully identifying the objectives of instruction, stating these objectives in terms of specific changes in pupil performance, and constructing or selecting evaluation instruments that satisfactorily measure the learning outcomes sought. Thus, content validation and the logical analysis involved in construct validation will be especially important to the teacher's evaluation of pupil learning.

Construct-Related Evidence

The types of validation approaches thus far described provide validity evidence that is directly applicable to specific practical test uses. Content-related evidence helps us determine how well test scores represent a given domain of tasks and is especially useful in both the preparation and evaluation of achievement tests. Criterion-related evidence indicates how well test scores predict or estimate performance on some criterion measure. In addition to these more specific and immediately practical uses, we usually wish to interpret test scores in terms of more general individual characteristics. These characteristics may be labeled in a variety of ways (e.g., abilities, psychological traits, personal qualities), but regardless of the label, they involve some inference about the person that go beyond the factual statement that he or she obtained a particular score on a particular test. For example, rather than speak about a pupil's score on a particular mathematics test or how well it predicts grades in future mathematics courses, we might want to infer that the pupil possesses a certain degree of *mathematical reasoning ability*. This provides a broad general description of pupil performance that has implications for many different uses.

Whenever we wish to interpret test performance in terms of some psychological trait or quality, we are concerned with construct-related evidence. A *construct* is a psychological quality that we assume exists in order to explain some aspect of behavior. Mathematical reasoning is a construct and so are intelligence, creativity, reading comprehension, and such personality characteristics as sociability, honesty, and anxiety. These are called *constructs* because they are theoretical constructions that are used to explain behavior. When we interpret test scores as a measure of a particular construct, we are implying that there is such a construct, that it differs from other constructs, and that the test scores provide a measure of the construct that is little influenced by extraneous factors. Verifying such implications is the task of construct validation.

There is an obvious advantage in being able to interpret test performance in terms of psychological constructs. Each construct has an underlying theory that can be brought to bear in describing and predicting a person's behavior. If, for example, we say a person is highly intelligent, has good reading comprehension, or is sociable, we know what type of behavior might be expected in various specific situations.

Construct validation may be defined as the process of determining the extent to which test performance can be interpreted in terms of one or more psychological constructs. Although construct validation has been commonly associated with theory building and theory testing,[5] it also has implications for the practical use of test results. Whenever a test is to be interpreted as a measure of a particular construct, the various types of evidence useful for construct validation should be considered during its development or selection. This will usually include evidence from both content- and criterion-referenced validation studies plus other types of evidence. The most appropriate types of evidence will be dictated by the particular construct to be measured.

In general, the process of construct validation involves (1) identifying and describing, by means of a theoretical framework, the meaning of the construct to be measured; (2) deriving hypotheses regarding test performance from the theory underlying the construct; and (3) verifying the hypotheses by logical and empirical means. Construct validation takes place primarily during the development and tryout of a test and is based on an accumulation of evidence from many different sources. When selecting a published test that presumably measures a particular construct, such as math reasoning or reading comprehension, the test manual should be examined to determine what evidence is presented to support the validity of the proposed interpretations.

An illustration of some types of evidence that might be used in the construct validation of a math reasoning test is shown in Figure 3.8. Although other types of studies could be added, this listing is sufficient to clarify the *variety* of types of evidence needed to support the claim that the test scores can be interpreted as measures of math reasoning. Notice that both content-related and criterion-related evidence are included, along with other comparisons and correlations. No single type of evidence is sufficient, but the accumulation of various types of evidence helps describe what the test scores measure and how they relate to other significant variables. This clarifies the meaning of the test performance and aids in determining how validly math reasoning is being measured by the test.

In theory building and theory testing, the accumulation of evidence for construct validation may be endless. As new data are gathered, both the theory and the test

[5]L. J. Cronbach and P. E. Meehl, "Construct Validity in Psychological Tests," *Psychological Bulletin* 52 (1955): 281–302.

FIGURE 3.8
An illustration of some types of evidence used in construct validation.

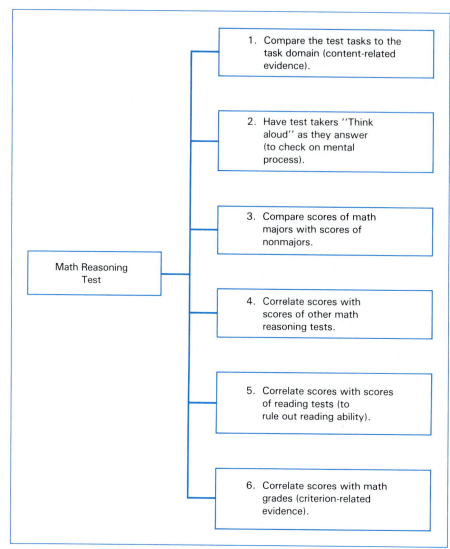

1. Compare the test tasks to the task domain (content-related evidence).

2. Have test takers "Think aloud" as they answer (to check on mental process).

3. Compare scores of math majors with scores of nonmajors.

Math Reasoning Test

4. Correlate scores with scores of other math reasoning tests.

5. Correlate scores with scores of reading tests (to rule out reading ability).

6. Correlate scores with math grades (criterion-related evidence).

are likely to be modified, and the testing of hypotheses continues. For the practical use of test results, however, we need to employ a more restricted framework when considering construct validation. During the development and selection of tests, our focus should be on the types of evidence that it seems reasonable to obtain, giving special attention to those data that are most relevant to the types of interpretations to be made. We can thus increase our understanding of what the test measures and how validly it does so without becoming involved in an endless task of data gathering.

Methods Used in Construct Validation

Construct validation depends on logical inferences drawn from a variety of types of data. As noted earlier, both content-related and criterion-related evidence provide partial support for our interpretations, but this must be supplemented by various studies that further clarify the meaning of the test scores. Although it is impossible to describe all of the specific procedures that might be used in construct validation, the following exemplify some of the more commonly used methods.

1. Defining the domain of tasks to be measured. The test specifications should be so well defined that the meaning of the construct is clear and it is possible to judge the extent to which the test provides a relevant and representative measure of the task domain (content validation). If a single construct is being measured, the items should evoke similar types of responses and be highly interrelated.

2. Analyzing the mental process required by the test items. The mental process called forth by the test items can be determined both by examining the test items themselves and by administering the test to individual pupils and having them "think aloud" as they answer. Thus, examination of the items in a reading comprehension test may indicate that literal comprehension is emphasized, with relatively few items devoted to inferential comprehension. This judgment can be checked by administering the test to individual pupils and having them explain how they obtain their answers. Similarly, "thinking aloud" on a math reasoning test, as in Figure 3.8, may verify that the items call for the intended reasoning process, or it may reveal that most problems can be solved by a simple trial-and-error procedure.

3. Comparing the scores of known groups. In some cases it is possible to predict that scores will differ from one group to another. These may be age groups, trained and untrained, adjusted and maladjusted, and the like. For example, most abilities increase with age (at least during childhood and adolescence). Also, it is reasonable to expect that achievement test scores will discriminate among groups with different amounts of training and that scores on adjustment inventories will discriminate between groups of adjusted and maladjusted individuals. Thus, a prediction of differences for a particular test can be checked against groups that are known to differ and the results used as partial support for construct validation.

4. Comparing scores before and after some particular treatment. Some test scores can be expected to be fairly resistant to specific training (e.g., intelligence), whereas others can be expected to increase (e.g., achievement). Similarly, some test scores can be expected to change as certain types of experimental treatment are introduced. For example, we would expect the scores on an anxiety test to change when individuals are subjected to an anxiety-producing experience. Thus, from the theory underlying the trait being measured, we can predict that the scores of a particular test will change (or remain stable) under various conditions. If our predictions are verified, the results will be further support for construct validation.

5. Correlating the scores with other measures. The scores of any particular test can be expected to correlate substantialy with the scores of other tests that presumably measure the same thing. By the same token, the test scores can be expected to have lower correlations with tests designed to measure a different ability or trait. For example, we would expect scholastic aptitude test scores to correlate rather highly with those of another scholastic aptitude test, but much lower with the scores of a musical aptitude test. Thus, for any given test, we would predict higher correlations with *like* tests and lower correlations with *unlike* tests. In addition, we might also predict that the test scores would correlate with various practical criteria. Scholastic aptitude scores, for example, should correlate satisfactorily with school grades, achievement test scores, and other measures of achievement. This latter type of evidence is, of course, obtained by criterion-related studies. Our interest here, however, is not in the immediate problem of prediction, but rather in using these correlations to support the claim that the test measures scholastic aptitude. As indicated earlier, construct validation depends on a wide array of evidence, including that provided by the other validation procedures.

In construct validation, our interest is not limited to the construct the test was designed to measure. Any factor that might influence the test scores is of legitimate concern. For example, we might ask how much the scores on a reading test depend on speed of reading or to what extent scores on a math reasoning test are influenced by computation skill and reading ability. Broadly conceived construct validation is an attempt to account for the differences in test scores. During test development, an attempt is made to rule out extraneous factors that might distort the meaning of the scores, and follow-up studies are conducted to verify the success of these attempts. The aim is to clarify the meaning of the test performance by identifying the nature and strength of all factors influencing the scores on the test.

Construct validation is important to all types of testing — achievement, aptitude, and personal–social development. Whether constructing or selecting a test, the meaning of the test scores is dependent on the care with which the test was constructed and the array of evidence supporting the types of interpretations to be made. Construct validation is emphasized in most recent discussions of validity in the technical and theoretical literature, in part, because, as we have seen, construct-related evidence subsumes content and criterion-related evidence and, in part, because *meaning* is crucial in our uses and interpretations of the scores. The latter point was stressed by Messick, who stated, "The meaning of the measure, and hence its construct validity, must always be pursued — not only to support test interpretation but also to justify test use."[6]

Factors Influencing Validity

Numerous factors tend to make test results invalid for their intended use. Some are rather obvious and easily avoided. No teacher would think of measuring knowledge of social studies with an English test. Nor would a teacher consider measuring

[6]S. Messick, "Validity," in *Educational Measurement*, 3d ed., ed. R. L. Linn (New York: Macmillan, 1989), p. 17.

problem-solving skills in third-grade arithmetic with a test designed for sixth-graders. In both instances, the test results would obviously be invalid. The factors influencing validity are of this same general nature but much more subtle in character. For example, a teacher may overload a social studies test with items concerning historical facts, and thus the scores are less valid as a measure of achievement in social studies. Or a third-grade teacher may select appropriate arithmetic problems for a test but use vocabulary in the problems and directions that only the better readers are able to understand. The arithmetic test then becomes, in part, a reading test that invalidates the results for their intended use. These examples show some of the more subtle factors influencing validity for which the teacher should be alert, whether constructing classroom tests or selecting published tests.

Factors in the Test Itself

A careful examination of test items will indicate whether the test appears to measure the subject-matter content and the mental functions that the teacher is interested in testing. However, any of the following factors can prevent the test items from functioning as intended and thereby lower the validity of the interpretations from the test scores.

1. Unclear directions. Directions that do not clearly indicate to the pupil how to respond to the items, whether it is permissible to guess, and how to record the answers will tend to reduce validity.

2. Reading vocabulary and sentence structure too difficult. Vocabulary and sentence structure that is too complicated for the pupils taking the test will result in the test's measuring reading comprehension and aspects of intelligence, which will distort the meaning of the test results.

3. Inappropriate level of difficulty of the test items. In norm-referenced tests, items that are too easy or too difficult will not provide reliable discrimination among pupils and will therefore lower validity. In criterion-referenced tests, the failure to match the difficulty specified by the learning outcome will lower validity.

4. Poorly constructed test items. Test items that unintentionally provide clues to the answer will tend to measure the pupils' alertness in detecting clues as well as those aspects of pupil performance that the test is intended to measure.

5. Ambiguity. Ambiguous statements in test items contribute to misinterpretations and confusion. Ambiguity sometimes confuses the better pupils more than it does the poor pupils, causing the items to discriminate in a negative direction.

6. Test items inappropriate for the outcomes being measured. Attempting to measure understanding, thinking skills, and other complex types of achievement with test forms that are appropriate only for measuring factual knowledge will invalidate the results.

7. Inadequate time limits. Time limits that do not provide pupils with enough time to consider the items and provide thoughtful responses can reduce the validity of interpretations of test scores. Rather than a measure of what a pupil knows about a topic or is able to do given adequate time, the test may become a measure of the speed with which the student can respond. For some measures (e.g., a typing test), speed may be important. However, for most achievement tests we would like to minimize the effects of speededness on pupil performance.

8. Test too short. A test is only a sample of the many questions that might be asked. If a test is too short to provide a representative sample of the performance we are interested in, its validity will suffer accordingly.

9. Improper arrangement of items. Test items are typically arranged in order of difficulty, with the easiest items first. Placing difficult items early in the test may cause pupils to spend too much time on these and prevent them from reaching items they could easily answer. Improper arrangement may also influence validity by having a detrimental effect on pupil motivation. This influence is likely to be strongest with young pupils.

10. Identifiable pattern of answers. Placing correct answers in some systematic pattern (e.g., T, T, F, F or A, B, C, D, A, B, C, D) will enable pupils to guess the answers to some items more easily, and this will lower validity.

In short, any defect in the test's construction that prevents the test items from functioning as intended will help invalidate the interpretations to be drawn from the results. Much of what is written in the following chapters is directed toward helping teachers improve the validity of their interpretations of test scores and other evaluation results.

Functioning Content and Teaching Procedures

In the case of achievement testing, the functioning content of test items cannot be determined merely by examining the form and content of the test. For example, the following item may appear to measure arithmetical reasoning if examined without reference to what the pupils have been taught:

EXAMPLE

If a 40′ pipe is cut so that the shorter piece is ⅔ as long as the longer piece, what is the length of the short piece?

However, if the teacher has taught the solution to this particular problem before giving the test, the test item now will measure no more than memorized knowledge. Similarly, tests of understanding, critical thinking, and other complex learning outcomes will provide valid measures in these areas only if the test items function as intended. If the pupils have previously been taught the solutions to the particular problems included in the test or have been taught mechanical steps for obtaining the solutions, the test results no longer can be considered valid indicators of the achievement of the more complex mental processes.

Factors in Test Administration and Scoring

The administration and scoring of a test may also introduce factors that have a detrimental effect on the validity of the interpretations from the results. In the case of teacher-made tests, such factors as insufficient time to complete the test, unfair aid to individual pupils who ask for help, cheating during the examination, and the unreliable scoring of essay answers tend to lower validity. In the case of published tests, failure to follow the standard directions and time limits, giving pupils unauthorized assistance, and errors in scoring similarly contribute to lower validity. For all types of tests, adverse physical and psychological conditions at the time of testing may also have a negative effect.

Factors in Pupils' Responses

In some instances, invalid test interpretations are caused by personal factors influencing the pupil's response to the test situation rather than to any shortcomings in the test instrument or its administration. Some pupils may be bothered by emotional disturbances that interfere with their test performance. Others may be frightened by the test situation and thereby are unable to respond normally, and still others may not be motivated to put forth their best effort. These and other factors that restrict and modify pupils' responses in the test situation will obviously distort the test results.

A less obvious factor that influences test results is *response set*, a consistent tendency to follow a certain pattern in responding to test items. For example, some persons will respond "true" when they do not know the answer to a true–false item, and others will tend to mark "false." A test with many true statements will consequently be to the advantage of the first type of person and to the disadvantage of the second type. Although some response sets, such as the one illustrated, can be offset by careful test construction procedures (e.g., including an equal number of true and false statements in the test), other response sets are more difficult to control. Typical of response sets in this latter category are the tendency to work for speed rather than accuracy, the tendency to gamble when in doubt, and the use of a particular style in responding to essay tests. These response sets reduce the validity of the test results by introducing into the test score factors that are not pertinent to the purpose of the measurement.

Nature of the Group and the Criterion

Validity is always specific to a particular group. An arithmetic test based on story problems, for example, may measure reasoning ability in a slow group and a combination of simple recall of information and computation skill in a more advanced group. Similarly, scores on a science test may be accounted for largely by reading comprehension in one group and by knowledge of facts in another. What a test measures is influenced by such factors as age, sex, ability level, educational background, and cultural background. Thus, in appraising reports of test validity included in test manuals or other sources, it is important to determine the nature of the validation group. How closely it compares in significant characteristics with the group of pupils we wish to test determines how applicable the information is to our particular group.

As noted earlier, in Figure 3.6, criterion-related validity coefficients will be smaller when (1) the characteristics measured by the predictor and the criterion are less alike, (2) the spread of scores is smaller, (3) the stability of scores is lower, and (4) the time span between measures is longer. Of these factors, probably the most frequently overlooked is the nature of the criterion being predicted. This is unfortunate, because knowing the specific nature of the criterion can help evaluate validity coefficients. For example, scores on a mathematics aptitude test are likely to provide a more accurate prediction of achievement in a science course in which quantitative problems are stressed than in one in which they play only a minor role. Likewise, we can expect scores on a critical thinking test to correlate more highly with grades in social studies courses that emphasize critical thinking than in those that depend largely on the memorization of the factual information. These examples simply illustrate the general rule that validity coefficients are influenced by the similarity between the performance measured by the test and the performance represented in the criterion. Thus, both need to be examined carefully for a full understanding of the relationship.

Because validity information varies with the group tested and the composition of the criterion measures used, published validation data should be considered as highly tentative. Whenever possible, the validity of the test results should be checked in the specific local situation.

This discussion of factors influencing the validity of test results should make clear the pervasive and functional nature of the concept validity. In the final analysis, the test users must make the final judgment concerning the validity of the test interpretations, for they best know how well the test fits the particular use, how well the testing conditions were controlled, and how typical the responses were to the testing situation.

Summary

The most important quality to consider when constructing or selecting a test (or other evaluation instrument) is validity, which refers to the meaningfulness and appropriateness of the interpretations to be made from test scores and other evaluation results. In using validity information, it is important to keep in mind that validity refers to the *interpretation of the test scores* rather than to the test itself, that its presence is a matter of *degree*, that it is always *specific* to some particular interpretation or use, and that it is a *unitary concept*.

Although validity is a unitary concept, it is based on various kinds of evidence. The three basic approaches to test validation are simply convenient categories for describing evidence of validity. Thus, content-related, criterion-related, and construct-related evidence all can contribute to the meaning of a set of test scores, and the strongest case for validity can be made when all three are present. For many specific and practical uses of test scores, however, just one or two types of evidence may be necessary or feasible to obtain.

Content validation is the process of determining the extent to which a set of test tasks provides a relevant and representative sample of the domain of tasks under consideration. This kind of validation procedure is especially important in achievement testing and is of primary concern in constructing classroom tests. The procedure involves writing test specifications that define a domain of instructionally relevant tasks and then constructing or selecting test items that provide a representative and relevant measure of the tasks. Content validation is also important in selecting published achievement tests. Here, the crucial question is how well the test measures the content and objectives of the *local instructional program*. The same types of test specifications used in constructing classroom tests can aid in selecting published tests that provide valid scores. The process of obtaining content-related evidence is also used as part of the procedure of construct validation.

Criterion-related validation is the process of determining the extent to which test performance is related to some other valued measure of performance (called a *criterion*). This may involve studies of how well test scores predict future performance (*predictive validation* study) or estimate some current performance (*concurrent validation* study). These validity studies are typically reported by means of a correlation coefficient called a *validity coefficient* or by use of an expectancy table. Criterion-related evidence of validity is of special significance in aptitude testing, but it is pertinent whenever test results are used to make predictions or to substitute for evaluation results obtained by more time-consuming methods. Because the meaning of test scores is enhanced by knowing what other measures they relate to, criterion-related studies are also used as partial evidence in construct validation.

Construct validation is the process of determining the extent to which test performance can be interpreted in terms of one or more constructs. Construct validation typically includes both content-related and criterion-related evidence plus other types of information. The procedure is one of clarifying what is being measured and what factors influence the test scores so that test performance can be interpreted most meaningfully. This involves both logical analysis and various comparative and correlational studies. Although the accumulation of evidence could be endless, in practical situations we need to focus on the types of evidence that it seems reasonable to obtain and that are most relevant to the types of interpretations to be made. The more complete the evidence is, however, the more confident we can be concerning the meaning of the test scores.

Many factors tend to influence the validity of test interpretations. Some of these influences can be found in the test instrument itself, some in the relation of teaching to testing, some in the administration and scoring of the test, some in the atypical responses of pupils to the test situation, and still others in the nature of the group tested and in the composition of the criterion measures used. A major aim in the construction, selection, and use of tests and other evaluation instruments is to control those factors that have an adverse affect on validity and to interpret the results in accordance with what validity information is available.

Learning Exercises

1. If a fellow teacher told you that a particular reading test had high validity, what types of questions would you ask?
2. A high school science teacher prepared a common test to be used in all sections of biology,

without consulting the teachers of the other sections. What effect might this have on the test's validity? Why?

3. Compare the relative difficulty of determining validity for a norm-referenced survey test in social studies and a criterion-referenced mastery test in arithmetic. For which one would a table of specifications be most useful? Why?

4. If you wanted to determine the validity of a published achievement test for use in a course you are teaching or plan to teach, what procedure would you follow? Describe your procedure step by step, and give reasons for each step.

5. Define a validity coefficient, and list several factors that will influence its size.

6. Describe how to prepare an expectancy table. What is the advantage of an expectancy table over a validity coefficient for making predictions?

7. What types of evidence might be useful in the construct validation of each of the following?
   a. Test of reading comprehension.
   b. Test of creativity.

8. Study the validity sections of a test manual for a published achievement test and a scholastic aptitude test. How does the information differ for these two types of tests? Why?

9. Consult the validity section of the latest edition of *Standards for Educational and Psychological Testing* (see the reading list for this chapter), and review the types of information that test manuals should contain. Compare a recent test manual with the *Standards*.

10. List and briefly describe as many factors as you can think of that might lower the validity of a classroom test.

Suggestions for Further Reading

AMERICAN PSYCHOLOGICAL ASSOCIATION. *Standards for Educational and Psychological Testing.* Washington, D.C.: APA, 1985. See the first technical section on test validity for descriptions of the basic validation procedures and the nature of validity information to be sought in test manuals.

ANASTASI, ANNE. *Psychological Testing*, 6th ed. New York: Macmillan, 1988. Chapter 6, "Validity: Basic Concepts," describes the standard procedures for test validation.

CRONBACH, L. J. *Essentials of Psychological Testing*, 4th ed. New York: Harper & Row, 1984. Chapter 5, "Validation," describes and illustrates the procedures of test validation.

HAMBLETON, R. K. "Validating the Test Scores." In R. A. Berk, ed., *A Guide to Criterion-Referenced Test Construction*. Baltimore: Johns Hopkins University Press, 1984. Reviews the technique of content validation and methods for establishing the validity of the scores.

MESSICK, S. "Validity." In R. L. Linn, ed., *Educational Measurement*, 3d ed. New York: Macmillan, 1989, Chapter 2. Provides a comprehensive and theoretically sophisticated discussion of validity.

Chapter 4

Reliability and Other Desired Characteristics

Next to validity, reliability is the most important characteristic of evaluation results. . . . Reliability (1) provides the consistency that makes validity possible and (2) indicates how much confidence we can place in our results. . . . The practicality of the evaluation procedure is, of course, also of concern to the busy classroom teacher.

In Chapter 3 we emphasized that validity is the most important consideration in the selection and construction of evaluation procedures. First and foremost, we want evaluation results to serve the specific uses for which they are intended. Next in importance is *reliability*, and following that is a host of practical features that can be best classified under the heading of *usability*.

Nature of Reliability

Reliability refers to the *consistency* of measurement—that is, how consistent test scores or other evaluation results are from one measurement to another. Suppose, for instance, that Miss Jones had just given an achievement test to her pupils. How similar would the pupils' scores have been had she tested them yesterday or tomorrow or next week? How would the scores have varied had she selected a different sample of equivalent items? If it were an essay test, how much would the scores have differed had a different teacher scored it? These are the types of questions with which reliability is concerned. Test scores merely provide a limited measure of performance obtained at a particular time. Unless the measurement can be shown to be reasonably consistent (that is, generalizable) over different occasions or over different samples of the same performance domain, we can have little confidence in the results.

On the other hand, we cannot expect test results to be perfectly consistent. There are numerous factors other than the quality being measured that may influence test scores. If a single test is administered to the same group twice in close succession, some variation in scores can be expected because of temporary fluctuations in memory, attention, effort, fatigue, emotional strain, guessing, and the like. With a longer time period between tests, additional variation in scores may be caused by intervening learning experiences, changes in health, forgetting, and less comparable testing conditions. If we use a different sample of items in the second test, still another factor is likely to influence the results. Individuals may find one test easier than the other because it happens to contain more items on topics with which they are familiar. Such extraneous factors as these introduce a certain amount of *measurement error* into *all* test scores. Methods of determining reliability are essentially means of determining how much measurement error is present under different conditions. In general, the more consistent our test results are from one measurement to another, the less error there will be and, consequently, the greater the reliability.

The meaning of reliability, as applied to testing and evaluation, can be further clarified by noting the following general points:

1. Reliability refers to the *results* obtained with an evaluation instrument and not to the instrument itself. Any particular instrument may have a number of different reliabilities, depending on the group involved and the situation in which it is used. Thus, it is more appropriate to speak of the reliability of the "test scores" or of the "measurement" than of the "test" or the "instrument."

2. A closely related point is that an estimate of reliability always refers to a particular type of consistency. Test scores are not reliable in general. They are reliable (or generalizable) over different periods of time, over different samples of questions, over different raters, and the like. It is possible for test scores to be consistent in one of these respects and not in another. The appropriate type of consistency in a particular case is dictated by the use to be made of the results. For example, if we wish to know what individuals will be like at some future time, constancy of scores over time will be important. On the other hand, if we want to measure an individual's shifts in anxiety from moment to moment, we shall need a measure that lacks constancy over occasions in order to obtain the information we desire. Thus, for different interpretations we need different analyses of consistency. Treating reliability as a general characteristic can only lead to erroneous interpretations.

3. Reliability is a necessary but not a sufficient condition for validity. A test that produces totally inconsistent results cannot possibly provide valid information about the performance being measured. On the other hand, highly consistent test results may be measuring the wrong thing or may be used in inappropriate ways. Thus, low reliability can be expected to restrict the degree of validity that is obtained, but high reliability does not ensure that a satisfactory degree of validity will be present. In short, *reliability merely provides the consistency that makes validity possible*.

4. Reliability is primarily statistical. The logical analysis of a test will provide little evidence concerning the reliability of the scores. The test must be administered, one or more times, to an appropriate group of persons, and the consistency of the results determined. This consistency may be expressed in terms of shifts in the relative standing of persons in the group or in terms of the amount of variation to be expected in an individual's score. Consistency in the first case is reported by means of a correlation coefficient called a *reliability coefficient* and in the second case is reported by means of the *standard error of measurement*. Both methods of expressing reliability are widely used and should be understood by persons responsible for interpreting test results. Because both methods require variability in scores, these procedures for estimating reliability are primarily useful with *norm-referenced* measures. Procedures for estimating the reliability of criterion-referenced mastery tests will be considered later in the chapter.

Some Basic Terminology

Correlation coefficient	A statistic that indicates the degree of relationship between any two sets of scores obtained from the same group of individuals (e.g., correlation between height and weight).
Validity coefficient	A *correlation coefficient* that indicates the degree to which a measure predicts or estimates performance on some criterion measure (e.g., correlation between scholastic aptitude scores and grades in school).
Reliability coefficient	A *correlation coefficient* that indicates the degree of relationship between two sets of measures obtained from the same instrument or procedure (e.g., correlation between scores obtained from administrations of two forms of a test).

Determining Reliability by Correlation Methods

In determining reliability it would be desirable to obtain two sets of measures under identical conditions and then to compare the results. This procedure is impossible, of course, because the conditions under which evaluation data are obtained can never be identical. As a substitute for this ideal procedure, several methods of estimating reliability have been introduced.[1] The methods are similar in that all of them involve correlating two sets of data, obtained either from the same evaluation instrument or from equivalent forms of the same procedure. The correlation coefficient used to determine reliability is calculated and interpreted in the same manner as that used in determining the statistical estimates of validity. The only difference between a validity coefficient and a reliability coefficient is that the former is based on agreement with an outside criterion and the latter is based on agreement between two sets of results from the same procedure.

The chief methods of estimating reliability are shown in Table 4.1. Note that different types of consistency are determined by the different methods — consistency over a period of time, over different forms of the instrument, and within the instrument itself. The reliability coefficient resulting from each method must be

TABLE 4.1 Methods of Estimating Reliability	Type of Reliability Measure	Procedure
Test–retest method	Measure of stability	Give the same test twice to the same group with any time interval between tests, from several minutes to several years
Equivalent-forms method	Measure of equivalence	Give two forms of the test to the same group in close succession
(Test–retest with equivalent forms)	Measure of stability and equivalence	Give two forms of the test to the same group with increased time interval between forms
Split-half method	Measure of internal consistency	Give test once. Score two equivalent halves of test (e.g., odd items and even items); correct correlation between halves to fit whole test by Spearman–Brown formula
Kuder–Richardson method	Measure of internal consistency	Give test once. Score total test and apply Kuder–Richardson formula

[1]American Psychological Association, *Standards for Educational and Psychological Testing* (Washington, D.C.: APA, 1985).

interpreted according to the type of consistency being investigated. Each of these methods of estimating reliability will be considered in further detail as we proceed. Although these methods will be discussed mainly with reference to testing procedures, they are also applicable to other types of evaluation techniques.

Test–Retest Method

To estimate reliability by means of the test–retest method, the same test is administered twice to the same group of pupils with a given time interval between the two administrations (see Figure 4.1). The resulting test scores are correlated, and this correlation coefficient provides a measure of stability; that is, it indicates how stable the test results are over the given period of time. If the results are highly stable, those pupils who are high on one administration of the test will tend to be high on the other administration, and the remaining pupils will tend to stay in their same relative positions on both administrations. Such stability is indicated by a large correlation coefficient. Recall from our previous discussion of correlation coefficients that a perfect positive relationship is indicated by 1.00 and a zero relationship by .00. Measures of stability in the .80s and .90s are commonly reported for standardized tests of aptitude and achievement over occasions within the same year.

One important factor to keep in mind when interpreting measures of stability is the time interval between tests. If this time interval is short, say a day or two, the constancy of the results will be inflated because pupils will remember some of their answers from the first test to the second. If the time interval is long, say about a year, the results will be influenced not only by the instability of the testing procedure but also by actual changes in the pupils over that period of time. In general, the longer the time interval is between test and retest, the more the results

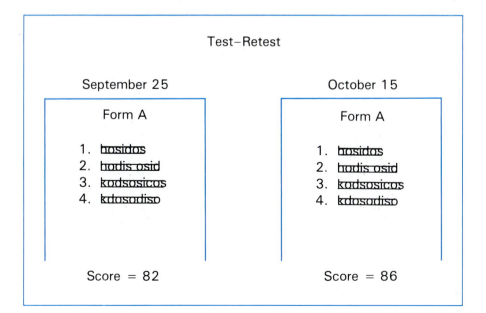

FIGURE 4.1
Test–retest method
(using same test forms).

will be influenced by changes in the pupil characteristic being measured and the smaller the reliability coefficient will be.

The best time interval between test administrations will depend largely on the use to be made of the results. If, for example, college admissions test scores can be submitted as part of an application to college several years after the test was taken, then stability over several years is quite important. But stability over a long period of time is neither important nor desirable for a unit test in a course designed to assess mastery of certain concepts and readiness to move on to new material. Thus, for some decisions we are interested in reliability coefficients based on a long interval between test and retest, and for others, reliability coefficients based on a short interval may be sufficient. The important thing is to seek evidence of stability that fits the particular interpretation to be made.

Most teachers will not find it possible to compute test–retest reliability coefficients for their own classroom tests. However, in choosing standardized tests, the stability of the scores serves as one important criterion. The test manual should provide evidence of stability, indicating the time interval between tests and any unusual experiences the group members might have had between testings. Other things being equal (such as validity), we shall favor the test whose scores have been shown to possess the type of stability we need to make sound decisions.

Information concerning the stability of test scores also has implications for the use of test results from school records and for the frequency of retesting. When using *any* test score from permanent records, one should check the date of testing and the stability data available to determine whether the results are still dependable. If there is doubt and the decision is important, retesting is in order.

Equivalent-Forms Method

Estimating reliability by means of the equivalent-forms method uses two different but equivalent forms of the test (also called *parallel* or *alternate forms*).[2] The two forms of the test are administered to the same group of pupils in close succession, and the resulting test scores are correlated. This correlation coefficient provides a measure of *equivalence*. Thus, it indicates the degree to which both forms of the test are measuring the same aspects of behavior.

The equivalent-forms method tells us nothing about the long-term stability of the pupil characteristic being measured but, rather, reflects short-term constancy of pupil performance and the extent to which the test represents an adequate sample of the characteristic being measured. In achievement testing, for example, there are thousands of questions that might be asked in a particular test. But because of time limits and other restricting factors, only some of the possible questions can be used. The questions included in the test should provide an adequate sample of the possible questions in the area. The easiest way to estimate if a test measures an adequate sample of the content is to construct two forms of the test and correlate the results. A high correlation indicates that both forms are providing similar results

---

[2]Equivalent forms are built to the same set of specifications (e.g., test content and difficulty) but are constructed independently.

and therefore are probably reliable samples of the general area of content being measured.

The equivalent-forms method of estimating reliability does away with the troublesome problem of selecting a proper time interval between tests, as is necessary with the test–retest method, though the need for two equivalent forms of the test restricts its use almost entirely to standardized testing. Here it is widely used because most standardized tests have two or more forms available. In fact, a teacher should be suspicious of any standardized test that has two forms available and does not report information concerning their equivalence. The comparability of the results of the two forms cannot be assumed unless such evidence is presented.

The equivalent-forms method is sometimes used with a time interval between the administration of the two forms of the test (see Figure 4.2). Under these test–retest conditions, the resulting reliability coefficient provides a measure of *stability and equivalence*. This is the most rigorous test of reliability because the stability of the testing procedures, the constancy of the pupil characteristic being measured, and the representativeness of the sample of tasks included in the test all are taken into account. Consequently, this is generally recommended as the soundest procedure for estimating the reliability of test scores. As with the ordinary test–retest method, the reliability coefficient must be interpreted in light of the time interval between the two forms of the test. For longer time periods, we should ordinarily expect smaller reliability coefficients.

Split-Half Method

Reliability also can be estimated from a single administration of a single form of a test. The test is administered to a group of pupils in the usual manner and then is divided in half for scoring purposes. To split the test into halves that are most equivalent, the usual procedure is to score the even-numbered and the odd-numbered items separately (see Figure 4.3). This produces two scores for each pupil, which, when correlated, provide a measure of *internal consistency*. This coefficient indicates the degree to which consistent results are obtained from the two halves of the test.

As noted, the preceding reliability coefficient is determined by correlating the scores of two half-tests. To estimate the scores' reliability based on the full-length test, the Spearman–Brown formula is usually applied:

$$\text{Reliability on full test} = \frac{\text{Two times correlation between half-tests}}{\text{One plus correlation between half-tests}}$$

The simplicity of the formula can be seen in the following example, in which the correlation coefficient between the test's two halves is .60:

$$\text{Reliability on full test} = \frac{2 \times .60}{1 + .60} = \frac{1.20}{1.60} = .75$$

This correlation coefficient of .75, then, estimates the reliability of a full test when the half-tests correlated .60.

FIGURE 4.2
Equivalent-forms
method (without and
with a time interval).

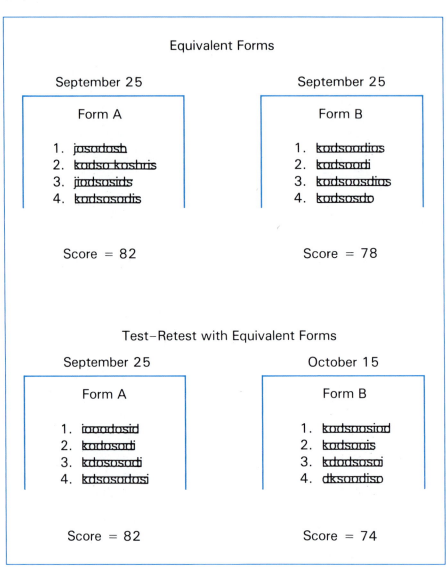

The split-half method is similar to the equivalent-forms method in that it indicates the extent to which the sample of test items is a dependable sample of the content being measured. A high correlation between scores on the two halves of a test denotes the equivalence of the two halves and consequently the adequacy of the sampling. Split-half reliabilities tend to be higher than equivalent-form reliabilities because the split-half method is based on the administration of a single test form. When two forms of a test are administered, even in close succession, more opportunity for inconsistency is introduced (e.g., differences from form to form in attention, speed of work, effort, fatigue, and test content). Because the equivalent-

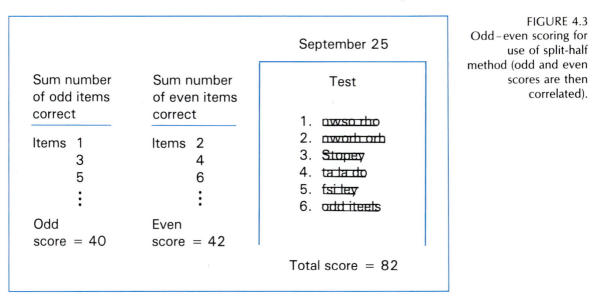

FIGURE 4.3
Odd – even scoring for
use of split-half
method (odd and even
scores are then
correlated).

forms method takes into account more sources of inconsistency, it provides a more stringent evaluation of reliability.

Kuder – Richardson Method

Another method of estimating the reliability of test scores from a single administration of a single form of a test is by means of formulas such as those developed by Kuder and Richardson. As with the split-half method, these formulas provide a measure of *internal consistency* but do not require splitting the test in half for scoring purposes. One of the formulas, called the Kuder – Richardson Formula 20, is based on the proportion of persons passing each item and the standard deviation of the total scores.[3] The computation is rather cumbersome, unless information is already available concerning the proportion passing, and few teachers are likely to do the computations involved. However, with the increasing availability of micro-computers and software for scoring and analyzing tests, it is much more feasible now than it once was to obtain Kuder – Richardson estimates of reliability at schools where these resources are available. In any event, our concern is with interpretation of the coefficients rather than the calculations.

Kuder – Richardson estimates of reliability provide information about the degree to which the items in the test measure similar characteristics. For a test with relatively homogeneous content (e.g., an arithmetic computation test), the reliability estimate generally will be similar to that provided by the split-half method. Indeed, the Kuder – Richardson estimate can be thought of as the average of all of the possible split-half coefficients for the groups tested. This is an advantage when

[3]A standard deviation is a measure of the spread of scores. See Appendix A for method of computing.

considering a test with relatively homogeneous content since the estimate does not depend on the way in which the items are assigned to the two half-tests as in the split-half method. For tests designed to measure more heterogeneous learning outcomes (e.g., a test covering ancient history, the Middle Ages, and modern history), however, the Kuder–Richardson estimate will be smaller than that provided by the split-half method and the latter method is to be preferred.

The simplicity of applying the split-half method and the Kuder–Richardson method has led to their widespread use in determining reliability. Such internal consistency procedures, however, have limitations that restrict their value. First, they are not appropriate for speeded tests — for tests with time limits that prevent pupils from attempting every item. If speed is a significant factor in the testing, the reliability estimates will be inflated to an unknown degree. This poses no great problem in estimating the reliability of test scores from teacher-made tests, because these are usually power tests. In the case of standardized tests, however, time limits are seldom so liberal that all pupils complete the test. Thus, measures of internal consistency reported in test manuals should be interpreted with caution *unless* evidence is also presented that speed of work is a negligible factor. For speeded tests, reliability obtained by the test–retest or equivalent-forms method should be sought.

A second limitation of internal consistency procedures is that they do not indicate the constancy of pupil response from day to day. In this regard, they are similar to the equivalent-forms method without a time interval. Only test–retest procedures indicate the extent to which test results are generalizable over different periods of time.

Comparing Methods

As stated earlier, each of the methods of estimating reliability provides different information concerning the consistency of test results. A summary of this information is presented in Table 4.2, which shows that most methods are concerned with only one or two types of consistency sought in test results. The test–retest method, without a time interval, takes into account only the consistency of the testing

TABLE 4.2		Type of Consistency		
Type of Consistency Indicated by Each of the Methods for Estimating Reliability	Method of Estimating Reliability	Consistency of Testing Procedure	Constancy of Pupil Characteristics	Consistency over Different Samples of Items
	Test–retest (immediate)	X	*	
	Test–retest (time interval)	X	X	
	Equivalent-forms (immediate)	X	*	X
	Equivalent-forms (time interval)	X	X	X
	Split-half	X		X
	Kuder–Richardson	X		X

*Short-term constancy of response is reflected in immediate retest, but day-to-day stability is not shown.

procedure and the short-term constancy of the response. If a time interval is introduced between the tests, the constancy of the characteristics of the pupil from day to day also will be included. However, neither of the test–retest procedures provides information concerning the consistency of results over different samples of items, because both sets of scores are based on the same test.

The equivalent-forms method without a time interval, the split-half method, and the Kuder–Richardson method all take into account the consistency of testing procedures and the consistency of results over different samples of items.

Only the equivalent-forms method with an intervening time period between tests takes into account all three types of consistency, which is the reason that this measure of stability and equivalence is generally regarded as the most useful estimate of test reliability.

Standard Error of Measurement

If it were possible to test a pupil over and over again on the same test, we would find that the scores would vary somewhat. The amount of variation in the test scores would be directly related to the reliability of the testing procedures. Low reliability would be indicated by large variations in the pupil's test scores, and high reliability would be indicated by little variation from one testing to another. Although it is impractical to administer a test many times to the same pupils, it is possible to *estimate* the amount of variation to be expected in test scores. This estimate is called the *standard error* of measurement.

Test manuals usually list the standard errors of measurement. Thus, all we need to do is take the standard error into account when interpreting individual test scores. For example, let us assume that we have just administered a standardized achievement test battery to a class of fourth-grade students and the results indicate that Mary Smith has a grade equivalent (GE) score of 5.2 on the mathematics test.[4] We find in the test manual that the standard error of measurement on the mathematics test is .4. What does the .4 tell us about Mary's mathematics achievement? In general, it indicates the amount of error that must be considered in interpreting Mary's score. More specifically, it provides the limits within which we can reasonably expect to find Mary's "true" mathematics achievement score. A true score is one that would be obtained if the test were perfectly reliable. If Mary Smith were tested repeatedly under identical conditions and there were no learning, practice, or fatigue effects, 68 percent of her obtained scores would fall within 1 standard error (.4) of her true score, 95 percent would fall within 2 standard errors (.8), and 99.7 percent would fall within 3 standard errors (1.2) (see diagram in box).[5] For practical purposes, these limits may be applied to Mary's obtained score of 5.2 to give us the following ranges within which we could be reasonably sure to find her true score.

---

[4]A grade equivalent score indicates the grade level that the average student has who has the same number of correct answers as Mary (see Chapter 14 for a discussion of grade equivalent scores).

[5]These percentages are based on the normal curve. See Chapter 14 for a description of the normal curve and Appendix A for a method of computing.

Hypothetical Distribution Illustrating the Standard Error of Measurement

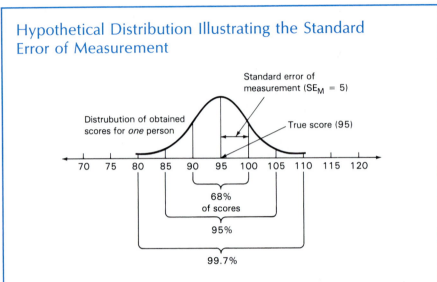

Theoretical Explanation of the Standard Error of Measurement

1. It is assumed that each person has a *true score* on a particular test, a hypothetical value representing a score free of error (true score = 95 on the diagram).
2. If a person could be tested repeatedly (without practice effects or other changes), the average of the obtained scores would approximate the *true score*, and the obtained scores would *be approximately normally distributed* around the true score (see diagram).
3. From what is known about the normal distribution curve, approximately 68% of the obtained scores would fall within 1 standard error of measurement of the person's true score; approximately 95% of the scores would fall within 2 standard errors; and approximately 99.7% of the scores would fall within 3 standard errors (see "The Normal Curve and the Standard Deviation Unit" in Chapter 14. The standard error of measurement is the standard deviation of the errors of measurement).
4. Although *the true score can never be known*, the standard error of measurement can be applied to a person's obtained score to set "reasonable limits" for locating the true score (e.g., an obtained score of 97 ± 5 = 92 to 102).
5. These "reasonable limits" provide *confidence bands* for interpreting an obtained score. When the standard error of measurement is small, the confidence band is narrow (indicating high reliability), and thus we have greater confidence that the obtained score is near the true score.

Number of Standard Errors	Score Units to Apply to Mary's GE Score of 5.2	Range of Scores
1	0.4	4.8–5.6
2	0.8	4.4–6.0
3	1.2	4.0–6.4

Although Mary's score of 5.2 indicates that she did better on this particular test than the typical fourth-grade student, the range of scores show that we cannot be certain that her true score is above that of the average fourth-grade student. One can be quite confident that her true score is somewhere between 4.4 and 6.0 because 95 percent of the observed scores fall within 2 standard errors of the true score. In interpreting individual test scores, however, the use of 1 standard error of measurement is more common. Thus, a range of 4.8 to 5.6 typically would be used to describe Mary's test performance.

The standard error of measurement shows why a test score should be interpreted as a "band of scores" (called a *confidence band*) rather than as a specific score. With a large standard error, the band of scores is large, and we have less confidence in our obtained score. If the standard error is small, the band of scores will be small and we will have greater confidence that our obtained score is a dependable measure of the characteristic. Viewing a test score as a band of scores makes it possible to interpret and use test results more intelligently. Apparent differences in test scores, between individuals and for the same individual over a period of time, often disappear when the standard error of measurement is considered. A teacher or counselor who is aware of the standard error of measurement finds it impossible to be dogmatic in interpreting minor differences in test scores.

The relationship between the reliability coefficient and the standard error of measurement can be seen in Table 4.3, which presents the standard errors of measurement for various reliability coefficients and standard deviations.[6] Notice that as the reliability coefficient increases, for any given standard deviation, the standard error of measurement decreases. Thus, large reliability coefficients are associated with small errors in specific test scores, and small reliability coefficients are associated with large errors.

If a test manual does not report the standard error of measurement, Table 4.3 can be used to estimate the standard error. In fact, this is the purpose for which the table was developed. All one needs to do to obtain an estimate of the standard error for a given test is to enter the column and the row nearest to the reliability coefficient and standard deviation reported in the test manual. For example, a reliability coefficient of .90 and a standard deviation of 16 would result in a standard error of 5.1, which is obtained by going down the second column (.90) to the row in which the standard deviation is 16.

---

[6]Standard deviation is a measure of the spread of scores. See Chapter 14 for a description and Appendix A for a method of computing.

Practical Applications of the Standard Error of Measurement in Test Interpretation

A confidence band 1 standard error above and below the obtained score is commonly used in test profiles to aid in interpreting individual scores and in judging whether differences between scores are likely to be "real differences" or differences caused by chance.

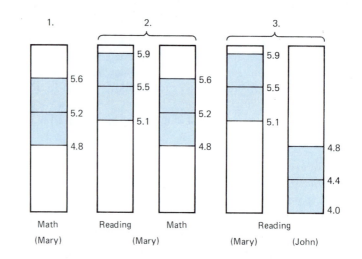

1. *Interpreting an individual score.* The confidence band indicates "reasonable limits" within which to locate the true score (Mary's math score probably falls somewhere between 4.8 and 5.6).
2. *Interpreting the difference between two scores from a test battery.* When the ends of the bands overlap, there is no "real difference" between scores (Mary's scores in reading and math show *no* meaningful difference).
3. *Interpreting the difference between the scores of two individuals on the same test.* When ends of bands do *not* overlap, there is a "real difference" between scores (Mary's reading score is higher than John's).

There are several precautions to be kept in mind when using Table 4.3 to estimate the standard error of measurement. First, the reliability coefficient and standard deviation must be based on the same group of persons. Second, entering the table with the reliability coefficient and standard deviation nearest to those in the manual gives only an approximation of the standard error of measurement. Third, the table does not take into account the fact that the standard error of measurement varies slightly at different score levels. Within these limitations,

| SD | Reliability Coefficient | | | | | | TABLE 4.3 |
	.95	.90	.85	.80	.75	.70	Standard Errors of Measurement for Given Values of Reliability Coefficient and Standard Deviation*
30	6.7	9.5	11.6	13.4	15.0	16.4	
28	6.3	8.9	10.8	12.5	14.0	15.3	
26	5.8	8.2	10.1	11.6	13.0	14.2	
24	5.4	7.6	9.3	10.7	12.0	13.1	
22	4.9	7.0	8.5	9.8	11.0	12.0	
20	4.5	6.3	7.7	8.9	10.0	11.0	
18	4.0	5.7	7.0	8.0	9.0	9.9	
16	3.6	5.1	6.2	7.2	8.0	8.8	
14	3.1	4.4	5.4	6.3	7.0	7.7	
12	2.7	3.8	4.6	5.4	6.0	6.6	
10	2.2	3.2	3.9	4.5	5.0	5.5	
8	1.8	2.5	3.1	3.6	4.0	4.4	
6	1.3	1.9	2.3	2.7	3.0	3.3	
4	.9	1.3	1.5	1.8	2.0	2.2	
2	.4	.6	.8	.9	1.0	1.1	

*This table is based on the formula $SE \text{ (Measurement)} = SD\sqrt{1 - r}$, where SD is the standard deviation of the test scores and r is the reliability coefficient. Reprinted from J. E. Doppelt, *How Accurate Is a Test Score?* Test Service Bulletin, no. 50 (New York: Psychological Corporation).

however, Table 4.3 provides a simple and quick method for estimating the standard error of measurement and an approximation accurate enough for most practical applications of test results.

So far we have discussed the standard error of measurement and its uses as if the magnitude of measurement errors were always the same regardless of the level of a person's score. Although this is common practice and works well most of the time, the assumption that the standard error of measurement is a constant throughout the score range does not hold up very well for extremely high or extremely low test scores. If a test is much too difficult for a student, for example, that student's score is apt to be based almost entirely on the luck he or she has in guessing the correct answers. Consequently, the standard error for that student will be considerably larger than the standard error for students for whom the test difficulty is more appropriate.

Because the standard errors of measurement tend to be larger for very high and very low test scores, some test publishers report standard errors of measurement separately for different ranges of scores. The procedures for estimating standard errors of measurement for different score levels are more complicated, but the concept and use of the information is no different except that the numerical value of the standard error that would be used depends on an individual's test score. This additional information makes it possible to have more accurate score bands for people with extreme scores. Suppose, for example, that the test manual reported the following standard errors of measurement for various ranges of GE scores for a fourth-grade reading comprehension test.

Grade Equivalent Score Range	Standard Error of Measurement
7.0 to 7.9	0.8
6.0 to 6.9	0.6
5.0 to 5.9	0.4
4.0 to 4.9	0.4
3.0 to 3.9	0.5
2.0 to 2.9	0.7

From these results we would recognize that scores indicating performance similar to that of the typical second- or seventh-grade student would be subject to much larger errors of measurement than scores similar to the typical fourth-grade student for whom the test was designed. The wide band for a student with a score of, say, 7.1 (6.3 to 7.9) would warn us that, although the student's performance is clearly well above that of the typical fourth-grade student, we cannot be very precise about how much higher.

The different standard errors by score level also help in selecting the level of a standardized test that will be most appropriate for a particular group of students. For example, if we know that most of the fourth-grade students in a school have scored far below the national average in earlier grades, we would know that the fourth-grade level of the test is apt to be too difficult and will result in large standard errors of measurement. In this case, we could expect that using the level of the test designed for third-grade students would result in scores with smaller standard errors of measurement and, thus, provide more dependable results.

The standard error of measurement has two special advantages as a means of estimating reliability. First, the estimates are in the same units as the test scores. This makes it possible to indicate directly the margin of error to allow for when interpreting individual scores. Second, the standard error is likely to remain fairly constant from group to group. This is not true of the reliability coefficient, which is highly dependent on the spread of scores in the group tested. Because the groups on which reliabilities are reported in test manuals will always differ somewhat from the group to be given the test, the greater constancy of the standard error of measurement has obvious practical value. The main difficulty encountered with the standard error occurs when we want to compare two tests that differ in length or that use different types of scores. Here the reliability coefficient is the only suitable measure.

Factors Influencing Reliability Measures

A number of factors have been shown to affect the conventional measures of reliability.[7] If sound conclusions are to be drawn, these factors must be considered when interpreting reliability coefficients. We have already seen, for example, that

[7]As noted earlier, these measures are primarily useful with *norm-referenced* tests, whose purpose is to discriminate among individuals.

speeded tests will produce a spuriously large reliability coefficient with the internal consistency methods of estimating reliability. We have also noted that test–retest reliability coefficients are influenced by the time interval between testings, with shorter time intervals resulting in larger reliability coefficients. Thus, in comparing the reliability coefficients of two or more tests, we must take such factors into account. Although we might want to favor the test with the largest reliability coefficient, we would not do so if we recognized that the reported coefficient was inflated by factors irrelevant to the consistency of the measurement procedure. Similarly, we might discount the difference between reliability coefficients reported for two different tests if the conditions under which they were obtained favored the test with the largest reliability coefficient.

Consideration of the factors influencing reliability not only will help us interpret more wisely the reliability coefficients of standardized tests but also should aid us in constructing more reliable classroom tests. Although teachers seldom find it profitable to calculate reliability coefficients for the tests they construct, they should take cognizance of the factors influencing reliability to maximize the reliability of their own classroom tests.

Length of Test

In general, the longer the test is, the higher its reliability will be. This is because a longer test will provide a more adequate sample of the behavior being measured, and the scores are apt to be less distorted by chance factors such as guessing. Suppose that to measure spelling ability, we asked pupils to spell *one* word. The results would be patently unreliable. Pupils who were able to spell the word would be *perfect spellers*, and pupils who could not would be *complete failures*. If we happened to select a difficult word, most pupils would fail; if the word was an easy one, most pupils would appear to be perfect spellers. The fact that *one* word provides an unreliable estimate of a pupil's spelling ability is obvious. It should be equally apparent that as we add more spelling words to the list, we come closer and closer to a good estimate of each child's spelling ability. Scores based on a large number of spelling words thus are more apt to reflect real differences in spelling ability and therefore to be more stable. By increasing the size of the sample of spelling behavior, therefore, we increase the consistency of our measurement.

A longer test also tends to lessen the influence of chance factors such as guessing. For example, on a ten-item true-and-false test, a pupil might know seven of the items and guess at the other three. A correct guess on all three items would result in a perfect score, and incorrect guesses on all three items would result in only seven correct. This would represent considerable variation in the test score resulting from guessing alone. However, if this same pupil were taking a test with 100 true-and-false items, the correct guesses would tend to be canceled by incorrect guesses, and the score would be a more dependable indication of actual knowledge.

The fact that a longer test tends to provide more reliable results was implied earlier in our discussion of the split-half method. You will recall that when scores from two halves of a test correlated .60, the Spearman–Brown formula estimated the reliability of the scores for the full-length test to be .75. This, of course, is equivalent to estimating the increase in reliability to be expected when the length of the test is doubled.

There is one important reservation in evaluating the influence of test length on the reliability of the scores, which is that the statements we have been making assume that the test will be lengthened by adding test items of the same quality as those already in the test. Adding ten spelling words that are so easy that everyone will get them correct or adding ten spelling words that are so difficult that no one will get them correct will not increase the reliability of the scores on a norm-referenced spelling test. In fact, there would be no influence on the reliability coefficient, because such additions would not influence the relative standing of the pupils in the group.

In constructing classroom tests, it is important to keep in mind the influence of test length on reliability and strive for longer tests. If short tests are necessary because of time limits or the pupils' age, more frequent testing may be used to obtain a dependable measure of achievement.

In using standardized tests, we should be wary of part scores based on relatively few items. Such scores are usually low in reliability and of little practical value. Before using such scores, the test manual should be checked for their reported reliabilities. If these are not reported or are very low, the part scores should be ignored, and only the total test score should be used.

Spread of Scores

As noted earlier, reliability coefficients are directly influenced by the spread of scores in the group tested. Other things being equal, the larger the spread of scores is, the higher the estimate of reliability will be. Because larger reliability coefficients result when individuals tend to stay in the same relative position in a group from one testing to another, it naturally follows that anything that reduces the possibility of shifting positions in the group also contributes to larger reliability coefficients. In this case, greater differences between the scores of individuals reduce the possibility of shifting positions. Stated another way, errors of measurement have less influence on the relative position of individuals when the differences among group members are large — that is, when there is a wide spread of scores.

This can be easily illustrated without recourse to statistics. Compare the following two sets of scores in terms of the probability that the individuals will remain in the same relative position on a second administration of the test. Even a cursory inspection of these scores will show that the persons in Group B are more likely to shift positions on a second administration of the test. With only a spread of 10 points from the top score to the bottom score, radical shifts in position can result from changes of just a few points in the test scores.

However, in Group A the test scores of individuals could vary by several points on a second administration of the test, with very little shifting in the relative position of the group members. The large spread of test scores in Group A makes shifts in relative position unlikely and thus gives us greater confidence that these differences among group members are real.

Group A	Group B
95	95
90	94
86	93
82	93
76	92
65	91
60	89
56	88
53	86
47	85

When constructing criterion-referenced mastery tests, a spread of scores is irrelevant because we would hope that all, or nearly all, pupils would get high scores. When measuring the degree to which pupils have progressed beyond the minimum essentials of a course, however, we should attempt to construct classroom tests that result in a wide spread of scores. In this way we can have greater assurance that the differences in pupil development (beyond the mastery level) reflect dependable differences in achievement and not differences due to chance factors such as guessing. To obtain a wider spread of test scores, most teachers need to construct more difficult tests. This can be done by stressing the measurement of more complex learning outcomes (e.g., transfer, problem solving). Such a procedure will tend to increase the reliability of the test scores and at the same time will have a favorable influence on validity. Arbitrarily manipulating the wording of test items simply to make them more difficult is likely to result in increased reliability at the expense of validity.

In selecting standardized tests, the effect of the spread of test scores on reliability coefficients also should be considered. For example, some test publishers report reliability coefficients calculated on test scores over several grade levels. Because the combined scores of pupils from several grade levels have a much larger spread than that found at a single grade level, such reliability coefficients are spuriously high. These reliability coefficients should be disregarded when selecting a test for a particular grade level. Every effort should be made to obtain reliability evidence on a group of pupils similar to the one to which we plan to administer the test. Only in this way can we have some assurance that the reliability coefficients reported in the test manual provide a satisfactory estimate of the test's reliability for our particular group of pupils.

Difficulty of Test

Norm-referenced tests that are too easy or too difficult for the group members taking it will tend to produce scores of low reliability. This is because both easy and difficult tests result in a restricted spread of scores. For the easy test, the scores are close together at the top end of the scale. For the difficult test, the scores are grouped together at the bottom end of the scale. For both, however, the differences among individuals are small and tend to be unreliable. A norm-referenced test of ideal difficulty will permit the scores to spread out over the full range of the scale.

The implications for classroom testing are obvious and were mentioned in the previous section. Classroom achievement tests designed to measure differences among pupils (norm referenced) should be so constructed that the average score is 50 percent correct and that the scores range from near zero to near perfect. Actually, the 50 percent correct applies only to the short-answer–type item. For selection-type items, the ideal average score would be higher because a proportion of the items could be answered correctly by guessing. On a true–false test, for example, pupils could be expected to get 50 percent of the items correct by guessing (chance score), and on a five-choice, multiple-choice test, the expected chance score would be 20 percent correct (one out of five). We can estimate a desirable average difficulty for a selection-type test by taking the point midway between the expected chance score and the maximum possible score. Thus, for a 100 item, true–false test the average difficulty would be 75 (midway between 50 and 100), and for a 100 item, five-choice, multiple-choice test, the average difficulty would be 60 (midway between 20 and 100). Constructing tests that match these levels of difficulty enables the full range of possible scores to be used in measuring differences among individuals. As noted earlier, the bigger the spread of scores is, the greater the likelihood is that the measured differences will be reliable.

The difficulty of test items in standardized tests should be carefully evaluated. If a test is designed for several grade levels, the difficulty level is usually most appropriate for the grades in the middle of the range. As we have already seen, the standard error of measurement, although relatively constant for students scoring in the central part of the score range, usually becomes larger for students scoring at the extremes. Thus, at the extreme grade levels, one can typically expect the differences among individuals to be less reliable.

In evaluating the difficulty of a standardized test, the teacher must also take into account the pupil's achievement level. As was previously indicated, a test that is of appropriate difficulty for average fourth-graders may be inappropriate for a fourth-grade class containing a disproportionate number of students who have a history of performing far below or far above the national average on achievement tests. More appropriate difficulty for a particular group often can be obtained by using the test designed for the next lowest or the next highest grade. Inspection of tables of standard errors of measurement by different score levels or, if these are unavailable, review of information concerning the difficulty of the test at different grade levels will help in making this judgment.

Objectivity

The objectivity of a test refers to the degree to which equally competent scorers obtain the same results. Most standardized tests of aptitude and achievement are high in objectivity. The test items are of the objective type (e.g., multiple choice), and the resulting scores are not influenced by the scorers' judgment or opinion. In fact, such tests are usually constructed so that they can be accurately scored by trained clerks and scoring machines. When such highly objective procedures are used, the reliability of the test results is not affected by the scoring procedures.

For classroom tests constructed by teachers, however, objectivity may play an important role in obtaining reliable measures of achievement. In essay testing and various observational procedures, the results depend to a large extent on the person doing the scoring. Different persons get different results, and even the same person may get different results at different times. Such inconsistency in scoring has an adverse effect on the reliability of the measures obtained, for the test scores now reflect the opinions and biases of the scorer as well as the differences among pupils in the characteristic being measured.

The solution is *not* to use only objective tests and to abandon all subjective methods of evaluation, as this would have an adverse effect on validity, and as we noted earlier, validity is the most important quality of evaluation results. A better solution is to select the evaluation procedure most appropriate for the behavior being evaluated and then to make the evaluation procedure as objective as possible. In the use of essay tests, for example, objectivity can be increased by careful phrasing of the questions and by a standard set of rules for scoring. Such increased objectivity will contribute to greater reliability without sacrificing validity.

Methods of Estimating Reliability

When examining the reliability coefficients of standardized tests, it is important to consider the methods that were used to obtain the reliability estimates. In general, the size of the reliability coefficient is related to the method of estimating reliability.

1. Test–retest method

    Typically provides *medium to large* reliability coefficients for a given test. May be larger than with the split-half method if the time interval is short. Coefficients become smaller as the time interval between tests is increased.

2. Equivalent-forms method (without time interval)

    Typically provides *medium to large* reliability coefficients for a given test. Coefficients tend to be lower than with the split-half method or the test–retest method using a short time interval.

3. Equivalent-forms method (with time interval)

    Typically provides *smallest* reliability coefficients for a given test. Coefficients become smaller as the time interval between tests is increased.

4. Split-half method (odd–even)

    Typically provides *largest* reliability coefficients for a given test. Spuriously high estimates are produced for speeded tests.

5. Kuder – Richardson methods

Typically provides reliability estimates that are *smaller* than those obtained by the split-half method. These estimates are also inflated by speed.

The variation in the size of the reliability coefficient resulting from the method of estimating reliability is directly attributable to the type of consistency included in each method. Recall that the equivalent-forms method with an intervening time interval took into account the most sources of variation in the test scores and consequently is the most rigorous method of estimating reliability. Thus, smaller reliability coefficients can be expected with this method, and it is unfair to compare directly such reliability coefficients with those obtained by less stringent methods.

At the other extreme, the larger reliability coefficients typically reported for the split-half method must be accepted cautiously. If speed is an important factor in the testing, split-half reliability coefficients should be disregarded entirely, and other evidence of reliability should be sought.

Reliability of Criterion-Referenced Mastery Tests

When we use criterion-referenced mastery tests, our desire for consistency of measurement is similar to that for norm-referenced tests. Thus, we would like an individual's performance to be consistent from (1) one item to another, when all items measure the same learning outcome (internal consistency); (2) one time to another, when the learning outcomes are expected to have a reasonable degree of constancy (stability); and (3) one form of the test to another, when the forms are intended to measure the same sample of learning tasks (equivalence). However, the focus is more often on the mastery decision than on the actual score. Also, because of the specificity of the tests and their close tie to instruction, they may have a narrower range of scores than is typically produced by norm-referenced tests. The focus on mastery decisions and the smaller variability in scores has led to different approaches to evaluating the reliability of criterion-referenced mastery tests.

Given the emphasis on the mastery decision, the most natural approach to reliability is to evaluate the consistency with which students are classified as masters or nonmasters. This type of reliability can be readily determined by computing the percentage of consistent decisions over two equivalent forms of a test. Although a number of more complicated approaches have been suggested, the simple calculation of the percentage of people who are consistently classified is the approach that is encouraged by the 1985 test *Standards*[8] for tests that are used to make dichotomous decisions such as master – nonmaster.

Let's assume that we have given two forms of a 20-item test to a classroom group of 30 pupils and set mastery at 16 items (80 percent correct). All pupils obtaining a

---

[8]American Psychological Association, *Standards for Educational and Psychological Testing* (Washington, D.C.: 1985).

score of 16 or higher on both forms of the test are classified as *masters* on both forms. All pupils obtaining a score of 15 or lower on both forms are classified as *nonmasters* on both forms. The remaining pupils are classified as masters on one form of the test and nonmasters on the other. If this latter group of reversals is relatively large, our test will obviously be inconsistent in classifying pupils. The data for such an analysis can be summarized in a two-by-two table like that in Figure 4.4.

By using the information in Figure 4.4, we can compute a percentage of consistency, using the following formula:

$$\% \text{ Consistency} = \frac{\text{Masters (both forms)} + \text{Nonmasters (both forms)}}{\text{Total number in group}} \times 100$$

$$\% \text{ Consistency} = \frac{20 + 7}{30} \times 100 = 90\%$$

Although the percentage agreement is conceptually simple and easy to compute, it does require two forms of the test. This is not a serious shortcoming, however, because mastery testing usually requires two or more forms of each test. It is seldom wise to permit pupils who do not demonstrate mastery on the first attempt to be retested with the same form of the test. Furthermore, procedures have been developed to estimate decision consistency based on the administration of a single test form; however, those procedures are relatively complex and are beyond the scope of this textbook.[9] Suffice it to say that they are intended to provide approximations to the percentage agreement based on equivalent forms from data available from the administration of a single test form.

When using criterion-referenced mastery tests in classroom instruction, we can increase the likelihood of reliable and valid results by using a sufficiently large sample of test items for each instructional objective or domain of learning tasks to be measured. If the intended outcome is very specific and highly structured (e.g.,

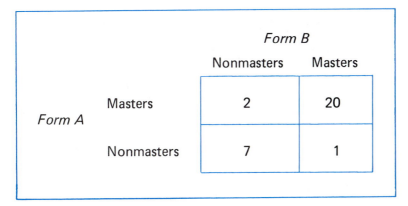

FIGURE 4.4
A classification of 30 pupils as masters or nonmasters on two forms of a test (mastery = 80% correct).

[9]M. J. Subkoviak, "Estimating the Reliability of Mastery–Nonmastery Classifications," in *A Guide to Criterion Referenced Test Construction*, ed. R. A. Berk (Baltimore: Johns Hopkins University Press, 1984).

"Adds two single-digit numbers"), a relatively small number of items (say, five) may be sufficient for a dependable judgment concerning mastery. For most mastery–nonmastery decisions, however, ten items for each separate domain of tasks are a more desirable minimum.[10] When instructional decisions are based on fewer than ten items, we should make only tentative decisions and seek verification from other available data and classroom observation.

In evaluating published tests that offer criterion-referenced interpretations *by objective*, it is important to check on the number of items measuring each objective. Although reliability estimates may be provided for the total test, it is the number of items measuring each objective that determines the reliability of our criterion-referenced interpretations with these tests.

How High Should Reliability Be?

The degree of reliability we demand in our educational measures depends largely on the decision to be made. If we are going to use test results to decide whether to review certain areas of subject matter, we may be willing to use a teacher-made test of relatively low reliability. Our decision will be based on the scores of the total group, and variation in individual scores will not distort our decision too much. Even if we do err in our decision, no catastrophe will result. The worst that can happen is that the pupils will get an unnecessary review of material or they will be deprived of a review that may be beneficial to them. On the other hand, if we are going to use a test to decide whether to award a high school diploma or a college scholarship, we should demand the most reliable measurement available. Such decisions have important consequences for the lives of the individuals involved.

It is not only a decision's importance that matters but also whether it is possible to confirm or reverse the judgment at a later time. Decision making in education is seldom a single, final act. It tends to be sequential, starting with rather crude judgments and proceeding through a series of more refined judgments. In the early stages of decision making, low reliability might be quite tolerable because test results are used primarily as a guide to further information gathering. For example, on the basis of classroom tests of questionable reliability, we might decide that some of our pupils are having such serious learning difficulties that they need special help. This decision can be confirmed or refuted by further testing with more dependable measures. Similarly, group scholastic aptitude scores of only moderate stability may be useful in grouping elementary pupils, because those who are misclassified can be easily shifted as new evidence becomes available. Opportunities for confirmation and reversal of judgments without serious consequences are almost always present in the early stages of educational decision making. Thus, the important thing when reliability is low or unknown is not to treat the scores as if they were highly accurate.

---

[10]For procedures for estimating the chances for incorrect decisions based on tests of different lengths, see J. Millman, "Criterion-Referenced Measurement," in *Evaluation in Education: Current Applications*, ed. W. J. Popham (Berkeley, Calif.: McCutchan, 1974), pp. 311–397.

Make tentative judgments, seek confirming data, and be willing to reverse decisions when wrong.[11]

Thus, when we ask how high reliability should be, several considerations must be taken into account. How important is the decision? Is it one that can be confirmed or reversed at a later time? How far reaching are the consequences of the action taken? For irreversible decisions that are apt to have great influence on the lives of individual pupils, we should make stringent demands on the reliability of the measures we use. For lesser decisions, especially for those that can be later confirmed or reversed without serious consequences, we should be willing to settle for less reliable measures. Thus, it depends largely on how confident we need to be about the decision being made. Greater confidence requires higher reliability (see box).

Reliability Demands and Nature of the Decision

High reliability is demanded when the
Decision is important.
Decision is final.
Decision is irreversible.
Decision is unconfirmable.
Decision concerns individuals.
Decision has lasting consequences.

Example
Select or reject
college applicants.

Low reliability is tolerable when the
Decision is of minor importance.
Decision making is in early stages.
Decision is reversible.
Decision is confirmable by other data.
Decision concerns groups.
Decision has temporary effects.

Example
Whether to
review a class-
room lesson.

Usability

In selecting tests and other evaluation instruments, practical considerations cannot be neglected. Tests are usually administered and interpreted by teachers with only a minimum amount of training in measurement. The time available for testing is almost always limited and is in constant competition with other important activities for its allotted time in the school schedule. Likewise, the cost of testing, although a minor consideration, is as carefully scrutinized by budget-conscious administrators

---

[11]Teacher-made tests commonly have reliabilities somewhere between .60 and .85, for example, but these are useful for the types of instructional decisions typically made by teachers.

as are other expenditures of school funds. These and other factors pertinent to the *usability* of tests and evaluation procedures must be taken into account when selecting evaluation instruments. Such practical considerations are especially important when selecting published tests.

Ease of Administration

If the tests are to be administered by teachers or others with limited training, ease of administration is an especially important quality to seek in a test. For this purpose, the directions should be simple and clear, the subtests should be relatively few, and the timing of the test should not be too difficult. Administering a test with complicated directions and a number of subtests lasting but a few minutes each is a taxing chore for even an experienced examiner. For a person with little training and experience, such a situation is fraught with possibilities for errors in giving directions, timing, and other aspects of the administration that are likely to affect the results. Such errors of administration can have, of course, an adverse effect on the validity and reliability of the test scores.

Time Required for Administration

With time for testing at a premium, we always favor the shorter test, other things being equal. But in this case, other things are seldom equal, because reliability is directly related to the test's length. If we attempt to cut down too much on the time allotted to testing, we may reduce drastically the reliability of our scores. For example, tests designed to fit a normal class period usually produce total test scores of satisfactory reliability, but their part scores, obtained from the subtests, tend to be unreliable. If we want reliable measures in the areas covered by the subtests, we need to increase our testing time in each area. On the other hand, if we want a general measure in some area, such as verbal aptitude, we can obtain reliable results in 30 or 40 minutes, and there is little advantage in extending the testing time. A safe procedure is to allot as much time as is necessary to obtain valid and reliable results and no more. Somewhere between 20 and 60 minutes of testing time for each individual score yielded by a published test is probably a fairly good guide.

Ease of Interpretation and Application

In the final analysis, the success or failure of a testing program is determined by the use made of the test results. If they are interpreted correctly and applied effectively, they will contribute to more intelligent educational decisions. On the other hand, if the test results are misinterpreted or misapplied or not applied at all, they will be of little value and may actually be harmful to some individual or group.

Information concerning the interpretation and use of test results is usually obtained directly from the test manual or related guides. Attention should be directed toward the clarity of score reports, the quality and relevance of norms, and the comprehensiveness of the suggestions for applying the results to educational problems. When the test results are to be presented to pupils or parents, ease of interpretation and application are especially important.

Availability of Equivalent or Comparable Forms

For many educational purposes, *equivalent* forms of the same test are often desirable. Equivalent forms of a test measure the same aspect of behavior by using test items that are alike in content, level of difficulty, and other characteristics. Thus, one form of the test can substitute for the other, making it possible to test pupils twice in rather close succession without their answers on the first testing influencing their performance on the second testing. The advantage of equivalent forms is readily seen in mastery testing in which we want to eliminate the factor of memory while retesting pupils on the same domain of achievement. Equivalent forms of a test also may be used to verify a questionable test score. For example, a teacher may feel that a scholastic aptitude or achievement test score is spuriously low for a given pupil and may easily check this by administering an equivalent form of the test.

Many tests also provide *comparable* forms. Published achievement tests, for example, are commonly arranged in a series that covers different grade levels. Although the content and level of difficulty vary, the tests at the different levels are made comparable by means of a common score scale. Thus, it is possible to compare measurements in grade 4 with measurements in grade 6 on a more advanced form of the test. Comparable forms are especially useful in measuring development in the basic skills.

Cost of Testing

The factor of cost has been left to the last because it is relatively unimportant in selecting tests. The reason for discussing it at all is that it is sometimes given far more weight than it deserves. Testing is relatively inexpensive, and cost should not be a major consideration. In large-scale testing programs in which small savings per pupil add up, using separate answer sheets, machine scoring, and reusable booklets will reduce the cost appreciably. To select one test instead of another, however, because the test booklets are a few cents cheaper is false economy. After all, validity and reliability are the important characteristics to look for, and a test lacking these qualities is too expensive at any price. On the other hand, the contribution that valid and reliable test scores can make to educational decisions seems to indicate that such tests are always economical in the long run.

Summary

Next to validity, reliability is the most important quality to seek in evaluation results. Reliability refers to the consistency of test scores and other evaluation results from one measurement to another. In interpreting and using reliability information, it is important to remember that reliability estimates refer to the *results* of measurement, that different ways of estimating reliability indicate different types of consistency, that a reliable measure is *not* necessarily valid, and that reliability is strictly a statistical concept. Reliability estimates are typically reported in terms of a *reliability coefficient* or the *standard error of measurement*.

Reliability coefficients are determined by several different methods, and each provides a different measure of consistency. The test–retest method involves giving the same test twice to the same group with an intervening time interval, and the resulting coefficient provides a measure of *stability*. How long the time interval should be between tests is determined largely by the use to be made of the results. We are primarily interested in reliability coefficients based on intervals comparable to the periods of time that the scores will be used and interpreted. The equivalent-forms method involves giving two forms of a test to the same group in close succession or with an intervening time interval. The first results in a measure of *equivalence*, and the second in a measure of *stability* and *equivalence*. The latter procedure is the more rigorous test of reliability because it includes multiple sources of variation in the test score. Reliability also can be estimated from a single administration of a single form of a test, either by correlating the scores on two halves of the test or by applying one of the Kuder–Richardson formulas. Both methods provide a measure of *internal consistency* and are easy to apply. However, they are not applicable to speeded tests and provide no information concerning the stability of test scores from day to day.

The standard error of measurement indicates reliability in terms of the amount of variation to be expected in individual test scores. It can be computed from the reliability coefficient and the standard deviation, but it is frequently reported directly in test manuals. The standard error is especially useful in interpreting test scores, because it indicates the "band of error" (called a *confidence band*) surrounding each score. It also has the advantage of remaining fairly constant from one group to another.

Reliability estimates may vary in accordance with the length of the test, the spread of scores in the group tested, the difficulty of the test, the objectivity of the scoring, and the method of estimating reliability. These factors should be taken into account when appraising reliability information. The degree and type of reliability to be sought in a particular instance depend mainly on the decision being made. For tentative reversible decisions, low reliability may be tolerable. But for final irreversible decisions, we should make stringent demands on the reliability of our measures.

Conventional measures of reliability depend on scores throughout the range and are influenced by the variability among scores. In criterion-referenced mastery testing, the classification of students as masters or nonmasters is the primary concern. Hence, the consistency of classifications for equivalent test forms is most relevant, and the simple percentage of times that consistent decisions are made provides the information needed to evaluate reliability of the decision.

In addition to validity and reliability, it is also important to consider the usability of tests and other instruments, including such practical features as ease of administration, time required, ease of interpretation and application, availability of equivalent or comparable forms, and cost of testing.

Learning Exercises

1. Define reliability, and describe its importance in testing.

2. Briefly describe the methods of estimating reliability. Can one method substitute for another? Why or why not?

3. Which method of estimating reliability provides the most useful information for each of the following? Why?

    a. Selecting a scholastic aptitude test for predicting future achievement.

    b. Retesting pupils for mastery.

    c. Determining whether a test measures a homogeneous trait.

4. What effect would the following most likely have on reliability?

    a. Increasing the number of items in a test.

    b. Removing ambiguous items.

    c. Changing from a multiple-choice test to an essay test covering the same material.

5. For which purpose is each of the following most useful? Why?

    a. Reliability coefficient.

    b. Standard error of measurement.

6. Using Table 4.3, determine the standard error of measurement for a set of test scores with a standard deviation of 16 and a reliability coefficient of .85.

7. Study the reliability sections of test manuals for a few scholastic aptitude tests. What types of reliability data are reported? Are these types of data valuable in deciding whether to choose the tests?

8. In the reliability section of the *Standards for Educational and Psychological Testing* (see the reading list for this chapter), review the types of information that test manuals should contain, and then compare a recent test manual with the *Standards*.

9. In reviewing the reliability data in a test manual, a teacher noted the following reliability coefficients:

    a. Correlation of Form A test scores over a one-month interval = .90.

    b. Correlation of Form A with Form B scores over a one-month interval = .85.

    c. Correlation of scores based on two halves (odd–even) of Form A = .95.

    How would you account for these differences in reliability coefficients (assume that the groups tested were the same)? Which estimate of reliability provides the most useful information? Why?

10. List and briefly describe as many things as you can think of that might be done to increase the reliability of a classroom test.

Suggestions for Further Reading

AMERICAN PSYCHOLOGICAL ASSOCIATION. *Standards for Educational and Psychological Testing.* Washington, D.C.: APA, 1985. See the section on reliability for descriptions of the basic types and for the kind of reliability information to be sought in test manuals.

ANASTASI, ANNE. *Psychological Testing,* 6th ed. New York: Macmillan, 1988. Chapter 5,

"Reliability," describes the various types of reliability coefficients, the standard error of measurement, and the factors influencing reliability.

CRONBACH, L. J. *Essentials of Psychological Testing*, 4th ed. New York: Harper & Row, 1984. Chapter 6, "How to Judge Tests," is an advanced treatment of reliability emphasizing the "generalizability" of test scores, methods of estimating error, and considerations in interpreting reliability estimates.

FELDT, L. S., AND BRENNAN, R. L. "Reliability." In R. L. Linn, ed., *Educational Measurement*, 3d ed. New York: Macmillan, 1989, Chapter 3. The chapter presents a comprehensive and technically advanced discussion of reliability.

Part 2
Constructing Classroom Tests

Part 2

Construction in Common Time

Chapter 5

Planning the Classroom Test

*Classroom tests play a central role in the evaluation of pupil
learning. . . . They provide relevant measures of many important
learning outcomes and indirect evidence concerning others. . . . The
validity of the information they provide, however, depends on the
care that goes into the planning and preparation of the tests.*

Our main goal in classroom testing is to obtain valid, reliable, and useful information concerning pupil achievement. This means determining *what* is to be measured and then defining it so precisely that test items can be constructed that evoke
the desired performance. It also means specifying the achievement domain in such
a manner that the sample of test tasks will represent the total domain of achievement tasks and that the results will be appropriate for the intended instructional
uses.

The likelihood of preparing valid, reliable, and useful classroom tests is greatly
enhanced if a series of steps is followed, as shown in Figure 5.1. In this chapter we
shall discuss those factors concerned with planning classroom tests. This includes
considerations in each of the following areas:

1. Determining the purpose of testing.
2. Developing the test specifications.

FIGURE 5.1
Basic steps in
classroom testing.

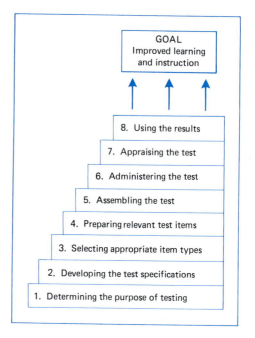

3. Selecting appropriate item types.
4. Preparing relevant test items.

Specific procedures for constructing each of the various types of test items will be described in Chapters 6 through 9, and Chapter 10 will be concerned with assembling, administering, and appraising classroom tests.

The Purpose of Classroom Testing

Classroom tests can be used for a variety of instructional purposes. These can be best described in terms of their location in the instructional process, which closely parallels the types of evaluation described in Chapter 1.

Pretesting

Tests may be given at the beginning of an instructional segment (e.g., unit or course) to determine (1) whether pupils have the prerequisite skills needed for the instruction (to determine *readiness*) or (2) to what extent pupils have already achieved the objectives of the planned instruction (to determine pupil *placement* or modification of instruction).

Readiness pretests are typically limited in scope. For example, a pretest in algebra might be confined to simple computational skills; a pretest in science might consist solely of basic science terms; and a pretest in German might be limited to knowledge of English grammar. In addition to being confined to a limited area, the pretest items tend to have a relatively low level of difficulty. Published readiness tests are available at the primary school level in the basic skill areas, but most teachers must develop their own readiness pretests if they are needed. These tests serve as a basis for remedial work or for the placement of pupils in special groups.

Pretests for determining the extent to which pupils have already achieved the objectives of the planned instruction are no different from the tests used to measure the outcomes of instruction. Thus, a test designed to measure final achievement in a course or unit may be given at the beginning to measure entry performance on the objectives. In this case, the final test should, of course, not be the same test used in pretesting but an equivalent form of it.

Testing During Instruction

Tests given during instruction (*formative* tests) are used to monitor learning progress, detect learning errors, and provide feedback to pupils and teacher.[1] These tests typically cover some predefined segment of instruction (e.g., chapter or particular set of skills) and thus encompass a rather limited sample of learning tasks. Ideally, the test will be constructed in such a way that corrective prescriptions can be given for missed test items or sets of items. When all pupils fail a set of items, a group review may be applicable. When a small number of pupils have errors, alternative methods of study may be prescribed (e.g., reading assignments, practice exercises, and the like).

Persistent learning difficulties may require the use of *diagnostic* tests. For this type of testing, a number of test items are needed in each specific area, with some slight variation from item to item. In diagnosing pupils' difficulties in adding whole numbers, for example, it would be necessary to include addition problems containing various number combinations, some *not* requiring carrying and some requiring carrying, to pinpoint the specific types of errors being made. Diagnostic testing is a highly specialized area that has been somewhat neglected in educational measurement. There are some published diagnostic tests but these are primarily in the basic skills area. In other areas, teachers have to depend more heavily on the diagnostic features of formative tests or make special efforts to prepare their own diagnostic tests.

End-of-Instruction Testing

At the end of a segment of instruction (e.g., unit or course), our main interest is in measuring the extent to which the intended learning outcomes have been achieved. Although these end-of-instruction tests (*summative* tests) are used primarily to certify mastery or assign grades, they also can serve other functions. The more restricted *end-of unit* test can be used for feedback to pupils, assigning of remedial work, and evaluating instruction.[2] In fact, it can serve the functions of both

---

[1] Teachers commonly call formative tests learning tests, practice tests, quizzes, unit tests, and the like.

[2] Some teachers use end-of-unit tests for grading purposes only, but they can and also should be used for improving learning and instruction.

formative and summative testing and in some cases serve as a pretest for the following unit (e.g., where the units are sequenced, as in math). The *end-of-course* test provides a broad survey of pupil learning over all of the intended outcomes of a course. In addition to its use in grading, it also can provide information for evaluating instructional effectiveness.

As a guide for test planning, a summary comparison of the various types of classroom testing is presented in Table 5.1.

Developing Test Specifications

To provide assurance that a classroom test will measure a representative sample of instructionally relevant tasks some type of test specifications should be used. When preparing a brief learning test on a limited area (e.g., spelling or capitalization) a simple listing of specific tasks, with an indication of the number of items measuring each task, may suffice. For most testing purposes, however, more elaborate test specifications are needed. One device that has been widely used for this purpose is a two-way chart, called a *table of specifications* (or *test blueprint*).

Building a Table of Specifications

Building a table of specifications includes (1) preparing a list of instructional objectives, (2) outlining the course content, and (3) preparing the two-way chart. These steps will be illustrated for a weather unit in junior high school science.

Preparing the List of Instructional Objectives.   Using the procedure for stating instructional objectives described in Chapter 2, the following list of general objectives and specific learning outcomes was prepared for the weather unit. Although the list is not exhaustive, it illustrates both the method of stating the objectives and the desired amount of detail. If this weather unit was being taught at a lower grade level, our objectives would be defined by fewer and simpler specific learning outcomes; at a higher grade level more complex learning outcomes would be included.

INSTRUCTIONAL OBJECTIVES FOR A WEATHER UNIT

1.   Knows basic terms.
   1.1.   Writes a definition of each term.
   1.2.   Identifies the term that represents each weather element.
   1.3.   Identifies the term that best fits a given weather description.
   1.4.   Matches the term to a picture of the concept.
   1.5.   Distinguishes between correct and incorrect uses of the term.
2.   Knows weather symbols.
   2.1.   Matches each symbol with the weather element it represents.
   2.2.   Draws the symbol for each weather element.
   2.3.   Identifies the meaning of each symbol.

TABLE 5.1

Summary Comparison of the Basic Types of Classroom Testing*

	Pretesting		Testing During Instruction		End Testing
	Readiness Pretest	Placement Pretest	Formative Test	Diagnostic Test	Summative Test
Focus of measurement	Prerequisite entry skills	Course or unit objectives	Predefined segment of instruction	Most common learning errors	Course or unit objectives
Nature of sample	Limited sample of selected skills	Broad sample of all objectives	Limited sample of learning tasks	Limited sample of specific errors	Broad sample of all objectives
Item difficulty	Typically has low level of difficulty	Typically has wide range of difficulty	Varies with the segment of instruction	Typically has low level of difficulty	Typically has wide range of difficulty
Time of administration	Beginning of course or unit	Beginning of course or unit	Periodically during instruction	As needed during instruction	End of course or unit
Type of instrument	Typically is criterion-referenced mastery test	Typically is norm-referenced survey test	Typically is criterion-referenced mastery test	Specially designed test to identify learning errors	Typically is norm-referenced survey test
Use of results	Remedy entry deficiencies or assignment to learning group	Instructional planning and advance placement	Improve and direct learning through ongoing feedback	Remedy errors related to persistent learning difficulties	Assign grades certify mastery, or evaluate teaching

*Adapted from P. W. Airasian and G. F. Madaus, "Functional Types of Student Evaluation," *Measurement and Evaluation in Guidance* 4(1972): 221–233.

3. Knows specific facts.

   3.1. Identifies the elements affecting weather.
   3.2. Names the instrument used for measuring each weather element.
   3.3. Identifies the unit of measurement used in reporting each weather element.
   3.4. Distinguishes between correct and incorrect procedures for determining each weather element.
   3.5. Matches the names of each cloud type with a description of its characteristics.
   3.6. Identifies the weather conditions associated with each type of front.

4. Understands the influence of factors on weather formation.

   4.1. Lists the characteristics of a given weather condition.
   4.2. Distinguishes between probable and improbable weather reports.
   4.3. Identifies the factors causing a given weather change.
   4.4. Predicts future weather from a change in conditions.

5. Interprets weather maps.

   5.1. Describes the weather for a given locality.
   5.2. Identifies the different types of fronts shown on a weather map.
   5.3. Describes the weather conditions surrounding each front shown on a weather map.
   5.4. Identifies the direction of movement for each front shown on a weather map.

The list of objectives is limited to those outcomes that can be measured by a classroom test. It does not include performance skills (e.g., using weather instruments, constructing weather maps) or affective outcomes (e.g., demonstrating scientific attitude). A more elaborate evaluation plan for a weather unit might contain a listing of all relevant outcomes with an indication of how each is to be evaluated. The advantage of that procedure is that testing is viewed in proper perspective and not likely to be overemphasized in evaluating learning outcomes.

Outlining the Instructional Content. The list of instructional objectives describes the types of performance the pupils are expected to demonstrate, and the instructional content indicates the area in which each type of performance is to be shown. Thus, the second step in preparing test specifications is to make an outline of the instructional content. The amount of detail to include in the content outline is somewhat arbitrary, but it should be detailed enough to ensure adequate sampling during test construction and proper interpretation of the results. The following list of topics and subtopics for our illustrative weather unit illustrates an adequate outline for test preparation.

CONTENT OUTLINE FOR A WEATHER UNIT

A. Air pressure.

   1. Measuring and reporting air pressure.
   2. Factors affecting air pressure.
   3. Relation to weather changes.

B. Air temperature.

    1. Measuring and reporting air temperature.
    2. Factors affecting air temperature.
    3. Relation to weather formations.

C. Humidity and precipitation.

    1. Measuring and reporting humidity.
    2. Factors affecting humidity.
    3. Forms of precipitation.
    4. Measuring and reporting precipitation.

D. Wind.

    1. Measurement of speed and direction.
    2. Factors affecting speed and direction.
    3. Symbols for reporting speed and direction.

E. Clouds.

    1. Types of clouds.
    2. Characteristics of cloud types.
    3. Factors causing cloud formations.
    4. Relation to weather conditions.
    5. Symbols for cloud types.

F. Fronts.

    1. Types of fronts.
    2. Formation of fronts.
    3. Weather related to fronts.
    4. Symbols for fronts.

For instructional purposes, some teachers prefer to expand the above outline to include all terms, symbols, and specific facts that the students are expected to learn. Where this is done, the more elaborate outline used for instruction, of course, also may be used for testing purposes.

Preparing the Two-Way Chart.   The final step in building a table of specifications is to prepare a two-way chart that relates the instructional objectives to the instructional content and, thus, specifies the nature of the test sample. An example of the chart for our weather unit in junior high school science is presented in Table 5.2. This table indicates both the total number of test items and the percentage of test items allotted to each objective and each area of content. For classroom testing, using the number of items only may be sufficient but the percentages are useful in determining the amount of emphasis to give to each area.

Table 5.2 was prepared by using the following steps.

1. List the general instructional objectives across the top of the table.

2. List the major content areas down the left side of the table.

3. Determine what proportion of the test items should be devoted to each objective and each content area.

Objectives	Knows			Understands	Interprets		
TABLE 5.2 Table of Specifications for a Weather Unit in Junior High School Science						Total Number of Items	Percent of Items
Content	Basic Terms	Weather Symbols	Specific Facts	Influence of Each Factor on Weather Formation	Weather Maps		
Air pressure	2	2	2	3	3	12	20
Wind	1	4	2	8	2	17	28
Temperature	2	2	2	2	2	10	17
Humidity and precipitation	3	2	1	2	5	13	22
Clouds	4	2	2			8	13
Total number of items	12	12	9	15	12	60	
Percent of items	20	20	15	25	20		100

By looking at the bottom row in Table 5.2, it can be seen that 20 percent of the items are to be devoted to "knowledge of basic terms," 20 percent to "knowledge of weather symbols," 15 percent to "knowledge of specific facts," and so on across the row. Similarly, the column on the far right shows that 20 percent of the items are to be concerned with "air pressure," 28 percent with "wind," 17 percent with "temperature," and so on down the column. Typically these percentages are assigned first to indicate the relative emphasis to be given to each objective and each content area. The total number of items for each area is then determined. For example, because this is to be a 60-item test, 12 of the items (20 percent) are to measure "knowledge of basic terms" and 12 of the items (20 percent) are concerned with "air pressure." Thus, the total number of items is computed and listed across the bottom of the chart and down the right-hand side of the chart. These numbers are then used as a *guide* to assign test items to each cell. For example, 2 items (approximately 20 percent of 12) have been assigned to the cell in the upper left-hand corner, indicating that the test will contain 2 items measuring "knowledge of terms" concerning "air pressure." The assignment of items to each cell is not strictly a matter of following the percentages, however. Some cells may be left blank, as shown in the chart, because items in those areas are inappropriate. Similarly, some cells may receive a larger number of items because the learning tasks for that cell may have received greater emphasis in teaching. Despite these adjustments to the distribution of items, the number of items in the cells of the table should approximate the desired distribution and must add up to the total number of items indicated for each column and row.

The final distribution of items in the table of specifications should reflect the emphasis given during the instruction. Objectives considered more important by the teacher should be allotted more test items. Similarly, areas of content receiving more instruction time should be allocated more test items. Although the decisions involved in making the table are somewhat arbitrary and the process is time consuming, the preparation of a table of specifications is one of the best means for ensuring that the test will measure a representative sample of instructionally relevant tasks. As noted in Chapter 3, this provides content-related evidence that the test will provide a valid measure of the intended learning outcomes. When desired, the table of specifications can be expanded to include those objectives not measured by tests (see Appendix F).

Other Examples of Test Specifications

Because of its broad coverage, a table of specifications is especially useful in constructing a test over a unit or course. Here the table provides some assurance that each of the diverse types of learning tasks will receive appropriate emphasis in the test. Whether a table of specifications is useful in constructing a test over a more limited area, however, depends on the scope of learning tasks to be covered by the test. If the domain of tasks is very limited, such as "adds fractions with the same denominator," a table of specifications might be unnecessary. Here we could simply list all, or nearly all, of the specific tasks encompassed by this learning outcome, as follows:

Adds two fractions with same denominator where the answer is less than one ($\frac{1}{3} + \frac{1}{3}$).

Adds two fractions with same denominator where the answer equals one ($\frac{1}{3} + \frac{2}{3}$).

Adds two fractions with same denominator where the answer is greater than one ($\frac{2}{3} + \frac{2}{3}$).

Adds two fractions with same denominator and reduces answer to lowest terms ($\frac{4}{6} + \frac{4}{6}$).

Adds more than two fractions with same denominator and reduces answer ($\frac{3}{8} + \frac{5}{8} + \frac{6}{8}$).

A list of learning tasks such as this specifies quite clearly the precise nature of the performance involved in "adding fractions with the same denominator." We could obtain a fairly representative sample of such tasks by simply constructing five or more items for each task, using various number combinations.

   If our arithmetic test were to cover a slightly larger achievement domain, say, "addition of fractions," we might now find a table of specifications quite useful. An illustration of such a table for a 50-item test is shown in Table 5.3. The use of such a table does not mean, of course, that we should not make the type of detailed breakdown illustrated for "adding fractions with the same denominator." Such a detailed listing of tasks aids in teaching, in detecting learning errors, and in constructing test items. The table of specifications, however, supplements such lists by

Content Area \ Instructional Objectives	Adds Fractions	Adds Fractions and Mixed Numbers	Adds Mixed Numbers	Total Items
Denominators are alike	5	5	5	15
Denominators are unlike (with common factor)	5	5	5	15
Denominators are unlike (without common factor)	6	7	7	20
Total items	16	17	17	50

specifying the sample of tasks to be included in the test. As noted earlier, this provides greater assurance that the intended learning outcomes will be measured in a balanced manner.

Using a One-Way Classification System. For tests in some areas, a one-way classification of items may be all that is needed. In planning for a reading test, for example, a list of the reading skills and the number of test items for measuring each skill may be sufficient for specifying what the test is to measure. The content (e.g., passages read) may vary from time to time, but the skill outcomes remain fairly constant. Thus, a master list of skills can be prepared for use with various types of reading material. An example of such a list is presented in Table 5.4.

It should be noted that each skill in Table 5.4 is stated in specific performance terms and that ten items are used to measure each skill. This provides for criterion-referenced interpretation and, if a standard of mastery is to be set, it can be done for each specific skill in term of a percentage-correct score. Although the material to be read is not included in the specifications, it will, of course, need to be carefully selected in terms of interest and readability level.

Using Detailed Specifications. In some cases, basic skill tests are developed by committees of teachers, either for schoolwide use in the instructional program or for some special need (e.g., minimum-competency testing). When committees are

Reading Skill	Number of Items
Identifies details stated in a passage	10
Identifies the main idea of a passage	10
Identifies the sequence of actions or events	10
Identifies relationships expressed in a passage	10
Identifies inferences drawn from a passage	10
Total number	50

used, detailed specifications should be prepared for each specific skill tested. As a guide for the item writers, the specifications should state the specific skill being measured and describe and illustrate the nature of the test items to be used. The detailed description of the item characteristics indicates the essential elements to consider in preparing the items and places restrictions on the structure of the item. An illustrative set of specifications for one of the specific reading comprehension skills listed in Table 5.4 is presented in Figure 5.2.

Using detailed specifications such as this provides greater assurance that all of the items that are written to measure a particular skill will have the same characteristics and thus will be functionally equivalent. If several forms of the test are being prepared, the specifications also aid the item writers in preparing equivalent forms.

An even more detailed set of test specifications has been suggested by Popham for use in criterion-referenced testing. He proposes that separate test specifications should be prepared for each set of items that purportedly measures the same class of behavior and that the test specifications should contain the following components:[3]

1. *General description*: A brief depiction, in general terms, of the behavior being assessed by the test.

General Outcome: Reading comprehension.

Specific Skill: Identifies details stated in a passage.

Type of Test Used: Multiple-choice (10 items).

Reading Passage: The reading passage will consist of from one to three paragraphs of material that is (1) of special interest to children, and (2) at the fifth-grade reading level.

Item Characteristics: Each test item will be in the form of a question or an incomplete statement, followed by four alternative answers. The item will require the pupil to identify such facts as names, dates, places, or the characteristics of important elements in the passage. The *correct answer* is based on information that has been explicitly stated in the passage. The *distracters* (incorrect alternatives) are to be made plausible by using words or phrases from the passage, or from content similar to the passage, and by matching the correct answer in terms of length and grammatical structure. The reading level of the test item will be no higher than the reading level of the passage.

Sample Item: (Passage describes United States space explorations). Which one of the astronauts was first to ride in a space capsule?

    A. Scott Carpenter
    B. John Glenn
    C. Virgil Grissom
    D. Alan Shepard (correct answer)

FIGURE 5.2
Illustrative specifications for a 10-item test measuring a specific reading skill.

[3]W. J. Popham, *Criterion Referenced Measurement* (Englewood Cliffs, N.J.: Prentice-Hall, 1978), pp. 121–122. For detailed descriptions of these components and for illustrative test specifications, see Chapter 6 in this book and Chapter 2 in R. A. Berk, ed., *A Guide to Criterion-Referenced Test Construction* (Baltimore: Johns Hopkins University Press, 1984).

2. *Sample item*: An illustrative item that reflects the test-item attributes to be delimited in the following two components.
3. *Stimulus attributes*: A series of statements that attempt to delimit the class of stimulus material that will be encountered by the examinee.
4. *Response attributes*: A series of statements that attempt either to (a) delimit the classes of response options from which the student makes *selected responses* or (b) explicate the standards by which an examinee's *constructed responses* will be judged.
5. *Specification supplement*: In certain cases it may be necessary to add an appendix or supplement to the preceding four components. This supplement typically provides a more detailed listing or explanation of eligible content.

Checklist for Reviewing Test Specifications

REVIEW QUESTIONS	YES	NO
1. Are the specifications in harmony with the purpose of the test?	___	___
2. Do the specifications indicate the nature and limits of the achievement domain?	___	___
3. Do the specifications indicate the *types* of learning outcomes to be measured?	___	___
4. Do the specifications indicate the *sample* of learning outcomes to be measured?	___	___
5. Is the *number* of test items indicated for the total test and for each subdivision?	___	___
6. Are the *types* of items to be used appropriate for the outcomes to be measured?	___	___
7. Is the *difficulty* of the items appropriate for the types of interpretation to be made?	___	___
8. Is the *distribution* of items adequate for the types of interpretation to be made?	___	___
9. If sample items are included, do they illustrate the desired attributes?	___	___
10. Do the specifications, as a whole, indicate a representative sample of instructionally relevant tasks that fits the use to be made of the results?	___	___

Some of these components are similar to those illustrated in Figure 5.2, but Popham's specifications are much more comprehensive and detailed. Each set of test specifications may run five or more pages in length. Although this may discourage their routine use, they provide the type of structure needed for preparing sets of test items that are both functionally equivalent and relevant to the domain to be tested. They, of course, not only provide guidelines for item writing, but also provide the "descriptive rigor" needed for sound criterion-referenced interpretations. The detailed descriptions help clarify the specific types of performance that the test scores represent.

Selecting Appropriate Item Types

The items used in classroom tests are typically divided into two general categories: (1) the objective item, which is highly structured and requires the pupils to supply a word or two or to select the correct answer from a number of alternatives, and (2) the essay question, which permits the pupils to select, organize, and present the answer in essay form. There is no conflict between these two item types. For some instructional purposes, the objective item may be most efficient, whereas for others the essay question may prove most satisfactory. Each type should be used where most appropriate, with appropriateness determined by the learning outcomes to be measured and by the advantages and limitations of each item type.

The Objective Test Item

The objective item includes a variety of different types, but they can be classified into those that require the pupil to *supply* the answer and those that require the pupil to *select* the answer from a given number of alternatives. These two general classes are commonly further divided into the following basic types of objective test items:

SUPPLY TYPES: EXAMPLES

1. Short answer.

What is the name of the author of *Moby Dick*?   (Herman Melville)
What is the formula for hydrochloric acid?   (HCl)
What is the value of X in the equation $2X + 5 = 9$?   (2)

2. Completion

Lines on a weather map joining points with the same barometric pressure are
  called (isobars).
The formula for ordinary table salt is (NaCl).
In the equation $2X + 5 = 9$; $X =$ (2)

SELECTION TYPES:

1. True-false or alternative response.

(T)   F   A virus is the smallest known organism.
T   (F)   An atom is the smallest particle of matter.
Yes   (No)   In the equation $2X + 5 = 9$, X equals 3.
(Yes)   No   Acid turns litmus paper red.

121

2. Matching.

(C)	1. And	A	Adjective
(D)	2. Dog	B	Adverb
(G)	3. Jump	C	Conjunction
(F)	4. She	D	Noun
(B)	5. Quickly	E	Preposition
		F	Pronoun
		G	Verb

3. Multiple-choice.

In the equation $2X + 5 = 9$, the 2X means

A   2 plus X.
B   2 minus X.
C   2 divided by X.
Ⓓ   2 multiplied by X.

In which of the following sentences do the subject and verb disagree?

A   When they win, they are happy.
Ⓑ   Politics are hard to understand.
C   The majority is always right.
D   One or the other is to be elected.

In addition to these basic types of objective test items, there are numerous modifications and combinations of types. However, there is little to be gained from listing all the possible variations, as many are unique to particular objectives or subject-matter areas. Some of the more common variations used to measure understanding, thinking skills, and other complex learning outcomes will be illustrated later. These, plus an understanding of the general principles of test construction and the principles that apply to each of the specific types of objective test items, should enable teachers to make adaptations that best fit their particular purposes.

The various types of objective test items have one feature in common that distinguishes them from the essay test. They present the pupils with a highly structured task that limits the type of response they can make. To obtain the correct answer, the pupils must demonstrate the specific knowledge, understanding, or skill called for in the item; they are not free to redefine the problem or to organize and present the answer in their own words. They must select one of several alternative answers or supply the correct word, number, or symbol. This structuring of the problem and restriction on the method of responding contribute to objective scoring that is quick, easy, and accurate. On the negative side, this same structuring makes the objective test item inappropriate for measuring the ability to select, organize, and integrate ideas. To measure such outcomes we must depend on the essay question.

The Essay Question

The essay question is commonly viewed as a single item type. A useful classification, however, is one based on the amount of freedom of response allowed the pupil. This includes the *extended response* type, in which the pupils are given almost complete freedom in making their responses, and the *restricted response* type, in which the nature, length, or organization of the response is limited. These types are illustrated as follows:

1. *Extended response type*:
   Describe what you think the role of the federal government should be in maintaining a stable economy in the United States. Include specific policies and programs, and give reasons for your proposals.

2. *Restricted response type*:
   State two advantages and two disadvantages of maintaining high tariffs on goods from other countries.

Notice in these examples, that the *extended response* type question permits pupils to decide which facts they think are most pertinent, to select their own method of organization, and to write as much as seems necessary for a comprehensive answer. Thus, such questions tend to reveal the ability to evaluate ideas, to relate them coherently, and to express them succinctly. To a lesser extent, they also reflect individual differences in attitudes, values, and creative ability.

Despite the apparent virtues of the extended response type of question, it has two weaknesses that severely limit its use: (1) it is inefficient for measuring knowledge of factual material because the questions are so extensive that only a small sample of content can be included in any one test, and (2) the scoring is difficult and apt to be unreliable because the answers include an array of factual information of varying degrees of correctness, organized with varying degrees of coherence, and expressed with varying degrees of legibility and conciseness.

The *restricted response* type of question minimizes some of the weaknesses of the extended response type. Restricting the type of response called for makes it more efficient for measuring knowledge of factual material and reduces somewhat the difficulty of the scoring. On the other hand, the more highly structured task presented by the restricted response type of question makes it less effective as a measure of the ability to select, organize, and integrate ideas, which is one of the unique purposes to be served by the essay test.

As with the various forms of objective test items, neither the extended response type question nor the restricted response type question can serve all purposes equally well. The type to use in a particular situation depends mainly on the learning outcomes to be measured and to a lesser extent on such practical considerations as the difficulty of scoring.

Comparative Advantages of Objective and Essay Questions

From our previous discussion, it is apparent that both the objective-item and the essay question can provide valuable evidence concerning pupil achievement. Each has advantages and limitations which make it more appropriate for some purposes than for others. A comparison of the relative merits of tests based on these two item types, with regard to a number of important characteristics, is presented in Table 5.5.

TABLE 5.5 Comparative Advantages of Objective and Essay Tests		Objective Test	Essay Test
	Learning outcomes measured	Is efficient for measuring knowledge of facts. Some types (e.g., multiple-choice) can also measure understanding, thinking skills, and other complex outcomes. Inefficient or inappropriate for measuring ability to select and organize ideas, writing abilities, and some types of problem-solving skills.	Is inefficient for measuring knowledge of facts. Can measure understanding, thinking skills, and other complex learning outcomes (especially useful where originality of response is desired). Appropriate for measuring ability to select and organize ideas, writing abilities, and problem-solving skills requiring originality.
	Preparation of questions	A relatively large number of questions is needed for a test. Preparation is difficult and time consuming.	Only a few questions are needed for a test. Preparation is relatively easy (but more difficult than generally assumed).
	Sampling of course content	Provides an extensive sampling of course content because of the large number of questions that can be included in a test.	Sampling of course content is usually limited because of the small number of questions that can be included in a test.
	Control of pupil's response	Complete structuring of task limits pupil to type of response called for. Prevents bluffing and avoids influence of writing skill, though selection-type items are subject to guessing.	Freedom to respond in own words enables bluffing and writing skill to influence the score, though guessing is minimized.
	Scoring	Objective scoring that is quick, easy, and consistent.	Subjective scoring that is slow, difficult, and inconsistent.
	Influence on learning	Usually encourages pupil to develop a comprehensive knowledge of specific facts and the ability to make fine discriminations among them. Can encourage the development of understanding, thinking skills, and other complex outcomes if properly constructed.	Encourages pupils to concentrate on larger units of subject matter, with special emphasis on the ability to organize, integrate, and express ideas effectively. May encourage poor writing habits if time pressure is a factor (it almost always is).
	Reliability	High reliability is possible and is typically obtained with well-constructed tests.	Reliability is typically low, primarily because of inconsistent scoring.

In considering the comparative advantages of these two main types as a basis for building a classroom test, we must be careful not to fall into "either-or" thinking, that is, to use either objective items or essay questions. It is frequently better to use both types in a single test, with each measuring the particular learning outcomes for which it is best suited. This should also have a desirable influence on pupil learning because in preparing for such tests they must attend to both the specific types of learning outcomes measured by objective items and the synthesis type of outcomes measured by essay questions.

Selecting the Most Appropriate Item Types

A basic principle in selecting the type of test item to use is: *Select the item type that provides the most direct measure of the performance task described in the intended learning outcome*. If, for example, the task is one of *writing, naming,* or *listing,* the item should require the pupils to supply the answer. If the task calls for *identifying* a correct answer, a selection-type item should be used. In the accompanying box, based on the weather unit discussed earlier, note how each type of objective item provides a direct measure of the outcome it was designed to measure. In those cases where the specific learning outcome does not make clear which item type to use, selection-type items would be favored because of the greater control over the pupil's response and the objectivity of the scoring.

In deciding which selection-type item to use, a common practice is to use the multiple-choice item if it will measure the learning outcome as directly as the other two types. The use of true–false items is typically restricted to those special instances where there are only two possible alternatives (e.g., distinguishing be-

---

Selecting Appropriate Item Types to Match Learning Outcomes

SHORT-ANSWER ITEMS

Specific Learning Outcome: Writes a definition of each term.
  Directions: Write a one-sentence definition of each of the following terms.
> 1. Weather
> 2. Humidity
> 3. Occluded front

Specific Learning Outcome: Names the instrument used for measuring each weather element.
  1. The instrument used to measure the amount of precipitation in a given locality is called a (an) _____ .

Specific Learning Outcome: Lists the characteristics of a given weather phenomenon.
  1. List three main characteristics of a hurricane.

(continued)

MULTIPLE-CHOICE ITEMS

Specific Learning Outcome: Identifies the units of measurement used in reporting each weather element on a weather map.

1. United States weather maps indicate air pressure in

  A inches
  B feet
  C pounds
  ***D** milibars

TRUE–FALSE ITEMS

Specific Learning Outcome: Distinguishes between correct and incorrect procedures for determining each weather element.

T F 1. Dew point is determined by cooling a sample of air until it is
  *   free of moisture.
T F 2. Ceiling is determined by using balloons that rise at known rates.
*

*Correct answers.

MATCHING ITEMS

Specific Learning Outcome: Matches each weather instrument to the weather element it measures.

  Directions: On the line to the left of each weather element in *Column A,* write the letter of the weather instrument in *Column B* that is used for measuring it. Each instrument in Column B may be used once, more than once, or not at all.

Column A	*Column B*
(B) 1. Air pressure	A Anemometer
(E) 2. Air temperature	B Barometer
(C) 3. Humidity	C Hygrometer
(A) 4. Wind velocity	D Rain gauge
	E Thermometer
	F Wind vane

tween correct and incorrect procedures). The matching item is a specialized form of the multiple-choice item and should be used only where a series of homogeneous things are to be related (e.g., dates and events, authors and books, instruments and uses). The multiple-choice item is favored for most other selection-type tasks because the use of four or five alternatives reduces the chances of guessing the answer and provides clues to pupils' misunderstandings. See Appendix F for other examples of how to relate test items to intended learning outcomes.

Whether a test item actually measures the particular performance called for by a specific learning outcome depends, of course, to a large extent on the skill with which the test item is constructed. No amount of skill, however, will enable us to develop a valid test of achievement if the test items selected for use are inappropriate for measuring the intended outcomes.

Considerations in Preparing Relevant Test Items

As noted earlier, the construction of items for a classroom test should be preceded by a series of preliminary steps. First, the purpose of the test should be determined. Second, a set of specifications should be developed. Third, the most appropriate item types should be selected. Finally, the test items should be constructed in accordance with the specifications developed during the preceding steps. The rules for constructing each item type will be discussed in Chapters 6 through 9. Here we shall focus on some of the general considerations involved in preparing relevant items for a classroom test.

Matching Items to Intended Outcomes

A classroom test is most likely to provide a valid measure of the instructional objectives if the test items are designed to measure the performance defined by the specific learning outcomes. The process of matching test items to the learning outcomes to be measured was illustrated earlier. Essentially, it involves fitting each test item as closely as possible to the intended outcome, as follows:

Specific Learning Outcome: Identifies the function of a given body structure. EXAMPLE
Relevant Test Item:

  What is the function of the kidneys?
   A Eliminate waste products.
   B Improve the circulation of blood.
   C Maintain respiration.
   D Stimulate digestion.

Thus, the preparation of relevant test items means analyzing the performance described in the specific learning outcome (i.e., "Identifies the function of . . .") and the construction of a test item that calls forth that performance (i.e., "What is the function of . . . ?"). Note in our example that the specific learning outcome defines the *type of response* the pupil is expected to make, but it does not indicate the *specific body structure* (i.e., kidney) the pupil is to identify. Keeping the learning outcome free of specific course content, like this, makes it possible to key the intended response to various areas of content. For example, pupils could be asked to identify the function of the heart, the lungs, the muscles, or any other body structure pertinent to the course's content. The desired pupil performance stated in the specific learning outcome can be keyed to each specific area of content by means of the table of specifications.

In some cases it may be desirable to prepare a general *item pattern* as an intermediate step between the specific learning outcome and the test item. A general item pattern for our illustrative test item, for example, would be as follows:

EXAMPLE

What is the function of . . . ?

An item pattern such as this could be completed by adding the name of any body structure and using it as a short-answer question or, in addition, by listing appropriate alternatives and using it as a multiple-choice item. Thus, using the item pattern as a guide, we could generate large numbers of relevant test items for this particular learning outcome. This procedure is especially useful when a file of test items is being prepared or when more than one form of the test is needed (e.g., pretesting – posttesting, retesting in mastery learning).

When item patterns are used as a guide to test construction, they can be arranged by general type of learning outcome:

EXAMPLES

Knowledge Outcomes

1. What is the name of . . . ?
2. What is the location of . . . ?
3. What are the characteristics of . . . ?
4. What is the function of . . . ?

Understanding Outcomes

1. What is the reason for . . . ?
2. What is the relationship between . . . ?
3. Which of these is an example of . . . ?
4. Which of these best summarizes . . . ?

Application Outcomes

1. What method would be best for . . . ?
2. What steps should be followed to construct . . . ?
3. Which of these indicates correct application of . . . ?
4. Which of these solutions is correct for . . . ?

Item patterns like these should not, of course, be developed haphazardly. Rather, they should be derived from the specific learning outcomes they represent. Although it usually will not be possible to develop item patterns for all outcomes, listing them will help generate pools of relevant test items. The test construction time saved by using such a list can be profitably used to construct more effective items in those areas in which general item patterns are infeasible.

Obtaining a Representative Sample of Items

A test, no matter how extensive, is almost always a sample of the many possible test items that could be included. For example, we expect pupils to know thousands of facts, but we can test for only a limited number of them; we expect pupils to develop understanding applicable to innumerable situations, but we can test application to only a limited number of situations; and we expect pupils to develop thinking skills that will enable them to solve a variety of problems, but we can test their problem-solving ability with only a limited number of problems. In each area of content and for each specific learning outcome, then, we merely select a sample of pupil performance and accept it as evidence of achievement in that area. We assume that the pupils' responses to our selected set of test items are typical of what their responses would be to other test items drawn from the same area. This means, of course, that our limited samples must be selected in such a way that they provide as representative a sample as possible in each of the various areas for which the test is being developed.

Our sampling is most likely to be representative when test preparation is guided by a carefully prepared set of specifications. Unless a table of specifications, or some similar device, is used as a guide in test construction, there is a tendency to overload the test with items measuring knowledge of isolated facts and to neglect the more complex learning outcomes. In the social studies area, for example, it is not uncommon to include a disproportionately large number of items that measure knowledge of names, dates, places, and the like. In science, defining terms and naming structures and functions are commonly overemphasized. In mathematics, computational skill is frequently the only learning outcome measured. In language arts and literature, the identification of parts of speech, literary characters, authors, and the like is frequently too prominent. These learning outcomes are, generally, *not* stressed because we think knowledge of isolated facts is more important than understanding, applications, interpretations, and various thinking skills. Rather, they usually receive undue prominence because we find it easier to construct such test items. *Without a carefully developed test plan, ease of construction all too frequently becomes the dominant criterion in constructing test items. As a consequence, the test measures a limited and biased sample of learning tasks and neglects many learning outcomes of greater importance.*

Test Length.   The length of a test is, of course, also an important factor in obtaining a representative sample. Test length is determined when the set of specifications is built and depends on such factors as the purpose of testing, the types of test items used, the age of the pupils, and the level of reliability needed for effective test use. Thus, a mastery test over a third-grade social studies *unit* might contain 30 objective items, whereas a survey test over a tenth-grade social studies *course* might contain more than 100 objective items and several essay questions. Although there are no hard and fast rules for determining test length, an important consideration from a sampling standpoint is the number of test items devoted to each specific area being measured. We want our classroom tests to be long enough to provide an adequate sampling of each objective and each content area. As a rule of thumb, it is desirable when constructing a mastery test to use at least ten objective test items to measure each specific learning outcome.[4] This number, however, might be lowered to as few as five if the task is extremely limited (e.g., "Adds two single-digit numbers," "Capitalizes proper names") and the pupils are to supply the answers rather than to select them. For a survey test, where the sample of test items typically covers a broad area and emphasis is on the total score, using several objective test items for each specific learning outcome and ten or more for each general objective probably would be sufficient.

Special problems of sampling arise when complex learning outcomes are being measured, because here we must turn to more elaborate objective-type items and essay questions. Both item types require considerable testing time, but a single test exercise is still inadequate for measuring an intended outcome. One exercise calling for the interpretation of graphs, for instance, is not sufficient to measure adequately the ability to interpret graphs. The nature of the data or the type of graph may be the most influential factor in determining whether it is interpreted properly. When several graphs are used, the effect of such factors is minimized, and we obtain a more representative sample of the ability to interpret graphs. A similar situation occurs with the use of essay questions. The answer to any single question depends too heavily on the particular sample of information called for by the question, and thus the only feasible solution is to confine each test of complex outcomes to a rather limited area (e.g., graph interpretation, problem solving) and to test more often. In any event, our aim should be to obtain as representative a sample of pupil performance as possible in each area to be tested. Other things being equal, the greater the number of test items the greater the likelihood of an adequate sample and thus the more reliable the results.

Selecting Proper Item Difficulty[5]

The difficulty of the items to be included in a classroom test depends largely on whether the test is being designed to describe the specific learning tasks pupils can perform (i.e., criterion referenced) or to rank the pupils in order of their achievement (i.e., norm referenced). As noted previously, these two approaches to measurement place quite different emphases on the role of item difficulty in classroom testing.

---

[4]For a fuller discussion of test length for criterion-referenced tests, see J. Millman, "Criterion-Referenced Measurements," in *Evaluation in Education: Current Applications*, ed. W. J. Popham (Berkeley, Calif.: McCutchan, 1974), pp. 311–397.

[5]Item difficulty is expressed as the percentage of pupils answering the item correctly. See Chapter 10 for a fuller discussion.

Item Difficulty and Criterion-Referenced Interpretation. The difficulty of the test item in a criterion-referenced test is determined by the nature of the specific learning tasks to be measured. If the learning tasks are easy, the test items should be easy. If the learning tasks are of moderate difficulty, the test items should be of moderate difficulty. No attempt should be made to modify item difficulty or to eliminate easy items from the test in order to obtain a range of test scores. On a criterion-referenced test we would expect all, or nearly all, pupils to obtain high scores when the instruction has been effective.

This discussion does not imply, of course, that item difficulty can be ignored when constructing items for a criterion-referenced test. On the contrary, care must be taken to match item difficulty to the difficulty of the learning task described in the intended outcome. This also involves special precautions to avoid irrelevant barriers to the answer (e.g., ambiguity), unintended clues to the correct response, or any other factor that might alter the level of difficulty of the test task. In final analysis, we want the pupil's responses on each test item to serve as a valid indicator of the presence or absence of the specific performance defined in the intended learning outcome.

Item Difficulty and Norm-Referenced Interpretation. Because norm-referenced tests are designed to rank pupils in order of achievement, deliberate attempts are made to obtain a wide spread of test scores. This involves eliminating the easy items that all pupils are likely to answer correctly and favoring items that maximize the differences in pupils' test performance. Our aim is to obtain as reliable a ranking of pupils as possible so that the decisions based on relative achievement (e.g., classroom grouping, grading) can be made with a high degree of confidence.

Maximum differentiation among pupils in terms of achievement is obtained when the average score is near the midpoint of the possible scores, and the scores range from near zero to near perfect. With a 100-item short-answer test, for example, an average score of 50 and a range of scores from 5 to 95 would be ideal. The ideal average score for selection-type items falls above that point because of the guessing factor. As a rule of thumb, the point midway between the expected chance score (proportion of items marked correctly by guessing) and the maximum possible score (total number of items in the test) provides a desirable average score. Thus, the average difficulty to try for on a 100-item test for various choice-type items would be as follows:

	Chance Score	Average Difficulty
Two-choice item (e.g., true–false)	50	75
Three-choice multiple-choice item	33	67
Four-choice multiple-choice item	25	63
Five-choice multiple-choice item	20	60

Except for a few items at the beginning of the test, for motivational purposes, none of our items should be so easy that everyone answers it correctly. Similarly, none of our test items should be so difficult that everyone misses it. Neither type of item discriminates among pupils, and therefore neither contributes to more reliable norm-referenced interpretations. As we shall see in Chapter 10, maximum discrimination among levels of achievement is made possible using items of average difficulty.

In attempting to construct test items of average difficulty, we should avoid resorting to undesirable methods for obtaining difficulty. It is not uncommon, for example, to use more obscure, less important factual information to increase the difficulty of test items. This generally leads to a lessening of validity and may also be undesirable from a learning standpoint. Pupils are likely to concentrate their efforts on learning less important material and to neglect more important learning outcomes. A closely related method of achieving difficulty at the expense of validity is to require pupils to make difficult but unimportant discriminations. In the following test items, for example, note how the significance of the information decreases as the difficulty increases:

EXAMPLES

The government of the United States was declared in effect under the Constitution in

    A   1787.
    B   1788.
    Ⓒ   1789.
    D   1790.

The government of the United States was declared in effect under the Constitution in

    A   January.
    B   February.
    Ⓒ   March.
    D   April.

The government of the United States was declared in effect under the Constitution on

    A   Monday.
    B   Tuesday.
    Ⓒ   Wednesday.
    D   Thursday.

Asking pupils to make fine discriminations, of course, does not always lead to learning outcomes of less significance. However, we need to be on guard against such dangers when increasing the difficulty of our test items. We should rule out all forms of *irrelevant* difficulty. Other things being equal, the best way to increase the relevant difficulty of test items is to move toward the measurement of more complex learning outcomes, such as understanding principles or applying principles to new situations.

Eliminating Irrelevant Barriers to the Answer

When constructing items for a classroom test, care must be taken to eliminate any extraneous factors that might prevent pupils from responding. If pupils have achieved a particular learning outcome (e.g., knowledge of terms), we would want them to answer correctly those test items that measure the attainment of that learning outcome. We would be very unhappy (and so would they) if they answered such test items incorrectly merely because the sentence structure was too complex, the vocabulary too difficult, or the type of response called for unclear. These factors, which are extraneous to the central purpose of the measurement, limit and modify the pupil's responses, and prevent them from showing their true levels of achievement. Such factors are as unfair as determining a person's running ability when an ankle is sprained. Although a measure of running ability would be obtained, the performance would be restricted by a factor we did not intend to include in our measurement.

One way to eliminate factors that are extraneous to the purpose of a measurement is to be certain that all pupils have the prerequisite skills and abilities needed to make the response. These have been called *enabling behaviors* because they enable the pupil to make the response but are not meant to be critical factors in the measurement. That is, they are a necessary but not a sufficient condition for responding correctly. Probably the most important enabling behavior in objective testing is reading skill. In essay testing, skill in written expression is an additional factor to be considered. In measuring understanding, thinking skills, and other complex learning outcomes, knowledge of certain facts and simple computational skills also might be necessary prerequisites.

In constructing test items, then, we need to strive for items that measure achievement of the specific learning outcomes and not differences in enabling behaviors. Differences in reading ability, computational skill, communication skills, and the like should not influence the pupils' responses unless such outcomes are specifically being measured. The only functional difference between those pupils who get an item correct and those who miss it should be the possession of the knowledge, understanding, or other learning outcome being measured by the item. All other differences are extraneous to the purpose of the item, and their influence should be eliminated or controlled for valid test results.

A special problem in preventing extraneous factors from distorting our test results is avoiding ambiguity. Objective test items are especially subject to misinterpretation when long, complex sentences are used, when the vocabulary is unnecessarily difficult, and when words that lack precise meaning are used. Thus, from the viewpoint of both level of reading difficulty and preciseness of meaning, the antidote for ambiguity seems to be a careful choice of words and the use of brief, concise sentences. In some cases, ambiguity can be reduced by using pictures or other illustrative material in place of verbal descriptions. When this is done, the illustrative material must, of course, also be carefully checked to make sure it is clear and unambiguous.

An effort should also be made to avoid any racial, ethnic, or sexual bias in preparing the test items. The vocabulary and test situations should be acceptable to various racial and ethnic groups and to both males and females and should be free of stereotyping. For example, in presenting characters in a story problem, a reading passage, or other test situation, minorities should not be portrayed as having subservient roles. Similarly, test situations should not always place males in such traditional roles as athlete, business executive, and professional person and females in such traditional roles as homemaker, teacher, and nurse. A balanced use of different roles for minorities and males and females is necessary if we are to avoid bias as a possible barrier to maximum test performance.

Some Possible Barriers in Test Items

Ambiguous statements
Excessive wordiness
Difficult vocabulary
Complex sentence structure
Unclear instructions
Unclear illustrative material
Race, ethnic, and sex bias

Avoiding Unintended Clues to the Answer

Test items should be constructed so that pupils obtain the correct answer *only* if they have attained the desired learning outcome. This is the counterpart of the preceding principle. In that one, we were concerned with those factors that prevent pupils from responding correctly, even though they have attained the desired learning outcome. Here we are concerned with those factors that enable pupils to respond correctly, even though they *lack* the necessary achievement. These are the clues, some rather obvious and some very subtle, that inadvertently creep into test items during their construction. They lead the nonachiever to the correct answer and thereby prevent the items from functioning as intended. When test items are short-circuited in this manner, they provide invalid evidence of achievement. Note how *an* provides a clue to the following item:

EXAMPLE

A porpoise is an

    A   plant.
    B   reptile.
    Ⓒ   animal.
    D   bird.

Such clues are not limited to selection-type items, as shown in the following supply-type item:

A piece of land that is completely surrounded by water is known as an _____ .

The clue is much less obvious to the person constructing this test item than it was in our first illustration. To the pupil taking the test, however, it becomes readily apparent. The two most plausible answers are *island* and *peninsula*. Because *peninsula* begins with a consonant sound and does not follow the article *an*, it is ruled out as a possibility. This does not imply, of course, that pupils need to know the rules for good grammatical structure in order to use such clues, as most clues are not analyzed and evaluated in this way. Rather, they are responded to in terms of partial knowledge and hunches. *An peninsula* just does not sound right to the pupil so the word *island* is used and the correct answer is obtained.

Leads to the correct answer may also be provided by simple verbal associations. Note how the word *wind* in the following item provides a clue to the answer:

Which of the following instruments is used to determine the direction of the wind?

- A   Anemometer.
- B   Barometer.
- C   Hygrometer.
- Ⓓ   Wind vane.

Rather than lead the uninformed to the correct answer, such clues should lead the nonachiever away from the correct answer. In the following item the same clue makes *wind vane* a plausible (but incorrect) answer for those pupils who have not learned the uses of the various weather instruments.

Which one of the following instruments is used to determine the speed of the wind?

- Ⓐ   Anemometer.
- B   Barometer.
- C   Hygrometer.
- D   Wind vane.

Verbal clues need not be as obvious as these. In fact, the clues that appear in the final version of a test are usually rather subtle, as they are based on partial knowledge and verbal associations not readily apparent to the casual observer. For example, at first glance the following item appears to be free from clues:

Which one of the following is used to prevent polio?

- A   Gamma globulin.
- B   Penicillin.
- Ⓒ   Salk vaccine.
- D   Sulfa.

An examination of this item, however, will indicate that the word *vaccine* provides a clue to the answer. All the pupil needs to know to answer the item correctly is that *vaccine* is used to prevent disease. Because most pupils have been vaccinated at one time or another, they probably possess this partial knowledge needed to make the clue apparent to them. Some pupils also may have developed a verbal association between *Salk* and *polio* and respond correctly on that basis. In either case, partial knowledge can lead to the correct answer and prevent the item from functioning as intended.

Another type of subtle clue is one based on the words used to qualify statements. For example, true–false statements that include qualifiers such as *sometimes, usually, generally,* and the like are most often true, whereas statements containing absolutes such as *always, never, none,* and *only* are most often false. Such words have been called *specific determiners*. They are difficult to remove from true–false items because true statements generally must be qualified, and false statements frequently must be stated in absolute terms to make them clearly false.

Other common clues in selection-type items include (1) stating correct answers in textbook language or in greater detail than incorrect answers are, (2) making correct answers longer than incorrect answers, and (3) placing the correct answers in some identifiable pattern (e.g., T, F, T, F). Some of these clues are more likely to be detected by low-achieving pupils who are desperately searching for some basis for answering.

Some Common Clues in Test Items

Grammatical inconsistencies
Verbal associations
Specific determiners (e.g., *always*)
Phrasing of correct responses
Length of correct responses
Location of correct responses

General Suggestions for Writing Test Items

In preparing a set of items for a test, there are some general rules of item writing that apply to all item types. These will be listed here. The specific rules for writing each item type will be described and illustrated in the following chapters.

1. Use your test specifications as a guide to item writing. The test specifications describes the performance to be measured and the sample of tasks to include. Thus, they serve as an aid for selecting the types of items to prepare, for item writing, and for determining how many items are needed for each section of the test.

*2. **Write more test items than needed.*** Preparing more test items than needed for a particular test will permit the weaker items to be discarded during later item review. It will also make it easier to match the final set of items to the specifications.

*3. **Write the test items well in advance of the testing date.*** Setting the items aside for several days and then reviewing them with a fresh outlook will reveal any lack of clarity or ambiguity that was overlooked during their preparation. It is frequently surprising how many defects slipped through during the original item writing.

*4. **Write each test item so that it calls forth the performance described in the intended learning outcome.*** Both during item writing and later item review, compare the test task to the performance it is designed to measure to make sure the two match.

*5. **Write each test item so that the task to be performed is clearly defined.*** Clarity is obtained by carefully formulating the question, using simple and direct language, using correct punctuation and grammar, and avoiding unnecessary wording.

*6. **Write each test item at an appropriate reading level.*** Keeping the reading difficulty and vocabulary level as simple as possible will prevent these factors from distorting the results. Pupils' responses should be determined by the performance being measured and not by some factor the item was not designed to measure.

*7. **Write each test item so that it does not provide help in answering other items in the test.*** Unless care is taken during item writing, one item may provide information that is useful in answering another item. For example, a name, date, or fact called for in a short-answer item might be inadvertently included in the stem of a multiple-choice item in another part of the test.

*8. **Write each test item so that the answer is one that would be agreed upon by experts.*** This rule is easy to satisfy when measuring factual knowledge but more difficult when measuring complex outcomes calling for the best answer. Thus, when asking for the "best reason," the "best method," the "best interpretation," and the like, be sure that experts would agree that the answer is clearly best.

*9. **Write each test item so that it is at the proper level of difficulty.*** Be sure the difficulty of the item matches the performance to be measured and the purpose of the test. Do not increase difficulty by adding unimportant or irrelevant material.

*10. **Whenever a test item is revised, recheck its relevance.*** When reviewing test items for appropriateness, clarity, difficulty, and freedom from clues and bias, some revision is often needed. After revising an item, check to be sure that it still provides a relevant measure of the intended learning outcome. Even slight changes can sometimes modify the function of a test item.

Focusing on Improving Learning and Instruction

The ultimate purpose of testing, as with all classroom procedures, it to improve pupil learning. Thus, as we construct classroom tests we should keep in mind the extent to which it is likely to contribute, directly or indirectly, toward this end. A well-constructed classroom test should increase both the quantity and quality of pupil learning.

1. Tests can have a desirable influence on pupil learning if attention is paid to the breadth of content and learning outcomes measured by the tests. When we select a representative sample of content from *all* of the areas covered in our instruction, we are emphasizing to the pupils that they must devote attention to *all* areas. They cannot neglect some aspects of the course and do well on the tests. Similarly, when our tests measure a variety of types of learning outcomes, the pupils soon learn that a mass of memorized factual information is not sufficient. They must also learn to interpret and apply facts, develop conceptual understandings, draw conclusions, recognize assumptions, identify cause-and-effect relations, and the like. This discourages the pupils from placing sole dependence on memorization as a basis for learning and encourages them to develop the use of more complex mental processes.

2. Constructing tests that measure a variety of learning outcomes should also lead to improved teaching procedures and, thus, indirectly to improved pupil learning. As we translate the various learning outcomes into test items, we develop a better notion of the mental processes involved. Thus, the functional nature of understandings, thinking skills, and other complex learning outcomes becomes increasingly clear to us. This clarification of how achievement is reflected in terms of mental processes enables us to plan the learning experiences of pupils more effectively. Furthermore, we also are more apt to emphasize understandings, thinking skills, and other complex learning outcomes in our teaching when we include them in our testing. This may seem a case of the cart pulling the horse, but a well-constructed test frequently leads to a review of teaching procedures and to the abandonment of those that encourage rote learning.

3. Finally, a test will contribute to improved teacher–pupil relations (with a beneficial effect on pupil learning) if pupils view the test as a fair and useful measure of their achievement. We can make fairness apparent by including a representative sample of the learning tasks that have been emphasized during instruction by writing clear directions, by making certain that the intent of each test item is clear and free of any type of bias that would prevent a knowledgeable person from answering correctly, and by providing adequate time limits for the test. Pupil recognition of usefulness, however, depends as much on what we do with the results of the test as on the characteristics of the test itself. We make the usefulness apparent by using the results as a basis for guiding and improving learning.

Summary

Planning the classroom test involves (1) determining the purpose of testing, (2) developing a set of test specifications, (3) selecting appropriate item types, and (4) preparing a set of relevant test items.

Classroom tests can be used for a variety of instructional purposes. The majority of specific uses can be best described in terms of their location in the instructional sequence. Thus, we have (1) pretesting at the beginning of a course or unit to determine learning readiness, to aid in instructional planning, and to make advanced placements; (2) testing during instruction (formative and diagnostic testing) that is used to improve and direct pupil learning and to identify and remedy learning errors; and (3) end-of-instruction testing (summative testing) that is used at the end of a course or unit to assign grades, certify mastery, or evaluate teaching. Each of these types of classroom testing places different demands on item sampling, item difficulty, and the type of interpretation used (i.e., criterion referenced or norm referenced).

A sample of pupil performance is more likely to be representative if a set of specifications is used in planning the test. Test specifications define and delimit the achievement domain to be measured and describe the sample of test items to be prepared. One form of specifications is a two-way chart called a table of specifications. Building the table involves (1) obtaining the list of instructional objectives, (2) outlining the course content, and (3) preparing the two-way chart that relates the instructional objectives to the course content and specifies the nature of the desired test sample. Although a table of specifications is especially useful in preparing summative tests (because of the broad coverage), it is also useful in preparing some formative tests. In other cases, however, a test plan might be limited to a brief list of specific and precisely stated learning outcomes, or it might contain a comprehensive and detailed set of test specifications with illustrative sample items.

The tests constructed by classroom teachers may be classified as objective tests or essay tests. These may be further subdivided into the following basic types of test items:

Objective Test:

    A. Supply type

        1. Short answer
        2. Completion

    B. Selection type

        1. True–false or alternative–response
        2. Matching
        3. Multiple choice

Essay Test:

    A. Extended response
    B. Restricted response

The objective test presents pupils with a highly structured task that limits their response to supplying a word, brief phrase, number, or symbol or to selecting the answer from among a given number of alternatives. The essay test permits pupils to respond by selecting, organizing, and presenting those facts they consider appropriate. Both types of tests serve useful purposes in measuring pupil achievement. The type to use in a particular situation is best determined by the learning outcomes to be measured and by the unique advantages and limitations of each type. A common practice is to include both objective test items and essay questions in classroom tests.

The preparation of a set of relevant test items involves (1) matching the items to the learning outcomes as directly as possible, (2) obtaining a representative sample of all intended outcomes, (3) selecting the proper level of item difficulty, (4) eliminating irrelevant barriers to the answer, (5) preventing unintended clues to the answer, and (6) focusing on improving learning and instruction. The rules for constructing each item type will be described in the chapters that follow.

Learning Exercises

1. Describe the nature of a readiness pretest and how the results might be used in teaching.
2. Describe how a formative test and a summative test differ.
3. What are the advantages of using a two-way chart when preparing test specifications? For what type of testing is it most useful? Why?
4. Describe what a set of test specifications should include where a group of teachers are preparing a mastery test of basic skills for use in several classes.
5. Why is it important for a classroom test to measure a representative sample of intended learning outcomes?
6. What types of information should be considered during each of the following steps in test construction?
    a. Developing a set of test specifications.
    b. Selecting the types of test items to use.
    c. Writing the test items.
7. List several learning outcomes that are best measured with objective test items. List several that require the use of essay questions.
8. List as many specific factors as you can think of that might prevent a pupil from getting an item correct even though he possessed the knowledge the item was designed to measure.
9. List as many specific factors as you can think of that would enable a pupil to answer an item correctly even though he lacked the knowledge the item was designed to measure.
10. Assume that you are going to prepare a brief mastery test for a unit of work in a course in your major teaching area. How would you proceed? How would your procedure differ if it were to be an end-of-course summative test?

Suggestions for Further Reading

MEHRENS, W. A., AND LEHMANN, I. J. *Measurement and Evaluation in Education and Psychology*, 3d ed. New York: Holt, Rinehart and Winston, 1984. Chapter 4, "Classroom Testing: The Planning Stage," describes the factors to consider in planning teacher-made achievement tests.

MILLMAN, J., AND GREENE, J. "The Specification and Development of Tests of Achievement and Ability." In R. L. Linn, ed., *Educational Measurement*, 3d ed. New York: Macmillan, 1989, Chapter 8. A comprehensive and advanced treatment of test development.

POPHAM, W. J. "Specifying the Domain of Content or Behaviors." In R. A. Berk, ed., *A Guide to Criterion-Referenced Test Construction*. Baltimore: Johns Hopkins University Press, 1984, Chapter 2. Describes and illustrates specifications for criterion-referenced tests.

ROID, G. AND HALADYNA, T. *A Technology for Test-Item Writing*. New York: Academic Press, 1981. Reviews and describes a number of new approaches for developing criterion-referenced achievement tests.

Chapter 6

Constructing Objective Test Items: Simple Forms

*Each type of test item has its own unique characteristics . . .
uses . . . advantages . . . limitations . . . and rules for
construction. . . . Here these are considered for the objective-test
forms that typically measure relatively simple learning outcomes: (1)
the short-answer item, (2) the true–false item, and (3) the matching
exercise.*

The preliminary test planning described in the last chapter provides a sound basis for developing classroom tests that can be used for a variety of instructional purposes. The test specifications clarify the sample of achievement to be measured, and the various considerations in test planning form a general framework within which to proceed. The next step is the actual construction of test items. This step is crucial because the validity of a classroom test is ultimately determined by the extent to which the performance to be measured is actually called forth by the test items. Selecting item types that are inappropriate for the learning outcomes to be measured, constructing items with technical defects, or unwittingly including irrelevant clues in the items can undermine all of the careful planning that has gone on before.

The construction of good test items is an art. The skills it requires, however, are the same as those found in effective teaching. Needed are a thorough grasp of subject matter, a clear conception of the desired learning outcomes, a psychological understanding of pupils, sound judgment, persistence, and a touch of creativity. The only additional requisite for constructing good test items is the skillful application of an array of simple but important rules and suggestions. These techniques of test construction are the topic of this and the next several chapters. The rules for constructing test items, described in these chapters, are applicable to all types of classroom tests.

In this chapter we shall limit our discussion to the simpler forms of objective test items, namely, the (1) short-answer item, (2) true–false or alternative-response item, and (3) matching exercise. These item types are treated together, as their use in classroom testing is largely restricted to the measurement of simple learning outcomes in the knowledge area. The discussion of each item type will be followed by a checklist for reviewing the items.

Short-Answer Items

The short-answer item and the completion item both are supply-type test items that can be answered by a word, phrase, number, or symbol. They are essentially the same, differing only in the method of presenting the problem. The short-answer item uses a direct question, whereas the completion item consists of an incomplete statement.

EXAMPLES

Short answer: What is the name of the man who invented the steamboat? (Robert Fulton)

Completion: The name of the man who invented the steamboat is (Robert Fulton).

Also included in this category are problems in arithmetic, mathematics, science, and other areas, whose solution must be supplied by the pupil.

Uses of Short-Answer Items

The short-answer test item is suitable for measuring a wide variety of relatively simple learning outcomes. The following outcomes and test items illustrate some of its common uses:

EXAMPLES

Knowledge of terminology
Lines on a weather map that join points of the same barometric pressure are called (isobars).
Knowledge of specific facts
A member of the United States Senate is elected to a term of (6) years.
Knowledge of principles
If the temperature of a gas is held constant while the pressure applied to it is increased, what will happen to its volume? (It will decrease.)

143

Knowledge of method or procedure

What device is used to detect whether an electric charge is positive or negative? (electroscope)

Simple interpretations of data

How many syllables are there in the word *Argentina?* (4)

In the number 612, what value does the 6 represent? (600)

In the triangle below, what is the number of degrees in each angle? (60)

If an airplane flying northwest made a 180-degree turn, what direction would it be heading? (southeast)

More complex interpretations can be made when the short-answer item is used to measure the ability to interpret diagrams, charts, graphs, and pictorial data.

Even more notable exceptions to the general rule that short-answer items are limited to measuring simple learning outcomes are found in the areas of mathematics and science where the solutions to problems can be indicated by numbers or symbols. The following examples illustrate this use:

EXAMPLES

Ability to solve numerical problems

Milk sells for $.96 a quart and $3.68 a gallon. How many cents would you save on each quart of milk if you bought it by the gallon? (4)

Skill in manipulating mathematical symbols

If $\dfrac{x}{b} = \dfrac{3}{b-1}$, then $x = \dfrac{(3b)}{(b-1)}$.

Ability to complete and balance chemical equations

$$\underline{\quad} Mg + (2)\ HCl \rightarrow (MgCl_2 + H_2)$$
$$\underline{(2)}\ Al + \underline{(6)}\ HCl \rightarrow (2AlCl_3 + 3H_2)$$

For outcomes similar to those in these last examples, the short-answer item is clearly superior. The performance described in the learning outcomes is identical with the performance called forth by the test items. To obtain correct answers, pupils must actually solve problems, manipulate mathematical symbols, and complete and balance equations.

Attempts are sometimes made to measure such problem-solving activities with selection-type test items, commonly resulting in test items that do not function as intended or that measure quite different learning outcomes. In the following multiple-choice items, for example, note how the division problem can be solved by working it backwards (multiplying 2 × 43, or merely 2 × 3) and how in the second problem the value of *x* can be determined by substituting each of the alternative answers in the equation on a trial-and-error basis. Such problems obviously do not demand the problem-solving behavior we are attempting to measure.

$2\overline{)86}=$

 A 41
 B 42
 Ⓒ 43
 D 44

If $\dfrac{x}{4} + \dfrac{x}{16} = 10$, then x equals

 A 16
 B 24
 Ⓒ 32
 D 48

Similar difficulties are encountered when we substitute selection items measuring the ability to "recognize balanced chemical equations" for short-answer items measuring the ability to "complete and balance chemical equations." The former task is a simple one requiring little more than a knowledge of arithmetic, but the latter one requires extensive knowledge of chemical reactions and their resulting products.

In summary, if the short-answer test item is most effective for measuring a specific learning outcome, it should be used. We should not discard it for items of the selection type unless we are fairly certain that the same learning outcomes will be measured. For many of the simpler learning outcomes, such as knowledge of factual information, changing to some form of selection item will *not* decrease the validity of the measurement and *will* result in increased objectivity and ease of scoring. For some of the more complex learning outcomes such as those in mathematics and science, however, discarding the short-answer test item may mean a change in the learning outcomes being measured. In deciding whether to use short-answer items or some other item type, our best guide is to follow this principle: *Each learning outcome should be measured as directly as possible, and the test-item type most appropriate for the purpose should be used.*

Advantages and Limitations of Short-Answer Items

The short-answer test item is one of the easiest to construct, partly because of the relatively simple learning outcomes it usually measures. Except for the problem-solving outcomes measured in mathematics and science, the short-answer item is used almost exclusively to measure the recall of memorized information.

A more important advantage of the short-answer item is that the pupils must supply the answer. This reduces the possibility that the pupils will obtain the correct answer by guessing. They must either recall the information requested or make the necessary computations to solve the problem presented to them. Partial knowledge, which might enable them to choose the correct answer on a selection item, is insufficient for answering a short-answer test item correctly.

There are two major limitations that restrict the use of the short-answer test item. One — unsuitability for measuring complex learning outcomes — has already been mentioned. The other is the difficulty of scoring. Unless the question is very carefully phrased, many answers of varying degrees of correctness must be considered for total or partial credit. For example, a question such as "Where was George Washington born?" could be answered by the name of the city, county, state, region, or continent. Although the teacher had the name of the state in mind when she wrote the question, she could not dismiss the other answers as incorrect. But even when this problem is avoided, the scoring is contaminated by the pupil's spelling ability. If full or partial credit is taken off for misspelled words, the pupils' test scores will reflect varying degrees of knowledge and spelling skill. If spelling is not counted in the scoring, the teacher must still decide whether misspelled words actually represent the correct answer. We all are familiar with misspellings so bad that it is difficult to determine what the pupil had in mind. The complications make scoring more time consuming and less objective than that obtained with selection-type items.

These limitations are less troublesome when the answer is to be expressed in numbers or symbols, as in problem solving in physical science and mathematics. Here, more complex learning outcomes can be measured, spelling is not a problem, and it is usually easier to write test items for which there is only one correct response.

Suggestions for Constructing Short-Answer Items

The short-answer item is subject to a variety of defects, even though it is considered one of the easiest to construct. The following suggestions will help you avoid possible pitfalls and will provide greater assurance that the items will function as intended.

1. **Word the item so that the required answer is both brief and specific.** As indicated earlier, the answer to an item should be a word, phrase, number, or symbol. This can be easily conveyed to the pupils through the directions at the beginning of the test and by proper phrasing of the question. More difficult is stating the question so that only one answer is correct.

EXAMPLES

Poor: An animal that eats the flesh of other animals is (carnivorous).

Better: An animal that eats the flesh of other animals is classified as (carnivorous).

The first version of this item is so indefinite that it could be completed with answers such as "the wolf," "a meat eater," or even "hungry." Asking the pupils to classify this type of animal, as called for in the improved version, better structures the problem and defines the type of response required.

2. Do not take statements directly from textbooks to use as a basis for short-answer items. When taken out of context, textbook statements are frequently too general and ambiguous to serve as good short-answer items. Note the vagueness of the first version of the following test item, which was taken verbatim from a chemistry textbook:

Poor: Chlorine is a (halogen).   EXAMPLES
Better: Chlorine belongs to a group of elements that combine with metals to form salt. It is therefore called a (halogen).

Pupils are most likely to respond to the first version of this test item with the word *gas*, because that is the natural state of chlorine, and there is nothing in the statement to imply that the word *halogen* is wanted. The only pupils who are apt to supply the intended answer are those who memorized the textbook statements. The revised version measures an important knowledge that does not depend on the phraseology of the textbook. Such items tend to discourage the pupils from developing little understood verbal associations based on textbook language and encourages them to achieve the learning outcomes being measured.

3. A direct question is generally more desirable than an incomplete statement. There are two advantages to the direct-question form. First, it is more natural to the pupils, as this is the usual method of phrasing questions in daily classroom discussions. This is especially important to elementary pupils when first exposed to short-answer tests. Second, the direct question usually better structures the situation and prevents much of the ambiguity that creeps into items based on incomplete statements. Just the phrasing of a question requires us to decide what it is we want to know.

Poor: John Glenn made his first orbital flight around the earth in (1962).   EXAMPLES
Better: When did John Glenn make his first orbital flight around the earth? (1962).
Best: In what year did John Glenn make his first orbital flight around the earth? (1962).

The first version of the item could, of course, be completed with "a space capsule," "Friendship Seven," "space," and similar answers. Putting it in question form forces us to indicate whether it is the time, place, or method we are interested in knowing. The last version is merely a refinement that makes the question even more specific and that naturally evolves from a consideration of the "when" aspect of the previous question.

4. If the answer is to be expressed in numerical units, indicate the type of answer wanted. For computational problems, it is usually preferable to indicate the units in which the answer is to be expressed. This will clarify the problem and will simplify the scoring.

Poor: If oranges weigh 5⅔ oz. each, how much will a dozen oranges weigh? Answer: (4 lb. 4 oz.).

Better: If oranges weigh 5⅔ oz. each, how much will a dozen oranges weigh? Answer: (4) lb. (4) oz.

Unless the type of unit is specified, as in the revised version, correct answers will include 68 oz., 4¼ lb., 4.25 lb., and 4 lb. 4 oz. This adds unnecessary confusion to the scoring.

When the problems do not come out even, it is also usually helpful to indicate the degree of precision expected in the answers. For example, specifying that the answers should be "carried out to two decimal places" or "rounded off to the nearest tenth of a percent" makes clear to the pupils how far to carry their calculations. This will ensure that they reach the degree of precision desired and also prevent them from wasting valuable testing time attempting to achieve a degree of precision not expected.

There are some instances, especially in science, when knowing the proper unit in which the answer is to be expressed and knowing the degree of precision to be expected are important aspects of the learning outcome to be measured. In such cases, the previous suggestions must, of course, be modified.

5. Blanks for answers should be equal in length and in a column to the right of the question. If blanks for answers are kept equal in length, the length of the blank space does not supply a clue to the answer. In the poor version of the following items, the length of the blank restricts the possible answers the pupils need consider. For the first item they need a long word and for the second item a short one.

Poor: What is the name of the part of speech that connects words, clauses, and sentences? (conjunction)
What is the name of the part of speech that declares, asserts, or predicts something? (verb)

Better: What is the name of the part of speech that connects words, clauses, and sentences?　　　　　(conjunction)
What is the name of the part of speech that declares, asserts, or predicts something?　　　　　(verb)

Placing the blanks in a column to the right of the question, as shown in the improved version, makes scoring quicker and more accurate.

6. ***When completion items are used, do not include too many blanks.*** If a statement is overmutilated, the meaning will be lost, and the pupil usually must resort to guessing what the teacher had in mind. Although some mutilated statements seem to measure rather complex reasoning abilities, such responses are more appropriate as measures of intelligence than achievement.

Poor: (Warm-blooded) animals that are born (alive) and (suckle) their young   EXAMPLES
          are called (mammals).
Better: Warm-blooded animals that are born alive
          and suckle their young are called   (mammals).

In the revised version, the blank is at the end of the statement, which is desirable, as the pupils are presented with a clearly defined problem before they come to the blank.

Checklist for Reviewing Short-Answer Items

REVIEW QUESTIONS	YES	NO
1. Is this the most appropriate type of item to use for the intended learning outcomes?	____	____
2. Can the items be answered with a number, symbol, word, or brief phrase?	____	____
3. Has textbook language been avoided?	____	____
4. Have the items been stated so that only one response is correct?	____	____
5. Are the answer blanks equal in length?	____	____
6. Are the answer blanks at the end of the items?	____	____
7. Are the items free of clues (such as *a* or *an*)?	____	____
8. Has the degree of precision been indicated for numerical answers?	____	____
9. Have the units been indicated when numerical answers are expressed in units?	____	____
10. Have the items been phrased so as to minimize spelling errors?	____	____
11. If revised, are the items still relevant to the intended learning outcomes?	____	____
12. Have the items been set aside for a time before reviewing them?	____	____

True – False or Alternative-Response Items

The alternative-response test item consists of a declarative statement that the pupil is asked to mark true or false, right or wrong, correct or incorrect, yes or no, fact or opinion, agree or disagree, and the like. In each case there are only two possible answers. Because the true – false option is the most common, this item type is most frequently referred to as the *true – false* test item. Some of the variations, however, deviate considerably from the simple true – false pattern and have their own characteristics. For this reason, some prefer the more general category, *alternative-response* item. We shall retain the more commonly used true – false designation.

Uses of True – False Items

Probably the most common use of the true – false item is in measuring the *ability to identify the correctness of statements of fact, definitions of terms, statements of principles, and the like*. For measuring such relatively simple learning outcomes, a single declarative statement is used with any one of several methods of responding.

EXAMPLES

Directions: Read each of the following statements. If the statement is true, circle the T. If the statement is false, circle the F.

Ⓣ F 1. The green coloring material in a plant leaf is called chlorophyll.
T Ⓕ 2. The corolla of a flower includes petals and sepals.
Ⓣ F 3. Photosynthesis is the process by which leaves make a plant's food.

Directions: Read each of the following questions. If the answer is yes, circle the Y. If the answer is no, circle the N.

Ⓨ N 1. Is 51% of 38 more than 19?
Y Ⓝ 2. Is 50% of ⁴⁄₁₀ equal to ⅔?
Y Ⓝ 3. If 60% of a number is 9, is the number smaller than 9?
Ⓨ N 4. Is 25% of 44 less than 12?

One of the most useful functions of the true – false item is in measuring the pupil's *ability to distinguish fact from opinion*. The following examples illustrate this use:

EXAMPLES

Directions: Read each of the following statements. If the statement is a fact, circle the F. If the statement is an opinion, circle the O.

Ⓕ O 1. The Constitution of the United States is the highest law of our country.
F Ⓞ 2. The first amendment to the Constitution is the most important amendment.
Ⓕ O 3. The fifth amendment to the Constitution protects people from testifying against themselves.

F ◎ 4. Other countries should adopt a constitution like that of the United States.

Directions: Read each of the following statements. If the statement is true, circle the T. If the statement is false, circle the F. If the statement is an opinion, circle O.

Ⓣ F O 1. The earth is a planet.
T Ⓕ O 2. The earth revolves around the moon.
T F ◎ 3. There are *no* plants or animals on Mars.

These items measure a learning outcome important to all subject-matter areas. If people are to think critically about a topic, they must first be able to distinguish fact from opinion.

All too frequently, true–false tests include numerous opinion statements to which the pupil is asked to respond merely true or false. This is extremely frustrating because there is no objective basis for determining whether a statement of opinion is true or false. The pupil must usually guess what opinion the teacher holds and mark the answers accordingly. This, of course, is undesirable from all standpoints — testing, teaching, and learning. It is much better to have the pupil identify the statements of opinion as such. An alternative procedure is to attribute the opinion to some source, making it possible to mark the statements true or false and measuring *knowledge concerning the beliefs held by an individual or the values supported by an organization or institution.*

Directions: Read each of the following statements. If the statement is true, circle the T. If the statement is false, circle the F.

T Ⓕ 1. Franklin D. Roosevelt believed that labor unions interfered with the United States free enterprise system.
Ⓣ F 2. The American Federation of Labor favors the closed shop.
T Ⓕ 3. The Supreme Court of the United States supports the principle of equal but separate facilities for the education of different racial groups.

Items such as the preceding can become measures of aspects of *understanding* if the opinion statements attributed to an individual or group are new to the pupil. The task then becomes one of interpreting the beliefs held by the individual or group and applying them to the new situation.

Another aspect of understanding that can be measured by the true–false item is the *ability to recognize cause-and-effect relationships.* This type of item usually contains two true propositions in one statement, and the pupil is to judge whether the relationship between them is true or false.

EXAMPLES

Directions: In each of the following statements, both parts of the statement are true. You are to decide whether the second part explains *why* the first part is true. If it does, circle Yes. If it does not, circle No.

Yes (No) 1. Leaves are essential   *because*   they shade the tree trunk.

Yes (No) 2. Whales are mammals   *because*   they are large.

(Yes) No 3. Some plants do *not* need sunlight   *because*   they get their food from other plants.

The true–false item also can be used to measure some *simple aspects of logic*, as illustrated by the following items that were developed for use in a science test:

EXAMPLES

Directions: Read each of the following statements. If the statement is true, circle the T; if it is false circle the F. *Also,* if the converse of the statement is true, circle the CT; if the converse is false, circle the CF. Be sure to give two answers for each statement.

(T) F CT (CF) 1. All trees are plants.
T (F) CT (CF) 2. All parasites are animals.
T (F) (CT) CF 3. All eight-legged animals are spiders.
(T) F (CT) CF 4. No spiders are insects.

A common criticism of the true–false item is that a pupil may be able to recognize a false statement as incorrect but still not know what *is* correct. For example, when pupils answer the following item as false, it does not indicate that they know what negatively charged particles of electricity are called; all the answer tells us is that they know they are *not* called neutrons:

EXAMPLE

T (F) Negatively charged particles of electricity are called neutrons.

This is a rather crude measure of knowledge, because there is an inestimable number of things that negatively charged particles of electricity are *not* called. To overcome such difficulties, some teachers prefer to have the pupils *change all false statements to true*. When this is done, the part of the statement it is permissible to change should be indicated.

EXAMPLES

Directions: Read each of the following statements. If a statement is true, circle the T. If a statement is false, circle the F *and* change the underlined word to make the statement true. Place the new word in the blank space after the F.

T (F) (electrons) 1. Particles of negatively charged electricity are called <u>neutrons</u>.

Ⓣ   F   _____   2. Mechanical energy is turned into electrical energy by means of the <u>generator.</u>

T   Ⓕ   <u>(store)</u>   3. An electric condenser is used to <u>generate</u> electricity.

Unless the key words to be changed are indicated in the correction type of true – false item, pupils are liable to rewrite the entire statement. In addition to the increase in scoring difficulty, this frequently leads to true statements that deviate considerably from the original intent of the item. A clever pupil may even change false statements to true by simply adding "not" in the appropriate place.

Advantages and Limitations of True – False Items

The advantages attributed to true – false items are not, unfortunately, very valid. One advantage cited most frequently is ease of construction. This has probably resulted from the common practice of taking statements from textbooks, changing half of them to false statements and submitting the product to pupils as a true – false test. Such test items are often so obvious that everyone gets them correct or so ambiguous that even the better pupils are confused by them. In short, it is easy to construct *poor* true – false items. To construct unambiguous true – false items, which measure significant learning outcomes, however, requires much skill.

A second advantage attributed to the true – false item, which is also more apparent than real, is that a wide sampling of course material can be obtained. Because a pupil can respond to many test items in a short period of time, it seems obvious that many areas can be covered. Less obvious, however, is that many types of subject matter do not lend themselves to true – false type items. True – false statements require course material that can be phrased so that the statements are true or false without qualification or exception. In all subject-matter fields there are areas in which such absolutely true or false statements cannot be made. In some fields, such as the social sciences, practically all significant statements require some qualification. Only the most trivial statements can be reduced to absolute terms.

One of the most serious limitations of the true – false item is in the types of learning outcomes that can be measured. As with the short-answer item, it is not especially useful beyond the knowledge area. The main exceptions to this seem to be distinguishing between fact and opinion and identifying cause-and-effect relationships. These two outcomes are probably the most important measured by this type of item. Many of the learning outcomes measured by the true – false item can be measured more effectively by other forms of selection items, especially the multiple-choice form.

Another factor that limits the usefulness of the true – false item is its susceptibility to guessing. With only two alternatives, a pupil has a fifty-fifty chance of selecting the correct answer on the basis of chance alone, and because of the difficulty of constructing items that do *not* contain clues to the answer, the pupil's chances of guessing correctly are usually much greater than 50 percent. With a typical 100-item true – false test, it is not unusual to have the lowest score somewhere above 80. Although an indeterminate amount of knowledge is reflected in such a score, many of the correct answers, beyond chance, can be accounted for by correct guesses guided by various clues that have been overlooked in constructing the items. A scoring formula utilizing a correction for guessing is frequently suggested as a solution for this problem. This formula takes into account only chance guesses, however, and does not include those guided by clues. In addition, such a scoring formula favors aggressive individuals willing to take a chance. Even when warned that there will be a penalty for guessing, they will continue to guess, using any clues available, and will do better than chance. Cautious pupils, on the other hand, will mark only those answers they are certain are correct and will omit many of the items they could mark correctly on the basis of clues and partial information. Thus, the scores tend to reflect personality differences as well as knowledge of the subject.

The great likelihood of successful guessing on the true–false item has several deleterious effects. (1) The reliability of each item is low, making it necessary to include many items in order to obtain a reliable measure of achievement. (2) The diagnostic value of such a test is practically nil because analyzing a pupil's response to each item is meaningless. (3) The validity of pupils' responses is questionable because of response sets. As noted earlier, a response set is a consistent tendency to follow a certain pattern in responding to test items. In taking a true–false test, for example, some pupils will consistently mark "true" those items they do not know, and others will consistently mark them "false." Thus, any given test will favor one response set over another and introduce an element into the test score that is irrelevant to the purpose of the test.

The limitations of the true–false item are so serious that it seems wise to use this item type only when other items are inappropriate for measuring the desired learning outcomes. This includes situations in which there are only two possible alternatives (e.g., right, left; more, less; who, whom; and so on) and special uses such as distinguishing fact from opinion, cause from effect, superstition from scientific belief, relevant from nonrelevant information, valid from invalid conclusions, and the like.

Suggestions for Constructing True–False Items

The main task in constructing true–false items is formulating statements free from ambiguity and irrelevant clues. This is extremely difficult, and the only guidance that can be given is of a negative sort—that is, a list of things to avoid when phrasing the statements.

1. Avoid broad general statements if they are to be judged true or false. Most broad generalizations are false unless qualified, and the use of qualifiers provides clues to the answer.

EXAMPLES Poor: T Ⓕ The president of the United States is elected to that office.
Poor: Ⓣ F The president of the United States is usually elected to that office.

In this example, the first version is generally true but must be marked false because there are exceptions, such as the vice president's taking office in event of the president's death. In the second version, the qualifier *usually* makes the statement true but provides a definite clue. Words such as *usually, generally, often,* and *sometimes* are most likely to appear in true statements, and absolute terms such as *always, never, all, none,* and *only* are more apt to appear in false statements. Although the influence of such clues sometimes can be offset by balancing their use in true–false statements, the simplest solution seems to be to avoid the use of broad generalizations that are obviously false or must be qualified by specific determiners.

2. Avoid trivial statements. In an attempt to obtain statements that are un-equivocally true or false, we sometimes inadvertently turn to specific statements of fact that fit this criterion beautifully but have little significance from a learning standpoint.

EXAMPLES

Poor: Ⓣ   F   Harry S Truman was the thirty-third president of the United States.

Poor: T   Ⓕ   The United States declared war on Japan on December 7, 1941.

The first item calls for a relatively unimportant fact concerning Truman's tenure as president, and the second item expects the student to remember that the United States did not declare war until December 8. Such items cause students to direct their attention toward memorizing minutiae at the expense of more general knowledge and understanding.

3. Avoid the use of negative statements, especially double negatives. Pupils tend to overlook negative words such as *no* or *not,* and double negatives contribute to the statement's ambiguity. Note the ambiguity in the following relatively simple statement, which uses two negatives.

EXAMPLES

Poor: Ⓣ   F   None of the steps in the experiment was unnecessary.

Better: Ⓣ   F   All of the steps in the experiment were necessary.

When a negative word must be used, it should be underlined or put in italics so that pupils do *not* overlook it.

4. Avoid long, complex sentences. As noted earlier, a test item should indicate whether a pupil has achieved the knowledge or understanding being measured. Long, complex sentences tend also to measure the extraneous factor of reading comprehension and therefore should be avoided in tests designed to measure achievement.

Poor: (T)   F   Despite the theoretical and experimental difficulties of determining the exact *pH* value of a solution, it is possible to determine whether a solution is acid by the red color formed on litmus paper when it is inserted into the solution.

Better: (T)   F   Litmus paper turns red in an acid solution.

As in the preceding example, it frequently is possible to shorten and simplify a statement by eliminating nonfunctional material and restating the main idea. If this is not possible, it may be necessary to change to another item form in order to avoid a complex sentence structure.

5. Avoid including two ideas in one statement, unless cause–effect relationships are being measured. Some difficulties arising from the inclusion of two ideas in one statement are apparent in the following example, which is one of many similar items a teacher actually used in a biology examination. In each instance, the pupils were asked to judge merely whether the statement was true or false.

Poor: T   (F)   A worm cannot see because it has simple eyes.

This item is keyed false because a worm does *not* have simple eyes. However, when this teacher asked one of his slow learners why he marked it false, the pupil said, "Worms can too see." This of course demonstrates why pupils can get such items correct with misinformation of the most erroneous sort. This is so because the first proposition can be true or false, the second proposition can be true or false, and the relationship between them can be true or false. Thus, when pupils mark the item false, there is no way of determining to which of the three elements they are responding. The best solution to this dilemma seems to be to use only true propositions and to ask the pupils to judge the truth or falsity of the relationships between them. Such items also might, of course, be divided into two simple statements, each containing a single idea.

6. If opinion is used, attribute it to some source, unless the ability to identify opinion is being specifically measured. As pointed out earlier, statements of opinion cannot be marked true or false, and it is unfair to expect pupils to guess how the teacher will score such items. It is, of course, also poor teaching practice to expect pupils to respond to opinion statements as statements of fact. Knowing whether some significant individual or group supports or refutes a certain opinion, however, can be important from a learning standpoint.

Poor: T   F   Adequate medical care can be best provided through socialized medicine.

Better: T   (F)   The American Medical Association favors socialized medicine as the best means of providing adequate medical care.

The first version cannot be answered true or false. It may serve a useful purpose in an attitude test, but there is no factual basis on which to decide the truth or falsity of the statement. The second version is clearly false.

7. ***True statements and false statements should be approximately equal in length.*** There is a natural tendency for true statements to be longer because such statements must be precisely phrased to meet the criterion of absolute truth. This can be overcome by lengthening the false statements through the use of qualifying phrases similar to those found in true statements. Thus, the length of the statement will be eliminated as a possible clue to the correct answer.

8. ***The number of true statements and false statements should be approximately equal.*** Constructing a test with the number of true statements and false statements approximately equal will prevent response sets from unduly inflating or deflating the pupils' scores. You will recall that some pupils consistently mark statements "true" when in doubt about an answer, whereas others consistently mark

Checklist for Reviewing True – False Items

REVIEW QUESTIONS	YES	NO
1. Is this the most appropriate type of item to use?	____	____
2. Can each statement be clearly judged true or false?	____	____
3. Have specific determiners (e.g., usually, always) been avoided?	____	____
4. Have trivial statements been avoided?	____	____
5. Have negative statements (especially double negatives) been avoided?	____	____
6. Have the items been stated in simple, clear language?	____	____
7. Are opinion statements attributed to some source?	____	____
8. Are the true and false items approximately equal in length?	____	____
9. Is there an approximately equal number of true and false items?	____	____
10. Has a detectable pattern of answers (e.g., T, F, T, F) been avoided?	____	____
11. If revised, are the items still relevant to the intended learning outcomes?	____	____
12. Have the items been set aside for a time before reviewing them?	____	____

them "false." Neither response set should be favored by overloading the test with items of one type.

In honoring this suggestion, the words *approximately equal* should be given special attention. If a teacher consistently uses "exactly" the same number, this will provide a clue to the pupil who is unable to answer some of the test items. The best procedure seems to be to vary the percentage of true statements somewhere between 40 and 60 percent. Under no circumstances should the statements be all true or all false. Pupils who detect this as a possibility can obtain perfect scores on the basis of one guess.

Matching Exercises

In its traditional form, the matching exercise consists of two parallel columns, with each word, number, or symbol in one column being matched to a word, sentence, or phrase in the other column. The items in the column for which a match is sought are called *premises*, and the items in the column from which the selection is made are called *responses*. The basis for matching responses to premises is sometimes self-evident but more often must be explained in the directions. In any event, the pupil's task is to identify the pairs of items that are to be associated on the basis indicated. For example, the pupil may be asked to identify important historical events, as in the following illustration:

EXAMPLES

Directions: On the line to the left of each United States space event in Column A, write the letter of the astronaut in Column B who achieved that honor. Each name in Column B may be used once, more than once, or not at all.

Column A	Column B
(G) 1. First United States astronaut to ride in a space capsule.	A Edwin Aldrin
(E) 2. First United States astronaut to orbit the earth.	B Neil Armstrong
(H) 3. First United States astronaut to walk in space.	C Frank Borman
(B) 4. First United States astronaut to step on the moon.	D Scott Carpenter
	E John Glenn
	F Wally Schirra
	G Alan Shephard
	H Edward White

This matching exercise illustrates an *imperfect match*; that is, there are more names in Column B than are needed to match each event in Column A. The directions also indicate that an item may be used once, more than once, or not at all. Both of these procedures prevent pupils from matching the final pair of items on the basis of elimination.

Two other factors are notable in our example. First, the items in the list of premises in Column A are homogeneous, as they all are concerned with important space events. Such homogeneity is necessary if a matching exercise is to function properly. Second, for each premise in Column A there are several plausible responses in Column B. Thus, the incorrect responses serve as attractive choices for those pupils who are in doubt about the correct answers. Both factors tend to minimize the opportunity for successful guessing.

Uses of Matching Exercises

The typical matching exercise is limited to measuring factual information based on simple associations. Whenever learning outcomes emphasize the *ability to identify the relationship between two things*, and a sufficient number of homogeneous premises and responses can be obtained, a matching exercise seems most appropriate. It is a compact and efficient method of measuring such simple knowledge outcomes. Examples of relationships considered important by teachers, in a variety of fields, include the following:

Persons. . . . . .Achievements
Dates. . . . . .Historical Events
Terms. .Definitions
Rules. . . . . Examples
Symbols. . . . . .Concepts
Authors. . . . . Titles of Books
Foreign Words. . . . . English Equivalents
Machines. . . . . Uses
Plants or Animals. . . . . .Classification
Principles. . . . . Illustrations
Objects. . . . . .Names of Objects
Parts. . . . . .Functions

   The matching exercise has also been used with pictorial materials in relating pictures and words and to identify positions on maps, charts, and diagrams. Regardless of the form of presentation, however, the pupil's task is essentially to relate two things that have some logical basis for association. This restricts the use of the matching exercise to a relatively small area of pupil achievement.

Advantages and Limitations of Matching Exercises

The major advantage of the matching exercise is its compact form, which makes it possible to measure a large amount of related factual material in a relatively short time. This is a mixed blessing, however, as it frequently leads to the excessive use of matching exercises and a corresponding overemphasis on the memorization of simple relationships.
   Another advantage often cited for the matching exercise is ease of construction. As with the true–false item, poor items can be rapidly constructed, but good items

require a high degree of skill. Much of the difficulty is because the correct response for each premise must also serve as a plausible response for the other premises. Any lack of plausibility will reduce the number of possible choices and provide clues to the correct answer. The matching exercise tends to have more such irrelevant clues than any other item type, with the possible exception of the true–false item.

The main limitations of the matching exercise are that it is restricted to the measurement of factual information based on rote learning and that it is highly susceptible to the presence of irrelevant clues. Another factor, somewhat related, is the difficulty of finding homogeneous material that is significant from the viewpoint of our objectives and learning outcomes. For example, we might start out with a few great scientists and their achievements, which we feel all pupils should know. In order to construct a matching item, it becomes necessary to add the names and achievements of other, lesser-known scientists. Thus, we find ourselves measuring factual information that was not included in our original test plan and that is far less important than other aspects of knowledge we had intended to include. In short, less significant material is introduced into the test because significant, homogeneous material is unavailable. This is a common problem in constructing matching exercises and one not easily avoided. One solution is to begin with multiple-choice items, because each item can be directly related to a particular outcome, and to switch to the matching form only when homogeneous material makes the matching exercise a more efficient method of measuring the same achievement.

Suggestions for Constructing Matching Exercises

Although the matching exercise has only limited usefulness in classroom tests, whenever it is used, special efforts should be made to remove irrelevant clues and to arrange it so that the pupil can respond quickly and without confusion. The following suggestions are designed to guide such efforts:

1. Use only homogeneous material in a single matching exercise. This has been mentioned before and is repeated here for emphasis. It is without a doubt the most important rule of construction and yet the one most commonly violated. One reason for this is that homogeneity is a matter of degree and what is homogeneous to one group may be heterogeneous to another. For example, let us assume that we are following the usual suggestion for obtaining homogeneity and develop a matching exercise that includes *only* men and their achievements. We might end up with a test exercise like the one on page 161.

Although the matching exercise in our example may be homogeneous for most pupils in the primary grades, the discriminations called for are so gross that pupils above that level will see it as a heterogeneous collection of inventors, explorers, and presidents. Thus, to obtain homogeneity at higher grade levels, it is necessary to have only inventors and their inventions in one matching exercise, explorers and their discoveries in another, and presidents and their achievements in another. At a still higher level, it may be necessary to limit matching exercises still further, such as to inventors whose inventions are in the same area, in order to keep the material homogeneous and free from irrelevant clues. As we increase the level of discrimina-

Directions: On the line to the left of each achievement listed in Column A, write the letter of the man's name in Column B who is noted for that achievement. Each name in Column B may be used once, more than once, or not at all.

Column A	*Column B*
(A) 1. Invented the telephone.	A Alexander Graham Bell
(B) 2. Discovered America.	B Christopher Columbus
(C) 3. First United States astronaut to orbit the earth.	C John Glenn
	D Abraham Lincoln
(F) 4. First president of the United States.	E Ferdinand Magellan
	F George Washington
	G Eli Whitney

tion called for in a matching exercise, significant homogeneous material becomes increasingly difficult to obtain. Take inventors, for example. How many significant inventions are there in any one area?

2. Include an unequal number of responses and premises, and instruct the pupil that responses may be used once, more than once, or not at all. This will make all the responses eligible for selection for each premise and will decrease the likelihood of successful guessing. When an equal number of responses and premises are used and each response is used only once, the probability for guessing the remaining responses correctly is increased each time a correct answer is selected. The odds for correct guessing increase as the list of available responses decreases, and the final response, of course, can be selected entirely on the basis of this process of elimination.

In most matching exercises, imperfect matching can be obtained by including more or fewer responses than premises. In either case, the directions should instruct the pupil that each response may be used once, more than once, or not at all.

3. Keep the list of items to be matched brief, and place the shorter responses on the right. A brief list of items is advantageous to both the teacher and the pupil. From the teacher's standpoint, it is easier to maintain homogeneity in a brief list. In addition, there is a greater likelihood that the various learning outcomes and subject-matter topics will be measured in a balanced manner. Because each matching exercise must be based on homogeneous material, a long list will require excessive concentration in one area. From the pupils' viewpoint, a brief list enables them to read the responses rapidly and without confusion. Approximately four to seven items in each column seems best. There certainly should be no more than ten in either column.

Placing the shorter responses on the right also contributes to more efficient test taking, as it enables pupils to read the longer premise first and then to scan rapidly the list of responses.

4. Arrange the list of responses in logical order. Place words in alphabetical order and numbers in sequence. This will contribute to the ease with which the pupils can scan the responses in searching for the correct answers. It will also prevent them from detecting possible clues from the arrangement of the responses.

EXAMPLES

Directions: On the line to the left of each historical event in Column A, write the letter from Column B that identifies the time period when the event occurred. Each date in Column B may be used once, more than once, or not at all.

Column A		Column B	
(B)	1. Boston Tea Party.	A	1765–1769
(A)	2. Repeal of the Stamp Act.	B	1770–1774
(E)	3. Enactment of the Northwest Ordinance.	C	1775–1779
(C)	4. Battle of Lexington.	D	1780–1784
(A)	5. Enactment of Townshend Acts.	E	1785–1789
(B)	6. First Continental Congress.		
(E)	7. United States Constitution drawn up.		

This matching exercise also demonstrates the use of *fewer* responses than premises and the desirability of placing the shortest items on the right.

Checklist for Reviewing Matching Items

REVIEW QUESTIONS	YES	NO
1. Is this the most appropriate type of item to use?	___	___
2. Is the material in the two lists homogeneous?	___	___
3. Is the list of responses longer or shorter than the list of premises?	___	___
4. Are the responses brief and on the right-hand side?	___	___
5. Have the responses been placed in alphabetical or numerical order?	___	___
6. Do the directions indicate the basis for matching?	___	___
7. Do the directions indicate that each response may be used more than once?	___	___
8. Is all of each matching item on the same page?	___	___
9. If revised, are the items still relevant to the intended learning outcomes?	___	___
10. Have the items been set aside for a time before reviewing them?	___	___

5. Indicate in the directions the basis for matching the responses and premises. Although the basis for matching is rather obvious in most matching exercises, there are advantages in clearly stating it. First, ambiguity and confusion will be avoided. Second, testing time will be saved because the pupil will not need to read through the entire list of premises and responses and then "reason out" the basis for matching.

Special care must be taken when stating directions for matching items. Directions that precisely indicate the basis for matching frequently become long and involved, placing a premium on reading comprehension. For younger pupils, it may be desirable to give oral directions, put an example on the blackboard, and have the pupils draw lines between the matched items rather than transfer letters.

6. Place all of the items for one matching exercise on the same page. This will prevent the disturbance created by thirty or so pupils switching the pages of the test back and forth. It also will prevent them from overlooking the responses appearing on another page and generally adds to the speed and efficiency of test administration.

Summary

The construction of classroom tests, like other phases of teaching, is an art that must be learned. It is not automatically derived from a knowledge of subject matter, a formulation of the learning outcomes to be achieved, or a psychological understanding of the pupils' mental processes, although all of these are prerequisites. The ability to construct high-quality test items requires, in addition, a knowledge of the principles and techniques of test construction and skill in their application.

In this chapter we discussed techniques for constructing short-answer items, true–false or alternative-response items, and matching exercises. These simple forms of objective test items are restricted almost entirely to measuring knowledge outcomes and are generally unsuitable for measuring understanding, thinking skills, and other complex achievements.

The short-answer item requires pupils to supply the appropriate word, number, or symbol to a direct question or incomplete statement. It can be used for measuring a variety of simple knowledge outcomes, but it is especially useful for measuring problem-solving ability in science and mathematics. The ease with which short-answer items can be constructed and their relative freedom from guessing favor their use. However, the areas in which they can be effectively used are restricted by the relatively simple learning outcomes measured and by the fact that the scoring is contaminated by spelling errors of varying degrees of magnitude. When short-answer items are used, the question must be stated clearly and concisely, be free from irrelevant clues, and require an answer that is both brief and definite. Problems requiring only a number or a symbol for an answer are particularly adaptable to the short-answer form.

The true–false item requires the pupil to select one of two possible answers. This item type is used for measuring simple knowledge outcomes when only two alternatives are possible or the ability to identify the correctness of statements of fact is important. It is also adaptable to measuring the ability to distinguish fact from opinion and the ability to recognize cause-and-effect relationships. The use of true–false items is limited by the difficulty of constructing clue-free items that measure significant learning outcomes, the susceptibility of this type to guessing, the low reliability of each item, and the general lack of diagnostic value. They may well be restricted to those areas for which other item types are inappropriate. When used, special efforts must be made to formulate statements that are free from ambiguity, specific determiners, and clues.

The matching exercises consist of two parallel columns of phrases, words, numbers, or symbols that must be matched. Examples of items included in matching exercises are persons and achievements, dates and historical events, and terms and definitions. The nature of the matching exercise limits it to measuring the ability to identify the relationship between two things. For this restricted use, it is a compact item type that can be used to measure many relationships in a short time. Its limitations include the difficulty of removing irrelevant clues and the difficulty of finding significant homogeneous material. When homogeneous material is available, including more items in one column than in the other, arranging the shorter responses on the right and in logical order, and indicating clearly the basis for matching all will contribute to the effectiveness of the matching exercise.

Learning Exercises

1. Defend the statement "Short-answer items should *not* be classified as objective items."
2. How would you handle the scoring of short-answer items when the answers were misspelled?
3. Marking a false statement false does not guarantee that the pupil knows what is true. How would you handle this problem?
4. You could expect 50 true–false items to have a lower reliability than would 50 short-answer items. Why?
5. Under what conditions is it preferable to use a matching item rather than some other item type? When should matching items be avoided?
6. In an area in which you are teaching or plan to teach, construct five short-answer items, five true–false items, and one five-alternative matching exercise. State the objectives being measured by the items.

Suggestions for Further Reading

BLOOM, B. S.; MADAUS, G. F.; AND HASTINGS, J. T. *Evaluation to Improve Learning*. New York: McGraw Hill, 1981. Chapter 7, "Item Writing and Item Selection," describes the various types of test items and suggestions for writing them. Includes numerous illustrative items and a summary checklist for item writing.

EBEL, R. L., AND FRISBIE, D. A. *Essentials of Educational Measurement*, 4th ed. Englewood Cliffs, N.J.: Prentice-Hall, 1986. In Chapter 9, "True–False Items," a strong case is made for their use and how to construct them is described and illustrated.

MEHRENS, W. A., AND LEHMANN, I. J. *Measurement and Evaluation in Education and Psychology*, 3d ed. New York: Holt, Rinehart & Winston, 1984. Chapter 6, "Writing the Objective Test Item: Short-Answer, Matching, and True–False," covers the same material as our Chapter 6 does but begins with general considerations for writing objective items.

NITKO, A. J. *Educational Tests and Measurement: An Introduction*. New York: Harcourt Brace Jovanovich, 1983. Chapter 7, "Developing True-False and Matching Items," describes and illustrates construction of these item types.

Chapter 7

Constructing Objective Test Items: Multiple-Choice Forms

Objective test items are not limited to the measurement of simple learning outcomes. . . . The multiple-choice item can measure at both the knowledge and understanding levels and is also free of many of the limitations of other forms of objective items.

The multiple-choice item is generally recognized as the most widely applicable and useful type of objective test item. It can more effectively measure many of the simple learning outcomes measured by the short-answer item, the true–false item, and the matching exercise. In addition, it can measure a variety of the more complex outcomes in the knowledge, understanding, and application areas. This flexibility, plus the higher quality items usually found in the multiple-choice form, has led to its extensive use in achievement testing.

Characteristics of Multiple-Choice Items

A multiple-choice item consists of a problem and a list of suggested solutions. The problem may be stated as a direct question or an incomplete statement and is called the *stem* of the item. The list of suggested solutions may include words, numbers, symbols, or phrases and are called *alternatives* (also called *choices* or *options*). The pupil is typically requested to read the stem and the list of alternatives and to select the one correct, or best, alternative. The correct alternative in each item is called merely the *answer*, and the remaining alternatives are called *distracters* (also called *decoys* or *foils*). These incorrect alternatives receive their name from their intended function — to distract those pupils who are in doubt about the correct answer.

Whether to use a direct question or incomplete statement in the stem depends on several factors. The direct-question form is easier to write, is more natural for younger pupils, and is more likely to present a clearly formulated problem. On the other hand, the incomplete statement is more concise, and if skillfully phrased, it too can present a well-defined problem. A common procedure is to start each stem as a direct question and shift to the incomplete statement form *only* when the clarity of the problem can be retained and greater conciseness achieved.

EXAMPLES

Direct-question form:
In which one of the following cities is the capital of California?

    A   Los Angeles
    Ⓑ   Sacramento
    C   San Diego
    D   San Francisco

Incomplete-statement form:
The capital of California is in

    A   Los Angeles.
    Ⓑ   Sacramento.
    C   San Diego.
    D   San Francisco.

In these examples, there is only one correct answer. The capital of California is in Sacramento and nowhere else. All other alternatives are wrong. For obvious reasons, this is known as the *correct-answer* type of multiple-choice item.

Not all knowledge can be stated so precisely that there is only one absolutely correct response. In fact, when we get beyond the simple aspects of knowledge, represented by questions of the who, what, when, and where variety, answers of varying degrees of acceptability are the rule rather than the exception. Questions of the *why* variety, for example, tend to reveal a number of possible reasons, some of which are better than the others. Likewise, questions of the *how* variety usually reveal several possible procedures, some of which are more desirable than the others. Measures of achievement in these areas, then, become a matter of selecting the *best answer*. This type is especially useful for measuring learning outcomes that require the understanding, application, or interpretation of factual information. Care must be taken, however, to be certain that the best answer is one agreed upon by experts, so that the answer can be defended as clearly best.

EXAMPLES

Best-answer type:

Which one of the following factors contributed most to the selection of Sacramento as the capital of California?

   Ⓐ   Central location
   B   Good climate
   C   Good highways
   D   Large population

(or)

Which one of the following factors is given most consideration when selecting a city for a state capital?

   Ⓐ   Location
   B   Climate
   C   Highways
   D   Population

What is the most important purpose of city zoning laws?

   A   Attract industry
   B   Encourage the building of apartments
   Ⓒ   Protect property values
   D   Provide school "safety zones"

The *best-answer* type of multiple-choice item tends to be more difficult than the *correct-answer* type. This is due partly to the finer discriminations called for and partly to the fact that such items are used to measure more complex learning.

Uses of Multiple-Choice Items

The multiple-choice item is the most versatile type of test item available. It can measure a variety of learning outcomes from simple to complex, and it is adaptable to most types of subject-matter content. It has such wide applicability and so many uses that many standardized tests use multiple-choice items exclusively.[1] Because we cannot illustrate all of the uses of the multiple-choice item, we shall show only its use in measuring some of the more common learning outcomes in the knowledge, understanding, and application areas. The measurement of more complex outcomes, using modified forms of the multiple-choice item, will be considered in the following chapter.

Measuring Knowledge Outcomes

Learning outcomes in the knowledge area are so prominent in all school subjects, and multiple-choice items can measure such a variety of these outcomes that

[1]This practice is not recommended for classroom testing. Despite the wide applicability of the multiple-choice item, there are learning outcomes, such as the ability to organize and present ideas, that cannot be measured with any form of selection item.

168

examples can be endless. Here we shall present some of the more typical uses of the multiple-choice form in measuring knowledge outcomes common to most school subjects.

Knowledge of Terminology.   A simple but basic learning outcome measured by the multiple-choice item is knowledge of terminology. For this purpose, pupils can be requested to show their knowledge of a particular term by selecting a word that has the same meaning as the given term or by choosing a definition of the term. Special uses of a term also can be measured by having pupils identify the meaning of the term when used in context.

Which one of the following words has the same meaning as the word *egress*?

    A   Depress
    B   Enter
    Ⓒ   Exit
    D   Regress

Which one of the following statements best defines the word *egress*?

    A   An expression of disapproval
    Ⓑ   An act of leaving an enclosed place
    C   Proceeding to a higher level
    D   Proceeding to a lower level

What is meant by the word *egress* in the following sentence: "The astronauts hope they can now make a safe *egress*"?

    A   Separation from the rocket
    B   Reentry into the earth's atmosphere
    C   Landing on the water
    Ⓓ   Escape from the space capsule

Knowledge of Specific Facts.   Another learning outcome basic to all school subjects is the knowledge of specific facts. It is important in its own right, and it provides a necessary basis for developing understanding, thinking skills, and other complex learning outcomes. Multiple-choice items designed to measure specific facts can take many different forms, but questions of the *who, what, when,* and *where* variety are most common. These various types are illustrated in the following examples. Although based on the space program, similar questions could be written in many other subject areas.

Who was the first United States astronaut to orbit the earth in space?

    A   Scott Carpenter
    Ⓑ   John Glenn
    C   Virgil Grissom
    D   Alan Shepard

What was the name of the missile that launched the first United States astronaut into orbital flight around the earth?

   Ⓐ   Atlas
   B   Mars
   C   Midas
   D   Polaris

When did a United States astronaut first orbit the earth in space?

   A   1960
   B   1961
   Ⓒ   1962
   D   1963

Where did the Friendship Seven capsule land after the first United States orbital flight around the earth?

   Ⓐ   Atlantic Ocean
   B   Caribbean Sea
   C   Gulf of Mexico
   D   Pacific Ocean

Knowledge of Principles. Knowledge of principles is also an important learning outcome in most school subjects. Multiple-choice items can be constructed to measure knowledge of principles as easily as those designed to measure facts.

EXAMPLES

The principle of capillary action helps explain how fluids

   A   enter solutions of lower concentration.
   B   escape through small openings.
   C   pass through semipermeable membranes.
   Ⓓ   rise in fine tubes.

Which one of the following principles of taxation is characteristic of the federal income tax?

   A   The benefits received by an individual should determine the amount of the tax.
   Ⓑ   A tax should be based on an individual's ability to pay.
   C   All citizens should be required to pay the same amount of tax.
   D   The amount of tax an individual pays should be determined by the size of the federal budget.

Knowledge of Methods and Procedures. Another common learning outcome readily adaptable to the multiple-choice form is knowledge of methods and procedures. This includes such diverse areas as knowledge of laboratory procedures; knowledge of methods underlying communication, computational, and perform- ance skills; knowledge of methods used in problem solving; knowledge of governmental procedures; and knowledge of common social practices. In some cases we might want to measure knowledge of procedures before we permit pupils to practice in a particular area (e.g., laboratory procedures). In other cases, knowledge of methods and procedures may be important learning outcomes in their own right (e.g., knowledge of governmental procedures). The following test items illustrate a few of these uses in different school subjects:

EXAMPLES

Which one of the following methods of locating a specimen under the microscope is most desirable?

    A   Start with the coarse adjustment up, and with your eye at the eyepiece, turn down the coarse adjustment.

    Ⓑ   Start with the coarse adjustment down, and with your eye at the eyepiece, turn up the coarse adjustment.

    C   Start with the coarse adjustment in the center, and with your eye at the eyepiece, turn up and down until you locate the specimen.

To make treaties, the president of the United States must have the consent of the

    A   Cabinet.

    B   House of Representatives.

    Ⓒ   Senate.

    D   Supreme Court.

Alternating electric current is changed to direct current by means of a

    A   condenser.

    B   generator.

    Ⓒ   rectifier.

    D   transformer.

If you were making a scientific study of a problem, your first step should be to

    Ⓐ   collect information about the problem.

    B   develop hypotheses to be tested.

    C   design the experiment to be conducted.

    D   select scientific equipment.

We have merely scratched the surface with our examples of multiple-choice items measuring knowledge outcomes. But as you develop items in the particular school subjects you teach, many other uses will occur to you.

Measuring Outcomes at the Understanding and Application Levels

Many teachers limit the use of multiple-choice items to the knowledge area because they believe that all objective-type items are restricted to the measurement of relatively simple learning outcomes. Although this is true of most of the other types of objective items, the multiple-choice item is especially adaptable to the measurement of more complex learning outcomes. The examples that follow illustrate its use in measuring various aspects of understanding and application.

In reviewing the following items, it is important to keep in mind that such items measure learning outcomes beyond factual knowledge *only if* the applications and interpretations are new to the pupils. Any specific applications or interpretations of knowledge can, of course, be taught directly to pupils as any other fact is taught. When this is done, and the test items contain the same problem situations and solutions used in teaching, it is obvious that the pupils can be given credit for no more than the mere retention of factual knowledge. To measure understanding and application, an element of novelty must be included in the test items. For illustrative purposes, it is necessary to assume that such novelty exists in the examples that follow.

Ability to Identify Application of Facts and Principles.   A common method of determining whether pupils' learning has gone beyond the mere memorization of a fact or principle is to ask them to identify its correct application in a situation that is new to the pupil. Application items measure understanding but they also include the ability to transfer learning to situations that have not been previously studied. Thus, the items can be designed to measure understanding at a relatively high level.

EXAMPLES

Which one of the following is an example of a chemical *element*?

    A   Acid
    B   Sodium Chloride
    Ⓒ   Oxygen
    D   Water

Directions: In each of the following sentences circle the word that makes the sentence correct.

                    that
  1. This is the boy (who) asked the question.
                    whom

                    (that)
  2. This is the dog   who   he asked about.
                    whom

Which one of the following best illustrates the principle of capillarity?

    Ⓐ   Fluid is carried through the stems of plants.
    B   Food is manufactured in the leaves of plants.
    C   The leaves of deciduous plants lose their green color in winter.
    D   Plants give off moisture through their stomata.

Pascal's law can be used to explain the operation of

    A   electric fans.
    Ⓑ   hydraulic brakes.
    C   levers.
    D   syringes.

Which one of the following best illustrates the law of diminishing returns?

A   The demand for a farm product increased faster than the supply of the product.

B   The population of a country increased faster than the means of subsistence.

C   A machine decreased in utility as its parts became worn.

Ⓓ   A factory doubled its labor force and increased production 50 percent.

Ability to Interpret Cause-and-Effect Relationships.   Understanding can frequently be measured by asking pupils to interpret various relationships among facts. One of the most important relationships in this regard, and one common to most subject-matter areas, is the cause-and-effect relationship. Understanding of such relationships can be measured by presenting pupils with a specific cause-and-effect relationship and asking them to identify the reason that best accounts for it.

Bread will not become moldy as rapidly if placed in a refrigerator because

EXAMPLES

Ⓐ   cooling retards the growth of fungi.

B   darkness retards the growth of mold.

C   cooling prevents the bread from drying out so rapidly.

D   mold requires both heat and light for best growth.

An increased quantity of carbon monoxide is produced when fuel is burned in a limited supply of oxygen because

A   carbon reacts with carbon monoxide.

Ⓑ   carbon reacts with carbon dioxide.

C   carbon monoxide is an effective reducing agent.

D   greater oxidation takes place.

Investing money in common stock protects against loss of assets during inflation because common stock

A   pays higher rates of interest during inflation.

B   provides a steady but dependable income despite economic conditions.

C   is protected by the Federal Reserve System.

Ⓓ   increases in value as the value of a business increases.

Ability to Justify Methods and Procedures.   Another phase of understanding important in various subject-matter areas is concerned with methods and procedures. A pupil might know the correct method or sequence of steps in carrying out a procedure, without being able to explain *why* it is the best method or sequence of steps. At the understanding level we are interested in the pupil's ability to justify the use of a particular method or procedure. This can be measured with multiple-choice items by asking the pupil to select the best of several possible explanations of a method or procedure.

Why is adequate lighting necessary in a balanced aquarium?

>   A   Fish need light to see their food.
>   B   Fish take in oxygen in the dark.
>   Ⓒ   Plants expel carbon dioxide in the dark.
>   D   Plants grow too rapidly in the dark.

Why do farmers rotate their crops?

>   Ⓐ   To conserve the soil.
>   B   To make marketing easier.
>   C   To provide for strip cropping.
>   D   To provide more uniform working conditions throughout the year.

Why is nickel used in the process of changing cottonseed oil to a solid fat?

>   A   It improves the texture and firmness.
>   B   It removes the nutlike odor.
>   C   It removes the brownish yellow color.
>   Ⓓ   It speeds up the process.

Although various aspects of understanding and application can be measured by single multiple-choice items, as shown in the preceding examples, a series of multiple-choice items based on a common set of data is even more adaptable to the measurement of complex achievement. Such items will be illustrated in the next chapter.

Advantages and Limitations of Multiple-Choice Items

The multiple-choice item is one of the most widely applicable test items for measuring achievement. It can effectively measure various types of knowledge and complex learning outcomes. In addition to this flexibility, it is free from some of the common shortcomings characteristic of the other item types. The ambiguity and vagueness that frequently are present in the short-answer item are avoided because the alternatives better structure the situation. In the following examples, note how the vague short-answer item becomes a clear-cut problem.

EXAMPLES   *Poor:*   Lincoln was born in _____ .
          Better: Lincoln was born in

>   A   Indiana
>   B   Illinois
>   Ⓒ   Kentucky
>   D   Ohio

Your first reaction to the short-answer item might be, "Why not put it in question form to make it clearer?" But even if we ask, "In what state was Lincoln born?" answers such as "poverty" could not be ruled out. In addition to clarifying the specific type of response called for, the multiple-choice item relieves us of the problem of deciding how to score misspelled answers. Although we may be interested in having pupils spell the names of states correctly, this should be done in a separate spelling test rather than letting it contaminate our measures of achievement.

One advantage of the multiple-choice item over the true–false item is that pupils cannot receive credit for simply knowing that a statement is incorrect; *they must also know what is correct*. Note the difference in the following two items:

T   Ⓕ   Lincoln was born in 1807.   EXAMPLES
            Lincoln was born in

                 A   1805
                 B   1807
                 Ⓒ   1809
                 D   1811

In the true–false version pupils will receive credit if they mark it false, even if they think Lincoln was born in some year other than 1809. In fact, if a pupil thought he was born in 1909, it would be marked false and the pupil would receive a 1-point credit for that response. Because marking statements false does *not* show that pupils know what is correct, the resulting scores tend to be inadequate measures of what pupils have learned. But this problem is not encountered with multiple-choice items because the pupils must select the correct answer to receive credit. Although the problem also could be resolved by having pupils change all false statements to true, that procedure is often cumbersome, especially when measuring complex learning outcomes.

Another advantage of the multiple-choice item over the true–false item is the greater reliability per item. Because the number of alternatives is increased from two to four or five, the opportunity for guessing the correct answer is reduced, and the reliability is correspondingly increased. The effect of increasing the number of alternatives for each item is similar to that of increasing the length of the test.

Using the *best-answer* type of multiple-choice item also circumvents a difficulty associated with the true–false item—obtaining statements that are true or false without qualification. This makes it possible to measure learning outcomes in the numerous subject-matter areas in which solutions to problems are not absolutely true or false but vary in degree of appropriateness (e.g., best method, best reason, best interpretation).

An advantage of the multiple-choice item over the matching exercise is that the need for homogeneous material is avoided. The matching exercise, which is essentially a modified form of the multiple-choice item, requires a series of related ideas to form the list of premises and alternative responses. In many content areas it is difficult to obtain enough homogeneous material to prepare effective matching exercises. But this problem is avoided with multiple-choice items because each item measures a single idea. Thus, it is possible to measure one or many relationships in a given area when the multiple-choice item is used.

Two other desirable characteristics of the multiple-choice item are worthy of mention. First, it is relatively free from response sets. That is, pupils generally do not favor a particular alternative when they do not know the answer. Second, using a number of plausible alternatives makes the results amenable to diagnosis. The kind of the incorrect alternatives pupils select provides clues to factual errors and misunderstandings that need correction.

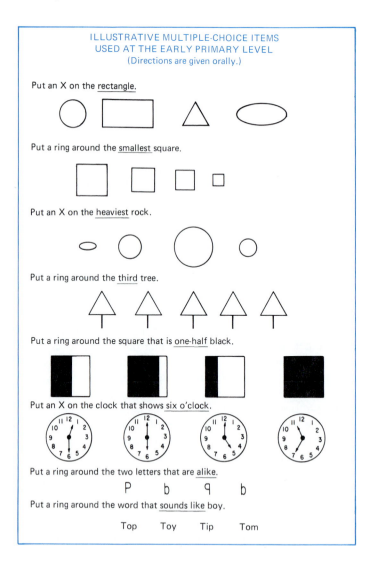

ILLUSTRATIVE MULTIPLE-CHOICE ITEMS
USED AT THE EARLY PRIMARY LEVEL
(Directions are given orally.)

Put an X on the rectangle.

Put a ring around the smallest square.

Put an X on the heaviest rock.

Put a ring around the third tree.

Put a ring around the square that is one-half black.

Put an X on the clock that shows six o'clock.

Put a ring around the two letters that are alike.

P   b   q   b

Put a ring around the word that sounds like boy.

Top   Toy   Tip   Tom

The wide applicability of the multiple-choice item, plus its advantages, makes it easier to construct high-quality test items in this form than in any of the other forms. This does not mean that good multiple-choice items can be constructed without effort. But for a given amount of effort, multiple-choice items will tend to be of a higher quality than short-answer, true-false, or matching-type items in the same area.

Despite its superiority, the multiple-choice item does have limitations. First, as with all other paper-and-pencil tests, it is limited to learning outcomes at the verbal level. The problems presented to pupils are verbal problems, free from the many irrelevant factors present in natural situations. Also, the applications pupils are asked to make are verbal applications, free from the personal commitment necessary for application in natural situations. In short, the multiple-choice item, like other paper-and-pencil tests, measures whether the pupil *knows* or *understands* what to do when confronted with a problem situation, but it cannot determine how the pupil actually *will* perform in that situation. Second, as with other types of selection items, the multiple-choice item requires selection of the correct answer, and therefore it is not well adapted to measuring some problem-solving skills in mathematics and science or to measuring the ability to organize and present ideas. Third, the multiple-choice item has a disadvantage not shared by the other item types: the difficulty of finding a sufficient number of incorrect but plausible distracters. This problem is especially acute at the early primary level because of the pupils' limited vocabulary and knowledge in any particular area. Even at this level, however, classroom teachers have been creative in adapting the multiple-choice item to the measurement of newly learned concepts (see box). As pupils move up through the grade levels and expand their vocabulary, knowledge, and understanding, plausible but incorrect answers become more available. It still takes a touch of creativity, however, to identify and state the most plausible distracters for use in multiple-choice items. This is the task that separates the good from the poor item maker. Fortunately, it gets easier with experience in constructing such items.

Suggestions for Constructing Multiple-Choice Items

The general applicability and the superior qualities of multiple-choice test items are realized most fully when care is taken in their construction. This involves formulating a clearly stated problem, identifying plausible alternatives, and removing irrelevant clues to the answer. The following suggestions provide more specific maxims for this purpose.

1. The stem of the item should be meaningful by itself and should present a definite problem. Often the stems of test items placed in multiple-choice form are incomplete statements that make little sense until all of the alternatives have been read. These are *not* multiple-choice items but, rather, a collection of true – false statements placed in multiple-choice form. A properly constructed multiple-choice item presents a definite problem in the stem that is meaningful without the alternatives. Compare the stems in the two versions of the test item in the following examples:

Poor: South America

    A   is a flat, arid country.
    B   imports coffee from the United States.
    C   has a larger population than the United States.
    Ⓓ   was settled mainly by colonists from Spain.

Better: Most of South America was settled by colonists from

    A   England.
    B   France.
    C   Holland.
    Ⓓ   Spain.

Formulating a definite problem in the stem not only improves the stem of the item, but it also has a desirable effect on the alternatives. In the preceding example, the alternatives in the first version are concerned with widely dissimilar ideas. This heterogeneity is possible because of the stem's lack of structure. In the second version, the clearly formulated problem in the stem forces the alternatives to be more homogenous.

A good check on the adequacy of the problem statement is to cover the alternatives and read the stem by itself. It should be complete enough to serve as a short-answer item. Starting each item stem as a direct question and shifting to the incomplete statement form only when greater conciseness is possible is the most effective method for obtaining a clearly formulated problem.

2. The item stem should include as much of the item as possible and should be free of irrelevant material. This will increase the probability of a clearly stated problem in the stem and will reduce the reading time required. The following examples illustrate how the conciseness of an item is increased by removing irrelevant material and including in the stem those words repeated in the alternatives. Notice that to obtain the conciseness of the final version, it is necessary to shift to the incomplete-statement form. The *best* version provides a slim-trim item that is easily read and focuses directly on the key element in the intended learning outcome.

Poor: Most of South America was settled by colonists from Spain. How would you account for the large number of Spanish colonists settling there?

    A   They were adventurous.
    Ⓑ   They were in search of wealth.
    C   They wanted lower taxes.
    D   They were seeking religious freedom.

Better: Why did Spanish colonists settle most of South America?
     A   They were adventurous.
     Ⓑ   They were in search of wealth.
     C   They wanted lower taxes.
     D   They were seeking religious freedom.

Best: Spanish colonists settled most of South America in search of
     A   adventure.
     Ⓑ   wealth.
     C   lower taxes.
     D   religious freedom.

There are a few exceptions to this rule. In testing problem-solving ability, irrelevant material might be included in the stem of an item to determine whether pupils can identify and select the material that is relevant to the problem's solution. Similarly, repeating common words in the alternatives is sometimes necessary for grammatical consistency or greater clarity.

3. Use a negatively stated item stem only when significant learning outcomes require it. Most problems can and should be stated in positive terms. This avoids the possibility of pupils' overlooking the *no, not, least,* and similar words used in negative statements. In most instances, it also avoids measuring relatively insignificant learning outcomes. Knowing the *least* important method, the principle that does *not* apply, or the *poorest* reason are seldom important learning outcomes. We are usually interested in pupils' learning the *most* important method, the principle that *does* apply, and the *best* reason.

Teachers sometimes go to ridiculous extremes to use negatively stated items because they appear more difficult. The difficulty of such items, however, is in the lack of sentence clarity rather than in the difficulty of the concept being measured.

EXAMPLES

Poor: Which one of the following states is not located north of the Mason–Dixon line?
     A   Maine
     B   New York
     C   Pennsylvania
     Ⓓ   Virginia

Better: Which one of the following states is located south of the Mason–Dixon line?
     A   Maine
     B   New York
     C   Pennsylvania
     Ⓓ   Virginia

Both versions of this item measure the same knowledge. But some pupils who can answer the second version correctly will select an incorrect alternative on the first version merely because the negative phrasing confuses them. Such items thus introduce factors that contribute to the invalidity of the test.

Although negatively stated items are generally to be avoided, there are occasions when they are useful, mainly in areas in which the wrong information or wrong procedure can have dire consequences. In the health area, for example, there are practices to be avoided because of their harmful nature. In shop and laboratory work, there are procedures that can damage equipment and result in bodily injury. And in driver training there are unsafe practices to be emphasized. When the avoidance of such potentially harmful practices is emphasized in teaching, it might well receive a corresponding emphasis in testing through the use of negatively stated items. When used, the negative aspects of the item should be made obvious.

EXAMPLES

Poor: Which one of the following is not a safe driving practice on icy roads?
    A   Accelerating slowly.
    Ⓑ   Jamming on the brakes.
    C   Holding the wheel firmly.
    D   Slowing down gradually.

Better: All of the following are safe driving practices on icy roads EXCEPT
    A   accelerating slowly.
    Ⓑ   jamming on the brakes.
    C   holding the wheel firmly.
    D   slowing down gradually.

In the first version of the item, the *not* is easily overlooked, in which case pupils would tend to select the first alternative and not read any further. In the second version, no pupil would probably overlook the negative element because it is placed at the end of the statement and is capitalized.

4. All of the alternatives should be grammatically consistent with the stem of the item. In the items in the following examples, note how the better version results from a change in the alternatives in order to obtain grammatical consistency. This rule is not presented merely to perpetuate proper grammar usage, however; its main function is to prevent irrelevant clues from creeping in. All too frequently the grammatical consistency of the correct answer is given attention, but that of the distracters is neglected. As a result, some of the alternatives are grammatically inconsistent with the stem and are therefore obviously incorrect answers.

EXAMPLES

Poor: An electric transformer can be used
    A   for storing up electricity.
    Ⓑ   to increase the voltage of alternating current.
    C   it converts electrical energy into mechanical energy.
    D   alternating current is changed to direct current.

Better: An electric transformer can be used to

    A   store up electricity.
    Ⓑ   increase the voltage of alternating current.
    C   convert electrical energy into mechanical energy.
    D   change alternating current to direct current.

How Many Alternatives Should Be Used in Multiple-Choice Items?

There is no "magic" number of alternatives to use in a multiple-choice item. Typically three, four, or five choices are used. Some favor 5-choice items to reduce the chances of guessing the correct answer.

	CHANCES OF A CORRECT GUESS	CHANCE SCORE ON 100-ITEM TEST
5-choice items	1 in 5	20
4-choice items	1 in 4	25
3-choice items	1 in 3	33

Reducing the chances of guessing the correct answers by adding alternatives enhances both reliability and validity, but *only if* all of the distracters are plausible and the items are well constructed. Our preference is for using 4-choice items because, with reasonable effort, three good distracters usually can be obtained (the fourth distracter tends to be difficult to devise and is usually weaker than the others). For young pupils, 3-choice items may be preferable in order to reduce the amount of reading.

The number of alternatives can, of course, vary from item to item. You might use a 5-choice item when four good distracters are available and a 3-choice item when there are only two. Don't give up too soon in constructing distracters, however. It takes time and effort to generate several good ones.

Similar difficulties arise from a lack of attention to verb tense, to the proper use of the articles *a* or *an*, and to other common sources of grammatical inconsistency. Because most of these errors are the result of carelessness, they can be detected easily by carefully reading each item before assembling them into a test.

5. An item should contain only one correct or clearly best answer. Including more than one correct answer in a test item and asking pupils to select all of the correct alternatives has two shortcomings. First, such items are usually no more than a collection of true–false items presented in multiple-choice form. They do not present a definite problem in the stem, and the selection of answers requires a mental response of true or false to each alternative rather than a comparison and selection of alternatives. Second, because the number of alternatives selected as correct answers varies from one pupil to another, there is no satisfactory method of scoring.

EXAMPLES					
	Poor:	The state of Michigan borders on			
		Ⓐ	Lake Huron.		
		B	Lake Ontario.		
		Ⓒ	Indiana.		
		D	Illinois.		
	Better:	The state of Michigan borders on			
		A	Lake Huron.	Ⓣ	F
		B	Lake Ontario.	T	Ⓕ
		C	Indiana.	Ⓣ	F
		D	Illinois.	T	Ⓕ

The second version of this item shows the pupils the type of response expected. They are to read each alternative and decide whether it is true or false. Thus, this is *not* a four-alternative, multiple-choice item, but a series of four statements, each of which has two alternatives — true or false. This second version, which is called a cluster-type true–false item, not only identifies the mental process involved, but it also simplifies the scoring. Each statement in the cluster can be considered as 1 point and scored as any other true–false item is scored. In contrast, how would you score a pupil who selected alternatives A, B, and C in the first version? Would you give him 2 points because he correctly identified the two answers? Would you give him only 1 point because he also selected one incorrect alternative? Or would you give him no points because he responded incorrectly to the item as a whole? How would you evaluate his response to alternative D? Assume that he knew Illinois did not border on Michigan and therefore did not select it, or assume that he was uncertain and left it blank. There is no method of scoring that will satisfactorily resolve these problems. Multiple-choice items, like the one in the first version, should be avoided or converted to the true–false form.

There is another important facet of this rule concerning single-answer multiple-choice items, that is, the answer must be agreed upon by authorities in the area. The best-answer type item is especially subject to variations of interpretation and disagreement concerning the correct answer. Care must be taken to make certain that the answer is clearly the best one. Frequently rewording the problem in the stem will correct an otherwise faulty item.

In the first version of the following item, different alternatives could be defended as correct, depending on whether the "best" refers to cost, efficiency, cleanliness, or accessibility. The second version avoids this problem by making the criterion of best explicit.

Poor: Which one of the following is the best source of heat for home use?
  A   Coal
  B   Electricity
  C   Gas
  D   Oil
Better: In the midwestern part of the United States, which one of the
  following is the most economical source of heat for home use?
  Ⓐ   Coal
  B   Electricity
  C   Gas
  D   Oil

---

*6. **Items used to measure understanding should contain some novelty, but beware of too much.*** The construction of multiple-choice items that measure learning outcomes at the understanding level requires a careful choice of situations and skillful phrasing. The situations must be new to the pupils, but not too far removed from the examples used in class. If the test items contain problem situations identical with those used in class, the pupils can, of course, respond on the basis of memorized answers. On the other hand, if the problem situations contain too much novelty, some pupils may respond incorrectly merely because they lack necessary factual information about the situations used. Asking pupils to apply the law of supply and demand to some phase of banking, for example, would be grossly unfair if they had not had a previous opportunity to study banking policies and practices. They may have a good understanding of the law of supply and demand but be unable to demonstrate this because of their unfamiliarity with the particular situation selected.

The problem of too much novelty usually can be avoided by selecting situations from the pupils' everyday experiences, by including in the stem of the item any factual information needed, and by phrasing the item so that the type of application or interpretation called for is clear.

*7. **All distracters should be plausible.*** The purpose of a distracter is to *distract* the uninformed away from the correct answer. To the pupil who has not achieved the learning outcome being tested, the distracters should be at least as attractive as the correct answer and preferably more so. In a properly constructed multiple-choice item, each distracter will be elected by some pupils. If a distracter is not selected by anyone, it is not contributing to the functioning of the item and should be eliminated or revised.

One factor contributing to the plausibility of distracters is their homogeneity. If all of the alternatives are homogeneous with regard to the knowledge being measured, the distracters are more likely to function as intended. Whether alternatives appear homogeneous and distracters plausible, however, also depends on the pupils' age level. Note the difference in homogeneity in the following two items:

EXAMPLES

Poor: Who discovered the North Pole?
    A   Christopher Columbus
    B   Ferdinand Magellan
    Ⓒ   Robert Peary
    D   Marco Polo

Better: Who discovered the North Pole?
    A   Roald Amundsen
    B   Richard Byrd
    Ⓒ   Robert Peary
    D   Robert Scott

The first version would probably appear homogeneous to pupils at the primary level because all four choices are the names of well-known explorers. However, pupils in higher grades would eliminate alternatives A, B, and D as possible answers because they would know these men were not polar explorers. They might also recall that these men lived several hundred years before the North Pole was discovered. In either case, they could quickly obtain the correct answer by the process of elimination. The second version includes only the names of polar

Ways to Make Distracters Plausible

1. Use the pupils' most common errors.
2. Use important-sounding words (e.g., "significant," "accurate") that are relevant to the item stem. But don't overdo it!
3. Use words that have verbal associations with the item stem (e.g., politician — political).
4. Use textbook language or other phraseology that has the "appearance of truth."
5. Use incorrect answers that are likely to result from pupil misunderstanding or carelessness (e.g., forgets to convert from feet to yards).
6. Use distracters that are homogeneous and similar in content to the correct answer (e.g., all are inventors).
7. Use distracters that are parallel in form and grammatically consistent with the item's stem.
8. Make the distracters similar to the correct answer in length, vocabulary, sentence structure, and complexity of thought.

Note of Caution

Distracters should distract the uninformed, but they should *not* result in "trick questions" that mislead the knowledgeable pupils (e.g., don't insert *not* in a correct answer to make it a distracter).

explorers, all of whom were active at approximately the same time. This homogeneity makes each alternative much more plausible and the elimination process much less effective. It also, of course, increases the item's level of difficulty.

In selecting plausible distracters, the pupils' learning experiences must not be ignored. In the foregoing item, for example, the distracters in the second version would not be plausible to pupils if Robert Peary was the only polar explorer they had studied. Obviously, distracters must be familiar to pupils before they can serve as reasonable alternatives. Less obvious is the rich source of plausible distracters provided by the pupils' learning experiences. Common misconceptions, errors of judgment, and faulty reasoning that occur during the teaching–learning process provide the most plausible and educationally sound distracters available. One way to tap this supply is to keep a running record of such errors. A quicker method is to administer a short-answer test to pupils and tabulate the most common errors. This provides a series of incorrect responses that are especially plausible because they are in the pupils' own language.

8. Verbal associations between the stem and the correct answer should be avoided. Frequently a word in the correct answer will provide an irrelevant clue because it looks or sounds like a word in the stem of the item. Such verbal associations should never permit the pupil who lacks the necessary achievement to select the correct answer. However, words similar to those in the stem might be included in the distracters to increase their plausibility. Pupils who depend on rote memory and verbal associations will then be led away from, rather than to, the correct answer. The following item, taken from a fifth-grade test on a weather unit, shows the incorrect and correct use of verbal associations between the stem and the alternatives:

EXAMPLES

Poor: Which one of the following agencies should you contact to find out about a tornado warning in your locality?

    A   State farm bureau
    Ⓑ   Local radio station
    C   United States Post Office
    D   United States Weather Bureau

Better: Which one of the following agencies should you contact to find out about a tornado warning in your locality?

    A   Local farm bureau
    Ⓑ   Nearest radio station
    C   Local post office
    D   United States Weather Bureau

In the first version, the association between "locality" and "local" is an unnecessary clue. In the second version, this verbal association is used in two distracters to make them more attractive choices. But if irrelevant verbal associations in the distracters are overused, pupils will soon catch on and avoid alternatives with pat verbal associations.

9. The relative length of the alternatives should not provide a clue to the answer. Because the correct answer usually needs to be qualified, it tends to be longer than the distracters unless a special effort is made to control the alternatives' relative length. If the correct answer cannot be shortened, the distracters can be expanded to the desired length. Lengthening the distracters also is desirable for another reason. The added qualifiers and greater specificity frequently contribute to their plausibility. The best we can hope for in equalizing the length of a test item's alternatives is to make them approximately equal. Consequently, we still have the problem of the length of the correct answer. Although it should not be consistently longer than the other alternatives, it also should not be consistently shorter or consistently of median length.

EXAMPLES

Poor: What is the major purpose of the United Nations?
Ⓐ   To maintain peace among the peoples of the world.
B   To establish international law.
C   To provide military control.
D   To form new governments.

Better: What is the major purpose of the United Nations?
Ⓐ   To maintain peace among the peoples of the world.
B   To develop a new system of international law.
C   To provide military control of nations that have recently attained their independence.
D   To establish and maintain democratic forms of government in newly formed nations.

The relative length of the correct answer should vary from one item to another in such a manner that no pattern is discernible to indicate the answer. This means, of course, that sometimes it will be the longest.

10. The correct answer should appear in each of the alternative positions an approximately equal number of times but in random order. Some teachers often bury the correct answer in the middle of the list of alternatives. As a consequence, the correct answer appears in the first and last positions far less often than it does in the middle positions. This, of course, provides an irrelevant clue to the alert pupil.

In placing the correct answer in each position approximately an equal number of times, care must be taken to avoid a regular pattern of responses. A random placement of correct answers can be attained with the use of any book. For each test item, open the book at an arbitrary position, note the number on the right-hand page, and place the correct answer for that test item as follows:

IF PAGE NUMBER ENDS IN	PLACE CORRECT ANSWER
1	First
3	Second
5	Third
7	Fourth
9	Fifth

An even simpler method for obtaining an undetectable placement of the correct answer is to place all verbal alternatives in alphabetical order and all numerical answers in numerical order.

11. Use sparingly special alternatives such as "none of the above" or "all of the above." The phrases "none of the above" or "all of the above" are sometimes added as the last alternative in multiple-choice items. This is done to force the pupil to consider all of the alternatives carefully and to increase the difficulty of the items. All too frequently, however, these special alternatives are used inappropriately. In fact, there are relatively few situations in which their use is appropriate.

The use of "none of the above" is restricted to the correct-answer type of multiple-choice item and consequently to the measurement of factual knowledge to which absolute standards of correctness can be applied. It is inappropriate in best-answer type items because the pupil is told to select the *best* of several alternatives of varying degrees of correctness.

Use of "none of the above" is frequently recommended for items measuring computational skill in mathematics and spelling ability. But these learning outcomes generally should not be measured by multiple-choice items, because they can be measured more effectively by short-answer items. When "none of the above" is used in such situations, the item may measure nothing more than a pupil's ability to recognize incorrect answers, a rather inadequate basis for judging computational skill or spelling ability.

The alternative "none of the above" should be used only when the measurement of significant learning outcomes requires it. As with negatively stated item stems, sometimes procedures or practices should be avoided for safety, health, or other reasons. When knowing what *not* to do is important, "none of the above" might be appropriately applied. When used for this purpose, it also must be used as an incorrect answer a proportionate number of times.

The use of "all of the above" is fraught with so many difficulties that it might best be discarded as a possible alternative. When used, some pupils will note that the first alternative is correct and select it without reading further. Other pupils will note that at least two of the alternatives are correct and thereby know that "all of the above" must be the answer. In the first instance, pupils mark the item incorrectly because they do not read all of the alternatives, and in the second instance, pupils obtain the correct answer on the basis of partial knowledge. Both types of response prevent the item from functioning as intended.

Examples of Misuse of the Alternative "None of the Above"

Which of the following is *not* an example of a mammal?

   *A. Bird
    B. Dog
    C. Whale
    D. None of the above

(It would be easy to prove that "D" is *not* an example of a mammal.)

When the temperature drops, tire pressure tends to

   *A. Decrease
    B. Increase
    C. Stay the same
    D. None of the above

(There may be something other than A, B, or C, but I can't think of what it might be.)

United States federal law requires that first offenders must be fined or imprisoned if they possess

    A. Amphetamine
    B. Heroin
    C. Marijuana
   *D. None of the above

(Sounds like a very unfair law. If you don't agree, read only the stem and answer "D.")

  *correct answer

---

12. Do not use multiple-choice items when other item types are more appropriate. When various item types can serve a purpose equally well, the multiple-choice item should be favored because of its many superior qualities. Sometimes, however, the multiple-choice form is inappropriate or at least less suitable than other item types. In certain problem-solving situations in mathematics and science, for example, supply-type short-answer items are clearly superior. When there are only two possible responses (e.g., fact or opinion), the true–false item is more appropriate. When there are enough homogeneous items but few plausible distracters for each, a matching exercise might be more suitable. Although we should take full advantage of the wide applicability of the multiple-choice form, we should not lose sight of a principle of test construction cited earlier — *select the item type that measures the learning outcome most directly and most effectively.*

13. Break any of these rules when you have a good reason for doing so. Although these rules provide valuable guidelines for constructing multiple-

Checklist for Reviewing Multiple-Choice Items

REVIEW QUESTIONS	YES	NO
1. Is this the most appropriate type of item to use?	____	____
2. Does each item stem present a meaningful problem?	____	____
3. Are the item stems free of irrelevant material?	____	____
4. Are the item stems stated in positive terms (if possible)?	____	____
5. If used, has negative wording been given special emphasis (e.g., capitalized)?	____	____
6. Are the alternatives grammatically consistent with the item stem?	____	____
7. Are the alternative answers brief and free of unnecessary words?	____	____
8. Are the alternatives similar in length and form?	____	____
9. Is there only one correct or clearly best answer?	____	____
10. Are the distracters plausible to nonachievers?	____	____
11. Are the items free of verbal clues to the answer?	____	____
12. Are verbal alternatives in alphabetical order?	____	____
13. Are numerical alternatives in numerical order?	____	____
14. Have "none of the above" and "all of the above" been avoided (or used sparingly and appropriately)?	____	____
15. If revised, are the items still relevant to the intended learning outcomes?	____	____
16. Have the items been set aside for a time before reviewing them?	____	____

choice items, you may encounter instances where an exception to the rule may improve the item.

Summary

The multiple-choice item consists of a problem and a list of alternative solutions. The pupil responds by selecting the alternative that provides the correct or best solution to the problem. The incorrect alternatives are called distracters because their purpose is to distract the uninformed pupil from the correct response. The problem can be stated as a direct question or an incomplete statement. In either case, it should be a clearly formulated problem that is meaningful without reference to the list of alternatives.

The multiple-choice form is extremely flexible and can be used to measure a variety of learning outcomes at the knowledge and understanding levels. Knowledge outcomes concerned with vocabulary, facts, principles, and methods and procedures all can be measured with the multiple-choice item. Aspects of understanding, such as the application and interpretation of facts, principles, and methods, also can be measured with this item type. Many other more specific uses occur in particular school subjects.

The main advantage of the multiple-choice item is its wide applicability in the measurement of various phases of achievement. It is also free of many of the limitations of other forms of objective items. It tends to present a more well-defined problem than the short-answer item does; it avoids the need for homogeneous material required by the matching item; and it reduces the clues and susceptibility to guessing characteristic of the true–false item. In addition, the multiple-choice item is relatively free from response sets and is useful in diagnosis.

Its limitations are mainly that it is a selection-type paper-and-pencil test and measures problem-solving behavior at the verbal level only. Because it requires selection of the correct answer, it is inappropriate for measuring learning outcomes requiring the ability to recall, organize, or present ideas.

The construction of multiple-choice items involves defining the problem in the stem of the item, selecting one correct or best solution, identifying several plausible distracters, and avoiding irrelevant clues to the answer. Items used to measure learning outcomes at the understanding level must also include some (but beware of too much) novelty.

Learning Exercises

1. Describe the advantages of the multiple-choice item over each of the other objective-type items. What are the comparative disadvantages?

2. In an area in which you are teaching or plan to teach, construct one multiple-choice item in each of the following areas: knowledge, understanding, and application.

3. Make a checklist for evaluating the plausibility of distracters. Put the criteria in question form so that they can be answered with a simple yes or no.

4. How does a multiple-choice item designed to measure knowledge outcomes differ from one designed to measure understanding?

5. Describe the relative merits of using the correct-answer type and the best-answer type of multiple-choice items. What types of learning outcomes are best measured by each?

Suggestions for Further Reading

BLOOM, B. S.; MADAUS, G. F.; AND HASTINGS, J. T. *Evaluation to Improve Learning*. New York: McGraw-Hill, 1981. Chapter 8, "Evaluation Techniques for Knowledge and Comprehension Objectives," and Chapter 9, "Evaluation Techniques for Application and Analysis Objectives," include numerous illustrations of modified forms of multiple-choice items.

EBEL, R. L., AND FRISBIE, D. A. *Essentials of Educational Measurement*, 4th ed. Englewood Cliffs, N.J.: Prentice-Hall, 1986. Chapter 10, "Multiple-Choice Items," offers numerous sample test items to illustrate desirable and undesirable characteristics of multiple-choice items, as well as suggestions for writing good items.

GRONLUND, N. E. *How to Construct Achievement Tests*, 4th ed. Englewood Cliffs, N.J.: Prentice-Hall, 1988. Chapter 3, "Constructing Selection Items: Multiple-Choice," describes and illustrates the use of multiple-choice items for measuring various types of outcomes. The appendix contains a comprehensive checklist for evaluating an achievement test.

NITKO, A. J. *Educational Tests and Measurement: An Introduction*. New York: Harcourt Brace Jovanovich, 1983. Chapter 8, "Developing Multiple-Choice Items: Basic Principles," describes and illustrates different types of multiple-choice items.

Chapter 8

Measuring Complex Achievement: The Interpretive Exercise

Complex achievement includes those learning outcomes based on the higher mental process, such as . . . understanding . . . thinking skills . . . and various problem-solving abilities. . . . Many aspects of complex achievement can be measured objectively.

We have already had some experience with measuring complex achievement, as this category encompasses all those learning outcomes requiring more than the mere retention of factual knowledge. The use of the short-answer item to measure problem-solving abilities in mathematics and science, the true–false item to measure the ability to recognize cause–effect relationships, and the multiple-choice item to measure various aspects of understanding and application all illustrate the measurement of complex achievement. These illustrations, however, were limited to the use of single, independent test items of the objective type. Greater range and flexibility in measuring complex achievement can be attained by using more complex forms of objective test items.

A variety of learning outcomes are included in complex achievement. Following are some typical examples:

Ability to apply a principle.

Ability to interpret relationships.

Ability to recognize and state inferences.

Ability to recognize the relevance of information.

Ability to develop and recognize tenable hypotheses.

Ability to formulate and recognize valid conclusions.

Ability to recognize assumptions underlying conclusions.

Ability to recognize the limitations of data.

Ability to recognize and state significant problems.

Ability to design experimental procedures.

These and similar learning outcomes have been classified under such categories as understanding, reasoning, critical thinking, scientific thinking, creative thinking, and problem solving. There is general agreement that these learning outcomes based on higher order thinking skills constitute some of the most significant outcomes of education. One of the most promising forms for measuring a variety of complex learning outcomes in school subjects is the interpretive exercise.

Nature of the Interpretive Exercise[1]

An interpretive exercise consists of a series of objective items based on a common set of data. The data may be in the form of written materials, tables, charts, graphs, maps, or pictures. The series of related test items may also take various forms but are most commonly multiple-choice or true–false items. Because all pupils are presented with a common set of data, it is possible to measure a variety of complex learning outcomes. Pupils can be asked to identify relationships in data, to recognize valid conclusions, to appraise assumptions and inferences, to detect proper applications of data, and the like.

The common set of materials used in interpretive exercises ensures that all pupils will be confronted with the same task. It also makes it possible to control the amount of factual information given to them. We can give them as much or as little information as we think desirable in measuring their achievement of a learning outcome. In measuring their ability to interpret mathematical data, for example, we can include the formulas needed or require the pupils to supply them. In other areas, we can supply definitions of terms, meanings of symbols, and other facts or expect pupils to supply them. This flexibility makes it possible to measure various degrees of proficiency in any particular area.

Forms and Uses of the Interpretive Exercise

As with other objective items, there are so many forms and uses of the interpretive exercise that it is impossible to illustrate all of them. Here we shall present representative examples of this item type as applied to the measurement of complex

[1]Variations of this item are also called "classification exercises," "key-type items," and "master-list items."

learning outcomes in a variety of school subjects at the elementary and secondary levels. Different types of introductory material and different methods of responding also will be used to illustrate the great flexibility of the interpretive exercise. The references at the end of this chapter offer additional illustrative exercises.

Ability to Recognize the Relevance of Information

A learning outcome important to all subject-matter areas and that can be measured at all levels of instruction is the ability to recognize the relevance of information. The exercise presented here was prepared for third-grade pupils. An example at the high school level may be found in Appendix F.

EXAMPLES

Bill lost his overshoe on the way to school. He wanted to put a notice on the bulletin board so that the other children could help him find it. Which of the following sentences tell something that would help children find the overshoe?
Directions: Circle yes if it would help. Circle no if it would *not* help.

(yes)	no	1.	The overshoe was black.
yes	(no)	2.	It was very warm.
(yes)	no	3.	It was for his right foot.
yes	(no)	4.	It was a Christmas present.
yes	(no)	5.	It was nice looking.
(yes)	no	6.	It had a zipper.
(yes)	no	7.	It had a gray lining.

Ability to Recognize Warranted and Unwarranted Generalization

The ability to recognize the validity of generalizations is of central importance in the interpretation of data. As a minimum, pupils should be able to determine which conclusions the data support, which the data refute, and which the data neither support nor refute. The data may be in the form of tables, charts, graphs, maps, or pictures, and the test items may be true–false or multiple-choice items. The use of the true–false format is shown in the following example:

EXAMPLES
Mortality of White Persons from Motor Vehicle Accidents in the United States, 1957–1958*

AGE PERIOD (YEARS)	DEATH RATE PER 100,000	
	MALES	FEMALES
All ages	32.9	11.1
1–4	10.5	8.0
5–14	10.4	5.4
15–19	54.2	16.4
20–24	76.3	12.7
25–44	35.6	9.1
45–64	33.1	12.9
65 and over	58.4	22.5

*Source of data: Statistical Bulletin, Metropolitan Life Insurance Company, vol. 42, February 1961.

Directions: The following statements refer to the data in the preceding table. Read each statement and mark your answer according to the following key.

Circle: S if the statement is *supported* by the data in the table.
    R if the statement is *refuted* by the data in the table.
    N if the statement is *neither* supported nor refuted by the data.

 Ⓢ R N 1. The death rate from motor vehicle accidents is higher for men than for women.

 S R Ⓝ 2. Motor vehicle accidents are a major cause of death among young men between the ages of 20 and 24.

 S R Ⓝ 3. Men over 65 years of age drive no more safely than do teenage boys between 15 and 19 years of age.

 S Ⓡ N 4. The largest number of people killed in motor vehicle accidents are 65 years of age or over.

 S Ⓡ N 5. When all ages are combined, only about 11 percent of female deaths can be attributed to motor vehicle accidents.

Ability to Apply Principles

The application of principles may be shown in many different ways. In the following example, pupils are asked to identify principles that explain a situation and to recognize illustrations of a principle:

EXAMPLE

Mary Ann wanted her rose bush to grow faster, and so she applied twice as much chemical fertilizer as was recommended and watered it every evening. About a month later she noticed that the rose bush was dying.
Directions: Which of the following principles is necessary in explaining why the rose bush was dying? If a principle is necessary, circle N, if unnecessary, circle U.

 N Ⓤ 1. A chemical compound is changed into other compounds by taking up the elements of water.

 Ⓝ U 2. Semipermeable membranes permit the passage of fluid.

 N Ⓤ 3. Water condenses when cooled.

 Ⓝ U 4. When two solutions of different concentration are separated by a porous partition, their concentration tends to equalize.

Ability to Recognize Assumptions

Another learning outcome pertinent to the interpretation of various types of information is the ability to identify unstated assumptions that are necessary to a conclusion or course of action. The following item illustrates this type of interpretive exercise.

195

EXAMPLE
Studies have shown that there is a relationship between vocabulary and crime. Crime rates are higher for people with poorly developed vocabularies and crime rates are lower for people with well-developed vocabularies. Older studies have also shown that there is a positive relationship between the number of years of Latin studied and the size and preciseness of an individual's vocabulary. *Conclusion:* Crime rates can be lowered by reintroducing the study of Latin in the schools.

Which one of the following assumptions is necessary to reach such a conclusion?

A   Correlational methods were used to determine these relationships.
B   These reported relationships were statistically significant.
Ⓒ   Relationships such as these imply causation.
D   Latin scholars have a low crime rate.

Ability to Recognize Inferences

In interpreting written material, it is frequently necessary to draw inferences from the facts given. The following exercise measures the extent to which pupils are able to recognize warranted and unwarranted inferences drawn from a passage:

EXAMPLE[2]
Directions: Assuming that the information below is true, it is possible to establish other facts using the ones in this paragraph as a basis for reasoning. This is called drawing inferences. There is, of course, a limit to the number of kinds of facts which may be properly inferred from any statement.

By writing the proper symbol in the space provided, indicate that a statement is TRUE, if it may be properly inferred from the information given in the paragraph. Indicate that it is UNTRUE, if the information given in the paragraph implies that it is false. Indicate that NO INFERENCE can be drawn if the statement cannot be inferred one way or the other. Use only the information given in the paragraph as a basis for your responses. . . .

Use the following symbols in writing your answers:

T — if the statement may be inferred as TRUE.
F — if the statement may be inferred as UNTRUE.
N — if no inference can be drawn about it from the paragraph.

PARAGRAPH A

By the close of the thirteenth century there were several famous universities established in Europe, though of course they were very different from modern ones. One of the earliest to be founded was one of the most widely known. This was the University of Bologna, where students from all countries came who wished to have the best training in studying Roman Law. Students especially interested in philosophy and theology went to the University of Paris. Those who wished to study medicine went to the Universities of Montpellier or Salerno.

[2]Horace T. Morse and George H. McCune, *Selected Items for the Testing of Study Skills and Critical Thinking*, p. 66, Bulletin No. 15, 5th ed. Copyright © 1971 by National Council for the Social Studies (Washington, D.C.: National Education Association). Used by permission of the publisher.

QUESTIONS ON PARAGRAPH A

(T)   1. There were law suits between people occasionally in those days.
(N)   2. The professors were poorly paid.
(F)   3. In the Middle Ages people were not interested in getting education.
(T)   4. There were books in Europe at that time.
(N)   5. Most of the teaching in these medieval universities was very poor.
(N)   6. There was no place where students could go to study.
(F)   7. There were no doctors in Europe at this time.
(F)   8. There was no way to travel during the Middle Ages.
(T)   9. If a student wanted to be a priest, he would probably attend the University of Paris.
(N)   10. There were no universities in Europe before the thirteenth century.
(N)   11. There was only one language in Europe at this time.

Use of Pictorial Materials

Pictorial materials can serve two useful purposes in interpretive exercises. (1) They can help measure a variety of learning outcomes similar to those already discussed simply by replacing the written or tabular data with a pictorial presentation. This use is especially desirable with younger pupils and when ideas can be more clearly conveyed in pictorial form. (2) Pictorial materials can also measure the ability to interpret graphs, cartoons, maps, and other pictorial materials. In many school subjects, these are important learning outcomes in their own right.

The following examples illustrate the use of pictorial materials:

EXAMPLE I

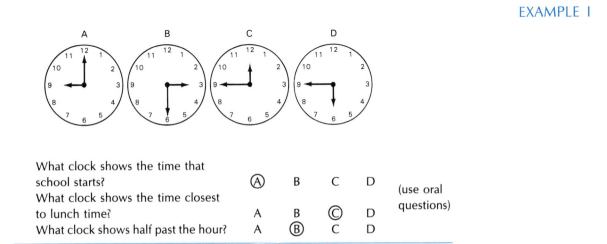

What clock shows the time that
school starts?   Ⓐ   B   C   D
                                                                    (use oral
What clock shows the time closest   questions)
to lunch time?   A   B   Ⓒ   D
What clock shows half past the hour?   A   Ⓑ   C   D

EXAMPLE II

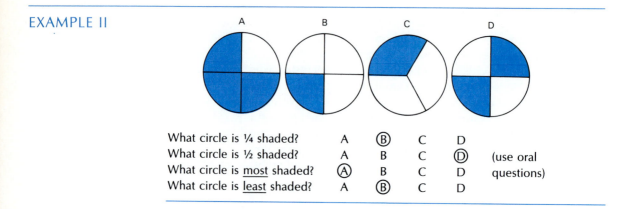

What circle is ¼ shaded?	A	Ⓑ	C	D
What circle is ½ shaded?	A	B	C	Ⓓ	(use oral
What circle is <u>most</u> shaded?	Ⓐ	B	C	D	questions)
What circle is <u>least</u> shaded?	A	Ⓑ	C	D

EXAMPLE III

At the right is a graph of Bill's weekly allowance distribution.

1. What is the ratio of the amount Bill spends for school supplies to the amount he spends for movies?

    A   7 : 2
    Ⓑ   1 : 3
    C   2 : 7
    D   3 : 1

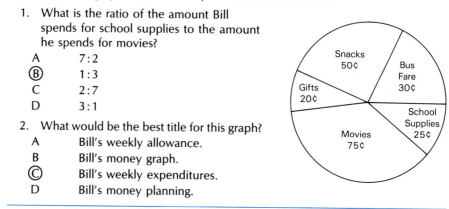

2. What would be the best title for this graph?

    A   Bill's weekly allowance.
    B   Bill's money graph.
    Ⓒ   Bill's weekly expenditures.
    D   Bill's money planning.

    These first three examples were designed for use in lower grades at the elementary level. They illustrate the use of pictorial materials that can be *drawn* by the teacher and items that are useful for measuring rather simple interpretations of concepts and relationships.

    The examples of interpretive exercises on the following pages were designed for higher grade levels. They are included here to illustrate the use of various types of pictorial materials, the measurement of different types of learning outcomes, and the use of both multiple-choice and true–false items. As noted in these examples, the pictures and diagrams used in an interpretive exercise frequently can be obtained from published sources. When this is done, care must be taken in reproducing the pictorial elements to make certain that they are clear and detailed enough for proper interpretation. It is also important, of course, to be aware of the copyright laws that govern the use of the material. However, there is seldom a problem in obtaining permission to reproduce copyrighted materials for classroom use.

EXAMPLE IV[3]

1. The cartoon illustrates which of the following characteristics of the party system in the United States?
   - Ⓐ Strong party discipline is often lacking.
   - B The parties are responsive to the will of the voters.
   - C The parties are often more concerned with politics than with the national welfare.
   - D Bipartisanship often exists in name only.

2. The situation shown in the cartoon is *least* likely to occur at which of the following times?
   - A During the first session of a new Congress
   - B During a political party convention
   - C During a primary election campaign
   - Ⓓ During a presidential election campaign

Cartoons like these can be found in newspapers and news magazines. Then simply prepare questions that require the desired interpretations. Either true–false or multiple-choice items might be used with this type of exercise. It is important to select a cartoon that illustrates a concept or principle that is relevant to the learning outcomes to be measured. Interpretive exercises of this type are especially useful in social studies.

[3]Educational Testing Service, *Making the Classroom Test: A Guide for Teachers*, p. 6. Copyright © 1973 by Educational Testing Service (Princeton, N.J.). Used by permission of the publisher.

EXAMPLE V[4]   In the following questions you are asked to make inferences from the data that are given you on the map of the imaginary country, Serendip. *The answers in most instances must be probabilities rather than certainties.* The relative size of towns and cities is not shown. To assist you, the map is divided into squares lettered vertically from A to E and numbered horizontally from 1 to 5.

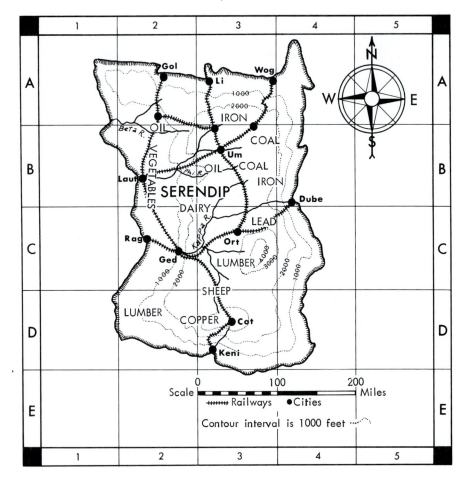

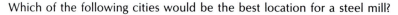

Which of the following cities would be the best location for a steel mill?

A   Li   (3A)
Ⓑ   Um   (3B)
C   Cot   (3D)
D   Dube (4B)

---

[4]Educational Testing Service, *Multiple-Choice Questions: A Close Look*, p. 5. Copyright © 1973 by Educational Testing Service (Princeton, N.J.). Used by permission of the publisher.

This question is based on the following situation:

A piece of mineral is placed in a bottle half-filled with a colorless liquid. A two-holed rubber stopper is then placed in the bottle. The system is then sealed by inserting a thermometer and connecting a glass tube to the stoppered bottle and a beaker of limewater as shown in the accompanying diagram:

EXAMPLE VI[5]

The following series of observations is recorded:

I. Observations during the first few minutes:
    1. Bubbles of a colorless gas rise to the top of the stoppered bottle from the mineral.

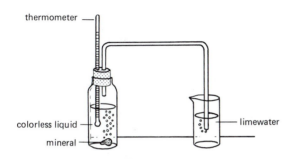

thermometer

colorless liquid

mineral

limewater

    2. Bubbles of colorless gas begin to come out of the glass tube and rise to the surface of the limewater.
    3. The limewater remains colorless throughout this period of time.
    4. The thermometer reads 20° C.
II. Observations at the end of thirty minutes:
    1. Bubbles of colorless gas continue to rise in the stoppered bottle.
    2. The piece of mineral has become noticeably smaller.
    3. There is no apparent change in the level of the liquid in the bottle.
    4. The colorless liquid in the bottle remains colorless.
    5. The thermometer reads 24° C.
    6. The limewater is cloudy.

Which one of the following is the best explanation for the appearance of gas bubbles at the end of the tube in the beaker of limewater?

A   The pressure exerted by the colorless liquid is greater than that exerted by the limewater.
Ⓑ   The bubbles coming from the mineral cause an increased gas pressure in the stoppered bottle.
C   The temperature increase at the end of thirty minutes causes an expansion of gas in the stoppered bottle.
D   The decrease in the size of the piece of mineral causes reduced pressure in the stoppered bottle.

EXAMPLE VII[6]   DISTRIBUTION OF SCIENTISTS BY UNITED STATES GEOGRAPHIC DIVISION, 1960

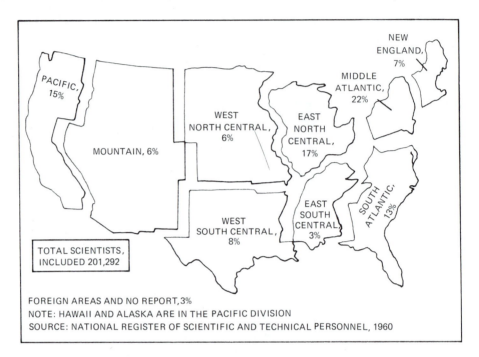

Directions: The following statements refer to the data in the above map. Read each statement, and mark your answer according to the following key.

Circle: T — if the data in the map are sufficient to make the statement *true.*

F — if the data in the map are sufficient to make the statement *false.*

I — if the data in the map are *insufficient* to determine whether the statement is true or false.

(T)   F   I   1. The South Atlantic division has more than twice as many scientists as the West North Central division.

T   F   (I)   2. More scientists are trained in the Middle Atlantic division than in any other division.

T   F   (I)   3. The number of scientists is increasing more rapidly in the eastern divisions than in the western divisions.

(T)   F   I   4. There are more than 6,000 scientists in the East South Central division.

T   (F)   I   5. There are fewer scientists per square mile in the New England division than in any other division.

T   F   (I)   6. There is less need for scientists in the Mountain division than in the Pacific division.

---

[6]The map on which this item is based was reproduced from *Scientific Manpower Bulletin*, No. 17, National Science Foundation (Washington, D.C.: April 1962). Used by permission of the publisher.

Advantages and Limitations of Interpretive Exercises

The interpretive exercise has several advantages over the single, independent objective test item. *First*, the introductory material makes it possible to measure the ability to interpret written materials, charts, graphs, maps, pictures, and other communication media encountered in everyday situations. The rapid expansion of knowledge in every subject-matter area has made it impossible to learn all of the important factual information in a given field, which has led to greater dependence on libraries, reference materials, self-study techniques, and, consequently, interpretive skills. *Second*, the interpretive exercise makes it possible to measure more complex learning outcomes than can be measured with the single objective item. Some data, such as those presented in the interpretive exercise are necessary if pupils are to demonstrate thinking and problem-solving skills. The inclusion of such data in individual test items is possible but awkward. In addition, by having a series of related test items based on a common set of data, both greater depth and breadth can be obtained in the measurement of intellectual skills. *Third*, the interpretive exercise minimizes the influence of irrelevant factual information on the measurement of complex learning outcomes. As we noted with the single multiple-choice item, pupils may be unable to demonstrate their understanding of a principle simply because they do not know some of the facts concerning the situation to which they are to be applied. This blocking of response, caused by a lack of detailed factual information not directly pertinent to the purpose of the measurement, can be largely eliminated with the interpretive exercise. In the introductory materials, we can give pupils the common background of information needed to demonstrate understanding, thinking skills, and problem-solving abilities.

The main advantage of the interpretive exercise over the essay test, in measuring complex achievement, is derived from its greater structure. Pupils are not free to redefine the problem or to demonstrate those thinking skills in which they are most proficient. The series of objective items forces them to use only the mental processes called for. This, of course, also makes it possible to measure separate aspects of problem-solving ability and to use objective scoring procedures.

As with all forms of test items, the interpretive exercise does have some limitations. Probably the greatest limiting factor, and one that may have occurred to you as you reviewed the sample items, is the difficulty of construction. Selecting printed materials that are new to the pupils but that are relevant to the instructional outcomes requires considerable searching. When pertinent material is found, it usually must be edited and reworked to make it more suitable for testing purposes. Then, test items must be constructed that demand the specific behaviors indicated in the learning outcomes being measured. The final process is most often circular (i.e., goes back and forth between revising the introductory material and revising the test items until a satisfactory product is obtained). This entire procedure is time consuming and requires much greater skill than that needed to construct single objective test items. But three positive comments can be made regarding the difficulty of constructing interpretive exercises: (1) More and more items of this type now appear in various subject-matter fields. The references at the end of this chapter contain numerous examples that may serve as guides to test construction. (2) The greater instructional emphasis on complex learning outcomes resulting from the use of interpretive exercises offsets the additional effort required in test construction. (3) The task becomes easier with practice and experience.

A second limitation, especially pertinent when the introductory material is in written form, is the heavy demand on reading skill. The poor reader is handicapped by both the difficulty of the reading material and the length of time it takes to read each test exercise. The first problem can be controlled somewhat by keeping the reading level low and the second by using brief passages. Both of these are only partial solutions, however, because the poor reader will still be at a decided disadvantage. In the primary grades and in classes that contain many poor readers, interpretive exercises might be better limited to the use of pictorial materials.

Compared to the essay test, the interpretive exercise has two shortcomings as a measure of complex achievement. First, it cannot measure a pupil's overall approach to problem solving. It is efficient for measuring specific aspects of the problem-solving process, but it does not indicate whether the pupil can integrate and use these skills when faced with a particular problem. Thus, it provides a diagnostic view of the pupils' problem-solving abilities, in contrast with the holistic view of essay questions. Second, because the interpretive exercise usually uses selection items, it is confined to learning outcomes at the recognition level. To measure the ability to *define* problems, to *formulate* hypotheses, to *organize* data, and to *draw* conclusions, supply procedures such as the essay test must be used.

Suggestions for Constructing Interpretive Exercises

There are two main tasks in constructing interpretive exercises: (1) selecting appropriate introductory material and (2) constructing a series of dependent test items. In addition, care must be taken to construct test items that require analyzing the introductory material in terms of complex learning outcomes. The following suggestions will aid in constructing high-quality interpretive exercises:

1. Select introductory material that is relevant to the objectives of the course. Interpretive exercises, like other testing procedures, should measure the achievement of specific instructional outcomes. Success in this regard depends to a large extent on the introductory material, as this provides the common basis for the test items. If the introductory material is too simple, the exercise may become a measure of general information or simple reading skill. On the other hand, if the material is too complex or unrelated to instructional goals, it may become a measure of general reasoning ability. Both extremes must be avoided. Ideally, the introductory material should be pertinent to the course content and complex enough to evoke the mental reactions specified in the course objectives.

The amount of emphasis given to the various interpretive skills in the course objectives is also important. Care must be taken not to overload the test with interpretive items in any particular area. The selection of introductory material should be guided by the emphasis to be given to the measurement of complex achievement and each type of interpretive skill.

*2. **Select introductory material that is appropriate to the pupils' curricular experience and reading level.*** Many complex learning outcomes can be measured with different types of introductory material. The ability to recognize the validity of conclusions, for example, can be measured with written materials, tables, charts, graphs, maps, or pictures. The type used should be familiar to the pupils so that the nature of the material does not prevent them from demonstrating their achievement of the complex learning outcomes. It would be unfair, for example, to ask pupils to recognize the validity of conclusions based on data presented in graph form if they had not had experience in interpreting graphs similar to those used in the test.

When various types of introductory material will serve a purpose equally well and all are familiar to the pupils, we favor material that places the least demand on reading skill. For elementary pupils, pictorial materials are definitely favored. For higher grade levels, pictorial materials and verbal materials with a low vocabulary load and simple sentences are preferred. Although general reading skill is necessary in all written tests, it can become prominent in interpretive exercises unless efforts are made to minimize its influence.

*3. **Select introductory material that is new to pupils.*** In order to measure complex learning outcomes, the introductory material must be new. Asking pupils to interpret materials identical to those used in instruction does not ensure that the exercise will measure anything other than rote memory. Too much novelty, however, must be avoided. Materials similar to those used in class but that vary slightly in content or form are the most desirable. Such materials can be obtained by modifying selections from textbooks, newspapers, news magazines, and various reference materials pertinent to the course content.

*4. **Select introductory material that is brief but meaningful.*** Another method of minimizing the influence of general reading skill on the measurement of complex learning outcomes is to keep the introductory material as brief as possible. Digests of articles are frequently available and are good raw material for interpretive exercises. If digests are unavailable, the summary of an article or a key passage may be sufficient. In some cases, the relevant information is summarized better in a table, diagram, or picture.

In striving for brief introductory material, be careful not to omit elements that are crucial to the interpretive skills being measured. The material also should, of course, be complete enough to be meaningful and interesting to the pupils.

*5. **Revise introductory material for clarity, conciseness, and greater interpretive value.*** Although some materials (for example, graphs) can be used without revision, most selections require some adaptation for testing purposes. Technical articles frequently contain long, detailed descriptions of events. On the other hand, news reports and digests of articles are brief but often present exaggerated reports of events to attract the reader's interest. Although such reports provide excellent material for measuring the ability to judge the relevance of arguments, the need for assumptions, the validity of conclusions, and the like, the material must usually be modified to be used effectively.

Revision of the introductory material and construction of the related test items tend to be interdependent procedures. Rewriting material often suggests questions to be used, and the construction of test questions often necessitates revisions of the material. In revising a description of an experiment, for example, assumptions, hypotheses, or conclusions explicitly stated in the description may be deleted and used as a basis for questions. Likewise, a question calling for application of the experimental findings may require the addition of new material to the selection. Thus, the revision of the introductory material and the construction of test items proceed in a circular fashion until a clear, concise interpretive exercise evolves.

6. Construct test items that require analysis and interpretation of the introductory material. There are two common errors in the construction of interpretive exercises that invalidate them as a measure of complex achievement. One is to include questions that are answered directly in the introductory material —that is, asking for factual information explicitly stated in the selection. Such questions measure simple reading skill. The second is to include questions that can be answered correctly without reading the introductory material — that is, requiring answers based on general information. These questions, of course, merely measure simple knowledge outcomes.

If the interpretive exercise is to function as intended, it should include only those test items that require pupils to read the introductory material and to make the desired interpretations. In some instances, the interpretations will require pupils to supply knowledge beyond that presented in the exercise. In others, the interpretations will be limited to the factual information provided. The emphasis on knowledge and interpretive skill will be determined by the learning outcomes being measured. Regardless of the emphasis, however, the test items should be dependent on the introductory material, while at the same time calling forth mental reactions of a higher order than those related to simple reading comprehension.

7. Make the number of test items roughly proportional to the length of the introductory material. It is inefficient to have pupils analyze a long, complex selection of material and then answer only one or two questions about it. Although it is impossible to specify the exact number of questions that should accompany a given amount of material, the items presented earlier in this chapter show a desirable balance. Other things being equal, we always favor the interpretive exercise that has brief introductory material and a relatively large number of test items.

8. In constructing test items for an interpretive exercise, observe all pertinent suggestions for constructing objective items. The form of test item used in the interpretive exercise will determine the rules for construction. If the multiple-choice or true–false items are used, the suggestions for constructing these item types should be followed. When modified forms are used, suggestions for constructing each of the various types of objective items should be reviewed for their applicability in construction. Freedom from irrelevant clues and technical defects is as important in interpretive exercises as it is in single, independent test items.

   9. In constructing key-type test items, make the categories homogeneous and mutually exclusive. The key-type item, which is used rather often in interpretive exercises, is a modified multiple-choice form that uses a common set of alternatives. In this regard, it is also similar to the matching item and so should be constructed in the same way, with special attention devoted to the categories used in the key. All of the categories in any one key should be homogeneous; that is, they all should be concerned with similar types of judgment. At the same time, there should be no overlapping of categories. Each alternative should provide a separate category so that there is a clear-cut system of classification and each item has only one correct answer.

The majority of dental scientists agree that fluoridated water reduces tooth decay. A number of cities have fluoridated their water supply, and reports indicate that fluoridated water is both safe and inexpensive. Despite an intensive educational campaign pointing out the benefits of fluoridated water, many cities do not yet have it.
Resolved: In the interests of national health, all cities should be required to fluoridate their water supply.
Directions: Read each of the following statements carefully. In front of each statement mark

   KEY: A — if the statement supports the resolution.
            B — if the statement contradicts the resolution.
            C — if the statement is a fact.
            D — if the statement is an opinion.
   _____1. The long-range effects of fluoridated water on an individual's
                  health have not been studied.
                      (Similar items complete the exercise.)

EXAMPLE

   In this example, the key includes two overlapping categories, one concerned with the relationship of each statement to the resolution and the other with the nature of the statement itself. This makes it impossible to have only one correct answer for each statement. Item 1, for example, would have to be marked category B because it contradicts the resolution and category C because it is a statement of fact.
   The above key could be improved by limiting the categories to the relevance of the statements to the resolutions, as illustrated in the following key:

   KEY: A — if the statement *supports* the resolution.
         B — if the statement *contradicts* the resolution.
         C — if the statement neither supports nor contradicts the resolution.

EXAMPLE

If judging both the factual nature of a statement and its relevance is important, these two elements can be combined to form discrete categories as follows:

> KEY: A — if it is a statement of *fact* that *supports* the resolution.
> B — if it is a statement of *opinion* that *supports* the resolution.
> C — if it is a statement of *fact* that *contradicts* the resolution.
> D — if it is a statement of *opinion* that *contradicts* the resolution.

The main drawback to combining two types of judgment in one category is the greater complexity of the key. This is especially undesirable with younger pupils.

10. **In constructing key-type test items, develop standard key categories where applicable.** Despite the usefulness of the interpretive exercise for measuring complex achievement, classroom teachers have not used it extensively, often because of the difficulty of construction. The popularity of the key-type item in interpretive exercises is probably because it uses a common set of alternatives. This makes it easier to construct than the regular multiple-choice form, which requires a different set of alternatives for each item.

It is often possible to simplify further the construction of key-type interpretive exercises by preparing key categories that can be reused with different content. For example, a learning outcome such as the ability to recognize assumptions might lead to the following key:

EXAMPLE

> KEY: A — an assumption that is necessary to make the conclusion valid.
> B — an assumption that would invalidate the conclusion.
> C — an assumption that has no bearing on the validity of the conclusion.

This key could be used with a brief description of a situation, a conclusion based on the situation, and a list of assumptions. Both the key and the form of the item could be used repeatedly, with only the content varying. Although selecting new content material is still a problem, the framework of the standard key categories simplifies the process.

Standard key categories, of course, cannot be used in all areas and their use should not be permitted to determine which learning outcomes receive emphasis. Rather, the time and effort saved by such procedures should free the teacher to explore more creative applications of the interpretive exercise in other areas.

Summary

Complex achievement refers to those learning outcomes based on the higher mental processes. Such outcomes are classified under various general headings, including understanding, reasoning, thinking, and problem solving. The attainment

Checklist for Reviewing Interpretive Exercises

REVIEW QUESTIONS	YES	NO
1. Is this the most appropriate item format to use?	___	___
2. Is the material to be interpreted relevant to the intended learning outcomes?	___	___
3. Is the material to be interpreted appropriate to the pupils' curricular experience and reading level?	___	___
4. Have pictorial materials been used whenever appropriate?	___	___
5. Does the material to be interpreted contain some novelty (to require interpretation)?	___	___
6. Is the material to be interpreted brief, clear, and meaningful?	___	___
7. Are the test items based directly on the introductory material (cannot be answered without it), and do they call for *interpretation* (not just recall or simple reading skills)?	___	___
8. Has a reasonable number of test items been used in each interpretive exercise?	___	___
9. Do the test items meet the relevant criteria of effective item writing?	___	___
10. When key-type items are used, are the categories homogeneous and mutually exclusive?	___	___
11. If revised, are the interpretive exercises still relevant to the intended learning outcomes?	___	___
12. Have the interpretive exercises been set aside for a time before reviewing them?	___	___

of goals in these areas can be measured by both objective and subjective means. The most commonly used objective item is the *interpretive exercise.*

The interpretive exercise consists of a series of objective questions based on written materials, tables, charts, graphs, maps, or pictures. The questions require pupils to demonstrate the specific interpretive skill being measured. For example, pupils might be asked to recognize assumptions, inferences, conclusions, relationships, applications, and the like. The structure of the interpretive exercise makes it possible to obtain independent measures of each aspect of thinking and problem-solving skill. Although it is efficient for measuring such learning outcomes, it does not measure pupils' ability to integrate and use these skills in a global attack on a problem. Thus, it is limited to a diagnostic analysis of problem-solving skills.

Probably the main reason for not using the interpretive exercise is the difficulty of construction. This process involves (1) selecting appropriate introductory material, (2) revising the material so as to fit the outcomes to be measured, and (3) constructing a series of dependent test items that call forth the desired behavior. Although these steps are admittedly time consuming, the rewards in improved teaching – learning practices seem to justify the time and effort.

Learning Exercises

1. What are the advantages of the interpretive exercise over the essay test for measuring complex achievement? What are the disadvantages?
2. For which types of learning outcomes is the interpretive exercise most likely to be appropriate? Why?
3. Discuss the relative merits of the interpretive exercise and the single-item multiple-choice question. For which situation would each be most useful? What are the limitations of each?
4. Construct one interpretive exercise for each of the following:
    a. A paragraph of written material.
    b. A picture or cartoon.
    c. A chart or graph.
5. What steps would you follow in examining an interpretive exercise to determine whether it had been properly constructed?
6. What are some of the factors to consider when you are deciding whether to use interpretive exercises in a classroom test?

Suggestions for Further Reading

MEHRENS, W. A., AND LEHMANN, I. J. *Measurement and Evaluation in Education and Psychology*, 3d ed. New York: Holt, Rinehart & Winston, 1984. See Chapter 7, "Writing Objective Test Items: The Multiple-Choice and Context-Dependent Items," for sample interpretive exercises and suggestions for construction.

NITKO, A. J. *Educational Tests and Measurement: An Introduction*. New York: Harcourt Brace Jovanovich, 1983. See Chapter 9, "Writing Items to Test Higher Level Cognitive Abilities," for item construction using pictures, graphs, maps, and printed material.

WESMAN, A. G. "Writing the Test Item." In R. L. Thorndike, ed., *Educational Measurement*. Washington, D.C.: American Council on Education, 1971. An extended treatment of the topic of item writing. See pages 120 – 128 for the construction of interpretive exercises.

ILLUSTRATIVE TEST ITEMS

MORSE, H. T., AND McCUNE, G. H. *Selected Items for the Testing of Study Skills and Critical Thinking*. Washington, D.C.: National Council for the Social Studies, 1971.

Multiple-Choice Questions: A Close Look. Princeton, N.J.: Educational Testing Service, 1973. Illustrates the use of the multiple-choice item for measuring complex achievement in a variety of fields. Maps, graphs, pictures, diagrams, and written materials are used. Each item is followed by a statistical and logical analysis of its effectiveness.

Chapter 9

Measuring Complex Achievement: The Essay Test

Some aspects of complex achievement are difficult to measure objectively. . . . Learning outcomes that indicate pupils are to originate ideas . . . to organize and express ideas . . . and to integrate ideas in a global attack on a problem . . . require the greater freedom of response provided by the essay test.

Up to this point, our main concern has been with objective test items. We noted that such items can measure a variety of learning outcomes, from simple to complex, and that the interpretive exercise is especially useful for measuring complex achievement. Despite this wide applicability of objective-item types, there remain significant instructional outcomes for which no satisfactory objective measurements have been devised. These include such outcomes as the ability to recall, organize, and integrate ideas; the ability to express oneself in writing; and the ability to supply rather than merely identify interpretations and applications of data. Such outcomes require less structuring of response than that imposed by objective test items, and it is in the measurement of these outcomes that the essay question serves its most useful purpose.

Forms and Uses of Essay Questions

We shall limit our discussion of the essay question to its use in the measurement of complex achievement although we recognize that many teachers use essay questions to measure knowledge of factual information. Unfortunately, this is probably one of its principal uses in classroom testing, but using essay tests to measure factual knowledge is seldom warranted. The distinctive feature of essay questions is the freedom of response. Pupils are free to select, relate, and present ideas in their own words. Although this freedom enhances the value of essay questions as a measure of complex achievement, it introduces scoring difficulties that make them inefficient as a measure of factual knowledge. For most purposes, knowledge of factual information can be more efficiently measured by some type of objective item.

Essay questions should be primarily used to measure those learning outcomes that cannot be measured by objective test items. The special features of essay questions can be utilized most fully when their shortcomings are offset by the need for such measurement. Learning outcomes concerned with the abilities to select, organize, integrate, relate, and evaluate ideas require the freedom of response and the originality provided by essay questions. In addition, these outcomes are of such great educational significance that the expenditure of energy in the difficult and time-consuming task of evaluating the answers can be easily justified.

The freedom of response provided by essay questions is not an all-or-nothing affair but, rather, a matter of degree. At one extreme, the response is almost as restricted as that in the short-answer objective item, in which a sentence or two may be all that is required. At the other extreme, pupils are given almost complete freedom in making their responses, and their answers may require several pages. Although variations in freedom of response tend to fall along a continuum between these extremes, essay questions can be conveniently classified into two types, the restricted response type and the extended response type referred to earlier.

Restricted Response Questions

The restricted response question usually limits both the content and the response. The content is usually restricted by the scope of the topic to be discussed. Limitations on the form of response are generally indicated in the question.

EXAMPLES

State the main differences between the Korean War and previous wars in which the United States has participated.

Why is the barometer one of the most useful instruments for forecasting weather? Answer in a brief paragraph.

Describe two situations that demonstrate the application of the law of supply and demand. Do not use those examples discussed in class.

Another way of restricting responses in essay tests is to base the questions on specific problems. For this purpose, introductory material like that used in interpretive exercises can be presented. Such items differ from objective interpretive exercises only by the fact that essay questions are used instead of multiple-choice or true–false items.

The majority of dental scientists agree that flouridating a city's water supply is a safe and inexpensive method of preventing tooth decay. However, many cities have not fluoridated their water because the residents voted against it. One of the main arguments against fluoridation is that *fluoridating a city's water supply violates the individual's freedom of choice.*

   (A) Indicate whether you agree or disagree with the italicized part of the last statement.
   (B) List reasons that support your position.

Because the restricted response question is more structured, it is most useful for measuring learning outcomes requiring the interpretation and application of data in a specific area. In fact, any of the learning outcomes measured by an objective interpretive exercise also can be measured by a restricted response essay question. The difference is that the interpretive exercise requires pupils to select the answer, whereas the restricted response question requires them to supply it. In some instances, the objective interpretive exercise is favored because of the ease and reliability of scoring. In other situations, the restricted response question is better because of its more direct relevance to the learning outcome (e.g., the ability to *formulate* valid conclusions).

   Although restricting pupils' responses to essay questions makes it possible to measure more specific learning outcomes, these same restrictions make them less valuable as a measure of those learning outcomes emphasizing integration, organization, and originality. Restricting the scope of the topic to be discussed and indicating the nature of the response desired limit the pupil's opportunity to demonstrate these behaviors. For such outcomes, greater freedom of response is needed.

Extended Response Questions

The extended response question allows pupils to select any factual information that they think is pertinent, to organize the answer in accordance with their best judgment, and to integrate and evaluate ideas as they deem appropriate. This freedom enables them to demonstrate their ability to select, organize, integrate, and evaluate ideas. On the other hand, this same freedom makes the extended response question inefficient for measuring more specific learning outcomes and introduces scoring difficulties that severely restrict its use as a measuring instrument.

Compare developments in international relations in the administrations of
President Eisenhower and President Kennedy. Cite examples when possible.

Evaluate the significance of the sea captain's pursuit of the white whale in
Moby Dick.

Describe the influence of Mendel's laws of heredity on the development of
biology as a science.

Write a scientific evaluation of the Copernican theory of the solar system.
Include scientific observations that support your statements.

The need to measure a pupil's global attack on a problem, like that demanded by the extended response question, can be easily defended. The thinking and problem-solving skills measured by objective interpretive exercises and restricted response essay questions seldom function in isolation. In a natural situation they operate together in a manner that includes more than a sum of the skills involved. These skills interact with one another and with the knowledge and understanding the problem requires. Thus, it is not just the skills we are interested in measuring but also how they function together.

Both teachers and test specialists agree that the extended response question does require complex behaviors that cannot be measured by more objective means. But they disagree as to the extent to which the scoring can satisfactorily measure these behaviors. Test specialists point out that the scoring is so unreliable that such questions should not be used for measurement but as teaching devices only. With little regard for the opinions and evidence of test specialists, many teachers continue to use the extended response question to measure pupil achievement. Unfortunately, they frequently do so without regard to the learning outcomes being measured or to the complexities involved in the construction and scoring of such questions. Neither the "head in the sand" position of the test specialists nor the "everything is coming up roses" attitude of the teachers seems to contribute much to the valid measurement of pupil achievement. It seems more sensible to identify the complex behaviors we want to measure, formulate questions that elicit these behaviors, evaluate the results as reliably as we can, and then use these admittedly inadequate data as the best evidence we have available.

Summary Comparison of Learning Outcomes Measured

As noted earlier, the restricted response question can measure a variety of complex learning outcomes similar to those measured by the objective interpretive exercise. The main difference is that the interpretive exercise requires pupils to *select* the answer, and the restricted response question requires the pupil to *supply* the answer. In comparison, the extended response question measures more general learning outcomes, such as the abilities to select, organize, integrate, and evaluate ideas. A summary comparison of the types of complex learning outcomes measured by each of these essay types in comparison with the objective interpretive exercise is presented in Table 9.1.

Type of Test Item	Examples of Complex Learning Outcomes That Can Be Measured	TABLE 9.1 Types of Complex Learning Outcomes Measured by Essay Questions and Objective Interpretive Exercises
Objective Interpretive Exercises	Ability to— identify cause–effect relationship identify the application of principles identify the relevance of arguments identify tenable hypotheses identify valid conclusions identify unstated assumptions identify the limitations of data identify the adequacy of procedures (and similar outcomes based on the pupil's ability to *select* the answer)	
Restricted Response Essay Questions	Ability to— explain cause–effect relationships describe applications of principles present relevant arguments formulate tenable hypotheses formulate valid conclusions state necessary assumptions describe the limitations of data explain methods and procedures (and similar outcomes based on the pupil's ability to *supply* the answer)	
Extended Response Essay Questions	Ability to— produce, organize, and express ideas integrate learnings in different areas create original forms (e.g., designing an experiment) evaluate the worth of ideas	

The learning outcomes in Table 9.1, of course, *merely suggest the types of learning outcomes that can be measured.* With slight modifications in wording, an infinite variety of outcomes can be stated in each area. The essay question's freedom of response is a matter of degree, and thus, the functions of the restricted response question and the extended response question often overlap near the middle of the range.

Advantages and Limitations of Essay Questions

The main advantage of the essay question is that it measures complex learning outcomes that cannot be measured by other means. But the use of essay questions does not guarantee the measurement of complex achievement. To do so, essay questions must be constructed as carefully as are objective test items. The course objectives pertinent to complex achievement must be defined in terms of specific learning outcomes, and the essay questions must be phrased so as to produce the desired behavior. When a table of specifications is used in planning for the test, it is, of course, simply a matter of constructing the questions in accordance with the specifications.

A second advantage of the extended response question is its emphasis on the integration and application of thinking and problem-solving skills. Although objective items such as the interpretive exercise can be designed to measure various aspects of complex achievement, the ability to integrate and apply these skills in a general attack on a problem requires the features of the essay question.

Because the pupils must present their answers in their own handwriting, the essay test is often regarded as a device for improving writing skills. Everyone would agree that the ability to express oneself in writing is an important educational objective. However, there is some question whether the tensions and pressures of test taking provide a good climate for developing writing skills. Written assignments that could be completed under more favorable conditions would contribute more to the attainment of this objective.

Another commonly cited advantage of the essay question is its ease of construction. This factor, probably more than any other, has led to its widespread use by classroom teachers. In a matter of minutes, most teachers can formulate several essay questions, an attractive feature for the busy teacher. This apparent advantage can be very misleading, however. Constructing essay questions that require the specific behaviors emphasized in a particular set of learning outcomes takes considerable time and effort. When ease of construction is stressed, it usually refers to the common practice of dashing off questions at the last minute, with little regard for the course objectives. In such cases there is some question whether ease of construction can be considered an advantage. In addition to the invalidity of the measurement, evaluating the answers to carelessly developed questions tends to be a confusing and time-consuming task.

The limitations of the essay test are so severe that it would probably be discarded entirely as a measuring instrument did it not measure significant learning outcomes that cannot be measured by other means. The most serious limitation is the unreliability of the scoring. Over the years various studies have shown that answers to essay questions are scored differently by different teachers and that even the same teachers score the answers differently at different times. Such results hardly foster confidence in the essay test. In all fairness, however, we should point out that in most studies of the reliability of scoring essay questions, the learning outcomes being measured were not clearly identified. Evaluating essay questions without adequate attention to the learning outcomes being measured is comparable to the "three blind men appraising an elephant." One teacher stresses factual content, one organization of ideas, and another writing skill. With each teacher evaluating the degree to which different learning outcomes are achieved, it is not surprising that their scoring diverges so widely. Even variations in scoring by the same teacher can probably be explained to a large extent by inadequate attention to learning outcomes. When the evaluation of answers is not guided by clearly defined outcomes, it tends to be based on less stable, intuitive judgments. Although the subjective scoring of essay questions will always include some uncontrollable variations, the scoring reliability can be greatly increased by clearly defining the outcomes to be measured, properly framing the questions, carefully following scoring rules, and obtaining practice in scoring.

A closely related limitation of essay questions is the amount of time required for scoring the answers. If the scoring is done conscientiously and helpful comments are written on the papers, even a small number of papers may require several hours of scoring time. If the classes are large and several essay questions are used, conscientious scoring becomes practically impossible. Ironically, most of the suggestions for improving the scoring of essay questions require more time, not less, as might be hoped. The only practical solution is to reserve the use of essay questions for those learning outcomes that cannot be measured objectively. With fewer essay questions to score in a given test, more time will be available for reading and evaluating the answers.

Another shortcoming of essay questions is the limited sampling they provide. So few questions can be included in a given test that some areas are measured thoroughly, but many others are neglected. This inadequate sampling makes essay questions especially inefficient for measuring knowledge of factual information. For such outcomes we can use objective test items and reserve essay questions for measuring complex achievement. This does not eliminate the sampling problem, however, because we would also like an adequate sample of complex behaviors. When we must use essay questions, despite their limited sampling, we should try to obtain as representative a sample as possible. One way of doing this is to accumulate evidence from a series of essay questions administered at different times throughout the school year.

Suggestions for Constructing Essay Questions

The improvement of the essay question as a measure of complex learning outcomes requires attention to two problems: (1) how to construct essay questions that call forth the desired behavior and (2) how to score the answers so that achievement is reliably measured. Here we shall suggest ways of constructing essay questions, and in the next section, we shall suggest ways of improving scoring, although these two procedures are interrelated.

1. Restrict the use of essay questions to those learning outcomes that cannot be satisfactorily measured by objective items. Other things being equal, we always favor objective measurement over subjective measurement. There appears to be little justification for using essay questions to measure learning outcomes that can be satisfactorily measured by more objective means. Likewise, the problems of scoring and the inadequacy of sampling are ample justification for not using essay questions. But when other things are *not* equal, the use of essay questions may be desirable. When objective items are inadequate for measuring the learning outcomes, the use of essay questions can be defended, despite their limitations. Some of the complex learning outcomes, such as those pertaining to the organization, integration, and expression of ideas, will be neglected unless essay questions are used. By restricting its use to these areas, the essay questions' contribution to the evaluation of pupil achievement can be most fully realized.

2. Formulate questions that will call forth the behavior specified in the learning outcomes. As with objective items, essay questions should measure the achievement of clearly defined instructional objectives. If the ability to apply principles is being measured, for example, the questions should be phrased in such a manner that they call forth that particular behavior. Essay questions should never be hurriedly constructed in the hope that they will measure broad, important (but unidentified) educational objectives. Each essay question should be carefully designed to elicit particular aspects of behavior defined in the desired learning outcomes (see box on page 219). The item stems shown in the box are, of course, simply illustrative of the many types of questions that might be asked, and the phrasing of any particular question will vary somewhat from one subject to another.

Constructing essay questions in accordance with particular learning outcomes is much easier with restricted response questions than with extended response questions. The restricted scope of the topic and the type of response expected make it possible to relate a question directly to one or more of the outcomes. For the extended response question, the extreme freedom makes it difficult to phrase the question so that the pupil's responses will reflect the particular learning outcomes desired. This difficulty can be partially overcome by indicating the bases on which the answer will be evaluated.

EXAMPLE

Write a two-page statement defending the importance of conserving our natural resources. (Your answer will be evaluated in terms of its organization, its comprehensiveness, and the relevance of the arguments presented.)

Informing the pupils that they should pay special attention to organization, comprehensiveness, and relevance of arguments defines the task and makes it possible to key the item to a particular set of learning outcomes. These directions alone will not, of course, ensure that the appropriate behaviors will be exhibited. It is only when the pupils have been taught how to organize ideas, how to treat a topic comprehensively, and how to present relevant arguments that such directions will serve their intended purpose.

3. Phrase each question so that the pupil's task is clearly indicated. The purpose a teacher had in mind when formulating a question is often not conveyed to the pupil because of the ambiguous phrasing of the question. As a result, pupils interpret the question differently and give a hodgepodge of answers. Because it is impossible to determine which of the incorrect answers are due to misinterpretation and which to lack of achievement, the results are worse than worthless: They may

Some Types of Thought Questions and Sample Item Stems

1. *Comparing*
   Describe the similarities and differences between . . .
   Compare the following two methods for . . .

2. *Relating cause and effect*
   What are major causes of . . . ?
   What would be the most likely effects of . . . ?

3. *Justifying*
   Which of the following alternatives would you favor, and why?
   Explain why you agree or disagree with the following statement.

4. *Summarizing*
   State the main points included in . . .
   Briefly summarize the contents of . . .

5. *Generalizing*
   Formulate several valid generalizations from the following data.
   State a set of principles that can explain the following events.

6. *Inferring*
   In light of the facts presented, what is most likely to happen when . . . ?
   How would (Senator X) be likely to react to the following issue?

7. *Classifying*
   Group the following items according to . . .
   What do the following items have in common?

8. *Creating*
   List as many ways as you can think of for . . .
   Make up a story describing what would happen if . . .

9. *Applying*
   Using the principle of . . . as a guide, describe how you would solve the following problem situation.
   Describe a situation that illustrates the principle of . . .

10. *Analyzing*
    Describe the reasoning errors in the following paragraph.
    List and describe the main characteristics of . . .

11. *Synthesizing*
    Describe a plan for proving that . . .
    Write a well-organized report that shows . . .

12. *Evaluating*
    Describe the strengths and weaknesses of . . .
    Using the given criteria, write an evaluation of . . .

actually be harmful if used to measure pupil progress toward instructional objectives.

One way to clarify the question is to make it as specific as possible. For the restricted response question, this means rewriting it until the desired response is clearly defined.

EXAMPLE

Poor: Why do birds migrate?

Better: State three hypotheses that might explain why birds migrate south in the fall.

Indicate the most probable one and give reasons for your selection.

The improved version presents the pupils with a definite task. Although some pupils may not be able to give the correct answer, they all will certainly know what type of response is expected. Note also how easy it would be to relate such an item to a specific learning outcome such as "the ability to formulate and defend tenable hypotheses."

When an extended response question is desired, some limitation of the question may be possible, but care must be taken not to destroy its function. If it becomes too narrow, it will be less effective as a measure of the ability to select, organize, and integrate ideas. The best procedure for clarifying the extended response question seems to be the one suggested earlier, that is, to give the pupil explicit directions concerning the type of response desired.

EXAMPLE

Poor: Compare the Democratic and Republican parties.

Better: Compare the current policies of the Democratic and Republican parties with regard to the role of government in private business. Support your statements with examples when possible. (Your answer should be confined to two pages. It will be evaluated in terms of the appropriateness of the facts and examples presented and the skill with which it is organized.)

The first version offers no common basis for responding and, consequently, no frame of reference for evaluating the answer. Even if the only learning outcome being measured is the "ability to organize," greater structure is needed. If pupils interpret a question differently, their answers also will be organized differently, because organization is partly a function of the content being organized. Also, some pupils will narrow the problem before answering thereby give themselves a much easier task of organization than will pupils who attempt to treat the broader aspects of the problem.

The improved version gives pupils a clearly defined task without destroying their freedom to select and organize the answer. This is achieved both by limiting the scope of the question and by including directions concerning the type of answer desired.

The Importance of Writing Skill

Performance on an essay test depends largely on writing ability. If pupils are to be able to demonstrate their achievement of higher-level learning outcomes, they must be taught the thinking and writing skills needed to express themselves. This means teaching them how to select relevant ideas, how to compare and relate ideas, how to organize ideas, how to apply ideas, how to infer, how to analyze, how to evaluate, and how to write a well-constructed answer that includes these elements. Asking pupils to "compare," "interpret," or "apply" has little meaning unless they have been taught how to do it. The answer is not to give more essay tests, as pupils will just repeat their thinking and writing errors. The answer calls for some direct teaching and practice in writing in an atmosphere that is less stressful than an examination period.

4. Indicate an approximate time limit for each question. Most essay questions place a premium on speed of writing, because inadequate attention is paid to time limits during the test's construction. As each question is constructed, the teacher should estimate the approximate time needed for a satisfactory response. In judging the response time to be allotted to a question, keep in mind the slower pupils' writing speed. Most errors in judging the amount of time needed are in the direction of too little time. It is better to use fewer questions and more generous time limits than to put some pupils at a disadvantage.

The time limits allotted to each question should be indicated to the pupils so that they can pace their writing on each question and not be caught at the end of the testing time with "just one more question to go." If the test contains both objective and essay questions, the pupils should, of course, be told approximately how much time to spend on each part of the test. This may be done orally or included on the test form itself. In either case, care must be taken not to create overconcern about time. The *adequacy* of the time limits might very well be emphasized in the introductory remarks, so as to allay any anxiety that might arise.

5. Avoid the use of optional questions. A fairly common practice in the use of essay questions is to give pupils more questions than they are expected to answer and to permit them to choose a given number. For example, the teacher may include six essay questions in a test and direct the pupils to write on any three of them. This practice is generally favored by pupils because they can select those questions they know most about. Except for the desirable effect on pupil morale, however, there is little to recommend the use of optional questions.

If pupils answer different questions, it is obvious that they are taking different tests, and so the common basis for evaluating their achievement is lost. Each pupil is demonstrating the achievement of different learning outcomes. As noted earlier, even the "ability to organize" cannot be measured adequately without a common set of responses because organization is partly a function of the content being organized.

The use of optional questions might also influence the validity of the test results in still another way. When pupils anticipate the use of optional questions, they can prepare answers on several topics in advance, commit them to memory, and then select questions to which the answers are most appropriate. During such advance preparation, it is also possible for them to obtain help from others in selecting and organizing their answers. Needless to say, this provides a distorted measure of the pupil's achievement, and it also tends to have an undesirable influence on study habits, as intensive preparation in a relatively few areas is encouraged.

Checklist for Reviewing Essay Questions

REVIEW QUESTIONS	YES	NO
1. Is this the most appropriate type of item to use?	___	___
2. Are the questions designed to measure higher-level learning outcomes?	___	___
3. Are the questions relevant to the intended learning outcomes?	___	___
4. Does each question clearly indicate the task to be performed?	___	___
5. Are pupils told the bases on which their answers will be evaluated?	___	___
6. Are generous time limits provided for answering the questions?	___	___
7. Are pupils told the time limits and/or point values for each question?	___	___
8. Are all pupils required to respond to the same questions?	___	___
9. If revised, are the questions still relevant to the intended learning outcomes?	___	___
10. Have the questions been set aside for a time before reviewing them?	___	___

Suggestions for Scoring Essay Questions

Improving the reliability of scoring answers to essay questions begins long before the test is administered. The first step is to decide what learning outcomes are to be measured. This is followed by phrasing the questions in accordance with the learning outcomes and including explicit directions concerning the types of answers desired. Only when both the pupils and the teacher understand the task to be performed can reliable scoring be expected. No degree of proficiency in evaluating answers can compensate for poorly phrased questions.

When the necessary preliminary steps have been taken in constructing essay questions, the following suggestions can be used effectively to increase the reliability of the scoring:

1. Prepare an outline of the expected answer in advance. This should contain the major points to be included, the characteristics of the answer (e.g., organization) to be evaluated, and the amount of credit to be allotted to each. For a restricted response question calling for three hypotheses, for example, a list of acceptable hypotheses would be prepared, and a given number of scoring points would be assigned to each. For an extended response question, the major points would be outlined. In addition, the relative amount of credit to be allowed for such characteristics as the accuracy of the factual information, the pertinence of the examples, and the skill of the organization would be indicated.

Preparing a scoring key provides a common basis for evaluating the pupils' answers and increases the likelihood that our standards for each question will remain stable throughout the scoring. If prepared during the test's construction, such a scoring key also helps us phrase questions that clearly convey to the pupils the types of answers expected.

2. Use the scoring method that is most appropriate. There are two common methods of scoring essay questions. One is called the *point method* and the other the *rating method*. With the point method, each answer is compared with the ideal answer in the scoring key, and a given number of points is assigned according to the adequacy of the answer. With the rating method, each paper is placed in one of a number of piles as the answer is read. These piles represent degrees of quality and determine the credit assigned to each answer. If eight points are allotted to the question, for example, nine piles might be used ranging in value from eight points to none. Usually between five and ten categories are used with the rating method.

Restricted response questions generally can be satisfactorily scored by the point method. The restricted scope and the limited number of characteristics included in a single answer make it possible to define degrees of quality precisely enough to assign point values. The extended response question, however, usually requires the rating method. Only gross judgments can be made concerning the relevance of ideas, the organization of the material, and similar qualities evaluated in answers to extended response questions. Classifying such characteristics into ten categories is probably as precise as we can expect to be.

When the rating method is used, it is desirable to rate each characteristic separately. This provides for greater objectivity and increases the diagnostic value of the results.

3. Decide how to handle factors that are irrelevant to the learning outcomes being measured. Several factors influence our evaluations of answers to essay questions that are not directly pertinent to the purposes of the measurement. Prominent among these are legibility of handwriting, spelling, sentence structure, punctuation, and neatness. We should make an effort to keep such factors from influencing our judgment when evaluating the content of the answers. In some instances, such factors may, of course, be evaluated for their own sake. When this is done, you should obtain a separate score for written expression or for each of the specific factors. As far as possible, however, we should not let such factors contaminate the extent to which our test scores reflect the achievement of other learning outcomes.

Another decision concerns the presence of irrelevant and inaccurate factual information in the answer. Should you ignore it and score only that which is pertinent and correct? If you do, some pupils will write everything that occurs to them, knowing that you will sort out and give them credit for anything correct. This discourages careful thinking and desirable evaluative abilities. On the other hand, if you take off points for irrelevant and inaccurate material, the question of how much to lower the score on a given paper is a troublesome one. Probably the best procedure is to decide in advance approximately how much the score on each question is to be lowered when the inclusion of irrelevant material is excessive. The pupils should then be warned that such a penalty will be imposed.

4. Evaluate all answers to one question before going on to the next one. One factor that contributes to unreliable scoring of essay questions is a shifting of standards from one paper to the next. A paper with average answers may appear to be of much higher quality when it follows a failing paper than when it follows one with near-perfect answers. One way to minimize this is to score all answers to the first question, shuffle the papers, then score all answers to the second question, and so on, until all of the answers have been scored. A more uniform standard can be maintained with this procedure because it is easier to remember the basis for judging each answer, and answers of various degrees of correctness can be more easily compared. When the rating method is used and the papers are placed in several piles on the basis of each answer, shifting standards also can be checked by reading each answer a second time and reclassifying it if necessary.

Evaluating all answers to one question at a time helps counteract another type of error that creeps into the scoring of essay questions. When we evaluate all of the answers on a single paper at one time, the first few answers create a general impression of the pupil's achievement that colors our judgment concerning the remaining answers. Thus, if the first answers are of high quality, we tend to overrate the following answers; whereas if they are of low quality, we tend to underrate them. This "halo effect" is less likely when the answers for a given pupil are not evaluated in continuous sequence.

5. Evaluate the answers without looking at the pupil's name. The general impression we form about each pupil during our teaching is also a source of bias in evaluating essay questions. It is not uncommon for a teacher to give a high score to a poorly written answer by rationalizing that "the pupil really knows that material, even though she didn't express it too clearly." A similar answer by a pupil regarded less favorably will receive a much lower score, with the honest conviction that the

Bluffing—A Special Scoring Problem

It is possible for pupils to obtain higher scores on essay questions than they deserve by means of clever bluffing. This is usually a combination of writing skill, general knowledge, and the use of common "tricks of the trade." Following are some ways that pupils might attempt to influence the reader and, thus, inflate their grades.

1. Writing something for every question—even if it is only a restatement of the question. (Pupils figure they might get some credit. Blank spaces get none.)
2. Stressing the importance of the topic covered by the question, especially when short on facts (e.g., "This battle played a significant role in the Civil War.").
3. Agreeing with the teacher's views whenever it seems appropriate (e.g., "The future of mankind depends on how well we conserve our natural resources.").
4. Being a name dropper (e.g., "This is supported by the well-known experiment by Smith." The reader assumes that the pupil knows Smith's "well-known" experiment.).
5. Writing on a related topic and fitting it to the question (e.g., prepared to write on President Harry Truman but asked to write about General Douglas MacArthur, the pupil might start with: "Harry Truman was the president who fired General MacArthur. . . ."—from here on there is more about President Truman than General MacArthur.).
6. Writing in general terms that can fit many situations (e.g., in evaluating a short story, the pupil might say: "This was an interesting story. The characters were fairly well developed, but in some instances more detail would be welcome. . . ." This might be called the *fortune teller* approach.)

Although bluffing cannot be completely eradicated, carefully phrasing the questions and following clearly defined scoring procedures can reduce it.

pupil deserved the lower score. This halo effect is one of the most serious deterrents to reliable scoring by classroom teachers and is especially difficult to counteract.

When possible, the identity of the pupils should be concealed until all answers are scored. The simplest way to do this is to have the pupils put their names on the back of the papers. In some cases, when our curiosity cannot be easily controlled, it is better to identify the papers by numbers rather than names. If a pupil's identity cannot be concealed because of familiar handwriting, the best we can do is make a conscious effort to eliminate any such bias from our judgment.

6. If especially important decisions are to be based on the results, obtain two or more independent ratings. Sometimes essay questions are included in tests used to select pupils for awards, scholarships, special training, and the like. In such cases, two or more competent persons should score the papers independently, and their ratings should be compared. After any large discrepancies have been satisfactorily arbitrated, the independent ratings may be averaged for more reliable results.

Summary

The essay question is especially useful for measuring those aspects of complex achievement that cannot be measured by more objective means. These include (1) the ability to supply rather than merely identify interpretations and applications of data and (2) the ability to select, organize, and integrate ideas in a general attack on a problem. Outcomes of the first type are measured by *restricted response* questions and outcomes of the second type by *extended response* questions.

Although essay questions provide a relevant measure of significant learning outcomes, they have several limitations that restrict their use: (1) the scoring tends to be unreliable; (2) the scoring is time consuming; and (3) only a limited sampling of achievement is obtained. Because of these shortcomings, essay questions should be limited to testing those outcomes that cannot be measured by objective items.

The construction and scoring of essay questions are interrelated processes that require attention if a valid and reliable measure of achievement is to be obtained. Questions should be phrased so that they measure the attainment of definite learning outcomes and clearly convey to the pupils the type of response expected. Indicating an approximate time limit for each question and avoiding the use of optional questions also contributes to more valid results. Scoring procedures can be improved by (1) using a scoring key, (2) adapting the scoring method to the type of question used, (3) controlling the influence of irrelevant factors, (4) evaluating all answers to each question at one time, (5) evaluating without looking at the pupils' names, and (6) obtaining two or more independent ratings when important decisions are to be made.

Learning Exercises

1. In an area in which you are teaching or plan to teach, identify several learning outcomes that can be best measured with essay questions. For each learning outcome construct two essay questions.
2. Criticize the following essay questions, and restate them so that they meet the criteria of a good essay question.
   a. Discuss air transportation.
   b. Do you think the government should spend more on moon exploration?
   c. What is your attitude toward socialized medicine?

3. For each of the following, would it be more appropriate to use an extended response question or a restricted response question?

    a. Compare two periods in history.

    b. Describe the procedure for using a dictionary.

    c. Indicate the advantages of one procedure over another.

    d. Evaluate a short story.

4. Essay tests are frequently defended on the grounds that they give pupils an opportunity to learn to write. How do you react to this view?

5. What factors should be considered in deciding whether essay questions are to be included in a classroom test? Which of the factors are most important?

6. Describe how essay tests might be used to facilitate learning. What types of learning are most likely to be enhanced?

Suggestions for Further Reading

EBEL, R. L., AND FRISBIE, D. A. *Essentials of Educational Measurement*, 4th ed. Englewood Cliffs, N.J.: Prentice-Hall, 1986. Chapter 8, "The Use of Essay Tests," compares essay and objective tests and suggests how to prepare and grade essay questions.

HOPKINS, K. D., AND STANLEY, J. C. *Educational and Psychological Measurement and Evaluation*, 6th ed. Englewood Cliffs, N.J.: Prentice-Hall, 1981. Chapter 8, "Constructing and Using Essay Tests," discusses the limitations of essay tests and how to construct and score them.

MEHRENS, W. A., AND LEHMANN, I. J. *Measurement and Evaluation in Education and Psychology*, 3d ed. New York: Holt, Rinehart & Winston, 1984. Chapter 5, "The Essay Test: Preparing the Questions and Grading the Responses," presents examples of different types of essay questions, a review of the claims for using essay tests, and suggestions for construction and scoring.

NITKO, A. J. *Educational Tests and Measurement: An Introduction*. New York: Harcourt Brace Jovanovich, 1983. Chapter 6, "Developing Essay and Completion Items," describes the construction and scoring of essay items.

Chapter 10

Assembling, Administering, and Appraising Classroom Tests

Care in preparing a test plan and constructing relevant test items should be followed by similar care in . . . reviewing and editing the items . . . arranging the items in the test . . . preparing clear directions . . . reproducing the test . . . and administering and appraising the results. . . . Classroom tests also can be improved by applying simple methods of item analysis . . . and building a test-item file.

Effective classroom testing begins with a test plan that specifically describes the instructional objectives and content to be measured and the relative emphasis to be given to each intended learning outcome. This is followed by the selection of the most appropriate item formats (e.g., multiple choice, essay) and the preparation of test items that are relevant to the learning outcomes specified in the test plan. These steps have received considerable attention in the preceding chapters because they are crucial to the test's validity. The only way we can ensure that a classroom test will serve its intended purpose is to identify the learning outcomes we want to measure and then to construct test items that call forth the specific performance described in the learning outcomes. We must also assemble the items into a test, prepare directions, administer the test, score the test, and interpret and appraise the results.

Our goal throughout the preparation and use of classroom tests is to obtain valid evidence of pupil learning. In the final analysis, valid achievement testing is the end product of a systematically controlled series of steps, beginning with the identification of instructional objectives and ending with the scoring and interpretation of results. Although validity is *built in* during the construction of the test items, systematic procedures of assembly, administration, and scoring will provide greater assurance that the items will function as intended. Appraising the test items after the test has been administered can also help improve the quality of the items. Item analysis procedures provide information for evaluating the functional effectiveness of each item and for detecting weaknesses that should be corrected. This information is useful when reviewing the test with pupils, and it is indispensable when building a file of high-quality items.

Assembling the Classroom Test

The preparation of test items for use in a test is greatly facilitated if the items are properly recorded, if they are written at least several days before they are to be used, and if extra items are constructed.

Recording Test Items

When constructing the test items, it is desirable to write each one on a separate index card. In addition to the test item, the card should contain information concerning the instructional objectives, the specific learning outcome, and the content measured by the item. A space should also be reserved for item-analysis information, usually on the back of the card, to allow room to record the data each time the item is used. A card containing this information is presented in Figure 10.2.

Item cards provide flexibility. As the items are reviewed and edited, they can be eliminated, added, or revised with very little difficulty. The same holds true when arranging the items for the test: They can be arranged and rearranged merely by sorting the cards. The flexibility of this recording system also makes it easy to add the items to a computer item bank.

Reviewing Test Items

No matter how carefully test items have been prepared, defects inadvertently creep in during construction. As we concentrate on the clarity and conciseness of a question, a verbal clue slips in unnoticed. As we attempt to increase an item's difficulty, we unwittingly introduce some ambiguity. As we rework an item to make the incorrect choices more plausible, the behavior called forth by the item is unintentionally modified. In short, we focus so closely on some aspects of item construction that we overlook others. This results in an accumulation of unwanted errors that may distort the item's function. Such technical defects can be most easily detected by (1) reviewing the items after they have been set aside for a few days and (2) asking a fellow teacher to review and criticize them.

In reviewing test items, we should try to view the items from the pupil's viewpoint, as well as from that of the test maker. From these two vantage points, each item should be read carefully and its possible functioning effectiveness judged. The following questions will help you analyze the quality of each item.

1. Is the item format appropriate for the learning outcome being measured? If the learning outcome calls for the *definition* of a term, for example, a supply-type item (e.g., short-answer item) would be appropriate, and a selection-type item (e.g., multiple choice) would be clearly inappropriate. On the other hand, if the intended outcome was simply the *identification* of the correct definition, then a selection-type item would be adequate. Thus, the first step is to check whether the item format is suitable for the type of pupil performance described in the test plan. The action verb in the statement of each specific learning outcome (e.g., defines, describes, identifies) indicates which item format is more appropriate.

2. Does the knowledge, understanding, or thinking skill called forth by the item match the specific learning outcome and subject-matter content being measured? When a table of specifications has been used as a basis for constructing the test items, this is merely a matter of checking to see whether the item is still *relevant* to the same cell in the table. If the item's functioning content has shifted during construction, the item either should be modified so that it serves its original purpose or reclassified in light of the new purpose. In any case, the response called forth by an item should agree with the purpose for which the item is to be used.

3. Is the point of the item clear? A careful review of test items often reveals ambiguity, inappropriate vocabulary, and awkard sentence structure that were overlooked during their construction. Returning to test items after they have been set aside for a few days provides a fresh outlook that makes such defects more apparent. The difficulty of the vocabulary and the complexity of the sentence structure must, of course, be judged in terms of the pupils' maturity level. At all levels, however, ambiguity should be removed. In its final form, each item should be so clearly worded that all pupils understand the task. Whether pupils respond correctly should be determined solely by whether they possess the knowledge or understanding being measured.

4. Is the item free from excessive verbiage? Often, items become excessively wordy because of awkward sentence structure—mentioned in the previous section—or the inclusion of nonfunctional material. Some teachers prefer to justify the use of an item by including a statement or two concerning the problem's importance. Others expand a simple question into an elaborate story situation to make the item more interesting. Although adding such nonfunctional material may be useful in some instances, items are generally more effective when the problem is stated as concisely as possible. When reviewing items, the content of each item should be analyzed to determine the functional elements leading to the correct response. If there are any elements that the pupils may disregard entirely and still respond correctly, they probably should be removed.

Reviewing and Revising Test Items

1. Matching the learning outcome.
Specific Learning Outcome: Identifies the use of weather instruments.

     Item: Describe how the hygrometer works.

     Improved: The hygrometer is used to measure
         A. Air pressure.
        *B. Humidity.
         C. Rainfall.
         D. Wind velocity.

2. Clarifying the point of the item and the desired response.

     Item: Earthquakes are detected by _____.

     Improved: Earthquakes are detected by an instrument called
         (seismograph).

3. Removing excessive verbiage from multiple-choice stems.

     Item: In which one of the following regions of the United States
         can we expect annual rainfall to be the greatest?

     Improved: In which region of the United States is yearly rainfall
         greatest?
         A. Midwest
         B. New England
        *C. Pacific Northwest
         D. Southwest

4. Removing excessive verbiage from multiple-choice alternatives.

     Item: In which dirction do tornadoes move?
        *A. They move toward the Northeast.
         B. They move toward the Northwest.
         C. They move toward the Southeast.
         D. They move toward the Southwest.

     Improved: Tornadoes move toward the
        *A. Northeast.
         B. Northwest.
         C. Southeast.
         D. Southwest.

5. Keeping the reading level low.

     Item: *T F There is a dearth of information concerning the
               possibility that life exists on Mars.

     Improved: *T F There is a lack of information concerning life on
               Mars.

6. Removing verbal clues.

     Item: Evaporation is shown by water changing to
         A. Dew.
         B. Ice.
       *C. Water vapor.

     Improved: Evaporation is shown by water changing to
         A. Dew.
         B. Ice.
       *C. Steam.

5. *Is the item of appropriate difficulty?* If the test item is intended for a criterion-referenced mastery test, its difficulty should, of course, match the difficulty indicated by the statement of the specific learning outcome. No attempt should be made to alter item difficulty to fit some predetermined level. If the test item is to be used in a norm-referenced test, however, a difficulty level of 50 percent is desirable. As we shall see later, this level of difficulty provides the best discrimination between high and low achievers. In reviewing items for a test, all we can do is make our best judgment about item difficulty (unless item analysis data are available), taking into account the nature of the test and the educational background of the pupils.

6. *Does the item have an answer that would be agreed upon by experts?* This is seldom a problem with factual material, which usually can be judged as correct or incorrect. It is mainly a problem with selection-type items that ask for the best reason, the best method, the best interpretation, or whatever, in which the judgment of experts determines the answer. If experts agree on the best answer, fine, but do not include items that require pupils to endorse someone's unsupported opinion (even if it happens to be yours).

7. *Is the item free from technical errors and irrelevant clues?* The checklists for reviewing each of the item types, presented in Chapters 6 through 9, list points to consider in searching out technical errors and irrelevant clues. As noted earlier, an irrelevant clue is any element that leads the nonachiever to the correct answer and thereby prevents the item from functioning as intended. These include (1) grammatical inconsistencies, (2) verbal associations, (3) specific determiners (i.e., words such as *always* and *never*), and (4) some mechanical features, such as correct statements tending to be longer than incorrect ones. Most of these clues can be removed merely by trying to detect them during the item review. They somehow seem more obvious after the items have been set aside for a while.

8. *Is the item free from racial, ethnic, and sexual bias?* A final check should be made to make certain that the vocabulary and problem situation in each item would be acceptable to the members of all groups and would have a similar meaning to them. An effort should be made to remove any type of stereotyping, such as always portraying minorities in subservient roles, women in homemaking roles, and the like. A judicious and balanced use of different roles for minorities and males and females should contribute to more effective testing.

When it is possible to get fellow teachers to review the test items, they should be asked to read each item, indicate the answer, and note any technical defects. If an answer does not agree with the key, it may be because it is ambiguous. Asking another teacher to "think out loud" when deciding on the answer will usually reveal the misinterpretation of the question and the source of the ambiguity. This is how other persons can be most useful. Reviewers will be less helpful in evaluating the types of responses called forth by the items because this requires a knowledge of what the pupils have been taught. Only the teacher who prepared the item knows for sure whether an item measures understanding or merely the retention of a previously learned answer.

When the test items have been revised and those to be included in the test have been tentatively selected, the following questions should be asked:

1. Do the test items measure a representative sample of the learning outcomes and course content included in the test plan?
2. Are there enough test items for each interpretation to be made?
3. Is the difficulty of the test items appropriate for the purpose of the test and for the pupils for whom the test is intended?
4. Are the test items free from overlapping so that the information in one does not provide a clue to the answer in another?

Review of Test Items Selected from Item Banks

Test items selected from workbooks, teachers' guides, instructors' manuals, and item banks are seldom appropriate for use without modification. Thus, before they are used in a classroom test, they should be screened and modified to fit the local instructional program. Both the checklists for reviewing test items, presented in Chapters 6 through 9, and the list of review questions in this chapter are guides for this purpose. Our aim when *selecting* items for classroom use should be the same as when *constructing* them. We want the items to be both technically sound and relevant to what has been taught during the instruction.

The first question can be answered by comparing the final selection of items with the table of specifications or other test plan. Answers to the last three are determined by reviewing the test items in each section of the test and the test as a whole. Affirmative answers to these questions mean the items are ready to be arranged in a final test form.

Arranging Items in the Test

There are various methods of grouping items in an achievement test, and the method will vary somewhat with the use to be made of the results. For most classroom purposes, the items can be arranged by a systematic consideration of (1) the types of items used, (2) the learning outcomes measured, (3) the difficulty of the items, and (4) the subject matter measured.

First and foremost, the items should be arranged in sections by item type. That is, all true–false items should be grouped together, then all matching items, then all multiple-choice items, and so on. This arrangement requires the fewest sets of directions; it is the easiest for the pupils because they can retain the same mental set throughout each section; and it greatly facilitates scoring. When two or more item types are included in a test, there is also some advantage in keeping the simpler item types together and placing the more complex ones in the test, as follows:[1]

1. True–false or alternative-response items.
2. Matching items.
3. Short-answer items.
4. Multiple-choice items.
5. Interpretive exercises.
6. Essay questions.

Arranging the sections of the test in this order produces a sequence that roughly approximates the complexity of the learning outcomes measured, ranging from the simple to the complex. It is then merely a matter of grouping the items *within* each item type. For this purpose, items that measure similar outcomes should be placed together and then arranged in order of ascending difficulty. For example, the items in the multiple-choice section might be arranged in the following order: (1) knowledge of terms, (2) knowledge of specific facts, (3) knowledge of principles, and (4) application of principles. Keeping together the items that measure similar outcomes is especially helpful in determining the types of learning outcomes causing pupils the greatest difficulty.

If, for any reason, it is not feasible to group the items by the learning outcomes measured, it is still desirable to arrange them in order of increasing difficulty. Beginning with the easiest items and proceeding gradually to the most difficult has a motivating effect on pupils. Also, encountering difficult items early in the test often causes pupils to spend a disproportionate amount of time on such items. If the test is long, they may be forced to omit later questions that they could easily have answered.

With the items classified by item type, the sections of the test and the items within each section can be arranged in order of increasing difficulty. Some shifts in the first four item types may be warranted by the difficulty of the items used, but the interpretive exercises and essays tests certainly should be last.

In constructing classroom achievement tests, there is little to be gained by grouping test items according to subject-matter content. When it appears desirable to do so, such as in separating historical periods, these divisions should be kept to a minimum.

To summarize, the most effective method for organizing items in the typical classroom test is to (1) form sections by item type, (2) group the items within each section by the learning outcomes measured, and (3) arrange both the sections and the items within sections in an ascending order of difficulty. Use subject-matter groupings only when needed for some specific purpose.

---

[1] It is not expected that all item types will appear in the same test. Seldom are more than a few types used, but this is the general order.

Preparing Directions for the Test

Teachers sometimes devote considerable time and attention to the construction and assembly of test items and then dash off directions with very little thought. In fact, many teachers include no written directions with their tests, assuming either that the items are self-explanatory or that the pupils are conditioned to answering the types of items used in the test. Some teachers also use oral directions, but they frequently leave much to be desired. Whether written, oral, or both, the directions should include at least the following points:[2]

1. Purpose of the test.
2. Time allowed for answering.
3. Basis for answering.
4. Procedure for recording the answers.
5. What to do about guessing.

The amount of detail for each of these points depends mainly on the pupils' age level, the test's comprehensiveness, the test items' complexity, and the pupils' experience with the testing procedure used. Using new item types and separate answer sheets, for example, requires much more detailed directions than do familiar items requiring pupils merely to circle or underline the answer.

Purpose of the Test.   The purpose of the test is usually indicated when the test is announced or at the beginning of the semester when the evaluation procedures are described as a part of the general orientation to the course. Should there be any doubt whether the purpose of the test is clear to all pupils, however, it could be explained again at the time of testing. This is usually done orally. The only time a statement of the purpose of the test needs to be included in the written directions is when the test is to be administered to several sections taught by different teachers. Then a written statement of purpose ensures greater uniformity.

Time Allowed for Answering.   It is helpful to tell the pupils how much time they will have for the whole test and how to distribute their time among the parts. When essay questions are included, it is also good to indicate approximately how much time should be allotted to each question. This enables the pupils to use their time most effectively and prevents the less-able ones from spending too much time on questions that are particularly difficult for them.

Classroom tests of achievement should generally have liberal time allowances. Except for special computational skills, speed is not important. Our main concern is the level of achievement each pupil has attained. Were it not for practical considerations like the length of class periods and the pressure of other school activities, there would be no need for any time limits with most classroom achievement tests.

---

[2]N. E. Gronlund, *How to Construct Achievement Tests*, 4th ed. (Englewood Cliffs, N.J.: Prentice-Hall, 1988).

Judging the amount of time that pupils will need to complete a given test is not simple. It depends on the types of items used, the age and ability of the pupils, and the complexity of the learning outcomes measured. As a rough guide, the average high school student should be able to answer two true–false items, one multiple-choice item, *or* one short-answer item per minute of testing time. Interpretive test items take much more time; the exact amount depends on the length and complexity of the introductory materials. Also, elementary school pupils generally require more time per item than high school students do, and reading skill is an important determiner of the amount of time needed by a specific group. Experienced teachers familiar with the ability and work habits of a given group of pupils are in the best position to judge time allotments. It is better to err in the direction of allotting too much time than to deprive some of the slower pupils from demonstrating their maximum levels of achievement.

Basis for Answering.   The directions for each section of the test should indicate the basis for selecting or supplying the answers. With true–false, matching, and multiple-choice items, this part of the directions can be relatively simple. For example, a statement like "select the choice that best completes the statement or answers the question" might be sufficient for multiple-choice items. When interpretive exercises are used, however, more detailed directions are necessary because the basis for the response is much more complex. The directions must clearly indicate the type of interpretation expected. As stated in Chapter 8, each interpretive exercise usually requires its own directions.

It is sometimes good to include sample test items correctly marked so that pupils can check their understanding of the basis for answering. This practice is especially helpful to elementary school pupils and to pupils at other levels when complex item types are used.

As noted earlier, essay questions frequently require special directions concerning the type of response expected. If the selection and organization of ideas are emphasized, for example, this should be indicated to the pupils so that they have a more adequate basis for responding.

Procedure for Recording Answers.   Answers may be recorded on the test form itself or on separate answer sheets. If the test is short, the number of pupils taking the test is small, or the pupils are relatively young, answers are generally recorded directly on the test paper. For most other situations, separate answer sheets are preferred because they reduce the time needed for scoring, and they make it possible to use the test papers over again. The latter feature is especially useful when the test is to be given to pupils in different sections of the same course.

Directions for recording the answer on the test paper itself can be relatively simple. With selection items, it is merely a matter of instructing the pupils to circle, underline, or check the *letter* indicating the correct answer. For pupils in the primary grades, it is usually better to ask them to mark the answer directly by drawing a line under it. With supply items, the directions should indicate where to put the answer and the units in which it is to be expressed if the answer is numerical.

Course_____   Name_____

Section_____   Date _____

Test_____   Score: Part I_____

                                             Part II_____

                                             Total_____

DIRECTIONS: Read all directions on the test paper carefully and follow them exactly. For each test item, indicate your answer on this sheet by crossing out the appropriate letter (x) or filling the appropriate blank. Be sure that the number on the answer sheet is the same as the number of the test item you are answering.

True-False		Multiple-Choice		Short-Answer	
Item	Answer	Item		Item	Answer
1	T F	21	A B C D E	41	_____
2	T F	22	A B C D E	42	_____
3	T F	23	A B C D E	43	_____
4	T F	24	A B C D E	44	_____

FIGURE 10.1
Top portion of a teacher-made answer sheet.

Separate answer sheets are easily constructed, and the directions for their use can be placed on the test paper or on the answer sheet itself. A common type of teacher-made sheet is shown in Figure 10.1. The directions on this sheet are rather general, as they must cover instructions for recording various types of answers. Pupils are instructed to cross out rather than circle the letters indicating the correct answers, to facilitate scoring with a stencil key. Circled letters cannot be readily seen through holes in a stencil.

Special answer sheets for machine scoring can be used with classroom tests, but there is no advantage in using them unless machine scoring facilities are readily available and the number of papers to be scored warrants the expense. When machine scoring is used, special directions should be obtained from the company supplying the scoring service.

What to Do About Guessing.   When selection-type items are used, the directions should tell pupils what to do when they are uncertain of the answer. Should they guess or omit the item? If no instructions are given on this point, the bold pupils will guess freely, whereas others will answer only those items of which they are fairly certain. The bold pupils will select some correct answers just by lucky guesses, and thus their scores will be higher than they should be. On the other hand, if the pupils are merely instructed "Do not guess" or "Answer only those items of which you are certain," the more timid pupils will omit many items they could answer correctly. Such pupils are not very certain about anything, which prevents them from responding even when they are reasonably sure of the answers. With these directions, the bold pupils will continue to guess, although possibly not quite so wildly.

As Cronbach[3] pointed out, the tendency to guess or not to guess when in doubt about an item is determined by personality factors and cannot be entirely eliminated by directions that caution against guessing or that promise penalties to those who do guess. The only way to eliminate variations in the tendency to guess is to instruct pupils to answer every item. When this is done, no pupil is given a special advantage, and it is unnecessary to correct for guessing in the scoring. Directions such as the following are usually sufficient to communicate this to the pupils: "Because your score is the number right, be sure to answer every item."

Some teachers object to such directions on the grounds that encouraging guessing is undesirable from an educational standpoint. Most responses to doubtful items are not wild guesses, however, but are guided by some information and understanding. In this respect, they are not too different from the *informed* guesses we make when we predict weather, judge the possible consequences of a decision, or choose one course of action over another. Problem solving always involves a certain amount of this type of *informed* guessing.

A more defensible objection to directions that encourage guessing is that the chance errors introduced into the test scores lower the accuracy of measurement. Although this is certainly objectionable, it probably has less influence on the validity of the results than does the systematic advantage given to the *bold* guessers by the *do not guess* directions.

For liberally timed classroom tests, the *answer-every-item* directions are favored. But for speed tests and when teachers want to discourage guessing, directions such as the following are a good compromise:

> Answer all items for which you can find some reasonable basis for answering, even though you are not completely sure of the answer. *Do not guess wildly*, however, because there will be a correction for guessing.[4]

There seems to be a tendency in standardized testing to use the *make informed guesses but not wild guesses* type of directions. Speed, however, is more significant in standardized testing than in ordinary classroom testing, and the test items are not

---

[3]L. J. Cronbach, *Essentials of Psychological Testing*, 4th ed. (New York: Harper & Row, 1984).
[4]The correction-for-guessing formula and the rationale for its use will be discussed later in this chapter.

as closely keyed to the pupils' learning experiences. When the pupils are familiar with the test's content and have ample opportunity to consider every item, there is generally no need to warn against *wild* guesses or to correct for them.

Reproducing the Test

In preparing the test materials for reproduction, it is important that the items be spaced and arranged so that they can be read, answered, and scored with the least amount of difficulty. Cramming too many test items onto a page is poor economy. What little paper is saved will not make up for the time and confusion that results during the administration and scoring of the test.

All test items should have generous borders. Multiple-choice items should have the alternatives listed in a vertical column beneath the stem of the item, rather than across the page. Items should not be split, with parts of the item on two different pages. With interpretive exercises, the introductory materials can sometimes be placed on a facing page or separate sheet, with all of the items referring to it on a single page.

Unless a separate answer sheet is used, the space for answering should be down one side of the page, preferably the left. The most convenient method of response is

---

Helping Pupils Prepare for Tests

A. General preparation

1. Suggest ways of studying.
2. Give practice tests like those to be used.
3. Teach test-taking skills (see Chapter 13).
4. Teach how to write well-organized essay answers.
5. Stress the value of tests for improving learning.

B. Preparation for each test.

1. Announce in advance when the test will be given.
2. Describe the conditions of testing (e.g., one hour, closed book).
3. Describe the test's length and the types of items to be used (e.g., 20 multiple-choice and 3 essay items).
4. Describe the content and type of performance to be covered (a table of specifications is useful for this).
5. Describe how the test will be scored and how the results will be used.
6. Give the students sample items *similar* to those in the test (use a short practice test or present items orally and discuss answers).
7. Relieve anxiety by using a positive approach in describing the test and its usefulness.

circling the letter of the correct answer. With this arrangement, scoring is simply a matter of placing a strip scoring key beside the column of answers.

Test items should be numbered consecutively throughout the test. Each test item will need to be identified during discussion of the test and for other purposes such as item analysis. When separate answer sheets are used, consecutive numbering is, of course, indispensable.

The duplication of classroom tests is usually by mimeograph, Ditto machine, photo-offset method, or computer printing. Regardless of the process selected, it is desirable to proofread the entire test before it is administered. Charts, graphs, and other pictorial material must be checked to ensure that the reproduction has been accurate and the details clear.

Administering and Scoring Classroom Tests

The same care that went into the preparation of the test should be carried over into its administration and scoring. Here we are concerned with (1) providing optimum conditions for obtaining the pupils' responses and (2) selecting convenient and accurate procedures for scoring the results.

Administering the Test

The guiding principle in administering any classroom test is that *all pupils must be given a fair chance to demonstrate their achievement of the learning outcomes being measured*. This means a physical and psychological environment conducive to their best efforts and the control of factors that might interfere with valid measurement.

Physical conditions such as adequate work space, quiet, proper light and ventilation, and comfortable temperature are sufficiently familiar to teachers to warrant little attention here. Of greater importance, but frequently neglected, are the psychological conditions influencing test results. Pupils will not perform at their best if they are tense and anxious during testing. Some of the things that create excessive test anxiety are

1. Threatening pupils with tests if they do not behave.
2. Warning pupils to do their best "because this test is important."
3. Telling pupils they must work fast in order to complete the test on time.
4. Threatening dire consequences if they fail the test.

The antidote to test anxiety is to convey to the pupils, by both word and deed, that the test results are to be used to help them improve their learning. They also should be reassured that the time limits are adequate to allow them to complete the test. This, of course, assumes that the test will be used to improve learning and that the time limits are adequate.

The time of testing can also influence the results. If tests are administered just before the "big game" or the "big dance," the results may not be representative. Furthermore, for some pupils, fatigue, the onset of illness, or worry about a particular problem may prevent maximum performance. Arranging the time of testing accordingly and permitting its postponement when appropriate can enhance the validity of the results.

The actual administration of the test is relatively simple, because a properly prepared classroom test is practically self-administering. Oral directions, if used, should be presented clearly. Any sample problems or illustrations put on the blackboard should be kept brief and simple. Beyond this, suggestions for administering a classroom test consist mainly of things to avoid.

1. Do not talk unnecessarily before the test. When a teacher announces that there will be "a full forty minutes" to complete the test and then talks for the first ten minutes, pupils feel that they are being unfairly deprived of testing time. Besides, just before a test is no time to make assignments, admonish the class, or introduce next week's topic. Pupils are mentally set for the test and will ignore anything not pertaining to the test for fear it will hinder their recall of information needed to answer the questions. Thus, the well-intentioned remarks fall on "deaf ears" and merely increase anxiety toward the test and create hostility toward the teacher.

2. Keep interruptions to a minimum during the test. At times a pupil will ask to have an ambiguous item clarified, and it may be beneficial to explain the item to the entire group at the same time. Such interruptions are necessary but should be kept to a minimum. All other distractions outside and inside the classroom should, of course, also be eliminated when possible. It is sometimes helpful to hang a "Do not disturb — TESTING" sign outside the door.

Steps to Prevent Cheating

1. Take special precautions to keep the test secure — during preparation, storage, and administration.
2. Have pupils clear off the tops of their desks (for adequate work space and to prevent use of notes).
3. If scratch paper is used (e.g., for math problems), have it turned in with the test.
4. Proctor the testing session carefully (e.g., walk around the room periodically and observe how the pupils are doing).
5. Use special seating arrangements, if possible (e.g., leave an empty row of seats between pupils).
6. Use two forms of the test and give a different form to each row of pupils (for this purpose, use the same test but simply rearrange the order of the items for the second form).
7. Prepare tests that pupils will view as relevant, fair, and useful.
8. Create and maintain a positive attitude concerning the value of tests for improving learning.

3. *Avoid giving hints to pupils who ask about individual items.* If the item is ambiguous, it should be clarified for the entire group, as indicated earlier. If it is not ambiguous, refrain from helping the pupil to answer it. Refraining from giving hints to pupils who ask for help is especially difficult for beginning teachers. But giving unfair aid to some pupils (the bold, the apple polishers, and so on) decreases the validity of the results and lowers class morale.

4. *Discourage cheating, if necessary.* When there is good teacher-pupil rapport and the pupils view tests as helpful rather than harmful, cheating is usually not a problem. Under other conditions, however, it might be necessary to discourage cheating by special seating arrangements and careful supervision. Receiving unauthorized help from other pupils during a test has the same deleterious effect on validity and class morale as does receiving special hints from the teacher. We are interested in pupils doing their best; but for valid results, their scores must be based on their own unaided efforts.

Scoring the Test

Procedures for scoring essay questions were described in the last chapter. Here we shall discuss scoring objective items.

If the pupils' answers are recorded on the test paper itself, a scoring key can be made by marking the correct answers on a blank copy of the test. Scoring then is simply a matter of comparing the columns of answers on this master copy with the columns of answers on each pupil's paper. A strip key, which consists merely of strips of paper on which the columns of answers are recorded, may also be used if more convenient. These can easily be prepared by cutting the columns of answers from the master copy of the test and mounting them on strips of cardboard cut from manila folders.

When separate answer sheets are used, a scoring stencil is most convenient. This is a blank answer sheet with holes punched where the correct answers should appear. The stencil is laid over each answer sheet, and the number of answer checks appearing through the holes are counted. When this type of scoring procedure is used, each test paper should also be scanned to make certain that only one answer was marked for each item. Any item containing more than one answer should be eliminated from the scoring.

As each test paper is scored, mark each item that is answered incorrectly. With multiple-choice items, a good practice is to draw a red line through the *correct* answer of the missed items rather than through the pupil's wrong answers. This will indicate to the pupil those items missed and at the same time will indicate the correct answers. Time will be saved and confusion avoided during discussion of the test. Marking the correct answers of missed items is especially simple with a scoring stencil. When no answer check appears through a hole in the stencil, a red line is drawn across the hole.

In scoring objective tests, each correct answer is usually counted as one point, because an arbitrary weighing of items makes little difference in the pupils' final scores. If some items are counted two points, some one point, and some one-half point, the scoring will be more complicated without any accompanying benefits. Scores based on such weightings will be similar to the simpler procedure of counting each item one point.

When pupils are told to answer every item on the test, a pupil's score is simply the number of items answered correctly. There is no need to consider wrong answers or to correct for guessing. When all pupils answer every item on a test, the rank order of the pupils' scores will be same whether the *number right* or a correction for guessing is used. Some teachers prefer to correct for guessing because they feel the resulting scores are a more accurate indication of the pupil's actual achievement. As we shall see in the following section, however, this is debatable.

Correction for Guessing.   Correcting for guessing is usually done when pupils do not have sufficient time to complete all items on the test and when they have been instructed that there will be a penalty for guessing. The most common formula used for this purpose is the following:

$$\text{Score} = \text{Right} - \frac{\text{Wrong}}{n - 1}$$

In this formula, n is the number of alternatives for an item. Thus, the formula applies to various selection-type items as follows:

True-false items:

$$S = R - \frac{W}{2 - 1}$$

$$\text{(or)}$$

$$S = R - W$$

Multiple-choice items:

(A) Three alternatives $S = R - \dfrac{W}{2}$

(B) Four alternatives $S = R - \dfrac{W}{3}$

(C) Five alternatives $S = R - \dfrac{W}{4}$

Using a correction formula in the scoring makes it necessary to count both right and wrong answers. Omitted items are *not* counted in the scoring.

These correction-for-guessing formulas assume that when pupils do not know the answer to an item, they guess blindly among all alternatives and select the correct answer a given number of times on the basis of chance alone. Thus, if a pupil has 60 items right and 15 items wrong on a true-false test, it is assumed that there was blind guessing on 30 items on the test and that there was chance success in guessing (15 right and 15 wrong). The formula merely removes the lucky guesses from the score by subtracting the number wrong from the number right: Correct score $= 60 - 15 = 45$.

The same assumption is made in applying the formula to multiple-choice items, but the possibility of selecting the correct answer is smaller because there are more alternatives to choose from. For example, when a pupil has 60 items right and 15 items wrong on a four-alternative multiple-choice test, it is assumed that the pupil guessed blindly on 20 items and guessed successfully one fourth of the time. Thus, the blind guessing resulted in 5 right answers and 15 wrong answers. To remove the lucky guesses from the score, it is simply a matter of subtracting one third of the wrong answers. This is what the correction formula does, as illustrated below:

$$S = R - \frac{W}{3} \qquad S = 60 - \frac{15}{3} = 55$$

The correction-for-guessing (or correction-for-chance) formula provides a suitable correction when the basic assumption can be satisfied — that is, that pupils guess blindly when they do not know the answer. Such blind guessing seldom occurs in classroom testing, however. Some correct guesses are informed guesses based on partial information, and some wrong answers are due to misinformation or extremely plausible distracters. When pupils can eliminate some of the alternatives in items and make informed guesses among those remaining, the formula *under-corrects* for chance success. When pupils select incorrect alternatives because of misinformation or the plausibility of distracters, the formula *overcorrects* for chance success. Consequently, when the correction formula is used with classroom tests, an unknown amount of error is introduced into the scoring. Although it is hoped that the two types of error will cancel each other out, there is no way of determining the amount of distortion in the test scores.

Because of the questionable assumption on which the correction-for-guessing formula is based, it is recommended that it not be used with the ordinary classroom test. The only exception is when the test is speeded to the extent that pupils complete different numbers of items. Here its use is defensible because pupils can increase their scores appreciably by rapidly (and blindly) guessing at the remaining untried items just before the testing period ends.

Appraising Classroom Tests

Before a classroom test has been administered, it should be evaluated according to the points discussed earlier. The most important of these points are listed in Table 10.1, a convenient checklist for reviewing the test. A *yes* response to each of these questions indicates that the test has been carefully prepared and will probably function effectively.

After a classroom test has been scored and the pupils have discussed the results, a common practice is to discard the test. Except for the pupils' criticism during class discussion, which helps identify some of the defective items, the teacher has little evidence concerning the quality of the test that was used. In addition, by discarding

A. Adequacy of Test Plan
1. Does the test plan adequately describe the instructional objectives and the content to be measured?
2. Does the test plan clearly indicate the relative emphasis to be given to each objective and each content area?
B. Adequacy of Test Items
3. Is the format of each item suitable for the learning outcome being measured (*appropriateness*)?
4. Does each test item require pupils to demonstrate the performance described in the specific learning outcome it measures (*relevance*)?
5. Does each test item present a clear and definite task to be performed (*clarity*)?
6. Is each test item presented in simple, readable language and free from excessive verbiage (*conciseness*)?
7. Is each test item of appropriate difficulty for the type of test constructed (*ideal difficulty*)?
8. Does each test item have an answer that would be agreed upon by experts (*correctness*)?
9. Is each test item free from technical errors and irrelevant clues (*technical soundness*)?
10. Is each test item free from racial, ethnic, and sexual bias (*cultural fairness*)?
11. Is each test item independent of the other items in the test (*independence*)?
12. Is there an adequate number of test items for each learning outcome (*sample adequacy*)?
C. Adequacy of Test Format and Directions
13. Are test items of the same type grouped together in the test (or within sections of the test)?
14. Are the test items arranged from easy to more difficult within sections of the test and the test as a whole?
15. Are the test items numbered in sequence?
16. Is the answer space clearly indicated (on the test itself or on a separate answer sheet), and is each answer space related to its corresponding test item?
17. Are the correct answers distributed in such a way that there is no detectable pattern?
18. Is the test material well spaced, legible, and free of typographical errors?
19. Are there directions for each section of the test and the test as a whole?
20. Are the directions clear and concise?

TABLE 10.1
Checklist for Evaluating the Classroom Test

the test, much of the careful planning and hard work that went into its preparation is wasted. A better procedure is to appraise the effectiveness of the test items and to build a file of high-quality items for future use.

Determining Item Effectiveness

The effectiveness of each test item can be determined by analyzing the pupils' responses to it. This item analysis is usually designed to answer questions such as the following:

1. Did the item function as intended?
   a. Did *norm-referenced* test items adequately discriminate between high and low achievers?
   b. Did *criterion-referenced* test items adequately measure the effects of the instruction?

2. Were the test items of appropriate difficulty?

3. Were the test items free of irrelevant clues and other defects?

4. Were each of the distracters effective (in multiple-choice items)?

Answers to such questions are of obvious value in selecting or revising items for future use. The benefits of item analysis are not limited to the improvement of individual test items, however. There are a number of fringe benefits of special value to classroom teachers. The most important of these are the following:

1. Item-analysis data provide a basis for efficient class discussion of the test results. Knowing how effectively each item functioned in measuring achievement makes it possible to confine the discussion to those areas most helpful to pupils. Easy items that were answered correctly by all pupils can be omitted from the discussion, and the concepts in those items causing pupils the greatest difficulty can receive special emphasis. Similarly, misinformation and misunderstandings reflected in the choice of particular distracters can be corrected. Item analysis will also expose technical defects in items. During discussion, defective items can be pointed out to pupils, saving much time and heated discussion concerning the unfairness of these items. If an item is ambiguous and two answers can be defended equally well, both answers should be counted correct and the scoring adjusted accordingly.

2. Item-analysis data provide a basis for remedial work. Although discussing the test results in class can clarify and correct many specific points, item analysis frequently brings to light general areas of weakness requiring more extended attention. In an arithmetic test, for example, item analysis may reveal that the pupils are fairly proficient in arithmetic skills but are having difficulty with problems requiring the application of these skills. In other subjects, item analysis may indicate a general weakness in knowledge of technical vocabulary, in an understanding of principles, or in the ability to interpret data. Such information makes it possible to focus remedial work directly on the particular areas of weakness.

3. Item-analysis data provide a basis for the general improvement of classroom instruction. In addition to the preceding uses, item-analysis data can assist in evaluating appropriateness of the learning outcomes and the course content for the particular pupils being taught. For example, material that is consistently too simple or too difficult for the pupils might suggest curriculum revisions or shifts in teaching emphasis. Similarly, errors in pupil thinking that persistently appear in item-analysis data might direct attention to the need for more effective teaching procedures. In these and similar ways, item-analysis data can reveal instructional weaknesses and clues for their improvement.

4. Item-analysis procedures provide a basis for increased skill in test construction. Item analysis reveals ambiguities, clues, ineffective distracters, and other technical defects that were missed during the test's preparation. This information is used directly in revising the test items for future use. In addition to the improvement of the specific items, however, we derive benefits from the procedure itself. As we analyze pupils' responses to items, we become increasingly aware of technical defects and what causes them. When revising the items, we gain experience in rewording statements so that they are clear, rewriting distracters so that they are more plausible, and modifying items so that they are at a more appropriate level of difficulty. As a consequence, our general test construction skills will improve.

Simplified Item-Analysis Procedures for Norm-Referenced Classroom Tests

Because norm-referenced and criterion-referenced tests serve different functions, the method for analyzing the effectiveness of the test items differs. Here we shall consider item-analysis procedures used with norm-referenced tests, where special emphasis is placed on item difficulty and item discriminating power. A discussion of item-analysis procedures used with criterion-referenced mastery tests will follow in a later section.

For most norm-referenced classroom tests, a simplified form of item analysis is all that is necessary or warranted. Because most classroom groups range somewhere between 20 and 40 pupils, an especially useful procedure is to compare the responses of the 10 highest scoring pupils with the responses of the 10 lowest-scoring pupils. As we shall see later, keeping the upper and lower groups at 10 pupils each simplifies the interpretation of the results. It also is a reasonable number for analysis in groups that contain between 20 and 40 pupils. For example, with a small classroom group, like that of 20 pupils, it is best to use the upper and lower halves to obtain dependable data, whereas with a larger group, like that of 40 pupils, use of the upper and lower 25 percent is quite satisfactory.[5]

To illustrate the method of item analysis, let us suppose that we have just finished scoring 32 test papers for a sixth-grade science unit on "weather." Our item analysis might then proceed as follows:

1. Rank the 32 test papers in order from the highest to the lowest score.
2. Select the 10 papers within the highest total scores and the 10 papers with the lowest total scores.
3. Put aside the middle 12 papers as they will *not* be used in the analysis.
4. For each test item, tabulate the number of pupils in the upper and lower groups who selected each alternative. This tabulation can be made directly on the test paper or on the test item card, as shown in Figure 10.2.
5. Compute the *difficulty* of each item (percentage of pupils who got the item right).
6. Compute the *discriminating power* of each item (difference between the number of pupils in the upper and lower groups who got the item right).

[5]For more refined analysis, the upper and lower 27 percent is often recommended, and most statistical guides are based on this percentage.

FIGURE 10.2
Test item card with
item-analysis data
recorded on back.

COURSE ___Science_____ UNIT ___Weather_____

OBJECTIVE ___Identifies use of instruments_____

ITEM

Which of the following is most useful in weather forecasting?

    A. Anemometer
    B. Barometer
    C. Thermometer
    D. Rain gauge

(Back of Item Card)

ITEM ANALYSIS DATA

Dates Used	Pupils	A	Ⓑ	C	D	E	Omits	Diff.	Disc.
			Alternatives					Indexes	
4/25/80	Upper 10	0	10	0	0		0	70%	.60
	Lower 10	2	4	1	3		0		
	Upper								
	Lower								
	Upper								
	Lower								

Comment:

7.   Evaluate the *effectiveness of distracters* in each item (attractiveness of the incorrect alternatives).

The first steps of this procedure are merely a convenient tabulation of pupils' responses from which we can readily determine item difficulty, item discriminating power, and the effectiveness of each distracter. This latter information can frequently be obtained simply by inspecting the item-analysis data. Note in Figure 10.2, for example, that 10 pupils in the upper group and four pupils in the lower group selected the correct alternative (B). This makes a total of 14 out of the 20 pupils who got the item right, indicating that the item has a fairly *low level of difficulty*. Because more pupils in the upper group than in the lower group got the item right, it is *discriminating positively*. That is, it is distinguishing between high and low achievers (as determined by the total test score). Finally, because all the alternatives were selected by some of the pupils in the lower group, *the distracters (alternatives A, C, and D) appear to be operating effectively*.

Although item analysis by inspection will reveal the general effectiveness of a test item and is satisfactory for most classroom purposes, it is sometimes useful to obtain a more precise estimate of item difficulty and discriminating power. This can be done by applying relatively simple formulas to the item-analysis data.

Computing Item Difficulty.   The difficulty of a test item is indicated by the *percentage of pupils who get the item right.*[6] Hence, we can compute item difficulty by means of the following formula, in which R = the number of pupils who got the item right and T = the total number of pupils who tried the item.

$$\text{Item Difficulty} = \frac{R}{T} \times 100$$

Applying this formula to the item-analysis data in Figure 10.2, our index of item difficulty (P) is 70 percent, as follows:

$$P = \frac{14}{20} \times 100 = 70 \text{ percent}$$

In computing item difficulty from item-analysis data, our calculation is based on the upper and lower groups only. We assume that the response of pupils in the middle group follow essentially the same pattern. This estimate of difficulty is sufficiently accurate for classroom use and is easily obtained because the needed figures can be taken directly from the item-analysis data.

Note that because our item analysis is based on 10 in the upper group and 10 in the lower group, all we need to do to obtain item difficulty is to divide the number getting it right by 2 ($14 \div 2 = 7$), move the decimal point one to the right (70), and add the percent sign (70%). In other words, 14 out of 20 is the same as 7 out of 10, which is 70 percent. If 13 pupils were to get the item right, item difficulty would be 6.5 out of 10 ($13 \div 2 = 6.5$), or 65 percent. This may seem a bit confusing at first, but once you grasp the idea, you can mentally compute item difficulty very quickly. As noted earlier, the ease of interpreting item statistics is one of the advantages of using 10 in each group. If more than 10 are used (or fewer), the formula for computing item difficulty can, of course, still be used, but it is much more difficult to compute the results mentally.

Computing Item Discriminating Power.   As we have already stated, an item discriminates in a positive direction if more pupils in the upper group than the lower group get the item right. Positive discrimination indicates that the item is discriminating in the same direction as the total test score. Because we assume that the total test score reflects achievement of desired objectives, we would like all of our test items to show positive discrimination.

The discriminating power of an achievement test item refers to *the degree to which it discriminates between pupils with high and low achievement.* Item discriminating power can be obtained by subtracting the number of pupils in the *lower* group who get the item right (R_L) from the number of pupils in the *upper* group

---

[6]Some have suggested that this should be called item *ease* rather than item *difficulty* because the easier the item is, the larger the percentage getting it right will be. However, item difficulty is standard usage in this country.

who get the item right (R_U) and dividing by *one half of the total* number of pupils included in the item analysis ($\frac{1}{2}T$). Summarized in formula form, it is[7]

$$\text{Item Discriminating Power} = \frac{R_U - R_L}{\frac{1}{2}T}$$

Applying this formula to the item-analysis data in Figure 10.2, we obtain an index of discriminating power (D) of .60, as follows:

$$D = \frac{10 - 4}{10} = .60$$

This indicates approximately average discriminating power. An item with maximum *positive* discriminating power is one in which all pupils in the upper group get the item right and all the pupils in the lower group get the item wrong. This results in an index of 1.00, as follows:

$$D = \frac{10 - 0}{10} = 1.00$$

An item with no discriminating power is one in which an equal number of pupils in both the upper and lower groups get the item right. This results in an index of .00, as follows:

$$D = \frac{10 - 10}{10} = .00$$

With this formula it is also possible to calculate an index of *negative* discriminating power; that is, one in which more pupils in the lower group than the upper group get the item right. This is generally wasted effort, however, because we are not interested in using items that discriminate in the wrong direction. Such items should be revised so that they discriminate positively, or they should be discarded.

As with item difficulty, when our item analysis is based on 10 in the upper group and 10 in the lower group, the index of discriminating power can be mentally computed both easily and quickly. All we need to do in this case is to subtract the number in the lower group getting it right from the number in the upper group getting it right ($10 - 4 = 6$), move the decimal point one to the left (.6), and add a zero after it (.60). Because with 10 in each group we are always dividing by 10, our index of discrimination is essentially the difference between the number getting it right in the two groups with the decimal point moved one to the left. The zero is added simply because the index of discrimination is usually carried to two decimal places. With more than 10 in each group we, of course, could not make these simple mental calculations but would have to resort to use of the formula.

---

[7]Item discriminating power also can be expressed by means of a correlation coefficient obtained directly from charts prepared for this purpose. See D. C. Adkins, *Test Construction* (Columbus, Ohio: Charles E. Merrill, 1974). Computer item analysis data also use correlation coefficients.

Evaluating the Effectiveness of Distracters.   How well each distracter is operating can be determined by inspection, and so there is no need to calculate an index of effectiveness, although the formula for discriminating power can be used for this purpose. In general, a good distracter attracts more pupils from the lower group than the upper group. Thus, it should discriminate between the upper and lower groups in a manner opposite to that of the correct alternative. An examination of the following item-analysis data will illustrate the ease with which the effectiveness of distracters can be determined by inspection. Alternative A is the correct answer.

Alternatives	*A	B	C	D	Omits
Upper 10	5	4	0	1	0
Lower 10	3	2	0	5	0

*Correct answer.

First note that the item discriminates in a positive direction, because 5 in the upper group and 3 in the lower group got the item right. The index of discriminating power is fairly low ($D = .20$), however, and this may be partly due to the ineffectiveness of some of the distracters. Alternative B is a poor distracter because it attracts more pupils from the upper group than from the lower group. This is most likely due to some ambiguity in the statement of the item. Alternative C is completely ineffective as a distracter because it attracted no one. Alternative D is functioning as intended, for it attracts a larger proportion of pupils from the lower group. Thus, the discriminating power of this item can probably be improved by removing any ambiguity in the statement of the item and revising or replacing alternatives B and C. The specific changes must, of course, be based on an inspection of the test item itself, Item-analysis data merely indicate poorly functioning items, not the cause of the poor functioning.

In some cases an examination of the test item will reveal no obvious error in the structure of the item and it may be best to try it with a second group. The number of cases involved is so small that considerable variation in student response can be expected from one group to another. A casual comment by the teacher, or some other classroom event, may cause students to select or reject a particular alternative.

Recording Item-Analysis Data on the Test Paper.   There is some advantage in recording item-analysis data directly on the test paper that was used as a scoring key, as shown in Figure 10.3. In reviewing the test results with pupils, for example, the data on the key aid in determining how much discussion to devote to any particular item, the types of misconceptions pupils may have (by the distracters selected), and which items are so defective that they might be discounted. If the upper (U) and lower (L) groups each contain 10 pupils, as in our illustration, item difficulty and item discriminating power can be mentally computed following the steps suggested earlier. For example, for the items in Figure 10.3, the mental computation and results are as follows:

Item Difficulty Index

Steps (using numbers to left of answer)	Item 1	Item 2
1. Add $U + L$ and divide by 2.	$18 \div 2 = 9$	$15 \div 2 = 7.5$
2. Move decimal point one to the right.	90	75
3. Add the percent sign.	90%	75%

Item Discrimination Index

Steps (using numbers to left of answer)	Item 1	Item 2
1. Subtract $U - L$.	$10 - 8 = 2$	$9 - 6 = 3$
2. Move decimal point one to the left.	.2	.3
3. Add a zero after the number.	.20	.30

As mentioned earlier, once this simple method of mentally computing the two indexes is mastered, no written computation is necessary. During the discussion of the test results, you can quickly judge the difficulty and discriminating power of any item, as well as the effectiveness of each distracter.

FIGURE 10.3
Sample test scoring key with item-analysis data added (U = upper 10 pupils, L = lower 10 pupils).

WEATHER UNIT

Name _____ Date _____

Directions. This test will measure what you have learned during the unit on weather.

There are 40 objective questions in the test. You will have the entire class period to complete it.

For each question there are several possible answers. Select the *best* answer and indicate it by encircling the letter of your answer.

Your score will be the number of questions answered correctly, so *be sure to answer every question.*

KNOWLEDGE OF FACTS

U L 1. Which of these instruments is used to measure humidity?

0 1 A. Anemometer
0 1 B. Barometer
10 8 C. Hygrometer
0 0 D. Thermometer

U L 2. What does the Beaufort scale indicate on a weather map?

1 2 A. Air pressure
0 1 B. Air temperature
0 1 C. Precipitation
9 6 D. Wind velocity

Cautions in Interpreting Item-Analysis Data on Norm-Referenced Tests

Item analysis is a quick, simple technique for appraising the effectiveness of individual test items. The information from such an analysis is limited in many ways, however, and must be interpreted accordingly. The following are some of the major cautions to observe:

1. Item discriminating power does not indicate item validity. In our description of item analysis, we used the total test score as a basis for selecting the upper group (high achievers) and the lower group (low achievers). This is the most common procedure because comparable measures of achievement are usually not available. Ideally, we would examine each test item in relation to some independent measure of achievement. However, the best measure of the particular achievement we are interested in evaluating is usually the total score on the achievement test we have constructed because each classroom test is related to specific instructional objectives and course content. Even standardized tests in the same content area are

Item Analysis by Computer

Many schools now have computers (or have access to them) that can both score and analyze tests. The computer printout will provide item-analysis information, a reliability coefficient, standard error of measurement for the test, and various other types of information concerning the performance of the individuals tested and the characteristics of the test. The nature of the information depends on the sophistication of the computer and the program that is used.

When item analysis is done by computer, the scores of the entire group are usually used rather than just the scores of the upper and lower groups. The total set of scores might be divided into two, three, four, or five levels, depending on the size of the group and the types of analyses. Item-analysis data on a computer printout based on 50 pupils might appear as follows, for each item:

Item Response Pattern

ITEM 1	A	B	*C	D	E	OMIT	TOTAL	ITEM STATISTICS
Upper 30%	1	1	12	1	0	0	15	Difficulty 60%
Middle 40%	2	2	12	3	1	0	20	Discrimination .40
Lower 30%	2	3	6	3	1	0	15	
Total	5	6	30	7	2	0	50	

The item-response data indicate how many pupils, at each level, selected the correct answer (C) and how many selected each of the distracters. The item statistics at the right indicate the index of difficulty and the index of discrimination for this item. Some computer programs report only the item statistics, but the item-response pattern is especially valuable for evaluating the effectiveness of the distracters and planning for item revision. Alternative E, for example, should be examined to determine whether it can be replaced by a more effective distracter.

usually inadequate as independent criteria, because they are aimed at more general objectives than those measured by a classroom test in a particular course.

Using the total score from our classroom test as a basis for selecting high and low achievers is perfectly legitimate as long as we remember that we are using an internal criterion. In doing so, our item analysis offers evidence concerning the *internal consistency* of the test rather than its validity. That is, we are determining how effectively each test item is measuring whatever the whole test is measuring. Such item-analysis data can be interpreted as evidence of *item validity* only when the validity of the total test has been proven or can be legitimately assumed.

2. A low index of discriminating power does not necessarily indicate a defective item. Items that discriminate poorly between high and low achievers should be examined for the possible presence of ambiguity, clues, and other technical defects. If none is found and the items measure an important learning outcome, they should be retained for future use. Any item that discriminates in a positive direction can contribute to the measurement of pupil achievement, and low indexes of discrimination are frequently obtained for reasons other than technical defects.

Classroom achievement tests are usually designed to measure several different types of learning outcomes (knowledge, understanding, application, and so on). When this is the case, test items that represent an area receiving relatively little emphasis will tend to have poor discriminating power. For example, if a test has forty items measuring knowledge of facts and ten items measuring understanding, the latter items can be expected to have low indexes of discrimination. This is because the items measuring understanding have less representation in the total test score and there is typically a low correlation between measures of knowledge and measures of understanding. Low indexes of discrimination here merely indicate that these items are measuring something different from what the major part of the test is measuring. Removing such items from the test would make it a more homogeneous measure of knowledge outcomes, but it would also damage the test's validity because it would no longer measure learning outcomes in the understanding area. Because most classroom tests measure a variety of types of learning outcomes, low positive indexes of discrimination are the rule rather than the exception.

Another factor that influences discriminating power is the difficulty of the item. Those items at the 50 percent level of difficulty make maximum discriminating power possible, because only at this level of difficulty can all pupils in the upper half of the group get the item right, and all pupils in the lower half get it wrong.[8] As we move away from the 50 percent level of difficulty toward easier or more difficult items, the index of discriminating power becomes smaller. Thus, items that are very easy or very difficult have low indexes of discriminating power. Sometimes it is

---

[8] The 50 percent level of difficulty does not guarantee maximum discriminating power but merely makes it possible. If half of the pupils in the upper group and half of the pupils in the lower group got the item right, it would still be at the 50 percent level of difficulty, but the index of discrimination would be zero.

necessary or desirable to retain such items, however, in order to measure a representative sample of learning outcomes and course content.

To summarize, a low index of discriminating power should alert us to the possible presence of technical defects in a test item, but it should not cause us to discard an otherwise worthwhile item. A well-constructed achievement test will, of necessity, contain items with low discriminating power, and to discard them would result in a test that is less rather than more valid.

3. Item-analysis data from small samples are highly tentative. Item-analysis procedures focus our attention so directly on a test item's difficulty and discriminating power that we are commonly misled into believing that these are fixed, unchanging characteristics. This, of course, is not true. Item-analysis data will vary from one group to another, depending on the pupils' level of ability, their educational background, and the type of instruction they have had. Add to this the small number of pupils available for analyzing the items in our classroom tests, and the tentative nature of our item-analysis data becomes readily apparent. If just a few pupils change their responses, our indexes of difficulty and discriminating power can be increased or decreased by a considerable amount.

The tentative nature of item-analysis data should discourage us from making fine distinctions among items on the basis of indexes of difficulty and discriminating power. If an item is discriminating in a positive direction, all of the alternatives are functioning effectively, and it has no apparent defects, it can be considered satisfactory from a technical standpoint. The important question then becomes not how high the index of discriminating power is, but rather, whether the item measures an important learning outcome. In the final analysis, the worth of an achievement test item must be based on logical rather than statistical considerations.

When used with norm-referenced classroom tests, item analysis provides us with a general appraisal of the functional effectiveness of the test items, a means for detecting defects, and a method for identifying instructional weaknesses. For these purposes, the tentative nature of item-analysis data is relatively unimportant. When we record indexes of item difficulty or discriminating power on item cards for future use, we should interpret them as rough approximations only. As such, they are still superior to our unaided estimates of item difficulty and discriminating power.

Item-Analysis and Criterion-Referenced Mastery Tests

The item-analysis procedures used with norm-referenced tests are not directly applicable to criterion-referenced mastery tests. Because criterion-referenced tests are designed to describe pupils in terms of the types of learning tasks they can perform, rather than to obtain a reliable ranking of pupils, indexes of item difficulty and item discriminating power are less meaningful.

Item Difficulty. The desired level of item difficulty for a criterion-referenced mastery test is not based on the items' ability to discriminate between high and low achievers, as it is for norm-referenced tests. Instead, the difficulty of each test item is determined by the learning outcome it is designed to measure. If the learning task defined by the outcome is easy, the test item should be easy. If the learning task has a moderate level of difficulty, the test item should have a moderate level of difficulty. No attempt is made to alter arbitrarily item difficulty in order to increase discriminating power or to obtain a spread of test scores. The standard formula for determining item difficulty can be applied to criterion-referenced test items, but the results are not usually used to select test items or to manipulate item difficulty. Most items on a criterion-referenced mastery test will have a large difficulty index (high percentage passing) when the instruction has been effective.

Item Discriminating Power.   The ability of test items to discriminate between high and low achievers is not crucial to criterion-referenced test items. Some good items might have very low, or zero, indexes of discrimination. If all pupils answer a test item correctly (i.e., zero discrimination) at the end of instruction, for example, this may indicate that both the instruction and the item have been effective. Although such items would be eliminated from norm-referenced tests because they fail to discriminate, here they provide useful information concerning which learning tasks all pupils have mastered. Because the purpose of a criterion-referenced test is to describe what pupils can do, rather than to discriminate among them, our traditional indexes of discriminating power are of little value for judging the test items' quality.

Analysis of Criterion-Referenced Mastery Items.   A crucial question in evaluating a criterion-referenced mastery test is "To what extent did the test items measure the effects of the instruction?" To answer this, the same test must be given before instruction (pretest) and after instruction (posttest) and the results compared. A simple item-by-item comparison can be made by means of an item-response chart such as that shown in Table 10.2.

To prepare a chart like Table 10.2, simply list the numbers of the test items across the top of the chart and the pupil's names down the side of the chart, and then record correct (+) and incorrect (−) responses for each pupil on the pretest (B) and posttest (A). The results in our sample table have been deliberately distorted to illustrate some of the basic patterns of item response. An analysis of the effectiveness of each item as a measure of *instructional effects* is as follows:

Item 1.   This is an *ideal* item for a criterion-referenced mastery test. All pupils responded incorrectly before instruction and correctly after instruction. Both the item and the instruction were effective.

Item 2.   This item was *too easy* to measure the effects of instruction, because all pupils responded correctly both before and after instruction.

Item 3.   This item was *too difficult* to measure the effects of instruction, or the instruction was inappropriate.

Item 4.   This item indicates an extremely *defective* item or an easy item followed by incorrect instruction.

Item 5.   This item illustrates an *effective* item, with a fairly typical response pattern. Some pupils responded correctly before instruction, but a larger proportion did so after instruction.

Items →		1		2		3		4		5
Pretest (B)										
Posttest (A)	B	A	B	A	B	A	B	A	B	A
Jim Hart	−	+	+	+	−	−	+	−	−	+
Dora Larson	−	+	+	+	−	−	+	−	+	+
Lois Trent	−	+	+	+	−	−	+	−	−	+
Donna Voss	−	+	+	+	−	−	+	−	−	+
Dick Ward	−	+	+	+	−	−	+	−	+	+
Bob West	−	+	+	+	−	−	+	−	−	−

TABLE 10.2

A Portion of an Item-Response Chart Showing Correct (+) and Incorrect (−) Responses Before and After Instruction

Where an index of item effectiveness is desired for each item, the following formula can be used to obtain a measure of *sensitivity to instructional effects (S)*.[9]

$$S = \frac{R_A - R_B}{T}$$

where

R_A = number of pupils who got the item right *after* instruction.
R_B = number of pupils who got the item right *before* instruction.
T = total number of pupils who tried the item both times.

Applying this formula to the five test items in Table 10.2, we obtain indexes of sensitivity to instructional effects (S) as follows:

Item 1: $S = \frac{6-0}{6} = 1.00$

Item 2: $S = \frac{6-6}{6} = .00$

Item 3: $S = \frac{0-0}{6} = .00$

Item 4: $S = \frac{0-6}{6} = -1.00$

Item 5: $S = \frac{5-2}{6} = .50$

Thus, the ideal item for a criterion-referenced mastery test yields a value of 1.00. Effective items fall between .00 and 1.00, and the higher the positive value is, the more sensitive the item will be to instructional effects. Items with zero and negative values do not reflect the intended effects of instruction.

[9]T. M. Haladyna and G. Roid, "The Role of Instructional Sensitivity in the Empirical Review of Criterion-Referenced Test Items," *Journal of Educational Measurement*, 18 (Spring 1981): 39–53.

Because the values used to represent effective criterion-referenced test items (.00 to 1.00) are the same as those used to represent item discriminating power, care must be taken not to confuse the meaning of the two indexes. The traditional *index of discriminating power* (D) indicates the degree to which an item discriminates between high and low achievers on a single administration of the test, and the *index of sensitivity to instructional effects* (S) indicates the degree to which an item reflects the intended effects of instruction.

Effectiveness of Distracters.   How well each alternative functions in a multiple-choice item is also important in criterion-referenced tests. Ideally, pupils should choose one of the incorrect alternatives if they have not achieved the objective that the test item measures. Thus, you should check the frequency with which each distracter is selected by those failing an item. This type of analysis might best be done on the pretest, in which a relatively large proportion of pupils can be expected to fail the items. If some items contain distracters that are not selected at all, or only rarely, revision is needed.

Building a Test-Item File

A file of effective items can be built and maintained easily if items are recorded on cards like the one shown in Figure 10.2. By indicating on the item card both the objective and the content area the item measures, it is possible to file the cards under both headings. Course content can be used as major categories, with the objectives forming the subcategories. For example, our item in Figure 10.2 measures knowledge of weather instruments, and so it is placed in the first category under weather instruments, as follows:

WEATHER INSTRUMENTS:

Knowledge

Understanding

Application

This type of filing system makes it possible to select items in accordance with any table of specifications in the particular area covered by the file.

Building a test-item file is a little like building a bank account. The first several years are concerned mainly with making deposits; withdrawals must be delayed until a sufficient reserve is accumulated. Thus, items are recorded on cards as they are constructed; item-analysis information is added after the items have been used; and then the effective items are deposited in the file. At first it seems to be additional work, with very little return. However, in a few years it is possible to start using some of the items from the file and supplementing these with other newly constructed items. As the file grows, it becomes possible to select the majority of the items from the file for any given test without repeating them too frequently. To prevent using a test item too often, record on the card the date an item is used.

A test-item file assumes increasing importance as we shift from test items that measure knowledge of facts to those that measure understanding, application, and thinking skills. Items in these latter areas are difficult and time consuming to construct. With all of the other demands on our time, it is nearly impossible to construct effective test items in these areas each time we prepare a new test. We have two alternatives: Either we neglect the measurement of learning outcomes in these areas (which has been the usual practice), or we slowly build a file of effective items in these areas. The choice is obvious if the quality of pupil learning is our major concern.

For a test file to be most effective, pupils should not be permitted to keep their test papers after the test has been scored and discussed in class. This disturbs some teachers who feel that the pupils should have their test papers for later study and review. There is no particular advantage in permitting pupils to keep their test papers, however, *if* there has been adequate discussion of the test results in class and

Item Banking by Computer

Some schools use computers to maintain item files (or item pools) for each of the various subjects and grade levels. The items are coded and stored by the test builder for easy retrieval. The code includes such things as instructional level, subject area, instructional objective, content topic, and item statistics (e.g., difficulty and discrimination indexes). This makes it possible to select items and build a test that matches a particular set of test specifications. The coded information concerning each item also aids in arranging the items in the test (e.g., by objective, order of difficulty).

The computer will print out these custom-designed tests and will also score, report, and analyze them. Some test publishers provide courseware programs for use with microcomputers that include item banking, test generation, scoring, and related functions (e.g., *SRA Micro Test Administration System* by Science Research Associates). See test publishers' catalogues for details on the microcomputer programs each offers. Publishers' addresses are listed in Appendix C.

Computer item banks are like any other item pool — *you get out only what you put in.* If you store ineffective items, you will get back ineffective items. Thus, item banking by computer requires careful screening of the items before they are entered. This is usually done by a committee of teachers in each department or instructional area, using checklists like those presented earlier in this book.

If a school does not have computer item banking, teachers should be encouraged to maintain item files like those suggested in this section. This will provide a pool of items for beginning a computer item bank when a computer is bought. With the rapidly increasing use of microcomputers in schools, that day will arrive sooner than you might expect.

a general review in the particular areas of weakness revealed by the test. After all, our aim is to help pupils improve their general knowledge and understanding in a given area. The test is merely a sample of this achievement. Although a discussion of test results will contribute to improved learning, extended study of the answers to specific test items may actually detract from this aim. This certainly would be the case if pupils concentrated on learning the sample of material included in the test and neglected the larger area of achievement it represented.

Summary

The same care that goes into the construction of individual test items should be carried over into the final stages of test development and use. Attending to the procedures for (1) assembling the test for use, (2) administering and scoring the test, and (3) appraising the results will provide increased assurance that valid results are obtained.

The preliminary steps in preparing the test for use will be simpler if the items are recorded on cards. This facilitates the task of editing the items and arranging them in the test. The editing includes checking each item to make certain that the item format is appropriate, that the item is relevant to the specific learning outcome it measures, and that it is free from ambiguity, irrelevant clues, and nonfunctioning material. The final group of items selected for the test also should be checked against the table of specifications, or other test plan, to make sure that a representative sample of the learning outcomes and course content is being measured. In arranging the items in the test, all items of one type should be placed together in a separate section. The items within each section should be organized by the learning outcome measured and then placed in order of ascending difficulty. The directions for the test should convey clearly to the pupil the purpose of the test, the time allowed for answering, the basis for answering, the procedure for recording the answers, and what to do about guessing.

The procedures for administering the test should give all pupils a fair chance to demonstrate their achievement. Both the physical and the psychological atmosphere should be conducive to maximum performance. Unnecessary interruptions and unfair aid from other pupils or the teacher should be avoided.

Scoring the test can be facilitated by a scoring key or scoring stencil if separate answer sheets are used. Counting each right answer as one point is usually satisfactory. A correction for guessing is unnecessary with the typical classroom test in which pupils have sufficient time to consider all questions. Because assumptions underlying the use of correction-for-guessing formulas are debatable, it is recommended that they be used only with speeded tests. For most classroom tests, it is satisfactory to tell pupils to answer every question and then simply count the number of correct answers.

After the test has been scored, you should appraise the functioning effectiveness of each item by means of item analysis. For norm-referenced tests, use simple statistical procedures for determining the index of item difficulty (percentage of pupils who got the item right), item discriminating power (the difference between high and low achievers), and the effectiveness of each distracter (degree to which it attracts more low achievers than high achievers). Item-analysis indexes can be mentally computed both easily and quickly if the data are based on the 10 highest-scoring and 10 lowest-scoring pupils (which is appropriate for class sizes ranging anywhere from 20 to 40 pupils). Because criterion-referenced mastery tests are designed to describe the learning tasks that pupils can perform, rather than to discriminate among pupils, the traditional indexes of item analysis are not fully appropriate. More meaningful here is a comparison of the pupils' item responses before instruction (pretest) and after instruction (posttest). This can be accomplished by means of an item-response chart or by computing an index of sensitivity to instructional effects. This type of information is useful for determining the extent to which criterion-referenced mastery items measure the intended effects of instruction. The results of item analysis are valuable in discussing the test with pupils, in planning remedial work, in improving teaching and testing skills, and in selecting and revising items for future use. For these and other purposes, however, item-analysis data must be interpreted cautiously because of their limited and tentative nature.

Building a test file of effective items involves recording the items on index cards, adding item-analysis information, and filing the cards by both the content area and the objective that the item measures. Such a test-item file is especially valuable in the areas of complex achievement in which the construction of test items is difficult and time-consuming. When enough high-quality items have been assembled, the burden of test preparation is considerably lightened. Computer item banking makes the task ever easier and soon will be available in most schools.

Learning Exercises

1. What are the advantages of recording items on separate index cards during test construction?
2. List as many things as you can think of that might prevent a test item from functioning as intended. Compare your list with the checklist in Table 10.1.
3. In what ways might poorly arranged items in a test adversely influence the validity of test results? What arrangement is best for valid results? Why?
4. What factors should be included in the general directions for a comprehensive departmental examination? How would the directions for a teacher's unit test differ?
5. What special precautions might be taken to avoid ambiguity, irrelevant clues, and other errors in objective test items?
6. Under what conditions should a correction for guessing be used to score a test? What are some of the reasons a correction for guessing should *not* be used with the typical classroom test?
7. If item-analysis data for a norm-referenced test showed that an item was answered correctly by 7 out of 10 pupils in the upper group and 3 out of 10 pupils in the lower group, what would the index of item difficulty be? What would the index of discriminating power be? Would this item be considered effective or ineffective?
8. How can you increase the discriminating power of a norm-referenced test?

9. Why is the index of discriminating power of little value in evaluating items on a criterion-referenced mastery test? Could the index of sensitivity to instructional effects be used with norm-referenced tests?

10. What are some advantages in maintaining a test item file? What precautions are necessary in using such a file?

Suggestions for Further Reading

ANASTASI, A. *Psychological Testing*, 6th ed. New York: Macmillan, 1988. Chapter 8, "Item Analysis," describes item-analysis procedures for norm-referenced tests with a brief introduction to item-response theory.

BAKER, F. A. "Computer Technology in Test Construction and Processing." In R. L. Linn, ed., *Educational Measurement*, 3d ed. New York: Macmillan, 1989, Chapter 10. Describes the use of microcomputers for item writing, item banking, test construction, scoring, and reporting.

BERK, R. A. "Conducting the Item Analysis." In R. A. Berk, ed., *A Guide to Criterion-Referenced Test Construction*. Baltimore: Johns Hopkins University Press, 1984, Chapter 5. Reviews and critiques the various item-analysis procedures for criterion-referenced tests.

EBEL, R. L., AND FRISBIE, D. A. *Essentials of Educational Measurement*, 4th ed. Englewood Cliffs, N.J.: Prentice-Hall, 1986. Chapter 13, "Using Item Analysis to Evaluate and Improve Test Quality," describes item analysis and illustrates its use in item revision.

MEHRENS, W. A., AND LEHMANN, I. J. *Measurement and Evaluation in Education and Psychology*, 3d ed. New York: Holt, Rinehart & Winston, 1984. Chapter 8, "Assembling, Reproducing, Administering, Scoring, and Analyzing Classroom Achievement Tests," presents a discussion of topics like those covered in this chapter.

Part 3

Selecting and Using Published Tests

Chapter 11

Achievement Tests

There are hundreds of published achievement tests available for
use. . . . Some consist of a battery of tests, whereas others measure
an individual subject or skill . . . and some provide a general survey
of learning outcomes, whereas others provide descriptive and
diagnostic information. . . . Becoming familiar with these basic types
of achievement tests . . . representative examples of them . . . and
principles of selection and use should provide helpful guidelines for
effective achievement testing.

Achievement testing plays an important role in the school program, and published achievement tests are widely used at both the elementary and secondary school levels. Most published achievement tests are called *standardized* achievement tests. These typically have been norm-referenced tests that measure the pupils' level of achievement in various content and skill areas by comparing their test performance with the performance of other pupils in some general reference group (e.g., a nationwide sample of pupils at the same grade level). In recent years, a number of *criterion-referenced* achievement tests also have been published. Most of these have been in the basic skill area, especially reading and mathematics. These tests are typically interpreted by means of the extent to which a limited set of instructional objectives has been mastered. Thus, they describe in terms of specific educational tasks what each pupil has learned and has yet to learn in some clearly specified achievement domain.

Although norm-referenced achievement tests and criterion-referenced achievement tests can be considered distinct test types, often test publishers attempt to incorporate elements of each in the same test. For example, most newly developed standardized achievement tests provide for both norm-referenced interpretation and interpretation by objective or by skill area.[1] On the other hand, some criterion-referenced achievement tests provide norms for further interpretation. Despite this provision for dual interpretation of the results, the structure and function of each test type are quite different and therefore will be described separately.

Because standardized achievement tests still dominate the field of educational testing, we shall discuss them first. We shall begin by examining their characteristics and showing how they compare with teacher-made achievement tests. We then shall discuss the major types of published achievement tests used in schools. Although we shall give examples of some of the more widely used tests, there are many other published achievement tests of high quality. We hope that the tests referred to here will simply serve as a starting point for exploring the many good achievement tests available. As a minimum, you should become familiar with some of the better published tests in your teaching area. See Appendix D for a selected list of published tests.

Characteristics of Standardized Achievement Tests

A standardized achievement test has certain distinctive features, including a fixed set of test items designed to measure a clearly defined achievement domain, specific directions for administering and scoring the test, and norms based on representative groups of individuals like those for whom the test was designed. Standard content and procedure make it possible to give an identical test to individuals in different places at different times. The norms enable us to compare an individual's test score with those of known groups who also have taken the test. Thus, test norms provide a standard frame of reference for determining an individual's relative level of test performance on a particular test and for comparing test performance on several different tests (providing all were standardized on the same group).

Equivalent forms are included in many standardized achievement tests, which make it possible to repeat the test without fear that the test takers will remember the answers from the first testing. Because equivalent forms of a test are built according to the same specifications, they measure the same sample of achievement with different sets of test items. They therefore can be used interchangeably for such purposes as measuring educational growth, checking on questionable test results from an earlier testing, and the like.

Comparable forms are also included in some standardized tests. These are forms that measure the same aspects of behavior, but at different grade levels. For example, one form will cover grades 1 to 3, and other forms will cover grades 4 to 6, 7 to 9, and 10 to 12. Such forms are especially useful for maintaining a continuity

---

[1]Caution is needed when making these latter types of interpretations, however, because standardized tests usually cover such a broad area of achievement that there may be relatively few items for each objective or skill being measured.

of measurement in a schoolwide testing program and for studying long-term trends in educational growth.

In summary, the characteristics of a carefully constructed standardized achievement test include the following:

1. The test items are of a high technical quality. They have been developed by educational and test specialists; tried out experimentally (pretested); and selected on the basis of difficulty, discriminating power, and relationship to a clearly defined and rigid set of specifications (see box).

How Publishers Select Test Items*

Iowa Tests of Basic Skills, Levels 9–14
Selection Process for Test Questions

1. Research	Writing teams study curriculum guides, textbooks, latest professional literature and research to identify the skills to be tested and new ways of testing these skills.
2. Writing	Four times as many test questions are produced as will eventually be used.
3. Editing for Tryouts	Questions are checked for length, reading level, vocabulary, art, and space requirements; and changed or dropped as necessary.
4. Editing after Tryouts	Iowa Testing Program tries out questions on school population of over 300,000. Each question is tried out on at least 200 students. Those questions that do not measure well (almost half) are dropped.
5. Author Reviews	Test authors review questions' relationship to skills categories, review balance between skills categories, and check for freedom from bias, eliminating where necessary.
6. Publisher Reviews	Test editors review questions for all factors, especially balance (geographical, urban/rural, sex, race,

(continued)

	etc.) and recommend further changes, which are made.
7. Independent Reviews	National team of professionals, representing five ethnic and racial groups, review questions for all factors, particularly cultural fairness. More changes are made following their recommendations.
8. Final Editing for Standardization	Editors and authors make final reviews for all factors, and final choice of questions is made for national norming.

*Reproduced by permission of The Riverside Publishing Company.

2. Directions for administering and scoring are so precisely stated that the procedures are standard for different users of the test.

3. Norms based on representative groups of individuals are provided as aids in interpreting the test scores. These norms are based on various age and grade groups on a national, regional, or state level. Norms for special groups, such as private schools, also might be supplied.

4. Equivalent and comparable forms of the test are usually provided as well as information concerning the degree to which the forms are comparable.

5. A test manual and other accessory materials are included as guides for administering and scoring the test, evaluating its technical qualities, and interpreting and using the results.

Despite the common characteristics of standardized tests, no two are exactly alike. Each test measures somewhat different aspects of content and skill. Also, there is wide variation in the completeness and quality of materials from one test to another. To further complicate test selection, some tests with similar titles measure objectives that differ markedly. Thus, the intelligent selection of standardized achievement tests from among the literally hundreds of tests available in each area requires studying the test content and the test materials in light of the objectives to be measured and the uses to be made of the results.

Standardized Tests versus Informal Classroom Tests

Standardized achievement tests and carefully constructed classroom tests are similar in many ways. Both are based on a table of specifications, both have the same type of test items, and both provide clear directions to the pupils. The main differences between the two types are (1) the nature of the learning outcomes and content measured, (2) the quality of the test items, (3) the reliability of the tests, (4) the procedures for administering and scoring, and (5) the interpretation of scores. Comparative advantages of standardized and informal classroom tests of achievement are shown in Table 11.1.

A review of the comparative advantages of the two types of tests indicates that each is superior for certain purposes and inferior for others. The broader coverage of the standardized test, its more rigidly controlled procedures of administering and scoring, and the availability of norms for evaluating scores make it especially useful for the following instructional purposes:

1. Evaluating pupils' general educational development in the basic skills and in those learning outcomes common to many courses of study.

2. Evaluating pupil progress during the school year or over a period of years.

3. Grouping pupils for instructional purposes.

	Standardized Achievement Tests	Informal Achievement Tests	
Learning outcomes and content measured	Measure outcomes and content common to majority of United States schools. Tests of basic skills and complex outcomes adaptable to many local situations; content-oriented tests seldom reflect emphasis or timeliness of local curriculum.	Well adapted to outcomes and content of local curriculum. Flexibility affords continuous adaptation of measurement to new materials and changes in procedure. Adaptable to various-sized work units. Tend to neglect complex learning outcomes.	TABLE 11.1 Comparative Advantages of Standardized and Informal Classroom Tests of Achievement
Quality of test items	General quality of items high. Written by specialists, pretested, and selected on basis of effectiveness.	Quality of items is unknown unless test item file is used. Quality typically lower than standardized because of teacher's limited time and skill.	
Reliability	Reliability high, commonly between .80 and .95; frequently is above .90.	Reliability usually unknown; can be high if carefully constructed.	
Administration and scoring	Procedures *standardized*; specific instructions provided.	Uniform procedures favored but may be flexible.	
Interpretation of scores	Scores can be compared with those of norm groups. Test manual and other guides aid interpretation and use.	Score comparisons and interpretations limited to local school situation.	

4. Determining pupils' relative strengths and weaknesses in broad subject or skill areas.

5. Comparing pupils' general level of achievement with their scholastic aptitude.

The standardized test's inflexibility makes it less valuable for those purposes for which the informal classroom test is so admirably suited.

1. Evaluating the learning outcomes and content unique to a particular class or school.

2. Evaluating pupils' day-to-day progress and their achievement on work units of varying sizes.

3. Evaluating knowledge of current developments in such rapidly changing content areas as science and social studies.

The complementary functions of the two types of tests indicate that both are essential to a sound instructional program. Each provides a specific type of information regarding the pupils' educational progress. In both cases, however, the value of the information depends on the extent to which the tests are related to the instructional objectives of the school. Standardized achievement tests, like informal classroom tests, can serve the many worthwhile instructional purposes attributed to them only when they measure the particular outcomes and content deemed important by those responsible for the instructional program.

Standardized Achievement Test Batteries

Standardized achievement tests are frequently used in the form of survey test batteries. A battery consists of a series of individual tests all standardized on the same representative group of pupils. This makes it possible to compare test scores on the separate tests and thus determine the pupils' relative strengths and weaknesses in the different areas covered by the test. With an elementary school test battery, for example, it is possible to determine that a pupil is strong in language skills but weak in arithmetic skills, good in reading but less proficient in spelling, and so on. Such comparisons are not possible with separate tests that have been standardized on different groups of pupils because the base for comparison is not uniform.

One limitation of test batteries is that all parts of the battery are usually not equally appropriate for measuring a particular school's objectives. When a test battery is constructed, it is based on the objectives and the content considered important by the specialists building the test. Although a particular school's goals probably will agree with some sections of the battery, it is fairly certain that they will not agree with all sections. Variations in subject-matter content from one curriculum to another and differences in grade placement of instructional materials make it unlikely that the various sections of a test battery will be uniformly applicable to the instructional program of any given school. This limitation is especially pronounced in content-oriented test batteries. It is less important in batteries designed to measure basic skills and general educational development.

Achievement batteries have been used most often at the elementary school level. Most schools use an achievement battery in grades 3 through 6, and many also use a battery in grades 1 and 2. This extensive usage is understandable because there is considerable uniformity in the learning outcomes sought, especially in the basic skills.

Elementary school batteries focus on the basic skills and usually include sections on reading, language, mathematics, and study skills. To allow for increasing difficulty and for varying emphasis from one grade level to another, a series of comparable forms has been developed to cover the various grade levels. Each form in the series covers one or two grades at the primary level and two or more grades beyond grade 4.

The basic skills in an achievement battery are measured by a number of subtests. Although the names of the subtests vary somewhat from one test publisher to another, and the batteries at the primary level usually contain fewer subtests, there is considerable uniformity in the outcomes measured by the various basic skill batteries. The following subtests are typical of those used in each basic skill area:

READING

Decoding skills (discrimination, analysis)

Vocabulary (meaning of words)

Comprehension (meaning of paragraphs and other written material)

LANGUAGE

Mechanics (capitalization, punctuation)

Expression (correctness, effectiveness)

Spelling (from dictation or identifying misspelled words)

MATHEMATICS

Computation (fundamental operations)

Concepts (meaning of concepts)

Problem solving (solving story problems)

STUDY SKILLS

Library and reference skills

Reading maps, graphs, and tables

A list of skill objectives and sample test items for the reading comprehension subtest of a widely used basic skill battery is shown in Figure 11.1. Notice that each test item is designed to measure a specific skill objective. A similar set of objectives is used in the construction of each of the other subtests, which are included in the teachers' guide that accompanies the battery.

FIGURE 11.1
Objectives and sample items from the Reading Comprehension Test, *Iowa Tests of Basic Skills*, Forms 7 & 8, © 1982, 1978 by the University of Iowa. Used by permission of The Riverside Publishing Company.

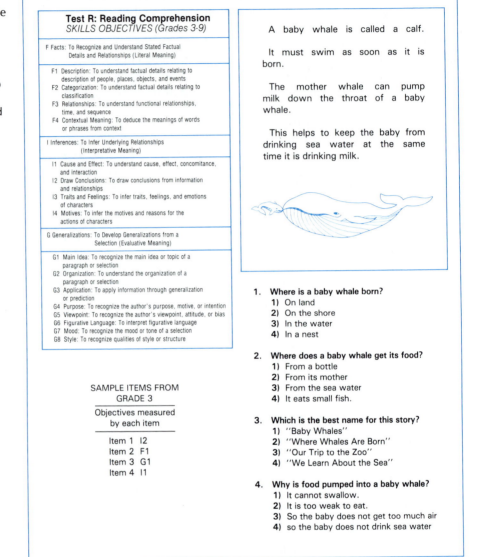

Test R: Reading Comprehension
SKILLS OBJECTIVES (Grades 3-9)

F Facts: To Recognize and Understand Stated Factual Details and Relationships (Literal Meaning)

F1 Description: To understand factual details relating to description of people, places, objects, and events
F2 Categorization: To understand factual details relating to classification
F3 Relationships: To understand functional relationships, time, and sequence
F4 Contextual Meaning: To deduce the meanings of words or phrases from context

I Inferences: To Infer Underlying Relationships (Interpretative Meaning)

I1 Cause and Effect: To understand cause, effect, concomitance, and interaction
I2 Draw Conclusions: To draw conclusions from information and relationships
I3 Traits and Feelings: To infer traits, feelings, and emotions of characters
I4 Motives: To infer the motives and reasons for the actions of characters

G Generalizations: To Develop Generalizations from a Selection (Evaluative Meaning)

G1 Main Idea: To recognize the main idea or topic of a paragraph or selection
G2 Organization: To understand the organization of a paragraph or selection
G3 Application: To apply information through generalization or prediction
G4 Purpose: To recognize the author's purpose, motive, or intention
G5 Viewpoint: To recognize the author's viewpoint, attitude, or bias
G6 Figurative Language: To interpret figurative language
G7 Mood: To recognize the mood or tone of a selection
G8 Style: To recognize qualities of style or structure

SAMPLE ITEMS FROM
GRADE 3

Objectives measured
by each item

Item 1 I2
Item 2 F1
Item 3 G1
Item 4 I1

A baby whale is called a calf.

It must swim as soon as it is born.

The mother whale can pump milk down the throat of a baby whale.

This helps to keep the baby from drinking sea water at the same time it is drinking milk.

1. **Where is a baby whale born?**
   1) On land
   2) On the shore
   3) In the water
   4) In a nest

2. **Where does a baby whale get its food?**
   1) From a bottle
   2) From its mother
   3) From the sea water
   4) It eats small fish.

3. **Which is the best name for this story?**
   1) "Baby Whales"
   2) "Where Whales Are Born"
   3) "Our Trip to the Zoo"
   4) "We Learn About the Sea"

4. **Why is food pumped into a baby whale?**
   1) It cannot swallow.
   2) It is too weak to eat.
   3) So the baby does not get too much air
   4) so the baby does not drink sea water

In addition to the traditional basic skills, some achievement batteries at the elementary school level include tests in listening comprehension and in the content areas of science and social studies. For these batteries it is usually possible also to obtain a separate partial battery limited to the measurement of basic skills. Batteries confined to the basic skills are generally preferred because content-oriented tests become outdated more quickly and are seldom well suited to the objectives of the local instructional program.

Achievement batteries have been less widely used at the high school level. The wide diversity of course offerings and the variations in course content within the same subject area have made it difficult to find a common core on which to base the tests. Most high school batteries focus on the same basic skills of reading, mathematics, language, and study skills that are covered by the elementary batteries (with the optional science and social studies tests). This provides for the continuous measurement of the basic skills throughout all grade levels. With the increasing emphasis on the teaching of basic skills and the widespread use of minimum-competency testing in the schools, high school basic skill batteries likely will be used more often.

Some high school batteries, such as the *Iowa Tests of Educational Development,* were designed to measure general educational development in intellectual skills and abilities that are not dependent on any particular series of courses. Instead, they assess analytical and evaluative skills that are needed in everyday life. The complete battery contains the following seven tests:

Correctness and Appropriateness of Expression

Ability to Do Quantitative Thinking

Analysis of Social Studies Materials

Analysis of Natural Science Materials

Ability to Interpret Literary Materials

Vocabulary

Use of Sources of Information

Interpretive-type exercises are used throughout the test battery. Sample items representing two of the tests are shown in Figure 11.2. In both tests, Part 1 focuses on understandings and thinking skills gained from the content area, and Part 2 stresses the ability to analyze and evaluate various types of material.

A list of representative achievement batteries that have been widely used in the schools is shown in Table 11.2. The grade range covered by each test series is indicated in the table. In some of the test series (e.g., STEP and *Stanford*), the tests at various levels have different names, but they are all part of a coordinated series that provide for continuous assessment throughout the grade range. Also, although *Tests of Achievement and Proficiency* (*TAP*) is listed separately, it is used in conjunction with the *Iowa Tests of Basic Skills* to form a coordinated program covering grades K–12. The *TAP* covers the same basic skill and content areas, with emphasis on ability to use information rather than on specific course content.

Although the batteries of tests designed to measure the basic skills are all somewhat similar in terms of the areas of skill covered, they vary considerably in terms of the nature of the test materials used and the specific abilities measured within each skill area. Therefore, in selecting an achievement battery, it is important to appraise carefully the specific test items to be certain that the abilities measured are relevant to the learning outcomes stressed in the school program. Any achievement battery will, of course, measure only some of the important outcomes of the school program. Other tests and evaluation procedures will be needed for a comprehensive coverage of a school's objectives.

FIGURE 11.2
Sample items like
those in the *Iowa Test
of Educational
Development.*
(Copyright © 1988 by
The Riverside Publishing
Company. Used by
permission.)

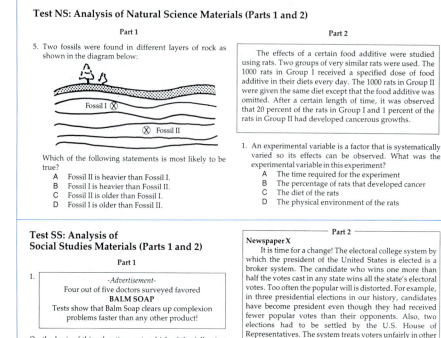

Test NS: Analysis of Natural Science Materials (Parts 1 and 2)

Part 1

5. Two fossils were found in different layers of rock as shown in the diagram below:

Fossil I ⊗

⊗ Fossil II

Which of the following statements is most likely to be true?
  A   Fossil II is heavier than Fossil I.
  B   Fossil I is heavier than Fossil II.
  C   Fossil II is older than Fossil I.
  D   Fossil I is older than Fossil II.

Part 2

The effects of a certain food additive were studied using rats. Two groups of very similar rats were used. The 1000 rats in Group I received a specified dose of food additive in their diets every day. The 1000 rats in Group II were given the same diet except that the food additive was omitted. After a certain length of time, it was observed that 20 percent of the rats in Group I and 1 percent of the rats in Group II had developed cancerous growths.

1. An experimental variable is a factor that is systematically varied so its effects can be observed. What was the experimental variable in this experiment?
  A   The time required for the experiment
  B   The percentage of rats that developed cancer
  C   The diet of the rats
  D   The physical environment of the rats

**Test SS: Analysis of
Social Studies Materials (Parts 1 and 2)**

Part 1

1.
-Advertisement-
Four out of five doctors surveyed favored
BALM SOAP
Tests show that Balm Soap clears up complexion problems faster than any other product!

On the basis of this advertisement, which of the following conclusions, if any, is valid?
  A   It has been scientifically demonstrated that the quickest way to get rid of any complexion problem is to use Balm Soap.
  B   Of the five leading brands of complexion soap, only one is better than Balm Soap from a medical point of view.
  C   Of all the doctors who recommend skin care products, four out of five recommend Balm Soap.
  D   None of these conclusions is valid.

Part 2
Newspaper X
It is time for a change! The electoral college system by which the president of the United States is elected is a broker system. The candidate who wins one more than half the votes cast in any state wins all the state's electoral votes. Too often the popular will is distorted. For example, in three presidential elections in our history, candidates have become president even though they had received fewer popular votes than their opponents. Also, two elections had to be settled by the U.S. House of Representatives. The system treats voters unfairly in other ways, too. Our lawmakers must be made to realize that the average person in this country is intelligent and capable of making a choice for president.

5. When Newspaper X speaks of the common people as intelligent and capable, what is being implied?
  A   The common people have been treated as equal to political leaders in the past.
  B   Only the common people can see the differernce between political candidates.
  C   The present electoral system assumes that the common people are unable to vote intelligently.
  D   The common people have a greater degree of intelligence and capability than political leaders.

Diagnostic Batteries for Instructional Use

Achievement test batteries have been traditionally designed as survey tests. That is, they provided a general, overall measure of the various areas of the curriculum. Typically, however, there were too few items measuring each skill to provide much help in making instructional decisions. The results might indicate a pupil's performance was low in reading or mathematics, for example, but they were of limited value for identifying the specific areas of strength and weakness. The few items in each area served as *indicators* of achievement but they were insufficient for *describing* what individual pupils had learned, what they had yet to learn, and the types of errors they were making.

In recent years test publishers have taken steps to make the test results of achievement batteries more useful to classroom teachers. Recent editions of the

	Grade Levels Covered													
Achievement Batteries	K	1	2	3	4	5	6	7	8	9	10	11	12	13
California Achievement Tests	X	X	X	X	X	X	X	X	X	X	X	X	X	
Comprehensive Tests of Basic Skills	X	X	X	X	X	X	X	X	X	X	X	X	X	
Iowa Tests of Basic Skills	X	X	X	X	X	X	X	X	X	X				
Metropolitan Achievement Tests	X	X	X	X	X	X	X	X	X	X	X	X	X	
Sequential Tests of Educational Progress (STEP + CIRCUS)	X	X	X	X	X	X	X	X	X	X	X	X	X	
SRA Achievement Series	X	X	X	X	X	X	X	X	X	X	X	X	X	
SRA Survey of Basic Skills	X	X	X	X	X	X	X	X	X	X	X	X	X	
Stanford Achievement Test Series	X	X	X	X	X	X	X	X	X	X	X	X	X	X
Iowa Tests of Educational Development										X	X	X	X	
Tests of Achievement and Proficiency (TAP)										X	X	X	X	

TABLE 11.2 Representative List of Achievement Batteries

Metropolitan Achievement Tests, for example, consist of an integrated series of *Survey Tests* and group-administered *Diagnostic Tests* covering the same areas of basic skills. The survey battery provides information about the pupils' relative performance in each of the areas, and the diagnostic tests in reading, mathematics, and language provide a more detailed description of the pupils' strengths and weaknesses in each skill area. This is accomplished, in part, by including a larger number of items in the diagnostic tests, using more subtests, and providing for criterion-referenced interpretation. The tests covered in each of the diagnostic batteries are presented in Table 11.3. The number of items in each test ranges from 15 to 60, but more commonly falls between 30 and 45. Sample items from four of the reading tests are shown in Figure 11.3.

In addition to the direct interpretation of strengths and weaknesses by subscores and instructional objectives, several special features were built into the Metropolitan Tests to aid instructional decisions.

1. An *Instructional Reading Level* can be determined by comparing the criterion-referenced reading comprehension score to graded basal readers.

2. An *Instructional Mathematics Level* can be determined by comparing criterion-referenced mathematics scores to graded levels of mathematics books.

3. Various comparisons between mathematics scores can be made to determine whether low problem-solving performance is due to lack of computational skills, low reading ability, or carelessness.

4. A *Research Skills Score* is obtained from items imbedded in various subject-matter tests.

TABLE 11.3	Reading	Mathematics
Tests Included in the Diagnostic Batteries of the Metropolitan Achievement Tests*	Visual Discrimination Letter Recognition Auditory Discrimination Sight Vocabulary Phoneme/Grapheme: Consonants Phoneme/Grapheme: Vowels Vocabulary in Context Word Part Clues Rate of Comprehension Skimming and Scanning Reading Comprehension	Numeration Geometry and Measurement Problem Solving Computation: Whole Numbers Computation: Decimals and Fractions Graphs and Statistics **Language** Listening Comprehension Punctuation and Capitalization Usage Written Expression Spelling Study Skills

*Has six levels for grades K–9.9, but, of course, not all diagnostic tests are used at each level.

5. A *Higher Order Thinking Skills Score* is obtained from critical thinking items used in several subject-matter tests.

6. Specific information is provided for instructional planning for those pupils needing remediation, as well as for those performing at or above average levels.

Similar diagnostic batteries in reading and mathematics are provided as separate components of the *Stanford Achievement Tests*, the *California Achievement Tests*, and the *Comprehensive Tests of Basic Skills*. This two-component system of survey and diagnostic tests, which are statistically linked, provides a sound approach for meeting both administrative and instructional needs. The survey tests provide a general measure of achievement for comparisons among schools and the diagnostic tests provide a more detailed measure of achievement for assessing the learning of individual pupils.

Although some achievement test batteries do not have a separate series of diagnostic tests, they typically aid instructional use by providing for analysis of results by objective, by specific skill area, or both. Whenever achievement test batteries (or any other test) provide for interpretation by objective, or specific skill, it is important to note the number of test items involved. It is not uncommon to base interpretation on as few as two or three test items. A lucky guess or careless error may be the deciding factor in determining whether success or failure is indicated. In such cases, it would be wiser to base instructional decisions on larger item clusters formed by combining items measuring similar objectives or skills.

Group-administered survey and diagnostic batteries are useful for identifying pupils who could benefit from remedial teaching and individual help. More serious learning problems, however, typically require the use of individually administered

FIGURE 11.3
Sample items
illustrating *Metropolitan
Achievement Tests:
Reading Diagnostic
Tests*, Intermediate
Level. (Copyright ©
1986, Harcourt Brace
Jovanovich. Used by
permission.)

Phoneme/Grapheme: Consonants
(Choose the word that has the same silent letter as the
underlined part of the key word)

knee

A king

B pink

C knit

D keen

Phoneme/Grapheme: Vowels
(Choose the word that has the same sound as the
underlined part of the key word)

boat

E hole

F land

G shoe

H got

Vocabulary in Context
(Choose the word that best completes the sentence)

Terry _____ to the park today.

A went   C home

B likes   D fast

Word Part Clues
(Choose the word that best completes the sentence)

Barry was very _____ when it
rained on Saturday.

E nonhappy   G dishappy

F unhappy   H rehappy

diagnostic tests and a careful study of the pupil's total development. The diagnosis
and remediation of severe learning disabilities is best left to the skilled clinician.

Achievement Tests in Specific Areas

In addition to achievement batteries, there are literally hundreds of separate tests
designed to measure achievement in specific areas. The majority of these can be
classified as tests of course content or reading tests of the general survey type. A

limited number of tests also have been developed for use in determining learning readiness.

Cautions in Selecting Achievement Batteries

1. Achievement batteries that focus on the basic skills measure important outcomes of the elementary school program, but these constitute only a portion of the outcomes of a modern curriculum.
2. At the high school level, basic skill batteries may serve both as learning readiness tests and as measures of learning outcomes in remedial basic skill programs. However, they provide only a limited measure of the many intended outcomes of the secondary school program.
3. Content-oriented tests in basic achievement batteries have broad coverage but limited sampling in each content area and may tend to become more quickly outdated than do the basic skills tests.
4. Achievement batteries differ in their emphasis on the various areas of basic skills, the different areas of content, and the specific types of learning outcomes measured. Thus, the selection of a battery should be based on their relevance to the school's objectives.
5. Diagnostic batteries should contain a sufficient number of test items for each type of interpretation to be made.

A separate test has certain advantages over a test battery. First, it is easier to select a separate test that fits the instructional objectives of a particular area. The difficulty of relating an entire battery of tests to instructional objectives was pointed out earlier. Second, a separate test is usually longer than a battery's subtests. This provides a more adequate sample of performance and more reliable part scores for instructional purposes. Third, the separate test's flexibility makes it easier to adapt to classroom instruction. Teachers can administer separate tests when they best fit their instructional needs, rather than following the rigid schedule of the school testing program.

One disadvantage of separate tests is that each one is usually standardized on a different groups of pupils. Because norm groups are not comparable, relative achievement of pupils in different areas cannot be compared. For example, it is not possible to determine whether a pupil has achieved more in science than in mathematics or in social studies than in English, if the tests were not standardized on the same representative group of pupils.

Separate Content-Oriented Tests

There are many achievement tests at the secondary level designed to measure the outcomes of specific courses. In fact, there are over a hundred separate tests in each of the major content areas of English, mathematics, science, and social studies. There are also separate tests in foreign language, business, and fine arts but not as many as those designed for the basic courses. All of these tests of specific course content are intended as "end of course" tests and thus are used primarily to measure the pupils' final levels of achievement. Although the tests vary in quality, many of them require pupils to demonstrate understanding and application as well as knowledge of factual information. For a complete listing of the separate tests available for use in schools, consult the catalogues of the test publishers in Appendix C. For critical reviews of the tests, see the latest *Mental Measurements Yearbooks* or *Test Critiques*.[2]

Cautions in Selecting Separate Tests in Specific Content Areas

1. Because separate tests are content oriented, the date of construction is especially important. Developments in some content areas, such as science and social studies, take place at such a rapid rate that some are soon out of date.
2. In addition to timeliness of test content, attention should be directed toward its appropriateness for the particular course in which it is to be used. Because a standardized test includes only the content common to many school systems, it may lack comprehensiveness and at the same time include questions on material that has not been covered in the local instructional program.
3. Many content-oriented tests emphasize the measurement of knowledge outcomes, although there are a number of exceptions. Standardized tests of specific knowledge are seldom as relevant and useful as are well-constructed teacher-made tests in the same area.
4. When a content-oriented test measures a variety of learning outcomes beyond those of specific knowledge (e.g., understanding, application, interpretation), it is important that the learning outcomes measured by the test complement those emphasized in the local instructional program.

---

[2]See Chapter 13 for descriptions of these guides.

Because of its flexibility and timeliness, the informal teacher-made test is frequently better suited to the measurement of instructional objectives in a particular course than is the standardized achievement test. However, when carefully selected according to course content and learning outcomes, the standardized test can serve as a valuable check on the teacher's informal classroom tests.

Reading Tests

One of the most widely used tests at all levels of instruction is the reading test. It occupies a prominent position in achievement test batteries and receives special emphasis in tests of general educational development. In addition, there are well over a hundred separate tests of reading ability.

Many reading tests are of the survey type, designed to measure a pupil's general level of reading ability. Such tests commonly measure vocabulary, reading comprehension, and rate of reading. The following list of reading skills is typical of those that reading survey tests attempt to measure.

Identifies the meaning of given words.

Identifies the meaning of words when used in context.

Identifies details directly stated in a passage or selection.

Identifies ideas implied in a passage or selection.

Identifies relationships (e.g., time, cause and effect) in a passage or selection.

Identifies the main thought or purpose of a passage or selection.

Identifies inferences drawn from a passage or selection.

Identifies conclusions drawn from a passage or selection.

Identifies the writer's tone, mood, and intent.

Reading tests differ greatly in the extent to which they cover these skills and in the degree of emphasis given to each. Some tests focus on the lower levels of comprehension (e.g., identifying directly stated details), whereas others stress the more complex interpretive skills (e.g., identifying relationships, inferences, and conclusions). Moreover, the last two reading skills in this list are more likely to be found in high school reading tests than in those designed for elementary school.

Reading tests also differ widely in the material to be read by the pupil. Some tests use short passages of a sentence or two, whereas others use extended passages. Some use stories only, and others use stories, letters, poems, and scientific articles. Still another source of difference among reading tests is the extensiveness with which each type of reading material and each reading skill is sampled. One test, for example, may have a relatively large number of test items measuring the ability to draw conclusions from scientific articles, whereas another test has just a few such items. These differences highlight the importance of defining what reading abilities are to be measured before selecting a test.

Reading tests may be selected for any of the following uses: (1) to evaluate the effectiveness of reading instruction, (2) to identify those pupils needing remedial work in reading, (3) to predict success in subject-matter courses, (4) to determine whether poor reading ability can account for low scores on scholastic aptitude tests, and (5) to help locate the causes of learning problems. Although a single reading test may not serve all of these uses equally well, how the results are to be used is an important consideration in test selection. The ideal reading test for a particular program is the one that best measures the instructional objectives and most effectively fulfills the uses to which the results will be put. See Appendix D for a list of reading tests.

Cautions in Selecting Reading Tests

1. No two reading tests are exactly alike. Although reading survey tests usually measure vocabulary, reading comprehension, and rate of reading, they differ in the material that the reader is expected to comprehend, in the specific reading skills tested, and in the adequacy with which each skill is measured.

2. Reading survey tests measure only some of the outcomes of reading instruction. The mechanics of reading (e.g., perceptual skills, word analysis) are typically measured by diagnostic reading tests. Some specialized reading skills (e.g., reading maps, graphs, charts) are more commonly measured by tests of study skills. Attitude toward reading and interest in reading, both of which are extremely important outcomes of reading instruction, must be determined by observation or other means.

3. Reading tests can serve many purposes in the school program. Thus, in addition to matching the objectives of instruction, test selection should take into account all of the possible uses to be made of the results.

Readiness Tests

Some tests have been designed to determine pupil readiness for learning school tasks. At the elementary level, reading readiness tests are probably the most familiar, but other types of tests are also used. Although readiness tests are essentially specialized scholastic aptitude tests, they are considered here because their test items are drawn from specific achievement areas. This has the advantage of providing diagnostic as well as predictive information. Thus, in addition to predicting learning success in a particular achievement area, test performance can provide information concerning the specific skills that pupils need to improve if their learning is to be effective.

Early School Readiness and Achievement Tests. Several tests have been developed to measure those basic concepts and skills considered essential for effective learning in the early school years. The tests are usually designed for preschool use (kindergarten or sooner) but also can be used in the early primary grades. A typical example is the *Boehm Test of Basic Concepts*. This test is based on a selection of verbal concepts (e.g., biggest, nearest, several) that are needed to understand oral communication and to profit most from school experiences. The test items are read to the pupils, and they answer by placing an X on the pictures designed to measure the concepts. See Figure 11.4 for a sample item.

Somewhat similar in makeup and purpose are the *Cooperative Preschool Inventory*, the *Stanford Early School Achievement Test*, and *Tests of Basic Experience*. These tests emphasize basic concepts, but they also tap other types of preschool learning (e.g., knowledge of environment). Although these tests are broader in scope than the *Boehm Test*, the intended use is the same — to determine the pupils' achievement of important concepts and skills and to detect deficiencies for which appropriate learning experiences might be supplied. These tests should be useful in planning for and evaluating preschool instruction and in designing remedial programs for individual pupils.

Reading Readiness Tests.   Tests of reading readiness are used at the kindergarten and first-grade level to help determine whether pupils have the necessary knowledge and skills to begin reading and to group pupils for beginning reading instruction. The following functions are commonly measured by reading readiness tests:

1. *Visual discrimination*. Identifying similarities and differences in words, letters, numbers, geometric figures, or pictures.

2. *Auditory discrimination*. Identifying similarities and differences in spoken words or sounds.

3. *Verbal comprehension*. Demonstrating or understanding the meaning of words, sentences, and directions.

4. *Recognition of letters, words, and numbers*. Identifying letters of the alphabet, words, and numerals.

FIGURE 11.4
Sample item from the
*Boehm Test of Basic
Concepts*. (Copyright ©
1967–1970, 1986 by The
Psychological
Corporation, San Antonio, ·
Texas. All rights reserved.
Reproduced by
permission.)

Mark the boat that is <u>farthest</u> from the shore.

5. *Recognition of words in sample lessons.* Identifying words that have been taught in sample lessons.
6. *Memory.* Reproducing a geometric figure, following instructions, or selecting a picture from memory.
7. *Drawing or copying.* Demonstrating skill in drawing or copying geometric forms, objects, letters, or numbers.

Not all reading readiness tests provide comprehensive coverage of the above areas. Some tests cover only a few readiness skills, whereas others include tasks from four or five of the areas. Thus, as in all types of testing, the first step is to decide what is to be measured. In this particular case, it means deciding what reading readiness skills are most relevant to the reading program. A clear description of the skills to be measured is a prerequisite to valid test selection and use.

A typical example of a widely used readiness test is the *Metropolitan Readiness Test*. It is available in two levels: Level 1 is used up to the middle of kindergarten, and Level 2 is used in the second half of kindergarten and the first half of grade 1. Level 2 contains the following eight tests:

1. Beginning Consonants.
2. Sound-Letter Correspondence.
3. Visual Matching.
4. Finding Patterns.
5. School Language.
6. Listening.
7. Quantitative Concepts.
8. Quantitative Operations.

Cautions in Selecting Readiness Tests

1. Because these tests are predictive instruments, the test manual should be examined concerning the effectiveness with which they predict success in the given area. Validity coefficients should be at least as high as those obtained with general scholastic aptitude tests and preferably higher.
2. In addition to their predictive value, these tests also have some general diagnostic value. Thus, the test's content should be evaluated in light of the type of readiness information desired and the uses to be made of the results.
3. These tests provide just a fraction of the information needed to determine readiness for learning in a given area. The pupil's social and emotional adjustment, past achievement in the area, motivation to learn, and cultural background also must be taken into account.

Sample items for some of the tests are shown in Figure 11.5. The items are orally administered with elaborate directions. The very abbreviated directions used here are simply to illustrate the nature of the task. If a test user is interested in reading readiness only, separate scoring and norms are available for tests 1 through 6.

Readiness for beginning reading involves more than the skills measured by readiness tests. Such factors as mental ability, physical development, experiential background, social and emotional adjustment, and desire to read also must be considered. The readiness test focuses on important prerequisite skills, but test performance must be interpreted in light of the pupil's total readiness for learning.

FIGURE 11.5
Sample items illustrating the *Metropolitan Readiness Test*, Level 2. (Copyright © 1986, Harcourt Brace Jovanovich. Used by permission.)

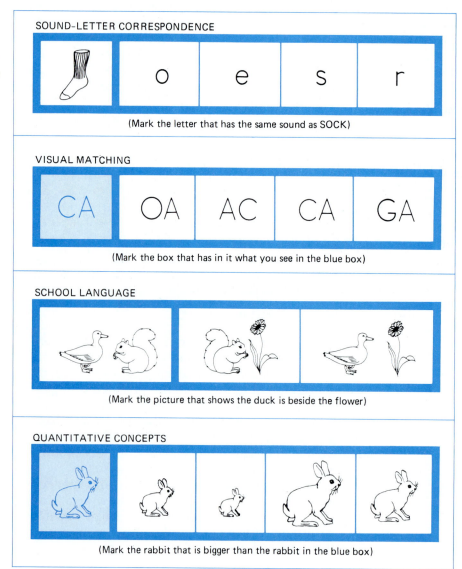

SOUND-LETTER CORRESPONDENCE

(Mark the letter that has the same sound as SOCK)

VISUAL MATCHING

(Mark the box that has in it what you see in the blue box)

SCHOOL LANGUAGE

(Mark the picture that shows the duck is beside the flower)

QUANTITATIVE CONCEPTS

(Mark the rabbit that is bigger than the rabbit in the blue box)

Customized Achievement Tests

Banks of objectives and related test items are maintained by most large test publishers and by some other organizations. These item banks are used for computer generation of customized tests. In some cases the tests are prepared by the test publisher. In others, the publisher will sell or lease computer software that includes the objective-item bank and a program for constructing and printing locally prepared customized tests.

When using *publisher-prepared* customized achievement tests, the test user typically selects the objectives to be measured from an objective catalogue and specifies the number of items to be used for measuring each objective. The test publisher then assembles and prints the test by taking from the item banks those items that measure the selected objectives. Scoring and reporting services are also available from the publisher for these tests. A typical example of such a customized program is the *Multiscore System*, by The Riverside Publishing Company. Currently it offers approximately 1,800 objectives and more than 5,500 test items in reading and language arts, mathematics, science, social studies, and life skills. The objectives are arranged by unit clusters in three catalogues, with the recommended grade level indicated for each objective. See Figure 11.6 for a sample listing. The

FIGURE 11.6
Sample Performance Objectives from *Multiscore*, Criterion-Referenced Testing Service Catalog. (Copyright © 1985 by The Riverside Publishing Company. Used by permission.)

UNIT CLUSTERS	PERFORMANCE OBJECTIVES	PERFORMANCE OBJECTIVE CODES	GRADE RANGE
Scientific Procedures A5A3	The student:		
	. . . classifies pictures by shape, sequence, function, symmetry, or other features.	5A01 / 5A02	3 – 4 / 7 – 8
	. . . identifies an object from various perspectives.	5A03	5 – 6
	. . . draws conclusions based on elapsed time, descriptions, and tabular data.	5A04	9 – 12
	. . . forms a hypothesis about an outcome.	5A05	3 – 4
	. . . forms a hypothesis or identifies a test for a hypothesis.	5A06 / 5A07 / 5A08	5 – 6 / 7 – 8 / 9 – 12
	. . . interprets visual or tabular data.	5A09 / 5A10 / 5A11	1 – 2 / 3 – 4 / 7 – 8
	. . . measures length in arbitrary units and/or solves problems involving measurement.	5A12 / 5A13 / 5A14	3 – 4 / 7 – 8 / 9 – 12

Scientific Methods — Grades 1 – 12 (9 objectives) — A SCIENCE service includes customized test booklets (either machine scorable or reusable), scoring, and reports (including class reports by objective and test item). Other test publishers have somewhat similar programs.

Locally-produced customized achievement tests can be prepared using microcomputer-based software products available from test publishers. An example of this type program is the *Academic Instructional Measurement System* (*AIMS*) by The Psychological Corporation. This is a large bank of objectives and test items in mathematics and reading and language arts developed from texts and curriculum materials used nationally. The preparation of locally constructed customized tests can be either done manually, from camera-ready printed materials, or by use of an optional microcomputer software system (see box). The system makes possible local test printing, scoring, and reporting of results.

Academic Instructional Measurement Systems (AIMS)

AIMS is a test development system for preparing locally developed tests for grades 1 to 12. It includes 989 objectives and 7,000 related test items in mathematics and reading and language arts. Steps in using the system include:

1. Selecting objectives that were taught in the classroom.
2. Selecting from among the 6 to 8 items for each objective.
3. Producing test booklets using camera-ready copy or the optional computer software system.
4. Producing answer keys and administration manuals.

AIMS Software Option

AIMS tests can be constructed by microcomputer with the *AIMS* software system. Objectives, test items, item statistics, and related materials are included on microcomputer diskettes. The program permits retrieval of text from the item bank for tests, administration manuals, and scoring keys. It also allows the deletion of items and the integration of locally written items and objectives into the bank. A demonstration disk with a tutorial booklet is available to show how *AIMS* software can make local test construction efficient and easy.

Adapted from The Psychological Corporation catalogue (1988).

Customized tests prepared by test publishers, or prepared locally, are especially useful for classroom testing because they can be designed to yield measurements of the specific knowledge and skills covered in the instructional program. Locally controlled microcomputer systems have the added advantage of being able to prepare tests as needed, without the time lag created when ordering customized tests from the publisher. In addition, a microcomputer system makes it easy to add locally prepared objectives and test items to the bank. In using customized tests, however they are prepared, it is important to select the objectives carefully and to include enough items for each instructional objective or skill cluster to provide for reliable interpretations. It is also necessary, of course, to make certain that the individual items are relevant to the instructional objectives they are to measure.

Information concerning customized test development and microcomputer software can be obtained from test publishers' catalogues. See Appendix C for test publishers' addresses and a list of objective-item banks available for school use.

Individual Achievement Tests

Because of the increased number of handicapped children in the regular classroom, it would seem desirable for classroom teachers to become familiar with some of the individual tests that are available for measuring achievement. These tests are

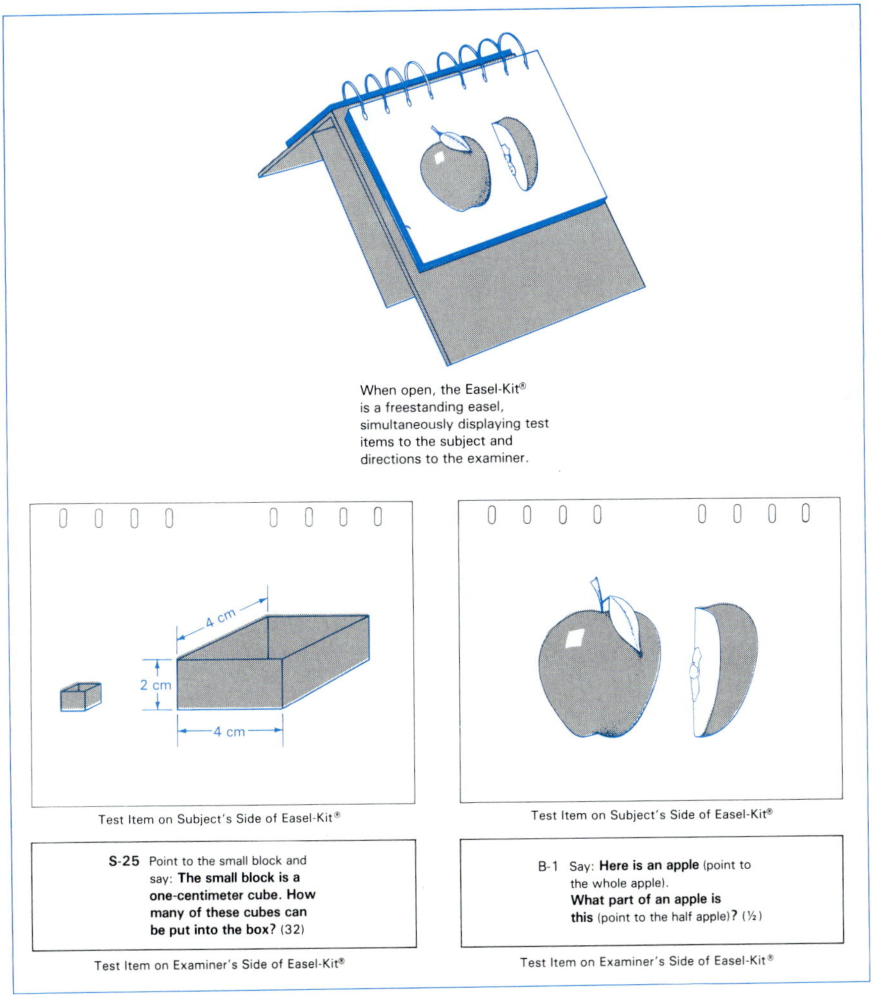

When open, the Easel-Kit® is a freestanding easel, simultaneously displaying test items to the subject and directions to the examiner.

Test Item on Subject's Side of Easel-Kit®

S-25 Point to the small block and say: **The small block is a one-centimeter cube. How many of these cubes can be put into the box?** (32)

Test Item on Examiner's Side of Easel-Kit®

Test Item on Subject's Side of Easel-Kit®

B-1 Say: **Here is an apple** (point to the whole apple). **What part of an apple is this** (point to the half apple)? (½)

Test Item on Examiner's Side of Easel-Kit®

FIGURE 11.7
Sample items from *KeyMath Diagnostic Arithmetic Test* illustrating use of Easel-Kit for Individual Testing. (Used by permission of AGS, American Guidance Service.)

administered to one pupil at a time and the questions are typically answered orally or by pointing, although some writing may be required. Some of the tests provide for norm-referenced interpretation, some use criterion-referenced interpretation, and still others provide for both types of interpretation. Typical examples of individual achievement tests include the following:

> *Basic Achievement Skills Individual Screener*
> (Grades 1 to 12)
>
> *Peabody Individual Achievement Test* – Revised
> (K to adult)
>
> *KeyMath Diagnostic Arithmetic Test* – Revised
> (K to grade 9)
>
> *Woodcock Reading Mastery Tests* – Revised
> (K to adult)

Each of these tests can be administered in 30 to 60 minutes, with much of the scoring completed during the administration. Other individual achievement tests can be obtained from test publishers' catalogues (see Appendix C). For reviews of these and other achievement tests discussed in this chapter, see the latest *Mental Measurements Yearbook* or *Test Critiques* described in Chapter 13.

Summary

Standardized achievement tests measure the common objectives of a wide variety of schools, have standard procedures for administration and scoring, and provide norms for interpreting the scores. A test manual and other accessory materials are typically provided to aid in the administration of the test and the interpretation and use of the results. The test items are generally of high quality because they have been prepared by specialists, pretested, and selected on the basis of their effectiveness and their relevance to a rigid set of specifications.

Despite their high technical quality, standardized achievement tests complement rather than replace teachers' informal classroom tests. They are especially useful for measuring general educational development, determining pupil progress from one year to the next, grouping pupils, diagnosing learning difficulties, and comparing achievement with learning ability. They are of less value for measuring learning outcomes unique to a particular course, the day-to-day progress of pupils, and knowledge of current developments in rapidly changing fields. These purposes are more effectively served by informal classroom tests.

Achievement test batteries are widely used at the elementary school level. They cover the basic skills (i.e., reading, language, mathematics, and study skills), and some batteries also include sections on listening comprehension and science and social studies. Test batteries are less widely used at the high school level because of the difficulty of identifying a common core of content. Batteries at this level are confined to the basic skills, to content included in the basic high school subjects, or to measures of general educational development. The main advantage of a test battery is that a pupil's strengths and weaknesses in different areas can be determined. Most test batteries provide for both norm-referenced interpretation and interpretation by objective or skill area. The complete test battery seldom fits all of the instructional objectives of the school, however, and this must be taken into account when one is interpreting the results.

The instructional use of achievement batteries has been enhanced by the publishing of sets of diagnostic batteries that are statistically linked to the survey batteries. The larger number of items and subtests in the diagnostic batteries make it possible to obtain a more detailed description of each pupil's strengths and weaknesses in learning.

In addition to achievement test batteries, there are many separate published tests designed to measure achievement in specific areas. These include tests on course content, reading tests, and readiness tests. Although these can be more readily adapted to the instructional program than complete batteries, the following cautions should be kept in mind during their selection and use: (1) published tests with similar titles may differ radically in terms of the type of test content and in terms of the emphasis given to the various skills measured; (2) published tests measure only a portion of the knowledge, skills, and abilities needed to evaluate, predict, or diagnose learning progress; (3) published tests are effective to the extent that they measure the instructional objectives and serve the intended uses of the particular school program in which they are administered.

To more adequately meet the needs of classroom teachers for individualized instruction and mastery learning, test publishers are now making available customized achievement tests. Some publishers also provide item banks and software programs that enable schools to produce their own customized tests with microcomputers. These customized achievement tests measure pupil mastery of locally selected instructional objectives and thus describe what learning tasks a pupil can and cannot perform in the local instructional program. The interpretations must be made with great caution, however, because there are frequently a small number of test items measuring each objective or skill.

There are now many handicapped pupils in regular classrooms. In testing these pupils, an individual achievement test may be more appropriate. These are administered on a one-to-one basis, and the questions are typically answered orally or by pointing. There are a number of such tests available for school use.

Learning Exercises

1. What are the similarities and differences in the making of a classroom test and a standardized test of achievement? How are the uses of the two tests likely to differ?

2. What are the advantages of using an achievement battery rather than separate achievement tests? What are the disadvantages?

3. Describe how a survey achievement battery and a related diagnostic battery differ in makeup and use.

4. If possible, study the manual of an achievement test battery. Review the information on how it was constructed. How complete is the information?

5. Examine two standardized achievement tests in an area you are teaching or plan to teach. How do the tests differ in terms of the learning outcomes and content each measures? What types of interpretations are suggested?

6. What are the advantages of using school readiness tests? What are some possible disadvantages?

7. For what situations might you use a customized achievement test instead of a standardized test?

8. What are the advantages of providing both norm-referenced interpretations and objective-referenced interpretations of published achievement tests? What are some of the cautions to be observed in making both types of interpretation for the same test?

Suggestions for Further Reading

ANASTASI, A. *Psychological Testing*, 6th ed. New York: Macmillan, 1988. Chapter 14, "Educational Testing," describes common types of achievement tests used in education with illustrative test items.

CHALL, J. S., AND STAHL, S. A. "Reading." In *Encyclopedia of Educational Research*, 5th ed. New York: Macmillan, 1982, vol. 3, pp. 1535–1559. Describes research on reading and its influence on practice. Reviews factors related to reading and learning disabilities. Extensive bibliography.

GORDON, N. J. "Readiness." In *Encyclopedia of Educational Research*, 5th ed. New York: Macmillan, 1982, vol. 3, pp. 1531–1535. Discusses the problem of learning readiness and the various measures used to determine readiness at the kindergarten and first-grade levels.

MEHRENS, W. A., AND LEHMANN, I. J. *Using Standardized Tests in Education*, 4th ed. New York: Holt, Rinehart & Winston, 1987. Chapter 8, "Standardized Achievement Tests," describes various types of achievement tests used in the schools and the uses of achievement test results.

SALVIA, J., AND YSSELDYKE, J. *Assessment in Special and Remedial Education*, 4th ed. Boston: Houghton Mifflin, 1988. Chapter 16, "Assessment of Academic Achievement: Screening Devices," describes specific tests and discusses how to get the most out of an achievement test. See Chapters 17, 18, and 21 for diagnostic testing in reading and mathematics and for school readiness testing.

Chapter 12

Aptitude Tests

Aptitude tests are designed to predict future performance in some activity. . . . Those used in schools range from the traditional scholastic aptitude tests to the more comprehensive differential aptitude tests. Attempts also have been made to develop special culture-fair tests . . . Typical examples of aptitude tests used in schools will be discussed and illustrated. . . . Group tests are commonly used but individual tests also have a place.

Because one of the school's major aims is to assist pupils to achieve the maximum of which they are capable, it is not surprising that standardized aptitude tests are so important. Some estimate of pupil ability is necessary in determining learning readiness, in individualizing instruction, in organizing classroom groups, in identifying underachievers, in diagnosing learning problems, and in helping pupils with their educational and vocational plans. Although the results of achievement tests are also useful for these purposes, aptitude tests make a special contribution.

Achievement and Aptitude Tests

Before we discuss the various types of aptitude tests, we shall consider some similarities and differences between achievement tests and aptitude tests. A common distinction is that *achievement* tests measure what a pupil has learned, and *aptitude* tests measure the ability to learn new tasks. Although this appears to be a clear distinction, it oversimplifies the problem and covers up some important similarities and differences. Actually both types measure what a pupil has learned, and both are useful for predicting success in learning new tasks. The main differences lie in (1) the types of learning measured by each test and (2) the types of prediction for which each is most useful.

Types of Learning Measured: The Ability Spectrum

The various types of learning measured by achievement and aptitude tests can be best depicted if they are arranged along a continuum, as shown in Table 12.1. In this spectrum of ability tests, achievement tests fall at Levels A and B and aptitude tests fall at Levels C, D, and E. The spectrum classifies the various types of tests according to the degree to which the test content depends on specific learning experiences. At one extreme (Level A) is the content-oriented achievement test that measures knowledge of specific course content. At the other extreme (Level E) is the culture-oriented nonverbal aptitude test that measures a type of learning little influenced by direct training. Thus, as we move through the different levels of the spectrum from A to E, the test content becomes less dependent on any particular set of learning experiences.

The closer that two tests are to each other in the spectrum, the more nearly alike will be the types of learning measured. Achievement tests designed to measure general educational development (Level B) and scholastic aptitude tests based on school-learned abilities (Level C), for example, both measure somewhat similar

TABLE 12.1	Level	General Test Type	Types of Learning Measured
Spectrum of Ability Tests According to Types of Learning Measured*	A	Content-oriented achievement tests (e.g., *Tests of Achievement and Proficiency*)	Knowledge of subject matter in courses such as social studies, English, mathematics, and science.
	B	Tests of general educational development (e.g., *Iowa Tests of Educational Development*, STEP)	Basic skills and complex learning outcomes common to many courses, such as the application of principles and interpretation of data.
	C	School-oriented aptitude tests (e.g., *Cooperative School and College Ability Tests*, SCAT)	Verbal, numerical, and general problem-solving abilities similar to those learned in *school*, such as vocabulary, reading, and arithmetic reasoning.
	D	Culture-oriented verbal aptitude tests (e.g., *Cognitive Abilities Test, Verbal Battery and Quantitative Battery*)	Verbal, numerical, and general problem-solving abilities derived more from the *general culture* than from common *school experiences*.
	E	Culture-oriented nonverbal aptitude tests (e.g., *Cognitive Abilities Test, Nonverbal Battery*)	Abstract reasoning abilities based on figure analogies, figure classification, and other nonverbal tasks unrelated to school experience.

*Adapted from L. J. Cronbach, *Essential of Psychological Testing*, 4th ed. (New York: Harper & Row, 1984).

abilities, and thus they can be expected to correlate rather highly. Likewise, the farther apart two tests are in the spectrum, the less they will have in common and consequently the lower the correlations will be between them. This information is useful in selecting and using aptitude tests. For instance, we can expect aptitude tests at Levels C and D to provide a better prediction of school achievement than those at Level E. On the other hand, if we are primarily interested in identifying pupils with undeveloped learning *potential*, tests at Level E will be more useful. When using this spectrum, however, remember that these are merely convenient categories for classifying the different types of ability tests and that some tests will cover two or more categories. Several wide-spectrum scholastic aptitude tests, for example, include a range of test content covering Levels C, D, and E in a single test score.

Types of Predictions Made with Achievement and Aptitude Tests

Achievement and aptitude tests also can be distinguished according to the types of predictions for which each is most useful. Because past achievement is frequently the best predictor of future achievement, both types of achievement tests are useful in predicting future learning. In general, the content-oriented achievement test (Level A) can predict how well a pupil will learn new knowledge in the same content area, but it is of less value in predicting future learning in other areas. For example, a test of first-semester English will be a good predictor of second-semester English but not of second-semester mathematics, science, or social studies. In other words, its value as a predictor of future learning depends largely on the relationship between the content being measured and the content in the future learning situation. Tests measuring general educational development (Level B) are much more effective predictors of future achievement than are content-oriented tests because they measure intellectual skills and abilities common to a variety of content areas.

If achievement tests are such good predictors of future learning, then why do we use aptitude tests (Levels C to E) in schools? There are several good reasons. (1) An aptitude test can be administered in a relatively short time (some as short as twenty minutes), whereas a comprehensive battery of achievement tests takes several hours. (2) In addition to time saved, aptitude tests can be used with pupils of more widely varying educational backgrounds. Because the type of learning measured is common to most pupils, an individual is less apt to be penalized because of specific weaknesses in past training. (3) Aptitude tests can be used before a pupil has had any training in a particular area. For example, success in a French course cannot be predicted by an achievement test in French until the person has had some training in it. (4) Another reason applies more to the culture-oriented aptitude test (Levels D and E). Because these are measures of aptitude least influenced by school-learned abilities, they can be used to distinguish low achievers working up to their ability from those with the potential for higher achievement. Identifying such underachievers with aptitude tests that depend heavily on school-learned abilities (Level C) is possible but less effective because the achievement skills required to respond to the test are those in which the underachiever is most apt to be weak.

In summary, both achievement tests and aptitude tests measure learned abilities, but achievement tests measure those that are more directly dependent on specific school experiences, whereas aptitude tests measure those based on a wide range of both in-school and out-of-school experiences. This is a matter of degree, however, and it is possible to arrange both types of test on a continuum, ranging from the measurement of specific course content (Level A) to the measurement of more broadly based abilities (Levels D and E). Achievement tests and aptitude tests become very much alike near the center of the continuum (Levels B and C). Achievement and aptitude tests are also similar in that they both are useful for predicting future achievement. In general, aptitude tests are a more convenient measure and one that predicts over a wide range of future experiences. As with types of learning outcomes measured, these differences are less pronounced near the center of the continuum.

Scholastic Aptitude and Learning Ability

Tests designed to measure learning ability traditionally have been called *intelligence tests*. This terminology is still used for some individually administered tests and for some group tests, but its use is declining. There are a number of reasons for this. (1) Many people have come to associate the concept *intelligence* with inherited capacity. (2) There is increasing controversy over the meaning of *intelligence* and the factors that should be included in the concept. (3) Tests in this area have been increasingly used for predicting achievement and describing learning abilities. In place of the term *intelligence test* have come such terms as *learning ability tests*, *school ability tests*, *cognitive ability tests*, and *scholastic aptitude tests*. All of these terms emphasize the fact that these tests measure developed abilities useful in learning and not innate capacity or undeveloped potential.

Pupils' scores on scholastic aptitude tests or ability tests are best interpreted as a measure of present learning ability. Test performance is influenced by such factors as inherited characteristics, experiential background, motivation, particular skills (e.g., reading, test taking), attention, persistence, self-confidence, and emotional adjustment. These factors are all a part of an individual's present ability to perform and, as such, affect both test scores and school achievement. Many of these factors can be modified by educational experiences, however, and therefore both learning ability and school achievement can be improved. It is when we interpret the test scores as unmodifiable measures of learning potential that we are apt to misuse the results.

Group Tests of Learning Ability

The majority of tests of learning ability administered in the schools are group tests. These are tests that, like standardized achievement tests, can be administered to many pupils at one time by persons with relatively little training in test administration. Some group tests yield a single score, whereas others yield two or more scores based on measures of separate aspects of ability. Here we shall briefly describe and illustrate the various types of group tests. Critical reviews of these and other ability tests can be found in the *Mental Measurements Yearbooks* and *Test Critiques*.

Single-Score Tests

Tests that yield a single score are designed to measure pupils' general learning ability. Typically, such a variety of types of items is included in the test that no particular ability or skill receives undue emphasis in the total score. Thus, the specific aspects of ability (such as verbal, numerical, and abstract reasoning) are blended together into one global measure of ability. These are sometimes called wide-spectrum tests and cover Levels C through E in the spectrum of abilities described earlier (see Table 12.1).

A common format for the single-score test is to arrange the items in a *spiral omnibus* pattern; that is, to mix together items of different types and arrange them in increasing order of difficulty. This makes it possible to have one set of directions and a relatively short testing time (thirty to forty minutes) because there are no separate subtests. An example of a widely used test of this type is the *Otis–Lennon School Ability Test*, 5th Ed. (grades 1–12). See Figure 12.1 for sample test items.[1]

Single-score tests are typically used to measure readiness for school learning and to predict success in future schoolwork. They are highly verbal in nature and this, of course, contributes to their predictive value because school learning is largely verbal. However, they do not provide for differential prediction for various types of

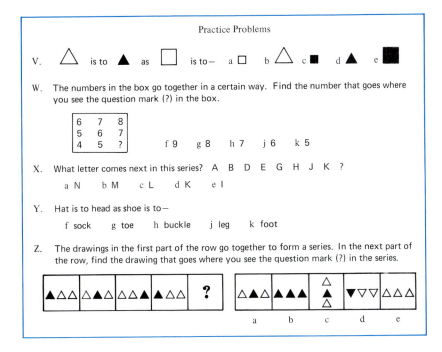

FIGURE 12.1
Sample items from the *Otis–Lennon School Ability Test*. (Reproduced from the *Otis–Lennon School Ability Test*. Copyright 1979, 1982, by Harcourt Brace Jovanovich, Inc. All rights reserved. Used by permission.)

---

[1] The publisher has indicated that the sixth edition will provide verbal, nonverbal, and total scores.

schoolwork. They are intended only as a general measure of current learning readiness. Thus, a low score will indicate a lack of readiness to perform well on school tasks, but the low score will reveal neither the nature nor the cause of the poor performance. Single-score ability tests provide a quick, effective, general measure of present learning ability.

Tests Yielding Separate Scores

A number of tests of learning ability yield two or more part scores as well as the total score. Some tests, like the *Educational Ability Series* (grades K to 12), have both verbal and nonverbal scores. The nonverbal score provides a check on the verbal score for those pupils who are deficient in verbal skills (e.g., poor readers). Other tests, like the *School and College Ability Tests* (SCAT, grades 3.5 to 12), provide verbal and quantitative scores. The purpose here is to obtain differential prediction of school success between courses stressing verbal concepts and those emphasizing mathematical concepts. Predictive studies indicate that verbal scores tend to be the best predictor of success in most courses, however, so interpretations concerning differential prediction must be cautiously made. A relatively large difference between verbal and quantitative scores is needed before it is meaningful. The test manual will indicate what size score difference is significant.

The *Cognitive Abilities Test* (grades K – 12) provides a measure of all three types of reasoning ability important in school learning. It provides scores for each of three different test batteries: Verbal, Quantitative, and Nonverbal. The test includes two primary levels for testing in kindergarten through grade 3, and eight higher levels for use in grades 3 through grade 12. These later eight levels are published in a single *multilevel edition* booklet that contains all three batteries. With the "multilevel" format, the items in each subtest are arranged in order of increasing difficulty and the examinees start and stop at different places, depending on their grade level. If the assigned level is inappropriate for a particular group (e.g., extremely good or poor readers) it is simply a matter of shifting to a higher or lower level within the test.

The primary levels of the *Cognitive Abilities Test* include the following six tests:

VERBAL BATTERY

Oral Vocabulary. Marks a picture that illustrates a word read aloud (e.g., the one that is *round*).

Verbal Classification. Marks a picture that belongs with three other pictures that are alike in some way (e.g., all are *toys*).

QUANTITATIVE BATTERY

Quantitative Concepts. Marks a picture illustrating a concept (e.g., *half* a pie).

Relational Concepts. Marks a picture illustrating a relation (e.g., *tallest* tree).

NONVERBAL BATTERY

Figure Matrices. Marks the figure that completes a four-cell matrix containing three geometric figures and one empty cell.

Figure Classification. Marks the figure that belongs with three other figures that are alike in some way (e.g., all are *triangles*).

Tests at the primary level are all administered with oral directions and a predetermined pattern of testing is followed. The order alternates the tests from different batteries to maintain interest and attention. Suggested time limits are given but they are power tests, not speed tests. The test administrator reads the instructions for each item and allows sufficient time for all children to try the item. No reading is involved.

The multilevel edition for grades 3–12 contains three tests in each of the three batteries—Verbal, Quantitative, and Nonverbal. The three tests in the Verbal Battery are illustrated by the sample items shown in Figure 12.2. The items in all three tests include verbal tasks that have not been directly taught in school but require the use of verbal concepts that have been learned both in and out of school. The instructions for our illustrative items are very abbreviated.

The Quantitative Battery contains three tests that require pupils to solve quantitative tasks that have not been directly taught in school. The sample items in Figure 12.3 illustrate the nature of these tests. Like the verbal battery, the emphasis is on reasoning abilities that require the use of concepts that have been learned both in and out of school.

The Nonverbal Battery consists of three tests using geometric shapes and figures, as illustrated in Figure 12.4. The concepts needed to solve the problems in these

---

Verbal Classification (Pick the word that is like the three words in **dark** type)

dog   rabbit   lion

A zoo   B cat   C wild   D pet   E feed

Sentence Completion (Pick the one word that makes a complete, sensible sentence)

We sailed the _____ in the bathtub

A dog   B doll   C boat   D towel   E rock

Verbal Analogies (Pick the word that is related to the third word in the same way that the second word is related to the first)

fire → hot: ice →

A cream   B melt   C box   D cold   E freeze

FIGURE 12.2
Sample items from the Verbal Battery of the *Cognitive Abilities Test,* Multi-Level Edition. (Copyright © 1986 by The Riverside Publishing Company. Used by permission.)

FIGURE 12.3
Sample items from the
Quantitative Battery of
the *Cognitive Abilities
Test*, Multi-Level
Edition. (Copyright ©
1986 by The Riverside
Publishing Company.
Used by permission.)

Quantitative Concepts (Compare the two coins and select the correct answer)

    I.   1 nickel   **A** I is more money than II

    II.   1 dime   **B** I is less money than II

                            C I is the same amount of money as II

Number Series (Figure out the rule used to arrange the numbers and choose the number that comes next in the series)

    10   8   6   4   2 → **A** 0 **B** 1 **C** 2 **D** 3 **E** 5

Equation Building (Arrange the numbers and signs in such a way as to produce one of the lettered answers)

    2   3   1   +   +   **A** 4 **B** 5 **C** 6 **D** 7 **E** 8

items are learned primarily from experiences out of school. Because the tests use neither words nor numbers, the nonverbal battery provides a poorer prediction of school success than the other two batteries. However, the nonverbal tests provide a more accurate measure of the reasoning abilities of poor readers and those deficient in language skills.

The scores on all batteries of the *Cognitive Abilities Test* are expressed as a *Standard Age Score* (SAS) that has a mean of 100 and a standard deviation of 16. Separate Verbal, Quantitative, and Nonverbal scores are reported, but no total score is reported for the combined batteries. It was felt that a total score could be misleading where skill development in the three areas was very uneven. For instructional purposes, it is better to focus on the strengths and weaknesses in cognitive skills than to conceal them with a total score.

In keeping with the current trend in ability testing, the authors make explicit that this test measures developed abilities that are modifiable by experience.

All users of the *Cognitive Abilities Test* should recognize that it measures developed abilities, not innate abilities. The cognitive skills measured by the test reflect the cognitive strategies and general cognitive control processes that an individual has developed, from experience both in and out of school, that enable him or her to learn new tasks or solve problems when instruction is absent or incomplete. Research has clearly shown that these skills change as individuals get older and as their experiences both in and out of school become broader and more varied.[2]

[2]R. L. Thorndike and E. Hagen, *Examiners Manual Cognitive Abilities Test*, Multilevel Edition. Boston: Riverside Publishing Company, 1986.

The use of Standard Age Scores, in place of the outmoded "deviation IQ" used in some older tests, helps avoid the many misinterpretations associated with IQ scores.

The *Cognitive Abilities Test* was described and illustrated in considerable detail because it shows the variety of item types used in group ability tests and it includes some of the current trends in testing (e.g., use of a multilevel format, elimination of the terms *intelligence* and *IQ scores*, and emphasis on power rather than speed of work). There are, of course, many other good tests of learning ability. See Appendix D for representative examples.

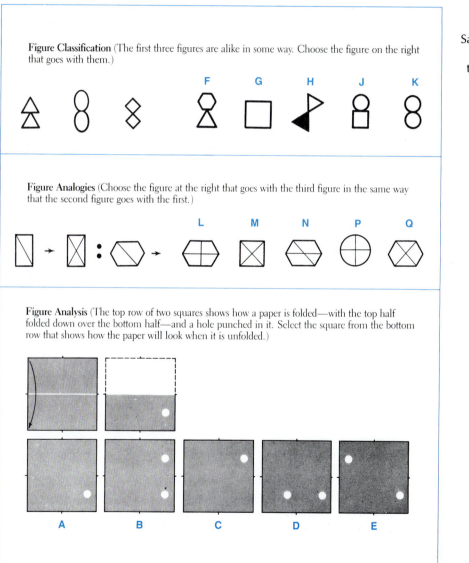

Figure Classification (The first three figures are alike in some way. Choose the figure on the right that goes with them.)

Figure Analogies (Choose the figure at the right that goes with the third figure in the same way that the second figure goes with the first.)

Figure Analysis (The top row of two squares shows how a paper is folded—with the top half folded down over the bottom half—and a hole punched in it. Select the square from the bottom row that shows how the paper will look when it is unfolded.)

FIGURE 12.4
Sample items from the Nonverbal Battery of the *Cognitive Abilities Test*, Multi-Level Edition. (Copyright © 1986 by The Riverside Publishing Company. Used by permission.)

Summary Comparison of Group Tests

The various types of group tests of learning ability that we have been discussing can be illustrated by circles, as shown in Figure 12.5. The single-score test provides a general measure of learning ability and thus is represented by a single circle with the letter G in it. The verbal (V)–nonverbal (NV) and verbal (V)–quantitative (Q) tests are both illustrated by two overlapping circles. The overlap in the circles (approximately 50 percent) represents the presence of a general ability factor common to both scores. The other portions of the circles represent the specific abilities (verbal, nonverbal, or quantitative) that are measured by each battery of subtests. In the multiscore battery the subtests also overlap to show that they reflect a general ability as well as the specific abilities they were designed to measure.

FIGURE 12.5
Summary comparison of types of group tests of learning ability. The Otis–Lennon School Ability Test illustrated here is for the fifth edition. The sixth edition will have verbal and nonverbal scores.

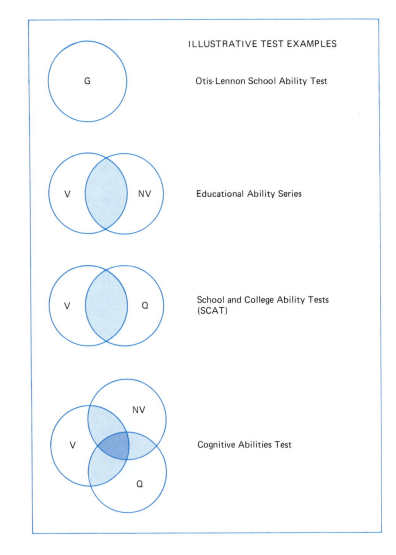

ILLUSTRATIVE TEST EXAMPLES

G — Otis-Lennon School Ability Test

V / NV — Educational Ability Series

V / Q — School and College Ability Tests (SCAT)

V / NV / Q — Cognitive Abilities Test

Choosing the Appropriate Test. The decision as to which type of test to select depends largely on the use to be made of the results. If the test is to be used only for an overall prediction of school success, a single-score test would suffice. However, if we want to obtain a more accurate measure of the reasoning abilities of poor readers or want to detect pupils weak in quantitative reasoning, then a test yielding separate scores would be favored. The single-score test provides a quick, easy to administer, global measure of reasoning ability, but multiscore tests provide information concerning several separate types of reasoning ability.

If the ability test is to be used in conjunction with an achievement test battery, it is important that the ability test and achievement battery both be standardized on the same population. This makes it possible to compare directly the two sets of scores and, thus, obtain a more complete description of educational progress and the factors affecting it. Most publishers of achievement test batteries publish a corresponding ability test, covering the same grade levels, and administer both to the same standardization groups. A list of such ability and achievement tests is presented in Table 12.2.

In some cases, it may be desirable to select the achievement battery first and then use the ability test that has been standardized on the same groups.

Individual Tests

Learning abilities are also measured by individual tests. These are typically called intelligence tests or intelligence scales but a broader interpretation is more defensible. Like the group tests, they measure present abilities that have been acquired through both in-school and out-of-school experiences.

Individual tests are administered to one examinee at a time in a face-to-face situation. The problems are presented orally by the examiner and the examinee

Ability Test	Grade Levels	Achievement Batteries
Otis-Lennon School Ability Test (OLSAT)	1–12	Metropolitan Achievement Tests Stanford Achievement Tests
Educational Ability Series	K–12	SRA Achievement Series SRA Survey of Basic Skills
Cognitive Abilities Test (CogAT)	K–12	Iowa Tests of Basic Skills (K–9) Tests of Achievement and Proficiency (9–12)
School and College Ability Tests (SCAT)	3.5–12.9	Sequential Tests of Educational Progress
Test of Cognitive Skills	2–12	California Achievement Tests (K–12) Comprehensive Tests of Basic Skills (K–12)

TABLE 12.2
Representative Ability Tests and Corresponding Achievement Batteries Standardized on the Same Populations

responds by pointing, giving an oral answer, or performing some manipulative task. The administration of individual tests requires extensive training. This is typically obtained in a special course in individual testing. A basic part of the course is extensive practice in test administration under supervision. No one should attempt to use individual tests without this special training.

Group tests provide a satisfactory estimate of learning abilities for the majority of pupils. However, individual tests have some special advantages over a group test. Because the individual test is administered to one pupil at a time, it is possible to control more carefully such factors as motivation and to assess more accurately the extent to which disabling behaviors are influencing the score. The influence of reading skill is deemphasized because the tasks are presented orally to the pupil. In addition, clinical insights concerning the pupil's method of attacking problems and persistence in solving them are more readily obtained with individual testing. These advantages make the individual test especially useful for testing young children, for retesting pupils whose scores on group tests are questionable, and for testing pupils with special problems. For example, in planning individualized programs for the mentally handicapped, the more dependable and informative individual measure of ability is preferred.

The two most highly regarded individual tests for use with school children are the *Stanford–Binet Intelligence Scale* and the *Wechsler Intelligence Scales*. Each of these will be briefly described. Although teachers would not be expected to administer such tests, some familiarity with the testing procedures should contribute to more effective interpretation and use of the test scores.

Stanford – Binet Scale: Fourth Edition

The fourth edition of the *Stanford–Binet Scale* is changed considerably from earlier editions. In the former editions (from 1908 on), the tests were arranged by age levels and the examiner presented a variety of item types as he or she moved from one age level to the next. The resulting measure of ability was expressed as a mental age that was then converted to a deviation IQ with a mean of 100 and a standard deviation of 16. The deviation IQ represented a highly verbal measure of general ability.

In the fourth edition, the grouping of items by age level has been replaced by the grouping of items into 15 separate tests. Each test consists of the same type items arranged in order of increasing difficulty, with two items at each level having approximately the same difficulty. The 15 tests include many of the item types of earlier editions but provide broader coverage of memory, quantitative, and spatial tasks. Six of the tests cover the full range of the scale, from age 2 to adult, but seven of the tests start above age 2 and two tests end below the adult level. The 15 tests are arranged into four cognitive areas, as follows:

VERBAL REASONING

Vocabulary — Defining terms.

Comprehension — Identifying and giving reasons for events.

Absurdities — Explaining what is wrong or silly about pictures.

Verbal Relations — Telling how three things are alike and differ from a fourth.

QUANTITATIVE REASONING

Quantitative — Counting, computation, and problem solving.

Number Series — Completing the next two items in a number sequence.

Equation Building — Arranging numbers and symbols to form an equation.

ABSTRACT/VISUAL REASONING

Pattern Analysis — Reproducing patterns using a form board and cubes.

Copying — Copying designs using blocks and drawings.

Matrices — Completing matrices that have portions missing.

Paper Folding and Cutting — Identifying pictures of unfolded paper after viewing it folded and cut.

SHORT-TERM MEMORY

Bead Memory — Identifying beads and bead patterns.

Memory for Sentences — Repeating sentences verbatim.

Memory for Digits — Repeating digits forward and backward.

Memory for Objects — Identifying proper sequences of pictures.

The tests are grouped under these four areas for scoring and profiling but are not administered in that order. The examiner follows a scheduled sequence that mixes the order of tests to maintain the examinee's interest. The examiner begins with the Vocabulary test, using chronological age for determining the *entry level* (i.e., where to begin the test). The Vocabulary test, along with chronological age, is then used as a routing test to determine the entry level on all other tests. On each test, the *basal level* is established (when all four items on two consecutive levels are passed) and then the test is continued until a *ceiling level* is reached (when three or more items are failed at two consecutive levels). This adaptive testing procedure, a carryover from earlier editions, eliminates the items that are too easy and too difficult for the examinee and administers only those of appropriate difficulty (see box).

The raw score for each test is obtained by subtracting the number of items failed from the number of the highest item administered. This procedure, of course, gives credit for those items below the basal level that were not administered. An individual's raw score on each test is converted, by means of tables, to standard scores with a mean of 50 and a standard deviation of 8. These scores are then combined to obtain *Standard Age Scores (SAS^s)* for each of the four cognitive areas and for the total scale. These *SAS^s* are normalized standard scores with a mean of 100 and a standard deviation of 16. The SAS units are the same as those used with the "deviation IQ" of earlier editions and, thus, provide for continuity of records. The elimination of the term *IQ* is a desirable move and one that is typical of newer ability tests.

An individual typically does not take all 15 tests. There are only 8 tests suitable

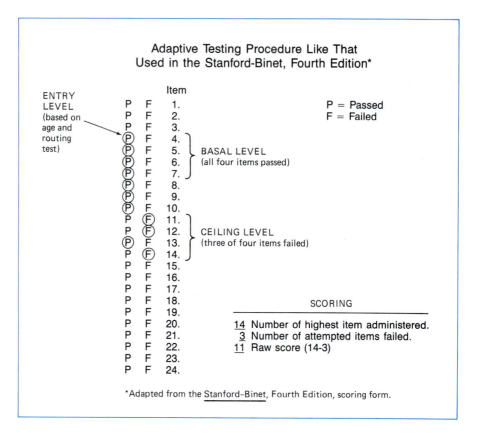

Adaptive Testing Procedure Like That
Used in the Stanford-Binet, Fourth Edition*

ENTRY LEVEL	Item

P = Passed
F = Failed

BASAL LEVEL (all four items passed)

CEILING LEVEL (three of four items failed)

SCORING

14 Number of highest item administered.
3 Number of attempted items failed.
11 Raw score (14-3)

*Adapted from the Stanford-Binet, Fourth Edition, scoring form.

for the youngest ages and only 13 tests that are suitable for the highest level. Also, in addition to the normal testing procedure, there are a number of abbreviated batteries for special purposes (e.g., quick screening, selecting gifted, assessing learning problems) and modifications in procedure for testing special populations (e.g., deaf, visually impaired, motor impaired, limited English proficiency). The changes from earlier editions make this fourth edition a more flexible and useful instrument.

In summary, the fourth edition of the *Stanford–Binet Scale* includes a variety of ability tests grouped into four cognitive areas. It is administered to one person at a time using an adaptive testing procedure. It provides four area scores and a full-scale score, called *Standard Age Scores*, that have a mean of 100 and a standard deviation of 16. The comprehensive coverage of the fourth edition and its flexibility of use make it an excellent measure of cognitive abilities when administered by a skillful and experienced examiner.

Wechsler Scales

The *Weschler Scales* include three tests that collectively cover all ages, from age 4 through adult:

1. *Wechsler Preschool and Primary Scale of Intelligence (WPPSI-R)* (ages 4 to 6.5).
2. *Wechsler Intelligence Scale for Children (WISC-R)* (ages 6.5 to 16.5).
3. *Wechsler Adult Intelligence Scale (WAIS-R)* (ages 16 to adult).

The *Weschsler* tests are organized by subtests. Each test consists of a Verbal Scale made up of five or six subtests and a Performance Scale made up of five subtests. Although the subtests vary slightly from one level to another, the following subtests from the *WISC-R* exemplify the test content in the *Wechsler tests*. The sample questions in parentheses were not taken from the *WISC-R* but are nevertheless similar.

VERBAL SCALE

1. *Information.* Answers questions based on general information (e.g., "How many legs does a cat have?").
2. *Similarities.* Explains in what way a series of paired things are alike (e.g., apple and orange).
3. *Arithmetic.* Solves problems similar to those used in school (e.g., "If two pencils cost a nickel, how many could you buy for a quarter?").
4. *Vocabulary.* Tells the meaning of words from a master list of 32, arranged in order of increasing difficulty.
5. *Comprehension.* Answers questions requiring common-sense comprehension (e.g., "Why should people tell the truth?").
    Digit Span (alternate test). Repeat series of digits forward and backward after hearing them once (e.g., 493). This test may substitute for any of the others in the Verbal Scale.

PERFORMANCE SCALE

6. *Picture Completion.* Tells what part is missing in incomplete pictures.
7. *Picture Arrangement.* Arranges sets of cartoon panels in proper sequence so that they tell a story.
8. *Block Design.* Arranges sets of blocks (colored red and white) so that they match pictures of designs on examiner's cards.
9. *Object Assembly.* Puts together jigsaw puzzles based on parts of objects (e.g., car).
10. *Coding.* Matches numbers and symbols by referring to a simple code that is kept in front of the examinee.
    Mazes (alternate for the coding test). Traces on a paper maze, within a set time limit.

Each subtest in the *WISC-R* is administered and scored separately. The tests are administered by alternating between the Verbal and Performance Scales (test order is 1, 6, 2, 7, and so on) to maintain greater interest and attention. The raw scores on the individual tests are converted to scaled scores with a mean of 10 and a standard deviation of 3. They are then combined to produce a Verbal IQ, a Performance IQ, and a total IQ. These are deviation IQ^s with a mean of 100 and a standard deviation of 15 (*Stanford–Binet* SAS^s use 16).

The three *Wechsler Scales* are all similar in test content and organization, and all three provide the same deviation IQ^s for the Verbal, Performance, and total scales. Like the *Stanford–Binet*, a number of abbreviated scales also can be used for various screening purposes.

Both the *Stanford–Binet* and the *Wechsler Scales* have been widely used for the individual testing of school children. Both yield highly reliable results (.90+ for the full-scale scores) when administered by competent examiners, and both are probably equally good for predicting success in school. However, the fourth edition of the *Stanford–Binet*, because of its broader coverage, it likely to be more useful for analyzing learning problems and for testing special populations.

Cautions in Interpreting and Using Learning Ability Scores

There are a number of cautions to keep in mind when interpreting and using learning ability tests. Here we shall highlight some of the main ones.

1. Allow for normal variation in the test scores. Learning ability, or scholastic aptitude, tests are some of our most reliable psychological tests. A reliability coefficient of .90 (which is typical), however, results in a standard error of measurement of approximately 5 points (SD = 16). Thus, a score of 100 should be interpreted as a band of scores ranging from 95 to 105, rather than as a precise point. When scores from different tests are compared we can expect differences larger than 5 points because the tests measure different aspects of ability and they are standardized on different populations. The largest variations in scores can be found at the elementary school levels because abilities are less stable during their formation and testing conditions are more difficult to control with elementary pupils.

2. Seek the causes of low scores. The scores on learning ability tests are based on the use of concepts acquired from both in-school and out-of-school experiences. Thus, inadequate motivation to do school tasks, a language handicap, or a barren home environment can prevent the learning of concepts required in the test. Similarly, poor reading ability, lack of test-taking skills, anxiety, and low self-esteem can lower scores by adversely influencing test performance. Many of these factors can be detected by simply looking for possible causes of low scores. Following up low scores on a group test with an individual test is also helpful. This reduces the influence of reading ability and provides for more careful observation of test-taking skills, language skills, motivation, and other relevant personal characteristics.

3. Verify test results by comparison with other information. More effective interpretation of learning ability test scores is likely to result when test performance is checked against teachers' observations, achievement test scores, and other evidence of learning and development. Discrepancies between the test scores and other information may suggest retesting or may simply clarify the nature of the factors influencing test performance.

4. Use the test results to improve learning. Learning ability tests provide a fairly good prediction of school success. Correlations between these test scores and school marks typically fall between .50 and .60. When correlated with scores on achievement test batteries, correlations of .60 to .80 are common. Unfortunately, the relationship between learning ability test scores and achievement is all too frequently used as a rationalization for inadequate school performance. For example, we might hear comments like, "These pupils aren't doing well in school because of their poor learning ability." Instead, why not alter the instruction for these children; slow the pace, introduce remedial programs that build up their verbal and quantitative concepts, and provide more direction and practice in problem solving. The same factors that lower school achievement (e.g., poor verbal and quantitative development) also lower scores on learning ability tests and both types of performance are modifiable. Thus, learning ability scores can be used, in conjunction with other information, to facilitate plans for improved learning rather than as an excuse for lack of school success.

5. Be cautious in identifying pupils as underachievers. Comparing a pupil's scores on a learning ability test and an achievement test and labeling the pupil an "underachiever" if the achievement test scores are lower is fraught with difficulties. Because both are measuring developed abilities, these discrepancies typically can be accounted for by such factors as the measurement error in both tests, the differences in content measured by the two tests, and variations in attitude and attention during test taking. If the two tests are normed on different populations, another basis for deviation is introduced. Discrepancies between learning ability and achievement test scores simply reflect the fact that the correlation between them is far from perfect. The safest procedure is to consider only very large discrepancies as possible signs of underachievement and then confirm these judgments by examining other types of information.

Culture-Fair Testing

Because all tests are measures of learned abilities, special problems arise when testing the aptitudes of individuals from different cultures and subcultures. There are numerous cultural differences that are likely to influence test performance. In addition to the more obvious one of language, there are such differences as motivation, attitude toward testing, competitiveness, speed, practice in test taking, and opportunity to learn the knowledges and skills measured by the test. Culture-fair testing is an attempt to obtain a measure of ability that is relatively free of all or most of these differences. Although various approaches have been used to accomplish this, the following procedures are typical: (1) The test materials are primarily nonverbal and include diagrams or pictures familiar to the various cultural groups for whom the test is intended. Sometimes translated verbal tests are used. (2) Attempts are made to use materials and methods that are interesting to the examinees, in order to encourage motivation. (3) Liberal time limits are typically provided to deemphasize speed as a factor. (4) The test procedures are kept simple in order to rule out differences in test-taking experience. (5) Test content is based on those intellectual skills common to the cultural groups being tested. Of course, culture-fair testing is more an ideal than a reality. Most attempts to remove cultural influences from tests have fallen short of their goal.

One of the best-known tests in this area is R. B. Cattell's *Culture-fair Intelligence Tests*. These are short, nonverbal tests that use pictures and diagrams common to many cultures. There are three scales available for different age levels. Scale 1 is for ages 4 to 8 and older retardates. It includes eight subtests, four of which must be administered individually. Scales 2 and 3 (age 8 to adult) each contain four subtests, involving the following perceptual tasks (see sample items in Figure 12.6):

1. *Series*. (Select the item that comes next in a series.)
2. *Classification*. (Select the item that does not belong with the others.)

FIGURE 12.6
Sample items from the *Culture-Fair Intelligence Tests*. (Reproduced by permission of the copyright owner, Institute of Personality and Ability Testing.)

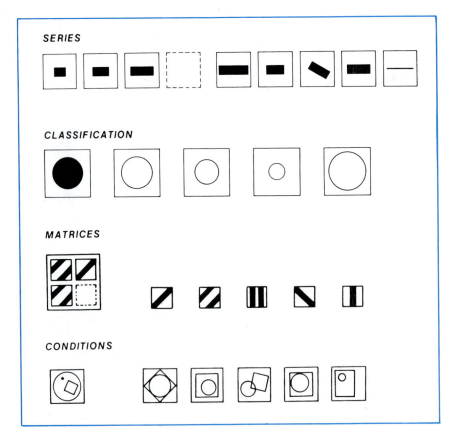

3. *Matrices*. (Select the item that completes a matrix.)
4. *Conditions*. (Match the conditions in a sample design by placing a dot in the appropriate place on one of several alternate designs. In the item in Figure 12.6, the dot must be in the circle but not in the small square.)

Scales 2 and 3 can be administered individually or as group tests. They have been given to individuals in a number of countries with mixed results. In general, test performance tended to differ most where the cultural differences were greatest. When used in schools in the United States, the Cattell tests can be expected to produce essentially the same results as does the Nonverbal Battery of the *Cognitive Abilities Test*.

Differential Aptitude Testing

The work of Guilford has been a major influence in moving testing from the measurement of a limited number of general mental abilities to the measurement of numerous specific abilities. On the basis of years of research, using the method of factor analysis, he proposed a three-dimensional model to provide a complete "structure of intellect."[3] His theoretical model is shown in Figure 12.7. The model

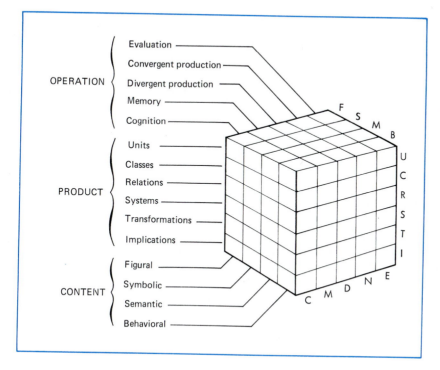

FIGURE 12.7
Guilford's structure of intellect model. (From J. P. Guilford, *The Nature of Human Intelligence*. New York: McGraw-Hill, 1967. Reproduced by permission.)

[3]J. P. Guilford, *The Nature of Human Intelligence* (New York: McGraw-Hill, 1967).

contains 120 cells ($5 \times 6 \times 4$), and each cell represents an ability that can be described by (1) what the person does (operation), (2) the nature of the material on which the operation is performed (content), and (3) the type of outcome or product involved (product). For example, a test based on figure analogies, like that in the Nonverbal Battery of the *Cognitive Abilities Test* (see Figure 12.4), would be classified in the Cognition-Figural-Relations cell because it calls for the recognition of figure relations. Similarly, a test using verbal analogies, such as those in the Verbal Battery of the *Cognitive Abilities Test* (see Figure 12.2), would be classified in the Cognition-Semantic-Relations cell because it calls for recognition of the relations between word meanings.

Tests have not been developed for each of the cells in the *structure of intellect*, but the model has served as a guide to Guilford and his coworkers in their search for specific abilities. It is assumed that someday there will be tests for all 120 cells, but this is not likely to happen without the model being modified in the process. From the standpoint of differential testing, the model emphasized the potentially large number of relatively independent factors that might be used to describe the various dimensions of human ability.

The experimental search for specific abilities by Guilford and others, combined with the increasing emphasis on educational and vocational guidance since the Second World War, has resulted in a number of multiaptitude batteries. Although such batteries are intended primarily for guidance purposes, they also can be useful in individualizing instruction and in planning courses that utilize a broader range of human abilities. As noted earlier, school learning is largely verbal learning, regardless of the name of the course. The differential testing of abilities provides an opportunity to develop learning experiences that take advantage of each individual's total pattern of aptitudes.

Multiaptitude batteries that measure both educational and vocational aptitudes have been designed primarily for the high school level and beyond. Among the most widely used tests of this type are the *Differential Aptitude Tests* (DAT) grades 8–12) and the *General Aptitude Test Battery* (GATB). The GATB was developed by the federal government for use in offices of the United States Employment Service (USES). It can be given in high schools, however, by special arrangement with USES. The GATB contains more vocationally oriented tests than the DAT does and is therefore especially well suited for the guidance of persons not going to college.

Here we shall describe the DAT in order to illustrate the nature and content of multiaptitude batteries. Information concerning other batteries available for use in the schools can be obtained from the *Mental Measurements Yearbooks* and *Test Critiques* (see Chapter 13).

Differential Aptitude Tests

The DAT battery includes eight tests, each measuring a separate set of abilities. Although some of the tests measure abilities specific enough to fit a particular cell in Guilford's model (see Figure 12.7), others measure a composite of abilities that have been found useful in educational and vocational guidance. The eight tests are

Verbal Reasoning (VR), Numerical Ability (NA), Abstract Reasoning (AR), Clerical Speed and Accuracy (CSA), Mechanical Reasoning (MR), Space Relations (SR), Spelling (S), and Language Usage (LU). In addition to separate scores for each of these tests, a combined verbal and numerical score (VR + NA) provides an index of scholastic aptitude similar to that obtained with group tests of learning ability. Sample items from the eight tests are shown in Figures 12.8 and 12.9.

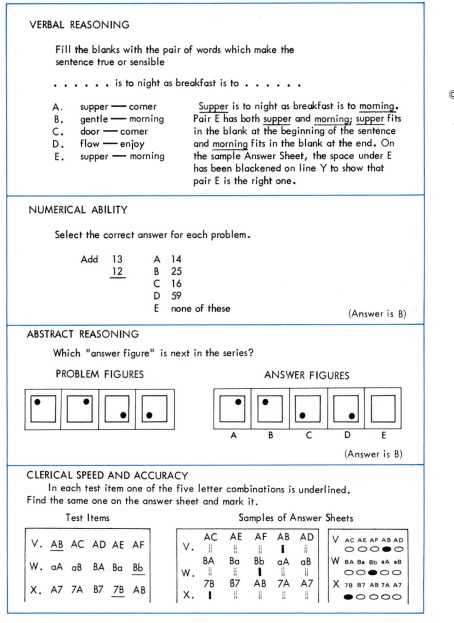

FIGURE 12.9
Sample items from the
*Differential Aptitude
Tests (DAT).*
(Reproduced by
permission. Copyright
© 1947, 1948, 1972, 1982
by The Psychological
Corporation, San Antonio,
Texas. All rights
reserved.)

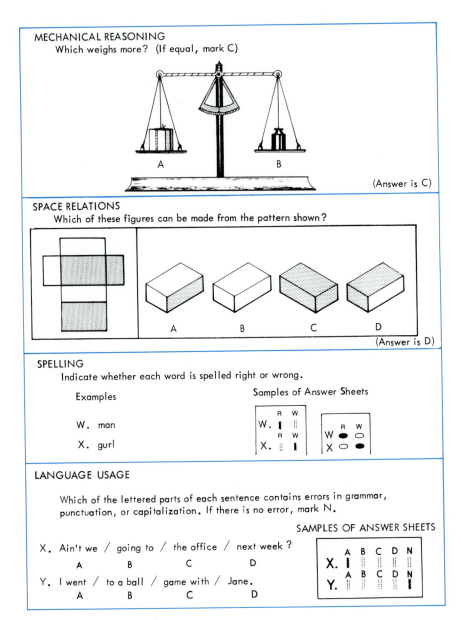

MECHANICAL REASONING
Which weighs more? (If equal, mark C)

A   B

(Answer is C)

SPACE RELATIONS
Which of these figures can be made from the pattern shown?

A   B   C   D

(Answer is D)

SPELLING
Indicate whether each word is spelled right or wrong.

Examples   Samples of Answer Sheets

W. man

X. gurl

LANGUAGE USAGE

Which of the lettered parts of each sentence contains errors in grammar,
punctuation, or capitalization. If there is no error, mark N.

SAMPLES OF ANSWER SHEETS

X. Ain't we / going to / the office / next week ?
         A   B   C   D

Y. I went / to a ball / game with / Jane.
        A   B   C   D

Using a battery of aptitude tests, like the *DAT*, has several advantages over using
a series of separate tests covering the same areas. First, because all tests have been
standardized on the same population, it is possible to compare a pupil's strengths
and weaknesses on the various measures of aptitude. Second, because all tests are
built for the same population of users, they are matched in difficulty and appropriateness for the grade levels for which they are intended. Separate tests covering the

same areas are apt to range widely in difficulty, especially the vocational tests. Third, using a common test format and uniform testing procedures for all tests simplifies test administration.

The scores for the *DAT* are plotted on a profile chart, as shown in Chapter 14, Figure 14.3. The profile chart is arranged so that differences between scores of *one inch or greater* are interpreted as significant. The use of *one-inch* score bands, like those in Figure 14.3, is the simplest method of profiling and lends itself to quick interpretation. When the bands do *not* overlap, the difference is significant; when they do overlap, it is not significant.

The tests in the *DAT* tend to be internally consistent (split-half reliabilities average about .90), and the intercorrelations between tests are low enough (average about .50) to indicate that each test measures a relatively independent ability. The evidence of differential prediction, however, is rather disappointing. One might expect the Verbal Reasoning scores to predict English achievement best, the Numerical Ability scores to predict mathematics and science achievement best, the Spatial Relations scores to predict achievement in mechanical drawing best, and so on. A review of the extensive data presented in the test manual, however, revealed only slight differences in prediction from one area to another. The best predictor of school marks in all courses turned out to be the general ability measure (VR + NA).

Computerized *DAT* Adaptive Edition

The computerized adaptive edition of the *Differential Aptitude Tests* (*DAT* Adaptive) is administered and scored by microcomputer. The "adaptive" feature permits each student to answer only the items appropriate for his or her ability level. Items that are too easy or too difficult for the individual are not administered. This individually tailored version reduces testing time. Although the *DAT* Adaptive is untimed, administration time is approximately half of that required for the paper-and-pencil edition. It has the added feature of providing a complete score report immediately following the completion of the testing.

An optional Career Planning Questionnaire (also available with the paper-and-pencil edition) can be administered and scored by computer, along with the *DAT* Adaptive. This questionnaire has students indicate their interest in school subjects and activities, their educational and career plans, their level of academic performance, and their interest in fields of work and specific occupations. A computer-generated Career Planning Report compares each student's interests and plans to the *DAT* scores and interprets and explains areas of agreement and disagreement. When a student's choices of occupation do not match the *DAT* scores, educational plans, and school subject preferences, a list of three occupational areas that do match them is added to the report. Thus, the *DAT* Adaptive can provide both a profile of *DAT* scores and a narrative report describing how the scores relate to the student's educational and career plans. With the aid of a school counselor, such reports should assist students in their vocational planning.

Summary

Standardized aptitude tests are designed to predict future performance in some activity, such as school learning. Like achievement tests, aptitude tests measure learned abilities. They differ from achievement tests, however, in that the test content is broader in scope, and test performance is less dependent on any specific set of learning experiences. This makes it possible to use the tests with pupils of varying educational backgrounds and to predict performance over a wide range of learning activities.

Group tests of learning ability (or scholastic aptitude) may yield a single score, separate verbal and nonverbal scores, separate verbal and quantitative scores, or several scores based on a series of specific aptitudes. The single-score test is designed to measure general learning ability only. In tests using verbal and nonverbal scores, the nonverbal score serves as a check on the learning ability of the poor reader. Tests with separate verbal and quantitative scores are used primarily for differential prediction. Which type of test to choose depends largely on the type of information desired and the use for which it is intended. For straightforward prediction of school success, a single-score test may suffice, but for helping pupils with learning problems and educational choices, tests with two or more scores are desirable.

Individual tests of learning ability deemphasize reading skill and provide more carefully controlled testing conditions. Thus, the individual test is especially valuable for testing young children and for checking on questionable scores obtained with group tests. Although extensive training and experience are required to administer individual tests, classroom teachers will likely encounter the scores on school records. It is therefore desirable to know the nature of the test content and the types of scores that are commonly used.

Most group and individual tests of learning ability report test performance in terms of standard scores with a mean of 100 and a standard deviation of 16 (15 for *Wechsler* tests). In interpreting and using the scores, it is important to allow for normal variation due to error, to seek causes of low scores, to verify the scores by comparison to other information, to use the results to improve learning, and to interpret underachievement cautiously.

Various attempts have been made to develop culture-fair tests by using nonverbal materials that are interesting and common to many cultures and by using simple procedures and liberal time limits. Although the instruments have not lived up to expectations, they have helped clarify the problems involved.

Comprehensive aptitude batteries, such as the *Differential Aptitude Tests (DAT)*, also have been developed for school use. These tests include reasoning ability tests as well as vocationally oriented tests. The computerized adaptive edition of the *DAT* is administered and scored by microcomputer and permits each student to answer only those items appropriate for his or her ability level. When combined with an optional Career Planning Questionnaire, a computer-generated profile of scores and a narrative report for career guidance is provided.

Learning Exercises

1. List the similarities and differences between achievement tests and aptitude tests.
2. What are the relative advantages and disadvantages of using group tests of learning ability rather than individual tests?
3. What are the main factors that might account for a difference in scores between two different group tests of learning ability?
4. List the similarities and differences between the *Stanford–Binet Scales* and the *Wechsler Scales*.
5. What cautions are necessary in interpreting and using group ability tests?
6. A pupil from a culturally different home received a score of 85 on the *Otis–Lennon School Ability Test*. What additional information would help you interpret the score? If you could have him take another test, what type of test would you want him to take? Why?
7. What tests in the *Differential Aptitude Tests* are most similar to the *Cognitive Abilities Test*?
8. What are the advantages of using the *Differential Aptitude Tests* instead of a group test like the *Cognitive Abilities Test*? What are the disadvantages?

Suggestions for Further Reading

ANASTASI, A. *Psychological Testing*, 6th ed. New York: Macmillan, 1988, Chapters 9–13. Includes descriptions of widely used individual, group, and multiple aptitude tests.

SALVIA, J., AND YSSELDYKE, J. *Assessment in Special and Remedial Education*, 4th ed. Boston: Houghton Mifflin, 1988. See Chapters 9–11 for descriptions of group and individual ability tests and difficulties of using them in current practice.

SATTLER, J. M. *Assessment of Children*, 3d ed. San Diego: Jerome M. Sattler, Publisher, 1988, Chapters 6–11. Describes the administration and interpretation of the *Stanford–Binet* and the *Wechsler Scales*.

Chapter 13

Test Selection, Administration, and Use

Published tests play an important role in the instructional program of the school. . . . They supplement and complement informal classroom tests and aid in many instructional decisions. . . . The task is to locate and select those tests that are most suitable . . . to administer and score them under carefully controlled conditions . . . and to make effective use of the results.

There are many published tests available for school use. The two types of most value to the instructional program of the school are the achievement tests and aptitude tests discussed in the last two chapters. There are hundreds of tests of each type, so great care is needed in selecting those tests that are most relevant to the objectives of the school program and most appropriate for the uses to be made of the results.

Some published tests are selected by individual teachers, but more frequently the tests are selected in accordance with the school testing program. In the latter case, teachers still should have a voice in the selection process, either through direct service on a test committee or through departmental and general staff meetings.

It is important that teachers participate actively in the selection of published tests. Their participation provides greater assurance that the tests are in harmony with the objectives of the instructional program and that the results will serve the various instructional uses for which they are intended. Although published tests can serve a variety of administrative and guidance functions, of central concern to any testing program is the effective use of tests in the instructional program.

In addition to familiarity with the procedures for selecting tests, teachers must also know the procedures for administering tests. In some schools they participate directly in these functions, while in others special personnel is used. In either case, however, the teacher's understanding of the procedures contributes to more effective interpretation and use of test results.

Obtaining Information about Published Tests

There are many available resources that are useful for locating and evaluating published tests in specific areas. These will aid in selecting tests that are most suitable and that are technically sound.

Buros Institute of Mental Measurements Guides

A basic source of information about tests is the *Mental Measurements Yearbook (MMY)*, that was started and edited by Oscar K. Buros for many years and is now published by the Buros Institute of Mental Measurements. The *MMY*s have been published periodically over the years but on no definite schedule.[1] Each *Yearbook* typically includes the following types of material:

1. Descriptive information concerning each test.
2. Critical reviews written by test specialists for the *MMY*.
3. Excerpts from test reviews published in professional journals.
4. Comprehensive bibliographies for many specific tests.
5. Listing of measurement books and book reviews.

The test reviews in the *Yearbooks* provide especially valuable information for evaluating the quality of published tests. Each test is typically reviewed by two or more specialists qualified by training and experience to evaluate the test. The reviewers do not hesitate to point out test weaknesses as well as any exaggerated claims made by test publishers. In addition, of course, they indicate the strengths of a test and the uses for which it is best suited.

Another useful Buros Institute guide for locating tests and information about tests is *Tests in Print*. This publication includes a descriptive listing of published tests, with extensive bibliographies for some. Although test reviews are not included, each test is indexed to those editions of the *Mental Measurements Yearbooks* that preceded it and contain reviews of the test.

As aids for locating tests for a particular use, *Tests in Print* provides an excellent guide to available tests, and the *Mental Measurements Yearbooks* provide the information needed to evaluate them. The cross-references to the *Yearbooks* in *Tests in Print* make it possible to locate numerous reviews for each test.

---

[1] The Buros Institute of Mental Measurements (University of Nebraska–Lincoln, 68588) now plans a biannual issue of *MMY*, with a *Supplement to MMY* to be published in alternating years.

Tests in Print has been published less frequently than the *Mental Measurements Yearbooks* and in the event a recent edition is not available, tests can be located by going directly to the *Yearbooks*. They are fully indexed and contain descriptions of the tests, as well as the test reviews. The *Yearbooks* can also be used, of course, for evaluating tests that have been located through test publishers' catalogues or other sources.

The Buros Institute of Mental Measurements also provides test information through a *Mental Measurements Yearbook* database. This computer database is updated monthly and, thus, provides the most recent information available (see box).

Mental Measurements Yearbooks and On-line Computer Service

The Buros Institute of Mental Measurements (University of Nebraska – Lincoln) has produced a database that is part of the on-line computer service offered by Bibliographic Retrieval Services, Inc. (BRS). The institute's database began with the test descriptions and reviews from *The Eighth Mental Measurements Yearbook* and includes updated descriptions and reviews of tests published after the *Eighth MMY* (search label MMYD). The institute's database is especially useful for obtaining current information on new and revised tests that appear between editions of the *Mental Measurements Yearbooks*. Computer searches of the database can be made through libraries that offer the BRS service.

Test Corporation of America Guides

Another useful source for locating and evaluating tests is in the publications of the Test Corporation of America.[2] One, titled *Tests: A Comprehensive Reference for Assessments in Psychology, Education, and Business*, describes more than 3,000 tests published in the English language. For each entry, there is a statement of the instrument's purpose, a brief description, and information concerning cost, scoring, and the publisher. *Tests* does not include evaluations of the instruments but serves as an excellent guide for locating tests. This is enhanced by the classification of tests into various categories and the use of numerous indexes.

Evaluations of tests in psychology, education, and business are provided in a series of volumes titled *Test Critiques*. Each critique is written by a measurement specialist and includes a detailed description of the test, practical applications of the test, technical information concerning the test, and a summarizing critique. There is special emphasis on aiding the test user, such as guidelines for administration, scoring, and interpretation. Technical terms are explained to make the information understandable to readers with little experience in testing. A separate publication,

---

[2]Test Corporation of America, 4050 Pennsylvania, Suite 310, Kansas City, Missouri 64111.

titled *Test Critiques Compendium*, contains reviews of the sixty most used psychology and education tests in a single volume.

Educational Testing Service (ETS) Test Collection

Educational Testing Service (Princeton, New Jersey) maintains a Test Collection that contains more than 14,000 tests. Annotated bibliographies are available in various areas that describe each test in detail. As new tests are added to the ETS Test Collection holdings, they are briefly described in a monthly newsletter, titled *News on Tests*. This newsletter provides a good source for locating new and recently revised tests. It also includes references to test reviews, lists of new publications, announcements of testing conferences, changes in publishers' addresses, and other news about testing.

The ETS Test Collection has established a database of its records that is part of the on-line computer service offered by Bibliographic Retrieval Services, Inc. (BRS). Computer searches for test information can be made through libraries that provide the BRS service. The ETS Test Collection will also provide computer searches for clients.

Test Publishers' Catalogues

Recent information concerning tests available for school use also can be obtained from test publishers' catalogues. These usually contain brief descriptions of each test, including possible uses of the test, cost, administration time, and similar information. If a publisher's claims for its tests are checked by independent reviews such as those presented in the *Mental Measurements Yearbooks* and *Test Critiques*, test catalogues provide a good source of information. They are especially useful for locating new tests and recent editions of earlier tests. A brief list of test publishers who will send catalogues upon request is included in Appendix C.

Testing Standards

An especially useful aid in evaluating and using published tests is the *Standards for Educational and Psychological Testing*. This set of standards was prepared by a joint committee of the American Psychological Association, the American Educational Research Association, and the National Council on Measurement in Education.[3] The *Standards* include recommendations intended for both test publishers and test users. Part I contains standards for the technical aspects of test instrumentation (validity, reliability, test development, norming, scaling, and related issues). Part II provides standards for the use of tests in various situations (clinical, educational, counseling, employment, professional licensure, and program evaluation). Part III covers standards for particular applications (linguistic minorities and handicapped). Part IV provides standards for test administration, scoring, reporting, and the rights of test takers.

Each recommendation in the *Standards* is classified as *primary* (to be met by all

[3]American Psychological Association, *Standards for Educational and Psychological Testing* (Washington, D.C.: APA, 1985).

319

tests), *secondary* (desirable), or *conditional* (classification depending on the conditions of testing). Comments following these standards are used to clarify or justify the recommendation or to describe the conditions under which the standard would apply (see box).

Illustrative Test Standard from the "Validity" Section*

Standard 1.1

"Evidence of validity should be presented for the major types of inference for which use of the test is recommended. A rationale should be provided to support the particular mix of evidence presented for the intended uses. (Primary)

Comment

Whether one or more kinds of validity evidence are appropriate is a function of the particular question being asked, the context, and the extent of previous evidence."

*From *Standards for Educational and Psychological Testing* (Washington, D.C.: American Psychological Association, 1985).

A review of the standards in Part I provides a good background for selecting and evaluating tests and the specific recommendations in Parts II, III, and IV provide excellent guidelines for effective test use.

Other Sources of Test Information

Test reviews and information concerning the nature and use of particular tests can frequently be found in professional journals (see list in Appendix B). Journal articles can be most easily located through the use of such bibliographic sources as the *Current Index to Journals in Education*, the *Education Index*, and *Psychological Abstracts*. In using these guides it is usually necessary to search under many different headings, such as aptitude testing, achievement testing, psychological tests, reading tests, tests and scales, and testing programs. In locating information on tests in a specific content area, it also may be necessary to look under that subject heading (e.g., English, science). Test reviews in professional journals can be most easily located by a computerized literature search.

Some textbooks in educational and psychological measurement include descriptions and evaluations of widely used tests and contain selected lists of tests in an appendix. Also, some textbooks in particular areas (e.g., reading, special education) describe tests that are especially useful in those areas. Although textbooks provide descriptive information concerning representative tests, this is mainly useful for orientation to the field of testing. Test selection for a particular situation includes a study of the situation to determine testing needs, searching for possible tests, consulting test reviews, and examining the test manuals and other test materials of the most likely prospects.

Selecting Appropriate Tests

Published tests play a vital role in the educational program of the school and therefore should be selected with the utmost of care. Hastily or casually selected tests seldom are in harmony with the objectives of the instructional program and, thus, may provide inadequate or inappropriate information on which to base educational decisions. The following sequence of steps provides general guidelines for a systematic approach to test selection.

Defining Testing Needs

The first task in selecting published tests is to define specifically the type of information being sought through testing. In selecting achievement tests, for example, it is insufficient to search for a test to evaluate "achievement in social studies" or to measure "reading comprehension." There are numerous tests in any given content area, and each measures somewhat different aspects of knowledge, under-

Publisher	Sources	Test Descriptions	Technical Information	Test Reviews	
Buros Institute of Mental Measurements	*Mental Measurements Yearbooks,* *Tests in Print*	X X	X	XX	TABLE 13.1 Sources for Locating and Evaluating Published Tests
Test Corporation of America	*Tests,* *Test Critiques*	X X	X	XX	
Educational Testing Service	*Test Collection,* *News on Tests*	X X(N)		X(S)	
(See publishers in Appendix C)	Test Publishers' Catalogues	X(N)			
American Psychological Association	*Standards for Educational and Psychological Testing*		XX		
(Varies)	Test Manuals	XX	XX		
(See list in Appendix B)	Professional Journals	X(N)	X(S)	X(S)	
(Varies)	Measurement Textbooks	X(S)	X(S)	X(S)	

XX = Most useful, X = Useful, X(N) = Useful for new tests, X(S) = Useful for some tests.

standing, and skill. To make a proper selection, we must first identify the objectives and specific learning outcomes of our instructional program. This is necessary in choosing relevant tests, whether selecting a single test for a particular course or a battery of tests for a schoolwide testing program.

Clarifying the type of information needed is equally necessary in selecting aptitude tests. It makes a difference whether we are going to use the results for determining reading readiness, for grouping pupils, for vocational planning, or for predicting success in science and mathematics courses. Each function requires different information and consequently a different type of aptitude measure. Thus, selection must be preceded by an analysis of the intended use of the results and the type of test data most appropriate for each use.

Narrowing the Choice

The need for published tests is usually considered in relation to the total measurement program. This makes it possible to choose tests that supplement and complement the other means of evaluating pupils. It is desirable to choose a test of general educational development, for example, if certain learning outcomes in the knowledge area already are being adequately measured by informal classroom tests. Similarly, if a scholastic aptitude test is to be used at a particular grade level for grouping purposes only, it may be desirable to group pupils on the basis of achievement test results and to replace the aptitude test with a diagnostic reading test. Such decisions can be made only when the need for testing is viewed in terms of the total measurement program.

Other factors in the school situation also help narrow the choice. If, for instance, the school lacks a person with the training and experience required to administer individual tests, only group tests need be considered. If the tests are to be administered by teachers without experience in test administration, those with simple directions are best. If the same type of achievement battery is desired for both the elementary and high school levels, only those batteries with tests at all grade levels need be examined. Considerations such as these offer additional criteria for determining the types of tests to seek.

Locating Suitable Tests

When the needs for testing have been identified, a list of possible tests can be compiled from test publishers' catalogues and the most recent edition of the *Mental Measurements Yearbook* and *Test Critiques*. The reviews in these guides are sufficiently detailed to weed out those tests that are clearly inappropriate or that have obvious technical weaknesses. Further evaluative information also can be found in other sources, such as those described earlier.

Obtaining Specimen Sets

When the list of tests has been reduced to a reasonable number, specimen sets should be obtained so that test manuals and the test items themselves can be evaluated. Test publishers generally supply specimen sets for each test they publish.

These can be purchased at relatively low cost and include a test manual, a test booklet, and scoring keys. Many universities, colleges, and large school systems maintain a file of such specimen sets.

Reviewing Test Materials

The test manual (sometimes accompanied by a technical manual and related aids) usually provides the most complete information for judging the appropriateness and the technical qualities of a test. A good test manual includes the following types of information:

1. Uses for which the test is recommended.
2. Qualifications needed to administer and interpret the test.
3. Evidence of validity for each recommended use.
4. Evidence of reliability for recommended uses and an indication of equivalence of any equivalent forms provided.
5. Directions for administering and scoring the test.
6. Adequate norms (including a description of the procedures used in obtaining them) or other bases for interpreting the scores.

Some test manuals (or supplements to the manuals) also contain suggestions and guides for interpreting and using the results. These are especially helpful for determining the functions for which the test is best suited.

In addition to reviewing the test manual, it is also wise to study the individual test items. The best method of doing this is to try to answer each item, as if you were taking the test. For achievement tests, it is also helpful to classify the items by means of a previously prepared table of specifications or other test plan. Although time consuming, there is no better means of determining how appropriate a test is for measuring the knowledge, skills, and understanding emphasized in the instructional program.

Using a Test Evaluation Form

Gathering information about specific tests is made easier if a test evaluation form is used. This provides a convenient means of recording significant data; it increases the likelihood that pertinent information will not be overlooked; and it provides for a summary comparison of each test's strengths and weaknesses (see box).

Although a test evaluation form provides a useful summary of information concerning tests, no test should be selected on the basis of this information alone. How well a test fits the school program and the particular uses for which it is being considered are always the main considerations.

Test Evaluation Form

Test title_____ Authors_____

Publisher_____ Publication date_____

Purpose of test_____

For grades (ages)_____ Forms_____

Scores available_____ Types of scoring_____

Administration time_____ Cost_____

Technical Features

Validity: Nature of evidence (content-, construct-, criterion-related).
Reliability: Nature of evidence (stability, internal consistency, equiva-
   lence). Standard error of measurement (size, type).
Norms: Type, adequacy, and appropriateness to local situation.
Criterion-referenced interpretation: Describe (if available).

Practical Features

Ease of administration (procedure and timing).
Ease of scoring and interpretation.
Adequacy of test manual and accessory materials.

General Evaluation

Comments of reviewers (see MMY and *Test Critiques*).
Summary of strengths.
Summary of weaknesses.
Recommendations concerning local use.

Administering Published Tests

Most group tests of achievement and scholastic aptitude can be successfully administered by any conscientious teacher. The main requirement is that the testing
procedures prescribed in the test manual be rigorously followed. To do this, it is
necessary to shift from being a teacher and helper to being an impartial test
examiner who will not deviate from the test directions.

Teachers sometimes wonder why it is important to follow the test procedures so
closely. What harm is there in helping pupils if they do not understand particular
questions? Why not give the pupils a little more time if they are almost finished?
Are not some of these directions a bit nit-picking, anyway? The answer is

A published test must be administered under standard conditions if the results are to be
meaningfully interpreted.

When a published norm-referenced test is given to representative groups of pupils
to establish norms, it is administered in exact accordance with the procedures

prescribed in the test manual. And so unless we adhere strictly to the same procedures, the standard conditions of measurement will be violated, and we cannot legitimately use the test norms to interpret our scores. Although not all published criterion-referenced tests have norms, the interpretation of the results according to an absolute standard (e.g., mastery – nonmastery) also depends on controlled conditions of administration. In short, when we alter the procedures for administering a published test, we lose the basis for a meaningful interpretation of the scores.

Test Administration

The administration of group tests is relatively simple: (1) motivate the pupils to do their best, (2) follow the directions closely (3) keep time accurately, (4) record any significant events that might influence test scores, and (5) collect the materials promptly.

1. Motivate the pupils. In testing, our goal should be to obtain maximum performance within the standard conditions set forth in the testing procedures. We want all pupils to earn as high a score as they are capable of achieving. This obviously means that they must be motivated to put forth their best effort. Although some pupils will respond to any test as a challenge to their ability, others will not work seriously at the task unless they are convinced that the test results will be beneficial to them.

In school testing, we can stimulate pupils to put forth their best effort by convincing them that the test results will be used primarily to help them improve their learning. We can also explain to them the value of the test results for understanding themselves better and for planning their future. But these need to be more than hollow promises made at the time of testing. Test results must be used in the school in such a manner that these benefits are clearly evident to the pupils.

Before administering a particular test, the teacher should explain to the pupils the purpose of the test and the uses to be made of the results. At this time, the teacher also should emphasize the advantages of obtaining a score that represents the pupils' best efforts but should not make the pupils overly anxious. Verbal reassurance that the size of the score is not as important as the fact that it represents one's best effort is usually helpful. The judicious use of humor can also somewhat offset test anxiety. The most effective remedy, however, is a positive attitude toward test results. When the pupils are convinced that valid test scores are beneficial to their own welfare, both their test anxiety and motivation tend to become minor problems.

2. Follow directions strictly. The importance of following the directions given in the test manual cannot be overemphasized. Unless the test is administered in exact accordance with the standard directions, the test results will contain an indeterminant amount of error and thereby prevent proper interpretation and use.

The test directions should be read *word for word* in a loud, clear voice. They should never be paraphrased, recited from memory, or modified in any way. The oral reading of directions will usually be more effective if the directions have been practiced beforehand.

After the directions have been read and during the testing period, some pupils are likely to ask questions. It is usually permissible to clarify the directions and to answer questions concerning mechanics (for example, how to record the answer), but the test manual must be your guide. If it is permissible to clarify the directions, you should not change or modify the directions in any way during your explanation.

Some teachers find it hard to refrain from helping pupils who are having difficulty in answering items on a published test. When questioned about a particular test item, they are tempted to say, "You remember, we discussed that last week," or to give similar hints to the pupils. This, of course, merely distorts the results. When asked about a particular test item during testing, the teacher should quietly tell the pupil: "I'm sorry, but I cannot help you. Do the best you can."

3. Keep time accurately. If a series of short subtests must be timed separately, it is desirable to use a stopwatch when giving the test. For most other purposes, a watch with a second hand is satisfactory. To ensure accurate timing, you should keep a written record of the starting and stopping times, the exact hour, minute, and second as follows:

	Hour	Minute	Second
Starting time	2	10	0
Time allowed		12	
Stopping time	2	22	0

4. Record significant events. The pupils should be carefully observed during testing and a record made of any unusual behavior or event that might influence the test scores. If, for example, a pupil appears overly tense and anxious, sits staring out of the window for a time, or seems to be marking answers randomly without reading the questions, a description of the behavior should be recorded. Similarly, if there are interruptions during the testing (despite your careful planning), a record should be made of the type and length of the interruption and whether it did or did not alter the testing conditions.

A record of unusual pupil behavior and significant events provides valuable information for determining whether test scores are representative of the pupils' best efforts and whether standard conditions have been maintained during testing. Questionable test scores should, of course, be rechecked by administering a second form of the test.

5. Collect test materials promptly. When the test has ended, all test materials should be collected promptly so that pupils cannot work beyond the time limits and so that all materials can be accounted for and secured.

Test Giver's Checklist

For those responsible for the testing program, from the ordering of the tests to their administration, the test giver's checklist summarizes the points that need to be considered (see box).

Test Giver's Checklist

1. Order and check test materials well in advance of the testing date.
   a. Were correct forms of the test sent?
   b. Is there the right number of tests and answer sheets?
   c. Have all needed materials been assembled (pencils, watch, etc.)?
   d. Have all test materials been securely stored until the testing date?
2. Select a suitable location for testing.
   a. Is there adequate work space?
   b. Is the lighting, heat, and ventilation satisfactory?
   c. Is the room in a quiet location?
   d. Is the seating arrangement satisfactory?
3. Take steps to prevent distractions.
   a. Will a TESTING IN PROGRESS sign be posted on the door?
   b. Will all needed materials be on hand before starting?
   c. Have arrangements been made to terminate distractions (e.g., bells)?
   d. Has the test been scheduled to avoid major school events?
4. Study the test materials and practice giving the test.
   a. Did you carefully read the test manual?
   b. Did you take the test yourself?
   c. Did you practice reading the directions?
   d. Did you anticipate questions pupils might ask?
5. Motivate the pupils.
   a. Was the purpose of the test explained to the pupils?
   b. Were the pupils told how the results would be used?
   c. Were the pupils encouraged to put forth their best effort?
   d. Has care been taken not to create test anxiety?
6. Follow test directions strictly and keep time accurately.
   a. Did you read the test directions *word for word*?
   b. Did you refrain from helping pupils (except with mechanics)?

(continued)

> c. Did you make a written record of starting and stopping times?
> d. Did you stick to the *exact* time schedule?
> 7. Record significant events.
>   a. Did pupils do anything that might affect the test results?
>   b. Were there any interruptions that might affect the scores?
> 8. Collect the test materials promptly when the testing has ended.
>   a. Were all test materials collected immediately?
>   b. Were the collected materials counted, checked, and secured?

Improving Pupil's Test-Taking Skills

Our suggestions for test administration, as summarized in the test giver's checklist, emphasize the importance of establishing the most suitable environment for the test taker and using methods that motivate the pupils to put forth their best efforts. Despite these procedures, however, some pupils might not perform at the level of which they are capable because they lack skill in test taking. It has been suggested by Sarnacki that all pupils be given training in test-taking skills to prevent such deficiencies from lowering their test scores.[4] This seems to be a sensible suggestion and one that could be easily handled in the regular classroom or through use of programed materials. Among the skills important in test taking are the following:

1. Listening to or reading directions carefully.
2. Listening to or reading test items carefully.
3. Setting a pace that will allow time to complete the test.
4. Bypassing difficult items and returning to them later.
5. Making informed guesses rather than omitting items.
6. Eliminating as many alternatives as possible on multiple-choice items before guessing.
7. Following directions carefully in marking the answer sheet (e.g., darken the entire space).
8. Checking to be sure the item number and answer number match when marking an answer.
9. Checking to be sure that the appropriate response was marked on the answer sheet.
10. Going back and checking the answers if time permits.

Test-taking skills such as these can be easily mastered, but pupils need practice to

[4]R. E. Sarnacki, "An Examination of Testwiseness in the Cognitive Domain," *Review of Educational Research* 49(Spring 1979):252–279.

develop them. Fortunately, many test publishers now provide practice tests that can be given before the regular test. This is of some help, but special training in test taking will provide even greater assurance that a pupil's test scores are not depressed by deficiencies in test-taking skills.

Using Results of Published Tests

Published achievement and learning ability tests can serve many different purposes in the school's educational program. All we shall attempt to do here is to describe briefly some of the possible uses and misuses of published tests that are of special interest to teachers.

Possible Uses of Published Tests

If they are selected and used with discretion, published tests of achievement and ability can play an important role in the school's evaluation program. As noted earlier, tests should be selected in accordance with the school's objectives and the purposes for which the results are to be used. When selected in this manner, they can contribute to more effective educational decisions in a number of areas.

Instructional Planning. Published tests of achievement and learning ability can aid instructional planning in a particular school or course in the following ways:

1. Identifying the level and range of ability among pupils. Among other things, instructional plans must take into account the pupils' learning ability and their present levels of achievement. Published tests can provide objective evidence on both of these points.

2. Identifying areas of instruction needing greater emphasis. If the published tests have been selected in accordance with the school's objectives, instructional weaknesses will be revealed by those areas of the test in which the pupils do poorly. Published tests are especially helpful in appraising strengths and weaknesses in learning (see Table 13.2).

3. Identifying discrepancies between learning ability and achievement. Although differences between learning ability and achievement must be interpreted with caution, large discrepancies can aid in identifying pupils who may be underachieving. In this as well as other areas, however, the results of published tests should be verified by other available evidence.

4. Identifying readiness for learning. There are a number of early school achievement tests and reading readiness tests that can aid in determining readiness for school instruction. These test results provide a good supplement to other evidence of learning readiness by indicating whether pupils have the concepts and skills needed for formal learning tasks. At higher grade levels, including high school,

TABLE 13.2	Teachers Were Asked to Indicate Which of These Uses They Made	Percentage Reporting Each Use
Percentage of Teachers Using Standardized Achievement Test Results in Various Ways*	Diagnosing Strengths and Weaknesses	74
	Measuring Student "Growth"	66
	Individual Student Evaluation	65
	Instructional Planning	52
	Class Evaluation	45
	Reporting to Parents	42
	Evaluation of Teaching Methods	37
	Reporting to Students	24

*Based on a survey of 3,306 teachers, grades K through 12 and adapted from J. P. Stetz and M. D. Beck, "Attitudes toward Standardized Tests: Students, Teachers, and Measurement Specialists," *NCME Measurement in Education* (Washington, D.C.: National Council on Measurement in Education, 12(1), 1981).

tests of basic skills can be interpreted and used as readiness tests. Learning at any level is enhanced if prerequisite skills have been mastered.

5. Diagnosing learning errors and planning remedial instruction. Published diagnostic tests are especially useful for pinpointing the learning errors that are handicapping a pupil's learning progress. Published tests provide a more systematic approach than that of informal methods, and the manuals typically provide suggestions for remediation. Unfortunately, these tests are limited almost entirely to the basic skills of reading and arithmetic.

6. Clarifying and selecting instructional objectives. The use of published tests aids in the clarification and selection of objectives in several ways. First, selecting the tests forces us to identify and state our objectives as clearly as possible. Second, an examination of the items in published tests tells us how different objectives function in testing. As we go back and forth (during test selection) between our objectives and the items in the tests under consideration, what a particular objective looks like in operational terms becomes clearer. Third, the results of published tests provide evidence that helps in selecting objectives at a particular grade level or in a particular course. If fall test results indicate that pupils in the sixth grade are weak in study skills, for example, sixth-grade teachers may want to include an objective in this area, even though they had not originally planned to devote much attention to study skills. Similarly, published test results might indicate that a particular objective is unnecessary because it has been satisfactorily achieved at an earlier grade level.

Sectioning and Grouping Pupils. One of the most common uses of published test results has been to organize groups that are similar in terms of learning ability. This ability grouping is frequently used in large schools when it is necessary to form several classes at each grade level or several sections of the same course. It is also used by teachers to form instructional groups within classes. Elementary teachers, for example, commonly form reading and arithmetic groups on the basis of pupil performance.

Forming school or classroom groups according to ability is often referred to as *homogeneous* grouping. This is somewhat of a misnomer, however, because pupils grouped according to one type of ability are apt to vary considerably in other abilities, interests, attitudes, and other characteristics significant from a learning standpoint. *Ability* grouping is a much more suitable term, but even here there is the danger of assuming that the pupils in a given group will be identical in ability. All we can hope is that the range of ability in the group will be smaller than it would be without such grouping.

Although ability grouping is practiced widely, there is still considerable criticism of its use. Two of the most common objections are (1) it does not adequately provide for individual differences, and (2) a stigma is attached to those in the slowest groups. The first objection is a valid one that has helped clarify the role of ability grouping that, by itself, it is inadequate in coping with individual differences. It merely reduces the range of ability in a group so that individualized instruction can be applied more effectively. The second objection describes a real danger that is difficult to avoid. Separate grouping in each subject has helped. When a pupil can be in a slow group in English, an average group in social studies and science, and an accelerated group in mathematics, there is less apt to be a stigma attached to those in the slow group. Flexible grouping that permits pupils to shift from one group to another, as performance improves, also helps counteract undesirable attitudes toward pupils in the slow group.

Individualizing Instruction. Despite the method of sectioning classes or grouping pupils within conventional classrooms, there will still be individual differences in aptitude and achievement in any given group. Thus, it is necessary to study the strengths and weaknesses of each pupil in class so that instruction can be adapted as much as possible to their individual learning needs. For this purpose (1) scholastic aptitude tests provide clues concerning learning ability; (2) reading tests indicate the difficulty of material the pupil can read and understand; (3) norm-referenced achievement tests point out general areas of strength and weakness; (4) criterion-referenced achievement tests describe how well specific tasks are being mastered; and (5) diagnostic tests aid in detecting and overcoming specific learning errors.

Criterion-referenced tests are especially well adapted to individualizing instruction because each set of test items is typically keyed to a specific objective. This makes it possible for a pupil to proceed through a given learning sequence by demonstrating mastery of the objectives one by one. Many publishers also provide references to books and other learning aids to guide the individual study of pupils who have failed to master a particular objective.

Identifying the Needs of Exceptional Children. Some pupils deviate so markedly from the group of normal pupils at their grade or age level that special treatment is needed. The gifted, mentally retarded, emotionally disturbed, physically handicapped, and similar exceptional children fall into this category. For this pupil, published tests are helpful in identifying their problems of learning and development so that special provisions can be made for meeting their exceptional needs. This use of tests is achieving growing importance now that *mainstreaming* (placing handicapped children in the least restrictive environment) has increased the number of exceptional children in regular classrooms. Mainstreaming requires that a detailed "individualized educational program" be written for each handicapped pupil.

Monitoring of Educational Progress over Extended Periods.

Published tests are especially useful in measuring learning progress over a given number of years. Comparable forms make it possible to measure the same learning outcomes annually and thus obtain a long-range picture of the pupils' educational development. Teacher-made tests are not as useful for this purpose because of the lack of uniformity from one year to the next.

In using published tests as one basis for determining pupils' educational development, care must be taken not to overgeneralize from the results. Tests that yield somewhat comparable measures of general educational progress throughout the school years must, of necessity, be confined to learning that is continuously developing and that is common to diverse curricula. In the main, this means the basic skills and those critical abilities used in the interpretation and application of ideas that cut across subject-matter lines. Although these are significant learning outcomes, they are only a partial indication of total educational development. Knowledge and understanding of specific subject-matter content, skills unique to each subject field, attitudes and appreciation, and similar learning outcomes that cannot be measured by survey tests of educational development are equally important.

Helping Pupils Make Educational and Vocational Choices.

At the high school level, published test results can contribute to more intelligent educational and vocational decisions. In deciding which curriculum to pursue, which courses to take, whether to plan for college, or which occupations to consider, pupils can be aided greatly by knowing their aptitudes and their strengths and weaknesses in achievement. Published tests are especially useful in educational and vocational planning because they indicate to pupils how they compare with persons beyond the local school situation. This is important because these are the persons with whom they will be competing after leaving high school.

Supplementary Uses.

In addition to the preceding uses of published tests, all of which are directly concerned with improving pupils' instruction and guidance, there are a number of supplementary uses to which they can be put, including (1) placing pupils transferred from other schools, (2) appraising the general effectiveness of the school program in developing basic skills, (3) identifying areas in the educational program in which supervisory aid and in-service training can be used most effectively, (4) evaluating new educational programs, (5) providing evidence for interpreting the school program to the public, and (6) gathering information for reports to other schools, colleges, and prospective employers. When published test results are presented to individuals and groups outside the school, it should be emphasized that these tests measure only some of the objectives of the school program.

Misuses of Published Tests

Published tests can be misused in any of the preceding areas if (1) there is inadequate attention to the educational objectives being measured; (2) there is a failure to recognize the limited position of tests in the total evaluation program; (3) there is unquestioning faith in the test results; or (4) the group tested is markedly different from the group for whom the test was intended. These factors contribute to the misapplication and misinterpretation of published test results in any situation. In addition, there are two misuses that warrant special attention.

Assignment of Course Grades.   Some teachers use the scores from published tests as a basis for assigning course grades. This is undesirable for at least two reasons: (1) published tests are seldom closely related to the instructional objectives of a particular course, and (2) they measure only a portion of the desired learning outcomes emphasized in instruction. Using these tests for grading purposes tends to overemphasize a limited number of ill-fitting objectives. In addition to the unfairness to the pupil, this practice encourages both teachers and pupils to neglect those objectives that are not measured by the tests.

In borderline cases, especially when promotion or retention is being decided, published test results can be a valuable supplement. Knowing a pupil's scholastic aptitude and general level of educational development contributes to a more intelligent decision concerning the best grade placement. Except for such special uses, however, published tests should play a minor role, if any, in determining course grades.

Evaluation of Teaching Effectiveness.   In some schools a teacher's effectiveness is judged by the scores pupils make on published tests. This is an extremely unfair practice because there are so many factors, other than teaching effectiveness, that influence test scores. Many of these, such as the class's level of ability, the pupils' cultural background, the pupils' educational experiences, and the relative difficulty of learning different course materials, cannot be controlled or equated with sufficient accuracy to justify inferring that the results are solely, or even largely, based on the teacher's efforts. Even if such factors could be controlled, published test results would be a poor criterion of teaching success because they are not closely related to the instructional objectives of particular courses and they measure only a portion of the learning outcomes teachers strive for in their instruction. At most, they should play only a minor role in teacher evaluation.

An especially undesirable side effect of using published tests as the sole or main measure of teaching effectiveness is that some teachers will obtain copies of the test and start teaching pupils the answers to specific test items. Although this unprofessional practice may begin with a few unethical teachers, subtle pressures (to avoid looking ineffective by comparison) soon cause the practice to spread. Such "teaching for the test," of course, not only will distort the measures of teaching effectiveness but also will invalidate the test scores for other school uses.

Summary

Teachers should know how to locate, select, administer, interpret, and use published tests. This contributes to more effective use of the test results in the instructional program. Two of the most useful sources for locating and evaluating tests are provided by Buros Institute for Mental Measurements (*Mental Measurements Yearbooks* and *Tests in Print*) and Test Corporation of America (*Tests and Test Critiques*). Both sets of publications provide comprehensive coverage of available tests. Other sources include the ETS Test Collection, *News on Tests*, test publishers' catalogues, and various professional journals and textbooks. The testing *Standards* helps determine what to look for in evaluating a test; the test manual provides useful information for the evaluation; and the *Yearbooks* and *Test Critiques* provide critical reviews by measurement experts.

To ensure that the most appropriate tests are selected, a systematic procedure should be followed. This includes (1) defining the specific type of testing information needed, (2) appraising the role of published tests in relation to other measurement procedures and to the practical constraints of the school situation, (3) locating suitable tests through the various guides and test publishers' catalogues, (4) obtaining specimen sets of those tests that seem most appropriate, (5) reviewing the test materials in light of their intended uses, and (6) summarizing the data and making a final selection. A summary of data concerning each test under consideration is simplified if a standard evaluation form is used when compiling the information.

Administration of published tests involves careful preparation beforehand and strict adherence to the set procedures during testing. In preparing for testing, (1) order and check the materials well in advance; (2) select a suitable location for testing; (3) make provisions to prevent distractions; and (4) practice administering the test. During test administration, (1) closely follow the directions and time limits; (2) encourage the pupils to do their best; and (3) keep a record of any event during the testing period that might affect the test scores. Also, our test results are more likely to be valid if questionable scores are checked by administering a second form of the test and pupils are given training in test taking skills.

Published test results can serve a number of useful purposes in the school. They can aid in instructional planning, sectioning and grouping of pupils, individualizing instruction, identifying the needs of exceptional children, monitoring educational progress over extended periods, educational and vocational planning, and appraising and reporting on the effectiveness of the school program. In general they should not be used for assigning course grades or as the sole or main basis for evaluating teaching effectiveness. Published tests are not closely enough related to the instructional objectives of particular courses and they measure too limited a sampling of the intended learning outcomes to be useful for these purposes. Using published test results to judge a teacher's effectiveness may lead to "teaching for the test" and invalidate the test scores for other school uses.

Learning Exercises

1. List the steps you would follow in locating and selecting the most recent suitable test in one of your teaching areas.

2. What types of information would you expect to find in each of the following: (a) *Mental Measurements Yearbooks*, (b) *Test Critiques*, (c) test manual?

3. Why is it important to follow the directions strictly when administering a published test?

4. Describe some of the ways that published tests might be used for instructional planning in one of your teaching areas.

5. Consult a test publisher's catalogue and read the descriptions of one achievement test and one scholastic aptitude test. What type of information is provided?

6. Consult the latest *Mental Measurements Yearbook* and study the reviews for one achievement battery, one reading test, and one scholastic aptitude test. What strengths and weaknesses do the reviewers emphasize?

7. Consult the *Standards for Educational and Psychological Testing* (see reading list for this chapter) and review the types of validity and reliability information that test manuals should contain. Compare a recent test manual against the *Standards* and evaluate its strengths and weaknesses.

8. Why shouldn't published achievement tests be used as the main basis for assigning course grades or determining teaching effectiveness?

Suggestions for Further Reading

AMERICAN PSYCHOLOGICAL ASSOCIATION. *Standards for Educational and Psychological Testing.* Washington, D.C.: APA, 1985. Presents recommendations for (1) the preparation of tests, manuals, and reports and (2) the selection and use of tests. An excellent set of guidelines for evaluating test materials and for using tests effectively.

ANASTASI, A. *Psychological Testing,* 6th ed. New York: Macmillan, 1988. For an orientation to psychological testing see Chapter 1, "Functions and Origins of Psychological Testing," Chapter 2, "Nature and Use of Psychological Tests," and Chapter 3, "Social and Ethical Considerations in Testing."

CONOLEY, J. C., AND KRAMER, J. J., EDS. *The Tenth Mental Measurements Yearbook.* Lincoln, Nebr.: Buros Institute of Mental Measurements, 1989. Provides test descriptions, critical reviews by measurement specialists, and references. Plans are to publish new editions biannually with a *Supplement* published in alternating years.

KEYSER, D. J., AND SWEETLAND, R. C., EDS. *Test Critiques Compendium.* Kansas City: Test Corporation of America, 1987. Descriptions and critiques of sixty widely used educational and psychological tests with special emphasis on practical user information. See also the various volumes of *Test Critiques*.

MEHRENS, W. A., AND LEHMANN, I. J. *Using Standardized Tests in Education,* 4th ed. New York: Longman, 1987. See Chapter 1, "Introduction to Measurement and Evaluation," for basic considerations in test selection and use.

MITCHELL, J. V., ED. *Tests in Print III.* Lincoln, Nebr.: Buros Institute of Mental Measurements, 1983. Includes brief descriptions of published tests, references on specific tests, and a directory of test publishers with an index to their tests. The test entries are cross-referenced to reviews in the *Mental Measurements Yearbooks*.

SALVIA, J., AND YSSELDYKE, J. *Assessment in Special and Remedial Education*, 4th ed. Boston: Houghton Mifflin, 1988. For an orientation to the selection, administration, and use of tests with elementary and secondary pupils with special problems, the entire book should be reviewed. Written for beginners.

SWEETLAND, R. C., AND KEYSER, D. J., EDS. *Tests: A Comprehensive Reference for Assessments in Psychology, Education and Business*, 2d ed. Kansas City: Test Corporation of America, 1986. Provides brief descriptions of 3,000 tests in psychology, education, and business. The easy to read entries include title, age or grade range, purpose, test description, time, scoring, cost, and publisher. Look for supplements or new editions of this reference.

Chapter 14

Interpreting Test Scores and Norms

Test results can be interpreted in terms of (1) the types of tasks that can be performed (criterion reference) or (2) the relative position held in some reference group (norm reference). . . . Both types of interpretation are useful. . . . The first describes what a person can do, and the second describes how the performance compares with that of others . . . Standardized tests traditionally emphasized norm-referenced interpretation, but many now include both types. . . . Interpreting test scores with the aid of norms requires (1) an understanding of the various methods of expressing test scores and (2) a clear grasp of the nature of the norm group. . . . Criterion-referenced interpretation requires analysis by objective or content cluster. . . .

Test interpretation would be greatly simplified if we could express test scores on scales like those used in physical measurement. We know, for example, that 5 feet means the same height whether we are talking about the height of a boy or a picket fence; that a 200-pound football player weighs exactly twice as much as a 100-pound cheerleader, and that 8 minutes is exactly one third as long as 24 minutes, whether we are timing a standardized test or a basketball game. This ability to compare measurements from one situation to another and to speak in terms of "twice as much as" or "one third as long as" is made possible by the fact that these physical measures are based on scales that have a true zero point and equal units.

The true zero point (e.g., the point at which there is "no height at all" or "no weight at all") indicates precisely where measurement begins and the equal units (e.g., feet, pounds, and minutes) provide uniform meaning from one situation to another and from one part of the scale to another. Ten pounds indicates the same weight to the doctor, the grocer, the farmer, and the housewife. Also, the difference between 15 and 25 pounds represents exactly the same difference as that between 160 and 170 pounds.

Unfortunately, the properties of physical measuring scales, with which we all are so familiar, are generally lacking in educational measurement. A pupil who receives a score of zero on a history test does not have zero knowledge of history; there are probably many simple questions that could be answered correctly but were not included in the test. A true zero point in achievement, where there is *no achievement at all*, cannot be clearly established. Even if it could, it would be impractical to start from that point each time we tested. What we do in actual practice is to assume a certain amount of basic knowledge and measure from there. This arbitrary starting point, however, prevents us from saying that a zero score indicates *no achievement at all* or that a score of 100 represents twice the achievement of a score of 50. Because we are never certain how far the zero score on our test is from the true zero point (i.e., the point of *no achievement at all*), test scores cannot be interpreted in the same way as physical measurements. We can speak of *more* or *less* of a given characteristic, but not *twice as much as* or *half as much as*.

The interpretation of test results is additionally handicapped by the inequality of our units of measurement. Sixty items correct on a simple vocabulary test does not have the same meaning as sixty items correct on a more difficult one; nor do either of the scores represent the same level of achievement as sixty items correct on a test of arithmetic, science, or study skills. Our test items simply do not represent equal units like feet, pounds, and minutes.

To overcome this lack of a definite frame of reference in educational measurement, a variety of methods of expressing test scores have been devised. As we shall see shortly, the methods vary considerably in the extent to which they provide satisfactory units of measurement. Much of our difficulty in the interpretation and use of test results is because we have so many different scoring systems — each with its own peculiar characteristics and limitations.

Methods of Interpreting Test Scores

Raw Scores

If a pupil responds correctly to sixty-five items on an objective test in which each correct item counts one point, the *raw score* will be 65. Thus, a *raw score* is simply the number of points received on a test when the test has been scored according to the directions. It does not make any difference whether each item is counted as one point, whether the items are weighted in some way, or whether a correction for guessing is applied; the resulting point score is still known as a *raw score*. We all are familiar with raw scores from our many years of taking classroom tests.

Although a raw score is a numerical summary of a pupil's test performance, it is not very meaningful without further information. If we are told that Michael Adams answered 35 items correctly on an arithmetic test, and therefore has a raw score of 35, our response is likely to be a question: "What does a 35 mean?" or "Is that a good score?" We might also have a list of more specific questions. "How many items were on the test?" "What kinds of arithmetic problems (e.g., addition of integers, multiplication of fractions, story problems) were presented?" "How difficult was the test?" "How does a score of 35 compare with the scores received by other pupils in Michael's class?"

Answers to these or similar questions are needed to make Michael's 35 or any other raw score meaningful. In general we can provide meaning to a raw score by either converting it into a description on the specific tasks that the pupil can perform (*criterion-referenced* interpretation) or converting it into some type of derived score that indicates the pupil's relative position in a clearly defined reference group (*norm-referenced* interpretation). Questions such as the one about the specific kind of arithmetic problems that are on the test are directed at a desire for criterion-referenced interpretations, while those such as the one asking for a comparison with the performance of other pupils are directed at the desire for norm-referenced interpretations. Often both types of interpretation are appropriate and useful.

Criterion-Referenced Interpretation

Criterion-referenced test interpretation permits us to describe an individual's test performance without referring to the performance of others. Thus, we might describe pupil performance in terms of the speed with which a task is performed (e.g., types 40 words per minute without error), the precision with which a task is performed (e.g., measures the length of a line within one sixteenth of an inch), or the percentage of items correct on some clearly defined set of learning tasks (e.g., identifies the meaning of 80 percent of the terms used to describe fractions). The *percentage-correct score* is widely used in criterion-referenced test interpretation. Standards for judging whether a pupil has mastered each of the instructional objectives or achievement domains measured by a criterion-referenced test are frequently set in these terms. The key, however, is in providing a clear description of what a pupil can and cannot do rather than in the use of a percentage-correct score. Knowing, for example, Michael Adams' raw score of 35 corresponds to percentage-correct score of 70 because there were 50 items on the arithmetic test provides relatively little help in understanding the meaning of the score. We still need to have a clear description of the domain of arithmetic items that the test represents in order to make a criterion-referenced interpretation of Michael's score.

Criterion-referenced interpretation of test results is most meaningful when the test has been specifically designed for this purpose (see Chapter 11). This typically involves designing a test that measures a set of clearly stated learning tasks. Enough items are used for each interpretation to make it possible to describe test performance in terms of a pupil's mastery or nonmastery of the tasks. The value of these descriptions of test performance is enhanced by the fact that the domain of measured achievement is delimited and clearly specified, the test items are selected on the basis of their relevance to the domain being measured, and there are enough test items to make dependable judgments concerning the types of tasks a pupil can and cannot perform.

Criterion-Referenced Interpretation of Standardized Tests. Although standardized tests have been typically designed for norm-referenced interpretations, it is possible to attach criterion-referenced meaning to the test results. This simply involves analyzing each pupil's test responses by item content and summarizing the results with descriptive statements (e.g., he solved all of the addition problems involving no carrying but solved only two of the ten problems requiring carrying). Some test publishers aid this type of interpretation by (1) providing the list of objectives measured by the test, with each item keyed to the appropriate objective, and (2) arranging the items into larger homogeneous content clusters for easy analysis.

Later in this chapter we shall describe and illustrate how criterion-referenced interpretations have been added to the norm-referenced interpretations of standardized tests. Because these tests are usually designed for norm-referenced testing, however, the criterion-referenced interpretations must be made with considerable caution (see box).

Cautions When Making Criterion-Referenced Interpretations of Standardized Tests

1. Are the achievement domains (objectives or content clusters) homogeneous, delimited, and clearly specified? *If not,* avoid *specific* descriptive statements.
2. Are there enough items (say 10) for each type of interpretation? *If not,* make tentative judgments and/or combine items into larger content clusters for interpretation.
3. In constructing the test, were the easy items omitted to increase discrimination among individuals? *If so,* remember that the descriptions of what low achievers "can do" will be severely limited.
4. Does the test use selection-type items only? *If so,* keep in mind that a proportion of correct answers may be based on guessing (this is especially crucial when only a few items are used to measure a specific content domain).
5. Do the test items provide a directly relevant measure of the objectives? *If not,* base interpretation on what the items actually measured (e.g., "ability to identify misspelled words" rather than "ability to spell." They are related but are not the same process).

Grouping items in standardized tests by objective and by larger content clusters enhances the instructional use of the results, but criterion-referenced interpretations must be made cautiously.

Expectancy Tables.   The use of expectancy tables, as discussed in Chapter 3, also falls within the province of criterion-referenced interpretation. The expectancy table makes it possible to interpret raw scores in terms of expected performance on some measure other than the test itself. As illustrated in Chapter 3, the scores on an aptitude test can be used to predict the probability of earning a particular letter grade (A, B, C, D, F) in a course. Similarly, expectancy tables can be used to predict the probability of success in a training program, on a job, or in any other situation of interest. The use of an expectancy table makes it possible to interpret a raw score simply and directly without the aid of test norms.

Norm-Referenced Interpretation

Norm-referenced test interpretation tells us how an individual compares with other persons who have taken the same test. The simplest type of comparison, one that is used in classroom testing, is to rank the scores from highest to lowest and to note where an individual's score falls. Noting whether a particular score is third from the top, about average, or one of the lowest scores in class provides a meaningful report to teacher and pupil alike. If a pupil's test score is third from the top in a classroom group of thirty pupils, it is a high score, whether it represents 90 percent of the items correct or 60 percent correct. The fact that a test is relatively easy or difficult for the pupils does not alter our interpretation of test scores in terms of *relative* performance. All that is required is a sufficient spread of test scores to provide a reliable ranking.

Derived Scores.   Although the simple ranking of raw scores may be useful for reporting the results of a classroom test, it is of limited value beyond the immediate situation because the meaning of a given rank depends on the number of group members. To obtain a more general framework for norm-referenced interpretation, raw scores are converted into some type of derived score. A *derived score is a numerical report of test performance on a score scale that has well-defined characteristics and yields normative meaning*. The most common types of derived scores are grade equivalents, percentile ranks, and standard scores. Grade equivalent scores, which are sometimes described as an example of a developmental score scale, report test performance in terms of the grade group in which an individual's raw score is just average. Percentile ranks and standard scores indicate the individual's relative standing within some particular group (see Table 14.1). Converting raw scores to derived scores is simple with standardized tests. Frequently the test publisher performs the conversions for us before reporting the scores. If not, however, all we need to do is consult the table of norms in the test manual and select the derived score that corresponds to the individual's raw score. Some derived scores are so easily computed that we can also develop local norms if desired.

There are, as we shall see, a variety of ways of expressing standard scores (e.g., T-scores, normal-curve equivalent scores, and standard age scores), but they are based on a common logic. They differ only in terms of the numerical values used and whether they are based on a normal distribution. There are also a number of approaches other than grade equivalents (e.g., age equivalents or publisher-specific extended score scales) to the definition of a developmental score scale. However, grade equivalents are by far the most common for educational achievement tests.

Norms. Tables of norms in test manuals merely present scores earned by pupils in clearly defined reference groups. The raw scores and derived scores are presented in parallel columns so that the conversion to derived scores can be easily made. These scores do not represent especially good or desirable performance but, rather, *normal* or *typical* performance. They were established at the time the test was standardized by administering the test to representative groups of pupils for whom the test was constructed. Thus, they indicate the typical performance of pupils in these standardization groups and nothing more. They should not be viewed as standards or goals to be achieved by other pupils.

Test norms enable us to answer questions such as the following:

1. How does a pupil's test performance compare with that of other pupils?
2. How does a pupil's performance on one test (or subtest) compare with performance on another test (or subtest)?
3. How does a pupil's performance on one form of a test compare with performance on another form of the test, administered at an earlier date?

These comparisons of test scores make it possible to *predict* a pupil's probable success in various areas, to *diagnose* strengths and weaknesses, to measure educational *growth*, and to use the test results for other instructional and guidance purposes. Such functions of test scores would be severely curtailed without the use of the derived scores provided by test norms.

A summary of the most common types of test norms is presented in Table 14.1. To interpret and use test results effectively, we need a good grasp of the characteristics, advantages, and limitations of each of these types of norms.

TABLE 14.1 Most Common Types of Test Norms	Type of Test Norm	Name of Derived Score	Meaning in Terms of Test Performance
	Grade norms	Grade equivalents	Grade group in which pupil's raw score is average.
	Percentile norms	Percentile ranks (or percentile scores)	Percentage of pupils in the reference group who fall below pupil's raw score.
	Standard score norms	Standard scores	Distance of pupil's raw score above or below the mean of the reference group in terms of standard deviation units.

Grade Norms

Grade norms have been widely used with standardized achievement tests, especially at the elementary school level. The grade equivalent that corresponds to a particular raw score identifies the grade level at which the typical pupil obtains that raw score. Grade equivalents are based on the performance of pupils in the norm group in each of two or more grades. For example, suppose the arithmetic test that Michael Adams took had been administered to 4th- and 5th-grade pupils in the norm group in October and in May. We would expect that the group who took the test in May of the 5th grade would generally get higher scores than the group who took the test in October of the 4th grade.

As we see in Table 14.2, this expected pattern is obtained. In October of grade 4, 50 percent of the pupils have raw scores below the *median* score of 28, but this value goes up to 35 in May of grade 4, to 37 in October of grade 5, and to 41 in May of grade 5. Thus, Michael would need to have a higher raw score (41) to obtain a grade equivalent of 5.8 (which corresponds to the typical performance of the grade 5 pupil in May) than he would to obtain a grade equivalent of 4.1 (the typical performance of the grade 4 student in October). Since Michael's raw score was actually 35, he would receive a grade equivalent score of 4.8: the grade at which the typical pupil receives a raw score of 35.

As is suggested by this example, grade equivalents are expressed by two numbers; the first indicates the year and the second, the month. Grade equivalents for the fifth grade, for example, range from 5.0 to 5.9, or if the decimal point is omitted, as is the practice for some tests, from 50 to 59. This division of the calendar year into tenths, starting with September = .0 and ending with June = .9, is based on the traditional school year and assumes little or no growth in achievement test performance during the summer vacation months.

Table 14.2 provides all that is needed to convert Michael's raw score to a grade equivalent because he happened to get a raw score equal to the median of one of the grade norm groups. To obtain grade equivalents for Bob Brown who got a raw score of 31 and Mary Carson who got a raw score of 45, however, we would need some more information. We could see that Bob should have a grade equivalent

Time of Administration		Median* Raw Score	Grade Equivalent	TABLE 14.2
Grade	Month			Illustration of the Construction of Grade Equivalent Scores
4	October (.1)	28	4.1	
4	May (.8)	35	4.8	
5	October (.1)	37	5.1	
5	May (.8)	41	5.8	

*50 percent of the pupils in the norm group score below and 50 percent score above the median raw score (see Appendix A).

somewhere between 4.1 and 4.8, but to determine a specific score we would need to *interpolate*, that is, decide how far to go above 4.1 toward 4.8 to account for the fact that Bob did better than the typical 4th-grade pupil did in October but not as well as the typical 4th-grade pupil in May. Similarly, we could see that Mary's raw score of 45 should be converted to a grade equivalent score above 5.8, but would have to *extrapolate*, that is, project the rate of increase with grade level beyond the point where data were collected, to give Mary a specific grade equivalent.

Fortunately, we don't need to know the details of interpolation or extrapolation to convert Bob's and Mary's raw scores to grade equivalents. Test publishers perform those operations and produce tables showing the grade equivalent corresponding to each possible raw score. To convert to grade equivalents with a table of grade norms, all one needs to do is find in the table the pupils' raw scores and read off the corresponding grade equivalents. Using this procedure, for example, we might find that Bob's grade equivalent is 4.4 and that Mary's grade equivalent is 6.5.

The popularity of grade norms is largely because test performance is expressed in units that are apparently easy to understand and interpret. To illustrate, assume that we obtained the following grade equivalents for John, who is in the *middle of the fifth grade*:

Arithmetic   5.5
Language   6.5
Reading   9.0

In examining these scores, teachers, parents, and pupils alike would recognize that John is exactly average in arithmetic, one year advanced in language, and three and a half years advanced in reading. Grade equivalents provide a common unit with which we all are familiar. The only difficulty is that this familiarity leads those who are unaware of the numerous limitations of grade norms to misleading or inaccurate interpretations. Concern about misinterpretations of grade equivalents has led to sharp criticisms of the scores. Indeed, an earlier version of the *Standards*[1] suggested that the use of grade equivalent scores should be discouraged. On the other hand, some measurement experts[2] have argued that grade equivalents are useful and no more subject to misinterpretation than other types of scores. In any event, there is no indication that their popularity is declining or that they are less used now than they once were. Hence, it is important to understand their limitations so that misinterpretations can be avoided.

Six possible misinterpretations of grade equivalents are worthy of consideration. Each of these misinterpretations is based upon an unjustified assumption about the meaning of the scores. These inappropriate assumptions are: (1) assuming that

[1]American Psychological Association, *Standards for Educational and Psychological Tests* (Washington, D.C.: APA, 1974).
[2]H. D. Hoover, "The Most Appropriate Scores for Measuring Educational Development in Elementary Schools: GE's," *Educational Measurement: Issues and Practice* 3, no. 4 (1984): 8–14.

norms are standards of what should be, (2) assuming that grade equivalents indicate the appropriate grade placement for a pupil, (3) assuming that all pupils should be expected to grow one grade equivalent unit per year, (4) assuming that the units are equal throughout the score range, (5) assuming that grade equivalents for different tests are comparable, and (6) assuming that the scores that are based on extrapolations to grades well above or below the test level are meaningful. Let's briefly consider each of these faulty assumptions and the resulting misinterpretation of grade equivalents.

1. Don't confuse norms with standards of what should be. For any particular grade equivalent, 50 percent of the pupils in the standardization group are above this norm, and 50 percent are below. Consequently, we should not interpret a particular grade norm as something all of our pupils should attain. If half of our pupils are above norm and half are below, we may conclude that our pupils compare favorably with the pupils in the norm group. Whether this is good or bad depends on a number of factors, such as our pupils' ability, the extent to which the learning outcomes measured by the test reflect our curriculum emphasis, and the quality of the educational facilities at our disposal. If we are teaching pupils with above-average ability under conditions comparable to those of schools in the norm group, merely matching the norm would be cause for concern. On the other hand, if our pupils have a history of low achievement in previous grades, reaching the norm might call for considerable pride. In any case, it is well to remember that the norm is merely an average score made by the pupils in the standardization group. As such, it represents the typical performance of average pupils in average schools and should not be considered a standard of excellence to be achieved by others.

2. Don't interpret a grade equivalent as an estimate of the grade where a pupil should be placed. One potential misinterpretation of grade norms, although not because of weaknesses in the scoring system itself, is to assume that pupils who earn certain grade equivalent scores are ready to do work at that level. For example, we might conclude that a fourth-grade pupil should be doing sixth-grade work in language skills if she earns a grade equivalent of 6.0 on a language skills test. This assumption overlooks the fact that she can obtain a grade equivalent score well above her grade level by doing the less-difficult test items more rapidly and accurately than the average fourth-grade pupil. The grade equivalent score of 6.0 may represent nothing more than a thorough mastery of language skills taught in the first four grades. Thus, grade equivalents should never be interpreted literally; at best, they are only rough guides to level of test performance. Pupils at different grade levels who earn the same grade equivalent score are apt to be ready for quite different types of instruction.

3. Don't expect that all pupils should gain 1.0 grade equivalent each year. It seems natural to think that if Jane and Sara had grade equivalents of 4.7 and 2.5, respectively, at the end of grade 3 that, with normal progress, they should be expected to each gain 1.0 and thus have scores of 5.7 and 3.5 at the end of grade 4. This expectation is inappropriate, not only because norms should not be confused with standards, but because that a gain of 1.0 per year is only typical of students scoring close to the average for their grade. On average, pupils who score well above their grade placement gain more than 1.0 grade equivalents per year, while pupils who score well below the norm gain less than 1.0 per year. Thus, if pupils in a remedial reading program show an average gain of 1.0 in a year's time, that actually would be better than is typical of students with low initial scores.

*4. **Don't assume that the units are equal at different parts of the scale.*** A year of growth in arithmetic achievement from grade 4.0 to 5.0, for example, might represent a much greater improvement than an increase from grade 2.0 to 3.0 or grade 8.0 to 9.0. Thus, being advanced or retarded in terms of grade units has a different meaning on different parts of the grade scale. Pupils who earn grade equivalents several grades above their grade placement might be demonstrating either vastly superior achievement or performance just slightly above average.

*5. **Don't assume that scores on different tests are comparable.*** A grade equivalent score of 8.0 on one test publisher's fifth-grade reading comprehension test may not represent the same degree of superior performance as an 8.0 on another publisher's fifth-grade reading comprehension test. We know that in both cases an 8.0 is well above the average for a fifth grader. However, an 8.0 might be one of the highest possible scores for one publisher's test, while the scores provided by the other publisher might go considerably higher.

The lack of comparability also applies to a single publisher's tests in different subjects. Patterns of growth vary from subject to subject, and so our grade equivalent units stretch and contract at different points on the scale for different subjects. Although it would be tempting to conclude that a fourth-grader who received a grade equivalent of 7.2 in reading and a grade equivalent of 6.3 in mathematics was better at reading than mathematics, such a conclusion is likely to be inappropriate. In comparison with other fourth grade pupils, the two scores may actually represent equally superior performance because the range of grade equivalent scores for fourth grade pupils is generally greater in reading than in mathematics.

*6. **Don't interpret extreme scores as dependable estimates of pupils' performance level.*** Grade equivalent scores that are several years above or below the pupil's actual grade placement and the grade levels where the test is normally used are based on extrapolation. This results in artificial units that do not correspond to the achievement of pupils in any particular group. Estimating these grade equivalents is frequently necessary because the younger pupils do not have the needed skills to take the test and because growth in the basic skills tends to level off in the eighth and ninth grades. In interpreting grade equivalents at the extremes, therefore, it is well to keep in mind that they do not represent the actual performance of pupils at these levels.

In summary, grade norms are based on the average performance of pupils at various grade levels. They are widely used at the elementary school level, largely because of the *apparent* ease with which they can be interpreted. As we have seen, however, grade equivalents have a number of limitations that can lead to misinterpretations. In general, grade norms are most useful for reporting growth in the basic skills during the elementary school period. They are least useful for comparing a pupil's performances on different tests. For whatever purpose grade norms are used, however, the inequality of grade units must be considered during interpretation of the results.

Percentile Rank

One of the most widely used and easily understood methods of describing test performance is percentile rank. A percentile rank (or percentile score) indicates a pupil's relative position in a group in terms of the percentage of pupils scoring *lower*. Thus, if we consult a table of norms and find that a pupil's raw score of 29 equals a percentile rank of 70, we know that 70 percent of the pupils in the reference group obtained a raw score lower than 29. Stating it another way, this pupil's performance surpasses that of 70 percent of the group.[3]

One method of presenting percentile norms is shown in Table 14.3. These norms are for the *Differential Aptitude Tests*. The raw scores for each subtest and for combined subtests are listed in columns across the table. The procedure for obtaining the percentile rank for any given raw score is to locate the score in the proper column and then to read the corresponding percentile rank at the side of the table. For example, a raw score of 37 on the Abstract Reasoning test is equivalent to a percentile rank of 80, and a raw score of 19 on the Numerical Ability test is equivalent to a percentile rank of 45. Only selected percentile ranks are given in the norm table, and it is suggested that these be considered as midpoints of a band of values. Thus, a percentile rank of 80 is interpreted as a percentile band ranging from 78 to 82 to allow for error in the measurement.

A desirable feature of percentile norms is that we can interpret a pupil's performance in terms of various groups. Most commonly, performance is reported in terms of relative standing in the pupil's own grade or age group. In some instances, however, we are more interested in how a pupil compares with those who have completed second-year French, are majoring in home economics, or are enrolled in the college-preparatory program. Such comparisons are possible with percentile norms. The interpretations of a particular score are limited only to the types of decisions we want to make and the availability of the appropriate sets of norms.

The wide applicability of percentile norms is not without its drawbacks. When interpreting a percentile rank, we must always refer to the norm group on which it is based. A pupil does not have a percentile rank of 80, but a percentile rank of 80 *in some particular group*. A raw score on a scholastic aptitude test, for example, may be equivalent to a percentile rank of 80 in a general group of high school seniors, 63 in a group of college-bound seniors, and 25 in a group of college freshmen in a highly selective college. Relative standing varies with the ability of the reference group used for comparison.

---

[3]Percentile rank is sometimes interpreted as the percentage of individuals receiving scores *equal to or lower than* a given score. The specific interpretation depends on the method of computation used, but for all practical purposes the meaning is essentially the same.

TABLE 14.3
Norms for the *Differential Aptitude Tests**

Percentile Norms for Forms V and W

Fall Grade 10

Males (N = 6150+)

Raw Scores

Percentile	Verbal Reasoning	Numerical Ability	VR + NA	Abstract Reasoning	Clerical S and A	Mechanical Reasoning	Space Relations	Spelling	Language Usage	Percentile
99	47–50	39–40	84–90	44–45	83–100	66–70	57–60	87–90	44–50	99
97	44–46	37–38	80–83	42–43	71–82	64–65	54–56	83–86	41–43	97
95	41–43	35–36	74–79	41	63–70	62–63	50–53	80–82	38–40	95
90	38–40	33–34	69–73	39–40	58–62	61	47–49	76–79	35–37	90
85	35–37	31–32	64–68	38	54–57	59–60	44–46	72–75	33–34	85
80	33–34	29–30	61–63	37	52–53	58	41–43	69–71	31–32	80
75	30–32	28	57–60	36	50–51	56–57	38–40	67–68	30	75
70	28–29	26–27	54–56	35	48–49	55	36–37	64–66	28–29	70
65	27	24–25	51–53	34	46–47	54	34–35	62–63	27	65
60	25–26	23	48–50	33	45	53	31–33	59–61	25–26	60
55	23–24	22	45–47	32	43–44	51–52	29–30	57–58	24	55
50	21–22	20–21	42–44	31	42	50	27–28	54–56	22–23	50
45	20	19	39–41	30	40–41	48–49	25–26	52–53	21	45
40	18–19	17–18	36–38	29	39	47	23–24	49–51	20	40
35	17	16	34–35	27–28	38	45–46	22	47–48	18–19	35
30	15–16	15	31–33	26	36–37	43–44	20–21	45–46	17	30
25	14	13–14	29–30	24–25	34–35	41–42	19	43–44	15–16	25
20	12–13	12	26–28	21–23	33	39–40	17–18	41–42	14	20
15	11	10–11	23–25	17–20	30–32	36–38	16	38–40	12–13	15
10	9–10	8–9	20–22	12–16	27–29	31–35	14–15	35–37	10–11	10
5	8	7	17–19	8–11	23–26	27–30	12–13	31–34	9	5
3	7	5–6	15–16	6–7	17–22	24–26	11	27–30	7–8	3
1	0–6	0–4	0–14	0–5	0–16	0–23	0–10	0–26	0–6	1
Mean	23.4	21.1	44.6	29.4	43.3	48.7	29.8	55.8	23.4	Mean
SD	10.8	8.9	18.3	9.6	13.7	10.8	12.5	15.5	9.5	SD

A related inconvenience with percentile norms is that numerous sets of norms are usually required. We need a set of norms for each group with which we wish to compare a pupil. This is not especially troublesome at the elementary school level where a pupil's own grade and age mates provide a suitable basis for comparison. At the high school level, however, where the curriculum becomes diversified and pupils pursue different courses, it becomes rather difficult. Here we need sets of norms for pupils who have completed varying numbers of courses in each subject area.

The main limitation of percentile norms is that percentile units are not equal on all parts of the scale. A percentile difference of 10 near the middle of the scale (e.g., 45 to 55) represents a much smaller difference in test performance than the same percentile difference at the ends (e.g., 85 to 95), because a large number of pupils receive scores near the middle, whereas relatively few pupils have extremely high or low scores. Thus, a pupil whose raw score is near average can surpass another 10 percent of the group by increasing the raw score just a few points. On the other hand, a pupil with a relatively high score will need to increase the raw score by a large number of points in order to surpass another 10 percent, simply because there are so few pupils at that level.

The inequality of units requires special caution when using percentile ranks. First, a difference of several percentile points should be given greater weight at the extremes of the distribution than near the middle. In fact, small differences near the middle of the distribution generally can be disregarded. Second, percentile ranks should not be averaged arithmetically. The appropriate average when using percentile norms is the 50th percentile. This is the midpoint of the distribution and is called the *median*, or counting average.

In summary, percentile norms are widely applicable, easily determined, and readily understood. A percentile rank describes a pupil's performance in terms of the percentage of pupils in some clearly defined group that earn a lower score. This might be a grade or age group, or any other group that provides a meaningful comparison (e.g., college freshmen). More than one set of norms is usually required, and percentile ranks must be interpreted in terms of the norm group on which they are based. The most severe limitation of percentile ranks is that the units are unequal. This can be offset somewhat by careful interpretation, however, because the inequality of units follows a predictable pattern.

Standard Scores

Another method of indicating a pupil's relative position in a group is by showing how far the raw score is above or below average. This is the approach used with standard scores. Basically, standard scores express test performance in terms of standard deviation units from the mean. The *mean (M)* is the arithmetical average, which is determined by adding all of the scores and dividing by the number of scores. The *standard deviation (SD)* is a measure of the spread of scores in a group. Because the method of computing the standard deviation is not especially helpful in understanding it, the procedure will not be presented here (see Appendix A for computation). The meaning of standard deviation and the standard scores based on it can best be explained in terms of the normal probability curve (also called the normal distribution curve or simply the normal curve).

The Normal Curve and the Standard Deviation Unit

The normal curve is a symmetrical bell-shaped curve that has many useful mathematical properties. One of the most useful from the viewpoint of test interpretation is that when it is divided into standard deviation units, each portion under the curve contains a fixed percentage of cases. This is shown in the idealized normal curve presented in Figure 14.1 (for the moment, disregard the raw scores beneath the figure). Note that 34 percent of the cases fall between the mean and +1 SD, 14 percent between +1 SD and +2 SD, and 2 percent between +2 SD and +3 SD.[4] The same proportions, of course, apply to the standard deviation intervals below the mean. Only 0.13 percent of the cases fall below −3 SD or above +3 SD. Thus, for all practical purposes, a normal distribution of scores falls between −3 and +3 standard deviations from the mean.

To demonstrate the value of standard deviation units for expressing relative position in a group, raw scores from two different tests have been placed beneath the row of deviations along the baseline of the curve in Figure 14.1. The tests have the following means and standard deviations:

	Test A	Test B
M	56	72
SD	4	6

FIGURE 14.1
Normal curve, indicating the approximate percentage of cases falling within each standard deviation interval.

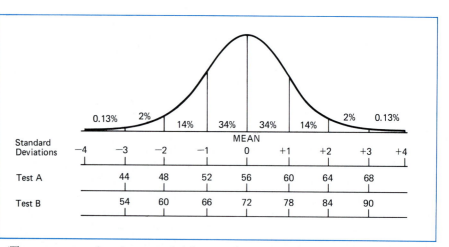

[4]These percentages have been rounded for ease of interpretation. See Figure 14.2 for precise figures.

In Figure 14.1 the mean raw scores of both tests have been placed at the zero point on the base line of the curve. Thus, they have been arbitrarily equated to zero. Notice that +1 *SD* is equivalent to 60 (56 + 4) on Test A and 78 (72 + 6) on Test B, and −1 *SD* is equivalent to 52 (56 − 4) on Test A and 66 (72 − 6) on Test B. If we convert all of the raw scores on the two tests to the standard deviation units in this manner, we can directly compare performance on the tests. For example, a raw score of 62 on Test A and 81 on Test B are equal because both are +1.5 standard deviation units above the mean. When converted to standard deviation units, the raw scores are, of course, no longer needed. A +2.5 *SD* on Test A is superior to a +2.0 *SD* on Test B, regardless of the size of the raw scores from which they were derived. The only restriction for such comparisons is that the conversion to standard deviation units must be based on a common group.

The utility of the standard deviation is that it permits us to convert raw scores to a common scale that has equal units and that can be readily interpreted in terms of the normal curve. At this point, it should be helpful to review a few of the characteristics of the normal curve that makes it so useful in test interpretation.

Referring to Figure 14.1 again, note that 68 percent (approximately two thirds) of the cases fall between −1 and +1 standard deviations from the mean. This provides a handy bench mark for interpreting standard scores and the standard error of measurement, as both are based on standard deviation units. The fixed percentages in each interval make it possible to convert standard deviation units to percentile ranks. For example, −2 *SD* equals a percentile rank of 2 because 2 percent of the cases fall below that point. Starting from the left of the figure, each point on the base line of the curve can be equated to the following percentile ranks:

$$-2\ SD = 2\%$$
$$-1\ SD = 16\%\ (\ 2 + 14)$$
$$0\ (M) = 50\%\ (16 + 34)$$
$$+1\ SD = 84\%\ (50 + 34)$$
$$+2\ SD = 98\%\ (84 + 14)$$

This relationship between standard deviation units and percentile ranks enables us to interpret standard scores in simple and familiar terms. When used for this purpose, we must, of course, be able to assume a normal distribution. This is not a serious restriction in using standard score norms, however, because the distribution of scores on which they are based usually closely approximates the normal curve. In many instances the standard scores are *normalized*; that is, the distribution of scores is made normal by the process of computing percentiles and converting directly to their standard score equivalents. Although it is generally safe to assume a normal distribution when using standard scores from tables of norms in test manuals, it is usually unwise to make such an assumption for standard scores computed directly from a relatively small number of cases, such as a classroom group.

Types of Standard Scores

There are numerous types of standard scores used in testing. Because they all are based on the same principle and are interpreted in somewhat the same manner, only the most common types will be discussed here.

z-Score. The simplest of the standard scores, and the one on which others are based, is the z-score. This score expresses test performance simply and directly as the number of standard deviation units a raw score is above or below the mean. In the previous section, we discussed z-scores but did not identify them as such. The formula for computing z-scores is

$$z\text{-score} = \frac{X - M}{SD}$$

where

X = any raw score
M = arithmetic mean of raw scores
SD = standard deviation of raw scores

You can quickly become familiar with this formula by applying it to various raw scores in Test A or Test B of Figure 14.1 and then visually checking your answer along the base line of the curve. For example, z-scores for the raw scores of 58 and 50 on Test A ($M = 56$, $SD = 4$) would be computed as follows:

$$z = \frac{58 - 56}{4} = .5 \qquad z = \frac{50 - 56}{4} = -1.5$$

A z-score is always minus when the raw score is smaller than the mean. Forgetting the minus sign can cause serious errors in test interpretation. For this reason, z-scores are seldom used directly in test norms but are usually transformed into a standard score system that uses only positive numbers.

T-Score. The term *T-score* was originally given to a type of normalized score based on a group of unselected twelve-year-old children. However, it has come to refer to any set of normally distributed standard scores that has a mean of 50 and a standard deviation of 10. T-scores (*linear* conversion) can be obtained by multiplying the z-score by 10 and adding the product to 50. Thus,

$$\text{T-score} = 50 + 10\,(z)$$

This formula will provide T-scores only when the original distribution of raw scores is normal because with this type of conversion (linear), the distribution of standard scores retains the same shape as the original raw score distribution.[5] Applying this formula to the two z-scores computed earlier ($z = .5$, $z = -1.5$), we would obtain the following results:

$$T = 50 + 10\,(.5) = 55 \qquad T = 50 + 10\,(-1.5) = 35$$

One reason that T-scores are preferred to z-scores for reporting test results is

[5]Some persons call any set of scores derived from this formula *T-scores*, whereas others call them *linear T-scores* or *Z-scores*, to distinguish them from *normalized T-scores*.

that, unlike the latter, only positive integers are produced. It seems preferable, for example, to report a person's test performance as a T-score of 33 than to report that same performance as a z-score of -1.7. The two scores are equivalent, however.

Because T-scores always have a mean of 50 and a standard deviation of 10, any single T-score is directly interpretable. A T-score of 55, for example, always indicates one-half standard deviation above the mean, and so on. Once the concept of T-scores is grasped, interpretation is relatively simple.

Normal-Curve Equivalent (NCE). In recent years, another normalized standard score, the normal-curve equivalent, which is commonly referred to as an NCE score, has come to be used for standardized achievement tests. NCE scores were introduced as part of the reporting and evaluation requirements of some federally supported compensatory education programs in order to avoid some of the pitfalls of grade equivalent scores. Because school districts needed NCE scores for this purpose, publishers of the major standardized achievement tests have added this score type to their list of score reporting options.

Like T-scores, NCE scores have a mean of 50. However, the standard deviation of NCE scores is 21.06 rather than the 10 that is used to define T-scores. This seemingly strange choice for a standard deviation was selected so that the NCE scores would range from 1 to 99. As can be seen from the following list of a few NCE scores and their corresponding percentile ranks, NCE scores of 1, 50, and 99 are equivalent to percentile ranks of the same numerical values. At other points on the scale, however, NCE scores have different numerical values than the corresponding percentile ranks. Compared to percentile ranks, they are more spread out at the extremes (e.g., an NCE difference of 90 to 99 corresponds to a percentile rank difference of only 97 to 99) and less spread out near the middle (e.g., an NCE difference of 50 to 75 corresponds to a percentile rank difference of 50 to 88).

NCE Score	Corresponding Percentile Rank	Percentile Rank	Corresponding NCE Score
99	99	99	99
90	97	90	77
75	88	75	64
50	50	50	50
25	12	25	36
10	3	10	23
1	1	1	1

Standard Age Scores. Another widely used standard score for ability tests is the Standard Age Score (SAS). Here the mean is set at 100 and the standard deviation at 16. Thus, a pupil with an SAS of 84 has scored 1 standard deviation below the mean (T-score = 40), and a pupil with an SAS of 116 has scored 1 standard deviation above the mean (T-score = 60). Scores on ability tests could just as easily be expressed as T-scores or NCEs. However, in the past these tests reported scores as deviation IQ scores with a mean of 100 and a standard deviation of 16 (15 on some tests). The SAS or similar scales such as the *Cognitive Skills Quotient* or *School Ability Index* have replaced deviation IQ scores in at attempt to avoid some of the misinterpretations associated with the terms *intelligence* and *IQ*.

Normalized Standard Scores

Normalized T-scores are calculated by (1) converting the distribution of raw scores into percentile ranks, (2) looking up the z-score each percentile rank would have in a normal distribution and assigning these z-scores to the corresponding raw scores, and (3) converting the z-scores to T-scores, using the formula presented earlier. The procedure of going from raw score to percentile to the corresponding z-score in a normal distribution is called an *area* conversion and yields normalized z-scores that are then transformed directly into normalized T-scores. This results in a normally distributed set of standard scores, regardless of the shape of the original distribution of raw scores. Normalizing is used by test publishers to remove minor irregularities in the raw score distributions.

Many other normalized standard scores are computed in the same way that normalized T-scores are determined, but different values are used for the mean and standard deviation. For example, standard scores with a mean of 100 and a standard deviation of 15 are used with some aptitude tests. Consequently, on these tests a score of 115 means 1 standard deviation above the mean, the same as a T-score of 60. Standard scores can be assigned any arbitrarily selected mean and standard deviation, and the interpretation will be the same because the basic frame of reference is the standard deviation unit.

Stanines. Some test norms are expressed as single-digit standard scores called *stanines* (pronounced *stay-nines*). This system of scores is so named because the distribution of raw scores is divided into nine parts (*stan*dard *nines*). Stanine 5 is precisely in the center of the distribution and includes all cases within one fourth of a standard deviation on either side of the mean. The remaining stanines are evenly distributed above and below stanine 5. Each stanine, with the exception of 1 and 9, which cover the tails of the distribution, includes a band of raw scores the width of one half of a standard deviation unit. Thus, for all practical purposes, stanines present test norms on a 9-point scale of equal units. These standard scores have a mean of 5 and a standard deviation of 2. The distribution of stanines in relation to the normal curve and the percentage of cases in each stanine are shown in Figure 14.2. (See later section in this chapter on local norms for the use of stanines.)

Comparison of Score Systems

The equivalence of scores in various standard score systems and their relation to percentiles and to the normal curve are presented in Figure 14.2. This figure illustrates the interrelated nature of the various scales for reporting relative position

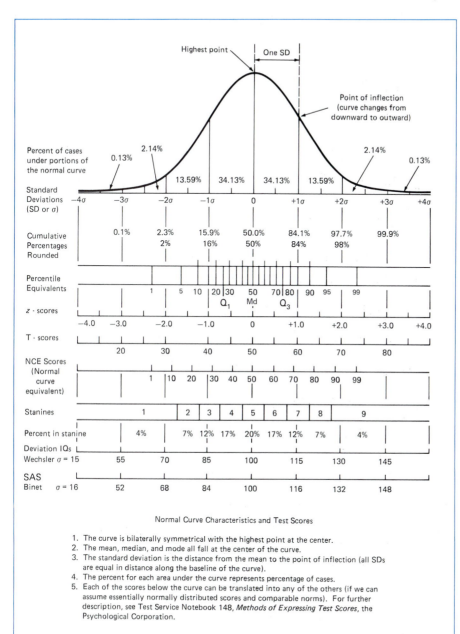

FIGURE 14.2
Corresponding
standard scores and
percentiles in a normal
distribution.

Normal Curve Characteristics and Test Scores

1. The curve is bilaterally symmetrical with the highest point at the center.
2. The mean, median, and mode all fall at the center of the curve.
3. The standard deviation is the distance from the mean to the point of inflection (all SDs are equal in distance along the baseline of the curve).
4. The percent for each area under the curve represents percentage of cases.
5. Each of the scores below the curve can be translated into any of the others (if we can assume essentially normally distributed scores and comparable norms). For further description, see Test Service Notebook 148, *Methods of Expressing Test Scores*, the Psychological Corporation.

in a normally distributed group. A raw score 1 standard deviation below the mean, for example, can be expressed as a z-score of -1.0, a percentile rank of 16, a T-score of 40, an NCE score of 29, a deviation IQ of 85, an SAS of 84, or a stanine of 3. Thus, the various scoring systems are merely different ways of saying the same thing, and we can readily convert back and forth from one scale to another (if we assume a normal distribution and comparable norm groups).

The relations among the scoring system shown in Figure 14.2 are especially helpful in learning to understand a particular standard score scale. Until we fully understand T-scores, for example, it is helpful to convert them, mentally, into percentile ranks. A T-score of 60 becomes meaningful when we note that it is equivalent to a percentile rank of 84. This conversion to percentile ranks, which are more easily understood, is also useful for interpreting standard scores to parents and pupils.

In summary, standard scores indicate a pupil's relative position in a group in terms of standard deviation units above or below the mean. In a normal distribution, the various standard score scales and the percentile scale are interrelated, making it possible to convert from one to another. Standard scores have the special advantage of providing roughly equal units. Thus, unlike percentiles, 10 standard score points represent approximately the same difference in test performance anywhere along the scale. In addition, standard scores can be averaged arithmetically. One drawback of standard scores is that they are not readily understood by pupils and parents. A more serious limitation is that interpretation is difficult unless the scores are normally distributed. This is not a problem in using standard score norms, however, because norm tables are generally based on normalized standard scores.

Profiles

One advantage of converting raw scores to derived scores is that a pupil's performance on different tests can be compared directly. This is usually done by means of a test profile, like the one presented in Figure 14.3. Such a graphic representation of test data makes it easy to identify a pupil's relative strengths and weaknesses. Most standardized tests have provisions for plotting test profiles.

The profile shown in Figure 14.3 indicates a desirable trend in profile construction. Instead of plotting test scores as specific points on the scale, test performance is recorded in the form of bands that extend one standard error of measurement above and below the pupil's obtained scores. Recall from our discussion of reliability that there are approximately two chances out of three that a pupil's true score will fall within one standard error of the obtained score. Thus, these *confidence bands* indicate the ranges of scores within which we can be reasonably certain of finding the pupil's true standings. Plotting them on the profile enables us to take into account the inaccuracy of the test scores when comparing performance on different tests. Interpreting differences between tests is simple with these score bands. If the bands for two tests overlap, we can assume that performance on the two tests does not differ significantly, and if the bands do *not* overlap, we can assume that there is probably a real difference in performance.

The score bands used with the *Differential Aptitude Tests* can be plotted by hand or by computer. The computer-produced profile shown in Figure 14.3 is based on the same-sex percentiles. These are recorded down the left side of the profile and were obtained from the percentile norms in Table 14.3. The opposite-sex percentiles are listed down the right side of the report also to show how the scores compare with the female norms. The difference in percentiles for some tests

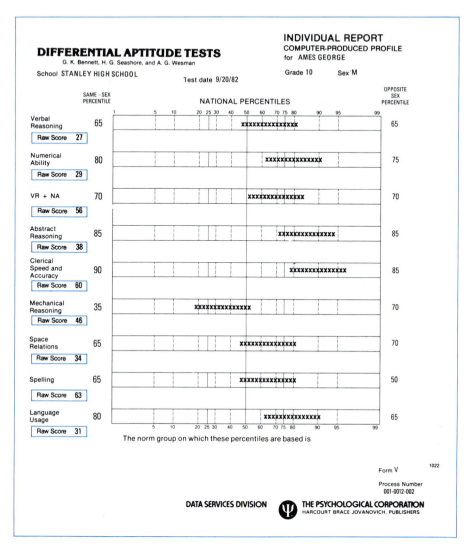

(e.g., Mechanical Reasoning and Language Usage) highlights the importance of reporting scores in terms of both male and female norms.

Not all test publishers make provisions for plotting score bands, but probably more will follow this practice in the future. There is no need to wait for special provisions, however, for it is possible to plot these bands for any test for which we have a standard error of measurement. All we need to do is determine the error band in raw score points and refer to the norm table with these figures. For example, if a pupil has earned a raw score of 74 and the standard error of measurement is 3, the error band in raw score points will range from 71 to 77. By locating these two numbers in the norm table we can obtain the corresponding range in percentiles, standard scores, or whatever derived score is being used, and plot the results directly on the profile. The use of such bands minimizes the tendency of test profiles to present a misleading picture. Without the bands we are apt to attribute significance to differences in test performance that can be accounted for by chance alone.

When profiles are used to compare test performance, it is essential that the norms for all tests be comparable. Many test publishers provide for this by standardizing a battery of achievement tests and a scholastic aptitude test on the same population.

Profile Narrative Reports

Some test publishers are now making available a profile of each pupil's scores, accompanied by a narrative report that describes how well the pupil is achieving. The graphic profile provides a quick view of the pupil's strengths and weaknesses, and the narrative report aids in interpreting the scores and in identifying areas in which instructional emphasis is needed. A typical report of this type, for a widely used test battery, is shown in Figure 14.4.

Narrative reports should be especially useful in communicating test results to parents. They are, of course, also helpful to those teachers who have had little or no training in the interpretation and use of scores from published tests.

Criterion-Referenced Skill Analysis

Some test publishers provide profiles that include both norm-referenced and criterion-referenced data. An example of such a report is shown in Figure 14.5. This pupil skills analysis report form, used with the *Standard Achievement Test*, presents a comprehensive and detailed description of each individual's test results. The norm-referenced scores and profile (using percentile bands) are shown in the top half of the report, and the criterion-referenced skill analysis by "content clusters" is shown in the bottom half.

Report forms like this yield a wealth of information for the instructional use of test results. The norm-referenced scores indicate how the pupil's test performance compares with that of others; the achievement/ability comparison indicates (in verbal form) how the pupil's achievement compares with that of other pupils of *similar ability*; the profile identifies strengths and weaknesses in each *general* content area; and the performance report, by content cluster, identifies strengths and weaknesses in *specific skills* in each general content area. As noted earlier in this chapter, however, caution is necessary when interpreting performance on content clusters based on a small number of test items. In these instances, the results are best interpreted as clues for further study.

In addition to detailed reports for individuals, many publishers also offer profile and skill analysis by class, school, and school system. By using computer scoring and reporting services, test results can be obtained in almost any form desired.

FIGURE 14.4 Illustrative Profile Narrative Report. (Reprinted by permission of Science Research Associates.)

Ⓐ   # A Personal Report to the Parents of   [ANDREWS TANYA]

ON APR 08, 1986, YOUR STUDENT TOOK THE SRA SURVEY OF BASIC SKILLS TEST, LEVEL 34 FORM P IN GRADE 4 AT METRO HIGH, PEORIA, IL.

Ⓑ FOR A COMPOSITE SCORE, YOUR STUDENT RECEIVED A 64 PERCENTILE, WHICH IS LISTED IN THE CHART BELOW. A 64 PERCENTILE MEANS THAT YOUR STUDENT SCORED BETTER THAN 64 PERCENT OF THE STUDENTS IN GRADE 4 WHO TOOK THE TEST DURING STANDARDIZATION. ON THE CHART, ON THE SAME LINE AS THE NUMBER 64, THERE IS A GROUP OF X'S. THESE X'S ARE CALLED A PERCENTILE BAND. YOUR STUDENT'S SCORE WOULD PROBABLY FALL WITHIN THIS RANGE IF THE TEST WAS TAKEN SEVERAL TIMES. THE POSITION OF THE BAND ON THE CHART DEPICTS GRAPHICALLY WHERE THE STUDENT'S SCORE FALLS IN RELATION TO BELOW AVERAGE, AVERAGE, OR ABOVE AVERAGE.

THE COMPOSITE SCORE IS LISTED ON THE CHART BELOW. BELOW THE COMPOSITE, YOU WILL FIND THE SCORES FOR THE DIFFERENT SUB-TESTS. THREE OF THESE SUB-TESTS CONTRIBUTE TO THE COMPOSITE SCORE: READING, MATHEMATICS, AND LANGUAGE. THE STUDENT RECEIVED A TOTAL SCORE IN READING OF 73, IN MATHEMATICS OF 52, AND IN LANGUAGE OF 63. THESE, LIKE THE COMPOSITE, ARE PERCENTILE SCORES.

Ⓓ TO SAY WHETHER A SCORE IS GOOD OR NOT, YOU HAVE TO REALLY KNOW THE INDIVIDUAL STUDENT AND HIS OR HER DAILY PERFORMANCE. WE CAN ONLY COMMENT ON THE STUDENT'S SCORES IN RELATION TO THE NATIONAL AVERAGE PERFORMANCE. THE TOTAL SCORES IN READING, MATHEMATICS, AND LANGUAGE ARE WITHIN THE NATIONAL AVERAGE.

Ⓔ A SIGNIFICANT DIFFERENCE OCCURS WHEN THE PERCENTILE BANDS OF X'S ON THE CHART DO NOT OVERLAP. THAT IS, THE HIGHEST X ON ONE BAND DOES NOT FALL IN A LINE WITH THE LOWEST X ON ANOTHER BAND. FOR YOUR STUDENT, YOU CAN SEE A SIGNIFICANT DIFFERENCE IN THE PERCENTILE BANDS BETWEEN MATHEMATICS TOTAL AND READING TOTAL.

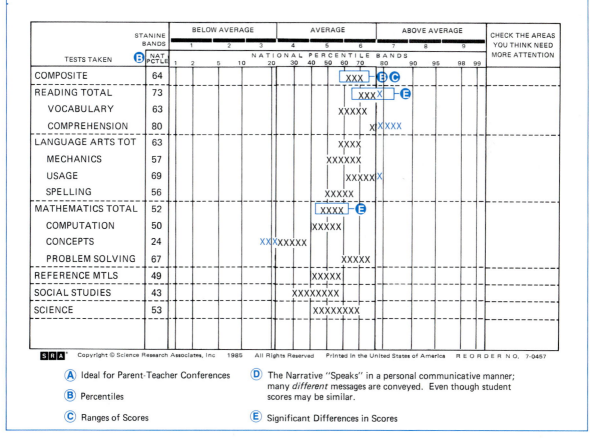

SRA® Copyright © Science Research Associates, Inc   1985   All Rights Reserved   Printed in the United States of America   REORDER NO. 7-0457

Ⓐ Ideal for Parent-Teacher Conferences

Ⓑ Percentiles

Ⓒ Ranges of Scores

Ⓓ The Narrative "Speaks" in a personal communicative manner; many *different* messages are conveyed. Even though student scores may be similar.

Ⓔ Significant Differences in Scores

FIGURE 14.5
Pupil Skills Analysis
Report Form. (Copyright
by The Psychological
Corporation. All rights
reserved. Reproduced by
permission.)

Stanford ACHIEVEMENT TEST WITH OTIS-LENNON SCHOOL ABILITY TEST

SKILLS ANALYSIS FOR CHARLES A BALLARD

TEACHER MS WELLENS
SCHOOL LAKESIDE ELEMENTARY GRADE 4 TEST DATE 10/12/82 COPY 1
SYSTEM NEWTOWN PUBLIC SCHOOLS STANFORD NORMS GR 4.1 LEVEL PRIM 3 FORM E
OLSAT NORMS GR 4 FALL LEVEL ELEM FORM S

TESTS NUMBER OF ITEMS	RAW SCORE	SCALE SCORE	NAT'L PR-S	GRADE EQUIV	ACHIEVMNT ABILITY COMPARISON
WORD STUDY SKILLS 54	35	142	50- 5	4.1	LOW
READING COMPREHENSION 60	49	143	50- 5	4.0	LOW
VOCABULARY 38	29	148	52- 5	4.3	LOW
LISTENING COMPREHENSION 40	31	139	44- 5	3.9	LOW
SPELLING 36	18	143	40- 5	3.8	LOW
LANGUAGE 46	37	148	60- 6	4.6	MIDDLE
CONCEPTS OF NUMBER 34	14	137	32- 4	3.5	LOW
MATH COMPUTATION 42	20	145	50- 5	3.9	MIDDLE
MATH APPLICATIONS 38	19	145	50- 5	4.0	LOW
SOCIAL SCIENCE 44	36	161	82- 7	5.5	MIDDLE
SCIENCE 44	19	130	34- 4	3.3	LOW
USING INFORMATION 40	27	160	77- 7	5.0	MIDDLE
TOTAL READING 114	84	143	50- 5	4.0	LOW
TOTAL LISTENING 78	60	144	48- 5	4.1	LOW
TOTAL LANGUAGE 82	55	146	52- 5	4.2	LOW
TOTAL MATHEMATICS 114	53	143	44- 5	3.8	LOW
BASIC BATTERY TOTAL 388	252	NA²	50- 5	4.0	NA²
COMPLETE BATTERY TOTAL 476	308	NA²	50- 5	4.0	NA²
OTIS-LENNON	AGE	PR-S	84-7	RS = 51	SAI = 116
SCHOOL ABILITY TEST	GRADE	PR-S	82-7		

NATIONAL PERCENTILE BANDS
1   5   10   20   30   40 50 60   70   80   90 95 99

AGE 9 YRS. 1 MO.

READING SKILLS GROUP—DEVELOPMENTAL

CONTENT CLUSTERS	RAW SCORE/NUMBER OF ITEMS	BELOW AVERAGE	AVERAGE	ABOVE AVERAGE
WORD STUDY SKILLS	35/54		√	
Structural Analysis	7/18	√		
Phonetic Analysis—Consonants	16/18			√
Phonetic Analysis—Vowels	12/18		√	
READING COMPREHENSION	49/60		√	
Textual Reading	15/20		√	
Functional Reading	17/20			√
Recreational Reading	17/20		√	
Literal Comprehension	28/30			√
Inferential Comprehension	21/30		√	
VOCABULARY	29/38		√	
LISTENING COMPREHENSION	31/40		√	
Retention	17/20		√	
Organization	14/20		√	
SPELLING	18/36		√	
Sight Words	6/ 8		√	
Phonetic Principles	4/16	√		
Structural Principles	8/12		√	
LANGUAGE	37/46		√	
Conventions	22/26		√	
Language Sensitivity	7/10		√	
Reference Skills	8/10			√
CONCEPTS OF NUMBER	14/34		√	
Whole Numbers and Place Value	8/18		√	
Fractions	1/ 5	√		
Operations and Properties	5/11		√	

WRITING TEST RESULTS:

CONTENT CLUSTERS	RAW SCORE/NUMBER OF ITEMS	BELOW AVERAGE	AVERAGE	ABOVE AVERAGE
MATHEMATICS COMPUTATION	20/42		√	
Addition with Whole Numbers	9/12		√	
Subtraction with Whole Numbers	8/ 9			√
Multiplication with Whole Numbers	2/12	√		
Division with Whole Numbers	1/ 9	√		
MATHEMATICS APPLICATIONS	19/38		√	
Problem Solving	9/18		√	
Geometry/Measurement	5/14	√		
Graphs and Charts	5/6			√
SOCIAL SCIENCE	36/44			√
Geography	6/ 6			√
History and Anthropology	6/ 9		√	
Sociology	5/ 6			√
Political Science	3/ 4			√
Economics	8/10			√
Inquiry Skills	8/ 9			√
SCIENCE	19/44		√	
Physical Science	4/11	√		
Biological Science	9/18		√	
Inquiry Skills	6/15		√	
USING INFORMATION	27/40			√

A. Names of subtests and number of items.
B. Types of scores and achievement/ability comparison.
(PR = Percentile Rank, S = Stanine, SAI = School
Ability Index)
C. Otis-Lennon School Ability Test scores by age
and grade.
D. Percentile bands (span ±1 standard error of
measurement).
E. Recommended reading group for instruction.
F. Number right/number possible and performance rating.

Judging the Adequacy of Norms

As noted earlier, test norms can be expressed in terms of several different types of derived scores. Regardless of the type of derived score used, the main purpose is to make possible an interpretation of pupils' test performance in terms of a clearly defined referenced group. This should not be just any reference group, however, but one that provides a meaningful basis for comparison.

The adequacy of test norms is a basic consideration during test selection and a factor to be reckoned with during the interpretation of test scores. The following criteria indicate the qualities most desired in norms:

1. Test norms should be relevant. Test norms are based on various types of groups. Some represent a national sample of all pupils at certain grade or age levels, whereas others are limited to samples from a given region or state. For special purposes, the norms also might be confined to a limited group such as high school pupils in independent schools, girls who have completed secretarial training in a commercial high school, or college freshmen in engineering. The variety of types of groups available for comparison makes it necessary to study the norm sample before using any table of norms. We should ask whether these norms are appropriate for the pupils being tested and for the decisions to be made with the results.

If we merely want to compare our pupils with a general reference group in order to diagnose strengths and weaknesses in different areas, national norms may be satisfactory. Here our main concern is with the extent to which our pupils are similar to those in the norm population on such characteristics as scholastic aptitude, educational experience, and cultural background. The more closely our pupils approximate those in the norm group, the greater will be our certainty that the national norms are a meaningful basis for comparison.

But when we are trying to decide such things as which pupils should be placed in an accelerated group, who should be encouraged to select the college preparatory curriculum, or whether a particular pupil should pursue a career in engineering, national norms are much less useful. For such decisions, we need norms for each of the specific groups involved. A pupil can have an above-average aptitude and achievement when compared with pupils in general and still fall short of the ability needed to succeed in highly select groups. When decisions involve predictions of future success in a particular area, comparing a pupil with potential competitors is more meaningful than comparisons with grade or age mates.

2. Test norms should be representative. Once we are satisfied that a set of test norms is based on a group with which comparisons are desired, it is appropriate to ask whether the norms are truly representative of that group. Ideally, the norms should be based on a random sample of the population they represent. This is extremely difficult and expensive, however, so we must usually settle for something less. As a minimum, we should demand that all significant subgroups of the population be adequately represented. For national norms, it is desirable to have a proper proportion of pupils from such subgroups as boys and girls, geographic regions, rural and urban areas, socioeconomic levels, racial groups, and schools of varying size. The most adequate representation in these areas is obtained when the norm sample closely approximates the population distribution reported by the United States Census Bureau.

3. Test norms should be up to date. One factor that is commonly neglected in judging the adequacy of norms is whether they are currently applicable. With the rapid changes that are taking place in education, we can expect test norms to become out of date much sooner than they did in the past.

It is generally unsafe to use the copyright date on the test manual as an indication of when the norms were obtained, as this date may be changed whenever the manual is altered (no matter how slightly). The description of the procedures used in establishing norms should be consulted for the year in which the norm groups were tested. When a test has been revised, also make certain that the norms are based on the new edition.

4. Test norms should be comparable. It is often necessary or desirable to compare directly scores from different tests, such as when we make profile comparisons of test results to diagnose a pupil's strengths and weaknesses or when we compare aptitude and achievement test scores to detect underachievers. Such comparisons can be justified only if the norms for the different tests are comparable. We can be assured of comparability when all tests have been normed on the same population. This is routinely done with the tests in an achievement battery, and test publishers also usually administer a scholastic aptitude test to the same norm group. Whenever the scores from different tests are to be compared directly, the test manuals should be checked to determine whether the norms are based on the same group and, if not, whether they have been made comparable by other means.

5. Test norms should be adequately described. It is difficult to determine whether these norms provide a meaningful basis of comparison unless we know something about the norm group and the norming procedures used. The type of information we might expect to find in a test manual includes (1) method of sampling; (2) number and distribution of cases in the norm sample; (3) characteristics of the norm group with regard to such factors as age, sex, race, scholastic aptitude, educational level, socioeconomic status, types of schools represented, and geographic location; (4) extent to which standard conditions of administration and motivation were maintained during the testing; and (5) date of the testing and whether in the fall or the spring. Other things being equal, we should always favor the test for which we have detailed descriptions of these and other relevant factors. Such information is needed if we are to judge the appropriateness of test norms for our particular purposes.

Using Local Norms

In some cases it may be desirable to compare pupils with local norms. If our pupils deviate markedly from those in the published norms on such characteristics as scholastic aptitude, educational experience, or cultural background, for example, comparison with a local group may be more meaningful. Local norms can also be useful for making within-class comparisons in special groups (e.g., retarded class in reading) and for determining how well particular children (e.g., handicapped children being mainstreamed) are succeeding in the regular classroom group. When we wish to make profile comparisons of scores obtained from tests standardized on different populations, local norms can also be used to obtain comparable scores by administering all tests to a common local group. Local norms can, of course, also be computed for classroom tests and are especially useful for departmental examinations used in several sections of a course.

Local norms are typically prepared using either percentile ranks or stanines. Most test publishers will provide local norms if requested, but they also can be prepared locally. The procedure for computing percentile ranks for local norms is illustrated in Figure 14.6. The procedure for preparing local stanine norms will follow a brief description of the stanine system.

Local Stanine Norms

Stanine scores are widely used for local norms because of the ease with which they can be computed and interpreted. The following points summarize their major strengths:

1. The stanine system uses a nine-point scale, in which 9 is high, 1 is low, and 5 is average. Thus, the system is easily explained to pupils and parents, and they can readily visualize where test performance falls (e.g., 7) on a scale of 1 to 9.

2. Stanines are normalized standard scores that make it possible to compare a pupil's performance on different tests (if based on a common group). Typically a difference of 2 stanines represents a significant difference in test performance between tests (assuming test reliability is satisfactory). Thus, a pupil with a stanine of 7 in arithmetic and 5 in spelling is probably demonstrating superior performance in arithmetic.

3. The stanine system makes it possible to readily combine diverse types of data (e.g., test scores, ratings, ranked data) because stanines are computed like percentile ranks but are expressed in standard score form. Thus, the conversion to stanines is simple, and the standard score feature makes it possible to add together stanine scores from various measures to obtain a composite score. A simple summing of stanines will give equal weight to each measure in the composite.[6]

4. Because the stanine system uses a single-digit score, it is easily recorded and takes up less space than other scores. (It was originally developed to fit into a single column on an IBM card.)

The main limitation of stanine scores is that growth cannot be shown from one

[6]In some cases, it may be desirable to form composite scores from weighted raw scores and then convert to stanines. Less error is introduced with this procedure.

FIGURE 14.6
Example of how local
norms are computed
using percentile rank.
(Adapted from
Educational Testing
Service Score Distribution
Sheet.)

COMPUTING PERCENTILE RANK

Score Group	Tally	Frequency	Cumulative Frequency	Percentile Rank
170 - 171	/	1	300	99
168 - 169		0	299	99
166 - 167	/	1	299	99
164 - 165	//	2	298	99
162 - 163	///	3	296	98
160 - 161	++++	5	293	97
158 - 159	++++ ///	8	288	95
156 - 157	++++ ++++ ///	13	280	91
154 - 155	++++ ++++ ++++ /	16	267	86
152 - 153	++++ ++++ ++++ ////	19	251	81
150 - 151	++++ ++++ ++++ ++++ /	21	232	74
148 - 149	++++ ++++ ++++ ++++ //	22	211	67
146 - 147	++++ ++++ ++++ ++++ ///	23	189	59
144 - 145	++++ ++++ ++++ ++++ ///	23	166	52
142 - 143	++++ ++++ ++++ ++++ //	22	143	44
140 - 141	++++ ++++ ++++ ++++ /	21	121	37
138 - 139	++++ ++++ ++++ ////	19	100	30
136 - 137	++++ ++++ ++++ ///	18	81	24
134 - 135	++++ ++++ ++++ /	16	63	18
132 - 133	++++ ++++ ////	14	47	13
130 - 131	++++ ++++ //	12	33	9
128 - 129	++++ ++++	10	21	5
126 - 127	++++ //	7	11	3
124 - 125	///	3	4	1
122 - 123	/	1	1	1

Total Number of Students 300

STEPS TO FOLLOW

1. Group scores by intervals (Column 1).
2. Make tally of the number of students earning scores falling in each score group (Column 2).
3. Add tallies and place in the frequency column (Column 3).
4. Add the frequencies in Column 3 from the bottom up (e.g., 1 + 3 = 4, 4 + 7 = 11, and so on) to determine the cumulative frequency (Column 4).
5. Compute the percentile rank (Column 5) for each score group as follows (using the score interval of 128-129 to illustrate):
   (a) Take half the frequency of the score group (½ x 10 = 5).
   (b) Add the result of (a) to the cumulative frequency for the score group just below it (5 + 11 = 16).
   (c) Divide the result of (b) by the total number of students in the norm group, and multiply by 100 (16 ÷ 300 = .05, .05 x 100 = 5).

year to the next. If a pupil's progress matches that of the norm group, the same position in the group will be retained and thus the same stanine assigned. This shortcoming is, of course, also characteristic of percentile ranks and of other standard scores used to indicate relative position in a particular group. To determine growth, we need to examine the increase in the raw scores or in developmental scale scores (e.g., grade equivalents).

Stanines are sometimes criticized on the grounds that they are rather crude units, because they divide a distribution of scores into only nine parts. On the plus side, however, these crude units prevent the overinterpretation of test scores. Although greater refinement might be desirable for some special purposes (e.g., identifying gifted pupils), stanines provide satisfactory discriminations in test performance for most educational uses of test results. With a more refined scoring system, there is always the danger that minor chance differences in scores will be interpreted as significant differences.

Assigning Stanines to Raw Scores. Transforming raw scores into stanines is relatively simple if the scores are ranked from high to low and there are no ties in rank. The top 4 percent of the raw scores are assigned a stanine score of 9; the next 7 percent of the raw scores are assigned a stanine score of 8; the next 12 percent, a stanine score of 7; and so on. The percentage of cases falling at each stanine level and the number of pupils to be assigned each stanine score for any size group from 20 to 100 are shown in Table 14.4. These figures, showing the number of pupils who should receive each stanine score, are determined by multiplying the number of cases in the group by the percentage of cases at each stanine level and rounding off the results.

Distributions of test scores usually contain a number of pupils with the same raw score. Consequently, we have ties in rank that prevent us from obtaining a perfect match with the theoretical distributions shown in Table 14.4. Because *all pupils with the same raw score must be assigned the same stanine score*, all we can reasonably expect to do is approximate the theoretical distribution in Table 14.4 as closely as possible. The step-by-step procedure for assigning stanines to test scores is shown in Table 14.5.

Cautions in Interpreting Test Scores

Interpreting test scores with the aid of norms requires an understanding of the type of derived score used and a willingness to study the characteristics of the norm group. In addition, however, we need to keep in mind the following general cautions that apply to the interpretation of any test score:

1. A test score should be interpreted in terms of the specific test from which it was derived. No two scholastic aptitude tests or achievement tests measure exactly the same thing. Achievement tests are especially prone to wide variation, and the differences are seldom reflected in the test title. For example, one arithmetic test may be limited to simple computational skills, whereas another may contain a number of reasoning problems. Similarly, one science test may be confined largely to items measuring knowledge of terminology, whereas another with the same title stresses the application of scientific principles. With such variation it is misleading to interpret a pupil's test score as representing general achievement in any particular area. We need to look beyond test titles and to evaluate the pupil's performance in terms of what the test *actually* does measure.

TABLE 14.4
Stanine Table Showing the Number of Pupils to Be Assigned Each Stanine for Groups Containing 20 to 100 Cases*

No. of Cases	Stanine Scores									No. of Cases	Stanine Scores								
	1	2	3	4	5	6	7	8	9		1	2	3	4	5	6	7	8	9
	Percentage of Cases										Percentage of Cases								
	4	7	12	17	20	17	12	7	4		4	7	12	17	20	17	12	7	4
20	1	1	2	4	4	4	2	1	1	61	3	4	7	10	13	10	7	4	3
21	1	1	2	4	5	4	2	1	1	62	3	4	7	11	12	11	7	4	3
22	1	2	2	4	4	4	2	2	1	63	3	4	7	11	13	11	7	4	3
23	1	2	2	4	5	4	2	2	1	64	3	4	8	11	12	11	8	4	3
24	1	2	3	4	4	4	3	2	1	65	3	4	8	11	13	11	8	4	3
25	1	2	3	4	5	4	3	2	1	66	3	4	8	11	14	11	8	4	3
26	1	2	3	4	6	4	3	2	1	67	3	5	8	11	13	11	8	5	3
27	1	2	3	5	5	5	3	2	1	68	3	5	8	11	14	11	8	5	3
28	1	2	3	5	6	5	3	2	1	69	3	5	8	12	13	12	8	5	3
29	1	2	4	5	5	5	4	2	1	70	3	5	8	12	14	12	8	5	3
30	1	2	4	5	6	5	4	2	1	71	3	5	8	12	15	12	8	5	3
31	1	2	4	5	7	5	4	2	1	72	3	5	9	12	14	12	9	5	3
32	1	2	4	6	6	6	4	2	1	73	3	5	9	12	15	12	9	5	3
33	1	2	4	6	7	6	4	2	1	74	3	5	9	13	14	13	9	5	3
34	1	3	4	6	6	6	4	3	1	75	3	5	9	13	15	13	9	5	3
35	1	3	4	6	7	6	4	3	1	76	3	5	9	13	16	13	9	5	3
36	1	3	4	6	8	6	4	3	1	77	3	6	9	13	15	13	9	6	3
37	2	3	4	6	7	6	4	3	2	78	3	6	9	13	16	13	9	6	3
38	1	3	5	6	8	6	5	3	1	79	3	6	10	13	15	13	10	6	3
39	1	3	5	7	7	7	5	3	1	80	3	6	9	14	16	14	9	6	3
40	1	3	5	7	8	7	5	3	1	81	3	6	9	14	17	14	9	6	3
41	1	3	5	7	9	7	5	3	1	82	3	6	10	14	16	14	10	6	3
42	2	3	5	7	8	7	5	3	2	83	3	6	10	14	17	14	10	6	3
43	2	3	5	7	9	7	5	3	2	84	4	6	10	14	16	14	10	6	4
44	2	3	5	8	8	8	5	3	2	85	3	6	10	15	17	15	10	6	3
45	2	3	5	8	9	8	5	3	2	86	3	6	10	15	18	15	10	6	3
46	2	3	5	8	10	8	5	3	2	87	4	6	10	15	17	15	10	6	4
47	2	3	6	8	9	8	6	3	2	88	3	6	11	15	18	15	11	6	3
48	2	3	6	8	10	8	6	3	2	89	4	6	11	15	17	15	11	6	4
49	2	4	6	8	9	8	6	4	2	90	4	6	11	15	18	15	11	6	4
50	2	3	6	9	10	9	6	3	2	91	4	6	11	15	19	15	11	6	4
51	2	3	6	9	11	9	6	3	2	92	4	6	11	16	18	16	11	6	4
52	2	4	6	9	10	9	6	4	2	93	4	6	11	16	19	16	11	6	4
53	2	4	6	9	11	9	6	4	2	94	4	7	11	16	18	16	11	7	4
54	2	4	7	9	10	9	7	4	2	95	4	7	11	16	19	16	11	7	4
55	2	4	7	9	11	9	7	4	2	96	4	7	11	16	20	16	11	7	4
56	2	4	7	9	12	9	7	4	2	97	4	7	12	16	19	16	12	7	4
57	2	4	7	10	11	10	7	4	2	98	4	7	12	16	20	16	12	7	4
58	2	4	7	10	12	10	7	4	2	99	4	7	12	17	19	17	12	7	4
59	3	4	7	10	11	10	7	4	3	100	4	7	12	17	20	17	12	7	4
60	3	4	7	10	12	10	7	4	3										

*Adapted from W. N. Durost, *The Characteristics, Use, and Computation of Stanines.* Copyright 1961 by Harcourt Brace Jovanovich, Inc. Used by permission.

TABLE 14.5 Procedure for Transforming Raw Scores to Stanines*

Stanine	(A) Score Interval	(B) Tallies	(C) Frequencies	Grouping Actual	Grouping Theoretical
9	58	I	1		
	57	–	–	4	4
	56	I	1		
	55	II	2		
8	54		–		
	53		–		
	52		–		
	51	I	1	7	6
	50	I	1		
	49	II	2		
	48		–		
	47	III	3		
7	46	I	1		
	45	III	3		
	44	II	2	12	11
	43		–		
	42	JHT I	6		
6	41	II	2		
	40	II	2		
	39	II	2	12	15
	38	I	1		
	37	JHT	5		
5	36	JHT	5		
	35	II	2		
	(E) 34	JHT II	7	20	18
	33	III	3		
	32	III	3		
4	31	JHT	5		
	30	I	1		
	29	III	3	14	15
	28	III	3		
	27	II	2		
3	26	IIII	4		
	25	JHT I	6	13	11
	24	III	3		
2	23	I	1		
	22	I	1	4	6
	21	II	2		
1	20	I	1		
	19		–	4	4
	18	I	1		
	17	II	2		
			90 (D)		

Illustration 1. Tally sheet for distribution of scores.

Directions for Illustration 1

1. Arrange test papers or answer sheets in rank order from high to low. On a separate piece of paper list every score in a column from the highest obtained score to the lowest, column (A). Opposite each score write the number of individuals who obtained that score. This may be done by counting the papers or answer sheets having the same score, or it may be done by tallying the scores in the manner shown in column (B).

2. Add the frequencies (C) and write the total at the bottom of the column (D). This is shown to be 90.

3. Beginning at the bottom, count up (cumulate) to one half the total number of scores, in this case 45 (one half of 90). This falls opposite the score of 34 (E), which is the median to the nearest whole number.

4. In the column at the extreme left of the Stanine Table (Table 14.4), look up the total number of cases (90). In this row are the theoretical frequencies of cases at each stanine level for 90 cases. In the middle of this row you will find the number of cases (18) to which a stanine of 5 should be assigned. Starting with median (in Illustration 1), lay off as nearly this number (18) of scores as you can. Here, it is 20.

5. Working upward and downward from scores falling in stanine 5, assign scores to stanine levels so as to give the closest approximation possible to the theoretical values. It is helpful to bracket these scores in the manner shown in column (A).

After having made a tentative assignment, make any adjustments necessary to bring the actual frequencies at each level into the closest possible agreement with the theoretical values. Remember, however, that all equal scores must be assigned the same stanines.

* Adapted from W.N. Durost, *The Characteristics, Use, and Computation of Stanines.* Copyright 1961 by Harcourt Brace Jovanovich, Inc. Used by permission.

2. A test score should be interpreted in light of all of the pupil's relevant characteristics. Test performance is influenced by the pupil's aptitudes, educational experiences, cultural background, emotional adjustment, health, and the like. Consequently, when a pupil performs poorly on a test, first consider the possibility of a cultural disadvantage, a language handicap, improper motivation, or similar factors that might have interfered with the pupil's response to the test.

3. A test score should be interpreted according to the type of decision to be made. The meaningfulness of a test score is determined to a considerable extent by the use to be made of it. For example, an IQ score of 100 would have different meanings if we were selecting pupils for a mentally retarded class, attempting to predict achievement in high school, or trying to decide whether a pupil should be encouraged to go to college. We will find test scores much more useful when we stop considering them as high or low *in general* and begin evaluating their significance in relation to the decision to be made.

4. A test score should be interpreted as a band of scores rather than as a specific value. Every test score is subject to error that must be allowed for during test interpretation. One of the best means of doing this is to consider a pupil's test performance as a band of scores one standard error of measurement above and below the obtained score. For example, if a pupil earns a score of 56 and the standard error is 3, the test performance should be interpreted as a band ranging from score 53 to score 59. Such bands were illustrated in the profiles presented earlier. Even when they are not plotted, however, we should make allowances for these error bands surrounding each score. This will prevent us from making interpretations that are more precise than the test results warrant. Treating small chance differences between test scores as though they were significant can only lead to erroneous decisions.

5. A test score should be verified by supplementary evidence. When interpreting test scores, it is impossible to determine fully the extent to which the basic assumptions of testing have been met (i.e., maximum motivation, equal educational opportunity, and so on) or to which the conditions of testing have been precisely controlled (i.e., administration, scoring, and so on). Consequently, in addition to the predictable error of measurement, which can be taken into account with standard error bands, a test score may contain an indeterminate amount of error caused by unmet assumptions or uncontrolled conditions. Our only protection against such errors is not to rely completely on a single test score. As Cronbach[7] pointed out:

> The most helpful single principle in all testing is that test scores are data on which to base further study. They must be coordinated with background facts, and they must be verified by constant comparison with other available data.

The misinterpretation and misuse of test scores would be substantially reduced if

---

[7]L. J. Cronbach, *Essentials of Psychological Testing*, 3d ed. (New York: Harper & Row, 1970), p. 381.

this simple principle were more widely recognized. But this caution should not be restricted to test scores; it is merely a specific application of the more general rule that no important educational decision should ever be based on one limited sample of performance.

Summary

Test interpretation is complicated because the raw scores obtained for a test lack a true zero point (point where there is *no achievement at all*) and equal units (such as feet, pounds, and minutes). In an attempt to compensate for these missing properties and to make test scores more readily interpretable, various methods of expressing test scores have been devised. In general, we can give meaning to a raw score either by converting it into a description of the specific tasks that the pupil can perform (*criterion-referenced* interpretation) or by converting it into some type of derived score that indicates the pupil's relative position in a clearly defined reference group (*norm-referenced* interpretation). In some cases both types of interpretation can be made.

Criterion-referenced test interpretation permits us to describe an individual's test performance without referring to the performance of others. This is typically done in terms of some universally understood measure of proficiency (e.g., speed, precision) or the percentage of items correct in some clearly defined domain of learning tasks. The *percentage-correct score* is widely used in criterion-referenced test interpretation, but it is primarily useful in mastery testing where a clearly defined and delimited domain of learning tasks can be most readily obtained.

Although criterion-referenced interpretation is frequently possible with standardized tests, such interpretations must be made with caution because these tests were typically designed to discriminate among individuals rather than to describe the specific tasks they can perform. Test publishers are now attempting to produce tests that are more amenable to criterion-referenced interpretation.

Expectancy tables also provide a type of criterion-referenced interpretation. Instead of describing an individual's performance on the test tasks, it indicates expected performance in some situation beyond the test (e.g., success in college). Expectancy tables provide a simple and direct means of interpreting test results without the aid of test norms.

Standardized tests typically have been designed for norm-referenced interpretation, which involves converting the raw scores to derived scores by means of tables of norms. These derived scores indicate a pupil's relative position in a particular reference group. They have the advantage over raw scores of providing more uniform meaning from one test to another and from one situation to another.

Test norms merely represent the typical performance of pupils in the reference groups on which the test was standardized and consequently should not be viewed as desired goals or standards. The most common types of norms are grade norms, percentile norms, and standard score norms. Each type has its own characteristics, advantages, and limitations, which must be taken into account during test interpretation.

Grade norms describe test performance in terms of the particular grade group in which a pupil's raw score is just average. These norms are widely used at the elementary school level, largely because of the apparent ease with which they can be interpreted. Depicting test performance in terms of grade equivalents can often lead to unsound decisions, however, because of the inequality of the units and the invalid assumptions on which they are based. Grade equivalent scores must be interpreted with extreme caution.

Percentile norms and standard score norms describe test performance in terms of the pupil's relative standing in some meaningful group (e.g., own grade or age group). A percentile rank indicates the percentage of pupils falling below a particular raw score. Percentile units are unequal, but the scores are readily understood by persons without special training. A standard score indicates the number of standard deviation units a raw score falls above or below the group mean. It has the advantage of providing equal units that can be treated arithmetically, but persons untrained in statistics find it difficult to interpret such scores. Some of the more common types of standard scores are z-scores, T-scores, NCE scores, standard age scores, and stanines.

With a normal distribution of scores, we can readily convert back and forth between standard scores and percentiles, making it possible to utilize the special advantages of each. Standard scores can be used to draw on the benefits of equal units, and we can convert to percentile equivalents when interpreting test performance to pupils, parents, and those who lack statistical training.

A pupil's performance on several tests that have comparable norms may be presented in the form of a profile, making it possible to identify readily areas of strength and weakness. Profile interpretation is more apt to be accurate when standard error bands are plotted on the profile. Some test profiles also include narrative reports and/or detailed analysis of the results by content or skill clusters. This criterion-referenced analysis is especially useful for the instructional use of test results.

The adequacy of test norms can be judged by determining the extent to which they are (1) relevant, (2) representative, (3) up to date, (4) comparable, and (5) adequately described. In some instances, it is more appropriate to use local norms than published norms. When local norms are desired, percentile and stanine norms can be readily computed.

In addition to a knowledge of derived scores and norms, the proper interpretation of test scores requires an awareness of (1) what the test measures, (2) the pupil's characteristics and background, (3) the type of decision to be made, (4) the amount of error in the score, and (5) the extent to which the score agrees with other available data. No important educational decision should ever be based on test scores alone.

Learning Exercises

1. Describe the cautions needed in making criterion-referenced interpretations of standardized achievement tests.
2. Describe the meaning of *raw* scores and *derived* scores.

3. A fifth-grade pupil received an average grade equivalent score of 6.8 on a standardized achievement battery administered in the fall of the year. What arguments might be presented for and against moving the pupil ahead to the sixth grade?

4. What advantages do stanines have over T-scores? What disadvantages?

5. Explain each of the following statements:

    a. Standard scores provide approximately *equal* units.

    b. Percentile scores provide *systematically unequal* units.

    c. Grade equivalent scores provide *unequal* units that vary unpredictably.

6. Assuming that all of the following test scores were obtained from the same normally distributed group, which score would indicate the highest performance? Which the lowest?

    a. z-score $= .65$.

    b. T-score $= 65$.

    c. NCE score $= 65$.

    d. Percentile score $= 65$.

7. Consult the section on norms in the 1985 *Standards for Educational and Psychological Testing*, and review the types of information that test manuals should contain. Compare a recent test manual with the *Standards*. (See the reference in "Suggestions for Further Reading.")

8. What is the difference between a norm and a standard? Why shouldn't test *norms* be used as *standards* of good performance?

9. What is the value of using national norms? Under what conditions is it desirable to use local norms?

10. What are the relative advantages and disadvantages of using local norms for disadvantaged pupils? For what purposes are more general norms (e.g., national) useful with these pupils?

Suggestions for Further Reading

AMERICAN PSYCHOLOGICAL ASSOCIATION. *Standards for Educational and Psychological Testing*. Washington, D.C.: APA, 1985. See the test standards in Part I for what to look for in test manuals and Parts II and III for material on the effective interpretation and use of tests in various areas.

ANASTASI, A. *Psychological Testing*, 6th ed. New York: Macmillan, 1988. Chapter 4, "Norms and the Interpretation of Test Scores," describes the various types of norms, computer interpretation of test scores, and criterion-referenced testing.

CRONBACH, L. J. *Essentials of Psychological Testing*, 4th ed. New York: Harper & Row, 1984. Chapter 4, "Scoring," includes the interpretation of test scores, descriptions of the various types of derived scores, and the characteristics of useful norms.

GRONLUND, N. E. *How to Construct Achievement Tests*, 4th ed. Englewood Cliffs, N.J.: Prentice-Hall, 1988. Chapter 8, "Interpreting Test Results," describes simplified methods for use with classroom tests.

LYMAN, H. B. *Test Scores and What They Mean*, 4th ed. Englewood Cliffs, N.J.: Prentice-Hall, 1986. A well-written and interesting description of the various types of test scores and how to interpret them, with emphasis on norm-referenced interpretation.

PETERSEN, N. S.; KOLEN, M. J.; AND HOOVER, H. D. "Scaling, Norming, and Equating." In R. L. Linn, ed., *Educational Measurement*, 3d ed. New York: Macmillan, 1989, Chapter 6. A comprehensive and technically advanced treatment of scales, norms, and equating scores.

Part 4

Evaluating Procedures, Products, and Typical Behavior

Chapter 15

Evaluating Learning and Development: Observational Techniques

Direct observation is the best means we have for evaluating some aspects of learning and development, . . . and it offers supplementary information concerning others. The problem is . . . how to get an objective record of the most meaningful behavior? This can be greatly facilitated by using such techniques as (1) anecdotal records, (2) rating scales, and (3) checklists.

As we have stated in previous chapters, many learning outcomes can be measured by paper-and-pencil tests. This is especially true of outcomes in the cognitive domain, such as those pertaining to knowledge, understanding, and thinking skills. The significance of these areas in all subject-matter fields has put paper-and-pencil testing in a prominent position in educational evaluation. This is as it should be, but we must be careful not to become dependent on it, as there are a number of important outcomes that require the use of other procedures.

Learning outcomes in skill areas and behavioral changes in personal-social development are especially difficult to evaluate with the usual paper-and-pencil test. A list of such outcomes, with representative types of pupil behavior, is presented in Table 15.1. This list is by no means complete, but it is comprehensive enough to show the great need to supplement paper-and-pencil testing with other methods of evaluation.

	Outcome	Representative Behaviors
TABLE 15.1 Outcomes Requiring Evaluation Procedures Beyond the Typical Paper-and-Pencil Test	Skills	Speaking, writing, listening, oral reading, performing laboratory experiments, drawing, playing a musical instrument, dancing, gymnastics, work skills, study skills, and social skills.
	Work habits	Effectiveness in planning, use of time, use of equipment, use of resources, demonstration of such traits as initiative, creativity, persistence, dependability.
	Social attitudes	Concern for the welfare of others, respect for laws, respect for the property of others, sensitivity to social issues, concern for social institutions, desire to work toward social improvement.
	Scientific attitudes	Open-mindedness, willingness to suspend judgment, sensitivity to cause–effect relations, an inquiring mind.
	Interests	Expressed feelings toward various educational, mechanical, aesthetic, scientific, social, recreational, vocational activities.
	Appreciations	Feeling of satisfaction and enjoyment expressed toward nature, music, art, literature, physical skill, outstanding social contributions.
	Adjustments	Relationship to peers, reaction to praise and criticism, reaction to authority, emotional stability, social adaptability.

Learning outcomes and aspects of development like those in Table 15.1 can generally be evaluated by (1) observing pupils as they perform and describing or judging that behavior (evaluating a speech), (2) observing and judging the quality of the product resulting from their performance (evaluating handwriting), (3) asking their peers about them (evaluating social relationships), and (4) questioning them directly (evaluating expressed interests). Although these *observational techniques*, *peer appraisals*, and *self-report methods* are more subjective than we would like, and their use frequently requires more time and effort than the typical testing procedures, they are the best means available for evaluating a variety of important behaviors. Our choice is simple: either we use these techniques to evaluate each learning outcome and aspect of development as directly and validly as possible, or we neglect those that cannot be measured by paper-and-pencil tests. From an educational standpoint, the choice seems obvious.

In this chapter, we shall describe those observational techniques found especially useful by teachers. These include

- Anecdotal records.
- Rating scales.
- Checklists.

The following chapter will be devoted to peer appraisals and self-report techniques.

Anecdotal Records

Teacher's daily observations give them a wealth of information concerning the learning and development of their pupils. For example, a third-grade teacher notices during oral reading that Mary mispronounces several simple words, that George sits staring out the window, and that Jane keeps interrupting the reading with irrelevant questions. Similarly, a high school chemistry teacher notices during a laboratory period that Bill is slow and inefficient in setting up his equipment, that John finishes his experiments early and helps others, and that Betty handles the chemicals in a careless and dangerous manner despite repeated warnings. Such daily incidents and events have special evaluative significance. They enable us to determine how a pupil typically performs or behaves in a variety of situations. In some instances, this information merely supplements and verifies data obtained by more objective methods. But in other cases, it is the only means we have for evaluating desired outcomes.

Impressions gained through observation are apt to provide an incomplete and biased picture, however, unless we keep an accurate record of our observations. A simple and convenient method of doing this is through *anecdotal records*.

Anecdotal records are factual descriptions of the meaningful incidents and events that the teacher has observed in the pupils' lives. Each incident should be written down shortly after it happens. The descriptions may be recorded on separate cards like the one shown in Figure 15.1, or as running accounts, one for each pupil, on separate pages in a notebook. A good anecdotal record keeps the objective description of an incident separate from any interpretation of the behavior's meaning. For some purposes, it is also useful to keep an additional space for recommendations concerning ways to improve the pupil's learning or adjustment. Such recommendations are seldom made, however, until several anecdotes have been recorded.

Class **4th Grade** Pupil **Bill Johnson**

Date **4/25/63** Place **Classroom** Observer **M.G.**

INCIDENT

As class was about to start, Bill asked if he could read a poem to the class —one he had written himself—about "spring." He read the poem in a low voice, constantly looked down at the paper, moved his right foot back and forth, and pulled on his shirt collar. When he finished, Jack (in the back row) said "I couldn't hear it. Will you read it again—louder?" Bill said "no" and sat down.

INTERPRETATION

Bill enjoys writing stories and poems and they reflect considerable creative ability. However, he seems very shy and nervous in performing before a group. His refusal to read the poem again seemed to be due to his nervousness.

FIGURE 15.1
Anecdotal record form.

Uses of Anecdotal Records

The use of anecdotal records has frequently been limited to the area of social adjustment. Although they are especially appropriate for this type of reporting, this is a needless limitation. Anecdotal records can be used for obtaining data pertinent to a variety of learning outcomes and to many aspects of personal and social development. The potential usefulness of the anecdotal method is revealed in the various areas of learning outcomes presented earlier in this chapter (see Table 15.1); you will see that many of the behaviors listed there can be appraised by means of direct observation.

The problem in using anecdotal records is not so much what *can* be evaluated as what *should* be evaluated with this method. It is obvious that we cannot observe and report on all aspects of pupil behavior, no matter how useful such records might be. Thus, we must be *selective* in our observations.

What Behaviors to Observe and Record

In general, our objectives and desired outcomes will guide us in determining what behaviors are most worth noting. In addition, we must also be alert to those unusual and exceptional incidents that contribute to a better understanding of each pupil's unique pattern of behavior. Within this general framework, there are several steps we can take to control our observations so that a realistic system of recording can be developed. They are

1. Confining our observations to those areas of behavior that cannot be evaluated by other means.
2. Limiting our observations of all pupils at any given time to just a few types of behavior.
3. Restricting the use of extensive observations of behavior to those few pupils who are most in need of special help.

There is no advantage in using anecdotal records to derive evidence of learning in areas in which more objective and practical methods are available. Knowledge, understanding, and various aspects of thinking skill can usually be evaluated by paper-and-pencil tests. Many learning outcomes of other types, such as the ability to give a speech, operate a microscope, or write a theme, are most effectively evaluated by rating methods or product evaluation. Records of actual behavior are best used to evaluate how a pupil typically behaves in a natural setting. How does the pupil approach a problem? How persistent in carrying out a task? How willing to listen to the ideas of others? What contributions are made to class activities? A pupil's verbal comments and actions in various natural situations reveal certain clues to attitudes, interests, appreciations, habits, and adjustment patterns that cannot be discovered by any other means. These are the types of behavior on which we should focus when keeping anecdotal records.

The best we can hope for with anecdotal records is a fairly representative sample of pupil behavior in the different areas for which we want information. This usually can be obtained more easily if we concentrate our observations on a few areas at a time. For example, an elementary teacher might pay particular attention to reading interests during the free reading period, to signs of appreciation during music and art, and to patterns of social relations during recess. Similarly, a high school science teacher might concentrate on incidents reflecting scientific attitude during certain class discussions and laboratory periods and on work habits and laboratory skills during others. In some cases the activity itself will indicate the types of observation most fruitful to focus on, whereas in others the emphasis at any given time may need to be determined arbitrarily. Despite the concentration of attention on certain areas at a particular time, however, we should always be alert to other incidents and events that have special significance for understanding a pupil's learning and development.

In addition to recording some information on all pupils, there are times when we need more comprehensive information regarding a relative few. The severely retarded reader, the socially rejected child, and the handicapped child are typical of those needing special attention. More extensive observations of such pupils are helpful in understanding their difficulties and in indicating remedial action. The most complete and useful information is obtained when we concentrate our observations on one or two pupils at a time. During such observations it also may be necessary to restrict further our record keeping on other pupils.

Some teachers become discouraged when they first use anecdotal records because they attempt to do too much. Limiting observations and reports to specific types of behavior, to specific pupils, or both is frequently necessary to make the procedure feasible. It is much better to have a clearly delimited and workable observational plan than to end up with an incomplete and atypical collection to unrelated incidents.

Advantages and Limitations of Anecdotal Records

Probably the most important advantage of anecdotal records is that they depict actual behavior in natural situations. The old adage that "actions speak louder than words" has a direct application here. A pupil may show good knowledge of health practices but violate them in everyday situations, may profess great interest in science but approach laboratory work in a haphazard and uninterested fashion, or may express great concern for the welfare of others but behave in a selfish manner. Records of actual behavior provide a check on other evaluation methods and also enable us to determine the extent of change in the pupil's typical patterns of behavior.

In addition to compiling descriptions of the most characteristic behavior of a pupil, anecdotal records enable gathering evidence on events that are exceptional but significant. Typical examples are the quiet pupil who speaks in class for the first time, the hostile pupil who makes a friendly gesture, the extreme conformist who shows a sign of originality, and the apathetic pupil who shows a spark of interest. These individually significant behaviors are apt to be excluded by other evaluation techniques. They are also likely to be overlooked by teachers unless a concerted effort is made to observe such incidents. Keeping anecdotal records makes us more diligent in observation and increases our awareness of such behaviors.

An advantage for the elementary teacher is that anecdotal records can be used with very young pupils and with those who are retarded in basic communication skills. They are especially valuable here because paper-and-pencil tests, self-report techniques, and peer appraisals are likely to be impractical or of limited use. Observational records of younger pupils are of value for still another reason. Because young children tend to be more spontaneous and uninhibited in their actions, their behavior is easier to observe and interpret.

One limitation of anecdotal records is the amount of time required to maintain an adequate system of records. Though this can be offset somewhat by limiting observations and reports, as suggested earlier, it is still a time-consuming task. If teachers keep anecdotal records for their own use only, they can work out a realistic plan by starting with a few anecdotes each day and gradually increasing it to a reasonable number. If the entire staff uses anecdotal records, it is good to have all teachers record as many anecdotes as is practical for a period of a few weeks and then hold a staff meeting to discuss the recorded anecdotes and to decide what constitutes a reasonable number. It is generally unwise to set a specific number that must be recorded each week, but an approximate minimum can serve as a general guide. When anecdotal records are used on a schoolwide basis, the most time-consuming aspect is summarizing the anecdotes and recording the summaries in the pupil's cumulative records. Of course, much of this work can be handled by the clerical staff.

Another serious limitation of anecdotal records is the difficulty of being *objective* when observing and reporting pupil behavior. Ideally, we would like a series of verbal *snapshots* that accurately represent the pupil's actual behavior. This goal is seldom attained, however, for teachers' own biases, hopes, and preconceived notions inevitably enter into their observations and reports. For example, they will tend to notice more desirable qualities in those pupils they like best and more undesirable qualities in those they like least. If they are evaluating the effectiveness of a new teaching technique in which they have great faith, they may notice positive results and ignore the negative. If they believe that boys are less well coordinated than girls, they will tend to perceive their performance skills as being of lower quality. Training in observation and reporting can reduce such distortions to a minimum, but they cannot be eradicated entirely. When anecdotal records are accumulated from a number of teachers, however, the biases of any particular one has less effect on the total pattern.

A related difficulty is obtaining an adequate sample of behavior. When a pupil is participating in class discussion, he may be so tense and anxious that he appears cold and unfriendly toward others and his ideas seem disorganized. But when observed in less formal settings, such as in the laboratory or on the playground, his behavior might be quite different. Similarly, a pupil may appear highly motivated and interested in mathematics class but bored and uninterested during English literature, or she may be attentive and inquisitive in science one day and apathetic the next. Everyone's behavior fluctuates somewhat from situation to situation and from one time to another. Therefore, to gain a reliable picture of a typical pattern of behavior we need to observe pupils over a period of time and a variety of situations. This also implies that general interpretations and recommendations concerning a pupil's adjustment should be delayed until a fairly adequate sample of behavior is obtained.

Effective Use of Anecdotal Records

In the previous sections, we stated or implied a number of ways to improve procedures for observing and reporting pupil behavior. These and other points are listed here as suggestions for the effective use of anecdotal records.

1. Determine in advance what to observe, but be alert for unusual behavior. We are more apt to select and record meaningful incidents if we review objectives and outcomes and decide which behaviors require evaluation by direct observation—that is, those that cannot be effectively evaluated by other means. We can further focus our observations by looking for just a few types of behavior at any given time. Although such directed observations are valuable for obtaining evidence of pupil learning, there is always the danger that unique incidents that have special value for understanding a pupil's development will be overlooked. Consequently, we must be flexible enough to notice and report any unusual behavior in the event that it may be significant.

2. Observe and record enough of the situation to make the behavior meaningful. It is difficult to interpret behavior apart from the situation in which it occurred. An aggressive action, such as pushing another child, for example, might reflect good-natured fun, an attempt to get attention, a response to direct provocation, or a sign of extreme hostility. Clues to the meaning of behavior frequently can be obtained by directing attention to the actions of the other pupils involved and the particular setting in which the behavior took place. The record, therefore, should contain those situational conditions that seem necessary for understanding the pupil's behavior.

3. Make a record of the incident as soon after the observation as possible. In most cases it is infeasible to write a description of an incident when it happens. However, the longer we delay in recording observations, the greater the likelihood that important details will be forgotten. Try to make a few brief notes at opportune times following behavioral incidents and complete the records after school.

4. Limit each anecdote to a brief description of a single incident. Brief and concise descriptions take less time to write, less time to read, and are more easily summarized. Just enough detail should be included to make the description meaningful and accurate. Limiting each description to a single incident also simplifies the task of writing, using, and interpreting the records (see box).

5. Keep the factual description of the incident and your interpretation of it separate. The description of an incident should be as accurate and objective as you can make it. This means stating exactly what happened in clear and nonjudg-

Writing Anecdotal Records

Write brief, specific descriptions.
Include a concise description of what the pupil said or did and the situation in which it occurred. (Example: On the playground today, Mary and Helen were choosing sides for softball. Betty said, "I want to be on Mary's team and play first base, or I won't play.")

1. *Do not write generalized descriptive anecdotes.* These describe the behavior in general terms, as being typical of the pupil. (Example: On the playground today, Betty again showed that she always wants her own way.)
2. *Do not write evaluative anecdotes.* These judge the behavior as acceptable or unacceptable, good or bad. (Example: Betty was selfish and disruptive on the playground today.)
3. *Do not write interpretive anecdotes.* These explain the reasons for the behavior, usually in terms of a single general cause. (Example: Betty can't play well with others because she is an overprotected, only child.)

mental words. Avoid such terms as *unhappy, shy, hostile, sad, ambitious, persistent,* and the like. If used at all, reserve such words for the separate section in which you give your tentative interpretations of the incident. There is no need to interpret each incident, but when interpretations are given they should be kept separate and labeled as such.

6. Record both positive and negative behavioral incidents. Teachers are often more apt to notice those behaviors that disturb them personally and that interfere with the process in the classroom. The result is that anecdotal records frequently contain a disproportionate number of incidents that indicate the *lack* of learning or development. For evaluation purposes, it is equally important to record the less dramatic incidents that provide clues concerning the growth that *is* taking place. Thus, a conscious effort should be made to observe and record these often more subtle positive behaviors as well as the more obvious negative reactions.

7. Collect a number of anecdotes on a pupil before drawing inferences concerning typical behavior. A single behavioral incident is seldom very meaningful in understanding a pupil's behavior. We all have our moments of *peak performance* and *extreme error-proneness,* elation and despair, confidence and self-doubt. It is only after observing a pupil a number of times in a variety of settings that the basic pattern of behavior begins to emerge. Consequently, we should generally delay making any judgments concerning learning or development until we have a sufficient sample of behavior to provide a reliable picture of how the pupil typically behaves in different situations.

8. Obtain practice in writing anecdotal records. At first, most teachers have considerable difficulty in selecting significant incidents, in observing them accurately, and in describing them objectively. Some training and practice are therefore desirable before embarking on the use of anecdotal records. If the entire school staff is involved, there should be a regular in-service training program. When one teacher wants to explore their use, a supervisor or fellow teacher can help appraise the quality of the records. It might be wise to start by observing pupil's study habits during a study period, as this will allow sufficient time to observe and record significant behavior.

Rating Scales

In contrast with the unstructured descriptions of behavior gathered in anecdotal records, rating scales provide a systematic procedure for reporting observers' judgments. Typically, a rating scale consists of a set of characteristics or qualities to be judged and some type of scale for indicating the degree to which each attribute is present. The rating form itself is merely a reporting device. Its value in appraising the learning and development of pupils depends largely on the care with which it is prepared and the appropriateness with which it is used. As with other evaluation instruments, it should be constructed in accordance with the learning outcomes to be evaluated, and its use should be confined to those areas in which there is a sufficient opportunity to make the necessary observations. If these two principles are properly applied, a rating scale will serve several important evaluative functions: (1) it will direct observation toward specific aspects of behavior; (2) it will provide a common frame of reference for comparing all pupils on the same set of characteristics; and (3) it will provide a convenient method for recording the observers' judgments.

Types of Rating Scales

Rating scales may take many forms, but most of them belong to one of the types that we shall describe next. Each type will be illustrated by using two dimensions from a scale for rating *contributions to class discussion*.

Numerical Rating Scale. One of the simplest types of rating scales is that in which the rater checks or circles a number to indicate the degree to which a characteristic is present. Typically, each of a series of numbers is given a verbal description that remains constant from one characteristic to another. In some cases, the rater is merely told that the largest number is high, 1 is low, and the other numbers represent intermediate values.

The numerical rating scale is useful when the characteristics or qualities to be rated can be classified into a limited number of categories and when there is general agreement concerning the category represented by each number. As commonly used, however, the numbers are only vaguely defined, and so the interpretation and use of the scale vary.

EXAMPLES

Directions: Indicate the degree to which this pupil contributes to class discussions by circling the appropriate number. The numbers represent the following values: 5 — *outstanding,* 4 — *above average,* 3 — *average,* 2 — *below average,* and 1 — *unsatisfactory.*

1. To what extent does the pupil participate in discussions?
    1 2 3 4 5
2. To what extent are the comments related to the topic under discussion?
    1 2 3 4 5

Graphic Rating Scale.   The distinguishing feature of the graphic rating scale is that each characteristic is followed by a horizontal line. The rating is made by placing a check on the line. A set of categories identifies specific positions along the line, but the rater is free to check between these points.

EXAMPLES

Directions: Indicate the degree to which this pupil contributes to class discussions by placing an *x* anywhere along the horizontal line under each item.

1. To what extent does the pupil participate in discussion?

never   seldom   occasionally   frequently   always

2. To what extent are the comments related to the topic under discussion?

never   seldom   occasionally   frequently   always

The scale shown in this example uses the same set of categories for each characteristic and is commonly referred to as a *constant-alternatives* scale. When these categories vary from one characteristic to another, the scale is called, quite logically, a *changing-alternatives* scale.

Although the line in the graphic rating scale makes it possible to rate at intermediate points, using single words to identify the categories has no great advantage over the use of numbers. There is little agreement among raters concerning the meaning of such terms as *seldom, occasionally,* and *frequently.* What is needed are behavior descriptions that indicate more specifically how pupils behave who possess various degrees of the characteristic being rated.

Descriptive Graphic Rating Scale.   The descriptive graphic rating scale uses descriptive phrases to identify the points on a graphic scale. The descriptions are thumbnail sketches that convey in behavioral terms how pupils behave at different steps along the scale. In some scales, only the center and end positions are defined. In others, a descriptive phrase is placed beneath each point. A space for comments is also frequently provided to enable the rater to clarify the rating.

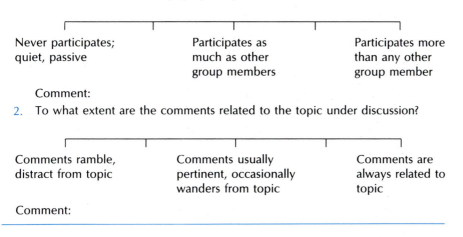

Directions: Make your ratings on each of the following characteristics by placing an x anywhere along the horizontal line under each item. In the space for comments, include anything that helps clarify your rating.

1. To what extent does the pupil participate in discussions?

| Never participates; quiet, passive | Participates as much as other group members | Participates more than any other group member |

Comment:

2. To what extent are the comments related to the topic under discussion?

| Comments ramble, distract from topic | Comments usually pertinent, occasionally wanders from topic | Comments are always related to topic |

Comment:

The descriptive graphic rating scale is generally the most satisfactory for school use. It explains to both the teacher and the pupil the types of behavior that represent different degrees of progress toward desired learning outcomes. The more specific behavior descriptions also contribute to greater objectivity and accuracy during the rating process. To aid scoring, numbers also may be added to each position on the scale.

Uses of Rating Scales

Rating scales can be used to evaluate a wide variety of learning outcomes and aspects of development. As a matter of convenience these uses may be classified into three evaluation areas: (1) procedure, (2) product, and (3) personal–social development.

Procedure Evaluation. In many areas, achievement is expressed specifically through the pupil's performance. Examples include the ability to give a speech, manipulate laboratory equipment, work effectively in a group, sing, play a musical instrument, and perform various physical feats. Such activities do not result in a product that can be evaluated, and paper-and-pencil tests are generally inadequate. Consequently, the procedures used in the performance itself must be observed and judged.

Rating scales are especially useful in evaluating procedures because they focus on the same aspects of performance in all pupils and have a common scale on which to record our judgments. If the rating form has been prepared in terms of specific learning outcomes, it also serves as an excellent teaching device. The dimensions and behavior descriptions used in the scale show the pupil the type of performance desired.

Two items from a typical rating scale for evaluating a speech are presented in Figure 15.2. The first part of the form is devoted to the content of the speech and how well it is organized. The second part is concerned with aspects of delivery such as gestures, posture, appearance, eye contact, voice, and enunciation. In developing such a scale, a teacher must, of course, include those characteristics that are most appropriate for the type of speaking ability to be evaluated and for the age level of the pupil to be judged.

Product Evaluation.   When pupil performance results in some type of product, it is frequently more desirable to judge the product rather than the procedures. The ability to write a theme, for example, is best evaluated by judging the quality of the theme itself. Little is to be learned by observing the pupil's performance. In some areas, however, such as typing, cooking, and woodworking, it might be most desirable to rate *procedures* during the early phase of learning and *products* later, after the basic skills have been mastered. In any event, product rating can provide evaluative information in many areas. In addition to those already mentioned, it is useful in evaluating such things as handwriting, drawings, maps, graphs, notebooks, term papers, book reports, and objects made in vocational courses.

A rating scale serves somewhat the same purpose in product evaluation that it does in procedure evaluation. It helps us judge the products of all pupils in terms of

FIGURE 15.2
Sample items from speech rating scale.

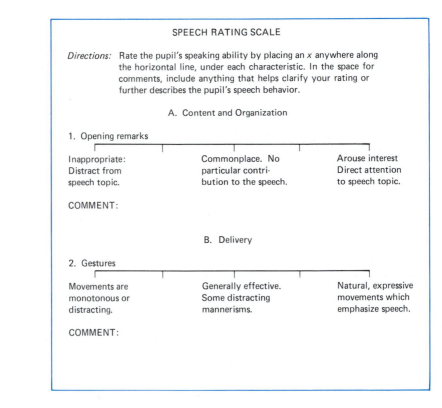

SPEECH RATING SCALE

Directions: Rate the pupil's speaking ability by placing an *x* anywhere along the horizontal line, under each characteristic. In the space for comments, include anything that helps clarify your rating or further describes the pupil's speech behavior.

A. Content and Organization

1. Opening remarks

| Inappropriate: Distract from speech topic. | Commonplace. No particular contri- bution to the speech. | Arouse interest Direct attention to speech topic. |

COMMENT:

B. Delivery

2. Gestures

| Movements are monotonous or distracting. | Generally effective. Some distracting mannerisms. | Natural, expressive movements which emphasize speech. |

COMMENT:

the same characteristics, and it emphasizes to the pupils those qualities desired in a superior product.

In some instances, it is necessary or desirable to judge a product according to its overall quality rather than its separate features. When this is the case, the products may be simply placed in rank order, or they may be compared to a product scale. A *product scale* is a series of samples of the product that have been graded to represent different degrees of quality. In evaluating handwriting, for example, a sample of handwriting is moved along the scale until the quality of the writing matches. The pupil's handwriting is then assigned the value indicated on the scale. See Figure 15.3 for a sample of a handwriting scale using a numerical rating from 0 to 10.

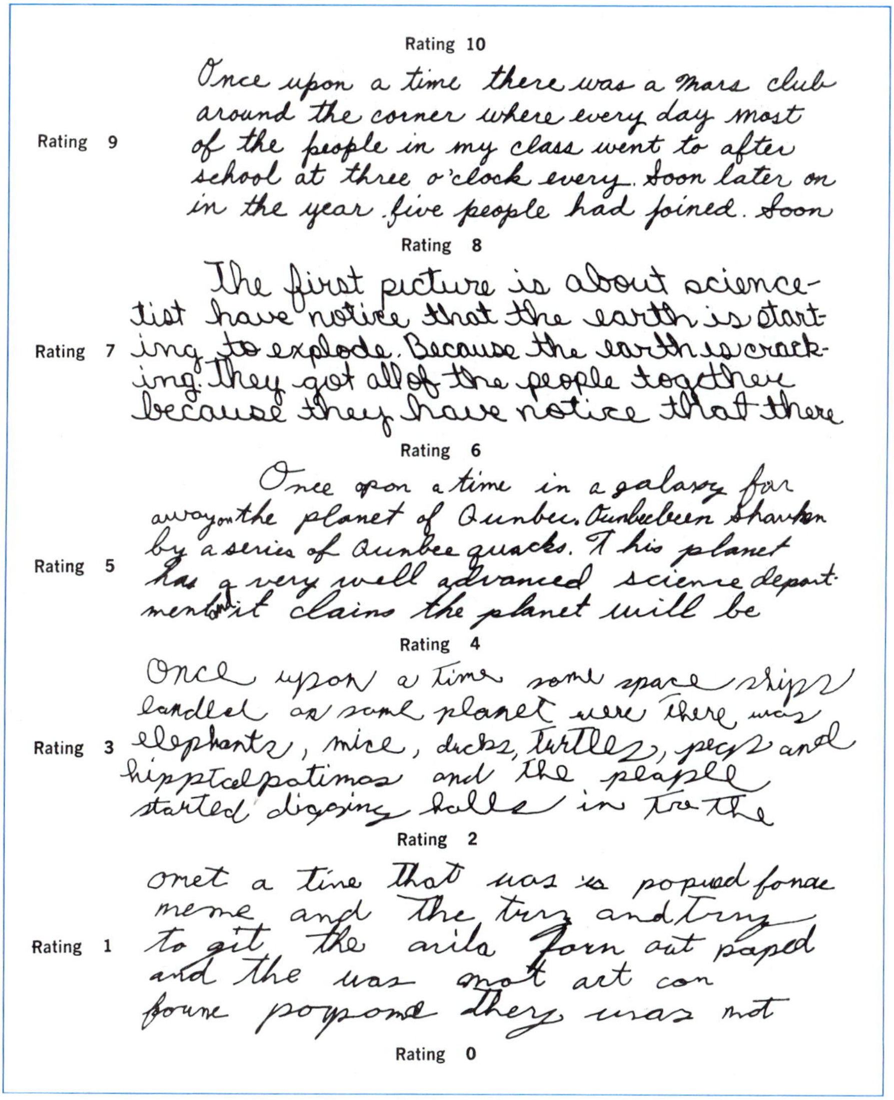

FIGURE 15.3
Handwriting scale used with the *Test of Written Language.* (Copyright 1983 by D. D. Hammill and S. C. Larsen. Used by permission of the publisher, PRO-ED, 5341 Industrial Oaks Blvd., Austin, Texas 78735.)

Product scales can be used in judging the quality of any product, but in most areas teachers will need to develop their own scales. This can be readily done by selecting samples of pupil work that represent from five to seven levels of quality and arranging them in order of merit. The levels can then be assigned a value from 1 to 7 and each of the remaining pupil products can be compared to the scale and rated in terms of the quality level it matches most closely. Such a scale might be developed each time a set of products is to be evaluated, or a more permanent scale might be developed and made available for pupil guidance. The latter procedure is favored when the product is fairly complex and difficult to construct.

Evaluating Personal–Social Development. One of the most common uses of rating scales in the schools is in rating various aspects of personal–social development. Most report cards have a special place for rating pupils on such attributes as citizenship, interest, classroom conduct, and cooperation. In addition, teachers may desire to rate each pupil on a standard rating form at periodic intervals. In this case, the rating scale items should be derived directly from the specific learning outcomes, as shown in Figure 15.4.

Rating personal–social characteristics is quite different from procedure and product evaluation. When judging procedures and products, the ratings are usually made during or immediately after a period of directed observation. In contrast, ratings of personal–social development are typically obtained at periodic intervals and represent a kind of summing up of the teacher's general impressions. The ratings are based on observation, to be sure, but the observations tend to be casual and spread over an extended period of time. We can generally expect such ratings to reflect more of the teachers' feelings and personal biases than those obtained at the end of a period of planned and directed observation.

Common Errors in Rating

Certain types of errors occur so often in ratings that special efforts are needed to counteract them. These include errors due to (1) personal bias, (2) halo effect, and (3) logical error.

Personal bias errors are indicated by a general tendency to rate all individuals at approximately the same position on the scale. Some raters tend to use the high end of the scale only, which is probably the most common type of bias and is referred to as the *generosity error*. Occurring much less frequently but persistently for some raters is the *severity error*, in which the lower end of the scale is favored. Still a third type of constant response is shown by the rater who avoids both extremes of the scale and tends to rate everyone as average. This is called the *central tendency error*. It also occurs much less often than the generosity error does, but it tends to be a fixed response style for some raters.

The tendency of a rater to favor a certain position on the scale has two undesirable results. First, it puts in doubt a single rating of an individual. A high or low rating might reflect the personal outlook of the rater rather than the personal characteristics of the person rated. This is not quite so serious if the ratings are used only in the local school setting. In a local school situation, we are apt to know the

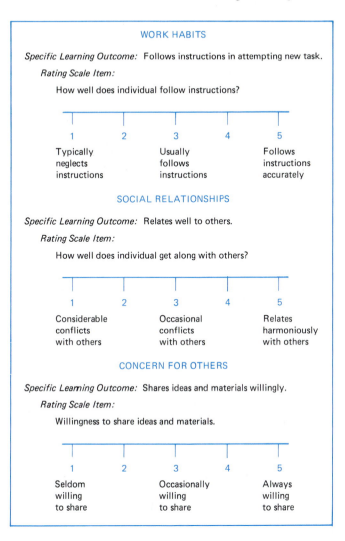

FIGURE 15.4
Sample rating scale
items for evaluating
specific outcomes in
various areas of
personal–social
development. (From N.
E. Gronlund, *Stating
Objectives for Classroom
Instruction*, 3d ed.
Copyright 1985,
Macmillan Publishing Co.,
Inc., New York. Used by
permission.)

rating habits of individual teachers and are thus able to discount their tendencies to overrate or underrate. Second, favoring a certain position on the scale limits the range of any individual's ratings. Therefore, even if we make allowances for a teacher's general tendency to rate pupils high, the ratings for different pupils may be so close together that they fail to provide reliable discriminations.

The *halo effect* is an error that occurs when a rater's general impression of a person influences the rating of individual characteristics. If the rater has a favorable attitude toward the person being rated there will be a tendency to give high ratings on all traits, but if the rater's attitude is unfavorable the ratings will be low. This differs from the generosity and severity errors in which the rater tends to rate everyone high or everyone low.

Because the halo effect causes a pupil to receive similar ratings on all characteristics, it tends to obscure strengths and weaknesses on different traits. This obviously limits the value of the ratings.

A *logical error* results when two characteristics are rated as more alike or less alike than they actually are because of the rater's beliefs concerning their relationship. In rating intelligence, for example, teachers tend to overrate the intelligence of pupils with high achievement because they expect the two characteristics to go together. Similarly, teachers who hold the common but false belief that gifted pupils have poor social adjustment will tend to underrate them on social characteristics. The errors, here, do not result from biases toward certain pupils or certain positions on the rating scale, but rather from the rater's assumption of a more direct relationship among traits than actually exists.

The various types of errors that appear in ratings are rather disconcerting to the classroom teacher who must depend on rating scales for evaluating certain aspects of learning and development. Fortunately, however, the errors can be markedly reduced by proper design and use.

Principles of Effective Rating

The improvement of ratings requires careful attention to selection of the characteristics to be rated, design of the rating form, and conditions under which the ratings are obtained. The following principles summarize the most important considerations in these areas. Because the descriptive graphic rating scale is the most generally useful form for school purposes, the principles are directed toward the construction and use of this type of rating scale.

1. Characteristics should be educationally significant. Rating scales, like other evaluation instruments, must be in harmony with the school's objectives and desired learning outcomes. Thus, when constructing or selecting a rating scale, the best guide for determining what characteristics are most significant is our list of intended learning outcomes. When these have been clearly stated in performance terms, it is often simply a matter of selecting those that can be most effectively evaluated by ratings and then modifying the statements to fit the rating format (see box).

2. Characteristics should be directly observable. There are two considerations involved in direct observation. First, the characteristics should be limited to those that occur in school situations so that the teacher has an opportunity to observe them. Second, they should be characteristics that are clearly visible to an observer. Overt behaviors like participation in classroom discussion, clear enunciation, and skill in social relations can be readily observed and reliably rated. However, less tangible types of behavior, such as *interest* in the opposite sex, *feeling* of inferiority, and *attitude* toward minority groups, tend to be unreliably rated because their presence must be inferred from outward signs that are indefinite, variable, and easily faked. Whenever possible, we should confine our ratings to those characteristics that can be observed and judged directly.

Preparing Rating Scales

The same basic principle guiding the construction of test items should be followed in preparing rating scales. That is, the instrument should be designed to measure the pupil performance described in the instructional objectives. Let us assume, for example, that a science teacher has listed the following outcomes as evidence of skill in one phase of laboratory performance.

Demonstrates Effective Use of Laboratory Equipment.

1. Selects proper equipment for a given experiment.
2. Sets up equipment quickly and correctly.
3. Manipulates equipment as needed during the experiment.
4. Measures accurately with each measuring device.
5. Follows safety rules when using equipment.
6. Cleans and returns equipment to its proper place.

This list of intended outcomes can then serve as the basis for preparing a rating scale to evaluate skill in using laboratory equipment. Each item in the list becomes an item in the rating form by simply adding some basis for recording degrees of effectiveness, as follows:

SELECTING LABORATORY EQUIPMENT

(1)	(2)	(3)	(4)	(5)
Cannot select equipment without help		Inconsistent in selecting proper equipment		Consistently selects proper equipment

The same procedure is followed when rating an educational product (theme, graph, painting, shop and home economics projects). The characteristics of a good product are listed and these then become the items in the rating scale. The instrument itself is simply a convenient form for recording observations and judgments concerning the extent to which pupils are meeting the criteria specified in the objectives.

3. Characteristics and points on the scale should be clearly defined. Many of the errors in rating arise from the use of general, vague trait characterizations and inadequate identification of the scale points. The brief descriptions used with the descriptive graphic rating scale help overcome this weakness. They explain both the points on the scale and each characteristic being rated. When it is infeasible or inconvenient to use a descriptive scale, as on the back of a school report card, a separate sheet of instructions can be used to provide the desired behavioral descriptions.

4. Between three and seven rating positions should be provided, and raters should be permitted to mark at intermediate points. The exact number of points to be designated on a particular scale is determined largely by the judgments to be made. In areas permitting only crude judgments, fewer scale positions are needed. There is usually no advantage in going beyond the seven-point scale, however. Only rarely can we make finer discriminations than this, and we can provide for those few situations by allowing the rater to mark between points.

5. Raters should be instructed to omit ratings when they feel unqualified to judge. Rating scales to evaluate personal–social adjustment are apt to contain some characteristics that the teacher has had little or no opportunity to observe. To require ratings on such traits merely introduces error into the descriptions. It is far better to permit the rater to omit these ratings. Some rating forms have a place to check *unable to judge* or *insufficient opportunity to observe* for each characteristic. Others have a space for comments after each characteristic, in which it is possible either to justify the rating given or to note the reason for not making a rating.

6. Ratings from several observers should be combined whenever possible. The pooled ratings of several teachers will generally be a more reliable description of pupil behavior than that obtained from any one teacher. In averaging ratings, the personal biases of individual raters tend to cancel out one another. Combined ratings are especially applicable at the high school level, where specific teacher–pupil contact is limited, but each pupil has classes with a number of teachers. They are less feasible at the elementary school level, because here we are apt to have only the ratings of the pupil's one regular teacher. The lack of additional raters at this level, however, is at least partially offset by the greater opportunity for the teacher to observe pupils in a variety of situations. Furthermore, the smaller number of elementary teachers in a school makes it easier to detect and allow for common biases, such as the tendency to overrate or underrate pupils.

Checklists

A checklist is similar in appearance and use to the rating scale. The basic difference between them is in the type of judgment needed. On a rating scale, one can indicate the *degree* to which a characteristic is present or the *frequency* with which a behavior occurs. The checklist, on the other hand, calls for a simple *yes–no* judgment. It is basically a method of recording whether a characteristic is present or absent or whether an action was or was not taken. Obviously, a checklist should not be used when degree or frequency of occurrence is an important aspect of the appraisal.

The checklist is especially useful at the primary level, where much of the classroom evaluation depends on observation rather than testing. A simple checklist for evaluating the mastery of mathematics skills at the beginning primary level is shown in Figure 15.5. If the intended learning outcomes are stated as specifically as this for each learning area, a checklist can be prepared by simply adding a place to check *yes* or *no*. As with rating scales, the stated learning outcomes specify the performance to be evaluated, and the checklist is merely a convenient means of recording judgments.

Checklists are also useful in evaluating those performance skills that can be divided into a series of specific actions. An example of such a checklist, for the proper application of varnish, is shown in Figure 15.6. The performance has been subdivided into a series of observable steps, and the observer simply checks whether each step was satisfactorily completed. The checklist in Figure 15.6 includes only those actions that are desired in a good performance. In some cases it may be useful to add those actions that represent common errors so that they can be checked if they occur. In our illustration, for example, we might add after item 4, "Stirs varnish before using." Because stirring paint is a necessary step when painting, some students might incorrectly carry over this action when using varnish. If the checklist is to be used by students, the incorrect actions should, of course, be clearly identified as such.

The following steps summarize the development of a checklist for evaluating a procedure consisting of a series of sequential steps.

1. Identify each of the specific actions desired in the performance.

2. Add to the list those actions that represent common errors (if they are useful in the evaluation, are limited in number, and can be clearly stated).

3. Arrange the desired actions (and likely errors, if used) in the approximate order in which they are expected to occur.

4. Provide a simple procedure for checking each action as it occurs (or for numbering the actions in sequence, if appropriate).

MATHEMATICS SKILLS CHECKLIST

Primary Level

Directions: Circle YES or NO to indicate whether skill has been demonstrated.

YES NO   1. Identifies numerals 0 to 10.
YES NO   2. Counts to 10.
YES NO   3. Groups objects into sets of 1 to 10.
YES NO   4. Identifies basic geometric shapes (circle, square, rectangle, triangle).
YES NO   5. Identifies coins (penny, nickel, dime).
YES NO   6. Compares objects and identifies bigger-smaller, longer-shorter, heavier-lighter.
YES NO   7. States ordinals for a series of 10 objects (1st, 2nd, 3rd, etc.).
YES NO   8. Copies numerals 1 to 10.
YES NO   9. Tells time to the half hour.
YES NO   10. Identifies one-half of an area.

FIGURE 15.5
Checklist for evaluating pupil's mastery of beginning skills in mathematics.

FIGURE 15.6

Checklist for evaluating the proper application of varnish.(From N. E. Gronlund, *Stating Objectives for Classroom Instruction,* 3d ed. Copyright 1985, Macmillan Publishing Co., Inc., New york. Used by permission.)

DIRECTIONS: On the space in front of each item, place a plus (+) sign if performance was satisfactory, place a minus (−) sign if it was unsatisfactory.

_____ 1. Sands and prepares surface properly.

_____ 2. Wipes dust from surface with appropriate cloth.

_____ 3. Selects appropriate brush.

_____ 4. Selects varnish and checks varnish flow.

_____ 5. Pours needed amount of varnish into clean container.

_____ 6. Puts brush properly into varnish (1/3 of bristle length).

_____ 7. Wipes excess varnish from brush on inside edge of container.

_____ 8. Applies varnish to surface with smooth strokes.

_____ 9. Works from center of surface toward the edges.

_____ 10. Brushes with the grain of the wood.

_____ 11. Uses light strokes to smooth the varnish.

_____ 12. Checks surface for completeness.

_____ 13. Cleans brush with appropriate cleaner.

_____ 14. Does *not* pour excess varnish back into can.

_____ 15. Cleans work area.

In addition to its use in procedure evaluation, the checklist can also be used to evaluate products. For this purpose, the form usually contains a list of characteristics that the finished product should possess. In evaluating the product, the teacher simply checks whether each characteristic is present or absent. Before using a checklist for product evaluation, you should decide whether the quality of the product can be adequately described by merely noting the presence or absence of each characteristic. If quality is more precisely indicated by noting the *degree* to which each characteristic is present, a rating scale should be used instead of a checklist.

In the area of personal–social development, the checklist can be a convenient method of recording evidence of growth toward specific learning outcomes. Typically, the form lists the behaviors that have been identified as representative of the outcomes to be evaluated. In the area of work habits, for example, a primary teacher might list the following behaviors (to be marked yes or no).

_____ Follows directions.

_____ Seeks help when needed.

_____ Works cooperatively with others.

_____ Waits turn in using materials.

_____ Shares materials with others.

_____ Tries new activities.

_____ Completes started tasks.

_____ Returns equipment to proper place.

_____ Cleans work space.

Although such items can be used in checklist form if only a crude appraisal is desired, they can also be used in rating scale form by recording the frequency of occurrence (e.g., *always, sometimes, never*).

Although we have described the individual use of checklists, rating scales, and anecdotal records, they are often used in combination when evaluating pupil performance (see Table 15.2).

Types of Proficiency	Examples of Performance to Be Evaluated	Assessment Techniques
Knowledge of experimental procedures	Describes relevant procedures. Identifies equipment and uses. Criticizes defective experiments.	Paper-and-pencil testing. Laboratory identification tests.
Skill in designing an experiment	Plans and designs an experiment to be performed.	Product evaluation (checklist).
Skill in conducting the experiment	Selects equipment. Sets up equipment. Conducts experiment.	Performance evaluation (anecdotal records or rating scale).
Skill in observing and recording	Describes procedures used. Reports proper measurements. Organizes and records results.	Product evaluation (analysis of report).
Skill in interpreting results	Identifies significant relationships. Identifies weaknesses in data. States valid conclusions.	Product evaluation and oral questioning.
Work habits	Manipulates equipment effectively. Completes work promptly. Cleans work space.	Performance evaluation (checklist).

TABLE 15.2

Combining Techniques to Evaluate Laboratory Performance in Science

Pupil Participation in Rating

In this chapter, we have limited our discussion to observational methods used by the teacher. We purposely omitted those checklists and rating scales used as self-report techniques by pupils because these will be considered in the following chapter. Before closing our discussion here, however, we should point out that most of the devices used for recording the teacher's observations also can be used by pupils to judge their own progress. From an instructional standpoint, it is often useful to have pupils rate themselves (or their products) and then compare the ratings with those of the teacher. If this comparison is made during an individual conference, the teacher can explore with each pupil the reasons for the ratings and discuss any marked discrepancies between the two sets.

Self-rating by a pupil and a follow-up conference with the teacher can have many benefits. It should help the pupil (1) understand better the instructional objectives, (2) recognize the progress being made toward the objectives, (3) diagnose more effectively particular strengths and weaknesses, and (4) develop increased skill in self-evaluation. Of special value to the teacher is the additional insight gained.

Pupil participation need not be limited to the *use* of the evaluation instruments. It is also useful to have pupils help *develop* the instruments. Through class discussion, for example, they can help identify the qualities desired in a *good speech* or a *well-written report* or the particular behaviors that characterize *good citizenship*. A list of these suggestions can then be used as a basis for constructing a rating scale or checklist. Involving pupils in the development of evaluation devices has special instructional values. First, it directs learning by causing the pupils to think more carefully about the qualities to strive for in a performance or product. Second, it has a motivating effect because pupils tend to put forth most effort when working toward goals they have helped define.

Summary

Observational techniques are especially useful in evaluating performance skills and certain aspects of personal–social development. In addition, the results of observation supplement and complement paper-and-pencil testing by indicating how pupils typically behave in natural situations.

The least structured observational technique is the anecdotal record. This is simply a method of recording factual descriptions of pupil behavior. To make anecdotal record keeping feasible, it is desirable to restrict observations at any given time to a few types of behavior or to a few pupils. Anecdotal records have the advantages of (1) describing behavior in natural settings, (2) highlighting evidence of exceptional behavior apt to be overlooked by other techniques, and (3) being usable with the very young and the retarded. Their limitations are (1) the time and effort required to maintain an adequate record system, (2) the difficulty of writing objective descriptions of behavior, and (3) the problem of obtaining an adequate sample of behavior. These advantages can be minimized by following specific procedures for observing and recording the behavioral incidents. Suggestions for improving anecdotal records include (1) determining in advance what to observe, (2) describing the setting in which the behavior occurred, (3) making the record as soon as possible after observing the behavior, (4) confining each anecdote to a single incident, (5) separating factual description from interpretation, (6) recording both positive and negative incidents, (7) collecting a number of anecdotes before drawing inferences, and (8) obtaining practice in observing and recording pupil behavior.

Rating methods are a systematic procedure for obtaining and recording the observers' judgments. Of the several types of rating scales available, the descriptive graphic scale seems to be the best for school use. In rating procedures, products, and various aspects of personal–social development, certain types of errors commonly occur. These include (1) personal bias, (2) halo effect, and (3) logical errors. The control of such errors is a major consideration in constructing and using rating scales. Effective ratings result when we (1) select educationally significant characteristics, (2) limit ratings to directly observable behavior, (3) define clearly the characteristics and the points on the scale, (4) limit the number of points on the scale, (5) permit raters to omit ratings when they feel unable to judge, and (6) combine ratings from several raters whenever possible.

Checklists perform somewhat the same functions as rating scales do. They are used in evaluating procedures, products, and aspects of personal–social development where an evaluation of the characteristics is limited to a simple "present–absent" judgment.

Having pupils help construct and use rating devices has special values from the standpoint of learning and aids in the development of self-evaluation skills.

Learning Exercises

1. Construct a rating scale for one of the following that would be useful for evaluating the effectiveness of the *performance*.
   a. Giving an oral report.
   b. Working in the laboratory.
   c. Participating in group work.
   d. Playing some type of game.
   e. Demonstrating a skill.
2. Construct a rating scale or checklist for one of the following that would be useful for evaluating the product.
   a. Constructing a map, chart, or graph.
   b. Writing a personal or business letter.
   c. Writing a theme, poem, or short story.
   d. Making a drawing or painting.
   e. Making a product in home economics.
   f. Making a product in industrial education.

3. Prepare a checklist for evaluating the ability to drive an automobile. Would a rating scale be better for this purpose? What are the relative advantages of each?

4. On which of the following characteristics would you expect teachers' ratings to be most accurate? Why?

   a. Appearance.

   b. Attitude toward school.

   c. Leadership.

   d. Self-confidence.

5. List some of the areas of evaluation in which *product scales* might be used for rating.

6. Observe a child at play and write an anecdotal record. Give both your descriptive account of the child's behavior and your interpretation of the behavior, but place these under separate headings.

7. What are the advantages and disadvantages of using observational techniques for evaluating pupil learning?

8. Briefly describe the steps you would follow if you were going to have pupils help evaluate the effectiveness of their class discussion.

Suggestions for Further Reading

BERK, R. A., ED. *Performance Assessment: Methods and Applications.* Baltimore: Johns Hopkins University Press, 1986. See chapters on "Writing Skills Assessment" and "Listening and Speaking Skills Assessment."

BOEHM, A. E., AND WEINBERG, R. A. *The Classroom Observer: A Guide to Developing Observation Skills,* 2d ed. New York: Teachers College Press, 1987. A brief guide to help preservice and in-service teachers make systematic observations of classroom situations and individual pupils at the preschool and grade-school levels.

COHEN, D. H.; STERN, V.; AND BALABAN, N. *Observing and Recording the Behavior of Young Children.* 3d ed. New York: Teachers College Press, 1983. Describes methods of studying children in various classroom situations. Includes numerous checklists and examples for preschool and primary levels.

CRONBACH, L. J. *Essentials of Psychological Testing,* 4th ed. New York: Harper & Row, 1984. Chapter 15, "Judgments and Systematic Observations," discusses ratings and means of improving them.

GRONLUND, N. E. *How to Construct Achievement Tests,* 4th ed. Englewood Cliffs, N.J.: Prentice-Hall, 1988. Chapter 6, "Constructing Performance Tests," covers steps in constructing a performance test and presents illustrative observational devices.

PRIESTLY, M. *Performance Assessment in Education and Training: Alternative Techniques.* Englewood Cliffs, N.J.: Educational Technology Publications, 1982. A comprehensive treatment of twenty-five types of performance assessment, including performance tests, work samples, identification tests, checklists, rating scales, and anecdotal records. Covers both test development and use.

STIGGINS, R. J. *Evaluating Students by Classroom Observation: Watching Students Grow.* Washington, D.C.: National Education Association, 1984. Step-by-step guidelines for using performance assessment to evaluate pupils' learning as reflected in their actual performance or products.

Chapter 16

Evaluating Learning and Development: Peer Appraisal and Self-Report

Judgments and reports made by pupils themselves are a valuable source of information in many areas of learning and development. (1) Peer judgments . . . determined by sociometric procedures . . . are especially useful in evaluating personal–social development. . . . (2) Self-report methods provide a fuller understanding of pupils' needs, problems, adjustments, interests, and attitudes . . . aid in assessing learning readiness . . . in curriculum planning . . . in pupil guidance.

Teachers' observations and judgments of pupil behavior are of special value in those areas in which the behavior is readily observable and the teachers have special competence to judge. In evaluating the ability to operate a microscope or the quality of handwriting, for example, the teacher is unquestionably in the best position to make the judgment. The procedure can be directly observed, or the product resulting from the procedure, and the teacher's knowledge in the area contributes to the validity and reliability of the judgments. There are some areas of pupil development, however, in which the teacher's evaluation of behavior is apt to be inadequate unless observations are supplemented and complemented by the pupils' judgments and reports.

Various aspects of personal–social development can be more effectively evaluated by including peer ratings and other *peer-appraisal* methods in the evaluation program. In the realms of leadership ability, concern for others, effectiveness in group work, and social acceptability, for example, pupils often know better than the teacher one another's strengths and weaknesses. The intimate interactions that occur in the give and take of peer relations are seldom fully visible to an outside observer. Some differences between teacher judgment and peer judgment also can be expected because each is using different standards. Children's criteria of social acceptability, for example, are apt to be quite different from adults' criteria.

Self-report techniques are also a valuable adjunct to the teacher's observations of behavior. A complete picture of pupils' adjustments, interests, and attitudes cannot be obtained without reports from them. Their expressed feelings and beliefs in these areas are at least as important as evidence obtained from observing their behavior. Although expressed feelings and observable behavior do not always completely agree, the self-report provides valuable evidence concerning the pupils' perceptions of themselves and how they want others to view them. In fact, a discrepancy between reported feelings and actual behavior is, in itself, significant evaluative information.

Though peer appraisal and self-report techniques are useful for understanding pupils better and guiding their learning, development, and adjustment, the results should *not* be used for marking and reporting or in any manner that interferes with honest responses. The pupils must be convinced that it is in their own best interests to respond as accurately and frankly as possible. Teachers who have good relations with their pupils and who have consistently emphasized the positive values of the evaluation information should have no difficulty in obtaining the pupils' cooperation in the effective use of these techniques. When only group results are needed, the pupils can, of course, respond anonymously.

Peer Appraisal

In some instances it is possible to have pupils rate their peers (fellow pupils) on the same rating device used by the teacher. At the conclusion of a pupil's oral report before the class, for example, the other pupils could rate the performance on a standard rating form. The average of these ratings is a good indication of how the group felt about the pupil's performance. Except for oral reports, speeches, demonstrations, and similar situations in which one individual performs at a time, however, the usual rating procedures are seldom feasible with pupils. If we ask pupils to rate their classmates on a series of personal–social characteristics, each pupil will be required to fill out thirty or more rating forms. This becomes so cumbersome and time consuming that we can hardly expect the ratings to be diligently made. When peer ratings and other methods of peer appraisal are used, we must depend on greatly simplified procedures. Some of the techniques are so simple that they can be used effectively with pupils at the primary school level.

The two most widely used techniques in this area are the (1) *guess who* technique and (2) sociometric technique.

Guess Who Technique

One of the simplest methods of obtaining peer judgments is by means of the *guess who* technique. With this procedure, each pupil is presented with a series of brief behavior descriptions and asked to name those pupils who best fit each description. The descriptions may be limited to positive characteristics or they may also include negative behaviors. The following items, taken from a form for evaluating *sociability*, are typical of the types of positive and negative descriptions used:

1. Here is someone who is always friendly.
2. Here is someone who is never friendly.

Some teachers prefer to use only the positive behavior descriptions because of the possible harmful effects of negative nominations on group morale. Teachers must make this decision for themselves, however, because they are the only ones who can determine what the effects might be on their pupils. When good relations have been established among pupils and between teacher and pupils, this is not likely to be a problem. But if there is doubt, it is usually better to sacrifice part of the evaluative data than to disrupt the morale of the class.

In naming persons for each behavior description, the pupils are usually permitted to name as few or as many as they wish. Directions and sample items from a form for evaluating *concern for others* are shown in Figure 16.1. The directions and behavior descriptions must, of course, be adapted to the pupils' age level. With very young pupils, the technique can be presented as a guessing game, with the items stated as follows: "Here is someone who talks a lot—guess who?" When the technique is used with older pupils, the *guess who* aspect is dropped, and the pupils are merely told to write the names of those who best fit each behavior description.

The *guess who* technique is based on the nomination method of obtaining peer ratings and is scored by simply counting the number of mentions each pupil receives on each description. If both positive and negative descriptions are used, such as friendly and unfriendly, the number of negative mentions on each characteristic is subtracted from the number of positive mentions. For example, 12 mentions as being friendly and 2 mentions of being unfriendly would result in a score of 10 on friendliness. The pattern of scores indicates each pupil's reputation in the peer group. This may not completely agree with the teacher's impressions of the pupil but it is nonetheless significant information concerning personal–social development. In fact, one of the great values of this type of peer appraisal is that it makes the teacher aware of feelings and attitudes among pupils that were undetectable through direct observation.

This nominating method can be used to evaluate any aspect of personal-social development for which pupils have had an adequate opportunity to observe. It is especially valuable for appraising personality characteristics, character traits, and social skills, but it is not limited to these areas. It is also useful in such areas as creativity, critical thinking, and problem solving. As with other evaluation techniques, the items used in any particular *guess who* form should be derived directly from the objectives to be evaluated.

FIGURE 16.1
Illustrative *Guess Who*
form for evaluating
pupils' "concern for
others."

DIRECTIONS

Listed below are descriptions of what some pupils in this room are like. Read the descriptions and write the names of the pupils who *best fit* each description. You may write the names of anyone in this room, including those who are absent. Your choices will not be seen by anyone else. Give first name and initial of last name.

Remember!

1. Write the names of pupils in this room who best fit each description.
2. Write as many names as you wish for each description.
3. The same person may fit more than one description.
4. You should write the first name and initial of last name.
5. Your choices will *not be seen* by anyone else.

Write the names below each description.

1. Here is someone who enjoys working and playing with others.

2. Here is someone who is willing to share materials with others.

3. Here is someone who is willing to help others with their schoolwork.

4. Here is someone who makes sure others are not left out of games.

5. Here is someone who encourages others to do well.

6. Here is someone who is kind to others who have a problem.

The items shown in Figure 16.2 were used to evaluate problem solving at the elementary school level and were derived directly from the stated objectives. More elaborate statements would, of course, be used at higher grade levels.

FIGURE 16.2
Sample *Guess Who*
items for evaluating
problem solving.

1. Who is best able to state the problem clearly?
2. Who asks the best questions?
3. Who is most willing to seek more information?
4. Who comes up with the best suggestions?
5. Who is most willing to consider different solutions?
6. Who comes up with the most complete plan?

The main advantage of the *guess who* technique is its usability. It can be administered in a relatively few minutes to pupils of all age levels, and scoring is a simple matter of counting the number of nominations received. Its main limitation is the lack of information it provides on the shy, withdrawn pupil. Such pupils are frequently overlooked when nomination methods are used. In effect, they have no reputation in their peer group and are simply ignored during the rating process.

Sociometric Technique

The sociometric technique is a method for evaluating the social acceptance of individual pupils and the social structure of a group. It is also a relatively simple technique, based on pupil's choices of companions for some group situation or activity. A typical sociometric form is shown in Figure 16.3. This form was used to measure pupils' acceptance as seating companions, work companions, and play companions at the later elementary school level. The directions illustrate several

FIGURE 16.3
Illustrative sociometric form.

Name _____ Date _____

    During the next few weeks we will be changing our seats around, working in small groups and playing some group games. Now that we all know each other by name, you can help me arrange groups that work and play best together. You can do this by writing the names of the children you would like *to have sit near you, to have work with you*, and *to have play with you*. You may choose anyone in this room you wish, including those pupils who are absent. Your choices will not be seen by anyone else. Give first name and initial of last name.
    Make your choices carefully so the groups will be the way you really want them. I will try to arrange the groups so that each pupil gets at least two of his choices. Sometimes it is hard to give everyone his first few choices so be sure to make five choices for each question.

Remember!

1. Your choices must be from pupils in this room, including those who are absent.
2. You should give the first name and the initial of the last name.
3. You should make all five choices for each question.
4. You may choose a pupil for more than one group if you wish.
5. Your choices will *not be seen* by anyone else.

I would choose to *sit near* these children:

1. _____ 3. _____
2. _____ 4. _____
                5. _____

I would choose to *work with* these children:

1. _____ 3. _____
2. _____ 4. _____
                5. _____

I would choose to *play with* these children:

1. _____ 3. _____
2. _____ 4. _____
                5. _____

important principles of sociometric choosing: (1) The choices should be real choices that are natural parts of classroom activities. (2) The basis for choice and the restrictions on the choosing should be made clear. (3) All pupils should be equally free to participate in the activity or situation. (4) The choices each pupil makes should be kept confidential. (5) The choices should be actually used to organize or rearrange groups. More spontaneous and truthful responses will be forthcoming when the pupils know that their choices will be used.

School activities abound with possibilities for sociometric choosing. Pupils can choose laboratory partners, fellow committee members, companions for group projects, and the like. Although some differences in choice can be expected from one situation to another, a large element of social acceptance runs through all choices. A pupil who is often chosen for one activity will also tend to be chosen often for other activities. The greatest variation in the choosing is when specific activities are used and skill and knowledge are important to successful performance. Even relatively unpopular pupils may be chosen as teammates for baseball if they are exceptionally good players. It is unlikely that they would be chosen as seating companions in the classroom, however, because this is almost a pure measure of social acceptance.

Sociometric experts disagree on the desirability of asking pupils to name also those whom they would *not* want as a companion. The arguments in favor of such negative choices are that rejected pupils can be identified and helped and that interpersonal friction can be avoided in arranging groups. The counterargument is that such questions make pupils more conscious of their feelings of rejection and that this may disturb both group morale and the emotional development of pupils. The safest procedure seems to be to avoid using negative choices unless they are absolutely essential to the purpose for which the technique is being used. If their use is essential, the approach should be casual and the pupils permitted, rather than required, to make such choices. A statement like the following will ordinarily suffice: "If there are pupils you would rather not have in your group, you may also list their names."

It is usually wise to restrict the number of choices each pupil makes on a sociometric question. For most purposes, five choices for each activity is a suitable number. Sociometric results have been shown to increase in reliability up to five choices, with no increase beyond that number. Also, five choices makes it easier to arrange sociometric groups because it is sometimes difficult to satisfy the first several choices for all pupils. At the lower elementary grades, it is usually necessary to limit the choices to two or three. Very young children find it difficult to discriminate beyond this number.

Tabulating Sociometric Results.

The pupil's sociometric choices must be organized in some fashion if we are to interpret and use them properly. A simple tally of the number of choices each pupil receives will indicate the degree of social acceptance. This may be all that is needed for some classroom uses, but it will not reveal who made the choices, whether two pupils chose each other, and what the social structure of the group is like. A complete record of the sociometric results can be made by tabulating the choices in a matrix table like the one shown in Figure 16.4. The pupils' names are listed down the side of the table and are numbered

FIGURE 16.4
Matrix table showing choices and rejections of work companions.

Pupils Chosen (matrix columns 1–20) — sociometric matrix of choices (ranked, some circled) and rejections (X).

Left-margin data (*Choices Given* and *Rejections Given*) and bottom-margin data (*Choices Received*, *Rejections Received*, *Mutual Choices*):

#	Name	Choices Given SS	Choices Given OS	Rejections Given SS	Rejections Given OS	Choices Received SS	Choices Received OS	Rejections Received SS	Rejections Received OS	Mutual Choices SS	Mutual Choices OS
1	John A.	4	1	2	0	1	0	0	0	0	0
2	Mike A.	5	0	2	0	4	0	0	0	3	0
3	Jim B.	5	0	0	0	3	0	0	0	3	0
4	Henry D.	4	1	0	0	2	0	2	0	1	0
5	Bob F.	4	1	0	1	3	1	3	1	1	0
6	Bill H.	2	3	0	1	8	4	0	0	2	2
7	George L.	5	0	2	0	7	0	0	0	4	0
8	Dick N.	4	1	0	0	5	2	2	0	2	0
9	Dale P.	5	0	1	0	4	0	0	0	3	0
10	Pete V.	4	1	0	0	5	2	0	0	1	0
11	Mary A.	3	2	0	0	7	1	0	0	3	1
12	Betty A.	5	0	0	0	8	4	0	1	5	0
13	Karen B.	4	1	1	1	6	0	0	1	3	0
14	Lois C.	4	1	0	0	5	2	1	0	4	0
15	Sharon J.	5	0	1	0	0	0	0	0	0	0
16	Ann K.	3	2	0	0	2	0	0	0	2	0
17	Margie M.	4	1	0	0	3	0	0	0	2	0
18	Sue R.	4	1	1	0	6	1	0	0	4	1
19	Pat S.	5	0	0	0	0	0	4	0	0	0
20	Carol W.	4	1	1	0	4	0	0	0	3	0

Central (School)
5A (Class)
F. R. Young (Teacher)

Note: SS = Same Sex   OS = Opposite Sex   X = Rejection

from 1 to 20. These same numbers, corresponding to the pupil's names, are then placed across the top of the table so that each pupil's choices can be recorded in the appropriate column. For example, the choices of John A. were as follows:

CHOSE		REJECTED
1. Bill H.	X	Henry D.
2. George L.	X	Bob F.
3. Mike A.		
4. Betty A.		
5. Pete V.		

These choices were recorded in the table to the right of John A.'s name by placing number 1 in column six to indicate Bill H. as his first choice, number 2 in column seven to indicate George L. as his second choice, and so on. The Xs represent rejection choices, and the circled numbers in the table indicate mutual choices. For example, Mike A. (number 2) chose Jim B. (number 3), and vice versa. Mutual choices are always an equal number of cells from the diagonal line, in each corresponding column and row.

In this particular tabulation form, the boys and girls are listed separately. This divides the main part of the table into four quarters. The boys' choices of boys fall into the upper left-hand quarter of the table, and the girls' choices of girls fall into the lower right-hand quarter. The diagonal line, which goes through the empty cells that are unused because pupils do not choose themselves, cuts through these two quarters. The upper right-hand quarter and the lower left-hand quarter, then, contain only cross-sex choices. This division of the table makes the number of choices given to the same sex and to the opposite sex readily apparent and easy to summarize.

In totaling the number of choices received, in Figure 16.4 each choice was given a value of one, regardless of level of choice. Some teachers prefer to weigh the choices so that a first choice counts more than a second choice, and so on, but there is no rational basis for assigning such weights. Various arbitrary weighting systems have been tried, but none has been shown to be superior to the method used here. Although it seems sensible to expect a pupil's first choice to have greater significance than the second, the degree to which choices differ cannot be predicted. One pupil may have a strong first preference, whereas another is equally attracted to several friends and finds it difficult to discriminate among the first several choices. Until a weighting system is found that handles such discrepancies, the simpler method of counting one for each choice should be used. The level of choice should still be recorded in the matrix table, however, because it is useful when the choices are used to organize groups.

The number of choices pupils receive on a sociometric question is used as an indication of their social acceptance by peers. When five choices are used, as in Figure 16.4, pupils who receive nine or more choices are called *stars*. Those who receive no choices are called *isolates*, and those who receive one choice are called *neglectees*. The remaining pupils, who fall somewhere above or below average, are given no special name. Pupils who receive only rejection choices are called *rejectees*. As noted earlier, when pupils choose each other, they are called *mutual choices*. This terminology is standard in describing and interpreting sociometric results.

The Sociogram.   The matrix table is useful for organizing sociometric data for future use and for determining the social acceptance of individual pupils. It does not depict the social structure of the group, however. When this is desired, the sociometric results are presented in a sociogram, a graphic picture of the social relations in a group, which may be plotted directly from the data recorded in the matrix table. A typical sociogram is shown in Figure 16.5. The sociometric data depicted here were taken from Figure 16.4.

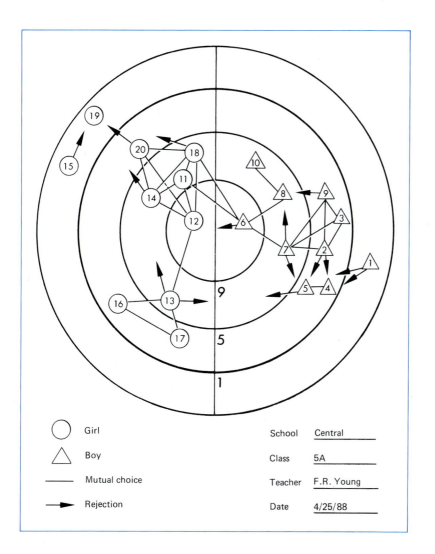

FIGURE 16.5
Sociogram depicting choices and rejections of work companions, based on data in Figure 16.4.

◯ Girl	School Central
△ Boy	Class 5A
—— Mutual choice	Teacher F.R. Young
⟶ Rejection	Date 4/25/88

The concentric circles form a target-type diagram on which to plot the sociometric data. Pupils in the star category (nine or more choices) are placed in the center of the target; isolates are placed in the outer ring; and the remaining pupils are placed between these extremes according to the number of choices received. The boys are represented by triangles and the girls by circles, with the numbers corresponding to each pupil's number in the matrix table (see Figure 16.4). The uncluttered appearance of this sociogram is because the use of lines is confined to mutual choices and rejections. Plotting all choices would result in such a maze of lines that the sociogram would be impossible to interpret.

In constructing a sociogram, it is helpful to start with the most often chosen pupils and work out from the center of the diagram. Pupils with mutual choices should be placed near each other. The original placement on the chart should be done lightly in pencil, as considerable rearrangement is necessary during the plotting to minimize the number of crossed lines. Plotting boys and girls on separate sides of the diagram also simplifies the process because the number of mutual cross-sex choices is usually small. When all pupils have been finally arranged on the diagram, check to be certain that each one is still in the proper position between the concentric circles because this indicates the approximate number of choices received.

The sociogram in Figure 16.5 illustrates the common social configurations you can expect in a group structure. Girls 12, 11, 14, 18, and 20 form a very cohesive *clique*, and girls 13, 16, and 17 form a *triangle*. Boys 10, 8, and 6 form a *chain* of mutual choices, and boys 4 and 5 from a mutual *pair*. In addition, there seems to be a social *cleavage* between boys and girls, except for the few mutual cross-sex choices of boy 6. Pupils 1, 15, and 19 are *isolated* from the group, and pupil 19 is actively *rejected* by four of her classmates.

Although sociograms depict in graphic form the social relations present in the group, *they do not indicate why* a particular social structure evolved nor *what should be done*, if anything, to change it. The sociogram is merely a starting point. To understand the cliques, cleavages, and social positions of individual pupils, it is necessary to supplement sociometric data with information obtained from observation, *guess who* techniques, and various other evaluation methods.

Uses of Sociometric Results.   The sociometric technique has been used for a variety of purposes in the school, including (1) organizing classroom groups, (2) improving individual pupils' social adjustment, (3) improving groups' social structure, and (4) evaluating the influence of school practices on pupils' social relations.

The first step in using sociometric results is to put the choices into effect. For example, if committees are to be formed, they should be patterned as closely as possible to the pupils' choices. This can usually be done most effectively by starting with the isolates and working toward the pupils receiving the largest number of choices. With five choices, it is usually possible to satisfy at least two choices for each pupil. By starting with the isolates, you are able to give them their two highest choices. This places them in contact with the pupils with whom they have the best chance for developing social relations. In arranging the groups, the sociometric choices should, of course, not be followed blindly. It may be desirable to place rural and urban pupils together to reduce an undesirable cleavage or to separate the members of a clique that has been disrupting the class. These adjustments can and should be made without violating your promise to give all of the pupils some of their choices.

Although sociometric results do not indicate how to improve social adjustment, they do help identify those pupils who are having difficulty in adjusting to the peer group. Isolated and rejected pupils are not apt to improve their social position without special help. If an isolated pupil is new to class, arranging opportunities for social contact may be all that is needed. In other cases, it may be a matter of helping isolated pupils improve their appearance, social skills, and apparent value to the group. In some instances, a pupil may be so socially withdrawn or aggressive toward others that the assistance of parents, the school counselor, and other special personnel may be required. Specific remedial procedures should be based on the causes of the pupil's isolation or rejection. The sociometric results merely alert us to the pupils most in need of further study and possible remedial action.

Sociometric measurement can contribute to the improvement of group structure in two ways. First, it helps pinpoint the cliques, cleavages, and mutual relations present in a group. Second, it provides the basic data for rearranging the group in a manner that is likely to result in a more cohesive social pattern. A disintegrated classroom structure, characterized by an overabundance of cliques, cleavages, and isolated pupils, commonly results in low group morale and a poor climate for learning. It is not expected that a simple rearrangement will eliminate cleavages along racial, religious, rural–urban, or socioeconomic lines. But it does offer an opportunity for interpersonal contacts, and if accompanied by other efforts to improve relations, these cleavages can be appreciably diminished.

In addition to its more common uses in the classroom, sociometric measurement is also useful in evaluating the effect of particular school practices on pupils' social relations. For example, it can be used to help answer questions like the following: Are the mainstreamed handicapped pupils being accepted by their peers in the regular classroom? Is our method of ability grouping creating a social cleavage between gifted and regular pupils? Does the competition we have built up between boys and girls in our elementary school result in an extreme sex cleavage? How does our activity program, which prevents bus-transported pupils from participating fully, influence the social relations between town and rural youth? The simplicity of the technique makes it usable with an entire school population as well as with a single classroom group.

Self-Report Techniques

Of various methods of obtaining information directly from an individual, the oldest and best known is the personal interview. The face-to-face contact gives it several advantages as a self-report procedure. First, it is flexible. Interviewers can clarify questions if they are not easily understood, they can pursue promising lines of inquiry, and they can give the interviewees an opportunity to qualify or expand on their answers, as needed. Second, interviewers can observe interviewees during the session, noting the amount of feeling attached to their answers, the topics on which they seem to be evasive, and the areas in which they are most expansive. Third, the interview makes possible not only collecting information from interviewees but also sharing information with them and, as in the case of the counseling interview, using the face-to-face contact as a basis for therapy.

The personal interview would be an almost ideal method of obtaining self-report information from pupils except for two serious problems. It is extremely time consuming, and the information gained is not standard from one person to another. Therefore, in the interests of both feasibility and greater comparability of results, the self-report inventory or questionnaire is commonly used in place of the personal interview. An inventory consists of a standard set of questions pertaining to some particular area of behavior, administered and scored under standard conditions. It is a sort of standardized, written interview that enables the collection of a large amount of information quickly and that provides an objective summary of the data collected.

The effective use of self-report inventories assumes that individuals are both *willing and able* to report accurately. Responses can usually be easily faked if individuals want to present a distorted picture of themselves. Even when they want to be truthful, their recollections of past events may be inaccurate and their self-perceptions biased. These limitations can be partly offset by using self-report inventories only when pupils have little reason for faking, by emphasizing the value of frank responses for self-understanding and self-improvement and by taking into account the possible presence of distortion when interpreting the results. When these inventories are used for evaluating affective behavior in the classroom, it may be wise to have the pupils respond anonymously.

Attitude Measurement

One of the areas in which self-report inventories are very useful in the classroom is attitude measurement. In some instances, attitudes may be important instructional outcomes in their own right (e.g., scientific attitude). In other cases, we may wish to obtain measures of pupils' attitudes toward certain classroom activities, the textbook, laboratory experiences, or our own instruction, so that needed adjustments can be made. Some information concerning attitudes can, of course, be discovered by observation, but a more complete evaluation requires that observation be supplemented by reports of the pupils' feelings and opinions.

One of the simplest self-report devices for measuring attitude is listing the activities or statements the pupils are expected to respond to and then devising some simple means of responding. The teacher-made form for measuring attitude toward mathematics activities at the lower primary level shown in Figure 16.6 illustrates this type of self-report form. The directions can be given orally and repeated for each activity, as follows: "Put an X in the box under the face that tells how you feel about *counting*."

Things We Do	I Like a Lot 😊	It's OK 😐	Don't Like It ☹
Counting			
Adding			
Subtracting			
Story Problems			
Math Games			
Drawing shapes			
Measuring			
Telling time			
Making change			

FIGURE 16.6
Teacher-made form for measuring attitude toward mathematics activities at the lower primary level.

Likert Scale

Another simple and widely used self-report method for measuring attitude is to list clearly favorable or unfavorable attitude statements and to ask the pupils to respond to each statement on the following five-point scale: strongly agree (SA), agree (A), undecided (U), disagree (D), and strongly disagree (SD). This is called a Likert scale, named after its originator, and it is very easily constructed and scored.

The construction involves the following steps:

1. Write a series of statements expressing positive and negative opinions toward some attitude object. For example, in preparing a scale to measure attitude toward school, a number of items like the following might be written.

   • School is exciting.

   • School is a waste of time.

   A good pool of such items can be obtained by having the pupils in your class each write several positive and negative statements.

2. Select the best statements (at least ten), with a balance of positive and negative opinions, and edit as needed.

3. List the statements, mixing up the positive and negative, and put the letters of the five-point scale (SA, A, U, D, SD) to the left of each statement, for easy marking. For pupils at the elementary level, it might be best to list the five points in multiple-choice fashion with the words written out (e.g., "strongly agree").

4. Add the directions telling pupils how to mark their answers, and include a key at the top of the page if letters are used for each statement (SA, A, U, D, SD).

5. Some prefer to drop the undecided category so that respondents will be forced to show agreement or disagreement. Others have expanded the scale by adding the

categories *slightly agree* and *slightly disagree*. Although such changes might be useful for some purposes, the five-point scale is quite satisfactory for most uses.

A Likert-type scale for measuring attitude toward a science course is shown in Figure 16.7. By lengthening the instrument and preparing separate scales, it is possible to obtain a more detailed measure of attitude toward specific parts of the course (e.g., textbook, visual aids, tests, laboratory work). Our example here simply shows the procedure and format.

The scoring of a Likert-type scale, like that in Figure 16.7, is based on assigning weights from 1 to 5 for each position on the scale. Favorable statements, like item 1 in Figure 16.7, are weighted 5, 4, 3, 2, 1, going from SA to SD. Unfavorable statements, like item 2 in Figure 16.7, have these weights *reversed*. Thus, they are weighted 1, 2, 3, 4, 5, going from SA to SD. An individual's total score on this type scale is the sum of the scores on all items, with the higher score indicating a more favorable attitude.

In using attitude scales like the one in Figure 16.7, it is usually best to ask for anonymous responses. This will indicate how the pupils in class feel about the course and, if separate scales are used, how they view the various activities in it. Such information is useful in making course revisions, and anonymous responses provide greater assurance that the replies will reflect the pupils' real feelings.

In interpreting the results of attitude scales, it is important to keep in mind that these are verbal expressions of feelings and opinions that individuals are willing to report. Good rapport with the respondents and a sincere belief on their part that frank responses are in their own best interests will help produce valid responses. Even under the most ideal conditions, however, it is wise to supplement attitudes determined by self-report methods with evidence from other sources. For example,

FIGURE 16.7
Illustrative Likert-type
attitude scale for
measuring attitude
toward a science
course.

Directions: Indicate how much you agree or disagree with each statement by circling the appropriate letter(s).

SA — Strongly Agree
A — Agree
KEY   U — Undecided
D — Disagree
SD — Strongly Disagree

SA	A	U	D	SD	1. Science classes are interesting.
SA	A	U	D	SD	2. Science laboratory is dull and boring.
SA	A	U	D	SD	3. It is fun working on science problems.
SA	A	U	D	SD	4. Class activities are good.
SA	A	U	D	SD	5. Reading the textbook is a waste of time.
SA	A	U	D	SD	6. The laboratory experiments are interesting.
SA	A	U	D	SD	7. Most class activities are monotonous.
SA	A	U	D	SD	8. I enjoy reading the textbook.
SA	A	U	D	SD	9. The problems we are studying are unimportant.
SA	A	U	D	SD	10. I am *not* very enthusiastic about science.

if pupils have reported a favorable attitude toward other ethnic groups, sociometric data can be used to determine how frequently members of those groups are chosen for classroom activities. Similarly, if favorable attitudes toward handicapped persons are reported, this might be checked by observing how the pupils interact with handicapped pupils in the classroom.

Published Attitude Scales

A number of published attitude scales are available for school use. An example is the *Estes Attitude Scales* (grades 3 through 12), designed to measure attitude toward school subjects. At the secondary level, the scales measure attitude toward English, mathematics, reading, science, and social studies. Items for two of the five subjects are shown in Figure 16.8. There is also an elementary form that measures attitude toward mathematics, reading, and science. Although the complete Likert scale is used at the secondary level, the elementary form uses only three categories (agree, don't know, disagree).

The items for each school subject were selected after extensive tryouts and statistical analyses of a larger number of items. The final selection of items resulted in an internally consistent scale for each school subject, with relatively low intercorrelations between the scales. Thus, the scales are fairly independent measures of attitude toward the various school subjects. Studies have also shown that the scores on these scales correlate with other measures of attitude, but the correlations are generally low.

Raw scores can be converted into both T-scores and percentile ranks (based on a limited norm sample).

Interest Inventories

As with attitude measurement, information about pupils' interests can be gathered from simple self-report devices prepared by the teacher. An interest inventory for reading, for example, might be no more than a list of types of books with the pupils asked to mark whether they like or dislike each type. An example of such an inventory is shown in Figure 16.9. A simpler version of this inventory could be developed for pupils at the primary level by using broader categories (e.g., animals, people, places).

Various methods of responding can be used with informal interest inventories. The simple *like–dislike* response method can be expanded to more points, such as a *like, indifferent, dislike* or *strongly like, like, indifferent, dislike, strongly dislike*. When there are relatively few items to be responded to, the pupils can rank them in order from *like most* to *like least*, as in the following example:

RANK   TYPE OF READING

_____ Fiction

_____ Nonfiction

_____ Poetry

_____ Drama

FIGURE 16.8
Portion of the *Estes
Attitude Scales.*
(Reprinted with
permission of PRO-ED.)

ESTES ATTITUDE SCALES

(Secondary Form)

DIRECTIONS: These scales measure how you feel about courses taught in school. On the front and back of this sheet are statements about school subjects. Read each statement and decide how you feel about it. Rate each statement on a scale of 1 to 5, as follows:

5 will mean "I strongly agree"
4 will mean "I agree"
3 will mean "I cannot decide"
2 will mean "I disagree"
1 will mean "I strongly disagree"

Use the separate answer sheet to indicate your feeling toward each statement. Show your answers by putting an X in the proper box. Please be as honest as possible in rating each statement. Your ratings will not affect your grade in any course.

English

1. Work in English class helps students do better work in other classes.
2. The study of English is a waste of time.
3. Writing papers for English class is good practice.
4. Almost any subject is better than English.
5. English courses are some of the worst courses.
6. Studying English is less tiring than studying other subjects.
7. English is a subject with very little real value.
8. English is boring.
9. Studying English in college would be valuable.
10. Students should be required to take English every year.
11. Most literature is dull.
12. English is fun.
13. Time spent in English class is time well spent.
14. English is one class I can do without.
15. English class is too short.

Mathematics

16. People who like math are often weird.
17. Working math problems is fun, like solving a puzzle.
18. It is easy to get tired of math.
19. Working math problems is a waste of time.
20. Studying math in college would be a good idea.
21. Being able to add, subtract, multiply, and divide is all the math the average person needs.
22. It is impossible to understand math.
23. Even though there are machines to work math problems, there is still a reason to study math.
24. Math is boring.
25. Only mathematicians need to study math.
26. Knowledge of math will be useful after high school.
27. Without math courses, school would be a better place.
28. A student would profit from taking math every year.
29. Math is easy.
30. Math is doing the same thing over and over again.

Continued ▶

A simple paired-comparison procedure also might be used to find out the pupils' reading preferences when there are relatively few items to respond to. Using these same four items, for example, we would have six pairs as follows:

_____ Fiction   _____ Fiction
_____ Nonfiction   _____ Drama

FIGURE 16.9
Illustrative inventory
for surveying reading
interests.

READING INTEREST INVENTORY

Directions: For each type of book listed below, circle L if you *like* reading that type of book and circle D if you *dislike* reading that type. List any other types of book you like to read on the lines below.

L D	1. Adventure		L D	10. Mystery
L D	2. Animal		L D	11. Politics
L D	3. Art		L D	12. Psychology
L D	4. Biography		L D	13. Romance
L D	5. Boating		L D	14. Science
L D	6. Car racing		L D	15. Science fiction
L D	7. History		L D	16. Sociology
L D	8. Hobbies		L D	17. Sports
L D	9. Music		L D	18. Western

List any others here _____

_____

_____ Fiction	_____ Nonfiction
_____ Poetry	_____ Drama

_____ Nonfiction	_____ Poetry
_____ Poetry	_____ Drama

The pupils are instructed to mark the type of reading that they most prefer in each pair. A simple tally of the number of marks for each type of reading will indicate the pupils' relative preference.

Using any of the preceding response methods, we can obtain an interest score for each individual pupil, or we can combine the results for the entire class. Although pupils can fake responses to informal interest inventories, they seldom do so. There are no right or wrong answers, and the results are usually used to plan classroom activities or to develop individual learning programs. In contrast with attitude scales, there is little reason to fear that one's responses to the inventory will influence grades.

Published Interest Inventories

There are a number of published interest inventories, but most of them have been designed for use in educational and vocational guidance. In some cases, however, the results can be used in planning more effective classroom instruction. Low interest scores in art and music, for example, might suggest that special activities are needed in these areas. Similarly, when a number of pupils have low interest scores in such areas as computation and science, a review of classroom activities and materials may be helpful. As with informal interest inventories, an individual's pattern of interests also may be useful in selecting reading material and planning individual learning programs.

One published interest inventory that has been widely used in the schools and that is adaptable to classroom use is the *Kuder General Interest Survey*. This inventory was designed for grades 6 to 12 and contains a number of activities arranged in groups of three. The pupils are forced to decide which one of the three activities they like most and which one they like least. The following items show the item format used in the *Kuder General Interest Survey* (but the items were not taken from that instrument).

	Most	Least
1. Build model airplanes.	M	L
Draw pictures of airplanes.	M	L
Write stories about airplanes.	M	L
2. Visit a farm.	M	L
Visit a library.	M	L
Visit a science museum.	M	L

By marking the activity liked *most* and the one liked *least* in each group of three, the individual is, of course, ranking them in order, because the unmarked one will fall in the middle. The same form is used for boys and girls, and the results are profiled using both male and female norms. The inventory can be hand scored by pupils or machine scored. Special Micro-E software provides for local computer scoring including the printing of a complete narrative report like that shown in Figure 16.10. The various parts of the report are indicated by circled letters and are described as follows:

A   V-score. Verifies that responses were carefully made.

B   Explains the test and its interpretation.

C   Scores are ranked by percentile for each norm group.

D   Each individual is compared to both male and female norms.

E   Graphic results are shown for each percentile.

F   High (above 75%), average, and low (below 25%) are indicated on graph.

G   Student is encouraged to look at both male and female norms.

H   Scores are converted to personality type codes.

The *Kuder General Interest Survey* is easy to administer, score, and interpret. Each student receives a narrative report form and an interpretive leaflet that describes the ten areas covered by the *Survey*. Although the report is designed to be self-interpreting, the aid of a teacher or counselor can contribute to the usefulness of the results.

There is also a *Kuder Occupational Interest Survey* for use in high school and beyond. It uses the same forced-choice method of responding to triad items (i.e., selecting the *most* and *least* liked) and also uses a verification score (V-score) for

FIGURE 16.10 Narrative Report Form for the *Kuder General Interest Survey*. (Reprinted by permission of Science Research Associates.)

SRA® KUDER GENERAL INTEREST SURVEY
Form E Narrative Report

Name	THOMPSON ALEX	Numeric Grid	343434343434343
Sex	M	Process Number	0001 00011
Level	GRADES 9 - 12	Norm Group	GRADES 9 - 12

Recently you took the KUDER GENERAL INTEREST SURVEY, FORM E. You were Ⓐ asked to indicate which of three activities you most preferred and which you least preferred. Your V score of 006 indicates that you marked your answers carefully and sincerely. This means that you can have confidence in the accuracy of your results.

Your results show how your interest in ten vocational areas compares to that of other students. The numbers in the charts below indicate the proportion of students whose interest in these ten areas is less than Ⓑ yours. Your scores are ranked from highest to lowest and grouped into HIGH, AVERAGE, and LOW interests. The charts below show which of the vocational areas fall within each of these groups. The vocational areas in which your interests are highest extend into the HIGH areas of the chart; those in which your interests are about the same as other students extend only into the AVERAGE area; and those that are lowest extend only into the LOW area.

Ⓓ Compared to other males: Compared to females:

Ⓕ Low....Avg..High....   Low....Avg..High....

Ⓒ Ⓔ
Persuasive 96-------:----:-----   Persuasive 98-------:----:-------
Literary   96-------:----:-----   Scientific 93-------:----:----
Scientific 78-------:----:-   Literary   88-------:----:---
Soc Serv   78-------:----:-   Computat'l 68-------:----:
Musical   66-------:----   Musical   54-------:---
Computat'l 60-------:----   Mechanical 36-------:-
Artistic   21-------   Soc Serv   33-------:-
Outdoor   18------   Outdoor   24-------
Clerical   14------   Artistic   18------
Mechanical 02-   Clerical   07----

Because there are differences in the interests of males and females, Ⓖ results are provided separately by sex. Generally you will be interested in the results for your own sex; however, if your interests are nontraditional, you may learn something from seeing how you compare with the other sex.

A number of reference books in which you may find occupational Ⓗ information are keyed to the following personality type codes: Realistic, Investigative, Artistic, Social, Enterprising, and Conventional. Your scores rank you highest on the following:

Compared to other males: Compared to females:

        Enterprising   Enterprising
        Investigative   Investigative
        Social   Social

For more information on the vocational areas and scores discussed here, read your Interpretive Leaflet. If you have any questions regarding these results, please see your counselor or teacher.

SRA® SCIENCE RESEARCH ASSOCIATES, INC.
155 North Wacker Drive, Chicago, Illinois 60606
1987, 1963 G. Frederic Kuder.
Printed in U.S.A. All rights reserved.   An IBM Company   Code 27-3898

determining whether the responses were carefully made. The results are reported in terms of 126 specific occupations and 48 college majors. The scores are expressed as correlations between an individual's pattern of interests and the interest pattern of each occupational and college group. The latest form of this instrument provides for both occupational scores and vocational area scores like those in the *Kuder General Interest Survey*.

Another interest inventory that has been widely used at the high school and college levels is the *Strong–Campbell Interest Inventory*. This inventory consists of 325 items grouped into seven sections. The items in the first five sections are marked like (L), indifferent (I), or dislike (D) for each item. In section 6 the individual chooses the preferred activity or marks an equal sign. In section 7 the rating is yes, no, or question mark. The seven sections, with illustrative items (but not taken from the inventory), are as follows:

1. *Occupations* (131 items).
   Airline pilot.
   Animal trainer.
2. *School subjects* (36 items).
   Astronomy.
   Auto mechanics.
3. *Activities* (51 items).
   Debating.
   Woodworking.
4. *Leisure Activities* (39 items).
   Swimming.
   Watching television.
5. *Types of people* (24 items).
   College students.
   Submissive people.
6. *Preference between two activities* (30 items).
   Ambulance driver – travel agent.
   Work with people – work alone.
7. *Your characteristics* (14 items).
   Get along well with others.
   Can speak effectively to groups.

The main part of the *Strong–Campbell Interest Inventory* is scored and interpreted in terms of the similarity between an individual's expressed interests and those of persons engaged in particular occupations. The answers are placed on answer sheets that must be machine scored. The results are printed out on a profile that contains 207 occupational scales, 23 basic interest scales, and 6 general occupational themes. The same inventory form is used by both males and females, and when scored on all scales, the profile indicates how an individual's interests compare to that of both sexes on each scale.

As with other self-report techniques, responses to published interest inventories can be easily faked. This is seldom a problem, however, where the emphasis is on self-understanding and educational and vocational planning. Pupils are anxious to find out about their interests and the inventories consist of items that tend to be psychologically nonthreatening.

The instability of pupils' interest during elementary and high school years suggests that we should use interest inventories with extreme caution at these levels. Interests typically are not very stable until approximately age seventeen. This does not mean that we must wait until this age to measure interests but that our interpretations must be highly tentative. In one sense the instability of interests among children and adolescents is highly encouraging, for it indicates that our efforts to broaden and develop interests through school activities have some chance of succeeding. It is mainly when we are attempting to use them in career planning that stability poses a serious problem. For vocational decisions, we should rely most heavily on interest measures obtained during the last two years of high school and later.

Another precaution to keep in mind is *not* to confuse interest scores with measures of ability. A strong interest in science, for example, may or may not be accompanied by the verbal and numerical abilities needed to pursue successfully a course of study or career in science. A scientific interest may be satisfied by collecting butterflies or by discovering a cure for cancer. Interest measures merely indicate whether an individual is apt to find satisfaction in a particular type of activity. Measures of ability determine the level of activity at which the individual can expect to function effectively.

Personality Measures

Classroom evaluations of pupils' personality characteristics and adjustment problems are probably best made through the use of anecdotal records, rating scales, and other observational and peer-appraisal techniques. However, there are two types of personality measures that classroom teachers should know about, *personality inventories* and *projective techniques*. These will be briefly described for general information only. To use them effectively requires special training in counseling or clinical psychology.

Personality Inventories

The typical personality inventory presents pupils with a series of questions like those used in a psychiatric screening interview. For example, an inventory might include items like the following:

- Do you daydream often?
- Are you frequently depressed?
- Do you have difficulty making friends?

- Do you usually feel tired?

Responses to such questions are commonly indicated by circling *yes, no,* or *?* (for uncertain). In some instances a forced-choice procedure is used, where the items are paired and the respondent must indicate which of the two statements is more characteristic of him.

Personality inventories vary considerably in the type of score provided. Some provide a single adjustment score, others have separate scores for particular adjustment areas (e.g., health, social, emotional) or for specific personality traits (e.g., self-confidence, sociability, ascendancy). In general, research has not supported the validity of separate scores for evaluating adjustment by means of inventories. Even using the total score for distinguishing between adjusted and maladjusted individuals is open to question.

All of the limitations of the self-report technique tend to be accentuated in the personality inventory. (1) The replies can be easily faked, and the threatening nature of many of the questions encourages presenting a distorted picture. Some inventories have "control keys" to detect faking, and others reduce it by means of the forced-choice procedure, but faking cannot be entirely eliminated. (2) In addition to honesty, accurate responses require good self-insight. But this is the very characteristic that poorly adjusted individuals are apt to lack, as they are prone to excessive use of adjustment mechanisms that tend to distort their perceptions of themselves and their relations with others. (3) The ambiguity of the items is also likely to distort the results. Questions like "Are you frequently depressed?" do not mean the same thing to different individuals. Although some ambiguity may be desirable in these inventories (as we are seeking *perceptions* rather than facts), words like *frequently* have such a broad range of meanings that error is likely to be introduced. In addition to these technical shortcomings, there is the *invasion of privacy* issue. Congressional investigators, parents, and others have raised the question of the school's right to ask pupils such personal questions. Primarily because of the invasion of privacy issue, the *routine* use of personality and adjustment inventories in schools has declined to near zero.

Psychologically trained counselors may find personality inventories useful for beginning counseling interviews. The client can be asked to fill out the inventory early in the counseling session, and the response to individual items can serve as a starting point for discussion. Even if the responses are not completely frank or insightful, this can be dealt with in the counseling sessions. When used in this way, the inventory simply serves as an *ice breaker*. Invasion of privacy is not an issue here because the client has voluntarily sought out a relationship in which revelation of inner feelings is a known requisite for obtaining help.

Projective Technique

Projective techniques are another method of evaluating personal–social adjustment with which the classroom teacher should be familiar. Because they generally require clinical training to administer and interpret, it is not expected that teachers will use them directly. It is more than likely, however, that they will encounter some clinical reports of pupils that contain interpretations of projective test results.

In contrast with the highly structured personality inventory, projective techniques provide almost complete freedom of response. Typically, individuals are presented with a series of ambiguous forms or pictures and asked to describe what they see. Their responses are then analyzed to determine what content and structure they have "projected" onto the ambiguous stimuli.

Two of the best known projective techniques are the *Rorschach Inkblot Test* and the *Thematic Apperception Test (TAT)*. The *Rorschach* consists of ten inkblot figures on cards, and the *TAT* includes a series of pictures. These tests are usually administered to one individual at a time, and the individual's responses are recorded during the testing. Analysis of the results requires both systematic scoring and impressionistic interpretation, with emphasis on the total personality pattern revealed. Projective techniques are used primarily as part of a complete clinical study of those individuals who are experiencing adjustment difficulties.

Summary

In some areas of learning and development, it is desirable to supplement the teacher's observations with information obtained directly from the pupils. We can ask the pupils to rate or judge their peers and to report on their own feelings, thoughts, and past behavior. Several peer-appraisal methods and self-report techniques have been developed for this purpose.

Peer appraisal is especially useful in evaluating personality characteristics, social relations skills, and other forms of typical behavior. The give and take of social interaction in the peer group provides pupils with a unique opportunity to observe and judge the behavior of their fellow pupils. Because these peer ratings are based on experiences that are seldom fully visible to adult observers, they are an important adjunct to teachers' observations.

Peer-appraisal methods include the *guess who* technique and the sociometric technique. The first of these techniques for obtaining peer ratings requires pupils to name those classmates who best fit each of a series of behavior descriptions. The number of nominations pupils receive on each characteristic indicates their reputation in the peer group. This nominating procedure can be used to evaluate any aspect of behavior that is observable to fellow pupils. The sociometric technique also calls for nominations, but here the pupils indicate their choice of companions for some group situation or activity. The number of choices pupils receive serves as an indication of their social acceptance, and the network of choices can be used to plot the social structure of the group. The results also can be used to rearrange groups, to improve the social adjustment of individual pupils, and to evaluate the influence of school practices on pupils' social relations.

Self-report techniques are used to obtain information that is inaccessible by other means, including reports on the pupil's attitudes, interests, and personal feelings. Such information can be obtained by means of a personal interview, but a self-report inventory is more commonly used. The inventory is a sort of standardized written interview that produces comparable results from one person to another. The effective use of self-report techniques assumes that the respondent is both *willing* and *able* to report accurately. Thus, special efforts must be made to meet these conditions.

Attitude scales can be used to gather information concerning pupils' feelings and opinions toward various classroom activities, situations, groups, and special events. Interest inventories contribute to a better understanding of pupils' preferences and are useful in educational and vocational planning. Personality inventories and projective techniques aid in evaluating pupils' personal–social adjustment but they are not recommended for use by the classroom teacher.

Both peer ratings and self-report inventories can provide useful information for understanding pupils better and for guiding their learning, development, and adjustment. These purposes are best served, however, when this information is combined with test results, observational data, and all other information concerning the pupils.

Learning Exercises

1. What types of behavior are best evaluated by peer appraisal? What are some of the necessary precautions in using peer-appraisal methods?
2. List several positive and negative statements that might be used on a *guess who* form for evaluating ability to work effectively in a group.
3. List three positive statements and three negative statements that might be used in a sociometric test for evaluating pupils' social acceptance by their peers. What are the advantages and disadvantages of using negative choices?
4. Describe the advantages and limitations of self-report inventories. What can be done to increase the validity of the results?
5. Write several statements that might be useful in a Likert-type attitude scale for evaluating pupils' attitudes toward homework.
6. What are the advantages and disadvantages of using each of the following for evaluating attitudes toward school?
    a. Attitude scale.
    b. Teacher observation.
    c. *Guess who* technique.
7. Why have so few interest inventories been developed for use at the elementary school level? How might interest inventories contribute to the instructional program?
8. What types of peer-appraisal and self-report methods might be used to determine whether ability grouping adversely affects pupil development? How would you develop each instrument?

Suggestions for Further Reading

ADAMS, G. S.. "Attitude Measurement." In *Encyclopedia of Educational Research*, 5th ed. New York: Macmillan, 1982, vol. 1, pp. 180–189. Describes the techniques of attitude measurement and discusses the validity and reliability of attitude measures.

ANASTASI, A. *Psychological Testing*, 5th ed. New York: Macmillan, 1988. Chapter 17, "Self-Report Inventories," and Chapter 18, "Measuring Interests, Values, and Attitudes," discuss the development and use of inventories and describe widely used instruments.

CRONBACH, L. J. *Essentials of Psychological Testing*, 4th ed. New York: Harper & Row, 1984. See Chapter 12, "Interest Inventories," Chapter 13, "General Problems in Studying Personality," and Chapter 14, "Personality Measurement Through Self-Report," for a comprehensive discussion of self-report measures, their validity, and the ethical issues involved.

MEHRENS, W. A., AND LEHMANN, I. J. *Using Standardized Tests in Education*, 4th ed. New York: Longman, 1987. See Chapter 9, "Interest, Personality, and Attitude Inventories," for a discussion of the problems of using self-report inventories and a description of representative instruments.

MUELLER, D. J. *Measuring Social Attitudes*. New York: Teachers College Press, 1986. Subtitled "A Handbook for Researchers and Practitioners," it describes and illustrates various methods of attitude scale construction. Includes an annotated bibliography of various sources of attitude scales.

Part 5

Test Uses and Concerns

Chapter 17

Marking and Reporting

Marking and reporting pupil progress is one of the more frustrating aspects of teaching. . . . There are so many factors to consider . . . and so many decisions to be made. . . . This chapter will remove some of the complexity by . . . describing the various types of marking and reporting systems . . . and providing guidelines for their effective use.

The task of reporting pupil progress cannot be separated from the procedures used in evaluating pupil learning and development. If instructional objectives have been clearly defined in performance terms and relevant tests and other evaluation procedures have been properly used, marking and reporting become a matter of summarizing the results and presenting them in understandable form. The task is still a perplexing one, however, because the evidence of learning and development must be presented on a very brief report form that is understandable to a variety of users (pupils, parents, teachers, counselors, administrators).

Reporting pupil progress becomes especially difficult when the vast array of evaluation data must be summarized as a single letter grade (e.g., A, B, C, D, F). Should the assigned grade represent achievement only or should effort and work habits be included? How should the various aspects of achievement (e.g., tests, reports, lab work) be weighted and combined? Should the achievement be judged in relation to other pupils, some absolute standard, or the individual's learning potential? What distribution of grades (i.e., A, B, C, D, F) should be used and how should this be determined? There are no simple answers to those questions.

Although some schools provide guidelines for assigning marks, practices vary from school to school and frequently from teacher to teacher within the same school. Many schools have circumvented the problems of using a single letter grade by supplementing it with a more elaborate reporting system. Some typical examples of these will be described shortly, but first let us consider some of the functions to be served by a marking and reporting system.

Functions of Marking and Reporting Systems

School marking and reporting systems are designed to serve a variety of functions in the school. These include (1) instructional uses, (2) reports to parents, and (3) administrative and guidance uses.

Instructional Uses

As with other facets of the instructional program, the main focus of the marking and reporting system should be the improvement of pupil learning and development. This is most likely to occur when the report (1) clarifies the instructional objectives, (2) indicates the pupil's strengths and weaknesses in learning, (3) provides information concerning the pupil's personal–social development, and (4) contributes to the pupil's motivation. These functions require a much more comprehensive report than the single letter grade.

The improvement of pupil learning is probably best achieved by the day-to-day evaluations of learning and the feedback from tests and other evaluation procedures. However, pupils also seem to need a periodic summary of their learning progress. They find it difficult to integrate test scores, ratings, and other evaluation results into a summary of how they are doing. A well-designed report form can provide this systematic summary of learning progress. If sufficiently detailed, it can pinpoint strengths and weaknesses in learning with implications for corrective action.

Periodic progress reports can contribute to pupil motivation by providing short-term goals and knowledge of results. Both are essential features of effective learning. How motivating the reports are likely to be, however, depends on the nature of the report and how it is used. If a single letter grade is used and pupils are threatened with low grades unless they study harder, the results are likely to be negative. However, if a comprehensive report of learning strengths and weaknesses is used and the report is presented as an opportunity to check on progress, motivation toward improved learning is likely to result.

Well-designed progress reports can also aid in evaluating the instructional procedures by identifying areas needing revision. When a majority of pupils have reports showing poor learning progress in a particular area, there may be a need to modify the instructional objectives or the classroom activities. In other cases, the reports may indicate that a remedial program would be beneficial for small groups or individuals.

Reports to Parents/Guardians

Informing parents (or guardians) of their children's school progress is a basic function of a marking and reporting system. These reports should help parents understand the objectives of the school and how well their children are achieving the intended learning outcomes of their particular program. This information is important from several viewpoints. First, by knowing what the school is attempting to do, parents are better able to cooperate with the school in promoting their children's learning and development. Second, information concerning their children's successes, failures, and special problems enables parents to give them the emotional support and encouragement needed. Third, knowing their children's strengths and weaknesses in learning provides a basis for helping them make more sound educational and vocational plans. To serve these purposes adequately, the reports should contain as much information and detail as parents can comprehend and use. At the elementary level, the report form is frequently supplemented by parent–teacher conferences.

Administrative and Guidance Uses

Marks and progress reports serve a number of administrative functions. They are used for determining promotion and graduation, awarding honors, determining athletic eligibility, and for reporting to other schools and prospective employers. For most administrative purposes, a single letter grade tends to be preferable, largely because such marks are compact and can be easily recorded and averaged.

There is little doubt that the convenience of the single mark in administrative work has been a major factor in retarding the development of more comprehensive and useful progress reports. This need not be the case, however. Where a new reporting system is being developed, it is possible to retain the use of letter grades for administrative purposes and to supplement them with the type of information needed by pupils, parents, teachers, and counselors. At the high school level, the retention of letter grades is almost mandatory because most college admission officers insist on them.

Counselors use reports on pupil achievement and development, along with other information, to help pupils make more realistic educational and vocational plans. Reports that include ratings on personal and social characteristics are also useful in helping pupils with adjustment problems. These guidance functions are best served by a reporting system that is both comprehensive and detailed.

In summary, the diverse functions to be served by a marking and reporting system indicate that more elaborate reports are needed than the traditional single letter grade. This does not mean that letter grades should be discarded. They are convenient, easily averaged, useful for administrative functions, and required for college admissions. Instead, letter grades should be *supplemented* by the type of information needed by the various users of the reports. When this is done, the letter grade can be retained as a pure measure of achievement, and such factors as effort, attitude, work habits, and personal–social characteristics can be reported on separately.

Types of Marking and Reporting Systems

Throughout the history of education, letter grades have been the primary method of reporting pupil progress in school. Various studies, over the years, have indicated that approximately 80 to 90 percent of the schools used letter grades. In some cases, especially at the elementary level, the report form also included a series of work habits and personal–social characteristics to be checked by the teacher. Various attempts have been made either to replace the traditional report form or to improve it. The modifications typically represent some type of compromise between the need for detailed information and the need for simplicity and conciseness.

Traditional Letter-Grade System

The traditional use of the letter-grade system is to assign a single letter grade (e.g., A, B, C, D, F) for each subject. In some cases a single number (e.g., 5, 4, 3, 2, 1) is used instead of a letter, but the marking system is essentially the same. This system is concise and convenient, the marks are easily averaged, and they are useful in predicting future achievement. However, they have several shortcomings when used as the *sole* method of reporting. (1) They typically are a combination of achievement, effort, work habits, and good behavior. (2) The proportion of pupils assigned each letter grade varies from teacher to teacher. (3) They do not indicate a pupil's strengths and weaknesses in learning. These limitations of the single letter grade make them difficult to interpret and use. A grade of C, for example, may represent good achievement but poor work habits and disruptive behavior or poor achievement accompanied by attentiveness, strong effort, and good behavior. In reacting to criticisms that the letter-grade system also fostered unfair competition among pupils, some schools reduced the number of marks to two (e.g., S = satisfactory, U = unsatisfactory) or three (e.g., by adding H = honors). These changes, of course, provide even less information than the traditional letter grade system.

Pass–Fail System

A two-category system (e.g., satisfactory–unsatisfactory, pass–fail) has been used in some elementary schools for many years. More recently, it has also found widespread use in high schools and colleges. As typically used at these levels, it serves as an option to the traditional letter grade in a limited number of courses. It permits students to take some courses, usually elective courses, under a *pass–fail* option that is not included in their grade-point average. The intent is to encourage students to explore new areas, even those for which they are not fully prepared. It also permits students to focus on those aspects of a course that relate most directly to their major field of study and to neglect those areas of little interest or relevance. Removing the fear of a lower grade point average gives students greater freedom to select their learning experiences.

As with any two-category system, the pass–fail option is easy to use but it offers less information than the traditional A, B, C, D, F system. It provides no indication of the level of learning and, thus, its value for describing present performance or predicting future achievement is lost. Also, study effort is frequently directed toward merely passing rather than a higher level of achievement. Despite its shortcomings, however, the pass–fail option can serve the purposes for which it is intended if its use is restricted to a minimum number of courses.

A special case for the use of a *pass–no grade* marking system can be made for courses taught under a pure mastery learning approach. Here, where pupils are expected to demonstrate mastery of all course objectives before receiving credit for a course, a simple pass is all that is needed to indicate mastery. The practice of assigning a letter grade of A to all pupils who complete a course under mastery conditions, as is frequently done, simply adds greater confusion to the meaning of letter grades. When the *pass–no grade* system is used, nothing is recorded on a pupil's school record until mastery of the course is demonstrated. The mastery learning approach presupposes that each pupil will be given as much time as he needs to attain mastery of the course objectives. Thus, the school record remains a blank until the course is successfully completed.

Checklists of Objectives

To provide more informative progress reports, some schools have replaced or supplemented the traditional marking system with a list of objectives to be checked or rated. These reports, which are most common at the elementary school level, typically include ratings of progress toward the major objectives in each subject-matter area. The following statements for reading and arithmetic illustrate the nature of these reports:

READING

1. Reads with understanding.
2. Works out meaning and use of new words.
3. Reads well to others.
4. Reads independently for pleasure.

ARITHMETIC

1. Uses fundamental processes.
2. Solves problems involving reasoning.
3. Is accurate in work.
4. Works at a satisfactory rate.

The symbols used to rate pupils on each of these major objectives vary considerably. In some schools the traditional A, B, C, D, F lettering system is retained, but more commonly there is a shift to fewer symbols, such as O (outstanding), S (satisfactory), and N (needs improvement).

The checklist form of reporting has the obvious advantage of providing a detailed analysis of the pupil's strengths and weaknesses so that constructive action can be taken to help improve learning. It also provides pupils, parents, and others with a frequent reminder of the objectives of the school. The main difficulties encountered with such reports are in keeping the list of statements down to a workable number and in stating them in such simple and concise terms that they are readily understood by all users of the reports. These difficulties are probably best overcome by obtaining the cooperation of parents and pupils during the development of the report form.

Letters to Parents/Guardians

Some schools have turned to the use of letters to provide for greater flexibility in reporting pupil progress to parents (or guardians). Letters make it possible to report on the unique strengths, weaknesses, and learning needs of each pupil and to suggest specific plans for improvement. In addition, the report can include as much detail as is needed to make clear the pupil's progress in all areas of development.

Although letters to parents might provide a good supplement to other types of reports, their usefulness as the *sole* method of reporting progress is limited by several factors. (1) Comprehensive and thoughtful written reports require an excessive amount of time and skill. (2) Descriptions of a pupil's learning weaknesses are easily misinterpreted by parents. (3) Letters fail to provide a systematic and cumulative record of pupil progress toward the objectives of the school. The flexibility of this method, which is one of its major strengths, limits its usefulness in maintaining systematic records. Because different aspects of development are likely to be stressed from one report to another, the continuity in reporting is lost.

When used in connection with a more formal reporting system, the informal letter can serve a useful role in clarifying specific points in the report and in elaborating upon various aspects of pupil development. It probably should be restricted to this supplementary role, however, and be used only as needed for clarification.

Tactful Remarks for Reporting to Parents

A teacher listed tactful ways of reporting to parents concerning their children's misbehavior in school. It included items like the following:

Lying — "Presents interesting oral reports but has difficulty in differentiating between factual and imaginary material."

Cheating — "Uses all available resources in obtaining answers but needs help in controlling resourcefulness during testing."

Bullying — "Has leadership qualities but needs to redirect them into more constructive activities."

Laziness — "Works on school tasks when given ample supervision but needs to develop independent work habits."

Parent–Teacher Conferences

To overcome the limited information provided by the traditional report card and to establish better cooperation between teachers and parents (or guardians), some schools have used regularly scheduled parent–teacher conferences. This reporting method has been most widely used at the elementary level, with its greatest use in the primary grades.

The parent–teacher conference is a flexible procedure that provides for two-way communication between home and school. Besides receiving a report from the teacher, parents have an opportunity to present information concerning the pupil's out-of-school life. In addition, the conference permits teachers and parents to ask questions, to discuss their common concerns in helping the pupil, and to cooperatively plan a program for improving the pupil's learning and development. The give and take in such a conference makes it possible to avoid, or overcome, any misunderstandings concerning the pupil's learning progress.

The parent–teacher conference is an extremely useful tool, but it shares two important limitations with the informal letter: (1) it requires an excessive amount of time and skill and (2) it does not provide a systematic record of pupil progress. In addition, some parents (or guardians) are *unwilling* or *unable* to come for conferences. Thus, it is most useful as a supplementary method of reporting.

Multiple Marking and Reporting Systems

Schools have used traditional letter grades (A, B, C, D, F) to report pupil progress for over seventy years, despite efforts to replace them with a more meaningful report. Their continued use indicates that they are serving some useful functions in the school (e.g., administrative). In addition, they are a simple and convenient means of maintaining permanent school records. Thus, rather than replace letter grades (or number grades), it seems more sensible to try to improve the letter grade system and *supplement* it with more detailed and meaningful reports of pupil learning progress. Some schools already use multiple marking and reporting systems.

The typical multiple reporting system retains the use of traditional marking (letter grades or numbers) and supplements the marks with checklists of objectives. In some cases, two marks are assigned to each subject: one for achievement and the other for effort, improvement, or growth. An example of a high school report form used for multiple marking is shown in Figure 17.1.

The report form in Figure 17.1 uses separate marks for achievement, effort, and ratings on two lists of objectives. The list at the upper left is of common school objectives appearing on all report forms. The list of objectives at the upper right is of those pertaining to the particular subject being marked, in this case social studies. This report form makes it possible to assign an achievement grade that solely measures achievement because effort and other personal characteristics are marked separately. It also informs both the pupil and parents of the progress being made toward the school's objectives and each subject's objectives. This report form was

FIGURE 17.1
A comprehensive report form that combines dual marking and checklists of objectives.

PROGRESS REPORT
University of Illinois High School
Urbana, Illinois

SOCIAL STUDIES

___ 1st quarter – November   ___ 3rd quarter – April

___ Semester – February   ___ Final Report – June

RATING SCALE: + Outstanding,   S – Satisfactory,   U – Unsatisfactory,   O – Inadequate basis for judgment.

S U O Respects rights, opinions, and abilities of others
S U O Accepts responsibility for group's progress
S U O Is careful with property
S U O Uses time to advantage
S U O Is-attentive
S U O Makes regular preparations as directed

+S U O Evidences independent thought and originality
+S U O Seeks more than superficial knowledge
+S U O Evidences growth in orderly and constructive group discussion
+S U O Keeps informed on current affairs
+S U O Discriminates in the selection and use of social studies materials
+S U O Demonstrates growth in the skills of critical thinking
+S U O Places people and events in their chronological and cultural setting.
+S U O Demonstrates social responsibility

ACHIEVEMENT

The grade is a measure of achievement with respect to what is expected of a pupil of this class in this school and in relation to what is expected in the next higher course in this subject.

___ 5 excellent   ___ 2 passing, but weak
___ 4 very good   ___ 1 failing
___ 3 creditable   ___ 0 inadequate basis for judgment

EFFORT

The grade below is an estimate, based on evidence available to the teacher, of the individual student's effort.

___ 5 excellent   ___ 2 weak
___ 4 very good   ___ 1 very weak
___ 3 creditable   ___ 0 inadequate basis for judgment

COMMENTS:

Teacher: ___

developed by committees of pupils, parents, teachers, and other school personnel and thus reflects the types of information these groups considered most useful.

Guidelines for Developing a Multiple Marking and Reporting System

No marking and reporting system is likely to be equally satisfactory in all schools. Each school system must develop methods that fit its particular needs and circumstances. The following principles for devising a multiple marking and reporting system are guidelines for this purpose:

1. The development of the marking and reporting system should be guided by the functions to be served. The type of information most needed by the report's users should be included. This typically requires a study of the functions for which the reports are to be used by pupils, parents, teachers, counselors, and administrators. Although it is seldom possible to meet all of their needs, a satisfactory compromise is more likely if they are known. It is helpful to supplement letter grades in each subject with separate reports on course objectives, effort, personal and social characteristics, and work habits. The letter grade should be retained as a *pure* measure of achievement, and any marks for improvement, effort, or growth should be made separately.

2. The marking and reporting system should be developed cooperatively by parents, pupils, and school personnel. School reports are apt to be most useful when all users have some voice in their development. This is usually done by organizing a committee consisting of representatives of parent groups, pupil organizations, elementary and secondary school teachers, counselors, and administrators. Ideas and suggestions are fed into the committee through the representatives, and the members carry back to their own respective groups, for modification and final approval, the committee's tentative plans. This cooperative participation not only will result in a more adequate reporting system, but it also increases the likelihood that the reports will be understood by those for whom they are intended.

3. The marking and reporting system should be based on a clear statement of educational objectives. The same objectives that have guided instruction and evaluation should serve as a basis for marking and reporting. Some of these will be general school objectives and others will be unique to particular courses or areas of study. Nevertheless, when devising a reporting system, the first question should be, "How can we best report pupil progress toward these particular objectives?" The final report form will be limited and modified by a number of practical considerations, but the central focus should be on the objectives of the school and course and the types of performance that represent the achievement of these objectives.

4. The marking and reporting system should be based on adequate evaluation. Teachers should not be expected to report on aspects of pupil performance when evidence is lacking or is very unreliable. By the same token, including items in a report form assumes that the performance will be evaluated as objectively as possible. Ratings on such items as critical thinking, for example, should be the end product of testing and controlled observation, rather than depend on snap judgments based on hazy recollections of incidental happenings. Therefore, in planning a marking and reporting system, it is necessary to take into account the types of evaluation data needed. The items included in the final report form should be those on which teachers can obtain reasonably reliable and valid information.

5. The marking and reporting system should be detailed enough to be diagnostic and yet compact enough to be practical. For guiding pupils' learning and development, we should like as comprehensive a picture of their strengths and weaknesses as possible. This desire for detail, however, must be balanced by such practical demands as (1) a reasonable amount of time required to prepare and use the reports; (2) reports that are understandable to pupils, parents, employers, and school personnel; and (3) reports that are easily summarized for school records. As noted earlier, a compromise between comprehensiveness and practicality is probably best obtained by supplementing the letter grade system with more detailed reports on other aspects of pupil development.

6. The marking and reporting system should provide for parent – teacher conferences, as needed. At the elementary school level, regularly scheduled conferences with parents might constitute part of the reporting system. At the high school level, such conferences are typically arranged, as needed, to deal with specific problems. At both levels, however, such conferences should supplement a more formal report form, rather than replace it. A uniform method of reporting pupil progress is needed for school records, and this is difficult to obtain from conference notes.

In summary, a multiple marking and reporting system takes into account the varied needs of pupils, parents, teachers, and other school personnel. The letter grade system (A, B, C, D, F) provides a simplified method of keeping a record of pupil achievement, the checklist of objectives provides a detailed report of pupil strengths and weaknesses in learning and development, and the parent – teacher conference helps maintain cooperation between home and school. When letter grades are supplemented by other methods of reporting, these grades themselves become more meaningful. Rather than being a conglomerate of achievement, effort, improvement, and personal behavior, letter grades can be confined to measuring achievement only. Multiple marking makes this possible by reporting separately on the other aspects of pupil development.

Assigning Letter Grades

Because most schools use the A, B, C, D, F marking system, most teachers will be faced with the problem of assigning letter grades. This involves questions such as the following:

1. What should be included in a letter grade?
2. How should achievement data be combined in assigning letter grades?
3. What frame of reference should be used in grading?
4. How should the distribution of letter grades be determined?

Each of these issues will be discussed in turn.

Determining What to Include in a Grade

As noted earlier, letter grades are likely to be most meaningful and useful when they represent achievement only. If they are contaminated by such extraneous factors as effort, amount of work completed (rather than quality of the work), personal conduct, and so on, their interpretation will become hopelessly confused. When letter grades combine various aspects of pupil development, not only do they lose their meaningfulness as a measure of achievement, but they also suppress information concerning other important aspects of development. A letter grade of B, for example, may represent average achievement with outstanding effort and excellent conduct or high achievement with little effort and some disciplinary infractions. Only by making the letter grade as pure a measure of achievement as possible and reporting on these other aspects separately can we hope to improve our descriptions of pupil learning and development.

If letter grades are to serve as valid indicators of achievement, they must be based on valid measures of achievement. This involves the process described earlier in this book — defining the course objectives as intended learning outcomes and developing or selecting tests and other evaluation devices that measure these outcomes most directly. How much emphasis should be given to tests, ratings, written reports, and other measures of achievement in the letter grades is determined by the nature of the course and the objectives being stressed. Thus, a grade in English might be determined largely by tests and writing projects, a grade in science by tests and evaluations of laboratory performance, and a grade in music by tests and ratings on performance skills. The types of evaluation data to include in a course grade and the relative emphasis to be given to each type of evidence are determined primarily by examining the instructional objectives. Other things being equal, the more important the objective is, the greater the weight it should receive in the course grade. In the final analysis, letter grades should reflect the extent to which pupils have achieved the learning outcomes specified in the course objectives, and these should be weighted according to their relative importance.

Combining Data in Assigning Grades

When the aspects of achievement (e.g., tests, written reports, performance ratings) to be included in a letter grade and the emphasis to be given to each aspect have been decided, our next step is to combine the various elements so that each element receives its intended weight. If we decide, for example, that the final examination should count 40 percent, the midterm 30 percent, laboratory performance 20 percent, and written reports 10 percent, we will want our course grades to reflect these emphases. A typical procedure is to combine the elements into a composite score by assigning appropriate weights to each element and then use these composite scores as a basis for grading.

Combining data into a composite score in order to produce the desired weighting is not as simple as it may appear at first glance. This can be illustrated by a simple example. Let us assume that we want to combine scores on a final examination and a term report and that we want them to be given *equal* weight. Our range of scores on the two measures are as follows:

	Range of Scores
Final Examination	80 to 100
Term Report	10 to 50

Because the two sets of scores are to be given equal weight, we may be inclined simply to add together the final examination score and the term report score for each pupil. We can check on the effectiveness of this procedure by comparing the composite score of a pupil who is highest on the final examination and lowest on the term report ($100 + 10 = 110$) with a pupil who is lowest on the final examination and highest on the term report ($80 + 50 = 130$). It is obvious from this comparison that simply adding together the two scores will not give them equal representation.

Another common but erroneous method of equating scores is to make the maximum possible score the same for both sets of scores. For our scores, this would mean multiplying the scores on the *term report* by 2, so that the top score on both measures would equal 100. Applying this procedure to the same two extreme cases we considered earlier, our first pupil would have a score of 120 ($100 + 20$) and our second pupil a score of 180 ($80 + 100$). It is obvious that this procedure does not equate the scores. In fact, there is now an even larger difference between the two composite scores. This is due to the fact that the influence each component has on the composite score depends on the variability, or spread, of scores and not on the total number of points. Thus, to weight properly the components in a composite score, the variability of the scores must be taken into account.

The range of scores in our example provides a measure of score variability, or spread, and this can be used to equate the two sets of scores. We can give the final examination and the term report equal weight in the composite score by using a multiplier that makes the two ranges equal. Because the final examination scores have a range of 20 ($100 - 80$) and the term report scores a range of 40 ($50 - 10$), we would need to multiply each *final examination* score by 2 to obtain the desired equal weight.[1] We can check on the effectiveness of this procedure by using the same two cases we considered earlier. The pupil highest on the final examination and lowest on the term report would now have a score of 210 ($200 + 10$), and the

---

[1] Note that this weighting is the reverse of the incorrect weighting procedure based on making the maximum possible scores equal.

pupil lowest on the final examination and highest on the term report would also have a score of 210 (160 + 50). Our check shows that the procedure gives the two sets of scores equal weight in the composite score. If we wanted our final examination to count twice as much as the term report, it would be necessary to multiply each final examination score by 4 rather than by 2.

A more refined weighting system can be obtained by using the standard deviation as the measure of variability,[2] but the range is satisfactory for most classroom purposes.

The components in a composite score also can be weighted properly by converting all sets of scores to stanines (standard scores, 1 through 9). When all scores have been converted to the stanine system (see Chapter 14), the scores in each set have the same variability. They then are weighted by simply multiplying each stanine score by the desired weight. Thus, a pupil's composite score would be determined as follows:

	Desired Weight	Pupil's Stanines	Weighted Score
Examination	2	9	18
Laboratory work	1	7	7
Written reports	1	8	8

Composite Score = 33

If desired, the composite score can be divided by the sum of the weights (in this case 4) to obtain a composite average (in this case 8.25). Although the composite average is not a stanine, it does indicate a pupil's relative position on a nine-point scale. These composite averages (or the composite scores) can be used to rank pupils according to an overall weighted measure of achievement in order to assign letter grades.

Selecting the Proper Frame of Reference for Grading

Letter grades are typically assigned on the basis of one of the following frames of reference:

1. Performance in relation to other group members (relative grading).
2. Performance in relation to prespecified standards (absolute grading).
3. Performance in relation to learning ability or amount of improvement.

Assigning grades on a *relative* basis involves comparing a pupil's performance with that of a reference group, typically one's classmates. With this system, the grade is determined by the pupil's *relative* ranking in the total group, rather than by some absolute standard of achievement. Because the grading is based on *relative*

---

[2]See R. L. Ebel and D. A. Frisbie, *Essentials of Educational Measurement*, 4th ed. (Englewood Cliffs, N.J.: Prentice-Hall, 1986).

performance, the grade is influenced by both the pupil's performance and the performance of the group. Thus, one will fare much better, gradewise, in a low-achieving group than in a high-achieving group.

Although relative grading has the disadvantage of a shifting frame of reference (i.e., grades depend on the group's ability), it is widely used in the schools, because much of classroom testing is norm referenced. That is, the tests are designed to rank pupils in order of achievement, rather than to describe achievement in absolute terms. Although position in the group is the key element in a relative system of grading, the actual grades assigned are also likely to be influenced to some extent by the achievement expectations that the teacher has acquired from teaching other groups. Thus, a high-achieving group of pupils is likely to receive a larger proportion of good grades than a low-achieving group will.

Assigning grades on an *absolute* basis involves comparing a pupil's performance to prespecified standards set by the teacher. These standards are usually concerned with the degree of mastery to be achieved by pupils and may be specified as (1) tasks to be performed (e.g., type 40 words per minute without error) or (2) the percentage of correct answers to be obtained on a test designed to measure a clearly defined set of learning tasks. Thus, with this system, letter grades are assigned on the basis of an *absolute* standard of performance rather than a relative one. If all pupils demonstrate a high level of mastery, all will receive high grades.

The absolute system of grading is much more complex than it first appears. To use absolute level of achievement as a basis for grading requires that (1) the domain of learning tasks be clearly defined, (2) the standards of performance be clearly specified and justified, and (3) the measures of pupil achievement be criterion referenced. These conditions are difficult to meet except in a mastery learning situation. When complete mastery is the goal, the learning tasks tend to be more limited and easily defined. In addition, percentage-correct scores, which are widely used in setting absolute standards, are most meaningful in mastery learning because they indicate how far a pupil is from complete mastery. All too frequently, schools use absolute grading based on percentage-correct scores (e.g., A = 95–100, B = 85–94, C = 75–84, D = 65–74, F = below 65) but the domain of learning tasks has not been clearly defined and the standards have been set in a completely arbitrary manner. To fit the grading system, teachers attempt to build tests (norm referenced) with scores in the 60 to 100 range. If the test turns out to be too difficult or too easy, they somehow adjust the scores to fit the absolute grading scale. But such grades are difficult to interpret because they represent an adjusted level of performance on some ill-defined conglomerate of learning tasks.

Although reporting pupil performance in relation to learning ability or amount of improvement shown has been fairly widely used at the elementary school level, this type of grading is fraught with difficulties. Making reliable estimates of learning ability, with or without tests, is a formidable task, because judgments or measurements of ability are likely to be contaminated by achievement to some unknown degree. Similarly, improvement (i.e., growth in achievement) over short spans of time is extremely difficult to estimate reliably with classroom measures of achievement. Thus, the lack of reliability in judging achievement in relation to ability, and in judging degree of improvement, will result in grades of low dependability. If used at all (e.g., to motivate low-ability pupils), such grades should be used as supplementary. In dual marking, for example, one letter grade might indicate level of achievement (relative or absolute), and the second letter grade might be used to represent achievement in relation to ability, or the degree of improvement shown since the last marking period.

Determining the Distribution of Grades

As noted in the previous section, there are two ways of assigning letter grades to measure the level of pupil achievement: the relative-grading system based on relative level of achievement and the absolute-grading system based on absolute level of achievement.

Relative Grading. The assignment of relative grades is essentially a matter of ranking the pupils in order of overall achievement and assigning letter grades on the basis of each pupil's rank in the group. This ranking might be limited to a single classroom group or might be based on the combined distributions of several classroom groups taking the same course. In any event, before letter grades can be assigned, the proportion of As, Bs, Cs, Ds, and Fs to be used must be determined.

One method of grading that has been widely used in the past is to assign grades on the basis of the normal curve. Grading on the normal curve results in an equal percentage of As and Fs and Bs and Ds. Thus, regardless of the group's level of ability, the proportion of high grades is balanced by an equal proportion of low grades. Such grading is seldom defensible for classroom groups because (1) the groups are usually too small to yield a normal distribution; (2) classroom evaluation instruments are usually not designed to yield normally distributed scores; and (3) the pupil population becomes more select as it moves through the grades and the less-able pupils fail or drop out of school. It is only when a course or combined courses have a relatively large and unselected group of pupils that grading on the normal curve might be defended. Even then, however, one might ask whether the decision concerning the distribution of grades should be left to a statistical model (i.e., normal curve) or should be made on a more rational basis.

The most sensible approach in determining the distributions of letter grades to be used in a school is to have the school staff set general guidelines for the approximate distributions of marks. This might involve separate distributions for introductory and advanced courses, for gifted and slow learning classes, and the like. In any event, the distributions should be flexible enough to allow for variation in the caliber of pupils from one course to another and from one time to another in the same course. Indicating ranges rather than fixed percentages of pupils who should receive each letter grade offers this flexibility. Thus, a suggested distribution for an introductory course might be stated as follows:

A = 10 to 20 percent of the pupils
B = 20 to 30 percent of the pupils
C = 30 to 50 percent of the pupils

D = 10 to 20 percent of the pupils

F = 0 to 10 percent of the pupils

These percentage ranges are presented for illustrative purposes only; there is no simple or scientific means of determining what these ranges should be for a given situation. The decision must be made by the local school staff, taking into account the school's philosophy, the pupil population, and the purposes of the grades. All staff members must understand the basis for assigning grades, and this basis must be clearly communicated to the users of the grades.

In setting an approximate distribution of grades for teachers to follow, the distribution should provide for the possibility of no failing grades. Whether pupils pass or fail a course should be based on their absolute level of learning rather than their relative position in some group. If all low-ranking pupils have mastered enough of the material to succeed at the next highest level of instruction, they all probably should pass. On the other hand, if some have not mastered the minimum essentials needed at the next highest level, these pupils probably should fail. Whether minimum performance has been attained can be determined by reviewing the low-ranking pupils' performance on tests and other evaluation instruments or by administering a special mastery test on the course's minimum essentials. Thus, even when grading is done on a relative basis, the pass – fail decision must be based on an absolute standard of achievement if it is to be educationally sound.

Absolute Grading. Absolute grading is most useful when a mastery learning approach is used, because mastery learning provides the necessary conditions for grading on an absolute basis. This includes delimiting the domain of learning tasks to be achieved, defining the instructional objectives in performance terms, specifying the standards of performance to be attained, and measuring the intended outcomes with criterion-referenced instruments.

If the course's objectives have been clearly specified and the standards for mastery appropriately set, the letter grades in an absolute system may be defined as the degree to which the objectives have been attained, as follows:

A = Outstanding. Pupil has mastered all of the course's major and minor instructional objectives.

B = Very Good. Pupil has mastered all of the course's major instructional objectives and most of the minor objectives.

C = Satisfactory. Pupil has mastered all of the course's major instructional objectives but just a few of the minor objectives.

D = Very Weak. Pupil has mastered just a few of the course's major and minor instructional objectives and barely has the essentials needed for the next highest level of instruction. Remedial work would be desirable.

F = Unsatisfactory. Pupil has not mastered any of the course's major instructional objectives and lacks the essentials needed for the next highest level of instruction. Remedial work is needed.

If the tests and other evaluation instruments have been designed to yield scores in terms of the percentage of correct answers, absolute grading then might be defined as follows:

A = 95 to 100 percent correct

B = 85 to 94 percent correct

C = 75 to 84 percent correct

D = 65 to 74 percent correct

F = below 65 percent correct

As noted earlier, defining letter grades in this manner is defensible only if the necessary conditions of an absolute grading system have been met. Using percentage-correct scores when the measuring instruments are based on some undefined hodgepodge of learning tasks produces uninterpretable grades.

With absolute grading systems such as these, the distribution of grades is not predetermined. If all pupils demonstrate a high level of mastery, all will receive high grades. If some pupils demonstrate a low level of performance, they will receive low grades.

Guidelines for Effective Grading

1. Describe your grading procedures to pupils at the beginning of instruction.
2. Make clear to pupils that the course grade will be based on achievement only.
3. Explain how other elements (effort, work habits, personal–social characteristics) will be reported.
4. Relate the grading procedures to the intended learning outcomes (i.e., instructional objectives).
5. Obtain valid evidence (e.g., tests, reports, ratings) as a basis for assigning grades.
6. Take precautions to prevent cheating on tests, reports, and other types of evaluation.
7. Return and review all test results (and other evaluation data) as soon as possible.
8. Properly weight the various types of achievement included in the grade.
9. Do *not* lower an achievement grade for tardiness, weak effort, or misbehavior.
10. Be fair. Avoid bias, and when in doubt (as with a borderline score) review the evidence. If still in doubt, assign the higher grade.

The absolute-grading system for reporting on pupil progress seldom uses letter grades alone. A comprehensive report generally includes a checklist of objectives to inform both pupil and parent which objectives have been mastered and which have not been mastered by the end of each marking period. In some mastery learning programs, letter grades (or numbers) are assigned to *each* objective to indicate the level of mastery that has been achieved. An example of such a report form, designed for use in a junior high school, is shown in Figure 17.2. On this report form, a numerical rating is assigned to each objective as follows:

HAS ACQUIRED

1 = Skill well developed, good proficiency.

2 = Skill developed satisfactorily, proficiency could be improved.

3 = *Basic* skill developed, low proficiency, *needs* additional work.

NOT ACQUIRED

4 = *Basic* skill not acquired.

FIGURE 17.2
Illustrative report form used for mastery learning. (Reproduced by permission of Roselle School District No. 12, Roselle, Illinois.)

**ROSELLE SCHOOL DISTRICT NO. 12
ROSELLE JUNIOR HIGHSCHOOL**

PROGRESS REPORT TO PARENTS 19____ – 19____

Pupil_____   Math____ Teacher_____

Basic Skills — Blank indicates skill not covered or evaluated

	HAS ACQUIRED	NOT ACQUIRED
1. Addition (Whole, decimal, fraction)		
2. Subtraction (whole, decimal, fraction)		
3. Multiplication (whole, decimal, fraction)		
4. Division (whole, decimal, fraction)		
5. Four operations applied to new work		
6. Knowledge of math formulas		
7. Ability to see relationships		
8. Ability to follow procedures		
9. Ability to formulate problems from word context		
10.		

Social Growth, Work Habits, Attitudes

+ indicates strength
Blank indicates acceptable development
− indicates need for improvement

1. Self-discipline
2. Acceptance of responsibility
3. Positive attitude toward authority
4. Class participation
5. Independence in doing assignments
6. Completion of assignments
7. Positive influence in class
8. Positive effort
9. School work affected by frequent absences
  (√) if applicable

If a parent desires a conference, call the school for an appointment — 529-1600

As with other types of absolute grading, the number of 1s, 2s, 3s, and 4s to be assigned to each objective is not predetermined but depends entirely on the absolute level of performance achieved by each pupil. If all pupils achieve good proficiency on a particular objective, all will receive 1s on that objective.

Conducting Parent – Teacher Conferences

Regardless of the type of marking and reporting system used in the school, the parent–teacher conference is an important supplement to the written report of pupil progress. The face-to-face conference makes it possible to share information with parents (or guardians), to overcome any misunderstanding between home and school, and to plan cooperatively a program of maximum benefit to the pupil. At the elementary school level, where parent–teacher cooperation is most important, conferences with parents are regularly scheduled. At the secondary level, the parent–teacher conference is typically used only when some special problem situation arises.

Conferences with parents are most likely to be productive when they are preceded by careful planning and the teacher has skill in conducting such conferences. Many schools offer in-service training for teachers to help them develop effective conference techniques. Typically, such training includes knowledge of how to conduct a parent–teacher conference and role playing to practice the use of conference skills. The following points provide helpful reminders when preparing for and conducting parent–teacher conferences.

1. Make plans for the conference. Determine ahead of time the goals of the conference. Your main purpose may be to inform parents of their pupil's progress, but you may also want to obtain information from parents, make suggestions for home study, or discuss how to solve a particular problem. It is helpful to review the pupil's record, organize the information you are going to present, and make a list of points you want to cover and questions you plan to ask.

2. Begin the conference in a positive manner. Starting the conference by making a positive statement about the pupil sets the tone for the meeting. Saying something like "Betty really enjoys helping others," "Derek is an expert on dinosaurs," or "Marie is always smiling" tends to create a cooperative and friendly atmosphere. Once established, this positive attitude should be maintained throughout the conference.

3. Present the pupil's strong points before describing the areas needing improvement. It is helpful to present samples of the pupil's work when discussing the pupil's performance. This keeps the focus on what the pupil can do and what he or she has yet to learn. Showing an arithmetic test to a parent is much more effective than simply saying the pupil "does addition problems well but has difficulty with division problems" or "is good with simple computation but needs help with story problems."

4. Encourage parents to participate and share information. Although as a teacher you are in charge of the conference, you must be willing to listen to parents and share information rather than "talk at" them. They may have questions and concerns about the school and about their child's behavior that need to be brought out before constructive, cooperative action can be taken.

5. Plan a course of action cooperatively. The discussion should lead to what steps can be taken by the teacher and the parent to help the pupil. A brief summary at the end of the conference should review the points discussed and the action to be taken at home and school.

6. End the conference with a positive comment. At the end of the conference thank the parents for coming and say something positive about the pupil, like "Erik has a good sense of humor and I enjoy having him in class." Any such statement should, of course, fit the pupil, and not be a vague generality that is used repeatedly.

7. Use good human relation skills during the conference. Some of these skills can be summarized by the following "do's" and "don'ts."

DO'S

Be friendly and informal.

Be positive in your approach.

Be willing to explain in understandable terms.

Be willing to listen.

Be willing to accept parents' feelings.

Be careful about giving advice.

DON'TS

Don't argue or get angry.

Don't ask embarrassing questions.

Don't talk about other pupils, teachers, or parents.

Don't bluff if you don't know an answer.

Don't reject parents' suggestions.

Don't be a "know it all" with pat answers.

Although one cannot expect to conduct an effective conference by reading about how to do it, these points serve as a helpful reminder of things to do and to avoid when preparing for a conference.

Reporting Test Results to Parents

Test results are commonly reported to parents during a parent–teacher conference. Although parents have a legal right to all information the school has concerning their children, it should be presented to them in an understandable and usable form.

This means avoiding technical jargon and presenting test results to parents in language that is meaningful to them. There also will be less chance of misunderstanding and more chance of being viewed in proper perspective if the test results are presented as part of the total pattern of information about the pupil.

In preparing for the report to parents, review the test results, and decide when and how they will be introduced into the conference. The meaningful communication of test results to parents includes:

1. Describing what the test measures.
2. Explaining the meaning of the test scores.
3. Clarifying the accuracy of the test scores.
4. Discussing the use of the test results.

The amount of detail you give in each of these areas will, of course, depend on the time available for the conference and the parents' ability to understand the test results. In general, it is best to keep the explanations brief and simple. Do not overwhelm parents with more test information than they can grasp in the short span of time that is typically available for presenting test information.

Describing What the Test Measures

In reporting on the results of a learning ability test, saying something like "this test measures skills and abilities useful in school learning" may be sufficient. If the test contains several scores (e.g., verbal, quantitative, and nonverbal), each section of the test may be described in similarly general terms. Test manuals usually contain general descriptions of the tests and subtests that can be used to explain the test to parents. The following list of things to avoid should help prevent misinterpretation.

1. Do not refer to learning ability tests as intelligence tests. The term *intelligence* is emotionally charged and often misunderstood.
2. Do not describe learning ability tests as measures of fixed abilities. They are not! They measure learned abilities.
3. Do not say, "These test scores predict how well your child will do in school." They won't! Predictions for individuals are hazardous at best, and many factors determine school success. It is better to say something like "Pupils with scores like these usually do well in school," or, for low scores —"usually find learning difficult."

Achievement tests are easily described in terms of the test content, and the names of the subtests usually indicate what the test measures. To say that a reading test measures "vocabulary and reading comprehension" or that a math test measures "computation and problem solving" is frequently sufficient. In some cases it may be desirable to describe the test results by objective or item clusters, and these are typically identified on the pupil's individual report form. When narrative report forms are used, the test content is included as part of the narrative report.

Interpretations of vocational interest inventories, personality inventories, and other guidance-oriented assessment devices are best interpreted by the school counselor or other guidance personnel. Parents should be referred to the appropriate staff member if they have questions about scores on these instruments.

Explaining the Meaning of Test Scores

In making norm-referenced interpretations of test scores, both the meaning of the score and the nature of the norm group should be explained to parents, both simply and understandably. Both *percentile ranks* and *stanines* are widely used in reporting to parents because they are easy to explain and misinterpretations are less likely to occur. Saying something like the following will usually suffice with these scores:

EXAMPLE

Interpreting percentile ranks: "On the reading vocabulary test, Mary scored higher than 85 percent of a national group of fourth-grade pupils." (It might also be necessary to point out that the 85 percent does *not* refer to the percentage of items answered correctly, but only to the percentage of pupils scoring lower.)

Interpreting stanines: "On a scale of 1 to 9, on which the average score is 5, Mary received a score of 7 on the reading vocabulary test, when compared with a national group of fourth-grade pupils." (In some cases it may be desirable to use verbal descriptions such as above average [7, 8, 9], average [4, 5, 6], or below average [1, 2, 3] in place of numbers.)

Figure 17.3 shows the relation among stanines, percentile ranks, and broad verbal descriptions that can be used in reporting to parents.

Grade equivalents require special care in reporting test results to parents because

FIGURE 17.3
Relation of stanines, percentile ranks, and broad verbal descriptions in a normal distribution.

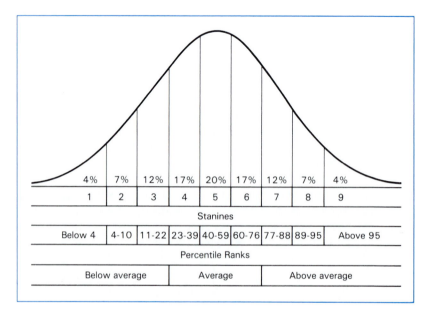

they are subject to so many misinterpretations (see Chapter 14). When using them, point out their shortcomings and explain that a grade-equivalent score does not necessarily indicate the grade-level work that the pupil can do.

It is wise to report all test results in terms of the same type of score (e.g., percentile ranks or stanines). This makes it easier to explain the scores to parents and makes comparisons among tests more understandable.

Although parents are interested in how their child's test performance compares with that of other children, they also want to know what the child has learned and has yet to learn. This type of criterion-referenced interpretation is more readily understood by parents and is typically reported in terms of relative degree of mastery. If you use percentage-correct scores, you may want to distinguish between percentile scores and percentage-correct scores. If you use mastery–nonmastery designations, describe the standard of mastery and explain how it was determined.

Clarifying the Accuracy of Test Scores

It is important to communicate to parents that all test scores contain some error. This can be done most easily if confidence bands (i.e., error bands) are used in interpreting test scores. Profiles using percentile rank frequently include confidence bands. If these are not available, percentile ranks should be interpreted as *estimates* that may vary up or down by several points on retesting.

Stanines contain broad units that allow for measurement error. Because each stanine is at least one-half standard deviation wide, a difference of 2 stanines usually represents a significant difference in test performance. Thus, if we had scores like these, we could make the following interpretation:

Mathematics   8

Reading   6

Science   5

"Performance is higher in mathematics than reading and science, but there is no difference in performance between reading and science." Parents should be told that a difference of 1 stanine is so small that it can be accounted for by errors of measurement alone.

When interpreting test results by objective or by item cluster, attention should be paid to the number of items on which each interpretation is based. If the number of items is small (say less than 10), make only tentative interpretations, and explain to the parents that these are simply clues to be verified by further study. When combined with the results of teacher-made tests and other classroom work, more dependable interpretations may be possible. It is always good practice to interpret test scores to parents in light of the other available data concerning the pupil.

Discussing Use of the Test Results

The interpretation of test results should be accompanied by an explanation of how the test results are to be used in the instructional program and a discussion of what action should be taken by both teacher and parent to improve the pupil's learning and development. This discussion, of course, should not be limited to the test results but should be based on all of the evidence concerning the pupil's learning and development. The value of test scores becomes clearer to parents when they are coordinated with all of the other information about the pupil and when they are seen as contributing to plans for constructive action.

Summary

School marks and progress reports serve various functions in the school. They provide information that is helpful to pupils, parents, and school personnel. Pupils find them useful as summary appraisals of learning progress that serve somewhat the same functions as other evaluation results. Parents, teachers, and counselors use the information in guiding learning and development and in helping pupils make realistic future plans. Administrators use the information to determine promotion, athletic eligibility, honors, and graduation. The reports also provide a basis for reporting to other schools and prospective employers.

The diverse functions of progress reports make it difficult to find a universally satisfactory reporting method. Some of the methods that have been tried include (1) the traditional marking system (e.g., A, B, C, D, F), (2) the pass–fail system, (3) checklists of objectives, (4) informal letters, and (5) parent–teacher conferences. Each method has rather severe limitations when used alone. Probably the best reporting system combines a concise mark for administrative functions with a more detailed report for teaching and guidance purposes. In any event, some combination of methods seems most appropriate.

The letter-grade system of marking (A, B, C, D, F) continues to be the most widely used system at both the elementary and secondary levels, despite attempts to replace it with a more meaningful report. This is probably because such grades are easily assigned and averaged and serve many useful administrative functions. Thus, it seems sensible to retain letter grades as a pure measure of achievement and to supplement them with more detailed and meaningful reports of learning progress. Such a multiple marking and reporting system should be developed cooperatively by parents, pupils, teachers, and other school personnel. Efforts should be made to develop a system that is in harmony with the functions to be served, the school's objectives, and the evaluation data available. Ideally, the report form should be as comprehensive and detailed as is practical and should be supplemented by parent–teacher conferences as needed.

Whether or not a multiple marking and reporting system is used in a school, most teachers will be responsible for assigning letter grades to pupils. This involves such considerations as determining what to include in the letter grade, how to combine the various achievement data into a composite, what frame of reference to use, and what distribution of letter grades to use. The letter grade is most likely to provide a meaningful measure of achievement (1) when it reflects the extent to which pupils have attained the learning outcomes specified in the instructional objectives, (2) when it is based on valid measures of achievement, and (3) when each component of achievement is weighted in terms of its relative importance. Assigning weights to each component requires that the variability (i.e., spread) of scores be taken into account.

Letter grades may be used to indicate a pupil's *relative* level of achievement or *absolute* level of achievement. When assigning relative grades, the normal curve is seldom an appropriate model for determining the distribution of grades. A more sensible approach is to have the school staff set up suggested distributions of grades that take into account the school's philosophy, the pupil population, and the purposes to be served by the grades. Absolute grading is most useful when a mastery learning approach is used. Here, the letter grades represent the degree to which the instructional objectives have been mastered. With this system, no predetermined distribution of letter grades is specified. If all pupils achieve a high degree of mastery, all will receive high grades. In some mastery systems, pupils receive a grade on each objective. Those who fail to achieve mastery on some of the objectives are usually given remedial help and enough additional learning time to achieve a satisfactory level of mastery.

Even when pupils are assigned grades on a relative basis, the pass–fail decision should be based on a pupil's absolute level of achievement. The important consideration is whether the pupil has the minimum knowledge and skills needed to succeed at the next highest level of instruction.

Letter grades are sometimes assigned on the basis of performance in relation to learning ability or amount of improvement. The problems of adequately judging learning ability apart from achievement and of reliably measuring learning gain over short spans of time restricts the use of these marking methods. If used at all (e.g., for motivation purposes), such grades should supplement grades based on the pupil's relative or absolute level of achievement.

Parent–teacher conferences provide an important method of sharing information with parents. Such conferences should supplement the more formal written report of pupil progress, however, rather than replace it. Effective conferences with parents require careful planning and sound conference techniques. It also includes knowing how to report test results to parents. Although guidelines are useful in preparing for conferences with parents, in-service training is usually needed to develop adequate conference skills.

Learning Exercises

1. What are the advantages and limitations of each of the following marking systems?
   a. Letter grade system (A, B, C, D, F).
   b. Pass–fail system.
   c. Checklist of objectives.
2. What types of information are most useful in a marking and reporting system designed to support the instructional program of the school? Why?
3. What are the advantages and limitations of a multiple marking and reporting system?
4. If you were to help set up a marking and reporting system for the level at which you plan to teach, what types of marks and reports would you want included? Why?

5. What procedures are involved in using an *absolute* basis for grading? What are some of the problems in using this system?

6. What are the advantages and limitations of assigning grades on a *relative* basis?

7. Describe the procedure for combining two test scores into a composite score where one of the scores is given twice the weight of the other.

8. List as many ways as you can think of for improving marking and reporting in the school.

9. What factors should be considered when deciding whether to pass or fail a pupil? Do you think the decision should be based on a relative standard or an absolute standard? Why?

10. What types of information should you have at hand during the parent–teacher conference? How would you explain to parents that their child was performing poorly in school? Describe the general approach that you would use in explaining test scores to parents.

Suggestions for Further Reading

Ebel, R. L., and Frisbie, D. A. *Essentials of Educational Measurement*, 4th ed. Englewood Cliffs, N.J.: Prentice-Hall, 1986. Chapter 14, "Grading and Reporting Student Achievement," discusses the problems of grading and describes the various grading systems. Also describes the procedure for weighting components when assigning grades.

Geisinger, K. T. "Marking Systems." In *Encyclopedia of Educational Research*, 5th ed. New York: Macmillan, 1982, vol. 3, pp. 1139–1149. Discusses the purposes of marking procedures and describes the various marking systems used in the schools.

Mehrens, W. A., and Lehmann, I. J. *Measurement and Evaluation in Education and Psychology*, 3d ed. New York: Holt, Rinehart and Winston, 1984. Chapter 19, "Marking and Reporting the Results of Measurement," describes the procedures for marking and reporting, including the reporting of test results.

Selden, S. "Promotion Policy." In *Encyclopedia of Educational Research*, 5th ed. New York: Macmillan, 1982, vol. 3, pp. 1467–1474. Reviews research findings on the differential effects of promotion and nonpromotion on pupil achievement and adjustment, and suggests that competency-based education may require a new promotion policy.

Chapter 18

School Testing, Trends, and Issues

Accountability . . . minimum-competency testing . . . mastery
learning . . . mainstreaming . . . national assessment programs
. . . all have contributed to increased testing in the schools . . .
and have both stimulated and reflected new trends in educational
measurement. The increased testing has also raised issues concerning
the nature, quality, and use of tests.

Testing in the schools has expanded rapidly. The growth in testing has been
stimulated by a variety of forces. In classroom instruction, the focus on tests for
improving learning has led to their increased use. This is especially apparent in
programs that emphasize mastery learning and individualized instruction. Even
greater increases in the use of tests, however, have come as the result of new testing
requirements that have been mandated by states and local school districts in efforts
to increase accountability and to reform education.

In the 1970s and early 1980s minimum-competency testing programs that
required students to pass tests for grade-to-grade promotion or for high school
graduation swept the nation. These were followed by the introduction of testing
requirements for teacher certification and, in some cases, recertification. Educational reformers of the mid- and late 1980s relied on test results to make the case
that reform was needed. More importantly, however, they have relied on tests as a
major mechanism of reform. These developments are combined with actions at the
national level that have resulted in more testing for evaluating federally sponsored
educational programs, for mainstreaming and planning individualized educational

programs for children with handicapping conditions, and, most recently, for comparing states in terms of scores their students achieve on tests. Some of these programs are likely to have a direct influence on your work as a teacher. Others you should know about so that you can serve as an informed professional in talking to pupils, parents, and the public.

The increased use of tests in the school and the varied functions they are expected to serve have contributed to a changing emphasis in educational measurement. They have also created public concern about the role of testing in the schools. Following a discussion of the various programs that have increased school testing in one way or another, we shall consider some of the major trends and critical issues in educational testing.

Accountability and Reform

Although expressions of concern about quality of education and calls for educational reform have been an almost constant part of the educational scene in this country, they reached new levels in the 1980s. The status of education was examined and found wanting in a large number of reports prepared by a variety of distinguished educators, commentators, and commissions. *A Nation at Risk: The Imperative for Educational Reform*,[1] issued by the National Commission on Excellence in Education, is probably the best known and most influential of these.

A Nation at Risk featured testing in two ways. Test scores, especially the decline in scores on college admissions tests that occurred between the early 1960s and 1980, were used to make the case that "the educational foundations of our society are presently being eroded by a rising tide of mediocrity that threatens our very future as a Nation and a people."[2] *A Nation at Risk* also stressed the importance of tests as instruments of improving education through their use to "(a) certify the student's credentials; (b) identify the need for remedial intervention; and (c) identify the opportunity for advanced work."[3]

A Nation at Risk was part of an educational reform movement in which testing played a major role that was actually already well under way in a number of states at the time of its publication. A majority of the states had already introduced some form of minimum-competency testing prior to 1983 when the report was published. These programs were stimulated by reports of high school graduates who were functionally illiterate and by the desire to ensure that all students at least achieve some agreed upon minimum standards of achievement before receiving a high school diploma.

Although, as the minimum-competency testing movement illustrates, many reforms were already under way when *A Nation at Risk* was published, it and related publications calling for reform stimulated a surge of activities in state legislatures,

---

[1]National Commission on Excellence in Education, *A Nation at Risk: The Imperative for Educational Reform* (Washington, D.C.: U.S. Government Printing Office, 1983).

[2]Ibid., p. 5.

[3]Ibid., p. 28.

state departments of education, and local school boards throughout the country.⁴ Once again, testing played a major role in the new surge in educational reforms. Chris Pipho, for example, who tracked these educational reforms, concluded that "nearly every large education reform effort of the past few years has either mandated a new form of testing or expanded use of existing testing."⁵

We shall briefly consider some of the characteristics of three of the uses of testing in the reforms of the 1970s and 1980s. These are (1) minimum-competency testing, (2) teacher testing, and (3) school building, district, and state report cards.

Minimum Competency Testing

Few educational trends have spread as fast as the minimum competency testing movement did in the late 1970s. Although requirements to pass tests in order to receive a diploma or to be promoted to the next grade have a fairly lengthy history, the tremendous growth took place in the mid- to late 1970s, particularly 1975 through 1978, during which time a total of twenty-six states enacted laws or broad rulings requiring some form of minimum-competency testing.⁶ These programs typically involve testing pupils on the basic skills of communication and computation and setting a satisfactory level of performance as a graduation requirement. Some of the more elaborate programs also include testing for competency in such basic life skills as citizenship, consumer education, career education, and health. In some programs, competency tests are also used as a basis for promotion at the lower grade levels.

By the beginning of the 1980s, the majority of states had either passed legislation or adopted state board-of-education rulings mandating some type of minimum-competency testing. In some states the programs are developed by local school districts but in others they are centrally controlled, and statewide competency tests are used. Pupils who fail the tests may be given remedial work, and those who fail repeatedly may be given a certificate of attendance or a special diploma rather than the regular high school diploma.

Although minimum-competency testing programs differ widely in origin and nature, they have some common problems that are not easily resolved. The following questions pertain to some of the more serious concerns:

1. What competencies should be assessed and when?

2. What types of tests and other evaluation instruments should be used?

3. How can we determine whether the evaluation instruments are providing dependable data?

⁴The April 27, 1988 issue of *Education Week* provides a listing of 32 major reports on educational reform since *A Nation at Risk*. Also see *American Education: Making It Work — A Report to the President and the American People*, by William J. Bennett, U.S. Secretary of Education (Washington, D.C.: U.S. Government Printing Office, April 1988).

⁵C. Pipho, "Tracking the Reforms, Part 5: Testing — Can It Measure the Success of the Reform Movement?" *Education Week* (May 22, 1985): 19.

⁶For a recent discussion of the nature of minimum-competency testing programs and the issues surrounding them, see R. M. Jaeger, "Certification of Student Competence," in *Educational Measurement*, 3d ed., ed. R. L. Linn (New York: Macmillan, 1989), Chapter 14.

4. How should we set the standards for passing or failing?

5. What type of remedial instruction is needed for those who fail?

6. How can we ensure fairness to minority group members and handicapped pupils?

7. How can we ensure that the program will contribute to pupil learning rather than detract from it?

Although the orientation is different, these are the same types of issues encountered in classroom testing and evaluation. Thus, whether you find yourself helping develop a local competency-testing program, participating in a statewide program, or merely serving as an informal critic, your knowledge of testing can be useful in making this type of testing program more effective.

Teacher Testing

The competency testing of students was soon followed by programs requiring the testing of prospective teachers and, in some states, the testing of practicing teachers. Test requirements for prospective teachers were common in the 1920s and 1930s but fell out of favor and were rarely used until recently. They came back into favor as part of the educational reform movement of the 1980s. Within a few years, what was once a practice of only a few states became the norm, and by 1987 all but two states had either implemented or enacted plans to implement teacher testing of some kind.[7]

Tests used for teacher certification are determined by individual states and, consequently, they vary in content coverage. Typically, however, the tests are intended to provide three general types of measures: basic skills, professional knowledge, and subject-matter knowledge. Basic skills tests are generally required for all prospective teachers in a state and usually cover general communication skills (e.g., reading, arithmetic, and writing). The professional knowledge tests usually cover topics such as instructional planning, student evaluation, and legal and professional standards affecting classroom practice. The subject-matter tests are tailored to the prospective teacher's area of certification (e.g., mathematics, reading specialist).

Not even proponents of teacher testing claim that paper-and-pencil tests of basic skills, professional knowledge, and subject-matter knowledge measure all that is required to be a successful teacher. Gregory Anrig, the president of Educational Testing Service, which publishes one of the most widely used teacher tests, for example, has noted that the tests do *not* assess such critical characteristics of good teachers as dedication, caring, and integrity.[8] Nor do they assess how well teachers can manage a classroom or how good they are at instilling a love of learning in their students.

[7]L. M. Rudner, "Teacher Testing—An Update," *Educational Measurement: Issues and Practice* (Spring 1988): 16–19.

[8]G. Anrig, "Teacher Education and Teacher Testing: The Rush to Mandate," *Phi Delta Kappan* (February 1986): 447–451.

The intent of the tests, like that of certification tests in other professions, is much more modest. They are intended to protect the public from teachers who lack the knowledge necessary to teach. Justification that the tests satisfy that goal depends almost entirely on content-related evidence of validity that is obtained by asking panels of teachers and teacher educators to judge the degree to which test objectives and test item content assess knowledge that is necessary for a minimally qualified teacher to know.

Controversy about teacher testing is greater where tests are required of practicing teachers for recertification or merit ratings than when they are used only for initial certification or admission into teacher training programs. In either case, however, the issues that generate the greatest controversy are validity, especially the lack of criterion-related evidence, the definition of minimum passing scores, and the disproportionate failure rates that have been observed for minority teachers and teacher candidates.

Partially as an outgrowth of the Carnegie Task Force on Teaching as a Profession, work has been undertaken to create a National Board for Professional Teaching Standards.[9] Major research efforts that would expand the assessment of teaching beyond paper-and-pencil measures to a wide range of performance tests and classroom observation measures are also under way.[10] It seems likely that these efforts will change the character of teacher assessment in the years to come.

Building, District, and State Report Cards

Policy makers at the local, state, and national levels have come to place greater and greater reliance on the results of standardized test scores to make educators more accountable for student achievement. Districts often compare schools in terms of scores on achievement tests, and it is not unusual to find the schools ranked from high to low in newspaper accounts of the test results. Similar comparisons among districts are made by states, and recently the practice has been moved up one more level with the publication of state-by-state reports by the United States Department of Education. Proponents of this use of test scores believe that by focusing on results they can encourage competition and greater efforts by educators to help students achieve.

The 19th annual Gallup Poll of attitudes toward education found that there is widespread support for the practice of using test results to compare schools and states. Gallup and Clark summarized their results as follows:

> In his 1984 State of the Union Address, President Reagan asserted, "Just as more incentives are needed within our schools, greater competition is needed among our schools. Without standards and competition there can be no champions, no records broken, no excellence — in education or any other walk of life." The public agrees. Seventy percent favor reporting the results of achievement tests by state and by school, so that comparisons

---

[9]Task Force on Teaching as a Profession, *A Nation Prepared: Teachers for the 21st Century* (Hyattsville, Md.: Carnegie Forum on Education and the Economy, 1986).

[10]See, for example, L. S. Shulman, "Knowledge and Teaching: Foundations for the New Reform," *Harvard Educational Review* 57 (1987): 1–22.

can be made. The public feels that such comparisons would serve as incentives to local public schools, whether the results showed higher or lower scores for local students.[11]

Test-based comparisons of schools, districts, and states have, as intended, increased the pressure on educators to make sure that their students do well on achievement tests. The degree to which the increased pressure has helped or hurt education, however, is quite controversial. Proponents argue that the tests measure objectives that are important for students to learn and that it is desirable for teachers to focus their attention on those objectives. They point with pride to the increases in test scores that have been observed in state and district testing programs during the last half of the 1980s.

Critics of the increased emphasis on test results for purposes of holding teachers accountable and the high stakes that are being attached to results, on the other hand, argue that the overreliance on test results distorts education. They argue that important objectives are being ignored because they are not included on the tests that count. Moreover, they claim that the increased scores paint a misleading picture because of teaching to the specifics of the tests rather than the more general content domains that the tests sample.

The proper role of tests in directing instruction is an issue that you are apt to have to struggle with, especially if the current emphasis on test results continues. What sort of preparation for taking tests should students have? How much time should be spent in test preparation activities such as taking practice tests and learning test taking strategies? To what degree should tested objectives be given more emphasis at the expense of objectives that are not tested? These are important educational questions that have no pat or simple answers. They require thought and reflection on the part of individual teachers and principals.

Consider, for example, the seemingly simple issues of "teaching to the test" and "teaching the test itself." We are almost always interested in making the inferences that go beyond the specific test that is used. We would like, for example, to be able to say something about a student's degree of understanding of mathematical concepts based on the score that is obtained on a math concepts test. Because the items on a test only sample the domain of interest, the test score and the inference about the degree of understanding are not the same. A generalization is required, and it is the generalization, not the test score, per se, that is important. When the specific items on the test are taught, the validity of the inference about the student's level of achievement is threatened. Teaching the specific test items is apt to result in an exaggerated view of student achievement in the overall domain of interest.

Teaching to the test, that is, emphasizing the objectives that are on the test without teaching the specific test items, has both potential advantages and disadvantages. Inasmuch as the objectives on the test are important, then emphasizing those objectives provides a desirable focus. On the other hand, multiple-choice, standardized tests do not cover all the important education objectives. Hence, a narrowing to only those objectives that are covered would be detrimental for education as a whole.

[11]A. M. Gallup and D. L. Clark, "The 19th Annual Gallup Poll of the Public's Attitudes Toward the Public Schools," *Phi Delta Kappan* (September 1987): 17–30.

Testing in Classroom Instruction

As we have seen, a variety of testing programs have been introduced with the explicit intent of influencing classroom instruction. However, an important distinction can be made between the externally imposed testing that has been put in place to achieve greater accountability and testing that is integrated with the day-to-day instructional program. A distinguishing characteristic of the externally imposed testing programs discussed in the preceding section is that they involve only summative evaluation, that is, an evaluation of the end result. The decisions to award or withhold a diploma based on a student's score on a minimum competency test or to give a prospective teacher a certificate are clearly summative. So too are the evaluations that are based on state-by-state, district-by-district, or school-by-school comparisons.

The test uses that are discussed in this section, on the other hand, stress formative evaluation and the integration of testing and instruction. In earlier chapters of this book we stressed that testing can help improve learning by assisting in (1) preassessing learners' needs, (2) monitoring learning progress, (3) diagnosing learning difficulties, and (4) determining the degree to which the intended learning outcomes have been obtained. While each of these uses of tests occurs in varying degrees in the use of teacher-made tests and informal observations, systematic reliance on all four functions is most clearly illustrated when mastery learning and individualized instruction are emphasized.

Mastery Learning

Mastery learning can be viewed as one aspect of conventional classroom instruction, as suggested in Chapter 2 that a course's intended learning outcomes be divided into *mastery* outcomes and *developmental* outcomes. The former are concerned with the minimum essentials of the course (e.g., basic skills) that must be mastered by all pupils and the latter with the more complex transfer-type objectives (e.g., application, problem solving) toward which pupils can show varying degrees of progress. Another way of viewing mastery learning in classroom instruction is as a basic strategy to be applied to *all* intended learning outcomes. This is the approach taken by B. S. Bloom, J. H. Block, and others.[12] Here, we shall describe Bloom's mastery learning strategy to illustrate how tests are used in monitoring and guiding pupil learning in such a program.

Essentially, Bloom's mastery learning approach is an instructional strategy designed to bring all, or nearly all, pupils to a specified level of mastery on *all* course objectives. It combines regular classroom instruction with feedback–corrective techniques for overcoming individual learning errors. Additional learning time is provided for those pupils who need it. Thus, the Bloom approach uses regular group-based instruction that is supplemented by carefully prescribed corrective

---

[12]J. H. Block, ed., *Mastery Learning: Theory and Practice* (New York: Holt, Rinehart & Winston, 1971); B. S. Bloom, G. J. Madaus, and J. T. Hastings, *Evaluation to Improve Learning* (New York: McGraw-Hill, 1981). See Chapter 3, "Learning for Mastery."

study for those pupils who fail to achieve mastery during the group-based instruction.

The following steps outline the essential features of Bloom's mastery learning strategy:

1. The course is subdivided into a series of learning units that includes a week or two of learning activity. These units might be chapters in a textbook or some other meaningful segment of course content.

2. The instructional objectives are identified and specified for each learning unit. A wide range of learning outcomes is stressed (e.g., knowledge, comprehension, application), and the objectives are defined in specific terms.

3. Mastery standards are set for the objectives in each learning unit, often as the percentage of test items a pupil is expected to answer correctly. Although the setting of mastery standards is somewhat arbitrary, the performance of pupils who have previously taken the course is used as a guide. Mastery is frequently set at 80 to 85 percent correct for each unit, but this must be adjusted to fit various learning and testing conditions.

4. The learning tasks in each unit are taught using the regular materials and methods of group-based instruction. This phase is similar to conventional classroom instruction.

5. Diagnostic-progress tests (*formative* tests) are given at the end of each learning unit. The results of these formative tests are used to reinforce the learning of pupils who have mastered the material and to diagnose the learning errors of those who have failed to achieve mastery. They are generally not used for assigning grades.

6. Procedures for correcting learning errors and additional learning time are prescribed for those pupils who do not demonstrate unit mastery. These prescriptive–corrective techniques include reading particular pages in an alternate textbook, using programmed materials, using audiovisual aids, individual tutoring, and small group study sessions. If one method does not prove successful with a particular learning problem, the pupil is encouraged to use another method. The pupil is usually retested after corrective study.

7. After completing all of the course units, an end-of-course test (*summative* test) is administered. The results of this test are used primarily to assign course grades. All grades are assigned on the basis of absolute standards that were set at the beginning of the course. Thus, if all pupils achieve the level of mastery prescribed for an A grade, all will receive that grade.

8. The results of the formative tests (unit tests) and the summative test (final examination) are used as a basis for evaluating and improving the instruction. Typically, the methods, materials, and sequencing of instruction are examined closely whenever a majority of pupils experience difficulty in mastering the learning tasks.

In summary, Bloom's mastery learning strategy is a group-based method that uses special techniques for adapting instruction to the needs of individual pupils. It differs from conventional classroom instruction in that it (1) emphasizes the mastery of all objectives in each of a series of learning units, (2) uses diagnostic-progress tests (formative tests) to identify each pupil's learning errors, (3) uses systematic feedback – corrective procedures and alternate learning resources (e.g., programmed material) for helping pupils overcome learning difficulties, and (4) provides additional learning time for those pupils who need it. Thus, instead of holding learning time constant and accepting a wide range of achievement, Bloom's approach allows for variation in learning time and emphasizes a high level of achievement for all pupils. Learning effectiveness and course grades are determined by the level of mastery pupils achieve, rather than by how their performance compares with that of their classmates.

As can be seen from the description of Bloom's mastery learning strategy, formative tests play a key role by (1) reinforcing the learning of high achievers, (2) pinpointing the errors of low achievers, and (3) indicating the type of corrective prescriptions needed to improve learning. The summative tests are used principally for assigning grades and evaluating the effectiveness of the instruction.

Individualized Instruction

Individualized instruction permits pupils to work on a series of individual learning units at their own pace and level of achievement. The pupil's work on each unit of study is commonly directed by a learning guide called an individual study unit, a teaching-learning unit, a learning package, a self-instructional unit, a student learning contract, or some similar name. Despite the variation in titles, learning guides are similar in content and design and typically include the following key elements:

1. One or more instructional objectives.
2. Pretest (or directions for obtaining it).
3. List of learning activities and materials.
4. Self-tests to aid the pupil in monitoring learning progress.
5. Posttest (or directions for obtaining it).

Thus, each learning guide consists of a self-contained instructional unit that permits a pupil to work through a program of study, unit by unit, with only a minimum of teacher guidance.

As noted in the learning guide outline, testing is a prominent part of each individual learning unit. The *pretest* aids in determining pupils' readiness for studying the unit and serves as a placement guide. If pupils do well on the pretest, they may be permitted to skip some of the objectives in the unit or may be directed to move on to the next unit. The *self-tests* are designed to measure mastery of each of the unit's instructional objectives. These tests help pupils decide when they should move on to the next objective and when they are ready to take the unit posttest. The *posttest* determines whether pupils have mastered the unit's objectives. If pupils perform satisfactorily on the posttest, they will move on to the next unit of study. If their performance is unsatisfactory, they will continue work on the unit and retake a second form of the posttest at a later date. The flow chart in

Figure 18.1 illustrates the use of testing in guiding pupils through units of individualized instruction. To read the chart, start with the UNIT PRETEST and simply follow the arrows.

Learning guides for individualized instructional units can be developed locally, or a school can participate in one of the comprehensive individualized instructional programs made available to schools. Regardless of the approach, there will be heavy emphasis on testing and evaluation. All such programs typically involve (1) pretesting to determine entry behavior and to place the pupil properly in the program, (2) testing during the program to monitor pupil progress, and (3) posttesting to determine the pupil's final mastery of the instructional objectives. Thus, the same types of testing used in conventional classroom instruction are also used in programs for individualizing instruction. Here, however, the testing function is even more crucial because periodic testing is used to guide and direct pupil progress on self-contained, individual learning units.

FIGURE 18.1
Flow chart for individualized instructional unit.

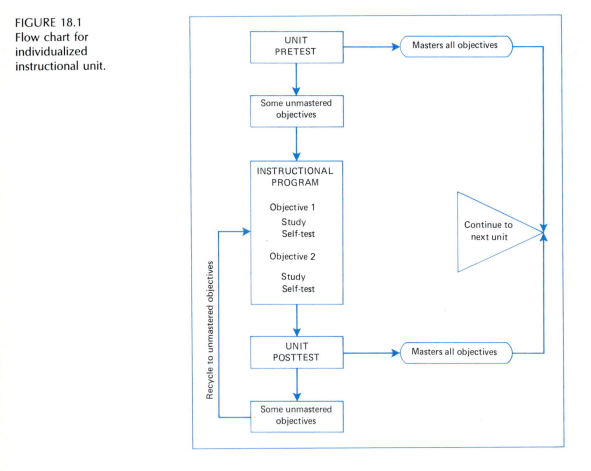

Mainstreaming

The Education for All Handicapped Children Act (Public Law 94-142) passed by the United States Congress in 1975 and put into effect in the fall of 1977 is having far-reaching effects on school practice.[13] This law has numerous provisions, but it is essentially designed to give the handicapped, from age 3 to 21, access to equal educational opportunity by placing them in the *least restrictive environment* and providing adequate resources and support. Handicapped pupils must be placed with their peers in the regular classroom unless other placement can be justified by suitable criteria. The term *mainstreaming* has been widely used to represent the educational provisions for helping handicapped pupils attain their rights under this law. Although mainstreaming requires shifting many pupils from special classes to regular classes, the term does not simply mean the placement of handicapped pupils in regular classrooms. Instead, it encompasses all activities for establishing an environment that is most conducive to the learning and development of the handicapped.

As might be expected, testing and evaluation play a significant role in the mainstreaming of handicapped pupils. They aid in assessing their special needs, planning *individualized educational programs* (IEPS) for them, determining their proper placement in the school program, and evaluating their learning progress and adjustment. Thus, as classroom teachers and other school personnel work more closely with the handicapped, they are likely to be exposed to a broader range of test data than in the past. The results of various psychological tests that were formerly used only by the school psychologist and special education teachers may now also need to be interpreted and used by regular classroom teachers. In addition, classroom teachers will likely be expected to assess and report periodically on the progress and adjustment of handicapped pupils placed in their classes. In short, mainstreaming requires more testing and demands that classroom teachers learn more about testing and evaluation.

National Assessment of Educational Progress

The National Assessment of Educational Progress (NAEP) is a nationwide testing program designed to obtain censuslike data for reporting to the public on the educational attainment of children and young adults in this country. Testing began in 1969 and has been continued annually, with reports to the public through the news media, professional associations, and various publications.

During the first twenty years of operation, assessments were administered to national samples of students in reading, writing, mathematics, science, citizenship, literature, social studies, career and occupational development, art, music, history, geography, and computer competence. In each area, test exercises are designed to

---

[13]P. S. Strain and M. M. Kerr, *Mainstreaming of Children in Schools* (New York: Academic Press, 1981).

measure specific objectives so that criterion-referenced interpretation of the data is possible. The exercises measure knowledge, understanding, skills, and attitudes and include a variety of item types. In addition to short-answer and essay questions, the exercises include performance tasks, observations, interviews, questionnaires, and sample products (e.g., art).

In the early days of NAEP, assessment exercises in one or more of the content areas were given to samples of 9-, 13-, and 17-year-old children each year. Exercises were also given to samples of young adults from age 26 to 35 on a regular basis. Since 1980 the assessments have taken place every other year, and in recent years samples have been selected to represent students in selected grades (3, 7, and 11 before 1988 and 4, 8, and 12 since that time) as well as age levels.

To determine changes in performance over time, some of the exercises in each area are repeated after a period of several years. Some of these items are used to report results after each assessment, while others are maintained as secure items for use in future assessments.

Prior to the 1984 assessment, results were reported separately by item. The reports simply indicated the percentage of individuals in each age group that gave the correct and incorrect answers to each exercise. Since 1984, the item level results have been supplemented by results on scales in each content area. Graphs of trends such as the one shown in Figure 18.2 plot the changes in typical performance of 9-, 13-, and 17-year-old children throughout the nation. Trends are also reported separately by geographic region, gender, and race/ethnicity. No results are given for individual students (each student completes only a sample of the exercises) or for individual schools. However, Congress passed legislation in 1988 that will allow state-by-state comparisons on a voluntary and experimental basis in 1990 and 1992.

The intent of the program is not to compare individuals or schools, but to report to the public, policy makers, and the profession on (1) what level of educational achievement is being attained by various age groups, (2) what changes in achievement have taken place over time, and (3) what differences there are in achievement and in changes in achievement for major regions of the country, gender, and racial/ethnic groups. Whether the list of purposes will be expanded to include state-by-state comparisons will depend on the reactions of Congress to the evaluations of the 1990 and 1992 effort to get states to volunteer to participate in such comparisons.

Current Measurement Trends and Issues

In recent years, numerous changes have taken place in educational measurement. In some instances, the various educational testing and assessment programs that we have been discussing have helped create or hasten these changes, whereas in others they have simply made the changes more visible. The rapidly expanding role of testing in education has also been paralleled by mounting criticisms of testing and its possible hazards to individuals and groups. In this section, we shall briefly

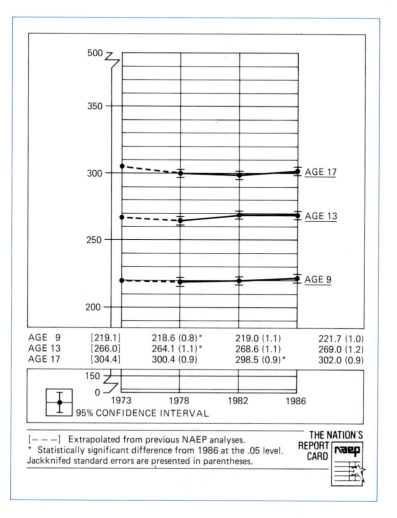

FIGURE 18.2
National Trends in
Average Mathematics
Proficiency for 9-, 13-,
and 17-year-olds:
1973–1986, from *The
Mathematics Report
Card: Are We
Measuring Up?*
Princeton, N.J.: The
National Assessment of
Educational Progress
(1988).

AGE 9	[219.1]	218.6 (0.8)*	219.0 (1.1)	221.7 (1.0)
AGE 13	[266.0]	264.1 (1.1)*	268.6 (1.1)	269.0 (1.2)
AGE 17	[304.4]	300.4 (0.9)	298.5 (0.9)*	302.0 (0.9)

95% CONFIDENCE INTERVAL

[− − −] Extrapolated from previous NAEP analyses.
* Statistically significant difference from 1986 at the .05 level.
Jackknifed standard errors are presented in parentheses.

THE NATION'S
REPORT
CARD

describe some of the more important trends and issues accompanying current developments in educational measurement.

Some Apparent Trends

Describing trends in any area is hazardous, and it is especially so in education. There seem to be so many new developments in education that turn out to be fads—which quickly rise and even more quickly fall. Be that as it may, the following changes in educational measurement seem to have enough breadth and staying power to represent trends. We have already considered changes that have taken place in the use of tests for purposes of accountability and the use of testing in classroom instruction. In addition to these trends in test use, significant changes are taking place in the technology of testing and in the public concern about testing.

Computerized Test Administration. With the rapid growth in the availability and power of relatively low-cost microcomputers, it is not surprising that the use of computers to administer tests is becoming increasingly common. Simply using a computer to administer items from a paper-and-pencil test can have some advantages (e.g., greater flexibility of administration, the speed with which scores can be returned, and the separation of speed and accuracy of responses). The potentially more significant changes, however, depend on using the computer to do things that cannot be reasonably accomplished with paper-and-pencil tests.

The most straightforward change that has the potential of improving both the efficiency with which information is handled and the quality of that information is the use of the computer to administer adaptive tests, that is, tests in which the choice of the next item to administer is based upon the previous responses of the test taker. The design of an adaptive test usually starts with the administration of an item that is expected to be of middle difficulty. The second and subsequent items to be administered are determined by the responses of the test taker. In general, if a test taker answers an item correctly, then the computer will select a somewhat more difficult item to administer next. Conversely, a somewhat easier item is administered following an incorrect answer. Testing is stopped when the estimates of the individual's performance reach some predetermined level of precision or when some pragmatic maximum number of items has been administered.

Adaptive testing is expected to enhance the efficiency and the precision with which certain types of knowledge, skills, and abilities are measured. But if adaptive tests just administer items of the type already in use in a better way, the full potential of the use of computers for the administration of tests still will not be realized. The appeal of computers as testing devices is not limited to doing better what we already do. Their potential to measure proficiencies that are not measured well by conventional paper-and-pencil tests is even more appealing.

Simulations can be used to present test takers with problems that have greater realism and more apparent relevance than problems that are commonly found on paper-and-pencil tests. Patient management problems that have been used for some time in medical education and in certification testing for physicians provide an illustration of the type of simulation tests that are apt to be seen in the future as computerized test administration becomes more common. Patient management problems simulate aspects of the job of a physician. The test taker is initially presented with a limited set of information about a patient, such as a verbal description of symptoms of the type that a patient might provide at the start of a visit. The test taker then has a variety of options such as getting a patient history, ordering laboratory tests, or deciding on a course of treatment. Requested information is provided and new options then can be followed by the test taker until a diagnosis is made and a course of treatment is prescribed.

Computer administered problem simulations along the lines of patient management problems have a number of potential advantages over current paper-and-pencil tests in many content areas. They provide a means of going beyond the sort of factual recall that is sometimes overemphasized on paper-and-pencil tests. They focus attention on the use of information to solve realistic problems. They can help assess not only the product of a student's thinking, but the process that the student uses to solve a problem, including the way in which the problem is attacked, the efficiency of the solution, and the number of hints that may be needed to solve the problem.

Item Response Theory.   Test development and test evaluation has depended heavily on mathematical models that have been in use since the early part of this century. These models, which are commonly referred to as classical test theory, have provided the basis for item analysis, the evaluation of test reliability, and the equating of scores from different forms of a test. While still useful and widely used, many of the functions that were once served by classical test theory are increasingly being taken over by item response theory.

Item response theory (IRT) focuses on responses to individual test items rather than total test scores. Using substantially more complicated mathematical models than those used in classical test theory, IRT provides a mathematical equation that predicts the probability of a correct response to a test item as a function of the test taker's "ability" (i.e., the level of an individual's proficiency or knowledge in the area being tested) and certain characteristics of the item. Item characteristics, or parameters, provide information that can be used in evaluating items, designing tests for specific purposes, and solving several important educational measurement problems that could not be solved within the confines of classical test theory. The specific item characteristics that are assessed depend on the specifics of the IRT model but may include a parameter for item difficulty, a parameter for item discriminating power, and a parameter to take into account the fact that an individual always has a nonzero probability of answering a multiple-choice item correctly simply by guessing.

Although the mathematics of IRT are beyond the scope of this book, the basic idea is straightforward, and the practical implications of the theory are substantial. The basic concepts are similar to a notion that Binet used in analyzing items for his intelligence test. Binet's concept was that the proportion of children who know the answer to a question should increase with age. IRT uses ability as defined by the total set of items on a test rather than age and is much more precise in specifying how the probability of a correct response should increase with ability. However, the idea that the probability of, say, answering an algebra item correctly should increase with increases in the mathematical knowledge of the test takers is intuitively reasonable.

IRT is now being used by a number of test publishers for some of the purposes that traditional item analysis and classical reliability estimation have served. For example, IRT provides statistics that can be used by the test developer to select tryout items to use on the final version of the test. It also provides a basis for estimating the standard error of measurement as a function of a person's estimated proficiency level.

In addition to providing an alternative means of doing what classical theory already does rather well, IRT provides the basis for doing some things that classical theory does not. It provides the basis, for example, of customized testing and computerized adaptive testing. Each of these uses is becoming increasingly common and important.

A customized test, for example, might be assembled to meet the particular specifications of a state or district but for which normative comparisons to the nation as a whole are desired. Since the customized test is administered only in the particular state or district for which it was specially constructed, there would seem to be no basis for comparing the performance of the state or district to the nation as a whole. However, if enough of the items with the right specifications are included on both the customized test and a nationally normed test, then IRT can be used to convert scores on the customized test to the scale of the norm-referenced test.

In computerized adaptive testing, different test takers are administered different test items, with the more able individuals being administered harder items. Just as it would be inappropriate to compare the ability of two high jumpers, both of whom cleared the bar on 7 out 10 attempts when the bar was set at heights between 6 feet and 7 feet for one jumper but set at heights of 5 feet to 6 feet for the second jumper, it also would be inappropriate to compare the performance of two individuals on a computerized adaptive test using a simple number-right score. Here, as with our customized test, IRT is needed to make the results comparable. It not only provides the basis for scoring the tests, but it also provides the basis for deciding which item should be administered next by the computer and when enough test items have been administered.

Public Concern About Testing. Decisions about the selection, administration, and use of educational tests are no longer left to the educator alone: The public has become an active and vocal partner. At the state level, mandated assessment programs have been imposed on the schools as a result of the public demand for evidence of the school programs' effectiveness. In some states, the public at large has participated, through selected groups, in determining the objectives and standards of the statewide assessment programs. In other states in which competency testing has been made the responsibility of the local school district, parent groups often help shape the programs. It is interesting to note that the concern of state legislators and the general public with the quality of school programs has created a demand for more testing in the schools—not less.

During the expansion of testing programs, there also has been some concern that there is too much testing in the schools, especially for high school students. In addition to taking the tests in the local school program, these students may also have to take one or more state competency tests and several college admissions tests. It is feared that the heavy demand on their time and energy might detract from their schoolwork and that the external testing programs may cause undesirable shifts in the school's curriculum. When teachers and schools are judged by how well students perform on state competency tests and by how many students are accepted by leading colleges, direct preparation for the tests is likely to enter into classroom activities and thereby distort the curriculum.

Probably the greatest public concern has been with the social consequences of testing, that testing may threaten the rights and opportunities of individuals and groups. This concern has shown up in the form of attacks on standardized tests and the testing industry, new legislation affecting testing, calls for a moratorium on standardized testing, and charges that tests are biased and discriminatory. Although there is certainly some justification for the public's concern with the social consequences of testing, much of the furor has been caused by the misinterpretation and misuse of test scores. Some of the current issues surrounding the testing controversy will be discussed in the following section.

Concerns and Issues

Although educational testing always has had its friendly and unfriendly critics, in recent years there has been increasing concern about the role of testing in the schools, especially the use of standardized tests. Critical issues concern the nature and quality of the tests, the possible harmful effects of testing on pupils, the fairness of the tests to minorities, and the potential hazards of testing to the individual's right to privacy.

Nature and Quality of Tests. A longstanding criticism of standardized tests is directed primarily at the use of multiple-choice items. In the early 1960s, critics such as Hoffmann[14] contended that the multiple-choice item, which is the main item type used in standardized tests, penalized the more intelligent original thinkers. He supported his claims by reviewing items from standardized tests and showing how the more brilliant and creative students were likely to see implications in the items that would question the correctness of the keyed answers. Although Hoffman obviously was able to discover some defective items that appeared in standardized tests, his criticisms seemed to go well beyond the evidence presented. On the positive side, he probably encouraged test publishers to supplement statistical item analysis with a more careful logical analysis of test items.

Multiple-choice questions continue to be the brunt of criticisms made by both specialists in educational measurement who seek ways of improving educational tests and by critics who would like to eliminate standardized testing. Frederiksen,[15] a major contributor to the field of measurement, for example, has argued that multiple-choice items place too much emphasis on "well-structured problems" when problems of greatest interest both in and out of school are often "ill structured" where skills such as problem identification and hypothesis generation are often as important as problem solution. Such criticisms have led to increased emphasis on open-ended questions and the design of computer simulation tests.

Critics such as Owen,[16] on the other hand, are more sweeping in their criticism. Owen's focus of criticism is frequently on Educational Testing Service and the Scholastic Aptitude Test, a test that he thinks lacks educational value and is more a measure of the degree to which the test taker knows the tricks of the test constructors and can think like they do than it is a measure of scholastic aptitude. In keeping with the latter view, he attempts to provide advice on how to beat the test, a topic that we will consider when we turn our attention to the coaching controversy.

[14]B. C. Hoffman, *The Tyranny of Testing* (New York: Crowell-Collier, 1962).

[15]N. Frederiksen, "The Real Test Bias," *American Psychologist* 39 (1984): 193–202.

[16]D. Owen, *None of the Above: Behind the Myth of Scholastic Aptitude* (Boston: Houghton Mifflin, 1985).

Owen's criticisms of multiple-choice items do not add that much of substance to the earlier criticisms of Hoffmann and others, but they are more strident in tone.

Another type of criticism, that tests measure only limited aspects of an individual, has also received considerable attention. This criticism is well founded. Tests do measure specific and limited samples of behavior. Aptitude tests typically measure samples of verbal and quantitative skills useful in predicting school success, and achievement tests measure samples of pupil performance on particular learning tasks useful in assessing educational progress. Both fulfill their limited functions quite well, but the difficulty arises when we expect more of them than was intended. For example, both the advocates and critics of college admissions testing sometimes assume that the tests measure all that is needed for success in college and beyond. This tendency to read into test scores more than they really tell has been called the *whole person fallacy* by W. W. Trunbull, the former president of the Educational Testing Service. A quotation from one of its publications makes clear the limited nature of these tests:

> Ability and academic achievement occupy an Olympian perch on the prestige ladder. Yet it is widely agreed that motivation, creativity, personal honesty, intuition, even the degree of social consciousness play significant roles in the struggle for the most cherished of American ideals — "success in life." Admission tests thus measure a relatively narrow segment of the human potential.[17]

Much of the misinterpretation and misuse of test scores would be avoided if the limited information that tests provide was more widely recognized. In college admission decisions, as well as in all other educational decisions, test scores provide just one type of information and always should be supplemented by past records of achievement and other types of assessment data. *No major educational decision should ever be based on test scores alone.*

The reliability and validity of tests also have been subject to criticism. This usually has been by uninformed critics who mistakenly believe that tests should be completely reliable and provide perfect predictions. These, of course, are unrealistic expectations. All measurement is subject to error, and predictions in all areas are fallible. Rather than compare the tests' reliability and validity with nonexistent ideal standards, they should be compared with the alternatives. Would our judgments of aptitude and achievement be more reliable without test results? Would our predictions of future school or occupational success be more valid without the additional information supplied by tests? Would our educational decisions be improved if we stopped using tests? We doubt it! Qualified users of tests take into account the possible error in test scores during test interpretation and use, and they combine test scores with other relevant information when making educational decisions. To argue that better educational decisions would be made without test scores is to argue that better decisions are made when less information is available. Test scores are certainly fallible, but probably less so than most of the other types of information that enter into educational decisions.

[17]*ETS Developments*, vol. 26 (Princeton, N.J.: Educational Testing Service, Spring 1979).

What Are the Consequences of Not Testing?*

"If the use of educational tests were abandoned, the encouragement and reward of individualized efforts to learn would be more difficult. Excellence in programs of education would become less tangible as a goal and less demonstrable as an attainment. Educational opportunities would be extended less on the basis of aptitude and merit and more on the basis of ancestry and influence; social-class barriers would become less permeable. Decisions on important issues of curriculum and method would be made less on the basis of solid evidence and more on the basis of prejudice or caprice. These, it seems to us, are likely to be the more harmful consequences, by far. Let us not forgo the wise use of good tests."

*R. L. Ebel, *Practical Problems in Educational Measurement* (Lexington, Mass.: Heath, 1980), pp. 34–35.

Effects of Testing on Pupils. Critics of testing have charged that testing is likely to have a number of undesirable effects on pupils. Some of the most commonly mentioned charges directed toward the use of aptitude and achievement tests are listed here with brief comments.

Criticism 1: Tests create anxiety. There is no doubt that anxiety increases during testing. For most pupils, it motivates them to perform better. For a relatively few, test anxiety may be so great that it interferes with test performance. These typically are pupils who are generally anxious, and the test simply adds to their already high level of anxiety. A number of steps can be taken to reduce test anxiety, such as thoroughly preparing for the test, taking practice exercises, and using liberal time limits. Fortunately, many test publishers in recent years have provided practice tests and shifted from speed tests to power tests. This should help, but it is still necessary to observe pupils carefully during testing and to discount the scores of overly anxious pupils. There is little likelihood, however, that test anxiety has any lasting influence on a pupil's mental health.

Criticism 2: Tests categorize and label pupils. Categorizing and labeling individuals is a serious problem in education, just as it is in our general society. It is all too easy to place individuals in pigeonholes and apply labels that then determine, at least in part, how they are viewed and treated. Classifying pupils in terms of levels of mental ability has probably caused the greatest concern in education. Critics contend that when pupils are classified as "mentally retarded," for example, it influences how teachers and peers view them, how they view themselves, and the kind of school program they are provided. When pupils are *mislabeled* as mentally retarded, as has been the case with some racial and cultural minorities, the problem is compounded. At least some of the support for mainstreaming handicapped pupils has come from the desire to avoid the categorizing and labeling that accompanies special education classes.

Classifying pupils into various types of learning groups can more efficiently use the teacher's time and the school's resources. However, any grouping system needs to take into account that tests measure only a limited sample of a pupil's abilities and that pupils are continuously changing and developing. Keeping the groupings tentative and flexible and regrouping for different subjects (e.g., reading, math) can avoid most of the undesirable features of grouping. It is when the categories are viewed as rigid and permanent that labeling becomes a serious problem. In such cases, it is not the test that should be blamed, but the user of the test.

Criticism 3: Tests damage pupils' self-concepts. This is one of the most serious charges against testing and requires the attention of teachers, counselors, and other users of tests. The improper use of tests may indeed contribute to distorted self-concepts. The stereotyping of pupils, mentioned in the previous section, is one misuse of tests that is likely to have an undesirable influence on a pupil's self-concept. Another is the inadequate interpretation of test scores that may cause pupils to overgeneralize from the results. It is certainly discouraging to receive low scores on tests, and it is easy to see how pupils might develop a general sense of failure unless the results are properly interpreted. Low-scoring pupils need to be made aware that aptitude and achievement tests are limited measures and that the results can change. In addition, the possibility of overgeneralizing from low test scores will be lessened if the pupil's positive accomplishments and characteristics are mentioned during the interpretation. When properly interpreted and used, tests can help pupils develop a realistic understanding of their strengths and weaknesses and, thereby, contribute to improved learning and a positive self-image.

Criticism 4: Tests create self-fulfilling prophecies. This criticism has been directed primarily toward intelligence or scholastic aptitude tests. The argument is that test scores create teacher expectations concerning the achievement of individual pupils; the teacher then teaches in accordance with those expectations, and the pupils respond by achieving to their expected level—a self-fulfilled prophecy. Thus, those who are expected to achieve more do achieve more, and those who are expected to achieve less do achieve less. This so-called *Pygmalion* effect received strong support from a widely heralded study by Rosenthal and Jacobsen,[18] even though the study was later challenged by other researchers.[19] The belief that teacher expectations enhance or hinder a pupil's achievement is widely held, and the role of testing in creating these expectations is certainly worthy of further research.

In summary, there is some merit in the various criticisms concerning the possible undesirable effects of tests on pupils. But these criticisms should be directed at the users of the tests rather than the tests themselves. The same persons who misuse test results are likely to misuse alternative types of information that are even less

[18]R. Rosenthal and L. Jacobsen, *Pygmalion in the Classroom* (New York: Holt, Rinehart & Winston, 1968).

[19]J. D. Elashoff and R. E. Snow, eds., *Pygmalion Reconsidered* (Worthington, Ohio: Charles A. Jones, 1971); C. K. West and T. H. Anderson, "The Question of Preponderant Causation in Teacher Expectancy Research," *Review of Educational Research* 46 (1976): 613–630.

accurate and objective. Thus, the solution is not to stop using tests, but to start using tests and other data sources more effectively. When tests are used in a positive manner, that is, to help pupils improve their learning and development, the consequences are likely to be desirable rather than undesirable.

Fairness of Tests to Minorities. The issue of test fairness to racial and cultural minorities has received increasing attention over the years. Concern with the fairness of tests has paralleled the general public concern with providing equal rights and opportunities to all United States citizens. Critics have charged that tests are biased and discriminatory and impede educational and occupational opportunities for minorities. The charge of test bias or unfairness can be examined from two viewpoints: (1) the possible presence of *bias* in the *test content* and (2) the possibly *unfair use* of test results. These factors are undoubtedly related, but we shall discuss them separately.

Much of the concern with bias in test content focuses on the fact that some minorities frequently earn lower test scores than do their more advantaged peers. As Gardner pointed out, however, low test scores do not *necessarily* indicate test bias:

> Lower scores *alone* on an achievement test do not signify bias. If they did, then every spelling test would be biased against poor spellers, every vocabulary test against persons who had poor vocabularies, and every shorthand test against persons who had never learned shorthand. . . .[20]

Thus, in evaluating the possible presence of bias in test content, it is important to distinguish between the performance the test is intended to measure and factors that may distort the scores unfairly. In testing arithmetic skills with story problems, for example, it is important to keep the reading level low so that the test scores are not contaminated by reading ability. If the reading is too difficult, poor readers will obtain lower scores than warranted, and thus, the test will be biased against them. Because a particular minority group may have a disproportionately large number of poor readers, the test may be more biased for that minority group than for other pupils. But if the test of arithmetic skill is *not* contaminated by reading or other factors, low scores will simply indicate lack of arithmetic skills. Such a test is fair to everyone even if the test scores indicate cultural differences in the mastery of arithmetic.

In the past, standardized tests typically emphasized content and values that were more familiar to white middle-class pupils than to racial or cultural minorities and pupils of lower socioeconomic status. Thus, the content of some scholastic aptitude tests contained vocabulary, pictures, and objects that minorities had less opportunity to learn in their culture. Similarly, some reading tests contained stories and situations that were unrelated to their life experiences. In addition, racial and cultural minorities were seldom represented in pictures, stories, and other test content. And when they were, it was sometimes in an offensive manner. How much these types of bias might have lowered the scores of individual pupils is impossible to say, but

---

[20]E. F. Gardner, "Bias," *NCME Measurement in Education*, National Council on Measurement in Education 9 (1978).

most persons familiar with testing would acknowledge some adverse effect. Fortunately, test publishers have taken steps to correct the situation. Test publishers now employ staff members representing various racial and cultural minorities, and new tests being developed are routinely reviewed for content that might be biased or offensive to minority groups. Statistical analysis is also being used to detect and remove biased test items.[21]

The most controversial problems concerning the fair use of tests with minority groups are encountered when aptitude tests are used as a basis for educational and vocational selection. Much of the difficulty here is with the definition of fair test use. One view is that a test is fair or unbiased if it predicts as accurately for minority groups as it does for the majority group. This traditional view, which favors a common cutoff score for selection, has been challenged as being unfair to minority groups because they often earn lower test scores, and thus, a smaller proportion of qualified individuals tends to be selected. Alternative definitions of test fairness favor some type of adjustment such as separate cutoff scores or bonus points for some minorities.[22]

Although the fair use of tests in selecting students and employees is widely debated in the professional literature, whether minority group membership is to be ignored or given special consideration in selection, the decisions will not be determined by educators or psychologists. The fair use of tests in selection is part of a larger issue that must be settled by society through court rulings. Stated in simplified form, the issue is how equal educational and occupational opportunities can be best provided for members of minority groups without infringing on the rights of other individuals.

Sex Bias. In recent years, considerable attention also has been given to the possibility of sex bias in tests. Critics have objected to the excessive use of masculine pronouns and to the portrayal of women mainly is such traditional roles as homemaker, nurse, and secretary. Although there is no question that such bias has been present in tests, as it has been in textbooks and other educational materials, the effect of the bias on test performance has not been established. A study of the influence of male and female references in reading passages, for example, showed no effect on test performance.[23] Despite such negative results, the removal of sex bias from all educational materials is desirable on other grounds, and test and book publishers are making concerted efforts to correct the situation.

The use of scores on tests such as the Preliminary Scholastic Aptitude Test (PSAT) and the Scholastic Aptitude Test (SAT) as the basis of awarding college scholarships has focused attention on the issue of sex bias in tests in recent years. On the mathematics section of the PSAT or the SAT the average score for boys has been higher than the average score for girls and there have been more boys than

[21]For a recent discussion of the use of these techniques and related issues, see N. S. Cole and P. A. Moss, "Bias in Test Use," in *Educational Measurement*, 3d ed., ed. R. L. Linn (New York: Macmillan, 1989).

[22]See, for example, N. S. Cole and P. A. Moss, "Bias in Test Use," for a discussion of these perspectives on bias.

[23]J. D. Moss and F. G. Brown, "Sex Bias and Academic Performance: An Empirical Study," *Journal of Educational Measurement* (1979): 197–201.

girls with very high scores for many years. In recent years, the average score for boys is also slightly higher than the average for girls on the verbal section of these tests. As a consequence, when the sum of the verbal and math scores are used to award scholarships, a substantially larger percentage of scholarships are awarded to boys than to girls. For example, in 1986, 61 percent of the National Merit Scholarship semifinalists were boys.

As in the case of differences in scores of racial/ethnic groups, the existence of a difference in average scores for boys and girls does not necessarily imply that the test is biased. There are, for example, differences in the amount of mathematics taken by girls and boys in high school and these differences may lead to differences in the scores on the mathematics tests. Whatever the cause of the differences, however, it does not change the fact that use of the tests alone results in a larger proportion of scholarships being awarded to boys than to girls, despite the fact that girls earn higher grades in school than boys on the average. Judgments about the proper use of test scores in making decisions about scholarships must rest on much more than technical evaluations of the tests and the degree to which the scores reflect real differences in knowledge, skills, and developed abilities rather than unintentional biases in the tests. Such judgments also involve questions of social values and social policy.

Although not a minority group, women have had some of the same problems as minorities have in attempting to obtain equal educational and occupational opportunities. Thus, in the use of test results in career planning, care needs to be taken so that test scores are not unfairly used to direct females away from certain occupations. For example, girls tend to score lower than boys on mechanical comprehension tests and to have lower mechanical interest scores. Although these differences probably reflect cultural influences rather than sex bias in the tests, it would be unfortunate if such results were used to limit the occupations girls might consider as possible careers.

Invasion of Privacy. The most frequently expressed concern with invasion of privacy has been with personality and adjustment inventories. Many of these instruments ask individuals to respond to questions concerning family relationships, sexual attitudes and behavior, and religious beliefs. Such questions are viewed as an invasion of privacy and, thus, ones that the school has no right to ask. The problem is most serious when such inventories are routinely administered to all pupils, as was once the practice in schools. The problem is less serious when the pupil is seeking help from a qualified counselor and is asked to respond to an inventory as part of the counseling process. Ever since the 1965 United States congressional investigations into the use of personality inventories in government, industry, and education, the routine use of personality inventories in school has practically disappeared. Their use is now restricted primarily to counseling situations, where they can be interpreted and used by psychologically trained counselors. In such cases, it is recommended that the completed inventory and scores be destroyed when they are no longer needed in counseling, to prevent them from falling into the hands of unqualified persons who might misinterpret or misuse the results.

The invasion of privacy issue is not limited to personality inventories but also affects personal information obtained for school records, college admission programs, and other external testing and data-gathering programs. When invasion of privacy is considered a possibility, *informed consent* should be obtained from pupils or parents. This involves making the interested persons aware of the purpose for which the information is being obtained, the nature of the information sought, and the ways in which the information might be used.

In protecting pupil privacy, it is also necessary to keep test scores and other personal information confidential. Test scores, grades, and other evaluative data should *not* be posted. They should be shared only with the pupil, the pupil's parents, and other qualified professionals in the school district who have a legitimate need for the information. Federal law states that information from school records must *not* be released to persons other than those mentioned without the written permission of parents or pupils if eighteen years of age or older. The law also gives parents, and pupils eighteen or older, the right to examine a pupil's school records and to challenge the contents. This legal right to review and dispute school records should aid in detecting errors in recording test scores and other evaluation data. It should also help remove biased, irrelevant, and obsolete material. Teachers and other school personnel are now under pressure to make sure that the information entered in pupils' records is objective, accurate, and relevant. Let us hope that the law does not inhibit teachers from entering useful information in pupils' files.

Coaching.   The degree to which coaching or short-term preparation for taking tests can improve scores has been a topic of considerable controversy for tests such as the SAT for a number of years. Coaching agencies make claims that dramatic increases in test scores can be achieved as the result of the short-term preparation that they provide. The College Board and Educational Testing Service, on the other hand, argue that gains from coaching are modest. Since both sides have a vested interest, it is difficult for parents and students to be able to evaluate the conflicting claims of the coaching and testing organizations.

A recent review of the available evidence regarding the effects of coaching led to the following conclusions.[24]

> Testing organizations, the College Board and Educational Testing Service in particular, insist that all verifiable evidence indicates that abilities measured by the SAT and similar admissions tests develop slowly, are largely insensitive to brief interventions involving drill and practice, and are quite valid for their intended purposes. The majority of the published evidence in the technical literature supports this view. It is unfortunate that the most dramatic claims to the contrary come, with rare exceptions, from outside the peer review process characteristic of modern scientific practice.
>
> Individual students must inevitably assess the data for themselves. The evidence, by no means conclusive, suggests that not all students benefit equally from special instruction. Highly motivated students, students whose high school record and other accomplishments

[24]L. Bond, "The Effects of Special Preparation on Measures of Scholastic Ability," in *Educational Measurement*, 3d ed., ed. R. L. Linn (New York: Macmillan, 1989).

are inconsistent with their test performance, and students who habitually use inefficient test taking strategies are likely to benefit most.

Apparently, intensive drill on sample test items is of limited value in preparing for SAT, but better test-taking skills and reviewing mathematics concepts might improve the performance of some students. It may be that the coaching schools that claim to increase scores do benefit students in these ways. It is also possible, of course, that some use such *extensive* tutoring that the students' general level of understanding of verbal and mathematical concepts is increased. This would not only improve test performance but would also improve performance later in college and, thus, be generally beneficial to the students. In such cases, the predictive value of the test scores would not be lessened because higher test scores would be accompanied by improved learning ability (see box).

Influence of Coaching on Student Performance and Test Validity*

There are three basic ways that coaching may improve test scores:

1. Coaching "may genuinely improve the abilities and skills measured by the test." This would enhance test validity because the increased test scores would be accompanied by increased learning ability and, thus, improved school performance.
2. Coaching "may enhance test-taking sophistication or reduce anxiety often associated with taking tests." This would enhance test validity because the improved "testwiseness" would result in "increased test scores that are now more accurate assessments of student ability."
3. Coaching "may teach test-taking stratagems and answer-selection tricks." This would have a negative effect on test validity because it would result in "increased test scores that are inaccurately high as assessments of student ability." This possibility is seldom a problem with professionally prepared tests because the items are well constructed and rarely contain extraneous clues, the directions clearly indicate test strategy, and "test-familiarization materials and practice tests" are provided to enhance and equate testwiseness.

"Thus, of the three main possible outcomes of coaching, two are good for both student performance and test validity while the third is a minor and rarely demonstrable problem with professionally developed tests."

*Adapted from S. Messick, "Issues of Effectiveness and Equity in the Coaching Controversy: Implications for Educational and Testing Practice," *Educational Psychologist* 17 (Summer 1982): 67–91.

Summary

There are a number of programs involving testing that you are likely to encounter in the school. As a teacher you may be directly involved in some of the programs. Others you may simply need to know about so that you can serve as an informed professional in dealing with pupils, parents, and the general public. These programs have generally contributed to expanded testing in the schools, which in turn have created new trends and raised concerns about testing.

Demands for accountability have led to substantial increases in the amount of testing in the schools and in the importance that is attached to the scores. Minimum-competency testing programs that required students to pass tests to receive high school diplomas or to be promoted to the next grade grew rapidly throughout the country in the late 1970s. These programs were soon followed by the introduction of testing requirements for teacher certification and, in some cases, recertification. Demands for comparisons of schools, school districts, and states in terms of pupil achievement test scores have led to the introduction of still more testing requirements and increased the stakes of testing for teachers and school administrators.

Increased testing in classroom instruction has resulted from the greater use of tests to improve learning. This is especially apparent in programs of mastery learning and individualized instruction. Both typically include (1) a pretest to determine entry behavior, (2) formative tests to monitor learning progress and provide diagnostic–corrective feedback, and (3) summative tests to measure final mastery. With the advent of microcomputers, much of the testing can be done with custom-designed tests that are printed by the computer. Test publishers now have software programs that provide these and other functions needed for instructional management systems.

Mainstreaming, which requires shifting handicapped pupils from special classes to regular classrooms unless adequate criteria can justify other placement, has become public law throughout the United States. It requires increased testing in the schools and greater knowledge about testing on the part of teachers and other school personnel.

The National Assessment of Educational Progress (NAEP) periodically tests a sample of children and young adults to obtain censuslike data concerning the nation's educational progress. The tests measure the attainment of specific objectives in all of the major areas of school learning, and the results are reported to the public through the news media, professional associations, and various publications. The most recent legislation concerning NAEP includes provisions for the use of the program to make state-by-state comparisons on a voluntary and experimental basis, a practice that, if continued, could increase the importance of NAEP in the future.

A number of changes in educational measurement have been broad enough and persistent enough to be identified as possible trends. In addition to the expanded uses of tests that have just been summarized, technological developments are changing the nature of testing. Most notable of these developments is the use of computers to administer tests and the use of item response theory. Computers provide a means of making tests adaptive to the individual test taker and the construction of realistic simulations to test problem solving skills. Item response theory provides the mathematical foundation for solving a number of practical testing problems.

Critics of testing have raised a number of issues concerning the possible consequences of testing in the schools. Most of the criticism has been directed toward standardized tests, including such issues as the nature and quality of the tests, the possible harmful effects of testing on pupils, the fairness of tests to minorities and women, the hazards of testing to the individual's right to privacy, and the effects of coaching. Although most of the criticisms of testing have some merit, most problems are *not* caused by the *use* of tests, but by the *misuse* of tests. In most cases, tests provide results that are more objective, accurate, and relevant than alternative sources of information. What is needed is a more professional use of tests, with greater emphasis on ways they can be used to improve pupil learning and development.

Learning Exercises

1. List the reasons for and against the use of a statewide minimum-competency testing program.
2. Discuss the potential effects of the pressure to compare schools, districts, and states in terms of pupil achievement test scores on instruction and pupil learning.
3. Describe the different uses that are made of tests in mastery learning and individualized instruction programs.
4. What is *mainstreaming*? Why does it require knowledge of testing and evaluation.
5. Describe the purpose and function of the National Assessment of Educational Progress. In what ways might this program influence school instruction?
6. What types of testing do you think should be increased or decreased in the schools? Why?
7. List possible advantages and disadvantages for each of the apparent trends in educational measurement cited in this chapter.
8. Which criticisms of testing do you consider to be most serious? What steps should be taken to correct them?
9. What are the advantages of the legal requirement that parents and pupils be given access to school records? What problems might arise from this, and what solutions would you suggest?

Suggestions for Further Reading

Anastasi, A. *Psychological Testing*, 6th ed. New York: Macmillan, 1988. Chapter 3, "Social and Ethical Considerations in Testing," discusses the qualifications of test users and the issues related to the effective and fair use of tests.

Berk, R. A., ed. *Handbook of Methods for Detecting Test Bias*. Baltimore: Johns Hopkins University Press, 1982. Contains a series of articles on strategies and techniques for detecting test bias, including the advantages and disadvantages of the various bias detection methods.

BOND, L. "The Effects of Special Preparation on Measures of Scholastic Ability." In R. L. Linn, ed., *Educational Measurement*, 3d ed. New York: Macmillan, 1989, Chapter 11. Provides a review of the literature on coaching.

BUNDERSON, C. V.; INOUYE, D. K.; AND OLSEN, J. B. "The Four Generations of Computerized Educational Measurement." In R. L. Linn, ed., *Educational Measurement*, 3d ed. New York: Macmillan, 1989, Chapter 9. Discusses the uses currently being made of computers to administer tests as well as uses that are likely to be seen in the future.

COLE, N. S., AND MOSS, P. A. "Bias in Test Use." In R. L. Linn, ed., *Educational Measurement*, 3d ed. New York: Macmillan, 1989, Chapter 5. Discusses a wide range of issues related to bias in test use and interpretation.

GARDNER, E. "Some Aspects of the Use and Misuse of Standardized Aptitude and Achievement Tests." In A. K. Widgor and W. R. Garner, eds., *Ability Testing, Part 2*. Washington, D.C.: National Academy Press, 1982, pp. 315–332. Lists and briefly discusses the major uses and misuses of tests.

HALL, K. A. "Computer-Based Education." In *Encyclopedia of Educational Research*, 5th ed. New York: Macmillan, 1982, vol. 1, pp. 353–367. Describes the development of computer-based instruction and an evaluation of its benefits in education.

JAEGER, R. M. "Certification of Student Achievement." In R. L. Linn, ed., *Educational Measurement*, 3d ed. New York: Macmillan, 1989, Chapter 14. Discusses measurement and policy issues involved in minimum-competency testing programs.

LINN, R. "Ability Testing: Individual Differences, Prediction, and Differential Prediction." In A. K. Widgor and W. R. Garner, eds., *Ability Testing, Part 2*. Washington, D.C.: National Academy Press, 1982, pp. 335–388. A comprehensive review of prediction studies in schools and occupations, with special attention to socioeconomic, sex, social, and ethnic differences.

MEYEN, E. L., AND ALTMAN, R. "Special Education." In *Encyclopedia of Educational Research*, 5th ed. New York: Macmillan, 1982, vol. 4, pp. 1739–1749. Focuses on Public Law 94-142 (Education for All Handicapped Children Act) and its impact on the education of the handicapped. Also discusses the effects of minimum-competency testing on programming for the handicapped.

WIDGOR, A. K., AND GARNER, W. R., EDS. *Ability Testing: Uses, Consequences, and Controversies, Part I*. Washington, D.C.: National Academy Press, 1982. A report by the Committee on Ability Testing convened by the National Academy of Sciences to study the role of testing in American life. Covers the controversies surrounding testing, the nature of ability testing, the use of tests in education and industry, and the social and legal issues in testing. The final chapter is a summary and review of the role of ability testing.

Appendices

Appendix A

Elementary Statistics

Statistics is concerned with the organization, analysis, and interpretation of test scores and other numerical data. As a minimum, teachers should know those statistical techniques that enable them to (1) analyze and describe the results of measurement obtained in their own classrooms, (2) understand the statistics used in test manuals and research reports, and (3) interpret the various types of derived scores used in testing.

Many teachers shy away from statistics because they think it requires advanced mathematics and tedious calculations. However, the elementary statistical concepts and skills we shall deal with require neither. The calculations that can be quite tedious if conducted by hand can be done quite readily with a simple, inexpensive, hand-held calculator. Because of the availability of calculators for $20 or so that not only can do all of the intermediate calculations but have built-in procedures for even the most complicated statistic we shall discuss (the correlation coefficient), we have reduced the emphasis on calculation that was present in previous editions. We also have kept the mathematics to a minimum and will emphasize interpretation.

The statistics that we shall be concerned with here are known as *descriptive statistics*. As the term suggests, the emphasis is on describing a set of scores. The description may take the form of tables, graphs, or a single number (e.g., an average). Some of these modes of description are seen routinely in newspapers, magazines, and the evening television news. The purpose of these statistics is to summarize sets of numbers so that interesting features may be seen and understood more easily. For example, given a list of the high and low temperatures for each of the 365 days of a year, it would be possible to read them all and get a sense of how temperate the climate was and of seasonal changes. However, a graph of the average high and low temperatures for each of the twelve months of the year could convey the information much more efficiently and effectively.

We shall begin with a brief discussion of organizing data and displaying results in tables and graphs. We shall then turn to a discussion of three types of statistical measures. These are

1. Measures of central tendency (averages).
2. Measures of variability (spread of scores).
3. Measures of relationship (correlation).

The first two measures provide a convenient means of analyzing and describing a single set of test scores, and the last measure can be used to indicate the agreement between two sets of test scores obtained for the same pupils. All three are widely used in educational measurement and should be mastered by anyone working with test data.

Organizing and Displaying Scores

When test scores are obtained for a group of pupils they are usually in haphazard order as shown in Table A.1.

TABLE A.1
Set of Scores for a Class of 24 Pupils

Pupil	Midterm	Final	Pupil	Midterm	Final
A	78	85	M	65	80
B	67	71	N	92	93
C	88	78	O	53	69
D	74	71	P	65	75
E	97	91	Q	83	76
F	84	88	R	79	74
G	57	76	S	45	63
H	65	68	T	95	80
I	81	94	U	62	58
J	58	67	V	74	80
K	70	72	W	85	96
L	81	87	X	76	81

After careful inspection of the scores on the midterm exam for the 24 pupils we could see that scores in the 70's and 80's are fairly common, that only 3 pupils had scores in the 90's, and that one pupil had a score less than 50. Similar statements might be made after inspecting the scores on the final exam. We might even note that there is a tendency for the scores on the final to be slightly higher than those on the midterm and that, as might be expected, there is a tendency for pupils with high scores on the midterm also to receive relatively high scores on the final, though the relationship is far from perfect. For example, pupil E, who had the highest score on the midterm, had the fourth highest score on the final, while pupil W, who had the fifth highest score on the midterm, had the highest score on the final.

From our detailed inspection of the scores in Table A.1 we could actually get a rough idea of all three of the statistical concepts that we are concerned with here. These are the central tendency, or score obtained by the average student, the variability of the scores (e.g., the midterm scores range from a high of 97 to a low of 45, but most of the pupils have scores between 60 and 90), and the relationship between performance on the midterm and performance on the final. None of these characteristics of the scores is very easy to see from the haphazard arrangement of the scores, however, nor are they very precise. If we were working with 200 scores for all seventh-grade pupils at a junior high school or 3,000 scores for all third-grade pupils in a school district, the difficulty of seeing interesting characteristics and communicating them in a precise way would be much greater than for our class of 24 pupils. But even for our 24 pupils, we need to organize and display the scores to see these characteristics more easily and we need to do some simple calculations to quantify the information in a more precise fashion.

Simple Ranking

For some uses, it may be sufficient to arrange a set of scores in order of size and to assign a *rank* to each score. This will indicate the relative position of each score in the group. Ordinarily, the largest score is given a rank of 1, the second largest a rank of 2, and so on until all scores are ranked. The midterm scores from Table A.1 have been rearranged in order of size and assigned ranks to illustrate the procedure. The results are presented in Table A.2.

Note that when two or more pupils have the same score (the two 81's, the two 74's, and the three 65's) the average of the ranks for those pupils is given to each. Thus, the two pupils who received scores of 81 on the midterm would have been ranked 8 and 9. They are both given the average of these two ranks (8.5) because

Midterm	Rank			Midterm	Rank		
97	1			74	13.5	}	Tied ranks 13 and 14
95	2			74	13.5		
92	3			70	15		
88	4			67	16		
85	5			65	18	}	Tied ranks 17, 18, and 19
84	6			65	18		
83	7			65	18		
81	8.5	}	Tied ranks 8 and 9	62	20		
81	8.5			58	21		
79	10			57	22		
78	11			53	23		
76	12			45	24		

TABLE A.2
Ranking Test Scores

485

there is no basis for giving one of the students a rank of 8 and the other one a rank of 9.

Using Table A.2, it is obviously much easier to find the highest and lowest midterm scores, the number of pupils with scores above 90 or below 70, and to see that scores in the 70's are obtained by pupils who rank close to the middle of the class than it was with Table A.1. It is also easy to see that half the pupils score above 75 and half of them score below 75. Creating a rank order list for the final exam scores would make it easy to see similar characteristics of those scores. For example, it would make it easier to see that while 9 pupils had scores below 70 on the midterm, only 5 had scores below 70 on the final.

Grouping Scores into Frequency Distributions

With only 24 scores there is not a great need to go beyond the rank order display of scores. With more scores, however, it is often helpful to construct grouped frequency distributions and graphs of the score distributions. Grouped frequency distributions of the midterm and final scores are shown in Table A.3. Note that the scores have been grouped into *class intervals*, the number of scores falling in each interval has been tallied, and the tallies have been counted to obtain the *frequency*, or number of scores in each interval. Thus, there were two pupils with midterm scores in the interval 95–99, one pupil with a score in the interval 90–94, and so on. The total number (N) is the sum of the numbers in the frequency column. In the finished table the tally column is usually omitted as it has been for the final exam scores.

To construct a grouped frequency distribution it is conventional to choose a class interval that is an odd number and that will result in approximately 10 to 12 intervals. This makes the midpoint of each interval an integer. For our example the

TABLE A.3	Midterm			Final	
Frequency Distributions of Midterm and Final Scores	Class Interval	Tally	Frequency	Class Interval	Frequency
	95–99	//	2	95–99	1
	90–94	/	1	90–94	3
	85–89	//	2	85–89	3
	80–84	////	4	80–84	4
	75–79	///	3	75–79	4
	70–74	///	3	70–74	4
	65–69	////	4	65–69	3
	60–64	/	1	60–64	1
	55–59	//	2	55–59	1
	50–54	/	1	50–54	0
	45–49	/	1	45–49	0
			N = 24		N = 24

class interval is 5 (e.g., 95, 96, 97, 98, and 99 in the highest interval) and the midpoint of each interval is an integer (e.g., 97 is the midpoint of the highest interval). The lower bound of each interval starts with a multiple of the width of the interval (e.g., the lowest interval starts with 45, the next with 50, and so on). All class intervals should be the same size.

To decide on the width of the interval that will result in a reasonable number of intervals, the range can be divided by 12 and the nearest odd number used as the width of the class interval. For example, the highest midterm score is 97 and the lowest is 45 for a range of 52 ($97 - 45 = 52$). Since $52/12 = 4.33$ the class interval was set at 5, the nearest odd number. Note that applying the same process for the final scores would have suggested that a class interval of 3 be used. However, using the same interval makes it easier to compare the two sets of scores.

The grouped frequency distributions provide a good summary of the results. Features of the two distributions that already have been mentioned can be easily seen. However, there is some loss of information. For example, from the grouped frequency distribution we see that two pupils had scores in the interval 95–99 on the midterm, but we can no longer tell that one of these pupils had a 95, while the other one had a score of 97.

Graphic Presentations of Frequency Distributions

A frequency distribution presents test data in a clear, effective manner, and it is satisfactory for most classroom purposes. But if we want to study the distribution of scores more carefully or to report the results to others, a graphic representation may be more useful. The two most commonly used graphs are the *histogram* (or bar graph) and the *frequency polygon* (or line graph). Both graphs are presented in Figure A.1, based on the midterm scores in Table A.3. The scores are shown along

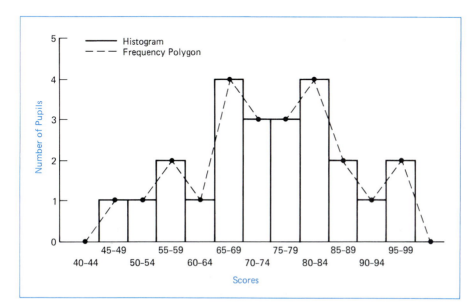

FIGURE A.1
Histogram and
frequency polygon
(plotted from midterm
exam scores in Table
A.3).

487

the base line, or horizontal axis, and are grouped into the same class intervals used in Table A.3. The vertical axis, to the left of the graphs, indicates the number of pupils earning each score and thus corresponds to the frequency column in Table A.3.

The *histogram* presents the data in the form of rectangular columns. The base of each column is the width of the class interval, and the height of the column indicates the frequency, or the number of pupils falling within that interval. It is as if each pupil earning a score within a given class interval were standing on the shoulders of the pupil beneath, to form a "human column."

The *frequency polygon* is constructed by plotting a point at the midpoint of each class interval at a height corresponding to the number of pupils, or frequency, within that interval and then joining these points with straight lines. As can be seen in Figure A.1, the frequency polygon and histogram are simply different ways of presenting the same data. In actual practice we would, of course, use only one of the graphs; the choice being somewhat arbitrary.

Histograms or frequency polygons allow us to see the shape of the distribution of scores as well as some to the features we have seen before. With a small number of pupils, such as the 24 in our example, the shape of the distribution is often jagged, going up and down and up again as you go from left to right. With a large number of scores, however, distributions of scores generally look smoother than the one shown in Figure A.1. Distributions of scores for many pupils on standardized tests often appear smooth and bell shaped, not unlike the shape of a normal distribution, and in many cases normal distribution is assumed or used as an approximation (see Chapter 14 for a description of the normal distribution and illustrations of some of its uses).

Stem-and-Leaf Display

An approach to displaying data that has become increasingly popular in recent years is the stem-and-leaf display. Like grouped frequency distributions, frequency polygons, and histograms, stem-and-leaf displays show the shape of a distribution of scores. In addition, they preserve all the information about the individual scores that is lost when scores are grouped into class intervals.

Tables A.4 and A.5 show two versions of stem-and-leaf displays for the midterm and final exam scores in Table A.1. The "stem" in Table A.4 is simply the tens digit for each score and the "leaf" is the units digit. On the midterm there were three scores in the 90's (92, 95, and 97). These three scores all have a stem of 9, and the individual scores are represented by the string of numbers 257 for the three leaves of 2, 5, and 7. Similarly, six pupils with scores in the 80's (81, 81, 83, 84, 85, and 88) are represented by the common stem of 8 and the string of numbers 113458 for the six leaves. The numbers in the columns labeled "count" simply record the number of scores with a given stem. As can be seen, the stem-and-leaf displays retain the detail that two pupils received a score of 81 while giving a general summary of the type provided by a grouped frequency distribution or frequency polygon.

Midterm Exam

Stem	Leaf	Count
9	257	3
8	113458	6
7	044689	6
6	25557	5
5	378	3
4	5	1
	N = 24	

Final Exam

Stem	Leaf	Count
9	1346	4
8	0001578	7
7	11245668	8
6	3789	4
5	8	1
4		
	N = 24	

The stem-and-leaf displays in Table A.5 show exactly the same information as is shown in Table A.4. The stems now correspond to 5-point intervals, however. Thus, 9* represents a stem for the numbers 95–99, 9: represents the stem for the numbers 90–94, and so on. By using two stems for each tens digit, the shape of the distributions can be seen more easily.

Midterm Exam

Stem	Leaf	Count
9*	57	2
9:	2	1
8*	58	2
8:	1134	4
7*	689	3
7:	044	3
6*	5557	4
6:	2	1
5*	78	2
5:	3	1
4*	5	1
	N = 24	

Final Exam

Stem	Leaf	Count
9*	6	1
9:	134	3
8*	578	3
8:	0001	4
7*	5668	4
7:	1124	4
6*	789	3
6:	3	1
5*	8	1
5:		
4*		
	N = 24	

Scatterplots

The graphs and displays we have presented have highlighted all but one of the features that was discussed concerning the data in Table A.1. Since the tables, graphs, and displays have focused on one type of score at a time, they have not done anything to make it easier to see the relationship between scores on the midterm and the final. To see the relationship better than can be seen from a simple listing of the scores, we need to construct a plot that displays pairs of numbers. Such a plot is called a scatterplot (or scattergram). The scatterplot for the scores in Table A.1 is shown in Figure A.2.

FIGURE A.2
Scatterplot of midterm
and final exam scores
(scores from Table A.1).

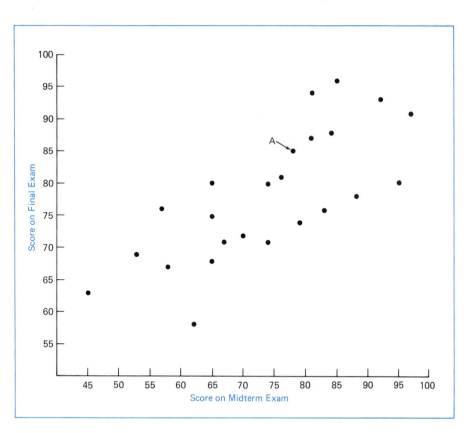

Each dot in Figure A.2 represents a pair of scores for an individual pupil. Thus, there are 24 dots corresponding to the pupils. A pupil's score on the midterm is shown on the horizontal, or X, axis and the pupil's score on the final is shown on the vertical, or Y axis. For example, pupil A had a score of 78 on the midterm and a score of 85 on the final. That pupil's score is represented by the dot that is shown by the arrow and the letter A. It is directly above the point on the horizontal line corresponding to a score of 78 and directly to the left of the point on the vertical axis corresponding to a score of 85. Points representing the remaining 23 pupils are plotted in a similar fashion.

By looking at the plot we see that there is a swarm of dots that tend to run from the lower left-hand corner to the upper right-hand corner of the figure. This shows that there is a positive relationship between the scores on the midterm and the scores on the final. That is, pupils with relatively low scores on one test tend to have relatively low scores on the other test while pupils with relatively high scores on one test tend to have relatively high scores on the other test. For example, there are 9 dots to the right of 80 on the horizontal axis. These represent the 9 pupils with midterm scores higher than 80. We see that all 9 of these points are above 75 on the vertical scale, indicating that no pupil who had a score of 80 or higher on the midterm had a score of 75 or less on the final. On the other hand, we can see by looking at the lower left-hand corner of the scatterplot that 6 of the 8 pupils who had midterm scores of 65 or less had scores of 75 or less on the final.

Although there clearly is a relationship between scores on the two tests, it is also clear that the relationship is far from perfect. That is, a pupil who has the highest or one of the highest scores on one test is not always ranked as highly on the other test. Indeed, the four pupils with scores of 90 or higher on the final had scores ranging all the way from 81 to 97 on the midterm, while one of the three pupils who had scores of 90 or higher on the midterm received a score of only 80 on the final.

Measures of Central Tendency

A measure of central tendency is simply an average or typical value in a set of scores. We all are familiar with the *arithmetic average* obtained by adding all of the scores in a set and dividing this sum by the number of scores. In statistics this type of average is called the *mean* and is represented by the letter M (or $\overline{X}$). Two other commonly used measures of central tendency are the *median* (represented by Mdn or P_{50}) and the *mode*. The median is the midpoint of a set of scores, that is, the point on either side of which half the scores occur. The mode (*fashion*) is the score that occurs most frequently. Because the mean, median, and mode are different types of averages the word *average* should be avoided when describing data. Preciseness requires that the specific type of average be indicated.

The method of determining each measure of central tendency will be described next and is illustrated in Table A.6.

The Mean (M or $\overline{X}$)

The *mean*, or arithmetic average, is the most widely used measure of central tendency. Because it is calculated by adding a series of scores and then dividing this sum by the number of scores, the computation from ungrouped data can be represented by the following formula:

$$M = \frac{\text{Sum of all scores}}{\text{Number of scores}} \qquad M = \frac{\Sigma X}{N}$$

in which

Σ = the sum of
X = any score
N = number of scores

Applying this formula to the scores in Table A.6 produces a mean of 73.92 for the midterm and 78.04 for the final. The mean takes into account the value of each score, and so one extremely high or low score could have an appreciable effect on it.

The Median (Mdn or P_{50})

The *median* is a *counting average*. It is determined by arranging the scores in order of size and counting up to (or down to) the midpoint of the set of scores. If the number of scores is *even* (as in Table A.6) the median will be halfway between

TABLE A.6
Measures of
Central Tendency*

	Midterm Score (X)		Final Score (Y)	
		97	96	
		95	94	
		92	93	
		88	91	
		85	88	
50% of	84		87	50% of
scores	83		85	scores
	81		81	
	81		80 ⎤	
	79		80 ⎬Mode = 80	
	78		80 ⎦	
	76		78	
Median = 75→			←Median = 77	
	74		76	
	74		76	
	70		75	
	67		74	
	65 ⎤		72	
50% of	65 ⎬Mode = 65		71	50% of
scores	65 ⎦		71	scores
	62		69	
	58		68	
	57		67	
	53		63	
	45		58	

Sum of X = 1,774   Sum of Y = 1,873
Mean = (1,774/24)   Mean = (1,873/24)
= 73.92   = 78.04

*Note that the scores are rank ordered separately for the midterm and the final.

the two middlemost scores. When the number of scores is *odd*, the median is the middle score.

The median is a *point* that divides a set of scores into equal halves, and thus the same number of scores falls above the median as below the median, regardless of the size of the individual scores. Because it is a counting average, an extremely high or low score will not affect its value.

The Mode

The *mode* is simply the most frequent or popular score in the set and is determined by inspection. In Table A.6 the mode is 65 for the midterm because the largest number of persons made that score. The mode is the least reliable type of statistical average and is frequently used merely as a preliminary estimate of central tendency. A set of scores sometimes has two modes and is called *bimodal*.

Measures of Variability

A set of scores can be more adequately described if we know how much they spread out above and below the measure of central tendency. For example, we might have two groups of pupils with a mean IQ of 110, but in one group, the span of IQs is from 100 to 120, and in the other, the span is from 80 to 140. These represent quite different ability groups. We can identify such differences by numbers that indicate how much scores spread out in a group. These are called measures of variability, or dispersion. The three most commonly used measures of variability are the *range*, the *quartile deviation*, and the *standard deviation*.

The Range

The simplest and crudest measure of variability is the range, calculated by subtracting the lowest score from the highest score. In the preceding example, the range of IQs in the first group is 20 points and in the second, 60 points. The range provides a quick estimate of variability but is undependable because it is based on the position of the two extreme scores. The addition or subtraction of a single end score can change the range significantly. In the preceding example, the ranges of the two groups would become equal if we added to the first group a pupil with an IQ of 80 and another with an IQ of 140. It is obvious that a more stable measure of variability would be desirable. For our example with the midterm and final exam scores, however, the smaller range for the final ($96 - 58 = 38$) than for the midterm (range $= 97 - 45 = 52$) accurately reflects the smaller variability in scores on the final exam that we have previously noted and that will be quantified by the other measures of variability.

The Quartile Deviation (Q)

The quartile deviation is based on the range of the middle 50 percent of the scores, instead of the range of the entire set. The middle 50 percent of a set of scores is called the *interquartile range*, and the *quartile deviation* is simply half of this range. The quartile deviation is also called the *semi-interquartile range*.

The middle 50 percent of the scores is bounded by the 75th percentile and the 25th percentile. These points are called *quartiles* and are indicated by Q_3 and Q_1, respectively. Quartiles are merely *points* that divide a set of scores into quarters. The middle quartile, or Q_2, is the median.

To compute the quartile deviation, we simply determine the values of Q_3 and Q_1 and apply the following formula:

$$Q = \frac{Q_3 - Q_1}{2}$$

We use the same counting procedure to locate Q_3 and Q_1 that we used to find the median. With the scores arranged in order of size, we start from the lowest score, and count off 25 percent of the scores to locate Q_1 and 75 percent of the scores to locate Q_3. Since we have 24 pupils in our example, Q_1 is equal to the score that is higher than that achieved by 6 students (25%) and lower than that achieved by 18 pupils (75%). For the midterm, $Q_1 = 65$ and for the final, $Q_1 = 71.5$. Note that Q_1 is 71.5 on the final because it falls halfway between 71, the 6th lowest score, and 72, the 7th lowest score. The values of Q_3 are 83.5 for the midterm (halfway between 83 and 84) and 86 for the final (halfway between 85 and 87).

Given the 75th and 25th percentiles (Q_1 and Q_3), the quartile deviation (Q) is easily computed. As would be expected from what we have already seen, Q is larger for the midterm scores ($Q = [83.5 - 65]/2 = 9.25$) than it is for the final scores ($Q = [86 - 71.5]/2 = 7.25$). These quartile deviation values simply quantify the fact that the midterm scores are more variable than the final scores.

Although quartiles are *points* on the scale (like averages and percentiles), the quartile deviation represents a *distance* on the scale. It indicates the distance we need to go *above* and *below* the median to include approximately the middle 50 percent of the scores.

The Standard Deviation (*SD*, s, or σ)

The most useful measure of variability, or spread of scores, is the *standard deviation*. The computation of the standard deviation does not make its meaning readily apparent, but essentially it is an average of the degree to which a set of scores deviates from the mean. Because it takes into account the amount that each score deviates from the mean, it is a more stable measure of variability than either the range or quartile deviation.

Because the procedure for calculating a standard deviation involves squaring each score, summing the scores and the squares of the scores, as well as taking a square root, the help of a hand-held calculator is highly desirable for any reasonably sized problem. Better yet, a calculator with built-in statistical procedures or a microcomputer with a simple statistical package is recommended for anyone who wants to compute statistics such as standard deviations and correlations on a routine basis. To perform the calculations by hand or with a hand-held calculator that does not offer statistical procedures, however, the following steps are involved.

1. Find the sum of the scores (ΣX) as was done to compute the mean.
2. Square each score (X^2).
3. Find the sum of the squared scores (ΣX^2).
4. Square the sum of the scores obtained in step 1, that is, multiply (ΣX) times (ΣX).
5. Divide the square obtained in step 4 by N, the number of pupils, ($\Sigma X)(\Sigma X)/N$.
6. Subtract the result in step 5 from the sum of the squared scores obtained in step 3, $\Sigma X^2 - (\Sigma X)(\Sigma X)/N$.
7. Divide the result in step 6 by ($N - 1$), one less than the number of pupils, $[\Sigma X^2 - (\Sigma X)(\Sigma X)/N]/(N - 1)$.
8. Find the square root of the result of step 7. This number is the standard deviation (SD) of the scores. Thus, the formula for the SD is

$$SD = \sqrt{\frac{\Sigma X^2 - (\Sigma X)(\Sigma X)/N}{N - 1}}.$$

The square of each midterm score and the square of each final score is listed in Table A.7. Also shown are the sums of the scores and of the squared scores. The last column of the table lists the product of the midterm score times the final score for each pupil. Those numbers are not used for calculating standard deviations but will be used later to calculate the correlation. Using the numbers for the midterm exam in the 8 steps just listed, the standard deviation is obtained as follows.

1. From Table A.7, $\Sigma X = 1,774$.
2. See Table A.7 for a listing of X^2 for each pupil.
3. From Table A.7, $\Sigma X^2 = 135,342$.
4. $(\Sigma X)(\Sigma X) = (1,774)(1,774) = 3,147,076$.
5. $(\Sigma X)(\Sigma X)/N = 3,147,076/24 = 131,128.1667$.

Pupil	Midterm Score (X)	X^2	Final Score (Y)	Y^2	XY
E	97	9409	91	8281	8827
T	95	9025	80	6400	7600
N	92	8464	93	8649	8556
C	88	7744	78	6084	6864
W	85	7225	96	9216	8160
F	84	7056	88	7744	7392
Q	83	6889	76	5776	6308
I	81	6561	94	8836	7614
L	81	6561	87	7569	7047
R	79	6241	74	5476	5846
A	78	6084	85	7225	6630
X	76	5776	81	6561	6156
D	74	5476	71	5041	5254
V	74	5476	80	6400	5920
K	70	4900	72	5184	5040
B	67	4489	71	5041	4757
H	65	4225	68	4624	4420
M	65	4225	80	6400	5200
P	65	4225	75	5625	4875
U	62	3844	58	3364	3596
J	58	3364	67	4489	3886
G	57	3249	76	5776	4332
O	53	2809	69	4761	3657
S	45	2025	63	3969	2835
Sum = 1,774		135,342	1,873	148,491	140,772
SD on midterm = 13.54			SD on final = 10.04		$r = .74$

TABLE A.7
Intermediate Calculations for Standard Deviation (SD) and Product-Moment Correlation Coefficient (r)

6. $\Sigma X^2 - (\Sigma X)(\Sigma X)/N = 135,342 - 131,128.1667 = 4,213.8333$.
7. $[\Sigma X^2 - (\Sigma X)(\Sigma X)/N]/(N - 1) = 4,213.8333/23 = 183.2101$.
8. $SD = \sqrt{183.2101} = 13.54$.

Applying the same steps to the scores on the final exam we find that the SD for the final is 10.04. What do these standard deviations of 13.54 on the midterm and 10.04 tell us? First, it should be no surprise that the midterm scores have a larger standard deviation than the final scores. We have already noted that the midterm scores are more spread out. The midterm scores have a larger range and a larger quartile deviation than the final scores. The larger standard deviation is one more way of quantifying the fact that the midterm scores have greater variability than the final scores do.

The standard deviation, like other measures of variability, represents a *distance*. If we move the distance equal to one SD above and below the mean we will find that somewhere between 60% and 75% of the scores fall in that region for most distributions of scores. In a normal distribution, 68% of the scores are included between the mean minus one SD and the mean plus one SD. For example, the midterm had a mean of 73.92 and a standard deviation of 13.54. Thus, the mean minus one SD is $73.92 - 13.54 = 60.38$ and the mean plus one SD is $73.92 + 13.54 = 87.46$. Looking at Table A.7, we see that 16 of the 24 pupils (67%) have midterm scores between these two limits. Although the distribution of midterm scores in not the same shape as a normal distribution the percentage of cases that fall between the mean plus and minus one SD is very close to the 68% that would be found for a true normal distribution. This result is not unusual and it is reasonable to expect that roughly two thirds of the cases will have scores between the mean minus one SD and the mean plus one SD.

Which Measure of Dispersion to Use

The quartile deviation is used with the median and is satisfactory for analyzing a small number of scores. Because these statistics are obtained by counting and thus are not affected by the value of each score, they are especially useful when one or more scores deviate markedly from the others in the set.

The standard deviation is used with the mean. It is the most reliable measure of variability, and is especially useful in testing. In addition to describing the spread of scores in a group, it serves as a basis for computing standard scores, the standard error of measurement, and other statistics used in analyzing and interpreting test scores.

Coefficient of Correlation

The final statistical measure that we shall consider is the *correlation coefficient*. The meaning of the correlation coefficient and its use in describing the validity and reliability of test scores can be found in Chapters 3 and 4. Basically, a coefficient of correlation expresses the degree of relationship between two sets of scores by numbers ranging from −1.00 to +1.00. A perfect positive correlation is indicated by a coefficient of +1.00 and a perfect negative correlation by a coefficient of −1.00. A correlation of .00 indicates no relationship between the two sets of scores. Obviously, the larger the coefficient (positive or negative), the higher the degree of relationship expressed.

Recall that from the scatterplot shown in Figure A.2 it was concluded that there was a positive relationship between scores on the midterm and scores on the final exam. The relationship was far from perfect, however. Thus, we should expect from an inspection of the scatterplot that the correlation coefficient should be greater than .00 but less than +1.00. As we shall see the correlation between the midterm and final scores is .74. This value reflects a relatively strong but less than perfect relationship between these two sets of scores.

Just as there are several measures of central tendency and several measures of variability, there are several different measures of relationship expressed as correlation coefficients. We shall consider only one of these, the *product–moment* correlation coefficient. This is by far the most commonly used and most useful correlation coefficient. It is the one that is most likely to be reported in test manuals and research studies. Indeed, if it is not specified otherwise when a correlation coefficient is reported, it is ordinarily assumed to be a product–moment correlation. The product–moment correlation coefficient is indicated by the symbol r.

As was true of a standard deviation, computation of a product–moment correlation coefficient is best done by a calculator or computer. Fortunately, much of the work for our example of 24 pupils with scores on a midterm and a final exam has already been done in Table A.7 because many of the intermediate values needed to compute the standard deviations of the two sets of scores are also used to compute the correlation coefficient. The following steps are involved in computing the correlation coefficient, r.

1. Begin by writing the pairs of scores to be studied in two columns, as was done in the columns labeled X and Y in Table A.7. Make certain that the pair of scores for each pupil is in the same row.

2. Square each of the entries in the X column and enter the result in the X^2 column, as was done to compute a standard deviation.

3. Square each of the entries in the Y column and enter the result in the Y^2 column.

4. In each row, multiply the entry in the X column by the entry in the Y column, and enter the result in the XY column (see the right-hand column of Table A.7).

5. Sum the entries in each column and note the number of (N) of pairs of scores. From Table A.7, then:

$$\Sigma X = 1{,}774 \qquad \Sigma Y = 1{,}873$$
$$\Sigma X^2 = 135{,}342 \qquad \Sigma Y^2 = 148{,}491$$
$$N = 24 \qquad \Sigma XY = 140{,}772$$

6. Substitute the obtained values in the formula:

$$r = \frac{[\Sigma XY - (\Sigma X)(\Sigma Y)/N]}{\sqrt{[\Sigma X^2 - (\Sigma X)(\Sigma X)/N][\Sigma Y^2 - (\Sigma Y)(\Sigma Y)/N]}}$$

This formula looks complex, but it requires only simple arithmetic. For the scores in Table A.7, the most tedious part of the calculations have already been done. All that remains is to substitute numerical values for the appropriate symbols in the previous formula for *r* and do the arithmetic operations. The substitutions and intermediate steps are illustrated by the following.

The numerator for *r* is

$$
\begin{aligned}
[\Sigma XY - (\Sigma X)(\Sigma Y)/N] &= 140{,}772 - (1{,}774)(1{,}873)/24 \\
&= 140{,}772 - 3{,}322{,}702/24 \\
&= 140{,}772 - 138{,}445.9167 \\
&= 2{,}326.0833.
\end{aligned}
$$

The part of the denominator involving X already has been used as part of the calculation of the standard deviation. It is

$$
\begin{aligned}
[\Sigma X^2 - (\Sigma X)(\Sigma X)/N] &= 135{,}342 - (1{,}774)(1{,}774)/24 \\
&= 135{,}342 - 3{,}147{,}076/24 \\
&= 135{,}342 - 131{,}128.1667 \\
&= 4{,}213.8333
\end{aligned}
$$

The part of the denominator involving Y is

$$
\begin{aligned}
[\Sigma Y^2 - (\Sigma Y)(\Sigma Y)/N] &= 148{,}491 - (1{,}873)(1{,}873)/24 \\
&= 148{,}491 - 3{,}508{,}129/24 \\
&= 148{,}491 - 146{,}172.0417 \\
&= 2{,}318.9583
\end{aligned}
$$

Putting these three parts together in the formula for *r* we have

$$r = \frac{2{,}326.0833}{\sqrt{(4{,}213.8333)(2{,}318.9583)}}$$

$$= \frac{2{,}326.0833}{\sqrt{9{,}771{,}703.706}} = \frac{2{,}326.0833}{3{,}125.9724}$$

$$= .74$$

Although it is not readily apparent from the preceding formula, the computations involve most of the steps needed to find the mean and the standard deviation of each set of scores (X and Y). Thus, the formula also can be written

$$r = \left(\frac{\dfrac{\Sigma XY}{N} - (M_x)(M_y)}{(SD_x)(SD_y)} \right) \left(\frac{N}{N-1} \right)$$

in which

M_x = mean of scores in X column
M_y = mean of scores in Y column
SD_x = standard deviation of scores in X column
SD_y = standard deviation of scores in Y column
Thus, for the same data

$$r = \left(\frac{5,865.5 - (73.92)(78.04)}{(13.54)(10.04)} \right)\left(\frac{24}{23} \right) = .74$$

If the means and standard deviations are already available for the two sets of scores, this latter formula will be easier to apply. If they are not available, the first formula can be used, and the means and standard deviations of the two sets of scores can also be computed during the process, if needed.

A Final Caution

Correlation indicates the degree of relationship between two sets of scores, but *not causation*. If X and Y are related, there are several possible explanations: (1) X may cause Y, (2) Y may cause X, or (3) X and Y may be the result of a common cause. For example, the increase in incidence of juvenile delinquency during the past decade has been paralleled by a corresponding increase in teachers' salaries. Thus, the correlation between these two sets of figures would probably be quite high. Obviously, further study is needed to determine the cause of any particular relationship.

References

COLADARCI, A., AND COLADARCI, T. *Elementary Descriptive Statistics: For Those Who Think They Can't*. Belmont, Calif.: Wadsworth, 1979. A witty and precise introduction to the basic concepts and procedures in elementary statistics.

DOWNIE, N. M., AND Heath, R. W. *Basic Statistical Methods*, 5th ed. New York: Harper & Row, 1984. An introductory textbook designed for nonmathematics majors.

HOPKINS, K. D., GLASS G. V., AND HOPKINS, B. R. *Basic Statistics for the Behavioral Sciences*, 2d ed. Englewood Cliffs, N.J.: Prentice-Hall, 1987. Provides an introduction to statistics with a good discussion of interpretations of correlation coefficients and factors that influence them.

JAEGER, R. *Statistics: A Spectator Sport*. Beverly Hills, Calif.: Sage Publications, 1983. Explains what statistics are, what they mean, and how they are used and interpreted. Emphasizes understanding rather than computation.

TOWNSEND, E. A., AND BURKE, P. J. *Using Statistics in Classroom Instruction*. New York: Macmillan, 1975. Offers step-by-step directions and practice in using simple descriptive statistics with test scores.

Appendix B

Lists of Professional Journals for Locating Measurement Articles

Articles on educational and psychological measurement appear in many different types of professional journals. List A includes those journals that focus most directly on measurement articles. List B contains journals that sometimes have measurement articles.

LIST A

Applied Measurement in Education
Applied Psychological Measurement
Educational Measurement: Issues and Practice
Educational and Psychological Measurement
Journal of Educational Measurement
Journal of Personality Assessment
Measurement and Evaluation in Guidance

LIST B

American Educational Research Journal
Journal of Applied Psychology
Journal of Counseling Psychology
Journal of Educational Psychology
Journal of School Psychology
Journal of Special Education
Psychology in the Schools
Review of Educational Research

Appendix C

A List of Test Publishers and Objective-Item Banks

Test Publishers

The following is a list of the test publishers and distributors whose tests were referred to earlier in this book (the tests are listed in Appendix D). All will provide catalogues of their current tests.

The names and addresses of other test publishers and distributors can be obtained from the latest volume of the *Mental Measurements Yearbook*.

1. American Guidance Service, Inc.
   Publishers Building
   Circle Pines, Minnesota 55014

2. C.P.S., Inc.
   P.O. Box 83
   Larchmont, New York 10538

3. CTB/McGraw-Hill
   Del Monte Research Park
   Monterey, California 93940

4. Consulting Psychologists Press, Inc.
   577 College Avenue
   Palo Alto, California 94306

5. Educational Testing Service
   Princeton, New Jersey 08540

6. Institute for Personality and Ability Testing
   P.O. Box 188
   Champaign, Illinois 61820

7. Psychological Assessment Resources (PAR)
   P.O. Box 998
   Odessa, Florida 33556

8. PRO-ED
   5341 Industrial Oaks Blvd.
   Austin, Texas 78735

9. Psychological Corporation
   555 Academic Ct.
   San Antonio, Texas 78204

10. Riverside Publishing Company
    8420 Bryn Mawr Drive
    Chicago, Illinois 60631

11. Scholastic Testing Service
    480 Meyer Road
    Bensenville, Illinois 60106

12. Science Research Associates,
    Inc.
    155 North Wacker Drive
    Chicago, Illinois 60606

Objective-Item Banks

Collections of instructional objectives and related test items are maintained by test publishers and others. These are usually in the form of a customized test development service, a complete test development system that has computer software for sale or lease, or both. Some of the larger item banks that cover all grade levels are listed below.

CTB/McGraw-Hill
  CTB/McGraw-Hill Item Bank
  Objective-Referenced Bank of Items and Tests (ORBIT)
Psychological Corporation
  Academic Instructional Measurement System (AIMS)
Riverside Publishing Company
  MULTISCORE
Science Research Associates
  SRA Objective/Item Bank
Tescor, Inc. (461 Carlisle Drive, Herndon, VA 22070)
  First National Item Bank & Test Development System

Objective-item banks are also maintained by some state departments, colleges, public schools, and private organizations. For a list and descriptions of a large number of objective-item banks, see Richard W. Naccarato, *A Guide to Item Banking in Education*, 3d ed., 1988 (Northwest Regional Education Laboratory, 101 S.W. Main Street, Suite 500, Portland, Oregon 97204). This volume consists of a detailed item bank data sheet for each system that describes the objective-item collection and how the system functions.

Appendix D

A Selected List of Published Tests

Test Name (Publishers' No.)*	Grade** Level Covered
Achievement Batteries	
California Achievement Tests (3)	K–12
Comprehensive Tests of Basic Skills (3)	K–12
Iowa Tests of Basic Skills (10)	K–9
Iowa Tests of Educational Development (12)	9–12
Metropolitan Achievement Tests (9)	K–12
SRA Achievement Series (12)	K–12
SRA Survey of Basic Skills (12)	K–12
Sequential Tests of Educational Progress (3)	K–12
Stanford Achievement Tests (9)	1–12
Tests of Achievement and Proficiency (10)	9–12
The 3-R^s Test (10)	K–12
Diagnostic Tests	
California Diagnostic Mathematics Tests (3)	1–12
California Diagnostic Reading Tests (3)	1–12
Metropolitan Achievement Tests	
Language Diagnostic Tests (9)	1–9.9
Mathematics Diagnostic Tests (9)	1–9.9
Reading Diagnostic Tests (9)	K.5–9.9
Stanford Diagnostic Mathematics Test (9)	1.5–12
Stanford Diagnostic Reading Test (9)	1.5–12

Test Name (Publishers' No.)*	Grade** Level Covered
Individual Achievement Tests	
Basic Achievement Skills Individual Screener (9)	1–A
Peabody Individual Achievement Test-R (1)	K–A
Key Math Diagnostic Arithmetic Test-R (1)	P–6
Woodcock Reading Mastery Test-R (1)	K–12
Criterion-Referenced Tests	
DMI Mathematics System (3)	K–8.9
National Proficiency Survey Series (10)	8–12
PRI Reading Systems (3)	K–9
(For Customized Testing, see objective item banks in Appendix C.)	
Reading Tests	
Gates–McGinitie Reading Tests (10)	K–12
Iowa Silent Reading Tests (9)	6–14
Nelson Reading Skills Test (10)	3–9
Nelson–Denny Reading Test (10)	9–16, A
(See also Achievement Batteries and Diagnostic Tests.)	
Learning Ability Tests	
Cognitive Abilities Test (10)	K–12
Culture-Fair Intelligence Test (6)	4–16, A
Educational Ability Series (12)	K–12
Henmon–Nelson Tests of Mental Ability (10)	K–12
Otis–Lennon School Ability Tests (9)	1–12
School and College Ability Tests, SCAT (3)	3–12
Tests of Cognitive Skills (3)	2–12
Multiaptitude Batteries	
Differential Aptitude Tests (9)	8–13, A
Readiness Tests	
Boehm Test of Basic Concepts (9)	K–2
Cooperative Preschool Inventory (3)	P–K
Metropolitan Readiness Test (9)	K–1
Stanford Early School Achievement Test (9)	K–1
Tests of Basic Experience (3)	P–1
Attitude Scales	
Estes Attitude Scales (8)	3–12
School Interest Inventory (10)	7–12
Survey of School Attitudes (9)	1–8
Interest Inventories	
Kuder General Interest Survey (12)	6–12
Kuder Occupational Interest Survey (12)	10–A
Strong–Campbell Interest Inventory (9)	11–A

*The publishers' numbers (in parentheses) refer to the list in Appendix C.
**Gives total span only, not the number of separate levels available (P = preschool, K = kindergarten,
    A = adult).

Taxonomy of Educational Objectives (Major Categories and Illustrative Objectives)

TABLE E.1

Major Categories in the Cognitive Domain of the Taxonomy of Educational Objectives (Bloom 1956)

Descriptions of the Major Categories in the Cognitive Domain

1. **Knowledge.** Knowledge is defined as the remembering of previously learned material. This may involve the recall of a wide range of material, from specific facts to complete theories, but all that is required is the bringing to mind of the appropriate information. Knowledge represents the lowest level of learning outcomes in the cognitive domain.

2. **Comprehension.** Comprehension is defined as the ability to grasp the meaning of material. This may be shown by translating material from one form to another (words or numbers), by interpreting material (explaining or summarizing), and by estimating future trends (predicting consequences or effects). These learning outcomes go one step beyond the simple remembering of material and represent the lowest level of understanding.

3. **Application.** Application refers to the ability to use learned material in new and concrete situations. This may include the application of such things as rules, methods, concepts, principles, laws, and theories. Learning outcomes in this area require a higher level of understanding than those under comprehension.

4. **Analysis.** Analysis refers to the ability to break down material into its component parts so that its organizational structure may be understood. This may include the identification of the parts, analysis of the relationships between parts, and recognition of the organizational principles involved. Learning outcomes here represent a higher intellectual level than comprehension and application because they require an understanding of both the content and the structural form of the material.

5. **Synthesis.** Synthesis refers to the ability to put parts together to form a new whole. This may involve the production of a unique communication (theme or speech), a plan of operations (research proposal), or a set of abstract relations (scheme for classifying information). Learning outcomes in this area stress creative behaviors, with major emphasis on the formulation of *new* patterns or structures.

6. **Evaluation.** Evaluation is concerned with the ability to judge the value of material (statement, novel, poem, research report) for a given purpose. The judgments are to be based on definite criteria. These may be internal criteria (organization) or external criteria (relevance to the purpose) and the student may determine the criteria or be given them. Learning outcomes in this area are highest in the cognitive hierarchy because they contain elements of all of the other categories plus value judgments based on clearly defined criteria.

Illustrative General Instructional Objectives	Illustrative Verbs for Stating Specific Learning Outcomes
Knows common terms Knows specific facts Knows methods and procedures Knows basic concepts Knows principles	Defines, describes, identifies, labels, lists, matches, names, outlines, reproduces, selects, states
Understands facts and principles Interprets verbal material Interprets charts and graphs Translates verbal material to mathematical formulas Estimates consequences implied in data Justifies methods and procedures	Converts, defends, distinguishes, estimates, explains, extends, generalizes, gives examples, infers, paraphrases, predicts, rewrites, summarizes
Applies principles to new situations Applies theories to practical situations Solves mathematical problems Constructs charts and graphs Demonstrates correct usage of a procedure	Changes, computes, demonstrates, discovers, manipulates, modifies, operates, predicts, prepares, produces, relates, shows, solves, uses
Recognizes unstated assumptions Recognizes logical fallacies in reasoning Distinguishes between facts and inferences Evaluates the relevancy of data Analyzes the organizational structure of a work (art, music, writing)	Breaks down, diagrams, differentiates, discriminates, distinguishes, identifies, illustrates, infers, outlines, points out, relates, selects, separates, subdivides
Writes a well-organized theme Gives a well-organized speech Writes a creative short story (or poem) Proposes a plan for an experiment Integrates learning from different areas into a plan for solving a problem Formulates a new scheme for classifying objects (or events or ideas)	Categorizes, combines, compiles, composes, creates, devises, designs, explains, generates, modifies, organizes, plans, rearranges, reconstructs, relates, reorganizes, revises, rewrites, summarizes, tells, writes
Judges the consistency of written material Judges the adequacy with which conclusions are supported by data Judges the value of a work (art, music, writing) by use of internal criteria Judges the value of a work (art, music, writing) by use of external standards	Appraises, compares, concludes, contrasts, criticizes, describes, discriminates, explains, interprets, justifies, relates, summarizes, supports

TABLE E.2

Examples of General Instructional Objectives and Clarifying Verbs for the Cognitive Domain of the Taxonomy

TABLE E.3

Major Categories in the Affective Domain of the Taxonomy of Educational Objectives (Krathwohl 1964)

Descriptions of the Major Categories in the Affective Domain

1. **Receiving.**   Receiving refers to the student's willingness to attend to particular phenomena or stimuli (classroom activities, textbook, music, etc.). From a teaching standpoint, it is concerned with getting, holding, and directing the student's attention. Learning outcomes in this area range from the simple awareness that a thing exists to selective attention on the part of the learner. Receiving represents the lowest level of learning outcomes in the affective domain.

2. **Responding.**   Responding refers to active participation on the part of the student. At this level he not only attends to a particular phenomenon but also reacts to it in some way. Learning outcomes in this area may emphasize acquiescence in responding (reads assigned material), willingness to respond (voluntarily reads beyond assignment), or satisfaction in responding (reads for pleasure or enjoyment). The higher levels of this category include those instructional objectives that are commonly classified under *interest*; that is, those that stress the seeking out and enjoyment of particular activities.

3. **Valuing.**   Valuing is concerned with the worth or value a student attaches to a particular object, phenomenon, or behavior. This ranges in degree from the more simple acceptance of a value (desires to improve group skills) to the more complex level of commitment (assumes responsibility for the effective functioning of the group). Valuing is based on the internalization of a set of specified values, but clues to these values are expressed in the student's overt behavior. Learning outcomes in this area are concerned with behavior that is consistent and stable enough to make the value clearly identifiable. Instructional objectives that are commonly classified under *attitudes* and *appreciation* would fall into this category.

4. **Organization.**   Organization is concerned with bringing together different values, resolving conflicts between them, and beginning the building of an internally consistent value system. Thus, the emphasis is on comparing, relating, and synthesizing values. Learning outcomes may be concerned with the conceptualization of a value (recognizes the responsibility of each individual for improving human relations) or with the organization of a value system (develops a vocational plan that satisfies his need for both economic security and social service). Instructional objectives relating to the development of a philosophy of life would fall into this category.

5. **Characterization by a Value or Value Complex.**   At this level of the affective domain, the individual has a value system that has controlled his behavior for a sufficiently long time for him to have developed a characteristic *life style*. Thus, the behavior is pervasive, consistent, and predictable. Learning outcomes at this level cover a broad range of activities, but the major emphasis is on the fact that the behavior is typical or characteristic of the student. Instructional objectives that are concerned with the student's general patterns of adjustment (personal, social, emotional) would be appropriate here.

Illustrative General Instructional Objectives	Illustrative Verbs for Stating Specific Learning Outcomes	
Listens attentively Shows awareness of the importance of learning Shows sensitivity to social problems Accepts differences of race and culture Attends closely to the classroom activities	Asks, chooses, describes, follows, gives, holds, identifies, locates, names, points to, selects, sits erect, replies, uses	**TABLE E.4** Examples of General Instructional Objectives and Clarifying Verbs for the Affective Domain of the Taxonomy
Completes assigned homework Obeys school rules Participates in class discussion Completes laboratory work Volunteers for special tasks Shows interest in subject Enjoys helping others	Answers, assists, complies, conforms, discusses, greets, helps, labels, performs, practices, presents, reads, recites, reports, selects, tells, writes	
Demonstrates belief in the democratic process Appreciates good literature (art or music) Appreciates the role of science (or other subjects) in everyday life Shows concern for the welfare of others Demonstrates problem-solving attitude Demonstrates commitment to social improvement	Completes, describes, differentiates, explains, follows, forms, initiates, invites, joins, justifies, proposes, reads, reports, selects, shares, studies, works	
Recognizes the need for balance between freedom and responsibility in a democracy Recognizes the role of systematic planning in solving problems Accepts responsibility for own behavior Understands and accepts own strengths and limitations Formulates a life plan in harmony with his abilities, interests, and beliefs	Adheres, alters, arranges, combines, compares, completes, defends, explains, generalizes, identifies, integrates, modifies, orders, organizes, prepares, relates, synthesizes	
Displays safety consciousness Demonstrates self-reliance in working independently Practices cooperation in group activities Uses objective approach in problem solving Demonstrates industry and self-discipline Maintains good health habits	Acts, discriminates, displays, influences, listens, modifies, performs, practices, proposes, qualifies, questions, revises, serves, solves, uses, verifies	

TABLE E.5
A Classification of
Educational Objectives
in the Psychomotor
Domain (Simpson 1972)

Description of the Major Categories in the Psychomotor Domain

1. **Perception.**   The first level is concerned with the use of the sense organs to obtain cues that guide motor activity. This category ranges from sensory stimulation (awareness of a stimulus), through cue selection (selecting task-relevant cues), to translation (relating cue perception to action in a performance).

2. **Set**.   Set refers to readiness to take a particular type of action. This category includes mental set (mental readiness to act), physical set (physical readiness to act), and emotional set (willingness to act). Perception of cues serves as an important prerequisite for this level.

3. **Guided Response.**   Guided response is concerned with the early stages in learning a complex skill. It includes imitation (repeating an act demonstrated by the instructor) and trial and error (using a multiple-response approach to identify an appropriate response). Adequacy of performance is judged by an instructor or by a suitable set of criteria.

4. **Mechanism.**   Mechanism is concerned with performance acts where the learned responses have become habitual and the movements can be performed with some confidence and proficiency. Learning outcomes at this level are concerned with performance skills of various types, but the movement patterns are less complex than at the next higher level.

5. **Complex Overt Response.**   Complex overt response is concerned with the skillful performance of motor acts that involve complex movement patterns. Proficiency is indicated by a quick, smooth, accurate performance, requiring a minimum of energy. This category includes resolution of uncertainty (performs without hesitation) and automatic performance (movements are made with ease and good muscle control). Learning outcomes at this level include highly coordinated motor activities.

6. **Adaptation.**   Adaptation is concerned with skills that are so well developed that the individual can modify movement patterns to fit special requirements or to meet a problem situation.

7. **Origination.**   Origination refers to the creating of new movement patterns to fit a particular situation or specific problem. Learning outcomes at this level emphasize creativity based upon highly developed skills.

References*

BLOOM, B. S., ED., ET AL. *Taxonomy of Educational Objectives: Handbook I, Cognitive Domain.* New York: D. McKay, 1956. Describes the cognitive categories in detail and presents illustrative objectives and test items for each.

HARROW, A. J. A *Taxonomy of the Psychomotor Domain.* New York: D. McKay, 1972. Provides

*Tables E.1–E.6 are from N. E. Gronlund, *Stating Objectives for Classroom Instruction*, 3d ed. (New York: Macmillan, 1985).

Illustrative General Instructional Objectives	Illustrative Verbs for Stating Specific Learning Outcomes	
Recognizes malfunction by sound of machine Relates taste of food to need for seasoning Relates music to a particular dance step	Chooses, describes, detects, differentiates, distinguishes, identifies, isolates, relates, selects, separates	TABLE E.6 Examples of General Instructional Objectives and Clarifying Verbs for the Psychomotor Domain
Knows sequence of steps in varnishing wood Demonstrates proper bodily stance for batting a ball Shows desire to type efficiently	Begins, displays, explains, moves, proceeds, reacts, responds, shows, starts, volunteers	
Performs a golf swing as demonstrated Applies first aid bandage as demonstrated Determines best sequence for preparing a meal	Assembles, builds, calibrates, constructs, dismantles, displays, disects, fastens, fixes, grinds, heats, manipulates, measures, mends, mixes, organizes, sketches	
Writes smoothly and legibly Sets up laboratory equipment Operates a slide projector Demonstrates a simple dance step	(Same list as for Guided Response)	
Operates a power saw skillfully Demonstrates correct form in swimming Demonstrates skill in driving an automobile Performs skillfully on the violin Repairs electronic equipment quickly and accurately	(Same list as for Guided Response)	
Adjusts tennis play to counteract opponent's style Modifies swimming strokes to fit the roughness of the water	Adapts, alters, changes, rearranges, reorganizes, revises, varies	
Creates a dance step Creates a musical composition Designs a new dress style	Arranges, combines, composes, constructs, creates, designs, originates	

a model for classifying learning outcomes in the psychomotor domain and presents illustrative objectives.

KRATHWOHL, D. R., ED., ET AL. *Taxonomy of Educational Objectives: Handbook II, Affective Domain.* New York: D. McKay, 1964. Describes the affective categories in detail and presents illustrative objectives and test items for each.

SIMPSON, E. J. "The Classification of Educational Objectives in the Psychomotor Domain." *The Psychomotor Domain*, vol. 3. Washington: Gryphon House, 1972. Describes the psychomotor domain in detail and presents illustrative objectives.

Appendix F

Relating Evaluation Procedures to Instructional Objectives

Instructional objectives encompass a variety of learning outcomes, and evaluation includes a variety of procedures. The key to effective evaluation of pupil learning is to relate the evaluation procedures as directly as possible to the intended learning outcomes. This is easiest to accomplish if the general instructional objectives and the specific learning outcomes have been clearly stated in terms of pupil performance. It is then simply a matter of constructing or selecting evaluation instruments that provide the most direct evidence concerning the attainment of the stated outcomes.

The sequence of steps shown in Figure F.1 summarizes the general procedure for relating evaluation techniques to instructional objectives.

Relating Test Items to Instructional Objectives

Preparing test items that are directly relevant to the instructional objectives to be measured requires matching the performance measured by the test items to the types of performance specified by the intended outcomes. Stating the outcomes as specifically as possible is useful in this regard, but good judgment is still needed. If the intended learning outcomes call for *supplying* the answers (e.g., *name, define*), the test items should also require that the answers be supplied rather than selected. If the intended learning outcomes call for *identifying* a procedure, the test items should be concerned only with identifying rather than with more complex out-

FIGURE F.1
Relation of evaluation
techniques to
objectives.

GENERAL INSTRUCTIONAL OBJECTIVES
(Intended outcomes that direct our teaching)

↓

SPECIFIC LEARNING OUTCOMES
(Types of pupil performance we are willing to accept as
evidence of the attainment of objectives)

↓

EVALUATION TECHNIQUES
(Procedures for obtaining samples of pupil performance
like those described in the specific learning outcomes)

comes. If the intended learning outcomes call for *performing* a procedure, the test items should require actual performance rather than a verbal description of how to do it. Issues such as these highlight the care needed in determining whether there is a good match between the stated outcomes and the expected responses to the test items.

Constructing relevant test items was considered in earlier chapters. Here we are simply pointing out the importance of matching test items as closely as possible to the learning outcomes they are intended to measure. The following examples, from various content areas, show reasonably good matches between intended outcomes and test items. In each example, the specific learning outcome describes the performance the pupil is to demonstrate, and the test item presents a task that demands that type of performance.

EXAMPLES

Specific Learning Outcome: Defines common terms. (Elementary Mathematics)
   Directions: In one or two sentences, define each of the following words:

1. Interest
2. Premium
3. Dividend
4. Collateral
5. Profit

Specific Learning Outcome: Identifies procedure for converting from one measure to another. (Elementary Mathematics)

1. The area of a rug is given in square yards. How should you determine the number of square feet?

   A   Multiply by 3
   (B) Multiply by 9
   C   Divide by 3
   D   Divide by 9

Specific Learning Outcome: Differentiates between relative values expressed in fractions. (Elementary Mathematics)

1. Which of the following fractions is smaller than one half?

   A   ⅔/4
   B   ⅘/6

C   ⅜
D   ⁹⁄₁₆

Specific Learning Outcome: Distinguishes fact from opinion. (Elementary Social Studies)

Directions: Read each of the following statements carefully. If you think the statement is a *fact*, circle the F. If you think the statement is an *opinion*, circle the O.

Ⓕ   O   1. George Washington was the first president of the United States.

F   Ⓞ   2. Abraham Lincoln was our greatest president.

Ⓕ   O   3. Franklin Roosevelt was the only president elected to that office three times.

Ⓕ   O   4. Alaska is the biggest state in the United States.

F   Ⓞ   5. Hawaii is the most beautiful state in the United States.

Specific Learning Outcome: Identifies common uses of weather instruments. (Elementary Science)

1. Which one of the following instruments is used to determine the speed of the wind?

A   Wind vane
Ⓑ   Anemometer
C   Altimeter
D   Radar

Specific Learning Outcome: Identifies cause-and-effect relationships. (Elementary Science)

Directions: In each of the following statements, both parts of the statement are true. Decide whether the second part explains *why* the first part is true. If it does, circle Yes. If it does not, circle No.

Examples:

Ⓨⓔⓢ   No   1. People can see   *because*   they have eyes.

Yes   Ⓝⓞ   2. People can walk   *because*   they have arms.

In the first example, the second part of the statement explains *why* "people can see," and so Yes was circled. In the second example, the second part of the statement does *not* explain *why* "people can walk," and so No was circled. Read each of the following statements and answer in the same way.

Yes   Ⓝⓞ   1. Some desert snakes are hatched from eggs   *because*   the weather is hot in the desert.

Ⓨⓔⓢ   No   2. Spiders are very useful   *because*   they eat harmful insects.

Ⓨⓔⓢ   No   3. Some plants do not need sunlight   *because*   they get their food from other plants.

Yes   Ⓝⓞ   4. Water in the ocean evaporates   *because*   it contains salt.

Ⓨⓔⓢ   No   5. Fish can get oxygen from the water   *because*   they have gills.

Specific Learning Outcome: Identifies reasons for an action or event. (Biology)

1. Which one of the following best explains why green algae give off bubbles of oxygen on a bright sunny day?

    A   Transpiration

    B   Plasmolysis

    Ⓒ   Photosynthesis

    D   Osmosis

Specific Learning Outcome: Identifies the relevance of arguments. (Social Studies)

   Directions: The items in this part of the test are to be based on the following resolution:

   Resolved: *The legal voting age in the United States should be lowered to eighteen.* Some of the following statements are arguments *for* the resolution, some are arguments *against* it, and some are *neither* for nor against the resolution. Read each of the following statements and circle

   F if it is an argument *for* the resolution.

   A if it is an argument *against* the resolution.

   N if it is *neither* for nor against the resolution.

Ⓕ	A	N	1.	Most persons are physically, emotionally, and intellectually mature by the age of eighteen.
F	A	Ⓝ	2.	Many persons are still in school at the age of eighteen.
F	A	Ⓝ	3.	In most states it is legal to drive an automobile by the age of eighteen.
F	Ⓐ	N	4.	The ability to vote intelligently increases with age.
F	A	Ⓝ	5.	The number of eighteen-year-old citizens in the United States is increasing each year.

   These examples are sufficient to show how test items should be related to specific learning outcomes. Although not all subject-matter areas and all types of learning outcomes are represented, the basic principle is the same. *State the desired learning outcomes in measurable terms, and select or develop test items that demand that specific type of performance.*

Relating Nontest Procedures to Instructional Objectives

There are many areas in which testing procedures are not useful. In evaluating some performance skills (e.g., singing, dancing, speaking), it is necessary to observe the pupils as they perform and to judge the effectiveness of the performance. In other instances it is possible to evaluate pupils' skill by judging the quality of the product resulting from the performance (e.g., a theme, a painting, a typed letter, a baked cake). In evaluating pupils' social adjustment it may be necessary to observe the pupils in formal and informal situations in order to judge their tendencies toward aggression or withdrawal, relations with peers, and the like. In fact, whenever we evaluate how pupils typically behave in a situation, some type of observational procedure is usually called for.

As with testing procedures, the selection or development of an observational technique should evolve from the objectives and specific learning outcomes. In the case of rating scales or checklists, the specific learning outcomes become the dimensions to be observed. In the following examples, note how the specific learning outcomes require only a slight modification to become items in a rating scale:

Speech

Specific Learning Outcome: Maintains good eye contact with audience.

Rating Scale Item

How effective is the speaker in maintaining eye contact with the audience?

1	2	3	4	5
Ineffective	Below average	Average	Above average	Very effective

Theme Writing

Specific Learning Outcome: Organizes ideas in a coherent manner.

Rating Scale Item

Organization of ideas.

1	2	3	4	5
Poor organization		Fair organization		Clear, coherent organization

Group Work

Specific Learning Outcome: Contributes worthwhile ideas to group discussion.

Rating Scale Item

How often does the pupil contribute worthwhile ideas to group discussion?

1	2	3	4	5
Never	Seldom	Occasionally	Fairly often	Frequently

More complete rating scales and checklists are presented in Chapter 15. It is our purpose here merely to illustrate how nontest procedures can be related to the learning outcomes we wish to evaluate. The specific learning outcomes specify the characteristics to be observed, and the rating scale provides a convenient method of recording our judgments. Such judgments are, of course, still subjective, but we have made them as objective as possible by defining the samples of pupil responses we wished to observe and then observing those responses.

Relating Evaluation Procedures Using an Expanded Table of Specifications

When using multiple techniques to evaluate classroom learning, it is usually desirable to expand the table of specifications used in test construction to include both test and nontest procedures. This provides an overall plan that clarifies how each evaluation technique relates to the instructional objectives. Including all objectives and evaluation procedures in a single table makes clear the relative emphasis given to each objective and each method of evaluation and prevents an overemphasis on testing procedures. A simplified version of such a table is presented in Table F.1.

TABLE F.1   Table of Specifications for Evaluation of a Weather Unit in Junior High School Science

Content	Knows		Understands	Interprets	Skill in		Total Number of Items
	Symbols and Terms	Specific Facts	Influence of Each Factor on Weather Formation	Weather Maps	Using Measuring Devices	Constructing Weather Maps	
Air pressure	2	3	3	3	Observe pupils using measuring devices (rating scale)	Evaluate maps constructed by pupils (checklist)	11
Wind	4	2	8	2			16
Temperature	2	2	2	2			8
Humidity and precipitation	2	1	2	5			10
Clouds	2	2	1				5
Total number of items	12	10	16	12			50
Percentage of evaluation	12%	10%	16%	12%	25%	25%	100%

Author Index

Subject Index

Norm-referenced test, 13–16, 18, 247–255
Norms
  grade, 342–47
  judging adequacy of, 361–362
  local, 362–367
  meaning of, 342
  percentile, 342, 347–349, 355, 364
  standard score, 342, 349–356
  types of, 342
Numerical rating scale, 383

Objective-referenced test, 14, 285–287
Objective test items
  alternative-response, 150–158
  interpretive exercise, 192–210
  matching, 158–163
  multiple choice, 166–191
  short answer, 143–149
  true–false, 150–158
  types of, 121–122
  versus essay, 19, 123–124
  see also Test items
Objective-item banks, 32, 502
Objectives
  reading, 271, 280
  taxonomy of, 31–32, 505–511
  types of, 26–32, 505–511
  see also Instructional objectives, Learning
    outcomes
Objectivity, 19, 96–97
Observational techniques
  anecdotal records, 377–383
  checklists, 392–395
  learning outcomes measured, 376
  rating scales, 383–392
Odd-even reliability, *see* Split-half method
Option, *see* Distracters
Organizing scores, 484–489
Otis–Lennon School Ability Test, 295–296,
    300, 301, 504
Outcomes, *see* Instructional ojbectives,
    Learning outcomes, Objectives

Parallel forms, *see* Equivalent forms
Parent–teacher conference, 433, 445–446
Pass–fail grading, 430–431
Peabody Individual Achievement Test, 287, 504
Peer appraisal
  "guess who" technique, 401–403
  nature of, 400
  sociometric technique, 403–409
Percentage-correct score, 14–15
Percentile norms, 342, 347–349, 355, 364
Percentile rank, 342, 347–349, 355, 364
Performance evaluation, 19, 385–388, 392–395

Performance terms
  meaning of, 24, 36–38
  in stating learning outcomes, 36–38, 39–43
  Taxonomy examples, 507, 509, 511
Personality inventories, 419–420
Personal–social development, evaluation of,
    377–383, 388, 389, 394–395, 400–409,
    419–421
Pictorial materials in testing, 197–202
Placement evaluation
  in classroom instruction, 12, 110–111, 113,
    459–461
  meaning of, 12, 110–111
Placement testing, 110–111, 113
Power test, 19
Practicality, *see* Usability
Preassessment, 9, 12, 110–111, 113, 461–462
Predictions
  with achievement and aptitude tests, 293–294
  differential, 296, 313
  validity of, 57–61, 64–65
Predictive validation, 57–61
Preparing pupils for tests, 239, 325, 328
Pretest, 9, 12, 110–111, 113, 461–462
PRI Reading Systems, 504
Procedure evaluation, 385–386, 392–394
Product evaluation, 386–388, 394
Product–moment correlation, 58–61, 496–499
Product scale, 387–388
Profile narrative report, 358–359, 417
Profiles, 356–360, 417
Projective techniques, 420–421
Psychological Abstracts, 320
Psychomotor domain (Taxonomy), 510–511
Published tests, *see* Criterion-referenced tests,
    Standardized tests
Published tests, in print, 317–319
Publishers of tests, 501–502
Pygmalion effect, 472

Quartile deviation, 493–494
Questionnaires, *see* Interest inventories,
    Personality inventories

Range, 493
Ranking test scores, 59, 485–486
Rating, pupil participation in, 396
Rating scales
  characteristics of, 383
  common errors in, 388–390
  in evaluating personal–social development,
    388–389
  in evaluating procedures, 385–386
  in evaluating products, 386–388
  principles of effective use, 390–392